CONTROVERSIES IN U.S. CONSTITUTIONAL LAW

미국 헌법 쟁점론

美 연방 수정헌법 제2조 총기 권리

안경환 임지봉 박창모 지영환 윤대현 외

박영사

Prologue

미국을 "총기가 지배하는 국가(gunocracy)"라 칭할 만큼 총기는 미국인들의 독특한 역사와 문화 속에 뿌리를 내리고 있다. 미국인들에게 화약 냄새는 집과 가족의 냄새처럼 친근하다. 집안 장식장에 총기를 진열해 놓고 어려서부터 자녀들에게 총을 쏘는 법을 가르치기도 한다. 미국에서 개인이 소유한 총기는 3억정에 이르고 있다. 미국 전체 인구를 무장시킬 수 있는 규모이다. 총이 미국의 생활 양식이며, 문화의 한 형태로 자리 잡고 있는 것이다.

미국에서 개인이 무기를 소유하고 휴대할 권리는 1791년 제정된 미국 연방 수정헌법 제2조에 규정되었다. 그러나 총기 소유는 신대륙 정착 초기부터 하나의 관습으로 용인된 제도였다. 식민지 정착민들은 영국의 관습법에 따라 제약 없이 총기를 소유할 수 있었다. 총은 외부의 적으로부터 가족의 생명과 재산을 지키는 무기였으며, 육류 공급을 위한 사냥이나 여가를 위한 사격의 도구였다.

미국이 영국으로부터 독립을 쟁취하는 과정에서 식민지인들은 자발적으로 '민병대(Militia)'를 조직하였다. 이는 정규군이 부족했던 초기 미국에서 국가의 안보를 지키는 중요한 역할을 하였다. 미국 건국의 아버지들은 이러한 경험을 바탕으로 정부의 독재에 맞서 국민 스스로가 무장할 권리가 보장되어야 한다고 믿었다.

이어진 서부개척 시기에 개인의 자유와 무력 방어의 개념이 더욱 확산되었다. 프런티어의 척박한 자연환경, 야생동물이나 인디언의 습격, 그리고 법과 질서가 확립되지 못한 상태에서 총은 생존을 위한 필수적인 도구였다. 남북전쟁 이후전쟁의 경험과 군복무자들의 귀향으로 총기가 더욱 일상화되었다. 20세기 중반 이후 NRA(전미총기협회)는 정치로비와 선거자금 지원을 통해 총기규제 반대 세력을 결집, 총기 소지의 자유를 미국의 정체성과 연결시키는 역할을 하였다. 반면, 연이어 발생하는 수많은 총기 범죄와 난동사건, 요인 암살과 정치적 테러를 방지하기 위해서 총기규제를 더욱 강화해야 한다는 주장이 제기되었다. 그러나 이러한 총기규제를 둘러싼 지속적인 찬반 논쟁에도 불구하고 총기소유는 개인의 자유와 권리를 보장하고, 정부의 권력 확대를 견제하는 수단으로 보장되어야 한다는 인식이 강하게 작용하고 있다.

우리는 미국에서 총기를 쉽게 구입하고 휴대할 수 있다는 사실은 잘 알고 있다. 그러나 언제부터, 왜, 어떤 근거로 총기의 소유와 휴대가 용인되었는지, 그리고 연이은 총기 난동과 요인 암살 사건에도 총기에 대한 규제가 효율적으로 이루어지지 못하는 이유가 무엇인지 아는 사람은 그리 많지가 않다. 이 저서는 이에 대한 대답을 제시하고자 하였다.

이 저서는 미국에서 총기문화가 뿌리를 내리게 된 역사, 문화적 배경, 수정헌법 제2조의 의미와 해석, 총기규제를 둘러싼 찬반 논쟁, 총기 사고와 폭력으로 발생되는 사회적 문제 등을 다각도로 살펴보고 있다. 이를 통해 총기문화가 "미국의 예외적인 특성"으로 자리를 잡게 된 과정을 이해할 수 있을 것이다.

이 저서는 또한 총기소유권에 대한 미국연방 대법원의 주요 판결과 법리적 해석, 미연방 수사국(FBI) 자료를 통한 총기 관련 범죄의 특성과 원인 분석, 미국 역대 대통령에 대한 암살(피격)과 주요 총기 사건의 실태와 영향, 미국 정부의 총기 관리와 감독 현황, 그리고 더 나아가 한국 총기 관리의 문제점과 개선 방안에 대한 제안 등 다양한 세부적인 주제들을 포함하였다.

여러 저자들의 다양한 연구 분야나 주제를 취합하여 〈미국 헌법 쟁점론〉이란 제목으로 이 저서를 출간을 하게 되었다. 이로 인해 통합적인 논지와 체제의 완성도에서 다소 미흡한 점도 있으리라 사료된다. 앞으로 지속적인 추가 연구와 독자들의 제언을 통해 좀 더 완성도 높은 내용으로 수정 보완될 수 있기를 기대한다.

마지막으로 이 저서의 출간을 처음으로 기획하고, 학자들과의 의견 교환을 통한 논문 선정, 출판사와의 협의 과정 등을 통해 이 저서가 원만히 출간되기까지 애써주신 지영환 박사의 노력과 헌신에 깊은 감사를 드린다.

2026년 1월 1일

손영호

베트남 호치민 국립대 인문사회대학 교수 · 청주대학교 역사문화학과 명예교수

The United States has often been described as a "gunocracy" — a nation governed, in part, by the gun itself. Firearms are deeply rooted in the unique history and culture of the American people. To many Americans, the scent of gunpowder is as familiar and comforting as the smell of home and family. Guns are displayed in household cabinets, and children are often taught to shoot from an early age. The number of privately owned firearms in the United States now exceeds three hundred million—enough to arm the entire population. The gun has thus become not merely a weapon, but a way of life and a distinctive expression of American culture.

The right of individuals to keep and bear arms was formally codified in 1791 through the Second Amendment to the U.S. Constitution. Yet, the practice of private gun ownership long predated this amendment. From the earliest days of colonial settlement, firearms were accepted as a customary institution under English common law. For the settlers, the gun was a vital instrument — defending family and property from external threats, providing meat for the table, and serving as a tool for recreation and marksmanship.

During America's struggle for independence from Britain, the colonists voluntarily organized militias, which played a crucial role in defending the nascent nation when regular troops were few. The Founding Fathers, shaped by this experience, came to believe that citizens must retain the right to arm themselves as a safeguard against tyranny and the overreach of government power.

As the frontier expanded westward, the concept of personal freedom and armed self-defense became even more deeply entrenched. In the harsh and untamed wilderness — amid attacks from wild animals and Native tribes, and in the absence of established law and order — the gun was indispensable for survival. After the Civil War, the experience of battle and the return of soldiers further normalized the presence of firearms in everyday life.

From the mid-twentieth century onward, the National Rifle Association(NRA) emerged as a powerful political force, mobilizing opposition to gun control through lobbying and campaign financing, and embedding the right to bear arms into the very fabric of American identity. At the same time, the rise in gun-related crimes, mass shootings, assassinations, and political violence gave rise to strong calls for stricter firearm regulation. Yet, despite these tragedies and the persistent public debate, the prevailing view remains that gun ownership is an essential element of individual liberty and a vital check on governmental power.

While many know that it is relatively easy to purchase and carry firearms in the United States, few understand when, why, and on what grounds this right became accepted—or why, despite repeated massacres and assassinations, effective gun control remains so elusive. This book seeks to provide an answer to those questions.

It examines the historical and cultural foundations of America's gun culture, the meaning and interpretation of the Second Amendment, the ongoing debates surrounding gun regulation, and the social problems arising from gun-related violence. Through these inquiries, readers will better understand how gun culture has come to embody one of the most distinctive and paradoxical aspects of American society.

In addition, this volume presents major rulings and doctrinal interpretations of the United States Supreme Court concerning the right to bear arms; analytical studies based on FBI data regarding the characteristics and causes of gun-related crimes; accounts of presidential assassinations and other key firearm incidents; assessments of governmental oversight and regulation; and, finally, proposals addressing challenges and potential reforms for firearm management in the Republic of Korea.

This work brings together diverse fields of study and research topics under the collective title Constitutional Issues in the United States. As such, there may be certain limitations in the unity of argument and structure. It is our hope that, through ongoing research and the thoughtful feedback of readers, future editions may achieve even greater refinement and completeness.

Lastly, I wish to express my deepest gratitude to Dr. Pyeong-jeong Ji Young-hwan(平靜 池榮鋎), whose vision first inspired this publication. His unwavering dedication — from conceptual planning and coordination among scholars to negotiation with the publisher — was indispensable in bringing this book to completion.

January 1, 2026

Son Young-ho

Professor, Faculty of Humanities and Social Sciences,
Ho Chi Minh City National University (Vietnam)
Professor Emeritus, Department of History and Culture, Cheongju University

Introductory Remarks — Purpose and Background of This Volume

The United States of America is a nation defined not only by its founding ideals but also by the controversies that continually shape their interpretation. Among the most enduring and consequential of these constitutional controversies is the right to keep and bear arms, as enshrined in the Second Amendment to the U.S. Constitution. This volume, *Controversies in U.S. Constitutional Law: The Right to Bear Arms under the Second Amendment*, explores the multiple dimensions — historical, legal, political, cultural, and philosophical — of one of the most debated constitutional provisions in U.S. history.

The Second Amendment emerged from a unique confluence of historical circumstances. The Founding Fathers, deeply influenced by the English Bill of Rights of 1689 and shaped by colonial experiences under British rule, codified the right to bear arms as a means of ensuring liberty, deterring tyranny, and empowering a citizen-based militia. At its core, the Second Amendment reflects the early American distrust of standing armies and a belief in the civic virtue of an armed populace.

However, the Amendment's meaning has been subject to continuous re-interpretation and legal challenge. What began as a broadly understood right tied to collective security and self-governance has become the focal point of legal and political debate over whether the Second Amendment protects an individual right, a collective right, or something in between. The controversies surrounding its interpretation have generated passionate arguments on all sides — from constitutional originalists and civil libertarians to public safety advocates and policy makers grappling with gun violence in American society.

This collection brings together scholarship that critically engages in these ongoing debates. The volume is organized around several major themes. First, it examines the historical foundations and cultural evolution of gun ownership in the United States. These chapters provide context on how gun culture became embedded in the American psyche — not merely as a matter of utility or defense, but as a symbol of freedom, frontier individualism, and resistance to centralized power. Drawing on history, literature, and film, these essays trace how deeply firearms are woven into the narrative of American identity.

Second, the book explores the legal and constitutional interpretations of the Second Amendment over time. A particular focus is placed on landmark Supreme Court cases such as *District of Columbia v. Heller*(2008) and *McDonald v. Chicago* (2010), which significantly reshaped the constitutional understanding of gun rights by affirming the individual's right to possess firearms for self-defense. These decisions reignited national conversations and inspired a new wave of academic and judicial engagement with the boundaries of governmental authority over gun regulation.

Importantly, the volume also addresses how the Second Amendment intersects with other constitutional values — federalism, separation of powers, the First Amendment, and evolving concepts of substantive due process and equal protection. Contributions examine the political influence of powerful advocacy groups such as the National Rifle Association(NRA) and analyze how public discourse around gun rights has shifted in response to mass shootings, domestic terrorism, and the emergence of armed protest movements.

Equally significant is the rise of digital and social media. Algorithm-driven platforms amplify emotional, partisan, and advocacy-driven content, deepening ideological divides while enabling new forms of activism. Empirical research shows that pro-gun advocacy online can directly influence firearm acquisition patterns, underscoring how media do not merely reflect public attitudes but shape them in tangible ways. This book situates the Second Amendment at the crossroads of constitutional law and media influence, recognizing that the meaning of rights cannot be divorced from the environments in which they are communicated, contested, and lived.

Finally, technological innovations present a new frontier. The spread of Internet of Things(IoT) home security systems — smart doorbells, cameras, and AI-enabled monitors — offers non-lethal alternatives to firearms in the domain of household protection. For many, particularly in younger and urban populations, such "tool media" reframe the meaning of security itself, suggesting that vigilance and deterrence can be achieved without personal armament. This shift challenges the symbolic and practical association between guns and safety that has long underpinned the Second Amendment debate.

The controversies explored in this book are not confined to the legal sphere; they are manifest in the daily lives of people. The frequency of gun violence in schools, neighborhoods, and public spaces underscores the urgent relevance of these debates. Yet at the same time, for many U.S. citizens, the right to bear arms remains an essential expression of personal liberty and constitutional heritage. This paradox — of rights exercised and rights constrained, of liberty upheld and lives lost — is at the heart of the American gun debate.

International readers, particularly in South Korea, will find in this volume a comprehensive introduction to an issue that has come to define American constitutional exceptionalism. In a global landscape where gun control is often more stringent and less politically charged, understanding the American case requires more than statistical comparison. It demands a nuanced exploration of constitutional text, founding philosophy, judicial doctrine, and political culture. This book aims to provide precisely that — an accessible, bilingual resource that invites comparative legal reflection and encourages transnational dialogue on rights, responsibility, and governance.

Another distinctive feature of this volume is its bilingual presentation. By offering both English and Korean versions of each essay, the book facilitates intellectual exchange between scholars and students of constitutional law in both countries. It recognizes that the meaning of legal texts is shaped by cultural context and that constitutional interpretation is never universal but always situated. The translation of constitutional controversy across linguistic and legal boundaries offers an opportunity for mutual learning and deeper understanding.

This volume does not seek to resolve the Second Amendment debate, nor does it advocate for a particular legal or policy solution. Rather, it seeks to present a balanced and rigorous foundation for informed inquiry. The aim is to empower readers — whether legal scholars, students, practitioners, or engaged citizens — to navigate the complexities of American constitutionalism with clarity, critical perspective, and contextual awareness.

We thank the contributors who brought this volume to life through their deep knowledge, careful research, and intellectual generosity. We also express our appreciation to those who helped with translation and proofreading, ensuring the clarity, accuracy, and accessibility of the bilingual format. This book stands as a testament to the value of cross-cultural legal scholarship and the importance of confronting constitutional controversies with openness and rigor.

In a time of deep division and heightened political tension, the question of what the Second Amendment means — and what it should mean — continues to resonate across courtrooms, legislatures, and communities. We hope this volume will serve as a meaningful contribution to that ongoing discourse and as a catalyst for deeper civic reflection on the nature of rights and responsibilities in democratic societies.

미국은 건국 이념으로 형성된 국가인 동시에, 그 이념의 해석을 둘러싼 끊임없는 논쟁 속에서 정체성을 만들어온 나라입니다. 그 가운데에서도 가장 지속적이고 영향력 있는 헌법적 논쟁 중 하나가 바로 연방헌법 수정조항 제2조, 즉 "무기를 소지하고 휴대할 국민의 권리"에 관한 것입니다. 본서『미국 헌법의 쟁점론: 수정헌법 제2조 총기권리』은 이 권리를 둘러싼 역사적 · 법적 · 정치적 · 문화적 논쟁을 다층적으로 조망하고, 그 헌법적 의미를 다각도로 탐색하는 연구 성과들을 집약한 것입니다.

수정헌법 제2조는 단순한 헌법 조항이 아니라, 식민지 시기와 독립 전쟁의 경험을 토대로 태동한 미국 특유의 정치철학과 시민윤리를 반영한 산물입니다. 영국의 1689년 권리장전에서 비롯된 무기소지의 전통과, 상비군에 대한 깊은 불신, 그리고 민병대 중심의 자치 방어 개념은 건국의 아버지들이 자유와 자치, 국가 권력에 대한 견제를 위해 무장권을 명문화하도록 이끌었습니다. 그러나 그 규정의 해석은 18세기 후반부터 오늘날까지 끊임없이 변모해왔고, 이제는 "개인의 권리인가, 집단의 권리인가?"라는 본질적 질문을 둘러싼 치열한 논쟁의 중심에 서게 되었습니다.

이 책은 바로 그 헌법적 논쟁의 현장을 다양한 관점에서 분석합니다. 전반부에서는 미국 총기문화의 역사적 기원과 문화적 전개 과정을 조명합니다. 개척시대의 생존 수단에서 시작된 총기는, 점차 자유의 상징, 개인 자율성의 상징, 중앙 권력에 대한 저항의 상징으로 자리 잡게 되었습니다. 문학, 영화, 대중문화 속 총기의 상징성은 미국인의 정체성과 가치관을 형성하는 데 큰 역할을 했으며, 오늘날에도 총기 보유에 대한 권리 의식을 지탱하는 서사로 기능하고 있습니다.

중반부에서는 수정조항 제2조의 법적 해석과 연방대법원의 주요 판례들을 분석합니다. 특히 2008년 *District of Columbia v. Heller* 판결과 2010년 *McDonald v. Chicago* 판결은 "자기방어를 위한 무기 소지가 개인의 헌법상 권리"임을 명시적으로 확인한 중대한 판례로 평가됩니다. 이 판결들은 미국 내 총기규제 입법, 사법 판단, 정치 담론 전반에 영향을 미쳤으며, 수정헌법 제2조를 다시금 공적 논의의 중심으로 이끌어냈습니다.

또한 본서는 총기 권리와 헌법상 타 권리들과의 관계도 심층적으로 탐색합니다. 예컨대, 총기 로비 단체인 미국총기협회(NRA)의 정치적 영향력, 총기를 중심으로 한 시민 저항운동, 표현의 자유와 결합된 무장 시위 등은 모두 수정조항 제2조 해석의 정치사회적 함의를 드러냅니다. 이처럼 무기소지권은 단순한 법적 권리를 넘어서, 미국 사회의 갈등 구조와 정치문화 속에서 살아 움직이는 헌법 원리로 작용하고 있음을 확인할 수 있습니다.

총기를 둘러싼 논쟁은 결코 법정 안에서만 벌어지는 것이 아닙니다. 이는 미국인의 일상 속으로 깊숙이 파고든 문제이며, 학교와 거리, 공공장소에서 발생하는 총기 난사 사건들은 이 권리가 초래할 수 있는 심각한 사회적 비용을 여실히 보여줍니다. 반면, 많은 미국인에게 총기 소지는 개인의 자유와 정체성, 헌법적 전통의 본질로 인식되고 있습니다. 바로 이 양면성 — 자유와 규제, 권리와 위험 사이의 긴장 — 이 미국의 총기 논쟁을 더욱 복잡하게 만드는 요인입니다.

동일하게 중요한 것은 디지털 및 소셜 미디어의 부상입니다. 알고리즘에 의해 구동되는 플랫폼들은 감정적이고 정파적이며 옹호적 성격의 콘텐츠를 증폭시켜 이념적 분열을 심화시키는 동시에 새로운 형태의 행동주의를 가능하게 합니다. 실증 연구는 온라인에서의 총기 옹호 활동이 직접적으로 총기 구매 패턴에 영향을 미칠 수 있음을 보여주며, 이는 미디어가 단순히 대중의 태도를 반영하는 데 그치지 않고 실제적인 방식으로 그것을 형성한다는 사실을 강조합니다. 본서는 수정헌법 제2조를 헌법 해석과 미디어 영향의 교차점에 위치시키며, 권리의 의미가 그것이 전달되고, 쟁점화되며, 실천되는 환경과 분리될 수 없음을 인식합니다.

마지막으로, 기술 혁신은 새로운 국면을 열고 있습니다. 사물인터넷(IoT) 기반의 가정 보안 시스템 — 스마트 초인종, 카메라, AI 기반 모니터 — 은 가정 보호 영역에서 총기에 대한 비치명적 대안을 제시합니다. 특히 젊은 세대와 도시 인구에게 이러한 '도구적 미디어'는 안전의 의미 자체를 재구성하며, 개인 무장을 통해서가 아니라 경계와 억제를 통해서도 안전을 달성할 수 있음을 시사합니다. 이러한 변화는 오랫동안 수정헌법 제2조 논쟁을 지탱해온 '총기와 안전' 간의 상징적 · 실질적 연계를 도전하는 흐름으로 작용합니다.

한국의 독자들에게 있어, 미국의 수정헌법 제2조는 종종 낯설거나 과도하게 느껴

질 수 있습니다. 그러나 이 헌법 조항이 형성된 역사적 맥락과 문화적 배경, 그리고 판례를 중심으로 한 사법적 해석의 흐름을 이해한다면, 미국 헌법의 독특성과 그 안에서 전개되는 논쟁의 깊이를 보다 정확히 파악할 수 있습니다. 본서는 이러한 비교법적 이해를 위한 토대를 제공하고자 하며, 동시에 헌법의 의미가 시대와 문화에 따라 어떻게 재구성되는지를 고찰하는 기회를 마련하고자 합니다.

본서의 또 하나의 특징은 바로 이중언어(영한 병기) 형식이라는 점입니다. 영어와 한국어로 구성된 이 책은 미국과 한국의 헌법학자, 법률가, 학생들이 서로의 시각을 공유하고 비판적으로 성찰할 수 있는 지적 장을 마련합니다. 헌법 해석은 언제나 문화적 맥락에 의존하며, 단일한 의미로 수렴되지 않는다는 점에서, 이러한 언어 간, 문화 간의 대화는 헌법적 사유의 지평을 넓히는 데 기여할 것입니다.

이 책은 수정헌법 제2조에 대한 논쟁을 종결하려는 시도도, 특정한 해석을 강변하려는 목적도 지니고 있지 않습니다. 오히려 그 반대로, 헌법적 논쟁이 지닌 복잡성과 층위를 충실히 드러냄으로써 독자가 스스로 판단하고 사고할 수 있도록 돕는 것이 본서의 진정한 목표입니다. 다양한 시각과 이론, 역사적 자료를 통해, 이 책은 독자들이 헌법과 시민의 권리에 대해 더욱 깊이 성찰할 수 있는 기회를 제공할 것입니다.

끝으로, 본서의 집필에 참여해주신 여러분께 깊은 감사의 말씀을 드립니다. 또한 번역, 교정, 감수에 애써주신 모든 분들의 노력과 헌신 덕분에 이 책이 완성될 수 있었습니다. 이 책이 한국과 미국의 헌법학 공동체에 기여가 되기를 바라며, 헌법적 논쟁을 분석하는 가운데 민주 사회에서의 진정한 권리와 책임이 무엇인지에 관한 범인류적 성찰의 촉매가 되기를 기대합니다.

January 7, 2026

2026년 1월 7일

C. Mo Bahk, Ph.D.

차 례

1. 미국의 총기문화에 대한 일 고찰

[손영호]

2. 미국 연방헌법 수정 제2조(무기소장권)의 의미

[안경환]

3. 미국 연방헌법 수정조항 제2조

[손영호]

4. 미국 수정헌법 제2조의 무기소지권과 총기규제

[임지봉]

5. 헌법상 민간부문총기관리·감독의 의미와 미국의 민간부문총기관리·감독현황 및 시사점

[장인호]

6. 총기난사요인이 대량살인 여부에 미치는 영향분석

[조현민]

7. 미국 연방 수정헌법 제2조 총기권리 위헌적 함의

[지영환·윤대현·조기환]

8. The Media and the Second Amendment to the Constitution of the United States

[박창모]

9. 國家의 法 對 人의 法哲學

[지영환]

부록 — 對談 : ChatGPT 對 평정(平静) 지영환(池榮鋎)

Chapters in Capsule 편별 캡슐요약

Chapter 1 (제1편)

The chapter presents a meticulously detailed exploration of the historical, cultural, and constitutional underpinnings of the United States' enduring gun culture, situating its origins in the nation's earliest colonial experience and tracing its evolution through the Revolutionary War, the westward expansion, popular culture, and modern constitutional law. The work's central contention is that American gun culture is not a recent or incidental phenomenon but rather a deeply rooted feature of the nation's identity—formed through lived necessity on the frontier, reinforced by the mythology of literature and film, and given legal sanction by the Second Amendment. This intertwining of practical survival needs, symbolic values, and legal protections helps explain the remarkable resilience of American gun ownership traditions in the face of recurring gun-related tragedies.

The study begins with a stark observation about contemporary America: gun violence, ranging from urban shootouts to mass school shootings, is a persistent feature of daily life. Incidents occur in high schools, universities, and even elementary schools, and armed confrontations between criminals and police are common. The United States records more than 200,000 violent crimes each year, with firearms responsible for approximately 70% of the resulting deaths — about 25,000 annually. Yet, despite the magnitude of the problem, the acquisition of firearms remains remarkably accessible. Federal law allows almost any adult over the age of twenty-one to purchase a gun after a minimal background check, and there is no nationwide requirement for individual gun registration. This makes it impossible to know precisely how many guns are in circulation or who owns them. The FBI estimates that private citizens collectively possess more than 250 million firearms, with numbers increasing by millions annually — enough to arm the entire population. It is for this reason that some observers describe the United States as a "Gunocracy," a nation dominated by its firearms.

The question the chapter poses is straightforward yet profound: why, in a country that once successfully enacted nationwide Prohibition on alcohol, is it so resistant to effective regulation of firearms, despite the high social costs? The answer, the author argues, lies in the unique historical and cultural development of the United States, where firearms have long been associated not only with physical survival but also with personal liberty, self-reliance, and national identity.

The historical analysis begins with the term "gun culture" itself, popularized by historian Richard Hofstadter in 1970, who described firearms as embedded in the American experience from colonial settlement through the western frontier era. Hofstadter's framing made "gun culture" a central concept in public debate whenever gun-related controversies arose. Yet, this consensus view was challenged by historian Michael Bellesiles, whose 2000 book *Arming America* argued that widespread gun ownership did not exist in the colonial or early republican periods. Drawing on probate records from 1765 to 1790 in New England and Pennsylvania, Bellesiles claimed that only about 10% of people owned guns at that time, and that many were broken or unusable. He maintained that the romanticized tradition of an armed citizenry was a constructed myth, promoted later to justify political agendas favoring legalized gun ownership.

While Bellesiles's argument attracted attention for its originality, it was also criticized for its narrow evidentiary focus and for neglecting broader considerations such as the symbolic and political role of arms. Critics noted that if gun ownership were measured solely by numbers and production, other nations — like England — would have been the true originators of "gun culture," which they were not. Moreover, Bellesiles paid insufficient attention to the constitutional protection of arms in the Second Amendment and the attitudes of the Founding Fathers toward an armed populace. Many historians have argued instead that American gun culture emerged organically from the lived realities of colonial settlement, the fight for independence, and the westward movement. It drew on English hunting traditions, the Revolutionary militia ethos, and the practical demands of frontier life.

From the colonial era, firearms were indispensable tools for settlers, who relied on them for protection against both wild animals and potential conflict with Native Americans, as well as for supplementing their diet through hunting. Given the great distance from England and the impossibility of providing full military or police protection, the Crown permitted colonists to keep arms for self-defense. Notable historians like Daniel Boorstin and Wesley Craven emphasized that nearly every able-bodied male in early settlements possessed a gun, and that knowledge of its use was considered an essential component of manhood. William C. Davis vividly described frontier fathers teaching their sons to shoot by the ages of nine or ten, combining hunting trips with instruction in self-defense, and celebrating the family's security and prosperity through shared use of the rifle.

Travel narratives from the seventeenth through nineteenth centuries confirm the centrality of firearms in American daily life. Harold L. Peterson noted that between 1620 and 1690, there was no period in which firearms were more essential. While colonial America lacked the capacity to manufacture guns in large numbers, imports from Europe ensured access to high-quality arms. The result, by the eighteenth century, was that American colonists were arguably the best-armed civilian population in the world. English common law guaranteed the right to bear arms, and on the frontier this right was closely tied to ideals of personal liberty and self-determination.

The Revolutionary War further strengthened this association. In response to British attempts to confiscate colonial arms — such as the 1774 ban on exporting military supplies to the colonies and the seizure of weapons from Boston residents — patriot leaders urged citizens to arm themselves. Volunteer militias, often composed of local farmers and tradesmen, organized rapidly into "minute men," ready to fight at a moment's notice. These citizen forces, under leaders like George Washington, played decisive roles in battles such as Saratoga and Yorktown, contributing significantly to the war's outcome. The war thus enshrined the belief that firearms were essential not only for personal defense but for the preservation of political liberty. In this vision, the gun was a guarantor of independence, a check against tyranny, and a symbol of citizenship.

The westward expansion in the nineteenth century reinforced and extended these values. The frontier was a lawless and often dangerous space, where settlers faced threats from hostile groups, outlaws, and predatory wildlife. Memoirs and travelogues from regions like Alabama, Tennessee, Missouri, and Pennsylvania depict communities where every household possessed one or more firearms, and where hunting and marksmanship were daily practices. In Alabama, Philip Gosse recorded competitive shooting games that demanded extraordinary skill, such as hitting the head of a nail from a distance sufficient to drive it flush into a plank. Alexis de Tocqueville, visiting Tennessee, observed that many farmers preferred hunting to agricultural labor, treating it as both sustenance and leisure. In Missouri's Ozarks, Henry Rowe Schoolcraft found boys as young as fourteen proficient in the use of rifles, with hunting viewed as both economically valuable and socially honorable. Firearms were also used in communal law enforcement — citizens armed themselves to pursue criminals or settle disputes, further blurring the lines between private and public uses of force.

Such customs were woven into social rituals as well. "Christmas shooting," in which groups would fire volleys outside homes before being invited in to celebrate, demonstrated the blending of festive tradition and gun culture. Firearms were inexpensive and widely available by the mid-nineteenth century, making ownership virtually universal in many frontier regions. Even in more settled eastern areas, shooting ranges and hunting remained popular, underscoring that gun culture was not solely a rural or western phenomenon.

The chapter devotes significant attention to the role of literature and entertainment in mythologizing and disseminating gun culture beyond its original geographic and practical contexts. Nineteenth-century novels by James Fenimore Cooper, particularly his "Leather stocking Tales" such as *The Last of the Mohicans*, romanticized the frontier and its armed protagonists. These works, rooted in distinctly American landscapes and conflicts, portrayed firearms as instruments of justice, survival, and moral choice. In the early twentieth century, Owen Wister's *The Virginian* crystallized the image of the cowboy — stoic, honorable, skilled with a gun—as an enduring American archetype. This image, replicated in films and later television, shaped generations of Americans' perceptions of firearms, linking them to themes of personal honor, courage, and individualism.

Real-life figures also contributed to this cultural construction. Annie Oakley, a sharpshooter who toured nationally in Buffalo Bill's Wild West shows from the 1880s, amazed audiences with feats of marksmanship, helping to popularize shooting as both sport and spectacle. In cinema, early Westerns like *The Great Train Robbery*(1903) and classics such as *Stagecoach*(1939) and *High Noon*(1952) embedded gunfights, lawmen, and outlaws into the national imagination. Later, gangster films of the Prohibition era and postwar action movies further developed the gun-wielding hero or antihero, from *Bonnie and Clyde to Dirty Harry, The*

Godfather, and *Robocop*. Even films depicting the grim realities of war or urban violence continued to present firearms as central to narratives of power, justice, and identity. Through these media, the gun was transformed from a practical tool into a potent cultural symbol recognized worldwide as part of the American image.

The legal core of this cultural system lies in the Second Amendment to the U.S. Constitution. Ratified in 1791 as part of the Bill of Rights, it reflects the compromises between Federalists, who sought a strong central government, and Anti-Federalists, who feared centralized power and insisted on protections for individual liberties. The amendment's text — linking a "well-regulated militia" to "the right of the people to keep and bear arms" — has generated intense debate over whether it protects a collective right associated with state militias or an individual right to own firearms. Gun control advocates often emphasize the "militia" clause, interpreting it as a collective guarantee, whereas gun rights supporters argue that the phrase "right of the people" is used consistently in the Bill of Rights to denote individual rights.

Historical context strongly supports the individual-rights interpretation. In the Revolutionary era, "militia" referred broadly to the body of armed citizens rather than to a formal standing force. Leading figures such as Jefferson, Madison, Mason, Adams, and Paine explicitly endorsed the principle that individual arms ownership was essential to resist tyranny. British attempts to disarm colonists before the Revolution — most notably in Boston — were seen as acts of oppression that underscored the necessity of an armed populace. Madison warned that disarming the people was a means of enslaving them; Mason defined the militia as comprising "the whole people" except a few officials. These views, echoed in public debates and writings of the time, establish that the Second Amendment was understood as affirming a personal right.

The chapter reinforces this conclusion by noting modern scholarly consensus. Of thirty-six legal articles published after 1980 analyzing the amendment, thirty-two argued for the individual-rights interpretation. The U.S. Supreme Court endorsed this view in *District of Columbia v. Heller*(2008), ruling 5–4 that the Second Amendment protects an individual's right to possess firearms for lawful purposes, such as self-defense in the home. Justice Antonin Scalia's majority opinion explicitly rejected the notion that the right is limited to militia service, emphasizing that constitutional protections cannot be abridged based on contemporary crime rates or policy preferences.

In its concluding analysis, the chapter stresses that American gun culture is the product of intertwined historical experiences, geographic realities, and cultural narratives. From colonial settlers defending isolated homesteads, through Revolutionary militias preserving liberty, to frontier families surviving in hostile environments, the gun has been both a practical necessity and a symbolic marker of independence and self-reliance. Literature, entertainment, and folklore have romanticized and perpetuated these associations, transforming firearms into icons of American identity recognized globally. The Second Amendment codified this ethos into constitutional law, ensuring its survival into the present.

This legacy helps explain the enduring resistance to sweeping gun control measures. For many Americans, the right to own and carry firearms is not merely a matter of policy but an unalienable aspect of citizenship — one inherited from the Founders, sanctified by history, and continually reinforced by cultural memory. Even in the face of repeated mass shootings and urban gun violence, the notion that "protecting myself and my family is my responsibility, not the government's" remains powerful. The persistence of this belief means that American gun culture, forged in the crucible of frontier survival and national independence, continues to define both domestic political debates and the nation's self-image. Guns remain, in this telling, not only tools of defense or instruments of violence but enduring symbols of freedom, autonomy, and the American spirit itself.

이 편은 미국 총기문화의 기원, 형성, 그리고 지속성을 역사적/문화적/헌법적 관점에서 심층적으로 분석하며, 그 뿌리가 식민지 시대 초기 경험에 놓여 있고, 독립전쟁과 서부개척, 대중문화, 그리고 현대 헌법 해석을 거쳐 발전해 왔음을 보여준다. 저자는 총기문화가 단순한 현대 정치적 산물이 아니라, 개척 시대의 생존 필요성, 개인 자유와 자립성에 대한 상징, 그리고 수정헌법 제2조라는 법적 보장을 통해 미국인의 정체성에 깊이 각인된 현상임을 강조한다. 이러한 실용적 필요, 상징적 가치, 그리고 제도적 보호가 결합되었기에, 반복되는 총기 사건과 비극에도 불구하고 총기 소유 전통은 미국 사회에서 쉽게 사라지지 않는다고 본다.

저자는 먼저 현대 미국의 현실을 직시한다. 도심의 총격전에서부터 초/중/고교와 대학 캠퍼스의 총기 난사 사건에 이르기까지, 총기 폭력은 일상적이다. 매년 약 20만 건이 넘는 폭력 범죄가 발생하고, 그중 약 2만 5천 명이 목숨을 잃는데, 이 중 70%는 총기 사용에 의한 것이다. 그럼에도 불구하고 미국에서 총기 구입은 비교적 간단하며, 21세 이상 성인은 최소한의 신원 조회만 거치면 총을 살 수 있다. 게다가 전국 차원의 총기 등록 의무가 없어 실제 총기 수와 소유자를 정확히 파악하기 어렵다. FBI 추산에 따르면, 민간이 소유한 총기는 2억 5천만 정을 넘어서며 매년 수백만 정씩 증가해, 전 국민을 무장시킬 수 있을 정도다. 이런 배경에서 미국을 '총기 지배 국가(Gunocracy)'라 부르는 표현도 등장했다.

그렇다면, 한때 금주법과 같은 전국적 규제를 시행했던 나라가 왜 총기 규제에는 실패하는가? 저자는 그 이유를 미국의 독특한 역사와 문화에서 찾는다. 총기는 단순한 무기가 아니라, 생존 도구이자 자유와 자립성의 상징, 그리고 국가 정체성의 핵심 요소로 자리 잡았기 때문이다.

총기문화라는 개념은 1970년 역사학자 리처드 홉스태터가 처음 대중화했다. 그는 총기가 식민지 개척 시대부터 서부 개척기를 거치며 미국인의 경험 속에 깊이 뿌리내렸다고 주장했다. 그러나 2000년 마이클 벨레사일즈는 『아밍 아메리카(Arming America)』에서 식민지 및 초기 공화국 시기에 총기 보급률이 극히 낮았다고 주장하며 전통적 관념을 뒤집었다. 그는 1765~1790년 뉴잉글랜드와 펜실베이니아의 유언검인기록을 분석해 총기 소유자가 10%에 불과했고, 그나마 절반 이상이 고장 난 상태였다고 밝혔다. 따라서 '무장한 국민'이라는 이미지는 후대 정치적 필요에 의해 만들어진 신화라고 보았다.

하지만 이러한 주장은 총기 소유의 상징적/정치적 기능을 간과했다는 비판을 받았다. 소유 수량과 생산량만으로 총기문화를 정의한다면, 오히려 영국이 먼저 총기문화를 창조했어야 한다. 무엇보다 벨레사일즈는 총기 소유권을 보장한 수정헌법 제2조의 역사적 배경과 건국 지도자들의 인식을 충분히 다루지 않았다. 반면 다수의 역사학자들은 총기문화가 영국의 사냥 전통, 독립전쟁의 민병대 정신, 서부 개척기의 생활 필요성 등에서 자연스럽게 형성되었다고 본다.

식민지 시대 총기는 야생동물과 원주민의 위협으로부터 자신과 가족을 지키고, 사냥으로 식량을 확보하는 필수품이었다. 영국 본토와의 거리 때문에 치안 유지가 어려웠고, 이에 따라 식민지 주민들에게 무기 소유가 허용되었다. 다니엘 부어스틴과 웨슬리 크레이븐 등은 초기 정착민 대다수가 총기를 소유했다고 기록한다. 윌리엄 C. 데이비스는 아버지가 아들에게 어린 나이부터 사격과 자기 방어를 가르치는 모습을 묘사하며, 총이 가정의 안전과 공동체 결속의 핵심임을 강조했다.

17-19세기 여행기와 회고록은 총기가 생활 전반에 깊이 스며 있었음을 보여준다. 해롤드 L. 피터슨은 1620-1690년이 총기가 가장 절실했던 시기라고 말하며, 당시 식민지 주민들이 유럽에서 수입한 고성능 총기를 다루는 데 능숙했다고 기록했다. 18세기 미국인은 세계에서 가장 잘 무장된 사람들이었고, 이는 자유와 자기결정권에 대한 신념과 직결되었다.

독립전쟁은 이러한 연관성을 더욱 공고히 했다. 영국이 무기 반출을 금지하고 식민지 무장을 해제하려 하자, 주민들은 민병대를 조직해 무장을 결의했다. '1분 대기반(minutemen)'이라 불린 이들은 렉싱턴과 콩코드 전투에서 첫 교전을 벌였고, 새러토가와 요크타운에서의 승리를 통해 독립을 쟁취했다. 이 경험은 총기를 자유와 생존의 보루로 인식하게 만들었다.

19세기 서부 개척에서도 총은 필수품이었다. 알라바마, 테네시, 미주리, 펜실베이니아 등지의 기록은 가정마다 총을 비치하고, 사냥과 사격을 일상적으로 즐기며, 명중률을 경쟁하는 놀이가 사회문화의 일부였음을 보여준다. 크리스마스 전야에 총을 쏘며 이웃을 방문하는 '크리스마스 사격' 같은 관습도 있었다. 중서부 · 남부의 프런티어 지역은 물론, 동부의 상업도시에서도 사격장은 1830년대 이미 운영되고 있었다.

문학과 대중문화는 총기문화를 신화화하고 전국적으로 확산시키는 데 중요한 역할을 했다. 제임스 페니모어 쿠퍼의 '가죽 장화 연작(Leatherstocking Tales)'은 미국 자연과 무기를 든 개척자의 삶을 낭만적으로 묘사했고, 오웬 위스터의 『버지니아인(The Virginian)』은 명예롭고 고독한 카우보이의 전형을 창조해 영화 · TV 서부극의 원형이 되었다. 애니 오클리와 같은 실존 명사수는 사격을 스포츠와 오락으로 대중화했다. 서부극, 갱스터 영화, 액션 영화에 이르기까지 미국 대중매체는 총을 정의, 용기, 또는 반항의 상징으로 그려왔다. 이로써 총기는 실용적 도구를 넘어 세계적으로 인지되는 미국 문화의 상징이 되었다.

헌법적 차원에서 총기문화의 핵심은 수정헌법 제2조다. 1791년 비준된 권리장전에 포함된 이 조항은 "규율 있는 민병대는 자유로운 주의 안보에 필요하므로, 국민이 무기를 소유하고 휴대할 권리를 침해해서는 안 된다"고 규정한다. 이를 두고 집단적 권리(주 방위군 등)에 한정된다는 해석과, 개인의 권리라는 해석이 대립해왔다. 그러나 역사적으로 '민병대'는 무기를 소유한 일반 시민 전체를 가리켰고, 제퍼슨, 매디슨, 메이슨, 애덤스, 페인 등 건국 지도자들은 개인 무장권을 자유 수호의 핵심으로 보았다.

영국의 무기 몰수 시도와 억압 정책은 무장한 시민의 필요성을 부각시켰다. 매디슨은 무장을 해제하는 것은 국민을 노예화하는 방법이라고 경고했고, 메이슨은 민병대가 곧 모든 시민이라고 정의했다. 현대 연구에서도 이러한 해석은 지지를 받는다. 1980년 이후 발표된 논문 36편 중 32편이 개인 권리 해석을 옹호했다. 2008년 연방대법원은 *District of Columbia v. Heller* 사건에서 5 대 4로 개인의 자기방어 목적 총기 소유를 합헌으로 판결하며 이 해석을 확정했다. 스칼리아 대법관은 총기 사건의 심각성을 인정하면서도, 헌법은 가정 내 개인용 총기 금지를 허용하지 않는다고 명시했다.

결론에서 저자는 미국 총기문화가 지리적 환경, 역사적 경험, 문화적 전승이 결합된 결과라고 강조한다. 식민지 개척민, 독립전쟁 민병대, 서부개척자, 그리고 대중문화 속 카우보이와 액션 영웅에 이르기까지, 총은 생존 도구이자 자유의 상징으로 기능해 왔다. 이 유산은 반복되는 비극에도 불구하고 총기 규제에 대한 강한 저항을 낳았다. 많은 미국인에게 총기 소유는 정책 문제가 아니라, 창건자들로부터 물려받은 불가침의 시민권이며, 국가 정체성의 일부다. 총은 단순한 무기나 폭력의 수단을 넘어, 자유, 자율성, 그리고 '미국적 정신' 자체를 상징하는 존재로 남아 있다.

Chapter 2 (제2편)

The chapter undertakes a comprehensive and meticulously sourced legal-historical examination of the Second Amendment to the United States Constitution, which provides that "A well regulated Militia, being necessary to the security of a free State, the right of the people to keep and bear Arms shall not be infringed." The analysis spans from the constitutional language's origins in English law and political thought to the modern controversies in American jurisprudence, focusing especially on the question of whether the provision secures an individual right or merely a collective right tied to state militias. The author weaves together the philosophical backdrop of the American founding, the legislative and political history surrounding the Amendment's adoption, the evolving attitudes of Congress in enacting federal firearms regulations, and the reluctance of the federal courts, especially the Supreme Court, to give a definitive interpretation for much of the nation's history. Through this approach, the chapter not only illuminates the legal meaning of the Amendment but also shows how it has become deeply entangled with American political identity, cultural attitudes toward arms, and the balance of governmental powers.

From the outset, the author emphasizes that several terms in the Amendment — such as "well regulated," "militia," "arms," "keep," "bear," and "free State" — remain linguistically and conceptually ambiguous, and their definitive legal content can only be established through the interpretive authority of the Supreme Court. Yet for over two centuries, despite the Second Amendment's symbolic importance, the Court largely refrained from clarifying its scope. This institutional silence left open questions that are deeply consequential in a society marked by high rates of violent crime, pervasive firearm availability, and a longstanding cultural belief in the propriety, even necessity, of private gun ownership. For American observers, these questions are bound up with contemporary politics; for outside observers, they offer a window into how American constitutionalism accommodates, and sometimes resists, the regulation of potentially dangerous rights.

The intellectual and political lineage of the Amendment reaches back to the 1776 Declaration of Independence, whose text proclaims that people have an inherent right to alter or abolish any form of government that becomes destructive of their fundamental rights. This principle is directly traceable to the political philosophy of John Locke, who argued that the legitimacy of government rests on the consent of the governed and that when rulers become tyrannical, the people retain a residual right to resistance. The Second Amendment, ratified in 1791 as part of the Bill of Rights, translated this revolutionary ethos into a constitutional guarantee: it codified the people's ability to maintain arms not merely for hunting or self-defense but as a safeguard against governmental tyranny. In this sense, the right to keep and bear arms was not only about individual protection from crime but also about collective protection from oppression.

Nevertheless, the Amendment languished in relative obscurity in legal discourse for much of American history. For most of the 19th and 20th centuries, it was treated more as a constitutional ornament than as a subject of substantive legal development. Major constitutional treatises either omitted serious discussion of the provision or relegated it to a brief mention. Only toward the end of the 20th century did the Second Amendment reemerge as a central topic in constitutional debate, catalyzed by scholarly interventions such as Sanford Levinson's influential 1989 Yale Law Journal article, "The Embarrassing Second Amendment." Levinson argued that the provision should be understood within the framework of civic republicanism, a political tradition that values an armed citizenry as a means of preserving a free republic and maintaining the ultimate check on governmental overreach. His claim that the Amendment embodied a constitutionalized "right to revolution" provoked vigorous responses from other scholars. Critics like Wendy Brown questioned whether civic republican ideals — requiring high levels of civic virtue — could plausibly be invoked to justify widespread civilian armament in a modern pluralistic democracy. This exchange broadened the terms of the debate, drawing in historians, legal theorists, and political scientists.

The broader public's engagement with the Second Amendment was fueled by political events and legislative measures in the 1990s. The 1994 federal ban on assault weapons symbolized, for many gun owners, a direct infringement on lawful firearms use. The following year, the Oklahoma City bombing, perpetrated by individuals associated with anti-government "militia" movements, linked the constitutional term "militia" in the public imagination to extremist violence. These events gave the Amendment renewed salience, not only in academic circles but also in political rhetoric, advocacy campaigns, and public discourse.

At the heart of the controversy is the divide between the "collective-right" and "individual-right" interpretations. The collective-right view maintains that the Amendment protects only the prerogative of states to maintain militias and does not secure any personal right to arms. This view draws heavily on Article I, Section 8 of the Constitution, which grants Congress authority over organizing, arming, and disciplining the militia. Proponents argue that the Second Amendment was meant to prevent Congress from disarming the state militias and thereby eliminating a critical counterbalance to federal military power. In this interpretation, the "right of the people" is exercised collectively through state institutions. By contrast, the individual-right view holds that the Amendment protects personal ownership and use of firearms, independent of militia service. Supporters of this reading note that the phrase "the right of the people" appears elsewhere in the Bill of Rights — in the First and Fourth Amendments, for example — where it clearly refers to individual rights. Even if one accepts that the framers sought to protect the states'militia systems, individual-right proponents argue that the most practical way to do so is to ensure that individual citizens are armed.

Closely tied to this debate is the question of incorporation — whether the

Second Amendment applies to state governments through the Fourteenth Amendment. Supreme Court decisions from the late 19th century, such as United States v. Cruikshank(1875) and Presser v. Illinois(1886), concluded that the Amendment restricted only federal action. These cases, however, predated the Court's incorporation of most of the Bill of Rights to the states in the 20th century. As such, their binding authority is limited, but they continue to shape the historical landscape of Second Amendment jurisprudence. Historically, the Court has confined its review to federal laws, leaving most state-level firearms regulations unchallenged at the national level.

The origins of the right to keep and bear arms lie deep in English constitutional history. Colonial charters promised American settlers the rights enjoyed by English subjects, explicitly incorporating the protections of the 1689 English Bill of Rights. That document had emerged from the Glorious Revolution and reflected a widespread distrust of standing armies and the Crown's disarmament of political opponents. It recognized the right of Protestant subjects to have arms for their defense. William Blackstone, the great commentator on English law, classified this as one of the absolute rights of individuals, justified not only for resisting tyranny but also for private purposes such as self-defense, hunting, and marksmanship. In the 17th century, republican political thinkers like James Harrington and Henry Neville further developed the idea that a populace capable of bearing arms was essential to preserving liberty and maintaining a republican form of government. John Locke's assertion of a natural right to self-preservation provided a philosophical bridge between English political theory and American constitutionalism.

These ideas profoundly influenced the framers of the U.S. Constitution. During the Constitutional Convention, although Federalists and Anti-Federalists disagreed on the balance of power between the national and state governments, both camps recognized the value of an armed citizenry. Federalists such as James Madison and John Adams and Anti-Federalists such as Thomas Jefferson and Patrick Henry agreed that widespread civilian armament was a bulwark of liberty. The pseudonymous "Federal Farmer" insisted that the entire population should be armed as a safeguard against tyranny. The relative scarcity of debate records on the Second Amendment likely reflects a broad consensus on its necessity rather than indifference.

In the Virginia ratification convention, however, disagreements arose over the precise allocation of militia-related powers. Madison and George Mason, despite both valuing the militia, differed over congressional control. Mason feared that Congress might neglect or refuse to arm the militia, creating an excuse for maintaining a standing army. He advocated for a constitutional amendment explicitly granting states the authority to arm their militias independently if Congress failed to act. While collective-right advocates see this as support for a state-centered interpretation, Mason's definition of "militia" encompassed the entire body of the people, not merely formal military units, suggesting that the right had an inherently popular dimension.

Despite the framers'expectation that Congress would act to preserve an armed citizenry, legislative history reveals a steady trend toward firearms regulation. The first major federal gun law, the National Firearms Act of 1934, relied on Congress's taxing power to regulate certain classes of weapons. The Federal Firearms Act of 1938, based on the commerce power, imposed licensing requirements on manufacturers and dealers. Subsequent decades saw little federal action until the tumultuous 1960s, when a wave of political assassinations, urban unrest, and rising crime spurred Congress to pass the Gun Control Act of 1968, which introduced sweeping regulations. Later statutes included the Firearm Owners' Protection Act of 1986, which both strengthened and rolled back aspects of prior laws, the Brady Handgun Violence Prevention Act of 1993, mandating background checks and waiting periods for handgun purchases, and the 1994 Public Safety and Recreational Firearms Use Protection Act, which banned certain semi-automatic "assault weapons." These measures often provoked constitutional challenges, though not all reached the Supreme Court.

Judicial interpretation of the Second Amendment has been sparse and, until recently, unsatisfactorily conclusive. In United States v. Miller(1939), the Court upheld a restriction on transporting a sawed-off shotgun across state lines, reasoning that the Second Amendment protects only those arms with a reasonable relationship to the preservation or efficiency of a well-regulated militia. Many took this as an endorsement of the collective-right view, though others argued it left open the possibility that individuals have rights to arms suitable for militia use. Lower federal courts, interpreting Miller, generally adopted a narrow reading, focusing on state authority rather than individual rights. The Supreme Court's decades-long silence thereafter allowed competing narratives to solidify: gun control advocates interpreted the absence of intervention as tacit approval of regulation, while gun rights proponents viewed it as implicit affirmation of an enduring individual right.

Later cases touched on the Amendment indirectly. In United States v. Verdugo-Urquidez(1990), the Court defined "the people" as members of the national community or those with sufficient connection to it, a formulation that individual-right advocates see as consistent with their position. In United States v. Lopez(1995), the Court struck down the federal Gun-Free School Zones Act on Commerce Clause grounds, signaling that Congress's regulatory powers over firearms have limits.

In conclusion, the prevailing judicial doctrine has tended to construe the Second Amendment as securing for the states, rather than for individuals, the right to maintain armed militias. However, the historical record and the philosophical foundations of the provision point to a dual purpose: first, to enable the people to defend the nation without reliance on a standing army, and second, to preserve the means for citizens to resist military or governmental oppression. While the first purpose has little relevance in the modern context of a permanent federal military, the second remains conceptually and politically potent. If the right to keep and bear arms is understood as a fundamental right rooted in self-defense, any restriction should be subject to the most exacting judicial scrutiny, permissible only if it serves a compelling governmental interest. Ultimately, the scope and meaning of the Second Amendment will hinge on the willingness of the Supreme Court to reconcile the framers'original intent with the complex realities of contemporary American society.

이 편은 미국 연방헌법 수정 제2조의 의미와 함의를 법사학적/역사적 관점에서 포괄적이고 심층적으로 분석한다. 수정 제2조는 "질서정연하게 규율된 민병대는 자유로운 주의 안보에 필요하므로, 국민이 무기를 보유하고 휴대할 권리를 침해해서는 안 된다"라고 규정하고 있으며, 이 간결한 문구는 18세기 말의 정치철학, 영국법 전통, 그리고 미국 건국기의 제헌 논의 속에 뿌리를 두고 있다. 저자는 이 조항이 개인의 권리를 보장하는지 아니면 주의 집단적 권리를 보장하는지를 둘러싼 오랜 논쟁을 중심축으로 삼아, 제정 배경과 역사적 맥락, 연방의회의 총기 규제 입법, 연방대법원을 포함한 법원의 태도 변화를 검토한다. 이를 통해 수정 제2조가 미국 정치문화와 국민 정체성, 권력분립 구조 속에서 어떻게 자리매김해 왔는지를 입체적으로 보여준다.

저자는 먼저 이 조항 속의 핵심 용어들이 본질적으로 모호하다는 점을 지적한다. "질서정연하게"(well regulated), "민병대"(militia), "무기"(arms), "보유"(keep), "휴대"(bear), "자유로운 주"(free State) 등의 개념은 각각의 역사적/법적 맥락에서 의미가 달라질 수 있으며, 최종적으로는 연방대법원의 해석을 통해 확정될 수밖에 없다. 그러나 미국 역사에서 200년 넘게 대법원은 이 조항의 의미를 명확히 밝히는 데 매우 소극적이었다. 그 결과, 총기 소유와 규제라는 문제는 헌법상 권리 보장과 공공안전이라는 상충하는 가치가 맞부딪히는 영역으로 남아, 오늘날 미국 사회에서 극심한 정치적 분열과 문화적 갈등을 야기하고 있다. 미국의 높은 강력범죄율, 총기의 광범위한 보급, 그리고 개인 총기 소유를 당연시하거나 심지어 의무로까지 보는 문화적 정서는 이 조항의 해석과 직결되며, 이는 외부 관찰자들에게도 미국 특유의 헌정주의가 어떻게 위험한 권리까지도 제도권 안에 수용하는지를 보여주는 흥미로운 사례가 된다.

수정 제2조의 사상적 뿌리는1776년 독립선언문에까지 거슬러 올라간다. 독립선언문은 정부가 국민의 기본권을 파괴할 때 국민은 이를 변경하거나 폐지할 권리가 있다고 선언했으며, 이는 존 로크의 사회계약론에서 유래한 사상이다. 로크에 따르면 정부의 정당성은 피치자의 동의에 기반하며, 통치자가 폭군이 될 경우 국민은 저항할 권리를 보유한다. 1791년 권리장전의 일부로 제정된 수정 제2조는 이러한 혁명적 정신을 헌법의 조문 속에 구체화한 것으로, 무기 소유권을 사냥이나 자기방어뿐만 아니라 전제적 권력에 맞서 자유를 지키는 집단적·개인적 수단으로 보장했다. 따라서 이 권리는 단순한 범죄 예방이나 생활방어를 넘어, 자유를 지키기 위한 헌법적 안전장치였다.

그러나 제정 이후 상당 기간 동안 수정 제2조는 헌법 해석과 판례에서 변방에 머물렀다. 19세기와 20세기 대부분의 기간 동안 주요 헌법 교과서나 주석서들은 이조항을 간략히 언급하는 수준에 그쳤으며, 실질적 해석 논의는 거의 전개되지 않았다. 전환점은 1989년 샌포드 레빈슨 교수가 발표한 「부끄러운 수정 제2조」라는 논문이었다. 레빈슨은 이 조항을 시민공화주의의 틀에서 이해해야 하며, 무장한 시민은 자유로운 공화국의 존속과 정부 권력 남용에 대한 최후의 억제 장치라고 주장했다. 그는 수정 제2조가 일종의 '헌법 속 혁명권'을 제도화한 것이라고 해석했으며, 이는 다른 학자들의 격렬한 반론을 불러일으켰다. 예컨대 웬디 브라운은 현대의 다원적 민주주의에서 시민공화주의가 전제하는 높은 수준의 공덕심이 결여되어 있다는 점을 지적하며, 이를 근거로 광범위한 민간 무장을 정당화하는 것은 무리라고 비판했다. 이러한 논쟁은 학문적 범위를 넘어 정치철학, 역사학, 법학을 아우르는 다층적 논의로 확산되었다.

1990년대에 들어 정치/사회적 사건들은 수정 제2조 논쟁을 일반 대중의 관심사로 끌어올렸다. 1994년 연방 차원의 공격용 무기 금지법 제정은 많은 총기 소유자들에게 합법적 권리 침해로 받아들여졌고, 1995년 오클라호마 연방청사 폭파 사건은 '민병대'라는 헌법 용어를 반정부 극단주의 집단과 연계시키는 계기가 되었다. 이런 사건들은 수정 제2조를 둘러싼 해석을 학계뿐 아니라 정치 수사와 대중 담론의 중심으로 올려놓았다.

논쟁의 핵심은 수정 제2조가 개인적 권리를 보장하는지 아니면 주의 집단적 권리를 보장하는지 여부다. 집단적 권리론은 헌법 제1조 제8항의 '민병대 조항'을 근거로,

이 조항이 주정부의 무장 민병대를 해체하지 못하도록 하는 장치라고 해석한다. 반면 개인적 권리론은 설령 주 민병대 보호가 목적이었다 해도, 이를 실질적으로 보장하는 방법은 개별 시민의 무장권을 인정하는 것이라고 본다. 특히 '국민의 권리'라는 표현이 권리장전 전반에서 일관되게 개인을 지칭한다는 점은 강력한 근거다. 또한 이 권리가 수정 제14조를 통해 주정부에도 적용되는지 여부, 즉 수용(incorporation) 문제도 쟁점이다. 19세기 후반 *Cruikshank*(1875), *Presser*(1886) 판결은 수정 제2조가 연방에만 적용된다고 했지만, 이는 수용이론 확립 이전의 판례로 현재는 법적 구속력이 약하다. 역사적으로 대법원은 연방법만을 심사 대상으로 삼아 왔으며, 주 차원의 규제에는 개입하지 않았다.

수정 제2조의 기원은 영국 헌정사에 깊이 뿌리내려 있다. 식민지 인허장은 영국 국민의 권리를 식민지 주민도 향유한다고 규정했고, 이는 1689년 영국 권리장전에 근거했다. 권리장전은 상비군에 대한 불신과 국왕의 무장 해제 정책에 맞서, 프로테스탄트의 무기 보유권을 인정했다. 블랙스톤은 이를 절대적 권리로 분류하며, 폭정 저항이라는 공적 목적뿐 아니라 자기방어, 사냥, 사격 등 사적 목적도 포함된다고 설명했다. 17세기 공화주의 사상가 해링턴과 네빌은 무장한 시민이야말로 자유를 지키는 핵심이라고 보았고, 로크는 자기보존권을 자연권으로 규정하며 이를 철학적으로 뒷받침했다. 이러한 사상은 미국 건국기의 자유주의와 결합하여, 민간 무장이 자유 사회의 필수 요소라는 미국적 신념을 형성했다.

제헌회의에서 연방주의자와 반연방주의자는 권력 구조 설계에서는 대립했지만, 무장 시민의 필요성에는 의견이 일치했다. 매디슨, 애덤스, 제퍼슨, 헨리 등은 모두 광범위한 민간 무장이 자유의 보루라고 보았다. '연방 농부'라는 필명은 전 국민의 상시 무장을 주장했다. 버지니아 비준회의에서 매디슨과 조지메이슨은 민병대에 대한 연방 권한을 두고 논쟁했는데, 메이슨은 연방이 민병대를 무장시키지 않거나 소집하지 않을 경우에 대비해 주정부에 독자적 권한을 부여해야 한다고 주장했다. 집단적 권리론은 이를 주 중심 해석의 근거로 보지만, 메이슨이 말한 '민병대'는 전 국민을 포함하는 개념이었다.

연방의회는 건국자의 기대와 달리 총기 소유를 촉진하기보다 규제하는 방향으로 입법을 이어왔다. 1934년 총기세법(NFA), 1938년 총기법(FFA)을 시작으로, 1968년 총기규제법(GCA), 1986년 총기소유자보호법, 1993년 브래디법, 1994년 공격용 무기 금지법 등 규제가 확대되었다. 이러한 법률들은 정치 암살, 도시 범죄, 총기 밀거래 등 사회문제에 대응하기 위한 것이었으나, 수정 제2조와의 관계에서 늘 논쟁을 불러왔다.

연방대법원은 수정 제2조 해석에 극히 소극적이었다. 1939년 *Miller* 판결은 잘 규율된 민병대 유지와 관련 없는 무기는 보호 대상이 아니라고 하여 집단적 권리론에 힘을 실었으나, 일부는 이를 개인 권리를 전제로 한 것으로 보았다. 이후 하급심은 이를 좁게 해석하여 개인 권리를 인정하지 않았고, 대법원의 장기간 침묵은 규제 옹호론자에게는 묵시적 승인으로, 권리 옹호론자에게는 묵시적 인정으로 해석되었다. 1990년 *Verdugo–Urquidez* 판결에서 '국민'을 국가 공동체 구성원으로 정의한 점은 개인 권리론을 뒷받침하며, 1995년 *Lopez* 판결은 상거래 조항의 한계를 들어 학교 인근 총기 금지법을 무효화했다.

결론적으로, 현행 판례는 수정 제2조를 주정부의 민병대 유지권으로 보는 경향이 강하지만, 역사적 기록과 철학적 토대는 이 조항이 상비군 없는 국가 방위와 군사적/정부적 압제 저항이라는 이중 목적을 지녔음을 시사한다. 첫째 목적은 현대의 상비군 체제에서는 실효성이 적지만, 둘째 목적은 여전히 의미가 크다. 만약 무기소지권이 자기방어에 뿌리를 둔 본질적 권리라면, 그 제한은 '중대한 공익' 요건을 충족하는 엄격심사를 거쳐야 한다. 궁극적으로 수정 제2조의 범위와 의미는 건국 당시의 원래 의도와 현대적 현실을 어떻게 조화시킬지에 대한 연방대법원의 판단에 달려 있다.

Chapter 3 (제3편)

The chapter examines in depth the origins, legal interpretations, and ideological foundations of the Second Amendment to the United States Constitution, centering on its guarantee of "the right of the people to keep and bear arms." It begins by situating the issue in the context of America's exceptionally high civilian gun ownership rates, the prevalence of gun-related crime, and the recurrent national debates that erupt in the wake of mass shootings and assassinations. Notable public events

— such as the assassinations of Martin Luther King Jr. and Robert F. Kennedy in 1968, and the Columbine High School massacre in 1999 — are presented as catalysts for intensified scrutiny of U.S. gun policy. These tragedies, alongside persistent gun violence that claims tens of thousands of lives annually, repeatedly push the question of regulation to the forefront. Yet, every attempt at legislative reform collides immediately with the constitutional language of the Second Amendment, which gun rights advocates interpret as an inviolable individual liberty.

The chapter carefully distinguishes between "amendment" in the technical sense — an addition to the Constitution — and the colloquial but inaccurate expression "amended constitution," clarifying that there is no separate "revised constitution," only the original Constitution supplemented by amendments. The Second Amendment, adopted in 1791 as part of the Bill of Rights, must be read against its legal ancestry in English common law and republican political thought. In the wake of the 1688 Glorious Revolution, the 1689 English Bill of Rights prohibited maintaining a standing army in peacetime without parliamentary consent and affirmed the right of subjects to possess arms for self-defense. This tradition crossed the Atlantic with the colonists, was reinforced during the American Revolution, and became codified in the Second Amendment. Thinkers such as James Harrington and James Burgh elaborated a republican ideology of an armed citizenry, ideas that profoundly influenced American founders like Thomas Jefferson and James Madison.

The text then surveys the emergence of scholarly and legal debate in the United States, especially from the 1970s onward, as assassinations and mass shootings brought the issue to public and academic prominence. While U.S. scholarship has explored the Second Amendment's legal interpretations, its historical and philosophical roots have often been under examined. This work emphasizes both: the long standing dispute over whether the Amendment protects an individual right or a state's right to maintain a militia, and the deeper ideological question of what core principle the Amendment was meant to serve. For the Founding Fathers, the chapter argues, that principle was the basic right of self-defense — a concept they understood in broader and more concrete terms than is common today.

The "states' rights" position interprets the Amendment as protecting state authority to maintain organized militias under their control, rather than granting individuals an unfettered right to own firearms. It rests heavily on Article I, Section 8 of the Constitution, which gives Congress the power to call forth, organize, arm, and discipline the militia, while reserving to the states the appointment of officers and training according to congressional rules. On this view, the "militia" is a collective body, and the right to keep and bear arms is instrumental to its preservation. Government regulation of individual gun ownership is therefore constitutionally unobjectionable. By contrast, the "individual rights" view insists that the Amendment's reference to "the right of the people" matches its use elsewhere in the Bill of Rights to denote personal liberties, and that personal armament is the most effective guarantee of a militia's vitality. Even if the framers intended to safeguard militias, that aim is best achieved by ensuring individual citizens are armed.

The Supreme Court's engagement with the Amendment has been sporadic and, until recently, narrow. In U.S. v. Cruikshank(1875) the Court held that the Second Amendment restricts only federal action, not that of the states, and does not bar regulation of firearms perse. In Presser v. Illinois(1886) the Court upheld a state law restricting unauthorized military drilling, again emphasizing the Amendment's application solely to federal authority. In U.S. v. Miller(1939) the Court sustained a federal restriction on transporting an unregistered short-barreled shotgun across state lines, reasoning that the Amendment protects only arms with a reasonable relation to the preservation or efficiency of a well-regulated militia. None of these cases recognized a free-standing individual right to gun ownership. Meanwhile, the practical role of militias faded; by the early twentieth century, state militias had been replaced by the National Guard, and private citizens no longer served as militia members in the Revolutionary-era sense.

From the 1960s through the 1980s, the states'rights interpretation dominated legal thought, endorsed by influential scholars like Laurence Tribe and organizations such as the ACLU. The individual-rights position gained academic traction with Stuart R. Hays's critique of militia-only interpretations and his framing of the Amendment as encompassing a broader "right of revolution" against tyranny. By the 1980s, surveys of legal scholarship — such as in the Encyclopedia of the American Constitution — showed that most authors favored recognizing the right to keep and bear arms as an individual fundamental right beyond the reach of ordinary regulation. This scholarship often drew on English common law traditions, colonial resistance to British arms seizures, and the Founders' expressed belief in the necessity of an armed populace.

An important modern turning point came with District of Columbia v. Heller (2008). Dick Anthony Heller, a security officer, challenged Washington D.C.'s ban on handgun possession in the home. In a 5–4 decision, the Supreme Court held that the Second Amendment protects an individual's right to possess firearms for lawful purposes such as self-defense within the home, striking down the D.C. law. Justice Antonin Scalia's majority opinion emphasized that the right predated the Amendment's adoption, was recognized historically, and could not be eliminated even in the face of modern gun violence. The dissent, by Justice Stephen Breyer, argued that the right was not absolute and could be subject to regulation in high-crime urban settings. Heller thus shifted the judicial center of gravity toward the individual-rights interpretation, though it left open questions about the permissible scope of regulation.

The chapter devotes substantial attention to the ideological roots of the Amendment in the natural law tradition's conception of self-defense. Locke framed self-defense as an inalienable right, grounded in the preservation of life, liberty, and property, and extending to collective resistance against oppressive government. Cesare Beccaria argued that disarming citizens harms victims more than it deters criminals, likening arms bans to prohibiting water to prevent drowning. Thomas Paine insisted that without arms, the virtuous are at the mercy of the vicious; arms protect not only individuals but the security of society. In the eighteenth-century American context — lacking formal police forces — personal defense was indistinguishable from community defense, and citizens often organized into posses or patrols to maintain order. Montesquieu and others extended the analogy from individual self-defense to the state's right to wage defensive war.

William Blackstone, the great expositor of English common law, treated the right to have arms as an absolute right of individuals, a final safeguard when legal remedies failed, applicable against both criminal violence and political oppression, and even for private purposes such as hunting. The symbolism of arms as a badge of free status dated back to Anglo-Saxon traditions, where freedmen ceremonially received weapons. Historical experience, the Founders believed, showed that tyrants first move to disarm the populace to secure domination. Jefferson urged his nephew to carry a gun as a means of cultivating independence and spirit. Adams and Madison likewise affirmed that the right to arms was essential to liberty.

The narrative also addresses counter arguments that widespread armament fosters disorder. Figures like Timothy Dwight and Joel Barlow replied that oppressive governments, not ordinary citizens, have cause to fear an armed populace, and that disarmament invites abuse. Historical anecdotes, such as Francis Place's account of declining anti-Semitic violence in England after Jewish youths learned boxing, illustrate the deterrent value of defensive capacity.

The revolutionary context reinforced these convictions. British attempts in the 1770s to impose taxes without representation, quarter troops, and disarm colonists — culminating in the Boston Massacre and weapons seizures — convinced Americans that arms were essential to safeguard liberty. The Declaration of Independence crystallized the principle that people have the right to alter or abolish a government destructive of their rights, a principle the Second Amendment would embody in concrete form.

The chapter concludes that the Second Amendment did not create a new right but reaffirmed a preexisting, fundamental right of self-defense that Americans had long exercised under common law and colonial practice. For the Founders, arms were the measure separating liberty from subjugation, a safeguard against both criminal threats and governmental tyranny. While modern conditions differ — professional police forces now exist, and the militia as the framers knew it is gone — crime and the potential for oppression remain. In this light, the right to keep and bear arms retains its character as a basic right, deeply embedded in America's constitutional tradition and political culture, and continues to animate the contentious debate over gun control.

이 편은 미국 연방헌법 수정조항 제2조가 보장하는 "국민이 무기를 소지하고 휴대할 권리"의 연원, 법적 해석, 그리고 이념적 기반을 심층적으로 분석한다. 논의는 미국의 압도적으로 높은 민간 총기 보유율, 빈발하는 총기 범죄, 그리고 대형 총기 참사 이후 반복적으로 격화되는 전국적 논쟁이라는 현실에서 출발한다. 1968년 마틴 루터 킹 목사와 로버트 F. 케네디 상원의원 암살, 1999년 콜럼바인 고등학교 총기 난사와 같은 사건들은 미국 총기 정책에 대한 비판과 재검토를 촉발시킨 계기로 제시된다. 매년 수만 명의 생명을 앗아가는 총기 폭력 속에서, 규제 입법 시도는 곧바로 수정조항 2조의 문구와 충돌하며, 총기 권리 옹호자들은 이를 절대 불가침의 개인 자유로 해석한다.

저자는 '수정헌법'과 '수정조항'의 용어를 엄밀히 구분하며, 미국에는 헌법 원문과 그에 부가된 수정조항만 존재한다는 점을 명확히 한다. 1791년 권리장전의 일부로 채택된 제2조는 영국 관습법과 공화주의 정치사상에서 그 법적 혈통을 찾을 수 있다. 1688년 명예혁명 후 채택된 1689년 영국 권리장전은 의회의 동의 없이 평시 상비군을 유지하는 것을 금지하고, 신민의 자기방어를 위한 무기 보유권을 인정했다. 이러한 전통은 식민지로 건너와 독립전쟁을 거치며 강화되었고, 제퍼슨, 매디슨 등 미국 건국의 아버지들에게 계승되어 수정조항 2조에 구체적으로 성문화되었다.

1970년대 이후 미국에서는 암살과 총기 난동이 사회적 쟁점으로 부각되며 학계와 법조계에서 무기소지권 논의가 활발해졌다. 그러나 국내외 연구들은 법률적 해석에 치중하는 경향이 강했고, 역사적/사상적 배경은 상대적으로 소홀히 다루어졌다. 본 장은 무기소지권 귀속을 둘러싼 '주의 권리' 대 '개인의 권리' 논쟁과, 수정조항 2조의 핵심 이념이 무엇인지에 대한 고찰을 함께 진행한다. 저자는 건국의 아버지들이 제1조의 신앙/표현의 자유에 이어 제2조에 무기소지권을 명시한 근본 목적이 자기방어의 기본권에 있었음을 강조한다.

'주의 권리'론은 제2조를 주정부가 통제하는 민병 유지권 보장으로 해석한다. 헌법 제1조 8절이 연방의회에 민병의 소집/무장/훈련 권한을 부여하되 장교 임명과 훈련은 주에 위임한 점을 근거로, 무기 보유는 집단적 필요에 종속된다고 본다. 반면 '개인의 권리'론은 '국민의 권리'라는 표현이 권리장전 전반에서 개인을 지칭하며, 개인 무장이야말로 민병의 실질적 기반을 지탱한다고 본다. 설령 민병 보호가 주목적이라 해도 그 실현은 시민 개개인의 무장을 통해서 가능하다는 것이다.

연방대법원의 판례는 드물고 제한적이었다. 1875년 *Cruikshank* 판결은 제2조가 연방정부만을 구속하며 주 규제에는 적용되지 않는다고 보았다. 1886년 *Presser* 판결도 주의 군사훈련 제한법을 인정하며 같은 입장을 반복했다. 1939년 *Miller* 판결은 등록되지 않은 단총 운송 금지를 합헌으로 보고, '잘 규율된 민병'과 합리적 연관이 있는 무기만이 보호 대상이라고 했다. 세 판결 모두 개인의 자유로운 총기 소지를 명시적으로 인정하지 않았다. 20세기 초 민병은 주 방위군으로 대체되었고, 개인이 민병 구성원으로 무기를 보유할 실질적 이유는 사라졌다.

1960~80년대에는 주의 권리 해석이 우세했으나, 스튜어트 헤이즈가 민병 한정 해석을 비판하며 제2조를 '국민혁명권'으로 확장 해석하면서 개인 권리론이 부상했다. 1980년대 이후 다수의 학술논문이 개인의 기본권으로서의 무기소지권을 지지했고, 이는 영국 관습법의 시민무장권, 식민지 시절 영국의 무기 몰수 저항, 건국 지도자들의 신념을 근거로 삼았다.

2008년 *Heller* 판결은 분수령이었다. 워싱턴 D.C.의 가정 내 권총 소지를 금지한 법률에 대해 대법원은 5대 4로 위헌을 선고하며, 자기방어 등 합법적 목적의 개인 무기소지권을 인정했다. 스칼리아 대법관은 이 권리가 제정 전부터 역사적으로 인정돼 왔다고 강조했고, 브레이어 대법관은 절대적 권리가 아니라고 반박했다. 판결은 개인 권리 해석을 강화했지만, 규제 가능 범위는 남겨두었다.

이 장은 제2조의 사상적 기원을 자연법상의 자기방어권에서 찾는다. 로크는 생명/자유/재산 보존을 위한 수단으로 자기방어를 규정했고, 베카리아는 무기 금지가 피해자만을 해친다고 비판했다. 페인은 무기 없는 선량한 시민은 악인의 희생물이 된다고 했으며, 18세기 미국에서는 경찰 부재 속에서 개인 방어가 곧 공동체 방어였다. 몽테스키외는 개인 방어와 국가 방위를 동일시했고, 블랙스톤은 무기소지권을 법적 구제가 실패할 때의 최후 수단이자 절대적 권리로 규정했다. 앵글로-색슨 전통에서 무기는 자유 신분의 상징이었고, 폭군은 권력 강화를 위해 국민을 무장 해제했다. 제퍼슨은 무장을 독립심과 기개를 기르는 수단으로 권했고, 애덤스와 매디슨도 자유의 필수 요소로 보았다.

시민 무장이 무질서를 초래한다는 주장에 대해 드와이트와 발로는 억압적 정부만이 무장 시민을 두려워한다고 응수했다. 프란시스 플레이스의 유대인 권투 일화는 방어 능력의 억제 효과를 보여준다. 혁명기의 식민지인들은 영국의 세금과 군 주둔, 무기 몰수에 맞서 무장이 필수임을 깨달았고, 독립선언서는 권리 파괴 정부를 전복할 국민의 권리를 선언했다. 제2조는 이를 구체적 권리로 형상화한 것이다.

결론적으로, 제2조는 새로운 권리를 창설한 것이 아니라 관습법과 식민지 경험 속에서 이미 존재하던 자기방어의 기본권을 재확인한 것이다. 건국 지도자들에게 무기는 자유와 예속을 가르는 척도였으며, 범죄와 폭정 모두에 맞서는 방패였다. 오늘날 민병은 사라지고 경찰력이 존재하지만, 범죄와 권력 남용의 가능성은 여전하다. 이런 맥락에서 무기소지권은 미국 헌정 전통과 정치문화 속에 깊이 뿌리내린 기본권으로서, 총기 규제를 둘러싼 논쟁의 핵심으로 남아 있다.

Chapter 4 (제4편)

This chapter offers a thorough, historically grounded, and legally detailed analysis of the right to keep and bear arms under the Second Amendment to the United

States Constitution, with particular attention to how that right has been interpreted by courts, especially the U.S. Supreme Court, in relation to contemporary gun control legislation. It begins by framing the issue in the urgent context of modern America's ongoing gun violence crisis. The catalyst is the horrific mass shooting on May 24, 2022, at Robb Elementary School in Uvalde, Texas, where an eighteen-year-old gunman murdered nineteen children and two teachers and injured seventeen others. This event, combined with the sobering statistic that in the first half of 2022 alone more than 1,350 people had been killed or injured in mass shootings in the United States, intensified calls for stricter regulation. Surveys indicated that a growing majority of Americans — 70 percent in one poll — prioritize new gun control measures over preserving unrestricted gun rights. Yet, these public sentiments collide with entrenched political opposition from the National Rifle Association(NRA), one of the most influential lobbying organizations in U.S. politics, and many Republican lawmakers. For them, the Second Amendment's guarantee of the right to bear arms is not just a historical relic but a constitutional bulwark that cannot be compromised, even in the face of recurring tragedies.

From there, the chapter turns to the historical and intellectual origins of the Second Amendment. The starting point is England's long-standing distrust of standing armies, which were seen as instruments of monarchical power and potential vehicles for tyranny. In that political culture, the defense of the realm and the maintenance of public order were entrusted instead to citizen militias. This arrangement was rooted in centuries-old common law traditions, which recognized the bearing of arms not merely as a military necessity but as a basic individual right. In Anglo-Saxon custom, the conferral of arms marked the transition from slavery to freedom, symbolizing the status of a free person endowed with rights. By the late seventeenth century, amid political upheavals like the Glorious Revolution, this right was given explicit statutory recognition in the English Bill of Rights of 1689, which barred the maintenance of a standing army in peacetime without parliamentary consent and affirmed that subjects could possess arms for self-defense. Political philosophers such as John Locke gave this right a theoretical foundation in the natural law tradition. In *Two Treatises of Government*, Locke argued that sovereignty derives from the people, government exists to secure their fundamental rights, and citizens have the right — indeed the duty — to resist oppressive rulers, even by force if necessary. Arms possession was, in this framework, the ultimate safeguard of life, liberty, and property. William Blackstone, in his *Commentaries on the Laws of England*, went further by classifying the right to have arms as both a means of securing absolute rights and itself an absolute right, a final remedy when other legal protections fail.

The American colonists inherited these traditions. The British Crown's promises that emigrants would enjoy the full rights of English subjects, including the right to arms, were part of the appeal of settlement in the New World. In the vast and sparsely governed colonies, firearms were indispensable: they protected against Native American raids, criminal violence, and wild animals, and were essential for hunting to supplement limited food supplies. The colonies lacked professional armies and formal police forces; law enforcement functions were carried out by local militias, posses, and sheriffs. Over time, British measures to tighten imperial control — stationing troops, quartering soldiers in civilian homes, and confiscating colonial arms — heightened fears of subjugation. The colonists' resolve to preserve their right to arms crystallized in 1775 when the First Continental Congress adopted a declaration on the necessity of taking up arms. After independence, most state constitutions incorporated explicit guarantees of the right to bear arms. The distrust of standing armies persisted into the drafting of the U.S. Constitution. Although Article I, Section 8, gave Congress the power to call forth and regulate militias, Anti-Federalists feared that without an explicit guarantee, militias would be dissolved and replaced by a national standing army loyal to federal power. Ratification was achieved only after Federalists promised to adopt a Bill of Rights, with the Second Amendment among its provisions. James Madison's initial proposal included a conscientious objector clause, but the final text combined the militia rationale and the individual right in a single sentence: "A well regulated Militia, being necessary to the security of a free State, the right of the people to keep and bear Arms shall not be infringed."

From its adoption, the Second Amendment has been understood in two fundamentally different ways. The "states' rights" interpretation emphasizes the prefatory clause, reading the Amendment as securing the authority of state governments to maintain and regulate organized militias, not as granting individuals a broad constitutional right to own firearms. Under this view, "the people" is a collective entity, and the right exists only within the context of service in a state-regulated military body. The "individual rights" interpretation, by contrast, focuses on the operative clause's explicit reference to "the right of the people," consistent with other provisions of the Bill of Rights that denote personal rights. On this reading, the Amendment protects individual ownership and use of firearms for lawful purposes, including but not limited to militia service.

For much of its history, the U.S. Supreme Court adhered to the states' rights view. In *United States v. Cruikshank*(1875), the Court held that the Second Amendment restricted only federal action, not state regulation, and did not create an unqualified individual right. *Presser v. Illinois*(1886) upheld state limits on unauthorized military drilling, again tying the Amendment to the militia context. *United States v. Miller*(1939) sustained a federal prohibition on transporting an unregistered short-barreled shotgun across state lines, reasoning that the Second Amendment protected only arms with a reasonable relationship to the preservation or efficiency of a well-regulated militia. In these decisions, the Court did not recognize an enforceable personal right to arms outside the militia framework.

This interpretive landscape changed dramatically with *District of Columbia v. Heller*(2008). Confronting a D.C. law that banned handgun possession and required lawful firearms in the home to be kept unloaded and disabled, the Court split 5–4. Writing for the majority, Justice Antonin Scalia distinguished between the Amendment's prefatory clause, which states a purpose, and its operative clause, which states a right. He concluded that "the right of the people" denotes an individual right, as in the First and Fourth Amendments, and that "keep and bear Arms" historically encompassed possession and carrying for self-defense, not solely for military service. The Court stressed that the right is not unlimited — laws barring possession by felons or the mentally ill, restricting guns in sensitive places, or regulating commercial sales remain valid — but held that a categorical ban on functional handguns in the home violates the Second Amendment under any level of scrutiny. The dissenters, led by Justices Stevens and Breyer, argued that the Amendment was intended to protect state militias, not to constitutionalize a broad self-defense right, and defended the D.C. law as a proportionate response to urban gun violence.

Two years later, in *McDonald v. City of Chicago*(2010), the Court addressed whether the Second Amendment applies to state and local governments. In another 5–4 decision, Justice Samuel Alito's majority opinion held that the right recognized in *Heller* is fundamental to the American scheme of ordered liberty and deeply rooted in the nation's history and tradition, and thus applies to the states via the Fourteenth Amendment's Due Process Clause. Justice Clarence Thomas concurred in the result but argued for incorporation through the Privileges or Immunities Clause, which he viewed as more faithful to the original understanding of the Fourteenth Amendment. The dissenters contended that the right was not fundamental in the constitutional sense and warned against imposing uniform federal standards that limit state regulatory autonomy.

The chapter notes the significance of these decisions in shifting the Court's stance from more than a century of states'rights orthodoxy to an individual rights doctrine that constrains both federal and state laws. However, important questions remain unresolved. Neither *Heller* nor *McDonald* articulated a clear standard of review for evaluating gun regulations, leaving lower courts to apply intermediate scrutiny, strict scrutiny, or other tests inconsistently. The scope of permissible regulation of weapons beyond handguns, restrictions on carrying firearms outside the home, and the constitutionality of many existing laws are still contested.

An important methodological point is that both the *Heller* majority and the principal dissent invoked originalism, interpreting the Amendment in light of its text and the public meaning at the time of its adoption, yet they emphasized different historical evidence and reached opposite conclusions. Scalia focused on founding-era linguistic usage, analogous state constitutional provisions, and early commentary, while Stevens emphasized militia-related history and structural considerations. This divergence within a shared interpretive framework underscores the role of judicial value judgments in constitutional adjudication.

The chapter also places these debates within the larger context of incorporation doctrine. Originally, the Bill of Rights applied only to the federal government; it was the Fourteenth Amendment's Due Process Clause that became the vehicle for applying most of these protections to the states. While *Heller* did not decide the incorporation question, *McDonald* did, extending the Second Amendment's individual right to state and local governments. The majority's reasoning reaffirmed that self-defense is central to the right and that this right is intertwined with America's historical experience of civilian arms-bearing.

In conclusion, the chapter emphasizes that for most of American constitutional history, the Supreme Court interpreted the Second Amendment as protecting only state authority over militias. The *Heller* decision in 2008 redefined it as safeguarding an individual right to possess functional firearms for lawful purposes such as self-defense in the home, and *McDonald* in 2010 extended that protection to the states. Yet the boundaries of the right are still being defined, and the Court has not settled on a uniform standard for assessing the constitutionality of gun regulations.

The author anticipates that future jurisprudence will refine these standards within an originalist interpretive framework. Finally, while South Korea currently has no constitutional right to keep and bear arms, the American experience — particularly the judicial reasoning in *Heller* and *McDonald* — may offer valuable comparative insights should such a debate arise in the Korean context, illustrating how courts balance constitutional text, historical meaning, and contemporary public safety concerns.

이 편은 미국 연방헌법 수정헌법 제2조가 보장하는 무기소지권의 역사적 기원, 해석상의 쟁점, 그리고 현대 총기규제와의 관계를 종합적으로 고찰한다. 특히 미국 연방대법원의 판례를 중심으로, 이 권리가 어떻게 이해되고 있는지, 그리고 총기규제법의 합헌성 심사와 어떤 연관을 갖는지를 심층적으로 분석한다. 논의의 출발점은 2022년 5월 24일 텍사스주 유발디(Uvalde) 롭 초등학교에서 발생한 총기 난사 사건이다. 당시 18세 청년이 학생 19명과 교사 2명을 살해하고 17명을 부상시킨 이 사건은 미국 전역에 충격을 주었고, 이미 매일 10여 명 이상이 총기 난사로 사상당하는 현실을 더욱 부각시켰다. 올해 상반기에만 1,350명 이상이 총기 난사로 죽거나 다친 것으로 집계되었으며, 여론조사 결과 미국인 70%가 총기소유권보다 새로운 총기규제법 제정을 우선해야 한다고 응답했다. 그러나 NRA(미국총기협회)와 이를 지지하는 공화당 정치인들은 수정헌법 제2조의 무기소지권을 내세워 규제에 반대하고 있다. 따라서 핵심적인 질문은 포괄적 총기규제가 반드시 헌법상 권리 침해로 귀결되는지 여부다.

저자는 먼저 수정헌법 제2조의 역사적/사상적 배경을 추적한다. 영국에서는 상비군이 국왕의 권력과 전제정치의 도구로 인식되어 오랫동안 불신의 대상이었다. 그 대신 시민들이 자발적으로 무장한 민병대가 국방과 치안 유지의 기능을 맡았다. 이러한 전통 속에서 무기소지권은 종교의 자유보다도 먼저 관습법으로 자리 잡았으며, 무기는 자유인의 신분을 상징하는 표지였다. 앵글로-색슨 시대에는 노예가 해방될 때 무기를 부여하는 의식이 있었고, 이는 자유와 권리의 회복을 상징했다. 17세기 말 명예혁명 이후 제정된 1689년 영국 권리장전은 평시 의회 동의 없는 상비군 유지 금지와 함께 신민의 자기방어용 무기소지권을 명문화했다. 존 로크는 『통치론』에서 국민이 생명 · 자유 · 재산을 지키기 위해 전제정부에 무력으로 저항할 권리를 강조했고, 윌리엄 블랙스톤은 『영국법 주해』에서 무기소지권을 절대적 권리이자 다른 절대적 권리를 수호하는 최종 수단으로 규정했다.

이러한 전통은 북미 식민지에 그대로 이식되었다. 영국 정부는 이주민과 그 자녀가 영국인의 모든 권리를 누린다고 약속했고, 치안이 취약한 신대륙에서 총기는 생존을 위해 필수적이었다. 원주민의 공격, 범죄, 야생동물로부터의 방어뿐 아니라 사냥을 통한 식량 확보에도 필요했다. 상비군이나 전문 경찰이 없던 시절, 건강한 성인 남성들이 자경단이나 보안관 역할을 하며 치안을 유지했다. 그러나 18세기 후반 영국은 식민지를 통제하기 위해 무기 몰수와 군 주둔을 확대했고, 이는 식민지인들에게 무기소지권이 자유를 지키는 핵심이라는 인식을 심어주었다. 1775년 대륙회의는 무장 선언을 채택했고, 독립선언 이후 다수의 주 헌법에 무기소지권이 명문화되었다. 연방헌법 제정 과정에서 연방주의자와 반연방주의자는 모두 무기소지권의 중요성에는 동의했지만, 이를 헌법에 명시할지 여부에서는 갈렸다. 결국 권리장전 채택을 조건으로 연방헌법이 비준되었고, 매디슨이 제안한 초안은 일부 수정되어 1791년 비준된 최종 제2조는 민병대 필요성과 개인의 권리를 결합한 형태로 명문화되었다.

그러나 해석에서는 '주의 권리'론과 '개인의 권리'론이 대립해왔다. '주의 권리'론은 "규율 있는 민병대"라는 문구를 강조해, 주정부가 조직/규율하는 민병대의 집단적 총기소유권만을 보장한다고 본다. 이에 따르면 '국민의 권리'는 집단 개념이며, 개인의 무기소유는 헌법상 보장되지 않는다. 반면 '개인의 권리'론은 '국민의 권리'가 권리장전 전반에서 개인권을 의미한다는 점에 주목해, 자기방어 등 민병대 외 목적의 무기소지도 보호된다고 본다.

연방대법원은 오랫동안 전자의 입장을 취했다. *Cruikshank*(1875)와 *Presser*(1886)에서 제2조는 연방정부만 구속하며 개인의 권리를 창설하지 않는다고 판시했고, *Miller*(1939)에서는 '잘 규율된 민병대'와 합리적 관련이 있는 무기만 보호된다고 보았다. 그러나 2008년 *Heller* 판결에서 대법원은 5대 4로 입장을 전환했다. 워싱턴 D.C.의 권총 전면 금지와 가정 내 방아쇠 잠금장치 의무를 위헌으로 판단하며, 민병대 복무와 무관한 개인의 무기소지권을 인정한 것이다. 스칼리아 다수의견은 서론부와 본문부를 구분하고, '국민의 권리'를 개인권으로 해석했으며, 'keep and bear arms'를 자기방어용 무기를 포함하는 역사적 개념으로 보았다. 다만 범죄자/정신질

환자의 소지 제한, 민감 장소 휴대 금지, 상업 판매 규제 등은 합헌 범위로 인정했다. 반대의견은 역사적으로 제2조의 목적이 민병대 보호였음을 강조하며, D.C. 법이 도시 범죄에 대한 합리적 대응이라고 주장했다.

2010년 *McDonald* 판결은 5대 4로 제2조를 수정헌법 제14조의 적법절차조항을 통해 주와 지방정부에도 적용된다고 판시했다. 알리토 다수의견은 자기방어권이 미국 역사와 전통에 깊이 뿌리내린 기본권이라고 보고, 이를 편입해 주법에도 적용해야 한다고 했다. 토머스는 특권/면책조항을 통한 편입이 더 적절하다고 주장했다. 반대의견은 무기소지권이 헌법상 근본권이 아니며, 각 주가 규제 자율성을 가져야 한다고 강조했다.

이 두 판결은 100여 년간 지속된 '주의 권리' 중심 해석을 '개인의 권리' 중심으로 전환시켰지만, 합헌성 심사의 구체적 기준은 제시하지 않았다. 하급심은 중간심사, 엄격심사 등 다양한 기준을 적용하고 있으며, 권총 외 무기, 공공장소 휴대, 기타 규제에 대한 판단은 여전히 남아 있다. 흥미로운 점은 다수/반대 모두 원의주의적 해석을 사용했지만, 인용하는 역사 자료와 강조점이 달라 결론이 갈렸다는 것이다. 다수의견은 제정 당시 언어 용례, 주헌법 규정, 초기 주석 등을 근거로 개인권을 강조했고, 반대의견은 민병대 역사와 구조적 논리를 중시했다.

장 후반부는 편입이론을 설명한다. 권리장전은 원래 연방정부만 구속했으나, 제14조 적법절차조항이 기본권을 주에도 적용시키는 통로가 되었다. *Heller*는 편입 여부를 다루지 않았지만, *McDonald*는 이를 인정하며 제2조 권리를 주법에도 적용시켰다. 다수의견은 자기방어권이 '질서 있는 자유' 체계에서 근본적 권리이자 미국 역사에 깊이 뿌리내린 권리임을 강조했고, 규제 위헌 여부 판단은 하급심에 환송했다. 토머스는 절차조항 대신 특권·면책조항을 통한 편입이 옳다고 보았다. 반대의견은 무기소지권이 본질적 자유가 아니라고 보았고, 총기규제 문제는 민주적 절차를 통해 주와 지방자치단체가 결정해야 한다고 주장했다.

결론적으로, 연방대법원은 오랫동안 제2조를 주정부 민병대 권한 보장 조항으로 보았으나, *Heller*는 이를 개인의 권리로 재해석했고, *McDonald*는 적용범위를 주정부로 확장했다. 그러나 심사기준 부재와 미해결 쟁점으로 인해 권리의 경계는 여전히 형성 중이다. 향후 판례는 원의주의 해석 틀 속에서 규제 허용범위를 구체화할 가능성이 크다. 한국은 총기소지 자유가 없지만, 향후 유사한 논의가 발생한다면 미국 판례는 헌법 해석과 공공안전의 균형이라는 측면에서 중요한 비교법적 시사점을 제공할 수 있다.

Chapter 5 (제5편)

The chapter delivers a comprehensive and deeply contextualized discussion of the meaning, history, and legal framework of civilian gun control and oversight, focusing on the South Korean system while drawing extensively on the American experience to identify weaknesses and suggest reforms. It begins by recounting a series of alarming firearm incidents that shook South Korea in early 2015, including shootings in Sejong City, Hwaseong, Okcheon, and Gimpo. In these cases, civilian-held firearms — often hunting rifles or air guns — were taken from storage, sometimes under the pretense of legal use, and then employed in deadly assaults on neighbors, family members, or bystanders. The events left multiple people dead or injured and sent waves of anxiety through the public. Such incidents are particularly troubling because Korea, unlike the United States, does not have a widespread civilian gun culture and already maintains comparatively strict controls under the "Guns, Swords, and Explosives Control Act." The law imposes a licensing system, prohibits certain categories of individuals from owning firearms, and requires all licensed civilian guns to be stored at police facilities, only to be checked out temporarily for specific lawful uses such as hunting or sport shooting. Even so, these safeguards have proved inadequate, as dangerous individuals have been able to retrieve firearms and commit violent crimes. In response to these tragedies, the National Assembly passed an amendment to the Act in February 2015, tightening some provisions, but the chapter argues that far deeper and more systematic reform is necessary to ensure public safety and fulfill constitutional obligations.

The work first clarifies what is meant by "civilian gun control and supervision." Civilian firearms, under Korean law, include pistols, rifles, shotguns, machine guns, air guns, and other lethal weapons capable of killing or seriously injuring. Control and supervision refer to the set of legal and administrative measures by which the state licenses, monitors, stores, and regulates such weapons in private hands, with the aim of preventing accidents, intentional killings, threats, and mass shootings. Because firearm misuse can cause irreversible harm, the constitutional right to life demands rigorous preventive oversight. The state's duty extends beyond protecting citizens from governmental abuse to shielding them from violence perpetrated by other private individuals. This constitutional duty to maintain safety and order binds both the legislature, which must create effective laws, and the executive, which must enforce them diligently. Article 37(2) of the Korean Constitution explicitly permits the restriction of freedoms and rights by law when necessary for national security, order maintenance, or public welfare—conditions easily met in the case of gun regulation.

The chapter then turns to the historical and philosophical background that informs modern gun regulation debates, beginning in England. Deep distrust of standing armies, which were viewed as tools of royal oppression, led to reliance on citizen militias. This tradition was supported by the English Bill of Rights of 1689, which not only forbade the maintenance of a standing army in peacetime without Parliament's consent but also affirmed the right of Protestant subjects to have arms for their defense. Arms possession was not only a means of resisting tyranny but also a badge of free status, symbolizing a citizen's rights and duties. In Anglo-Saxon practice, freedmen received weapons as a mark of liberty. By the seventeenth century, political thinkers like John Locke incorporated arms possession into the natural law right of self-defense, emphasizing the people's right to resist oppression. William Blackstone further described the right to have arms as an "absolute right," both as a tool to preserve life, liberty, and property, and as an ultimate safeguard when other legal protections failed.

This tradition crossed the Atlantic with the colonists and became embedded in American political culture. In the remote and lightly governed colonies, firearms were indispensable for personal protection, hunting, and community defense. There were no professional police forces or standing armies to maintain local security; instead, able-bodied men served in militias, posses, or as constables. British attempts in the 1770s to impose taxes without representation, quarter troops in civilian homes, and confiscate colonial arms intensified fears of subjugation. The colonists responded by forming militias and, in 1775, the First Continental Congress adopted a declaration on the necessity of taking up arms. After independence, most state constitutions included explicit protections for the right to bear arms. When the U.S. Constitution was drafted, Federalists and Anti-Federalists differed on the balance of national and state power, but both valued the militia system as a check on tyranny. The Second Amendment, ratified in 1791, combined a statement of militia necessity with a guarantee that "the right of the people to keep and bear Arms shall not be infringed."

In the United States, interpretation of the Second Amendment has long been divided. The "collective rights" view ties the right to the maintenance of state-regulated militias, while the "individual rights" view sees it as protecting personal firearm possession for self-defense and other lawful purposes. For more than a century, the U.S. Supreme Court favored the militia-focused interpretation. In *United States v. Cruikshank*(1875), the Court held that the Second Amendment limited only federal action, not state regulation. In *Presser v. Illinois*(1886), it upheld a state ban on unauthorized military drilling. In *United States v. Miller*(1939), it sustained a federal law restricting interstate transport of unregistered short-barreled shotguns, reasoning that the Amendment protected only arms with a reasonable relationship to a well-regulated militia. It was not until *District of Columbia v. Heller*(2008) that the Court recognized an individual right to possess firearms for self-defense in the home, striking down a D.C. handgun ban and certain storage requirements. Justice Antonin Scalia's majority opinion distinguished between the Amendment's prefatory clause and operative clause, concluded that "the right of the people" denotes individual rights, and held that this right extends to weapons commonly used for lawful purposes. In *McDonald v. City of Chicago*(2010), the Court incorporated this right against the states via the Fourteenth Amendment, emphasizing that self-defense is a fundamental right deeply rooted in American history.

Despite these rulings, the chapter notes that the United States continues to grapple with extreme gun violence. Civilian-owned firearms exceed the U.S. population, and mass shootings occur regularly in schools, workplaces, and public spaces. Legislative efforts to impose universal background checks, restrict assault weapons, and strengthen mental health reporting have repeatedly failed at the federal level, often due to NRA opposition and partisan gridlock, though some states have enacted their own stricter measures. The American experience demonstrates both the resilience of constitutional rights in the face of regulation and the persistent challenges of reconciling those rights with public safety.

From these observations, the author extracts key lessons for Korea's civilian gun control regime. First, loosening standards for gun possession or access can rapidly increase the risk of shootings; therefore, licensing, manufacturing, import, and storage requirements should be rigorously enforced and, where necessary, tightened. Second, gaps between constitutional norms and practical realities must be addressed by adapting oversight systems to evolving social and technological conditions. Third, illegal manufacturing, smuggling, and online sales must be targeted with aggressive enforcement and heavier penalties. Fourth, technological advances like 3D printing make it easier to produce firearms at home, requiring preemptive regulation of manufacturing methods and strict quality standards. Fifth, police staffing for gun supervision should be scaled proportionately to the number of civilian firearms in circulation. Sixth, systems for tracking, inspecting, and confiscating illegal firearms should be continuously improved, including voluntary surrender programs and regular audits of licensed firearms. Seventh, public education programs, especially for licensed hunters and sport shooters, should be expanded to promote legal compliance and safe handling.

The chapter's analysis of Korea's "Guns, Swords, and Explosives Control Act" identifies several shortcomings. While the law requires licensing, police storage of civilian guns, and penalties for violations, the actual vetting of applicants is often superficial, storage facilities are inadequate, record keeping is inconsistent, and dangerous individuals can sometimes retrieve firearms under legitimate pretenses. The author recommends raising the minimum age for gun ownership, permanently banning ownership by those with histories of violent crime, attaching GPS tracking devices to civilian firearms, imposing limits on the total number of guns an individual can own, fostering cooperation between police and civil organizations, requiring guarantors and psychological evaluations for firearm release, increasing penalties for gun crimes, and expanding the physical capacity for secure storage and inspections.

Ultimately, the chapter argues that because gun violence threatens the most basic constitutional right — the right to life — and imposes immense social costs, Korea must adopt a preventive approach to civilian gun control. Strengthening oversight under the Guns, Swords, and Explosives Control Act is essential to ensuring that firearms are used only for lawful, safe purposes and that the public can trust in the security of their communities. The American experience shows both the dangers of insufficient regulation and the complexity of balancing individual rights with collective safety. By combining strong preventive rules, effective enforcement, and adaptive regulation to meet emerging threats, Korea can create a system of civilian gun control that both protects constitutional rights and safeguards public order.

이 편은 대한민국의 민간 총기관리/감독 제도의 헌법적 의미와 역사적 배경, 그리고 현행 법제의 문제점을 진단하며, 미국의 총기관리 사례를 심층적으로 분석해 우리나라 법제 개선에 적용할 수 있는 시사점을 제시한다. 서두에서는 2015년 초에 연이어 발생한 충격적인 총기사건들이 언급된다. 세종시, 화성시, 옥천군, 김포시 등에서 발생한 사건들은 모두 민간이 소지한 엽총이나 공기총이 사용된 경우였으며, 이 과정에서 다수의 사망자와 부상자가 발생했다. 특히 경찰이 관리하는 보관창고에서 총기를 인출한 뒤 살인이나 협박에 사용한 사례들이 국민을 경악하게 했다. 현행 「총포/도검/화약류 등 단속법」은 일정 연령 미만자, 마약/알코올 중독자, 금고 이상 형 집행 종료 후 3년 미만 경과자 등의 총기 소지를 금지하고, 허가된 총기는 경찰관서에 보관하도록 규정하고 있음에도, 이러한 사고가 반복된다는 것은 제도 운영과 집행에 심각한 허점이 존재한다는 것을 보여준다. 2015년 2월 국회는 일부 규정을 강화하는 개정안을 통과시켰지만, 저자는 단편적 조치로는 총기사고를 예방할 수 없으며, 헌법상 생명권 보장과 질서유지 의무를 실현하기 위해서는 보다 전면적이고 체계적인 제도 개선이 필요하다고 강조한다.

저자는 먼저 '민간 총기관리/감독'의 개념을 명확히 한다. 우리 법에서 총기는 권총, 소총, 기관총, 엽총, 공기총, 그 밖에 사람을 살상할 수 있는 무기 전반을 포함한다. 민간 총기관리/감독이란 국가가 민간이 소지하는 이러한 살상 무기를 허가/저장/점검/규제하는 모든 절차를 의미하며, 목적은 살인, 협박, 무차별 난사와 같은 범죄를 예방하는 데 있다. 총기 사고는 단순한 부상이나 재산 피해를 넘어 생명을 위협하는 경우가 대부분이며, 일단 생명을 잃으면 회복할 수 없다는 점에서 사전 예방의 중요성은 아무리 강조해도 지나치지 않다. 헌법 제37조 제2항은 국가안전보장, 질서유지, 공공복리를 위해 필요할 경우 법률로 자유와 권리를 제한할 수 있다고 규정하며, 이는 총기규제의 헌법적 근거를 제공한다. 국가의 의무는 국민을 정부 권력의 남용으로부터 보호하는 데 그치지 않고, 타인의 불법행위나 폭력으로부터도 보호하는 것을 포함한다. 따라서 입법부는 효과적인 법률을 제정하고, 행정부는 이를 철저히 집행할 헌법적 의무를 진다.

이어 저자는 총기관리의 역사적 · 사상적 기원을 영국에서 찾는다. 영국은 오랫동안 상비군을 왕권 강화와 전제정치의 수단으로 인식하며 불신했고, 그 대신 무장한 시민 민병대가 국방과 치안을 맡았다. 이러한 전통은 1689년 '권리장전'에 반영되어,

의회의 동의 없이 평시 상비군을 유지하는 것을 금지하고, 신민의 자기방어를 위한 무기소지권을 명문화했다. 무기는 단순한 군사적 도구가 아니라 자유인의 지위를 상징하는 표식이었고, 앵글로색슨 관습법에서는 노예가 해방될 때 무기를 수여하는 의식이 있었다. 17세기 철학자 존 로크는 『통치론』에서 무기소지권을 자연권으로서의 자기방어권에 포함시키며, 국민이 생명/자유/재산을 수호하기 위해 전제정권에 저항할 권리를 이론적으로 정립했다. 윌리엄 블랙스톤 역시 『영국법 주해』에서 무기소지권을 다른 절대적 권리를 보호하는 수단이자 그것 자체로 절대적 권리로 규정했다.

이 전통은 식민지 시대의 북미로 이식되었다. 광활하고 치안이 불안정한 식민지에서 총기는 생존을 위해 필수적이었다. 원주민 공격, 범죄, 야생동물 위협으로부터 자신과 가족을 지키는 수단이었고, 식량 확보를 위한 사냥에도 필수였다. 당시에는 상비군이나 전문 경찰이 없었으므로, 성인 남성들이 민병대, 자경단, 보안관 등의 형태로 치안을 담당했다. 18세기 후반 영국이 무기 몰수, 군 주둔, 대표 없는 과세를 강화하자 식민지인들의 무장권 수호 의지는 더욱 강해졌다. 1775년 제1차 대륙회의는 '무장을 들 수밖에 없는 이유에 관한 선언'을 채택했고, 독립 이후 대부분의 주 헌법은 무기소지권을 명문화했다. 미국 연방헌법 제정 과정에서 연방주의자와 반연방주의자는 중앙정부와 주정부 권한 배분을 놓고 대립했지만, 무장 민병대의 필요성에는 동의했다. 그 결과 1791년 비준된 수정헌법 제2조는 "질서정연한 민병대"의 필요성과 "국민의 무기 보유 · 휴대권"을 결합한 문구로 채택되었다.

그러나 미국에서는 이 조항의 해석을 둘러싸고 오랫동안 '집단권' 해석과 '개인권' 해석이 대립했다. 전자는 무기소지권을 주정부가 규율하는 민병대의 집단적 권리로 본다. 후자는 이를 개인의 자기방어와 기타 합법적 목적을 위한 권리로 본다. 연방대법원은 19세기 후반과 20세기 전반 대부분의 기간 동안 전자의 입장을 취했다. *Cruikshank*(1875) 판결은 제2조가 연방정부만 구속한다고 보았고, *Presser*(1886)는 무허가 군사훈련을 금지한 주법을 합헌으로 인정했으며, *Miller*(1939)는 '잘 규율된 민병대'와 합리적 관련이 있는 무기만 보호된다고 판시했다. 그러나 2008년 Heller 판결에서 대법원은 워싱턴 D.C.의 권총 전면 금지와 방아쇠 잠금장치의무를 위헌으로 판단하며, 민병대 복무와 무관한 개인의 자기방어용 무기소지권을 인정했다. 스칼리아 다수의견은 서문과 본문을 구분해 해석하며, '국민의 권리'가 제1 · 4조에서처럼 개인권을 의미한다고 밝혔다. 2010년 *McDonald* 판결은 이 권리를 수정헌법 제14조의 적법절차조항을 통해 주와 지방정부에도 적용했다.

미국은 이러한 판례 변화에도 불구하고 총기 폭력이 심각하다. 민간 보유 총기 수는 인구 수를 초과하며, 학교 · 공공장소에서의 총기난사가 매년 발생한다. 연방 차원에서 보편적 신원조회, 공격형 무기 제한, 정신건강 보고 강화 등의 입법이 시도되었지만, NRA의 로비와 정치적 반목으로 무산된 경우가 많았다. 일부 주, 예를 들어 캘리포니아주는 가족이 법원에 위험 인물의 총기 일시 압수 명령을 청구할 수 있는 제도를 도입하는 등 자체 규제를 강화했다.

저자는 이러한 미국 사례에서 한국이 배워야 할 교훈을 도출한다. 첫째, 총기 규제 완화는 사고 증가로 직결되므로 제조/수입/허가/보관 규제를 강화해야 한다. 둘째, 헌법규범과 현실 간의 괴리를 줄이기 위해 사회/기술 변화에 대응하는 제도 개선이 필요하다. 셋째, 불법 제조/수입/온라인 거래에 대한 단속과 처벌을 강화해야 한다. 넷째, 3D 프린팅과 같은 기술로 인해 총기 제작이 용이해진 만큼 사전 통제와 품질 기준 설정이 필요하다. 다섯째, 민간 보유 총기 수에 비례해 총기관리 경찰 인력을 확충해야 한다. 여섯째, 불법 총기 추적/압수/회수 시스템을 지속적으로 개선하고, 자진 신고와 정기 점검을 병행해야한다. 일곱째, 수렵 허가자 등 합법 소지자를 대상으로 법규 준수와 안전 수칙 교육을 강화해야 한다.

또한 저자는 「총포/도검/화약류 등 단속법」의 허가/제조/판매/보관/점검/벌칙 규정을 면밀히 분석하며, 허가 심사의 부실, 보관시설 부족, 수입/제조 관리의 미흡, 기록관리의 부정확, 위험 인물에 대한 총기 반출 허용 등 문제를 지적한다. 이를 해결하기 위해 최소 소지 연령 상향, 폭력범죄 전과자의 영구적 소지 제한, 총기 GPS 부착, 개인 소지 총기 수 제한, 민간단체와의협력, 보증인 동행과 심리검사 의무화, 총기 범죄 형량 강화, 보관/점검시설 확충 등을 제안한다.

결론적으로, 총기범죄는 헌법상 생명권을 직접적으로 침해하고 사회적 비용을 초래하므로, 한국의 총기관리 정책은 사전 예방 중심으로 전환되어야 한다. 「총포/도검/화약류 등 단속법」을 강화하고, 강력한 규제와 집행, 변화하는 환경에 대한 유연한 대응을 결합하여, 합법적/안전한 총기 사용 환경을 조성하는 것이 국가의 의무다. 미국의 경험은 규제가 미흡할 경우 발생하는 위험과, 개인권과 공공안전의 균형이라는 복잡한 과제를 동시에 보여주며, 한국이 보다 안정적이고 안전한 사회를 만들기 위한 방향성을 제공한다.

Chapter 6 (제6편)

This chapter undertakes an extensive empirical investigation into the factors that influence whether an active shooting incident develops into a mass murder, focusing on the context of the United States and drawing on detailed data collected over nearly two decades. It defines "active shooting" as an event in which an offender engages in killing or attempting to kill people in a populated area using firearms, without a clear time limit, and with the potential for multiple casualties before intervention by law enforcement or others can stop the assault. The authors situate the study within the disturbing trend of rising active shooter incidents in the United States, noting that despite high-profile public debates and numerous policy proposals, such incidents have increased substantially, both in absolute numbers and in frequency. This trend is evidenced by FBI data showing that active shooter events have risen year after year, with a particularly sharp increase from 2020 to 2021 — ABC News reported a 50% jump in just that period. These incidents occur across varied settings — schools, workplaces, places of worship, commercial venues, and entertainment facilities — and can involve a wide range of perpetrators, from disgruntled employees and students to ideologically motivated assailants and individuals acting on personal grievances or in mental health crises.

The introduction emphasizes that active shootings, by their very nature, create the potential for mass casualties within minutes. This is due to the lethal efficiency of firearms, the density of potential targets in public spaces, and often, the element of surprise. The authors underline that understanding the factors that tip an active shooting toward mass murder is critical for designing effective prevention and mitigation strategies. Unlike many other forms of violent crime, active shootings often lack an immediate precipitating conflict between offender and victim; instead, they may involve strangers targeted solely because of their presence at a location chosen by the offender. This randomness increases public fear and the symbolic impact of such attacks.

The literature review synthesizes a broad body of scholarship on mass shootings and related forms of violence. Studies consistently confirm that firearms enable offenders to inflict far greater harm in a shorter period compared to other weapons, with higher rates of fatality and injury per incident. Research indicates that around one-third of mass shootings in the U.S. occur in designated "gun-free zones," although the interpretation of this statistic is contentious — critics note that such zones are often large public spaces where people congregate, making them attractive targets regardless of gun policy. Additional studies focus on mental illness, grievance accumulation, and situational triggers such as recent job loss, interpersonal conflict, or perceived injustice. The review also discusses the role of the media: extensive, sensational coverage of active shooters can, according to agenda-setting and attribution theories, inadvertently glamorize offenders and inspire copycat attacks, especially when attackers' names and manifestos are widely publicized.

The chapter engages with criminological and sociological theories that have been applied to explain such incidents. Social integration theory(Durkheim) considers the breakdown of social bonds and the resulting alienation as a driver of deviance. Social disorganization theory(Shaw & McKay) links crime rates to neighborhood instability and weakened informal controls. Strain theory (Merton) interprets mass violence as an extreme response to the gap between societal goals and legitimate means of achieving them. Routine activities theory(Cohen & Felson) emphasizes the convergence of motivated offenders, suitable targets, and absence of capable guardians in time and space. Other perspectives focus on situational opportunity structures, the availability and lethality of weapons, and the specific settings of attacks.

From this theoretical base, the study identifies four main variables hypothesized to significantly affect whether an active shooting results in mass murder. First is whether the offender commits suicide during or immediately after the attack. Prior research by Lankford(2012) found that approximately 96% of mass public shooters either commit suicide or attempt to do so, and suicide attempts often coincide with an intention to cause maximum harm before dying. The study hypothesizes that offender suicide correlates with higher lethality, as the offender may act without concern for escape or legal consequences.

The second variable is the relationship between the offender and the victims. Many mass shootings involve victims who are strangers to the offender; these attacks often take place in public venues and target groups indiscriminately, potentially increasing the number of casualties. Research by Fox & Levin and Böckler et al. indicates that when victims are strangers, the attacks tend to be less restrained and more indiscriminate, whereas targeted shootings involving acquaintances or family members may have fewer victims but can still be deadly. The study posits that incidents involving no prior relationship between offender and victim are more likely to meet the definition of mass murder.

The third variable is firearm characteristics, specifically caliber and type. Empirical studies(e.g., Braga & Cook, Jager & McCarty) have shown that higher-caliber firearms are more likely to produce fatal injuries than smaller-caliber weapons, even when controlling for number of shots fired and location of wounds. Semi-automatic and automatic firearms, especially with high-capacity magazines, allow rapid, sustained fire, giving victims less chance to escape or fight back. The hypothesis is that higher-caliber and higher-capacity firearms significantly increase the likelihood that an active shooting will escalate to mass murder.

The fourth variable is the strength of gun control laws in the jurisdiction where the incident occurs. The study uses indices such as the Giffords Law Center's

Annual Gun Law Scorecard to measure this, which rank states on the comprehensiveness of their regulations, including licensing requirements, background checks, restrictions on certain weapon types, and magazine capacity limits. Prior literature generally finds that stricter gun laws are associated with lower firearm homicide rates, though the relationship to mass shootings is less clear. The study hypothesizes that weaker gun laws will correlate with higher odds of mass murder in active shootings.

Methodologically, the authors draw on FBI data on active shooter incidents from 2000 to 2018, yielding 282 cases. They code each case for the four variables, supplementing FBI data with media reports, court documents, and other public sources to fill gaps. The dependent variable is whether the incident qualifies as mass murder — defined here as the killing of four or more people in a single event, excluding the offender. Binary logistic regression analysis is used to determine the statistical significance and strength of association for each variable.

Descriptive statistics show that 96.8% of offenders were male, with ages ranging widely but most frequently in their 30s. Nearly 40% of incidents involved offender suicide, and 37.1% involved semi-automatic handguns. Stranger shootings were common, and many incidents occurred in commercial or educational settings. The regression results indicate that offender suicide significantly increases the likelihood of mass murder, with an odds ratio of 2.23, meaning such incidents are more than twice as likely to meet the mass murder threshold. Victim relationship is also significant: stranger-involved shootings are more likely to be mass murders. Firearm caliber shows a positive association with mass murder likelihood, consistent with prior ballistics research. However, gun law strength, while in the expected direction, is not statistically significant in this analysis.

In interpreting these findings, the authors stress that offender suicide likely reflects a mind set oriented toward maximum damage without fear of capture, leading to riskier, more aggressive tactics. Stranger targeting often means attacks occur in crowded public places, increasing potential casualties. The caliber effect underscores that weapon lethality matters independently of other factors — high-caliber rounds cause more severe wounds and reduce survival chances even with prompt medical care. The lack of a statistically significant effect for gun law strength may reflect the complex reality that offenders can circumvent local laws by obtaining firearms in neighboring jurisdictions, or that state-level "scores" may not capture enforcement rigor or illegal market dynamics.

The policy implications are multifaceted. While broad gun control reforms remain politically polarized in the United States, the findings suggest targeted interventions: limiting civilian access to high-caliber and high-capacity firearms; improving early identification and intervention for individuals at risk of committing suicide; enhancing physical security in high-risk venues such as schools, shopping malls, and places of worship; and training staff and community members in rapid response measures. The authors note that situational prevention — such as controlled entry points, visible security presence, and real-time surveillance — can disrupt an attacker's plan or reduce their access to potential victims.

Beyond the U.S., the chapter argues that these insights are relevant internationally. Countries with strict gun laws, like South Korea, are not immune to the risk of mass casualty violence, even if the means differ. In Korea, for example, while civilian gun ownership is tightly restricted, incidents involving illegal firearms, modified air guns, or bladed weapons have occurred, and the potential for an active shooting event cannot be dismissed. The authors recommend that Korean authorities and policy makers monitor trends abroad, especially regarding offender behavior, suicide correlations, and weapon lethality, to inform domestic prevention strategies.

The chapter also underscores the importance of understanding the offender's planning process. Many active shooters engage in leakage behaviors — communicating intent, researching targets, or acquiring weapons and ammunition well in advance. Integrating threat assessment teams in schools, workplaces, and communities, with authority to act on credible threats, could prevent some attacks from materializing. Media guidelines that reduce the glorification of offenders while still informing the public could mitigate copycat risks.

Ultimately, the chapter concludes that active shootings are complex social phenomena that require integrated responses. Law enforcement, policy makers, mental health professionals, educators, and community organizations must coordinate to address both immediate threats and the deeper social and psychological factors that foster such violence. By isolating factors — suicide, victim relationship, firearm caliber — that have significant statistical associations with mass murder outcomes, this research provides an evidence-based foundation for targeted interventions. While the lack of significance for gun law strength in this model is notable, it does not negate the value of regulation; rather, it points to the need for nuanced, enforceable policies and multi-layered prevention strategies. The authors advocate for ongoing research that refines these models with updated data, explores interactions between variables, and considers the changing technological and social landscape of both firearms and public security.

이 편은 미국에서 발생한 총기난사 사건을 대상으로, 어떤 요인이 사건이 '대량살인'으로 이어질 가능성을 높이는지를 실증적으로 분석한 연구 결과를 제시한다. 여기서 '총기난사(active shooting)'란 범인이 공공장소에서 다수의 사람을 살해하거나 살해하려고 총기를 발사하는 사건으로, 시간적 제한이 명확하지 않고, 경찰이나 제3자의 개입으로 중단되기 전까지 다수의 사상자가 발생할 가능성이 높은 상황을 말한다. 저자들은 지난 20여 년 동안 미국에서 이러한 사건의 발생 빈도와 피해 규모가 증가해왔으며, 특히 최근 들어 급격한 증가세를 보이고 있음을 지적한다. FBI의 통계에 따르면, 미국 내 총기난사 사건은 매년 증가하고 있고, 2020년에서 2021년 사이에는 사건 수가 무려 50%나 증가했다는 ABC 뉴스의 보도도 인용된다. 이러한 사건은 학교, 직장, 예배당, 상업시설, 공연장 등 다양한 장소에서 발생하며, 범인의 유형도 전형적인 프로필로 한정되지 않는다. 학생, 직장인, 전직 군인, 범죄 전과자, 정신질환자 등 매우 다양하며, 동기는 개인적 원한, 사회적 불만, 정치/이념적 신념, 또는 단순한 보복 심리 등으로 폭넓게 분포한다.

서론에서는 총기난사의 특성이 다른 형태의 폭력 범죄와 구별되는 점을 강조한다. 우선 총기의 살상력과 발사 속도는 단시간에 대규모 피해를 초래할 수 있게 한다. 또한, 무차별적으로 목표를 정하는 경우가 많아 피해자가 범인과 아무런 관계가 없으며, 이는 사건의 무작위성과 불가예측성을 높인다. 특히 공공장소에서 발생할 경우, 현장에 있던 사람들이 단지 '그 자리에 있었다'는 이유만으로 희생자가 될 수 있다는 점에서 사회 전체의 불안을 심화시킨다.

문헌고찰 부분에서는 총기난사의 원인과 특성을 분석한 기존 연구들을 폭넓게 검토한다. 많은 연구가 총기의 특성, 특히 반자동/자동 화기나 대구경 탄환, 대용량 탄창 등이 피해 규모를 키운다는 점을 확인했다. '총기 없는 구역(gun-free zone)'에서 사건이 발생한 비율이 높다는 통계도 소개되지만, 이에 대한 해석은 논란이 있다. 일부 학자는 이러한 장소가 사람들의 밀집도가 높은 곳이어서 범인의 목표가 되기 쉽다고 설명한다. 또한, 범인의 정신적 상태, 오랜 기간 축적된 불만, 직업 상실이나 대인관계 갈등과 같은 상황적 촉발 요인도 중요한 변수로 거론된다.

이 장에서는 다양한 범죄학/사회학 이론이 적용된다. 뒤르켐의 사회통합이론은 사회적 유대의 약화와 소외감이 일탈 행동의 원인이 될 수 있음을 설명한다. 쇼와 매케이의 사회해체이론은 지역사회 붕괴와 비공식적 통제의 약화를 범죄율 상승의 요인으로 본다. 머튼의 아노미이론은 사회적으로 승인된 목표와 이를 달성할 합법적 수단의 괴리가 극단적 범행으로 이어질 수 있다고 본다. 코헨과 펠슨의 일상활동이론은 동기 있는 범인, 적합한 표적, 그리고 유능한 방어자의 부재가 시간과 공간상에서 동시에 발생할 때 범죄가 일어난다고 설명한다. 또한, 언론의 선정적 보도와 범인의 신원 공개가 모방 범행을 유발할 수 있다는 의제설정이론, 귀인이론, 소수자 스트레스 이론 등의 미디어 관련 관점도 검토된다.

이 연구는 네 가지 핵심 변수를 중심으로 총기난사가 대량살인으로 이어질 가능성을 분석했다. 첫째, 범인의 자살 여부다. 랭크퍼드(Lankford, 2012)는 다수의 대중 총기난사 범인들이 사건 도중이나 직후 자살하거나 자살을 시도한다고 보고했다. 이는 범인이 생존이나 법적 처벌에 대한 고려 없이, 최대한의 피해를 주고 죽으려는 의지를 반영할 수 있다. 따라서 범인 자살은 대량살인 가능성을 높이는 요인으로 설정되었다.

둘째, 범인과 피해자의 관계다. 피해자가 전혀 모르는 사람인 경우, 공격은 불특정 다수를 향해 무차별적으로 진행될 가능성이 크다. 폭스와 레빈(Fox & Levin), 뵈클러(Böckler) 등의 연구는 낯선 사람을 대상으로 한 총격이 더 높은 사망자 수를 기록하는 경향이 있음을 보여준다. 반면, 가족이나 지인, 동료를 대상으로 한 사건은 특정 목표에 집중하는 경향이 있어 피해 규모가 상대적으로 작을 수 있다.

셋째, 사용된 총기의 특성이다. 브라가와 쿡(Braga & Cook), 예거와 맥카티(Jager & McCarty) 등의 연구는 대구경 탄환이 소구경보다 훨씬 치명적 부상을 초래할 가능성이 높다고 입증했다. 반자동/자동 화기와 대용량 탄창은 발사 속도와 지속사격 능력을 높여 피해자의 도주나 반격 가능성을 줄인다. 연구에서는 총기의 구경과 발사 능력이 대량살인 가능성을 높일 것이라고 가정했다.

넷째, 사건 발생 지역의 총기규제 강도다. 기포즈 법률센터(Giffords Law Center)의 연례 '총기법 점수표' 등은 각 주의 규제 수준을 평가한다. 기존 연구(Kwon & Baack, Reeping et al., Chien & Gakh)는 강력한 총기규제가 총기 살인율을 낮추는 경향이 있다고 보고했지만, 대량살인 사건과의 관계는 명확하지 않다. 본 연구는 규제가 약한 지역에서 대량살인 가능성이 높을 것이라고 가정했다.

연구 방법으로는 FBI의 2000-2018년 총기난사 데이터 282건을 활용했다. 각 사건을 범인 자살 여부, 피해자와의 관계, 총기 특성, 총기법 강도 점수로 코딩했으며, 언론 보도와 법원 기록 등으로 보완했다. 대량살인은 범인을 제외하고 4명 이상의 사망자가 발생한 사건으로 정의했다. 분석에는 이항 로지스틱 회귀분석이 사용됐다.

기초 통계 분석 결과, 범인의 96.8%가 남성이었고, 연령은 30대가 가장 많았다. 범인 자살은 약 39%의 사건에서 발생했다. 무기의 경우 반자동 권총이 37.1%로 가장 많았으며, 사건 장소는 상업시설과 교육기관이 많았다. 회귀분석 결과, 범인 자살은 대량살인 발생 가능성을 2.23배 높였고, 피해자가 낯선 사람인 경우 대량살인 가능성이 유의하게 높았다. 총기의 구경 역시 대량살인과 정적 상관관계를 보였다. 반면, 총기규제 강도는 예측 방향과는 일치했으나 통계적으로 유의하지 않았다.

이러한 결과 해석에서, 범인 자살은 처벌 회피와 최대 피해 달성 의지가 결합된 행동으로, 사건 전개를 더 공격적이고 무차별적으로 만든다고 본다. 피해자가 낯선 경우, 장소 특성상 다수가 한꺼번에 공격받을 가능성이 커진다. 총기 구경의 영향은 탄환의 파괴력과 치명상 가능성을 높이는 물리적·의학적 연구와 부합한다. 반면, 총기 규제 강도의 효과가 미약한 것은 범인이 인접 주에서 무기를 구입하거나 불법 경로를 이용할 수 있고, 주별 규제 점수가 집행력이나 불법 시장의 영향을 충분히 반영하지 못하기 때문일 수 있다.

정책적 함의로, 미국에서는 광범위한 총기규제가 정치적으로 논란이 많지만, 대구경 및 대용량 탄창의 민간 접근 제한, 자살 위험군 사전 식별과 개입, 다중이용시설의 보안 강화 등이 대량살인 가능성을 줄일 수 있다고 제안한다. 또한, 출입 통제, 경비 인력 배치, 실시간 감시 등 상황적 예방책이 범인의 계획을 차단하거나 피해 규모를 줄일 수 있다.

저자들은 이러한 결과가 미국뿐 아니라 국제적으로도 유의미하다고 강조한다. 총기규제가 엄격한 한국이라 하더라도, 불법 총기, 개조된 공기총, 흉기 등을 통한 대규모 피해 가능성을 배제할 수 없다. 특히 범인의 자살 경향, 피해자와의 관계, 무기 치명성에 관한 분석은 한국의 예방 전략에도 적용 가능하다.

마지막으로, 범인의 사전 계획과 '유출 행동(leakage behavior)'을 모니터링하는 위협평가 체계의 필요성을 강조한다. 범행 전 의도 표명, 표적 조사, 무기/탄약 준비 등의 행동은 사전 차단의 기회를 제공한다. 학교, 직장, 지역사회 단위의 위협평가팀이 실질적 권한을 갖고 조기에 개입할 수 있도록 해야 한다. 언론은 범인의 이름과 구체적 수법 노출을 최소화해 모방 범죄를 방지해야 한다.

결론적으로, 총기난사는 단순한 치안 문제가 아니라 복합적인 사회현상으로, 경찰, 입법자, 정신건강 전문가, 교육자, 시민사회가 함께 대응해야 한다. 본 연구는 자살 여부, 피해자 관계, 총기 구경이라는 세 가지 주요 요인이 대량살인 가능성과 통계적으로 유의하게 연관된다는 점을 밝혀, 국가별로 상황에 맞는 예방정책을 설계하는 데 근거를 제공한다. 총기규제 강도의 통계적 유의성 부재는 규제 자체의 무용성을 뜻하는 것이 아니라, 보다 정교하고 집행력 있는 정책 설계가 필요함을 시사한다. 저자들은 향후 더 많은 데이터와 변수, 기술·사회 환경 변화를 반영한 심화 연구를 통해 이 모델을 발전시켜 나가야 한다고 강조한다.

Chapter 7 (제7편)

The chapter presents a deeply researched and integrated account of the American experience with firearms, combining the historical evolution of constitutional interpretation, the origins and contested meaning of the Second Amendment, the long trajectory of public mass shootings, and the rare but symbolically charged history of presidential assassinations and attempted assassinations. It argues that only by viewing these threads together — constitutional law, the lived history of violence, and the institutional responses — can one understand the entrenched and polarizing debate over guns in the United States and its implications for democratic governance.

The narrative begins with the U.S. Constitution, a document born of compromise in 1787, designed to balance power between the federal government and the states, and to embed a framework for liberty that could endure across generations. Interpretation of the Constitution has been shaped by two opposing philosophies. One is originalism, which insists that constitutional provisions must be read in light of their public meaning at the time of ratification. Originalists argue that the Second Amendment's meaning was fixed in 1791, rooted in the Founders' understanding of "militia" and "arms" in the context of their own day. The other is the living Constitution approach, which treats the document as a dynamic instrument that must be adapted to changing social realities and technological advances. Proponents of this view see the Second Amendment as open to reinterpretation in light of the vastly more lethal firearms of the modern era and the different nature of threats to public safety.

The Bill of Rights, added in 1791 to secure ratification and satisfy Anti-Federalist demands, enshrined individual liberties such as freedom of speech, religion, and assembly, the right to due process, and the prohibition of cruel and unusual punishment. Among these was the Second Amendment: "A well regulated Militia, being necessary to the security of a free State, the right of the people to keep and bear Arms shall not be infringed." This language fuses a collective rationale — the necessity of a well-regulated militia — with an operative guarantee — the right of the people to keep and bear arms. In the late 18th century, "militia" referred to the body of armed, able-bodied male citizens, and "arms" meant muskets, rifles, and pistols suitable for personal and militia use.

English legal heritage loomed large in this formulation. The 1689 English Bill of Rights recognized the right of Protestants to have arms for their defense, shaped by suspicion of standing armies and the perceived need for a citizenry capable of resisting tyranny. American colonists inherited this suspicion and it deepened in the years before the Revolution, when British authorities attempted to confiscate colonial arms, triggering confrontations at Lexington and Concord. In the Founders' view, an armed populace was not only a deterrent to foreign invasion but also a safeguard against domestic tyranny.

For most of U.S. history, however, the Supreme Court avoided deciding whether the Second Amendment guaranteed an individual right to own firearms unrelated to militia service. In *United States v. Miller*(1939), the Court upheld a federal restriction on sawed-off shotguns, reasoning that such a weapon had no reasonable relationship to the preservation or efficiency of a well-regulated militia. This decision was often interpreted as supporting the "collective rights" view — that the Amendment protected state militias rather than individual possession for private purposes.

That view prevailed in federal jurisprudence until *District of Columbia v. Heller*(2008). In Heller, the Court struck down Washington D.C.'s ban on handguns and requirement that lawful firearms in the home be kept inoperable, holding in a 5-4 decision that the Second Amendment protects an individual right to possess firearms unconnected to militia service, particularly for self-defense within the home. Justice Antonin Scalia's majority opinion treated the prefatory militia clause as announcing a purpose but not limiting the operative clause's scope. Two years later, in *McDonald v. City of Chicago*(2010), the Court extended this right to the states through the Fourteenth Amendment's Due Process Clause, making it clear that state and local governments are bound by the same constitutional constraints as the federal government. Yet these rulings left open questions about the extent to which firearms could be regulated—for example, whether bans on certain weapon types, limits on magazine capacity, or restrictions on carrying guns in public would pass constitutional muster.

From this legal foundation, the chapter moves to the lived experience of gun violence in America, tracing a chronology of public mass shootings from 1968 to 2025. The assassinations of Dr. Martin Luther King Jr. and Senator Robert F. Kennedy in 1968 were national traumas that spurred the Gun Control Act of 1968, which prohibited mail-order gun sales and restricted firearm ownership by certain categories of individuals. But in the decades that followed, mass shootings became distressingly frequent. The 1999 Columbine High School massacre, in which two students killed 13 people and injured 24, shocked the nation and redefined the public understanding of school shootings. In 2007, the Virginia Tech shooting claimed 32 lives, making it the deadliest shooting bya single gunman in U.S. history at the time. Sandy Hook Elementary in 2012 saw 20 children and 6 educators murdered, igniting a national debate over assault weapons and background checks. The 2016 Pulse nightclub attack in Orlando targeted the LGBTQ community and left 49 dead. In 2017, the Las Vegas shooting killed 60 and wounded hundreds from a hotel window overlooking an outdoor concert. In 2018, a gunman killed 17 at Marjory Stoneman Douglas High School in Parkland, Florida, catalyzing a youth-led movement for gun reform. The 2022 shooting at Robb Elementary in Uvalde, Texas, where 19 children and 2 teachers were killed, underscored once again the vulnerability of schools despite decades of "hardening" efforts.

The chapter also narrates the rarer but profoundly symbolic category of presidential assassinations and attempted assassinations, from Abraham Lincoln's murder by John Wilkes Booth in 1865, to the assassinations of James Garfield(1881), William McKinley(1901), and John F. Kennedy(1963). Each killing convulsed the nation, altered the course of history, and prompted security reforms. Attempts that failed are equally instructive: two in 1975 against President Gerald Ford, both by women armed with pistols; the 1981 shooting of Ronald Reagan by John Hinckley Jr., which seriously wounded the president and led to overhauls in Secret Service procedures; a 1994 attack on the White House by a man firing a semi-automatic rifle from the sidewalk; and more recent incidents involving threats or plots against presidents and major candidates in an era of deepening political polarization. These events reveal that even the most protected individuals are not immune to determined attackers, and they have driven continual adaptations in protective strategy.

By juxtaposing the mass shootings that have scarred civilian life with the targeted attacks on presidents, the chapter highlights the multifaceted nature of the American gun problem. In both contexts, firearms are the central instrument, but the motivations, settings, and symbolic resonances differ. Mass shootings often target strangers in public spaces, creating a spectacle of indiscriminate violence. Presidential attacks are highly focused and politically charged, aiming at the head of the executive branch and, symbolically, the nation itself. Yet both expose systemic vulnerabilities: failures to prevent dangerous individuals from obtaining guns, gaps in threat assessment, and the limits of reactive security measures.

The constitutional debate over firearms remains unresolved. Gun rights advocates, emboldened by *Heller*, argue that the Second Amendment guarantees a personal right to own and carry weapons for self-defense, hunting, and other lawful purposes, and that this right serves as a check on government overreach. Gun control proponents emphasize the "well regulated" language and the government's compelling interest in reducing gun violence, contending that rights are not absolute and can be subject to reasonable restrictions. This clash is not merely legal but cultural, with deep divisions along regional, political, and demographic lines. In some parts of the country, gun ownership is entwined with notions of independence, self-reliance, and heritage; in others, it is associated primarily with danger and tragedy.

The chapter situates the American debate in a global context, noting that many democratic nations, such as South Korea, Japan, the United Kingdom, and Australia, maintain strict firearms regulations and have far lower rates of gun violence. The differences, however, are not just legal but cultural and historical. In the United States, the Second Amendment is a constitutional anchor for gun rights, and its symbolic weight in political discourse is immense. This makes direct adoption of foreign regulatory models difficult, though not impossible. The author suggests that certain measures — universal background checks, licensing systems, safe storage laws, bans on high-capacity magazines and certain military-style weapons, and "red flag" laws that allow temporary removal of firearms from individuals deemed dangerous — are consistent with *Heller* and could be enacted without infringing on the core right.

In its integrated analysis, the chapter emphasizes that the gun issue in America is not a single policy challenge but a convergence of constitutional interpretation, public safety imperatives, historical legacy, and cultural identity. The transition from the militia-based armed citizenry of the 18th century to the highly individualized and technologically advanced gun culture of the 21st century has transformed the practical meaning of "keeping and bearing arms," even though the constitutional text has not changed. The persistence of mass shootings as a recurring trauma and the continuing threat of attacks on high-profile political figures both reinforce the urgency of finding a balance between rights and regulation.

The conclusion calls for a pragmatic path forward — one that acknowledges the enduring symbolic and constitutional significance of the Second Amendment, respects legitimate concerns about government overreach, but also confronts the demonstrable harms of gun violence. It advocates for evidence-based policy grounded in historical awareness, legal clarity, and practical enforcement capacity. By tracing the intertwined histories of constitutional doctrine, mass violence, and political assassination, the chapter offers a framework for understanding America's intractable firearms debate in all its dimensions and for exploring ways to reduce violence while preserving constitutional liberty.

이 편은 미국의 총기 문제를 헌법 해석의 역사, 수정헌법 제2조의 기원과 해석 논쟁, 대량 총기난사 사건의 역사적 전개, 그리고 대통령 암살 및 암살 시도의 사례를 모두 통합적으로 서술하며, 이를 통해 미국 사회에서 총기 권리와 규제를 둘러싼 뿌리 깊은 갈등을 조명한다. 저자는 헌법적 논의, 폭력의 역사, 제도적 대응을 함께 분석해야만 미국 총기 논쟁의 실체를 이해할 수 있으며, 민주주의 운영에도 함의를 찾을 수 있다고 주장한다.

이야기는 1787년 제정된 미국 헌법에서 시작된다. 헌법은 연방정부와 주정부 간 권력 균형을 설정하고, 세대를 넘어 지속 가능한 자유 보장 체계를 마련하기 위해 고안되었다. 헌법 해석에는 크게 두 가지 상반된 방법론이 존재한다. 하나는 '원전주의(originalism)'로, 헌법 조항은 제정 당시의 공적 의미에 따라 해석해야 한다는 입장이다. 원전주의자들은 수정헌법 제2조의 의미가 1791년 비준 당시 확정되었으며, 당시의 '민병대'와 '무기' 개념을 기준으로 이해해야 한다고 본다. 다른 하나는 '살아있는 헌법(living Constitution)' 접근으로, 헌법은 시대적 변화와 사회 현실, 기술 발전에 맞춰 해석이 확장되어야 한다고 본다. 이 입장은 현대의 고성능 · upheavals 대량살상 총기를 제정 당시의 권리 개념과 동일하게다루는 것은 불합리하다고 본다.

1791년 비준된 권리장전(Bill of Rights)은 언론/종교/집회의 자유, 적법절차 보장, 잔혹/비정상적 형벌 금지 등 핵심 자유를 명문화했고, 그 중 수정헌법 제2조는 "잘 규율된 민병대는 자유로운 주의 안보에 필요하므로, 국민이 무기를 보유하고 휴대할 권리를 침해해서는 안 된다"고 규정했다. 이 조문은 집단적 필요성(민병대)과 개인적 권리(무기 보유 · 휴대)를 한 문장에 결합했다. 18세기 말의 '민병대'는 무기를 지닌 평시 민간인들로, 필요 시 주 방위를 위해 소집되는 조직이었고, '무기'는 당시의 머스킷총,

소총, 권총을 의미했다.

이 개념의 배경에는 영국의 법적 전통이 있었다. 1689년 영국 권리장전은 상비군에 대한 불신과 종교적/정치적 상황 속에서 신민의 무기소지권을 인정했으며, 이는 폭정에 맞설 수 있는 시민의 권리로 이해되었다. 미국 식민지인들은 이를 계승했고, 영국이 독립 전 무기 압수를 시도하자 렉싱턴/콩코드 전투 등으로 맞섰다. 건국 지도자들에게 무장 시민은 외적 침입뿐 아니라 국내 폭정에 대한 억제 수단이었다.

그러나 미국 연방대법원은 20세기 중반까지 민병대와 무관한 개인적 무기소지권을 명확히 인정하지 않았다. *Miller*(1939) 판결은 잘 규율된 민병대의 효율성과 합리적 관련성이 없는 무기는 보호되지 않는다고 판시하며, 집단권 해석을 뒷받침하는 근거로 받아들여졌다. 이러한 경향은 *Heller*(2008) 판결에서 전환점을 맞았다. 워싱턴 D.C.의 권총 금지와 가정 내 총기 비장전 의무를 위헌으로 판단하며, 대법원은 민병대 복무와 무관한 개인의 자기방어용 무기소지권을 인정했다. 스칼리아 대법관은 민병대 조항을 목적 서문으로 보고, '국민의 권리'라는 표현은 제1・제4조에서처럼 개인권을 의미한다고 판시했다. 이어 *McDonald*(2010) 판결은 이 권리를 수정헌법 제14조를 통해 주와 지방정부에도 적용했다. 그러나 어떤 규제가 허용되는지에 대한 구체적 기준은 남겨져 있다.

법적 틀을 다진 뒤, 저자는 1968년부터 2025년까지의 주요 대량 총기난사 사건을 시간순으로 서술한다. 1968년 마틴 루서 킹 목사와 로버트 F. 케네디 상원의원 암살은 전국적 충격을 안겼고, 같은 해 총기규제법(Gun Control Act)이 제정되어 우편 주문 총기 판매 금지, 특정 범죄자의 총기 소지 금지 등 규제가 도입됐다. 그러나 이후에도 총기난사는 반복되었다. 1999년 콜럼바인 고교 사건에서는 학생 두 명이 13명을 살해하고 24명을 부상시켰으며, 이는 학교 총격 사건에 대한 대중 인식을 바꿨다. 2007년 버지니아텍 사건은 32명의 목숨을 앗아가 단일 범인 총격으로는 최악의 참사가 되었고, 2012년 샌디훅 초등학교에서는 6~7세 아동 20명과 교사 6명이 사망해 공격형 무기 금지 논쟁이 재점화됐다. 2016년 올랜도의 펄스 나이트클럽 총격은 LGBTQ 공동체를 겨냥해 49명이 사망했다. 2017년 라스베이거스에서는 호텔 창문에서 콘서트 관중을 향해 총격을 가해 60명이 사망하고 수백 명이 부상했다. 2018년 플로리다 파크랜드의 마조리 스톤맨 더글러스고교 사건(사망 17명)은 청소년 주도의 총기개혁 운동을 촉발했고, 2022년 텍사스 유발디의 롭 초등학교 사건(아동 19명/교사 2명 사망)은 학교 안전 강화에도 불구하고 취약성이 여전함을 보여줬다.

이어 저자는 대통령 암살 및 시도의 희귀하지만 상징성이 큰 사건들을 다룬다. 링컨 대통령(1865), 가필드 대통령(1881), 맥킨리 대통령(1901), 케네디 대통령(1963)은 모두 피격으로 사망했다. 각 사건은 국가적 충격과 경호 체계 변화로 이어졌다. 실패한 시도도 적지 않았다. 1975년 포드 대통령을 향한 두 차례의 권총 공격, 1981년 레이건 대통령을 중상을 입힌 힝클리의 총격은 경호 시스템 전면 개편을 불러왔다. 1994년 백악관을 향한 반자동 소총 사격, 그리고 최근 수년간의 정치적 양극화 속에서 나타난 위협과 모의 사건들은, 최고 수준의 경호를 받는 인물조차 무기 위협에서 완전히 자유롭지 않음을 보여준다.

민간인 대상 대량난사와 국가 최고지도자에 대한 공격을 나란히 보면, 두 유형 모두 총기가 중심 도구이며 사회와 정치에 깊은 상처를 남긴다는 공통점이 있다. 그러나 전자는 불특정 다수를 무차별 공격하며 공포와 무력감을 확산시키는 반면, 후자는 정치적으로 특정 인물을 겨냥해 국가 정체성과 통치 구조 자체를 상징적으로 흔든다. 두 경우 모두 위험인물의 총기 접근 차단 실패, 위협 평가의 미비, 사후 대응 위주의 경호/치안의 한계라는 구조적 문제를 드러낸다.

총기에 대한 헌법 논쟁은 여전히 결론나지 않았다. 총기권 옹호론자들은 *Heller* 판례에 힘입어, 제2조가 자기방어 · 사냥 · 기타 합법적 목적을 위한 개인의 무기소지권을 보장하며, 이는 정부 권력 남용을 억제하는 방파제라고 주장한다. 반면 규제론자들은 "잘 규율된"이라는 문구와 공공안전확보를 위한 권리 제한 가능성을 강조하며, 현대 총기의 살상력은 건국 당시 상상할 수 없던 수준이라고 지적한다. 이 대립은 법정뿐 아니라 입법부, 선거, 여론 속에서도 지역/문화/정파 간 균열을 심화시킨다. 일부 지역에서는 총기 소유가 독립심과 전통의 상징인 반면, 다른 지역에서는 총기가 위험과 비극의 원천으로 인식된다.

저자는 이를 국제적으로 비교하며, 한국/일본/영국/호주 등 다수 민주국가가 엄격한 총기규제와 낮은 총기 폭력률을 유지하고 있다고 지적한다. 미국은 제2조라는 헌법적 근거와 상징성이 커서 외국 모델을 단순 도입하기 어렵지만, *Heller*의 틀 안에서도 전면적 신원조회, 면허제, 안전 보관 의무, 대용량 탄창/특정 무기 금지, 위험인물 총기압수(red flag)법 등은 가능하며, 권리를 침해하지 않으면서 위험을 줄일 수 있다고 본다.

종합적으로, 미국의 총기 문제는 헌법 해석, 공공안전, 역사적 유산, 문화적 정체성이 교차하는 복합 현상이다. 18세기 민병대 중심의 무장 시민 개념에서 21세기 개인화/기술화된 총기문화로 변화하면서, "무기 보유/휴대"의 실질적 의미는 바뀌었지만 헌법 문구는 변하지 않았다. 반복되는 대량 총기난사와 대통령 암살 위협은 권리와 규제의 균형을 찾는 문제의 시급성을 보여준다.

결론에서 저자는 제2조의 상징성과 헌법적 의미를 존중하면서도, 현대 사회의 위험에 대응할 실용적 접근이 필요하다고 강조한다. 이는 정부 권력 남용과 무규제 상태 양쪽 모두에 대한 우려를 인정하고, 역사 인식과 법적 명확성, 실효성 있는 집행 능력에 기반한 정책을 수립하는 것을 포함한다. 헌법 해석, 폭력 사건의 유형별 특성, 예방/대응 전략을 종합적으로 고려한 이 장의 분석은, 미국 총기 논쟁을 다차원적으로 이해하고, 폭력을 줄이면서도 자유를 보존할 수 있는 길을 모색하는데 유용한 틀을 제공한다.

Chapter 8 (제8편)

The Second Amendment of the U.S. Constitution, ratified in 1791, affirms the right of the people to keep and bear arms within the context of a "well-regulated Militia." Originally grounded in concerns about tyranny and standing armies, its early interpretation emphasized collective rights tied to state militias. Over time, however, legal understanding has shifted toward individual gun ownership as a fundamental constitutional right. Landmark Supreme Court decisions such as *District of Columbia v. Heller*(2008) and *New York State Rifle & Pistol Association v. Bruen*(2022) have codified this view, affirming that individuals have a right to possess firearms for purposes such as self-defense, independent of militia service. These evolving legal interpretations have been shaped by media coverage, as the media play a crucial role in influencing how the public understands and debates the meaning and implications of the Second Amendment.

The Constitution provides the framework for governance and civil liberties, with the Bill of Rights enshrining protections including free speech, due process, and the right to bear arms. The Second Amendment, influenced by English common law and political philosophy, was crafted to ensure both state sovereignty and personal liberty. While originally tied to militia service, the meaning of the amendment has evolved significantly through judicial rulings and cultural shifts. This evolution has unfolded in a media-saturated environment where narratives, emotional appeals, and selective reporting strongly affect public opinion.

Media institutions — traditional and digital alike — serve as both mirrors and molders of public sentiment regarding the Second Amendment. In the wake of mass shootings or legislative debates, the media play a key role in highlighting gun-related issues and driving national conversation. When coverage focuses on tragedies and victims, public support for gun control tends to rise; when it emphasizes defensive gun use or constitutional liberties, it reinforces pro-gun rights views. These effects are driven by several well-established media theories: agenda-setting, which determines what the public pays attention to; framing, which influences how issues are interpreted; priming, which alters the standards people use to evaluate policies and political figures; and cultivation, which shapes long-term perceptions of reality and risk.

Agenda-setting helps explain the cyclical nature of public concern about gun laws — coverage spikes after high-profile incidents and fades without sustained attention. Framing adds another layer, with conservative media highlighting individual liberty and government overreach, while liberal outlets emphasize the public health toll of gun violence. These divergent frames do more than reflect audience preferences — they shape them, embedding ideological leanings within the narratives themselves. Media priming reinforces these leanings by repeatedly exposing audiences to specific frames and issues, subtly altering the way people evaluate policy debates and political leaders. Cultivation theory suggests that long-term exposure to violent media content(e.g., TV shows and movies) can create a distorted view of the world as dangerous, leading people to support gun ownership as a necessary means of personal protection.

Spiral of silence theory adds a social dimension to this analysis by explaining how individuals may silence their opinions when they perceive them to be in the minority. In regions where pro-gun sentiment is dominant, those who support regulation may withhold their views, and vice versa. This contributes to echo chambers and distorts perceptions of public opinion, making polarized positions seem more widely accepted than they may actually be. The result is a fractured and often adversarial public sphere, where consensus becomes increasingly difficult to achieve.

Supreme Court decisions like *Heller*, *McDonald v. Chicago*, and *Bruenhave* attracted significant media attention, often framed in highly polarized terms. These rulings have shifted the legal landscape in favor of individual gun rights, and media outlets have played a substantial role in shaping public interpretation of their significance. Coverage often reduces complex legal judgments to emotionally charged headlines, further polarizing the debate. Advocacy groups such as the NRA and Everytown for Gun Safety provide media-ready narratives that are widely reproduced, reinforcing partisan divisions and deepening the cultural rift over gun policy.

Digital and social media have amplified these effects, enabling advocacy groups and individuals to shape discourse in real time. Platforms like Twitter and Facebook create echo chambers that expose users primarily to ideologically aligned content. Research shows that anti-regulation groups, in particular, have effectively used fear-based messaging on social media to drive behaviors like increased firearm purchases. These strategies are often more emotionally resonant than data-driven public health messages, making them more influential in the short term.

The virality of such content also means that it reaches broad audiences quickly, shaping perception and policy conversations almost instantaneously.

Technological change adds yet another layer to this evolving landscape. The growing adoption of Internet of Things (IoT) devices — such as smart cameras and motion sensors — offers alternative means of home protection, especially among urban and younger populations. These devices serve the same function that many gun owners cite — home defense — yet do so without the risks associated with firearms. As these technologies become more widespread, they may gradually shift cultural attitudes toward what constitutes "protection," potentially reducing the perceived need for gun ownership for self-defense. The convenience and non-lethal nature of smart home security could lead to a reevaluation of security norms, especially among demographics that have historically been more supportive of gun control.

All of these dynamics — legal, cultural, technological, and communicative — converge to shape the modern American understanding of the Second Amendment. The media's role in this process is not passive; it is constitutive. Through mechanisms like framing and agenda-setting, media narratives influence not only what people think about gun rights and regulation, but also how they think about them. This has profound implications for public discourse, legal interpretation, and policy making.

Understanding these effects is essential for fostering a more informed and balanced debate on gun rights in the U.S. Enhancing media literacy among citizens, encouraging pluralistic news consumption, and promoting dialogue across ideological divides are necessary steps toward a healthier democratic discourse. Legal institutions, too, must be aware of how their decisions are portrayed and understood in the public arena, ensuring that legal communication is accessible and accurate. Cross-disciplinary research that integrates insights from law, communication, psychology, and technology is vital to addressing the full complexity of the

Second Amendment debate.

Ultimately, the Second Amendment discourse in U.S. society is not just a legal issue but a mediated struggle over identity, security, and democratic values. In a media environment defined by ideological fragmentation and emotional appeals, understanding how narratives are constructed and consumed is critical to shaping the future of gun policy. As society continues to embrace advanced safety-related digital and AI technologies, these innovations hold the potential to drastically transform public perceptions of the necessity of gun ownership in the years to come.

미국 헌법 제2수정안은 1791년에 비준되어 "잘 규율된 민병대는 자유로운 국가의 안보에 필요하므로, 국민이 무기를 소지하고 휴대할 권리는 침해되어서는 안 된다"고 명시하고 있다. 초기에는 주 방어와 관련된 집단적 권리로 이해되었으나, 시간이 지나면서 개인의 총기 소유권을 핵심으로 하는 해석으로 변화했다. 특히 2008년의 *District of Columbia v. Heller* 사건과 2022년의 *New York State Rifle & Pistol Association v. Bruen* 판결은 개인이 민병대와 무관하게 자위를 위해 총기를 소지할 권리를 헌법적으로 보호받는다고 판시했다. 이러한 법적 해석의 변화는 언론의 역할과 밀접하게 연결되어 있으며, 언론은 미국 사회의 총기 권리와 규제에 대한 담론과 인식을 형성하는 데 핵심적인 역할을 하고 있다.

미국 헌법은 국가의 통치 구조와 시민의 자유를 규정하는 기본 법률 문서로, 권리장전(Bill of Rights)을 포함한 27개의 수정헌법을 갖고 있다. 제2수정헌법은 영국의 관습법과 1689년의 권리장전에서 영향을 받아 주권 보장과 시민의 자유를 위한 민병대의 필요성을 반영하고자 했다. 그러나 시간이 지나며 이러한 해석은 개인의 권리 중심으로 변화하였고, 연방 대법원의 판례들은 이러한 해석을 확립하였다. 이 과정에서 언론은 단순한 정보 전달자를 넘어, 여론을 형성하고 사회적 의미를 부여하는 적극적인 참여자가 되었다.

언론은 전통 매체와 디지털 미디어를 포함하여 제2수정헌법에 대한 공공의 인식을 형성하는 데 중요한 역할을 한다. 대량 총격 사건이나 입법 논쟁 이후에는 총기 관련 이슈에 대한 언론 보도가 급증하며, 이는 여론과 정치적 관심을 유도한다. 언론이 피해자와 사건의 비극성을 강조할 경우, 총기 규제에 대한 지지가 증가하고, 반대로 자기 방어나 정부의 권한 남용에 초점을 맞추면 총기 권리에 대한 지지가 강해진다. 이러한 효과는 '의제 설정', '프레이밍', '프라이밍', '배양 이론' 등 다양한 미디어 이론에 의해 설명된다.

의제 설정 이론은 언론이 어떤 이슈를 중요하게 다루느냐에 따라 공중의 관심과 우선순위가 결정된다고 본다. 대형 사건 직후 언론의 관심이 집중되면 여론도 변동되지만, 지속적인 보도가 없을 경우 관심은 빠르게 식는다. 프레이밍 이론은 언론이 어떤 관점으로 이슈를 구성하느냐에 따라 해석 방식이 달라짐을 설명한다. 보수 언론은 총기 소지를 개인 자유와 헌법 수호의 문제로 다루는 반면, 진보적 언론은 이를 공공 보건과 사회적 피해의 관점에서 접근한다. 이러한 프레임은 단순히 의견을 반영하는 것이 아니라, 시청자의 인식과 정체성을 강화하고 극화시키는 역할을 한다.

프라이밍 이론은 언론 노출이 사람들의 평가 기준에 영향을 미친다는 것을 설명한다. 총기 사건이 반복적으로 보도되면, 사람들은 정치 지도자나 정책을 평가할 때 총기 관련 입장을 주요 기준으로 삼게 된다. 배양 이론은 장기적으로 폭력이나 범죄 관련의 미디어 콘텐츠(TV 프로그램, 영화 등)에 노출되면 세상이 위험하다는 인식을 갖게 되어, 개인의 총기 소유를 더 필요하다고 느끼게 된다는 점을 강조한다.

침묵의 나선 이론은 개인이 자신의 의견이 소수라고 느낄 때 표현을 자제하게 된다는 사회심리학적 설명을 제공한다. 총기 규제에 우호적인 지역에서는 총기 권리 지지자들이, 반대로 보수적인 지역에서는 규제 지지자들이 자신의 의견을 말하지 않고 침묵함으로써, 여론이 더 극단적으로 보이게 만든다. 이러한 침묵은 언론 보도, 사회적 압력, 소셜 미디어의 반응 등으로 강화되며, 결과적으로 공공 담론이 왜곡될 수 있다.

연방 대법원의 판결, 예를 들어 *Heller*, *McDonald*, *Bruen* 사건들은 언론에서 광범위하게 보도되었고, 이 과정에서 법적 복잡성은 단순한 문구로 축소되어 전달되었다. 보수 언론은 이를 자유의 승리로 묘사하고, 진보 언론은 공공 안전에 대한 우려를 강조하였다. 이들 판결은 실제로 미국 내 총기법에 큰 영향을 주었고, 언론 보도는 대중의 이해와 정책 결정 과정에 결정적인 영향을 끼쳤다. 언론은 종종 총기 관련 시민단체들의 주장과 자료를 그대로 인용함으로써, 정교한 분석 없이 편향된 시각을 강화하기도 한다.

디지털 미디어와 소셜 미디어는 이러한 현상을 더욱 가속화했다. 트위터, 페이스북, 유튜브와 같은 플랫폼은 실시간 논쟁과 여론 형성을 가능하게 했으며, 이념적으로 편향된 콘텐츠만을 보여주는 알고리즘 구조로 인해 이용자들이 자신의 견해를 확인하는 경향이 강화되었다. 특히 규제 반대 단체들은 공포를 자극하는 감성적 메시지를 활용해 총기 구매 행동까지 유도하는 데 성공하였다. 이러한 메시지는 공중 보건 프레임보다 더 빠르고 효과적으로 여론을 움직였으며, 실질적인 행동 변화로 이어졌다.

기술적 변화 또한 총기 소유에 대한 인식을 변화시키고 있다. 스마트 도어벨, 감지센서 등 IoT 기반 보안 기기들은 무력 충돌 없이도 효과적인 보호 수단을 제공하며, 특히 젊은 층과 도시 거주자들 사이에서인기를 끌고 있다. 이러한 기술은 총기 소유의 주요 이유 중 하나인 가정 방어를 대신할 수 있으며, 장기적으로는 총기 소유의 필요성에 대한 사회적 인식을 점차 변화시킬 수 있다. 무기 대신 기술을 통한 예방 중심의 보안 방식은 더 안전하고 현대적인 대안으로 인식되기 시작하고 있다.

이처럼 제2수정헌 논쟁은 단순한 법률 해석을 넘어, 문화적 정체성과 안보, 민주주의 가치에 대한 매개된 투쟁이다. 언론은 이 논의의 중심에서 여론을 형성하고 확대하며, 법적 판결과 정책 방향에 깊은 영향을 준다. 이러한 현상을 제대로 이해하기 위해서는 미디어 문해력 교육 강화, 이념을 초월한 대화 공간 마련, 법률 및 커뮤니케이션 분야의 학제 간 연구가 필요하다. 다양한 관점을 포용하고, 이슈에 대한 감정적 접근보다는 구조적 이해를 바탕으로 한 공공 논의가 이루어져야 한다.

궁극적으로, 총기 권리에 대한 미국 사회의 논쟁은 단순한 법적 쟁점이 아니라, 미디어 환경 속에서 끊임없이 재구성되는 문화적 담론이다. 이념적으로 분열된 언론 환경과 감성적인 소셜 미디어 콘텐츠가 주도하는 상황에서는, 담론의 방향성을 이해하고 건설적인 대화를 형성하는 것이 점점 더 중요해지고 있다. 특히 현재의 놀라운 수준의 안전 관련 디지털 및 AI 기술의 발전은, 미래에 사람들이 총기 소유의 필요성에 대한 인식을 근본적으로 변화시킬 수 있는 잠재력을 지니고 있다.

Chapter 9 (제9편)

This study explores how the Law of the State and the Law of Man reflect, confront, and ultimately converge upon each other in the search for the true meaning of "Law." The Law of the State begins with command, while the Law of Man originates in conscience. Yet these two are not separate or opposing systems; rather, they form a single philosophical structure of delegation and return. When the command of the State is delegated upward from human conscience, and when human conscience returns downward to the institutional order of the State, law is no longer a language of command but becomes a living moral order.

This study names this process "Delegated Secondary Reason," analysing the origin of law as both ethical memory and an act of testimony. The Law of the State is an institutional reason delegated from the Law of Man, and the Law of Man itself is a primary morality delegated from virtue (De) and conscience. This chain of delegation ultimately culminates in the intersection between Divine Love and Human Action—a sacred space of Justice, the Mandala of Law.

Horatio Nelson and Yi Sun-sin stand as historical embodiments of this delegated law. Nelson, through his final words — "Thank God, I have done my duty" — translated the command of the State into the language of human conscience. Yi Sun-sin, through his dying injunction — "戰方急, 愼勿言我死 (The battle is fierce; do not speak of my death)" — transformed human conscience into the command of the State. These two utterances testify to the same ethical structure in which nation and man, command and conscience, law and ethics converge. Nelson's Duty was the language of prayer directed toward God; Yi Sun-sin's Loyalty was the language of life directed toward humanity. At the moment their words meet, law is transfigured from the command of the State into the ethics of Man, and ethics, in turn, returns to the Love of God.

To visualize this cyclical structure, the paper presents the diagram "The Mandala of Delegation." Law arises from human virtue, justice is born from the memory of conscience, and salvation is fulfilled through the return of love. Thus, the Law of the State is delegated upward from the Law of Man, while the salvation of Man is bestowed downward from the Love of God. This structure reveals that the jurisprudence of the State is, in essence, a Delegated Secondary Reason derived from the jurisprudence of Man, whose foundation lies in the Conscience of Law—the ethical memory that sustains justice.

In particular, this study proclaims Yi Sun-sin (李舜臣) as the Fifth Saint of Humanity and defines his moral philosophy as a Jurisprudence of Action. While Confucius (Virtue), Jesus (Love), the Buddha (Enlightenment), and Socrates (Reason) laid the foundations of law, Yi Sun-sin completed that law through human life and ethical action. He extended Loyalty into an Ethics of Life, and his war was not a victory of empire but a redemption of humanity.

Ultimately, this study rediscovers the origin and destiny of law in the moral act of man. When the Law of the State is delegated from the Law of Man, law becomes a living conscience; when human action returns to Divine Love, ethics becomes salvation. The spirits of Nelson and Yi Sun-sin — through the Western virtue of Duty and the Eastern virtue of Loyalty — mark a civilizational coordinate where the law of nations and the law of humanity unite in one justice. This paper calls that convergence the Ethical Memory of Law, declaring that when law remembers virtue, justice is born; and when justice remembers humanity, salvation begins.

이 논문은 국가의 법(Law of the State)과 인간의 법(Law of Man)이 서로를 어떻게 비추며, 충돌과 합일의 지점에서 무엇이 진정한 '법'으로 완성되는가를 탐구한다. 국가의 법은 명령(Command)으로 시작하고, 인간의 법은 양심(Conscience)으로부터 비롯된다. 그러나 이 둘은 단절된 두 체계가 아니라, 서로를 향해 위임(Delegation)과 회귀(Return)의 순환을 이루는 하나의 철학적 구조를 형성한다. 국가의 명령이 인간의 양심으로부터 위로 위임되고, 인간의 양심이 다시 국가의 제도로 회귀할 때, 법은 단순한 명령의 언어가 아니라 살아 있는 윤리적 질서로 완성된다.

본 연구는 이 구조를 '위임된 2차적 이성(Delegated Secondary Reason)'이라 명명하고, 법의 근원을 도덕적 기억(Ethical Memory)과 행위의 증언(Act of Testimony)으로 분석한다. 국가의 법은 인간의 법으로부터 위임받은 제도적 이성이고, 인간의 법은 덕(德)과 양심으로부터 위임된 근원적 도덕이다. 이러한 위임의 사슬(Chain of Delegation)은 결국 신(神)의 사랑(Love)과 인간의 행위(Action)이 교차하는 정의(Justice)의 공간, 즉 법철학의 만다라(Mandala of Law)를 구성한다. Horatio Nelson과 李舜臣은 각각 서양과 동양의 문명사 속에서 이 '법의 위임'을 실천으로 증명한 인물이다. 넬슨은 "Thank God, I have done my duty."라는 언어로 국가의 명령을 인간의 양심으로 번역했고, 이순신은 "戰方急, 愼勿言我死."라는 마지막 유언으로 인간의 양심을 국가의 명령으로 승화시켰다. 두 문장은 국가와 인간, 명령과 양심, 법과 윤리가 교차하는 동일한 구조를 증언한다. 넬슨의 의무(Duty)는 신을 향한 기도의 언어였고, 이순신의 충의(Loyalty)는 인간을 향한 생명의 언어였다. 두 언어가 만나는 순간, 법은 국가의 명령을 넘어선 인간의 윤리로 승화되며, 윤리는 다시 신의 사랑으로 회귀한다.

이 논문은 이러한 순환적 구조를 시각화하기 위해 「위임의 도성(The Mandala of Delegation)」 도식을 제시한다. 법은 인간의 덕에서 발생하고, 정의는 양심의 기억 속에서 태어나며, 구원은 사랑의 회귀 속에서 완성된다. 이로써 국가의 법은 인간의 법으로부터 위로 위임되고, 인간의 구원은 신의 사랑으로부터 아래로 베풀어진다. 이러한 구조는 국가의 법철학이 인간의 법철학으로부터 위임된 2차적 이성임을 보여주며, 그 근원에는 '법의 양심(Conscience of Law)'이라는 윤리적 기억이 존재한다.

특히, 본 연구는 이순신(李舜臣)을 인류의 다섯 번째 성인(Fifth Saint of Humanity)으로 제시하며, 그의 윤리를 "행위의 법철학(Jurisprudence of Action)"으로 정의한다. 공자(덕), 예수(사랑), 석가(깨달음), 소크라테스(이성)의 가르침이 법의 기초를 세웠다면, 이순신의 행위는 그 법을 인간의 생명과 윤리 속에서 완성하였다. 그는 충의(Loyalty)를 넘어서 생명의 윤리(Ethics of Life)로 확장시켰고, 그의 전쟁은 제국의 승리가 아니라 인류의 구원이었다.

결론적으로, 본 논문은 '법의 기원과 귀결'을 한 인간의 행위 속에서 재발견한다. 국가의 법이 인간의 법으로부터 위임될 때 법은 살아 있는 양심이 되고, 인간의 행위가 신의 사랑으로 회귀할 때 윤리는 구원이 된다. 넬슨과 이순신의 영혼은 각각 서양의 의무와 동양의 충의 속에서, 국가의 법과 인간의 법이 만나 하나의 정의를 이루는 문명의 좌표를 남겼다. 본 연구는 그 만남을 "법의 기억(Ethical Memory of Law)"이라 부르며, 법이 덕을 기억할 때 정의가 태어나고, 정의가 인간을 기억할 때 구원이 시작된다고 선언한다.

1. 미국의 총기문화에 대한 일 고찰

- 총기문화의 기원과 형성을 중심으로 -

손 영 호*

Ⅰ. 머리말

미국에서는 크고 작은 총기 사건이 그칠 날이 없다. 중·고등학교나 대학가, 심지어 초등학교에서도 충격적인 총기사건이 자주 발생하고, 대낮에 총을 든 범인과 경찰의 총격전이 흔히 벌어지는 나라가 미국이다. 미국에서는 해마다 평균 200만 건이 넘는 폭력 범죄가 발생하고, 약 25만 명의 사람들이 목숨을 잃는데, 이 중에서 70%가 총기에 의한 사망이다. 미국에서 총기범죄나 사고가 일상적으로 일어나는 이유는 무엇일까? 대답은 간단하다. 21세가 되면 간단한 신원 조회만 통과하면 누구나 총기를 구입할 수 있기 때문이다. 흔히 미국을 "술보다 총이 더 사기 쉬운 나라"라고 일컫는 이유가 바로 여기에 있다.

미국에서는 개인의 총기 등록을 의무화하지 않는다. 때문에 정확한 총기의 수는 물론, 실제로 총기 소유자가 누구인지를 정확히 파악하기가 어렵다. 미 연방수사국(FBI)에 따르면 미국에서 개인이 소유한 총의 수는 2억 5천정에 이르고 있으며, 해마다 500만 정이 증가하는 것으로 나타났다.[1] 이것은 미국 전체 인구를 무장시킬 수 있는 규모이다. 미국을 '총기가 지배하는 국가(Gunocracy)'라 칭할 만큼 총기는 미국인들의 독특한 역사와 문화 속에 뿌리를 내리고 있다. 총기 소유자들은 대부분 총기가

---

* 베트남 호치민 국립대학교 인문사회대학 교수·청주대학교 인문대학 역사문화학과 교수, 이 글은 『역사와 담론』, 호서사학회, 2011에 게재된 논문임을 밝힌다.

1 Philip J. Cook and Jens Ludwig, *Evaluation Gun Policy: Effects on Crime and Violence* (Washington D.C., 2003), pp. 3-4.

범죄로부터 자신들을 보호할 수 있다고 믿으며, 사냥이나 사격 등 취미 생활을 즐기고 있다.

1920년부터 13년간 소위 '고상한 실험'이라고 불렸던 금주법까지 실시하였던 미국이지만, 엄청난 사회적 파장을 불러일으키고 있는 총기 소유에 대한 합리적인 규제를 취하지 못하는 이유는 무엇일까? 본고에서는 미국의 총기문화가 뿌리를 내리게 된 역사·문화적인 배경, 미국의 대중문학과 영화가 총기문화 형성에 끼친 영향, 그리고 총기 소유를 합법화 한 소위 수정헌법 제2조의 내용과 의미 등을 고찰해 보고자 한다. 이를 통해 총기문화가 "미국인들의 예외적인 특성"으로 자리를 잡게 된 과정을 파악할 수 있을 것이며, 더 나아가 미국인들의 생활양식과 가치관을 이해할 수 있을 것이다.

Ⅱ. 총기문화의 역사·문화적 기원

미국의 역사발전 과정에서 총기의 중요성을 인식하고 '총기문화(Gun Culture)'라는 단어를 처음으로 사용한 것은 미국의 역사가 리처드 홉스테터(Richard Hofstadter)였다. 그는 미국이 식민지 시대와 서부개척 시대를 거치면서 총은 미국의 독특한 문화로 자리 잡게 되었다고 언급하였다. 이후 총기를 둘러싼 논쟁이 있을 때마다, 총기문화라는 단어는 가장 핵심적인 키워드로 등장하게 되었다.[2]

미국 사학사에서 총기문화에 대한 논쟁을 촉발시킨 계기가 된 것은 조지아 대학의 역사학 교수인 마이클 벨레사일스(Michael A. Bellesiles)가 *Arming America: The Origins of a National Gun Culture* 라는 저서를 발표한 이후부터였다.[3] 벨레사일스는 1765-1790년 기간에 뉴잉글랜드와 펜실베이니아 지역의 유언검인기록(유언장, 유품목록, 회계 장부 등)을 통해 당시 총기 소유 인구는 전체 인구의 10%에 불과하였으며, 등록된 총기의 절반 이상이 무용지물이거나 고장 난 것이었다고 주장하였다.

이를 근거로 벨레사일스는 총기문화에 대한 전통적인 시각, 즉 총기는 식민지 시

---

2 Richard Hofstadter, "America as a Gun Culture," *American Heritage Magazine* (October, 1970).

3 Michael A. Bellesiles, *Arming America: The Origins of a National Gun Culture* (New York, 2000).

대부터 총은 미국인의 생활양식과 가치관을 형성하였으며, 더 나아가 독특한 미국의 문화로 자리 잡게 되었다는 주장에 반박하였다. 그에 따르면 19세기 중반까지도 총기의 양은 적었고, 그 활용도는 극히 미미한 수준이었다. 초기 정착과 식민지 시대의 미국인들의 주된 무기는 총이 아니라 도끼나 칼이었다. 독립전쟁시 민병대가 소지한 총기의 수는 극히 적어 사격훈련 조차 제대로 받지 못하였을 뿐만 아니라, 대부분 구식 소총으로 작동되지 않는 경우도 흔하였다. 남북전쟁 이전만 해도 미국의 총기산업이 발전되지 못하였고, 총기 제조업자도 드물었다. 벨레사일스는 "대부분 지역에서 총기 기술자가 드물어, 총을 수리하거나 보수하는데(총기기술자가 아니라) 대장장이에게 의존해야만 했다"라고 기록하였다.[4]

벨레사일스에 의하면 19세기 중반이후 기술혁신으로 총기 생산이 급격히 증가하고 값싼 총기가 널리 보급되면서 미국 특유의 총기문화가 생겨났다. 이 시기에 이르러 부유한 미국인들을 중심으로 영국 젠트리 계층을 본받아 사격과 사냥을 즐겼고, 총을 자신의 사회적 신분의 상징으로 삼기 시작하였다. 남북전쟁과 멕시코 전쟁으로 인해 총의 수요가 급증하였고, 전쟁이 끝난 후 퇴역병들이 총을 지닌 채 귀향하면서 총기문화는 전국적으로 확산되었다는 것이다. 따라서 벨레사일스는 미국에서 총기문화는 오랜 역사 발전과정에서 미국인들의 생활양식과 가치관으로 형성된 것이 아니라, 총기 소유를 합법화하려는 사람들에 의해 창조된 허구였다고 지적하였다. 즉 미국의 총기 문화는 "만들어진 전통"에 불과한 신화일 뿐이라는 것이다.

유언검인기록을 분석한 자료를 바탕으로 한 벨레사일스의 주장은 나름대로 독창적인 근거를 제시하고는 있으나, 전통적인 해석의 뒤엎을 만한 설득력을 보여주지 못한다. 왜냐하면 미국의 총기 문화는 총기의 소유와 생산만으로 설명하기엔 불충분하기 때문이다. 총기 소유와 생산량만으로 판단한다면 영국이 미국보다 먼저 총기문화를 창조하여야 하였을 것이다. 또한 벨레사일스의 저서는 총기의 소유와 휴대의 시민적 권리를 명시한 미국의 수정헌법 제2조가 왜 채택되었으며, 총기 소유에 대한 건국의 아버지들의 생각이 무엇이었는지에 대한 연구가 미흡한 것으로 지적되고 있다. 벨레사일스의 의견과는 달리 많은 역사학자들은 미국에서 총기문화는 식민지 정착

---

4 *Ibid.*, pp. 107, 228-229; Michael A. Bellesiles, "The Origins of Gun Culture in the United States, 1760-1865," *Journal of American History*, 83: 2 (September 1996), p. 443.

과 독립혁명, 그리고 서부 프런티어 시대를 거치면서 미국인들의 생활양식과 가치관으로 형성되어 왔음을 지적하고 있다. 즉 미국의 총기문화는 사냥과 스포츠의 오랜 전통, 영국과의 독립전쟁 당시 민병대의 활동, 그리고 서부 개척시대의 유습으로부터 유래되었다.[5] 우선 농업이 주요 생계 수단이었던 식민지 초기 정착민들에게 총은 야생동물이나 인디언의 위협으로부터 자신들을 보호하고, 사냥을 통해 부족한 육류원을 확보할 수 있었던 중요한 수단이 되었다. 영국 정부는 지리적으로 멀리 떨어진 식민지에 모국과 같은 수준의 치안과 질서 유지를 보장할 수 없었기 때문에 신대륙 정착민에게 자기방어를 위한 무기 소유를 허용하였다.

미국의 저명한 역사가이자 퓰리처상 수상자인 다니엘 부어스틴(Daniel J. Boorstine)은 "총기는 개척민들에게 자기 방어와 식량 확보를 위한 필수품이었기 때문에 당시엔 거의 누구나 총기를 보유하였다"라고 언급하였다.[6] 또 다른 역사학자인 웨슬리 크레이븐(Wesley F. Craven) 역시 "초기 영국 식민지 시대 거의 모든 능력 있는 남성들은 총기를 소유하였다"고 주장하였다.[7] 총은 개척민들과 항상 함께 하였고, 인디언이나 무법자, 야생동물로부터 생명과 재산을 보호하는 필수품이 되었다. 윌리엄 데브스(William C. Davis)는 프런티어 정착민들의 생활을 다음과 같이 묘사하였다.

> 정착민이 거처하는 오두막에는 적어도 한 두정의 라이플(소총)과 구식 피스톨(권총)이 있었다 … 총에 대한 기본 상식이 없거나 총에 적절히 사용할 줄 모르는 남자들은 진정한 남성으로 대접받지 못하였다 … 프런티어의 아버지는 아들이 9-10세에 이르면 총을 쏘고 스스로 방어하는 법을 가르쳤다 … 부자가 함께 사슴이나 곰 사냥을 즐겼고, 사냥 후에는 온 가족이 푸짐한 저녁상을 받을 수 있었다. 그리고 인디언들이 약탈을 하거나 싸움을 걸어오면, 강하게 키워진 사내아이는 아버지와 함께 가족의 생명과 재산을 지키는 용감한 전사가 되었다.[8]

총기 역사학자인 하롤드 패터슨(Harold L. Peterson)은 "미국에서 1620-1690년 기간

---

5 Robert J. Spitzer, *The Politics of Gun Control* (New York, 1995), chapter, 1.

6 Daniel J. Boorstine, *The Americans: The Colonial Experience* (New York, 1958), p. 353.

7 Wesley Frank Craven, *The Colonies in Transition, 1660-1713* (New York, 1968), pp. 30-31.

8 William C. Davis, *A Way Through the Wilderness: The Natchez Trace and the Civilization of the Southern Frontier* (New York, 1995), p. 88.

만큼 총기가 절실하게 필요했던 시기는 없었다"고 언급하였다. 총은 초기 정착민들에게 야생동물과 인디언들의 공격에 대비하고, 음식이나 옷가지, 다양한 일용품을 확보하는데 없어서는 안 될 도구였다. 당시 식민지에서는 총기를 생산할 기술과 자본이 부족하였지만, 유럽으로부터 다양한 종류의 총기를 수입하였으며, 그 결과 "미국인들은 유럽인을 능가하는 성능이 뛰어난 총기를 소유할 수 있었고, 능숙하게 총을 다루는 방법도 터득하였다."[9]

18세기 식민지 미국인들은 "세계에서 가장 잘 무장된" 사람들이었으며, 식민지는 모국인 영국의 관습법에 따라 무기를 소유하고 휴대하는 것을 법으로 보장하였다.[10] 손에는 총을 들고, 벨트에는 총탄을 두른 채, 프런티어 개척민들은 야생의 세계를 정복해 나갔고, 총기에서 뿜어 나오는 힘과 정의 가 새로운 사회 질서의 창출한다는 미국적 신화와 가치관을 형성하게 하였다.[11] 이러한 총기문화의 전통은 오늘날 미국에서 사냥이나 사격이 중요한 대중 스포츠의 하나로 자리 잡게 되는데 중요한 역할을 하였다. 사냥이나 사격은 도시나 산업화된 지역보다는 중서부나 남부의 농촌지역을 중심으로 성행하고 있는데, 이것은 미국의 총기문화가 도시보다는 농촌 지역(과거 프런티어 지역)에서 뿌리를 내리게 된 것에서 확인할 수 있다.[12]

독립혁명 당시의 민간인이 자발적으로 결성한 민병대는 총기문화의 정착에 상당한 기여를 하였다. 인지세법과 보스턴 차당사건을 계기로 영국의 식민지에 대한 노골적인 탄압이 가해지자, 식민지인들의 영국에 대한 불만이 가속화되었다. 영국 정부는 식민지가 본국과 지리적으로 멀리 떨어져 있어, 반란이 일어날 경우 식민지가 영국의 통제에서 벗어날 것을 두려워하였다. 이에 영국 의회는 1774년 10월 모든 총기와 납, 화약, 기타 군 장비에 대한 수출 금지령을 발표하였다.[13] 이것은 식민지에서의 무장 반란을 사전에 차단하기 위한 조치였다. 식민지 시대의 미국인들은 유럽에

---

9 Harold L. Peterson, "The Military Equipment of the Plymouth and Bay Colonies, 1620-1890," *The New England Quarterly* 20 (1947), p. 197.

10 John M. Dederer, *War in America to 1775: Before Yankee Doodle* (New York, 1990), pp. 116, 251.

11 Richard Slotkin, *Regeneration Through Violence: The Mythology of the American Frontier, 1600-1860* (Middletown, CT, 1973).

12 "A Look Inside America's gun culture," ABC News Online (April 17, 2007).

13 Margaret Marion Spector, *The American Development of the British Government*, 1768-1782 (New York, 1940), pp. 74-95.

서처럼 상비군을 유지할 수 있는 충분한 인적 자원과 재원을 갖추지 못하였다. 식민지인들은 사실상 그 때까지 단 한번도 통일을 이룩해 본적이 없었고, 전쟁을 수행하는 데 필요한 통일적인 기구도 없었다. 그러나 영국의 강압적인 통치에 대항하여 독립을 하여야 한다는 애국주의가 고조된 이후 자발적으로 무장할 것을 결의하였다. 각 주 식민지는 '1분 안에 즉각 출동할 수 있게 준비된 군인'이란 뜻의 '1분 대기반'이라는 민병(minute-man)을 조직하였다. 또한 전쟁 수행을 위해 무기고를 갖추었으며, 훈련과 동원 임무를 수행할 공안위원회도 조직하였다. 성인 백인 남성이면 누구나 조국의 위해 민병대에 가입하여 싸우는 것을 명예스럽게 생각하였다. 1775년 4월 보스턴 근교 렉싱턴과 콩코드에서 영국 정규군과 매사추세츠주 민병대 간에 무력 충돌로 마침내 독립전쟁이 시작되었다. 영국과의 교전상태에 돌입하자 식민지 대표들은 필라델피아에서 제2차 대륙회의를 개최하여 각 주의 민병대들을 통합하여 대륙 연합군을 조직, 독립을 위한 무력항쟁에 들어갔다. 연합군 총사령관에 임명된 조지 워싱턴의 지도 하에 각지에서 자발적으로 몰려든 민병의 수도 점차 증가되었다. 민병들의 장비는 부족하였고 제대로 된 훈련도 받지 못한 경우가 많았다. 그러나 13개 식민지 중에서 가장 막강했던 버지니아의 경우 만만치 않은 전력을 가지고 있었다. 혁명의 지도자였던 리처드 헨리 리(Richard Henry Lee)는 "버지니아에는 6,000명의 '라이플맨(Rifle Men)'으로 구성된 민병대가 있으며, 이들은 상당수는 정규적인 사격 훈련으로 200야드 밖의 오렌지를 명중시킬 수 있는 사격술을 보유하였다"고 언급하였다.[14]

민병대는 조국의 독립과 자유를 수호한다는 결의로 막강한 해군과 군사장비를 갖춘 영국군에 대항하여 많은 전공을 올렸다. 대륙 연합군은 1777년 가을 새러토가에서 영국군을 대파하여 승리를 위한 유리한 고지를 마련하였다. 그리고 마침내 1981년 10월 프랑스군의 지원을 받아 버지니아의 요크타운 전투에서 영국군에게 결정적인 승리를 거두고, 독립전쟁을 성공적으로 이끌었다. 자신의 생명과 재산을 지키고, 조국의 자유와 독립을 위해 총을 들고 영국군과 싸운 민병대의 정신은 미국인들에게 고귀한 전통으로 남아 있다. 이를 통해 미국인들은 총은 곧 자유와 생명을 지키는 수단이 된다는 신념을 갖게 되었던 것이다.

---

14 James Curtish Ballagh, ed., *The Letters of Richard Henry Lee*, 2 vols. (New York, 1911), pp. 130-131.

독립 후 서부개척 시대에 총은 인디언, 무법자, 그리고 야생동물의 위협으로부터 생명과 재산을 지키는 필수품이었다. 서부개척 시대 총기보유 현황을 확인할 수 있는 자료가 부족하여 정확한 총기보유 상황을 파악하기가 어렵다. 그러나 프런티어 여행자나 정착민들의 기행문과 서신, 회고록이나 자서전 등을 통해 19세기 초반 총기는 이미 보편화된 생활 도구였음을 확인할 수 있다.

1830년대 미국 남부의 알라바마 프런티어 지역을 방문했던 영국의 박물학자 필립 거스(Philip Gosse)는 "이곳 사람들은 스포츠와 육류 확보, 그리고 농작물을 보호하기 위하여 라이플로 다람쥐, 야생개, 여우 등을 사냥하는 것이 일상적인 생활이었다"고 하였다. 그는 알라바마인들의 사냥과 총기에 대한 태도를 다음과 같이 묘사하였다.

자기 방어와 자연에 대한 도전 정신은 이곳 사람들을 숙련된 사냥꾼으로 만들었다 … 누구든 장총을 지니고 있었으며, 총을 다루는 기술은 남부 남성들이 긍지를 느끼고 자랑스러워 할 만큼 아주 높은 수준이었다. 이곳에서는 나이가 아주 어린 아이들 조차도 총을 다루는데 뛰어난 기술을 가지고 있었다 … 젊은이들이 즐기는 게임은 사격이었다. 옛날 영국의 궁술(활쏘기)에서 볼 수 있는 것처럼 신출한 기술을 보여주었는데, 그것은 과녁에 못을 반쯤 박아 놓고 상당한 거리에서 총을 쏘아 못의 머리 부분을 조준하여 못이 판자에 완전히 박히게 하는 시합이었다. 못이 빗나가 휘거나 구부러진다면 물론 실격이었다.[15]

1831년 알라바마를 방문하였던 영국인 작가이며 사상가인 알렉시스 드 토크빌(Alexis de Tocqueville)은 테네시 지역에서 총기문화가 이미 보편화되었음을 한 농부의 말을 인용하여 다음과 같이 언급하였다.

이곳 사람들은 대체로 나태하고 노동을 악이라고 생각해요. 먹을 음식과 거처할 오두막만 있다면 그저 행복해 하며 담배를 피우거나 사냥하는 것만 생각한답니다. 여가 시간에는 농사는 돌보지 않고 어떻게 하면 좋은 총을 가지고 사냥을 할까 하는 데만 관심이 있지요.[16]

토크빌은 또한 이곳 '농부의 캐빈(Peasant's cabin)'에는 "잘 정돈된 침대와 의자, 그리고 몇 권의 책과 신문을 발견할 수 있으며, 거의 모든 가정에서 총을 볼 수가 있었으며, 사냥은 생활의 한 부분이었다"고 밝히고 있다.[17]

1818년 오자크(Ozarks) 지역(미주리, 알칸소, 오클라호마 세 주가 걸쳐 고원지대)을 방

---

15 Philip Gosse, *Letters from Alabama* (London, 1859), pp. 130-131.

16 Alexis de Tocqueville, trans. by George Lawrence, *Journey to America* (New Haven, 1960), p. 95.

17 *Ibid.*, p. 281.

문했던 영국인 여행자 헨리 로이 스쿨크래프트(Henry Rowe Schoolcraft)는 여가를 위한 스포츠 사냥이나 육류나 가죽을 얻기 위한 직업적인 사냥은 어디서나 목격할 수 있는 광경이라고 하였다. 이 지역 어린 아이들은 14세가 되면 라이플 사용법을 완벽하게 익혔으며, 동물의 가죽을 벗겨 신발이나 옷을 만드는 기술을 터득하였다.[18] 스쿨크래프트는 총이 사냥은 물론 생존을 위한 도구였음을 다음과 같이 묘사하였다.

오자크 지역 사람들의 일부는 농사를 짓고 일부는 사냥으로 살아간다 … 사냥은 중요하고 명예로운 것이며, 가계에 보탬이 되는 일이었다. 남성들의 가치와 평판은 사격 기술, 사냥에서의 민첩성과 강인함, 그리고 인내와 어려움을 극복하는 능력에 의해 평가되었다 … 사냥꾼들은 깊은 숲 속에서도 생존하는 능력을 터득하였고, 야생의 프런티어 곳곳에서 발생할 수도 있는 싸움에서도 효과적인 군사조직력을 형성할 수 있었다. 이들 훈련된 사냥꾼들은 곤경과 위험에 단련되었을 뿐만 아니라 완벽하게 라이플의 사용 기술을 터득하였다.[19]

1830-40년대 미국을 방문했던 유럽인들은 그들의 여행 기록이나 자서전을 통하여 미국을 방문한 목적의 하나가 사냥을 위한 것이었음을 증언하고 있다. 이들은 총은 미국인의 생활과 문화에 필수적인 요소였으며, 사냥과 사격은 어디서나 볼 수 있는 광경이었다고 언급하였다. 찰스 어거스터스 머레이(Charles Augustus Murray)는 버지니아의 한 농촌 지역을 방문한 경험을 다음과 같이 기록하였다.

나는 마을에서 7마일 정도 떨어진 외딴 농가에서 첫날밤을 보냈다. 이곳 사람들은 농사를 짓지만, 거의 모든 남성들은 라이플을 가지고 있었으며, 여가 시간에는 야생동물을 쫓아 사냥에 나섰다. 내가 런던에서 제작된 쌍 라이플총을 보여주자 사람들은 총의 구석구석을 살피면서 모양과 성능에 대하여 관심을 보였다. 그러나 총을 살펴본 뒤에 거의 모든 사람들은 '과녁 맞추기 시합을 한다면 난 당신을 이길 수 있다'고 이구동성 이야기하곤 하였다.[20]

미국에서 총기 소유와 사냥은 북부 지역보다는 서남부 지역에서 더 보편적으로 행해졌다. 그러나 북부에서도 총기문화가 널리 형성되었다는 사실을 다양한 기록을 통해 확인할 수 있다. 포테스큐 커밍(Fortescue Cuming)은 1807년부터 1809년까지 오하이오와 켄터키의 지역의 여행을 통하여 이곳 북부에서도 서남부 지역과 같이 스포츠

---

18 Henry Rowe Schoolcraft, intro. by Milton D. Rafferty, *Rude Pursuits and Rugged Peaks: Schoolcraft's Ozark Journey 1818-1819* (Fayetteville, Ark, 1996), p. 74.

19 *Ibid.*, p. 63.

20 Charles Augustus Murray, *Travels in North America* (London, 1838, reprinted New York, 1974), pp. 118-119.

나 사냥, 자기 방어를 위해 총이 널리 사용되고 있음을 확인하였다. 커밍은 자급자족을 위한 사냥과 시장에 내다 팔기 위한 상업적인 사냥을 구별하였는데, "상업적인 사냥보다는 자급을 위한 사냥이 일반적이었다"고 기록하였다.[21]

커밍은 사냥꾼인 자신조차도 놀라울 정도로 서부 펜실베이니아인들의 사격 솜씨에 감탄하며, 다음과 같이 기록하였다.

> 이곳 농촌 마을에서는 라이플 소총을 능숙하게 다루는 전문적인 사냥꾼이 많았다. 숲 속에서 배회하는 야생 칠면조나 나무 꼭대기에 매달려 있는 다람쥐의 머리를 정확히 가격하지 않으면 실패한 사격이라고 생각하였다. 이들은 작은 탄알 몇 개를 장재한 총으로 동물이나 새의 머리를 정확히 관통하는 신기에 가까운 사격 솜씨를 보여주었다.[22] 커밍은 몇몇 사례를 들어 총이 법을 집행하기 위한 도구로 사용되었다는 사실에 대해서도 언급하였다. 그는 서부 펜실베이니아 여행 중 한 마을에서 발생한 살인 사건을 목격하였는데, "이곳 주민들은 마을에서 살인 사건이 발생한 것을 확인한 후, 급히 이웃에게 알려 안전하게 대피시키고, 곧 이어 마을 사람들을 모아 무장한 채 범인을 추적하였다. 저항하는 범인 1명을 현장에서 사살하고, 다른 1명은 체포하였다"고 기록하였다.[23]

영국에서 미국으로 이민을 온 뒤 서부 펜실베이니아 산악지대를 여행했던 일라이어스 핌 포드햄(Elias Pim Fordham)은 "피스톨과 라이플로 무장한 40여 명으로 이루어진 강도단이 외딴 농가를 급습하여 옷가지와 가축을 약탈하였다"고 증언하였다.[24] 포드햄은 또한 채권자로부터 청탁을 받고 도주 중인 채무자를 추적하는 8명의 무장 총잡이들을 목격한 것과 "16-17세기 용기병(Dragoon Officer)처럼 구두 안창에다 피스톨을 숨기고 다니는" 치안 판사를 만난 경험을 기록하였다.[25] 이런 사례들은 당시 총이 자기 방어나 사냥뿐만 아니라, 살인이나 약탈의 도구로, 혹은 범법자를 응징하

---

21 Fortescue Cuming, *Sketches of a Tour to the Western Country Through the States of Ohio and Kentucky: A Voyage Down the Ohio and Mississippi Rivers* (Pittsburgh, 1810), pp. 30, 42, 113, 118, 135.

22 *Ibid.*, p. 30.

23 *Ibid.*, p. 54.

24 Elias Pim Fordham, ed., Frederic Austin Ogg, *Personal Narrative: Travels in Virginia, Maryland, Pennsylvania, Ohio, Indiana, Kentucky, and of a Residence in the Illinois Territory: 1817-1818*, (Cleveland, 1906), pp. 60-61.

25 *Ibid.*, p. 155.

는 수단으로도 사용되었음을 말해 주는 것이다. 또한 이런 기록을 통해 남북전쟁 이전에 이미 변방 프런티어 지역에서 강도나 순회 판사들 조차도 총기를 소유할 만큼 총기문화가 널리 퍼져 있다는 사실도 확인할 수 있다.

포드햄은 1817년 인디애나의 일리노이 지역의 야생지를 여행하는데 갖추어야 할 개인 소지품, 즉 총과 인디언 도끼, 숲 속에서 야영하는데 필요한 장비 등에 대해서도 상세한 기록을 남겼다. 그는 영국에 있는 동생에게 보낸 편지에서 "나는 창이 넓은 밀짚모자를 쓰고, 긴 바지에 모카신(Moccasins; 뒤축이 없는 인디언 신발)을 신고, 허리에는 탄약띠와 뿔모양의 화약 케이스를 차고, 어께에는 총을 멘 채, 온종일 말을 타고 이동하고 있다"고 말하였다.[26] 이것은 당시 프런티어 남성들의 통상적인 옷차림이었다. 이곳 사람들은 덫이 아니라 주로 총을 이용하여 사냥을 하였으며, 크리스마스 시즌에는 사냥한 야생 터키를 요리하여 밤새도록 먹고 마시며, 총을 쏘아대는 등 여흥을 즐겼다.[27]

이러한 '크리스마스 총포사격(Christmas shooting)' 행위는 1830년대 미주리 프런티어를 방문하였던 독일인 여행자 거트 고벨(Gert Göbel)의 증언에서도 확인되고 있다.

> 크리스마스 전날, 인근 마을에서 많은 젊은이들이 사냥용 라이플뿐만 아니라, 독립전쟁 때 사용하였던 구형 머스캣과 호스 피스톨(horse pistol, 가죽집에 넣는 대형 단총)을 들고 모여 들었다. 이들은 의기투합하여 총을 완전히 장전한 채 집집마다 돌아다녔다. 이들은 아주 조용하고 은밀하게 한 가옥에 접근하여 그 집의 부녀자나 아이들이 깜짝 놀랄 만큼 일시에 총을 쏘아 댔다. 총소리를 듣고 주인이 나타나지 않으면, 다시 총을 쏘아댈 참이었다. 그러나 보통 집 주인 남자는 즉시 문을 열고 답례로 자신의 총을 발사한 후, 이들 모두를 집안으로 초청하였다 … 잠시 머물러 잡담을 나눈 뒤, 일행은 이웃집으로 자리를 이동하여 같은 방법으로 총포 놀이를 즐겼다 … 마을 곳곳에서는 밤새도록 총 소리가 진동하였다.[28]

당시 프런티어 지역에서 크리스마스는 성스런 종교 축제일이기보다는, 먹고 마시

---

26 *Ibid.*, p. 109.

27 *Ibid.*, p. 147.

28 As quoted in Walter L. Robbins, "Christmas Shooting Rounds in America and Their Background," *Journal of American Folklore*, 86: 339 (1973), pp. 48-52.

며 여흥을 즐기는 세속적인 축제일처럼 보였다. 안식일도 역시 마찬가지였다. 1840년에 인디애나를 방문한 한 여행자는 "서부에서 안식일은 신성을 모독하는 일들로 가득하였다. 시장에서는 물건이 흥정되고, … 사람들은 오락과 유흥으로 마음이 들떠있었다. 사냥과 세속적인 이야기, 음주와 무절제한 행동은 프런티어에서 흔히 볼 수 있는 광경이었다"고 기록하였다.[29]

포드햄은 영국에 있는 동생에게 보낸 편지에서 "영국산 라이플은 이곳에서도 손쉽게 구할 수 있으니, 필요하다면 피스톨 한 두정만 가져오길 바란다"고 조언하였다.[30] 당시 미국에서는 성능이 뛰어나고 사용하기가 편리한 영국산 피스톨은 귀한 편이었으나, 라이플과 같은 총기류는 영국에서와 거의 같은 값이거나 오히려 더 싸게 구입할 수 있었다. 이것은 1810-1820년대 라이플이 프런티어 지역에서 흔히 사용되었으며, 그만큼 미국에서 총기가확산되어 대중화가 되었음을 말해주는 대목이다.[31] 실제로 1840년대에 이르러 프런티어 지역에서 총의 수요가 증가하였으며, 당시 성능이 우수한 라이플의 가격은 15-20불 정도에 구입할 수 있었기 때문에 누구든 원한다면 어렵지 않게 총을 구입할 수 있었다.[32]

감리교 목사인 피터 카트라이트(Peter Cartwright)는 1820년 미국 동부 애팔래치안 산맥을 넘어 볼티모어로 여행을 하였는데, 그의 증언에 따르면 당시 총기는 도처에서 흔하게 볼 수 있었으며, 심지어 길가에 놓여있는 총을 발견할 정도였다고 진술하였다.

산을 타고 내려오던 길에 서부로 이동하는 마차들을 여럿 목격하였다. 나는 마차들이 지난 간 후, 잘 손질된 소형 피스톨이 길거리에 떨어져 있는 것을 발견하였다. 총을 확인해 보니, 즉시 발사가 가능하도록 총탄이 장전되어 있었다. 마차를 이동하던 사람들이 부주위로 땅에 떨어뜨린 것이 분명해 보였다. 나는 동생에게 '이것은 신의 섭리야'라고 외쳤다. 왜냐하면 당시 산을 가로 지르는 길가에는 강도들이 득실 되었으며, 최근 이곳에서 살인과 강도사건이 자주 발생하였다는 소식을 들었기 때문이

---

29 Shirley S. McCord, ed., *Travel Accounts of Indiana, 1679-1916* (Indianapolis, 1970), p. 183.
30 *Ibid.*, pp. 223-225.
31 *Ibid.*, p. 237.
32 Ole Rynning, ed., *Ole Rynning's True Account of America* (Freeport, N.Y., 1971), p. 99.

었다.[33]

당시 프런티어 도처에는 항상 위험이 도사리고 있었기 때문에, 주운 피스톨은 여행 중에 강도들의 위협으로부터 신변을 보호하는 유익한 도구가 되었다. 카트라이트는 통행료 징수를 둘러싸고 강도들과 말다툼이 벌어졌으며, 강도들이 "총을 벗어 놓으라"고 으름장을 놓았는데, 이런 행위는 "우리 일행을 무장 해제시켜 물품을 빼앗거나 해치려는 의도가 있음을 보여주는 것"이라고 기록하였다.[34]

프런티어 여행자들이나 이주자들의 기행문이나 회고록, 그리고 서신 등을 통해 확인할 수 있듯이, 건국 초기부터 19세기 중엽에 이르는 기간에 미국에서 총기는 거의 모든 지역. 특히 서부와 남부 프런티어 지역에서 널리 보급되었다. 프런티어의 척박한 자연 환경, 야생 동물이나 인디언의 습격, 그리고 법과 질서가 확립되지 않은 곳인 까닭에 총은 생존을 위한 필수적인 도구였던 것이다.[35] 총은 외부의 적으로부터 자신과 가족을 방어하는 무기였으며, 육류 공급을 위한 사냥이나 여가를 위한 사격의 도구였다. 총은 더 나아가 무질서한 프런티어에서 범죄를 막고 법을 집행하기 위한 수단이 되었던 것이다. 이런 사실들은 남북전쟁 이전에 미국에서 총기는 널리 보급되어 이미 대중화되었음을 보여주는 것이다. 다시 말하면, 총기문화는 독특한 미국의 지리 환경과 역사 발전 과정에서 사회·문화적인 풍습의 한 형태로 발전되어 독특한 미국적 생활양식과 가치관을 형성하였던 것이다.

Ⅲ. 문학과 영화 속에 나타난 총기문화

앞서 살펴본 바와 같이 총기문화는 식민지 정착 이후부터 서부개척 시대를 거치면서 미국인들의 생활과 문화적 유습으로 자리를 잡게 되었다. 그러나 이러한 총기문화를 국민적 정서로 확산시키는 데는 미국의 문학과 영화 등 대중 매체가 중요한 역

---

33 Peter Cartwright, ed. by W. P. Strickland, *Autobiography of Peter Cartwright The Blakwoods Preacher* (Cincinnati, n.d.), p. 200.

34 *Ibid.*, pp. 201, 206.

35 이미 정착지가 형성된 동부 도시 지역에서도 총기 소유는 드문 일이 아니었다. 뉴욕 맨하턴에서는 이미 1830년대 상업용 사격 연습장이 생겨났을 정도로 총기는 널리 보급되었다.

할을 하였다. 서부개척 시대의 모험담은 미국의 대중문학에서 가장 인기 있는 소재가 되었다. 미국의 낭만주의 작가인 제임스 페니모어 쿠퍼(James F. Cooper)는 「개척자들」(*Pioneers*, 1823), 「모히칸족의 최후」(*The Last of the Mohican*, 1826), 「대평원」(*The Prairie*, 1827), 「길잡이」(*The Pathfinder*, 1840), 그리고 「밀렵자」(*The Deerslayer*, 1840) 등 소위 5편의 '가죽장화 소설'(Leatherstocking novels)을 통해 프런티어를 배경으로 낭만적이며 역동적인 서부 개척자들의 삶과 모험을 묘사하였다.[36] 이들 작품들은 유럽문화의 이식이 아닌, 미국 프런티어의 자연을 배경으로 문명과 야만, 원시림과 정착촌, 개인의 자유와 공동체의 질서 사이의 대립과 조화라는 주제를 다룬 작품들이다.

미국 서부문학의 효시로 꼽히는 「모히칸족의 최후」는 미국이 독립하기 직전 뉴욕주의 조지 호수와 허드슨강 상류를 무대로 인디언 모히칸족의 마지막 후예와 그들의 손에 의해 키워진 백인 청년의 모험과 투쟁, 그리고 사랑을 그린 대작이다. 미국의 초기 프런티어의 역사(영국과 프랑스간의 식민지 지배권을 둘러싼 전쟁, 개척민과 인디언과의 갈등과 투쟁 등)가 고스란히 녹아있는 이 소설은 후에 수차례 영화와 TV 드라마로 만들어져 일반 대중의 서부에 대한 관심과 향수를 느끼게 하였다.

19세기 후반 서부 개척시대를 살았던 미국인들은 자신의 기억과 마음속에 각기 다른 모습의 카우보이를 그리고 있었다. 이렇게 사람들의 생각 속에 흩어져 있던 카우보이의 존재가 소설가 오웬 위스터(Owen Wister)에 의해 미국인 모두가 공감할 수 있는 전형적인 모습으로 구체화되었다. 1860년 필라델피아에서 태어난 위스터는 청년시절 프런티어를 여행하면서 서부의 자연환경과 토양, 그리고 이곳 사람들의 생활과 전승문화에 매료되었다. 그는 이러한 서부에서의 다양한 경험과 생각을 일기로 기록하였으며, 이를 바탕으로 1902년 최초의 카우보이 소설 「버지니아인」(*The Virginian*)을 저술하였다.[37] 위스터는 「버지니아인」에서 "악에는 당당히 맞서지만 자존심과 명예를 지키려는 고독한 카우보이"의 모습을 그리고 있다. 흙먼지가 자욱한 거리에서 일정한 거리를 두고 적대적인 두 사람이 명예를 걸고 당당히 총을 뽑는 장면이 나오는데, 이것이 이후 고전 서부극에서 자주 등장하는 결투 장면의 기원이 되었다. 위스

---

36 James Fenimore Cooper (1789-1815) (http://www.kirjasto.sci.fi/jfcooper.html)

37 Randy F. Nelson, *The Almanac of American Letters* (Los Altos, California, 1981), p. 287.

터에 의해 창조된 카우보이의 특성 — 거칠고 자유 분망하며, 의협심이 강하고, 명예를 죽음보다 중요하게 여기는 신념 — 은 이후 다른 소설이나 영화 속에서 나타나는 카우보이의 전형적인 모습이 되었다.

위스터의 작품은 출간한지 8개월 만에 14번이나 증판을 거듭할 정도로 큰 호응을 불러일으켰다. 이 소설은 후에 수차례 각색되어 영화와 TV 드라마로 만들어져 서부와 카우보이에 대한 서정적인 향수를 불러일으켰다. 위스터의 딸은 아버지의 소설 「버지니아인」이 미국 역사에 미친 영향에 대하여 다음과 같이 언급하였다.

아무도 이 소설이 수많은 서부인들이 모델로 삼게 될 카우보이의 이상적인 모습을 만들어 냈다는 사실을 깨닫지 못하였다. 소설속의 카우보이는 일반대중들의 상상력을 사로잡은 최초의 카우보이였으며, 수백만 명의 젊은 여성들이 사랑에 빠져들게 한 인물이었다. 준수한 외모에다가 인간적이며 유머 감각도 있었다 …

「버지니아인」의 카우보이는 민간전승의 이야기에 나오는 카우보이의 원형이 되었다. 어린 아이들은 유행처럼 카우보이모자를 쓰고 장난감 권총을 허리에 차고 다니며, 자신이 카우보이라도 된 것처럼 행동하였다. 이 소설 하나가 모든 사람들의 마음속에 영원히 각인될 서부의 역사와 전통을 만들어 냈던 것이다. 자존심과 명예를 지키고, 사랑하는 연인을 보호하며, 정의를 위하여 불의한 악당에게 총을 뿜어대는 카우보이의 영웅적인 행동이 이후 수많은 서부 소설이나 영화, 라디오와 TV 드라마로 각색되었다 … 「버지니아인」은 단순히 작가의 상상력이 만들어 낸 허구의 이야기이지만, 미국의 역사와 가치관을 창조해 낸 작품이었다.[38]

서부개척 시대 최초의 여성 슈퍼스타는 애니 오컬리(Annie Oakley)였다. 오컬리는 오하이오 주 한 농촌 마을에서 태어나 고아로서 불우한 삶을 살았지만, 명사수로서 세계적인 명성을 얻은 전설적인 인물이었다. 그녀는 이미 12살 때 달아나는 다람쥐의 머리를 정확히 관통시킬 정도로 뛰어난 사격술을 보여 주었다. 그녀는 소총(22 caliber rifle)으로 27m 떨어진 과녁의 한 가운데를 정확히 맞추었다. 그녀의 사격 기술은 공중에 카드를 날려 땅에 닿기 전에 5, 6개의 구멍을 내어, 카드를 반으로 자를 수 있을 정도였다. 오컬리는 1885년부터 전국을 순회하며 공연한 「버팔로 빌의 와일드 웨스트 쇼」(*Buffalo Bill's Wild West*)」에서 현란한 총 솜씨로 대중의 인기를 한 몸에 받았으며, 당시 미국인들로 하여금 사격에 대

---

38 Frances Kimble Wister, ed., *Owen Wister out West: His Journals and Letters* (1958), as Quoted in http://en.wikipedia.org/wiki/Owen_Wister, p. 2.

한 관심과 흥미를 불러일으키는데 커다란 영향을 끼쳤다. 그녀의 이야기를 소재로 한 「애니여, 총을 들어라」(*Annie, Get Your Gun*)는 영화와 뮤지컬로도 상영되어 폭발적인 인기를 모았다.[39]

황야를 가로지르는 말과 마차, 대평원을 질주하는 버펄로 무리를 쫓는 인디언, 수천 마리의 소 떼를 몰고 다니는 카우보이, 돈과 황금을 위해 아무데나 총을 쏘아대는 총잡이, 그리고 일확천금을 꿈꾸는 노다지꾼, 무법자와 이를 쫓는 보안관의 대결 … 이런 것들을 소재로 한 서부극의 모험과 낭만, 그리고 격식을 벗어난 자유는 많은 미국인들에게 서부가 곧 미국인 정신적 고향이라는 가치관을 심어주기에 충분하였다. 피스톨로 무장하고 악한을 쳐부수는 영웅적인 서부극의 이야기는 수천 명의 사람들을 매혹시켰고, 미국에서 총기문화가 뿌리를 내리는데 커다란 역할을 하였다.

20세기 들어서도 「대열차 강도」(*The Great Train Robbery*, 1903)」, 존 웨인을 서부극의 우상으로 만든 「역마차」(*Stagecoach*, 1939), 보안관이 무법자를 상대로 외로이 목숨을 건 결투를 벌이는 「하이 눈」(*High Noon*, 1952) 등이 미국인들에게 서부의 향수를 불러일으키며 흥행에 성공하였다. 서부 야생지의 서정적인 풍광을 배경으로 펼쳐지는 인디언과 백인 정착민, 총으로 무장한 무법자와 보안관, 그리고 카우보이 등이 등장하는 서부 영화는 당시 미국인들에세 폭발적인 인기를 끌어 서부 영화가 널리 대중화되는 계기가 되었다.[40]

서부 개척자나 카우보이, 그리고 정의로운 보안관들을 소재로 한 문학 작품에 이어, 1910년대에는 미국 영화 산업 발달에 힘입어 갱 영화가 출현하기 시작하였다. 1912년 처음 시작된 갱 영화는 1920년대 금주법 시대를 거치면서 1930년대에 이르러 전성기를 구가하였다. 갱 영화는 당시 실존 인물이었던 알 카포네의 등장, 1929년 성 바란타인 대학살 사건, 뉴욕이나 시카고 등 대도시에서 벌어진 범죄 조직 간의 치열한 총격전 등 당시의 시대·사회적인 분위기에 힘입어 폭발적인 인기를 끌었다. 이러한 갱 영화들은 "거들먹거리며 공갈 협박하고, 잔인하고 교활한 수법으로 법질서에 도전하는 주류 밀매업자나 도시 갱단"을 주요 소재로 다루었다.[41]

2차 세계대전이 발발과 함께 할리우드는 전쟁이라는 국가적인 당면 과제를 맞이하여 미국인들의 단결과 애국심을 고양시키는 영화를 제작하였다. 과거 황야에서 외롭고 거친 삶을 살았던 카우보이나 조직을 위해 무장한 갱단의 무용담은 이제 국민적 화합과 애국심을 강조하고, 개인적인 가치보다는 집단의 단결을 강조하는 전쟁 영화로 대체되었다. 당시의

---

39 http://cakel,history,com/entry/annie-Oakley

40 "Western Films," Tim Dirks, *Filmsite, 1996-2007* (http://www.filmsite.org/westernfilms.html)

41 "Crime and Gangster Films," Tim Dirks, *Filmsite*, 1996-2007 (http://www.filmsite.org/crimefilms.html)

전형적인 전쟁영화는 다양한 인종으로 이루어진 전투 요원들이 분대나 소대 단위를 형성하여 막강한 인원과 장비를 소유한 적군에 대항하여 눈부신 전공을 세우는 것을 주요 내용으로 하였다.

20세기 후반 할리우드는 여전히 총과 폭력을 소재로 한 영화를 제작하여, 수많은 영웅과 악당을 만들어 냈다. 「보니와 클라이디」(*Bonnie and Clyde*, 1967)나 「대부」(*The Godfather*, 1972)와 같은 영화에서는 악명 높은 범죄자를, 「더티 하리」(*Dirty Harry*, 1971)와 「로버캅」(*Robocop*, 1987)에서는 법과 정의를 지키는 영웅의 모습을 만들어 냈다. 이어 1970년대에는 베트남 전쟁을 배경으로 한 영화가 제작되어 많은 관객으로부터 공감을 얻었다. 「택시드라이버」(*Taxi Driver*, 1976)와 「지옥의 묵시록」(*Apocalypse Now*, 1979)과 같은 영화에서는 전후 참전병들이 보호시설에서 사회 복귀를 위해 훈련 과정을 거치지만, 현실에 적응하지 못하고 점차 광인이 되어버린 귀환병들의 이야기를 담고 있다. 「귀향」(*Coming Home*, 1978)과 「사슴 사냥꾼」(*The Deer Hunter*, 1978)은 전쟁의 상흔으로 육체적, 정신적으로 고통 받는 전역병들의 처절한 삶을 사실적으로 묘사하였다.[42]

이후 액션 영화는 할리우드의 영화의 상당 부분을 차지하며 영웅적인 총잡이들을 때로는 사실적으로 때로는 환상적으로 그려냈다. 「두건을 쓴 보이지」(Boyz *in the Hood, 1991*) 나 「사회에 대한 협박」(*Menace to Society*, 1993)과 같은 1990년대 영화는 대도시에서 발생하는 폭력과 범죄물을 다루어 살인과 위협의 도구로 사용되는 총기의 부정적인 면을 부각시키기도 하였다. 현재에도 미국의 대중문화를 선도하고 있는 영화, 텔레비전, 음악, 서적, 잡지 등에서 총과 폭력, 그리고 전쟁은 중요한 소재로 등장하고 있다. 특히 대중적인 영향력이 큰 텔레비전의 경우 섹스 관련 영상이나 음란물 등은 엄격히 규제가 되는 반면, 총격사건이나 범죄 장면은 비교적 제약 없이 사실적으로 표현하고 있다.[43] 이런 영화를 통해 전 세계 사람들은 자연스럽게 미국은 카우보이의 나라이며, 총에서 뿜어대는 힘과 정의가 미국의 이미지라는 인상을 갖게 만들었다. 미국인들의 총기 소유에 집착적인 생각은 미국의 오랜 역사적 배경과 함께 대중 매체의 확산으로 국민적 정서와 공감대가 형성되면서 하나의 문화 형태로 자리 잡게 되었다.

---

42 "Hollywood as History: The New Hollywood," Digital History.

43 "Report Urges FCC to Regulate TV Violence," *The Washington Post* (February 16, 2007.

Ⅳ. 수정헌법 제2조의 내용과 의미

미국에서 총기문화가 정착하게 된 것은 무엇보다도 국민의 무장권을 보장한 수정헌법 제2조가 존재하기 때문이다. 수정헌법은 미국 헌법 제정 당시 강한 연방 정부를 세워 강력한 국가를 건설하려고 했던 연방주의자들(Federalists)과 연방정부의 통제로부터 벗어나 각주의 독립을 유지하려고 했던 반연방주의자들(Anti-Federalists) 간의 타협의 산물이었다. 헌법이 비준 과정에서 연방정부가 개인의 자유를 침해할 경우에 대책이 없다는 것이 헌법의 결함으로 지적되었다. 그 결과 제임스 매디슨(James Madison)의 주도하에 10개의 수정 조항이 원래의 헌법에 추가되었다. 이것은 새 헌법과 그에 따라 조직된 연방정부의 강력한 구속력을 탐탁지 않게 생각하던 반연방주의자들의 주장을 반영한 것이었다.

따라서 수정헌법은 연방정부나 연방의회에 대항하여 개인의 자유와 권리를 보호하고, 각 주의 독립성과 자율성을 보장하기 위한 조항들로 채워져 있다. 1조는 종교, 언론 및 출판의 자유와 집회와 청원의 권리, 2조는 개인의 무기 소유와 휴대의 권리, 3조는 민간인의 가택에서 군인의 숙영을 금지하는 조항을 담고 있다. 나머지 4-10소까지는 수색 및 체포영장, 형사 사건에서의 권리, 공정한 재판을 받을 권리, 민사사건에서의 권리, 그리고 국민이나 각 주가 보유하는 권한 등을 명시하였다.

수정헌법 제2조는 "규율을 갖춘 민병대(A well-regulated militia)는 자유로운 주 정부의 안보에 필요하므로, 무기를 소유하고 휴대할 수 있는 국민의 권리(the right of the people)는 침해를 받아서는 안 된다" 규정하고 있다. 이 조항을 둘러싼 해석의 차이로 인하여 학계는 물론 시민단체, 그리고 대법원의 판결에 이르기까지 총기를 둘러싼 논쟁이 제기될 때마다 서로 상반된 주장들이 제기되고 있다. 총기 규제론자들은 이 조항에서 주체는 개개인의 사람이 아니라, 집단으로서의 민병대라고 주장하고 있다. 즉, '규율을 갖춘 민병대'가 정부의 통제하에 집단적으로 총기를 보유하는 것을 의미하는 것이지, 개인의 총기소유를 허락한 것이 아니라는 것이다. 반면, 총기 옹호자들은 총기를 소유하고 휴대할 수 있는 것은 '국민의 권리'라고 해석한다. 이러한 '국민의 권리'는 수정헌법 1조, 3조, 그리고 4조에서 10조까지의 조항에서도 나타나며, 이것은 민병대와 같은 집단적인 조직체가 아닌 국민 개개인의 자유를 보장하기 위한 것이라고 주장한다. 따라서 총기 소유는 헌법에 명시된 국민의 기본권이며, 그 어떤 이유로든지 이를 침해할 수 없다는 것이다.

수정헌법 제2조에 대한 이런 논쟁의 근거와 타당성을 가리기 위해서는 건국초기 이 조항이 채택된 역사적인 배경과 목적을 살펴 볼 필요가 있다. 아메리카 신대륙에서의 주도권을 차지하기 위한 전쟁(프렌치-인디언 전쟁)에서 영국은 승리를 거두어 신대륙에 대한 지배권을 강화하였다. 그러나 영국은 전쟁으로 인한 엄청난 부채로 극심한 재정난에 시달리게 되었다. 이를 보충하기 위해 영국은 식민지에 각종 세법, 즉 설탕세법(1764), 인지세법(1785), 타운센드법(1767) 등을 통과시켜 식민지의 경제적 부담을 가중시켰다. 이에 대해 각 식민지는 "대표 없는 곳에 과세 없다"고 외치면서 식민지를 착취하는 각종 세법의 철폐를 요구하고, 영국 상품에 대한 대규모 불매운동을 전개하였다.

영국 의회는 식민지의 거센 항의에 부딪쳐 인지세법만은 철폐하였으나, 이미 식민지에 고조된 반영국 감정을 꺾을 수는 없었다. 영국과 식민지 간에 갈등과 분규가 점차 심화되자, 영국은 식민지에 상비군의 수를 증가시켰다. 뿐만 아니라, 영국은 군대민박법(1765)을 채택하여 식민지인들에게 영국 군대의 주둔에 필요한 숙식을 제공하도록 강요하였다. 영국이 취한 이러한 일련의 조치들은 식민지 미국을 착취하고 억압하려는 노골적인 의도로 보일 수밖에 없었다. 식민지인들의 저항과 불만이 점차 확대되자, 영국은 군사력을 더욱 증강시켜 식민지를 강압적으로 통치하려 하였다. 마침내 1770년 3월 보스턴 세관에 주둔하고 있던 영국군이 시위대를 향해 발포하여 5명이 사망하는 소위 '보스턴 학살(Boston Massacre)' 사건이 발생하였다. 이것은 독립전쟁의 서막을 알리는 사건이었다.

보스턴 학살 사건은 식민지인들도 자기 방어를 위하여 무장할 권리가 있다는 신념을 갖게 만든 계기가 되었다. 아이러니하게도 당시 미국인들은 영국의 관습법에 의하여 사실상 무기를 소유할 수 있는 권리를 부여받고 있었다. 이에 대해 영국 정부도 식민지인들도 자국민과 같이 무기를 소유하고 휴대할 수 있는 권리가 있음을 부인할 수는 없었다. 그러나 내심 미국인들의 무장에 대해서는 두려움을 느끼고 있었다. 결국 영국 정부는 식민지에서의 반란을 제압하고 효율적인 통치를 위해서 식민지인들의 무기 소유를 금지하는 한편, 식민지인들이 소유하고 있는 무기를 몰수하기에 이르렀다. 식민지인들은 그들 관할 지역의 행정청에 자신들이 소유한 무기를 반환한 후에야 도시를 떠날 수 있었다.[44]

식민지에서 무기를 몰수하려는 영국의 조치에 대하여 건국의 아버지들은 영국 상비군의 위협에 대한 심각한 우려를 제기하였다. 그리고 식민지인들도 영국의 압제와 탄압에 대항하기 위하여 스스로 무장하여야 한다는 신념을 갖게 하였다. 존 애덤스(John Adams)는 "모든 시민들은 공격을 위해서가 아니라, 자신을 스스로 방어하기 위해서 무장할 권리를 부여받았다"고 언급하였다.[45] 후에 수정헌법 제2조의 채택을 강력히 제창하였던 조지 메이슨(George Mason)은 당시 보스턴에서의 강압적인 무기 몰수에 분개하여 다음과 같이 말하였다.

… 일반 시민들로(특히, 유한 시민계급이나 자영 농민) 구성된 규율을 갖춘 민병대는 (영국) 상비군으로부터 우리 조상들이 세운 법을 지키고 자유를 수호하는데 필요하다. 우리 시민들 각자는 잘 정비된 화승총(Fire-lock), 1파운드의 화약과 4파운드의 납, 탄알대, 점화를 위한 부싯돌과 화약통 등을 신속하게 갖추고 무장할 것을 결의해야 한다.[46]

매디슨은 식민지인들의 자발적인 참여로 구성된 민병대와 영국 정부의 통제를 받는 상비군을 구별하였고, 상비군에 대항하여 일반 시민들은 무장할 권리가 있음을 천명하였다. 그는 더 나아가 "국민을 무장 해제시키는 것은 그들을 노예화시키는 가장 효과적인 방법이 될 것"이라고 언급하였다. 이러한 국민적 권리에 대한 견해가 가장 명확하게 나타난 것은 토머스 제퍼슨(Thomas Jefferson)이 초안한 독립선언서였다.

모든 사람은 평등하게 태어났으며, 조물주는 몇 개의 양도할 수 없는 권리를 부여했는데, 그 권리 중에는 생명과 자유와 행복의 추구가 있다. 이 권리를 확보하기 위해 인류는 정부를 조직했으며, 이 정부의 정당한 권력은 국민의 동의에서 유래된다. 또 어떠한 형태의 정부든지 이러한 목적(국민의 기본권)을 파괴할 때는 언제든지 정부를 변혁시키거나 폐지시킬 수 있으며, 국민이 가장 안전하고 행복할 수 있는 원칙에 기

---

44 Stephen P. Halbrook, *That Every Man Be Armed* (Albuquerque, N.M,, 1984) p. 59

45 Lyman H. Butterfield and Hilda B. Zobel, eds., *Legal Papers of John Adams*, III (Riverside, N,J, 1965), p. 248.

46 *Ibid.*, p. 61.

초를 둔 새로운 정부를 조직하는 것은 국민의 권리이다.[47] 제퍼슨뿐만 아니라, 다른 건국의 아버지들도 모든 미국인들이 무장하여 전제적인 정부에 저항할 것을 요구하였다. 유명한 『상식(*Common Sense*)』이라는 소책자를 저술하여 혁명의 불길을 당긴 토머스 페인(Thomas Paine)은 "만약에 무기가 존재하지 않는다면 세계의 모든 나라는 평등한 관계가 유지될 것이다 … 그러나 무력을 사용할 수 있는 힘을 가진 국가와 무기 사용을 박탈당한 국가가 충돌한다면 무서운 재앙이 닥칠 것이다. 왜냐하면 약자는 강자의 희생이 될 것이기 뻔 하기 때문이다"라고 언급하면서, 영국에 대항하여 무기를 들 것을 촉구하였다.[48]

미국 혁명의 경우에서는 오히려 강자가 약자의 먹이가 된 형국이었다. 막강한 전력과 경험을 가진 영국군은 결연한 독립의 의지로 무장한 식민지 미국인들에 의해 오히려 포위 공세를 받았다. 건국의 아버지들은 한 목소리로 이것은 무기를 소유하고 휴대할 수 있는 국민적 권리가 가져온 결과라고 하였다. 매디슨은 "그들 국민들이 무장하는 것을 두려워하는 다른 국가와는 달리 우리 미국인들은 무장할 수 있는 권리와 이점을 가지고 있다"라고 하였다.[49] 초대 대통령 조지 워싱턴은 제1차 연방의회에서 자유민인 성인 남성은 모두 의무적으로 민명대에 등록하도록 하는 법안을 채택하도록 촉구하였으며, 더 나아가 "자유민들은 무장을 하여야 할뿐만 아니라, 규율 있는 훈련도 받아야 한다"고 하였다.[50]

조지 메이슨은 헌법 비준을 둘러싼 버지니아 의회의 논쟁에서 민병의 자격 요건을 더욱 구체화하였다. 메이슨은 "민병은 누구인가? 그것은 관직에 있는 몇몇 공무원들을 제외하고 전체 국민을 의미한다"고 언급하였다.[51] 여기서 메이슨은 '몇몇 공무원을 제외하고'라는 표현을 사용함으로써 분명히 개인적으로 무장한 모든 시민들이 민병에 참여하여야 하며, '전체 시민의 무장화'가 바로 전제적인 정부에 대항하여 자유

---

47 Thomas Jefferson, *The Declaration of Independence*, 한국미국사학회 D9역음, 『사료로 읽는 미국사』(궁리출판, 2006), pp. 65-66.

48 Thomas Paine, *Writings*, III, ed. by M. Conway ed. (New York, 1896), p. 56.

49 James Madison, *The Federalist*, No. 46 (Rutland, VT, 1992), p. 245.

50 *Papers of President*, I, ed. by J. G., Richardson, p. 65.

51 Jonathan Elliot, *The Debates in the Several State Conventions on the Adoption of the Federal Constitution*, III (Washington D.C., 1836-45), pp. 425-427.

와 독립을 지키는 요체가 된다는 것을 분명히 밝히고 있다. 건국의 아버지들의 이러한 견해는 수정헌법 제2조에서 언급된 총기소유가 집단으로서 민명대에 한정된 것이 아니라, 국민의 개인적인 자발적인 권리라는 것을 보여주는 것이다.

총기소유가 국민의 개인적 권리라는 주장은 1980년 이후 수정헌법 제2조의 법률적 해석을 다룬 논문 36편을 분석한 『미국 헌법의 백과사전(*Encyclopedia of the American Constitution*)』이라는 저서를 통해서도 확인 할 수 있다. 이 저서에 따르면, 단지 4편만이 정부가 개인의 총기 소유를 규제하거나 통제할 수 있다는 견해를 낸 반면, 나머지 32편은 모두 총기 소유는 국민 개개인의 기본적인 권리에 속하며, 따라서 연방정부나 주정부가 국민의 무기 소유의 권리를 침해할 수 없다고 주장하였다.[52]

예일대 법과대학 교수인 아크힐 아마(Akhil Amar)는 다음과 같이 수정헌법 제2조에서 언급된 국민의 무장권에 대하여 언급하였다. 무기를 소유하고 휴대할 수 있는 권리는 각 주의 민병대가 아니라, 국민의 권리에 속한다. 수정헌법 제2조에 명시된 '국민(The people)'은 일반 시민들 개개인을 말하는 것으로, 이것은 (미국인을 통칭하여 일컫는) 'We the People'과 같은 의미를 지니는 것이다. 따라서 수정헌법 1조에서 명시한 종교, 언론 및 출판의 자유, 집회와 청원의 권리와 같이, 국민의 무기소유권도 개인적인 권리로 인정되어야 한다 … 수정헌법 제2조가 채택될 당시 민병대는 무기를 소유할 수 있는 모든 시민들을 통칭하여 언급한 것이며, 따라서 민병대는 국민과 동일한 개념이다.[53]

이런 견해는 무기 소유권을 개인의 기본권이라고 확신했던 건국의 어버지들의 생각과 정확히 일치하는 것이다. 제퍼슨은 "총을 가지지 못하는 인간은 자유인이라고 말할 수 없다"고 하였으며, 패트릭 헨리는 "누구나 무장해야 함이 우리의 목표이다"라고 하였다.[54] 또한 애덤스는 "모든 시민들은 공격을 위해서가 아니라, 자신을 스스로 방어하기 위해서 무장할 권리를 부여받았다"고 언급하였다.[55]

---

52 Leonard W. Levy and Dennis J. Mahoney, *Encyclopedia of the American Constitution* (Riverside, N.J., 1986). 이 저서에 실린 36편의 논문에 대하여 Wayne R. LaPierre, Guns, Crime, and Freedom (Washington, D. C., 1994), pp. 237-240 참조.

53 Alshil Amar, "The Bill of Rights As a Constitution," *Yale Law Journal* 100 (1991), pp. 1131, 1166.

54 *Debates and other Proceedings of the Convention of Virginia*, convened at Richmond, on the 2n day of June 1788 (Petersburg, VA., 1788).

여기서 우리는 국민의 총기 소유권에 관한 최근(2008년 6월 26일)의 미국 대법원 판례를 주목할 필요가 있다. 무장 경비대 소속의 딕 앤서니 헬러(Dick A. Heller)가 총기를 가정에서 소유하는 것을 금지한 워싱턴 당국의 조치에 반발하여 제기한 소위 *District of Columbia v. Heller* 소송 사건에서 미 대법원은 워싱턴 D.C가 개인의 총기 소유를 불법화하려는 것은 수정헌법 제2조의 정신에 배치되는 것으로 위헌이라고 5대 4로 판결하였다.[56] 워싱턴 D.C는 1976년 이래 32년간 샌프란시스코, 시카코 등과 함께 개인의 총기 소유를 가장 엄격히 금지하는 정책을 펴왔다. 워싱턴 D.C가 내세운 총기 규제의 근거는 수정헌법 제2조에 명시된 무기 소유권을 경찰 및 보안군의 "집단적 무기 소지권"으로 해석한 데 있었다.

수정헌법 제2조가 보장하고 있는 무기 소지권을 개인에게까지 인정할 수 있느냐 여부에 대해 대법원이 구체적인 판결을 내린 것은 이번이 처음이었다. 총기소유 합헌 결정을 내린 안토닌 스칼리아(Antonin Scalia) 대법관은 이번 판결에 찬성한 다른 4명의 대법관을 대표한 결정문에서 "이 나라에서 벌어지고 있는 총기 사건의 심각성을 잘 알고 있으나, 우리의 헌법은 가정에서 자기 방어를 위해 사용하는 개인용 총기를 금지하는 것을 허용하지 않는다"고 지적하였다. 즉, 총기 소유는 침해할 수 없는 미국인 개개인의 고유 권한이라는 것이다.[57]

V. 맺음말

미국에서 총기문화가 합법적으로 뿌리를 내리게 된 가장 중요한 요인은 무엇보다도 수정헌법 제2조에 총기를 소유하고 휴대할 수 있는 국민적 권리가 명시되었기 때문이었다. 건국의 아버지들은 개인의 무기 소유권이 전제 정부의 폭정과 상비군의 횡포로부터 미국의 자유를 수호할 수 있는 안전한 장치이며, 동시에 외부의 위협으로

---

55 Lyman H. Butterfield and Hilda B. Zobel, eds., *Legal Papers of John Adams*, III (Riverside, N.J., 1965), p. 248.

56 District of Columbus, et al., Petitions V. Dick Anthony Heller, 554 U. S. (2008).

57 조선일보」(2008. 6. 28).

부터 자기 보호와 방어를 위한 수단으로 확신하였다. 2세기가 지난 오늘날에도 많은 미국인들은 총기 소유는 침해할 수 없는 기본권이며, "나와 가족의 생명을 지키는 것은 경찰이 아니라, 내가 소유한 총"이라는 자기 방어의 철학을 신봉하고 있다. 이런 사실은 의회나 정부 차원에서 개인의 총기소유를 금지하는 것은 위헌이라는 최근의 미국 대법원 판례(*District of Columbia v. Heller*)에서도 확인되고 있다. 빈번히 발생하는 충격적인 총기 사건과 사고에도 불구하고, 총기규제를 위한 '원-포인트' 개혁이 이루어지지 못하는 이유가 바로 여기에 있다.

수정헌법 제2조의 채택으로 총기 소유의 합법성이 보장되었지만, 총기 소유는 신대륙 정착 초기부터 사실상 하나의 사회 관습으로 용인된 제도였다. 식민지 정착민들은 영국의 관습법에 따라 제약 없이 총기를 소유할 수 있었다. 총은 외부의 적으로부터 자신과 가족의 생명과 재산을 지키는 무기였으며, 육류 공급을 위한 사냥이나 여가를 위한 사격의 도구였다. 국민의 자발적인 무장으로 조직된 민병대는 영국에 대항하여 미국의 독립과 자유를 쟁취하였으며, 서부 개척자들은 장총을 허리에 차고 황야를 개척하였다.

서부개척 시대의 여행 기록이나 서신, 회고록이나 자서전 등을 통해 확인할 수 있듯이, 건국 초기부터 19세기 중엽에 이르는 기간에 총기는 프런티어 전 지역에 널리 보급되었다. 프런티어는 척박한 자연 환경, 야생 동물이나 인디언의 습격, 그리고 법과 질서가 확립되지 않은 곳인 까닭에 총은 생존을 위한 필수적인 도구였던 것이다. 총은 더 나아가 무질서한 프런티어에서 범죄를 막고 법을 집행하기 위한 수단이 되었던 것이다.

이러한 총기문화를 국민적 정서로 확산시키는 데는 미국의 문학과 영화 등 대중매체가 중요한 역할을 하였다. 서부개척 시대의 낭만과 모험을 그린 대중 문학이나 총이나 폭력을 소재로 한 영화들을 총기에 대한 미국인의 가치관을 형성하게 하였다. 이러한 작품들은 전 세계 사람들에게 자연스럽게 미국을 카우보이의 나라이며, 총에서 뿜어대는 힘과 정의가 미국의 이미지라는 인상을 갖게 만들었다. 오늘날 미국인들의 총기 소유에 집착적인 관념은 미국의 오랜 역사적 배경과 함께 대중 매체의 확산으로 인한 국민적 정서와 공감대가 만들어낸 결과이다. 다시 말하면 총기문화는 미국의 독특한 지리 환경과 역사발전 과정에서 사회 · 문화적인 풍습의 한 형태로 발전되어 미국적 생활양식과 가치관으로 형성된 것이다.

미국은 1898년 미서전쟁을 계기로 서부 프런티어 경계를 넘어 해외 팽창을 시도하였고, 그 결과 서구 열강으로 등장하게 되었다. 20세기에 들어서는 1차 세계대전과 2차 세계대전을 통해 미국은 군수산업을 발전시켜 결국 오늘날 세계 최강의 군사 대국으로 성장하게 된 기반이 되었다. 이런 역사 발전 과정에서 미국인들에게 총은 국가건설의 원동력이 되었을 뿐만 아니라, 미국적인 정서와 가치관을 형성하게 하였다. 총은 독립과 자유, 애국심의 상징이며, 더 나아가 힘과 남성다움을 표출하는 강대국 미국의 상징으로 인식되었던 것이다.

이러한 '와일드 웨스트'로부터 각인된 터프한 남성적 이미지는 아직도 미국인의 정서로 남아있다. 그 대표적인 예가 부시 대통령이 이라크와 북한을 '악의 축'으로 언급한 것이나, 9.11 테러 직후 "빈 라덴을 죽이든지, 아니면 사로잡아야 할 것"이라고 단오하게 언급한 대목에서도 찾아 볼 수 있다. 영화 「벤허」의 주연 배우이며 전미 총기협회(National Rifle Association, NRA) 회장을 역임하였던 찰턴 헤스톤의 말에서도 미국인들의 총기에 대한 강한 신념을 읽을 수 있다.

미국은 자신과 자신의 가정을 지키기 위해 총을 드는 용기로 건설된 나라이다. 난 죽어도 총을 포기 못한다. 이것은 이 나라를 건설한 현명한 백인 조상들이 물려준 권리이다. 난 장전을 선택했어.

2. 미국 연방헌법 수정 제2조(무기소장권)의 의미*

안 경 환**

I. 머리말

"질서정연하게 규율된(well-regulated) 민병대는 자유국가(free State)의 안전을 위해 필요한고로 무기를 보유하고 휴대할 국민의 권리는 이를 침해하지 못한다."[1] 1791년에 제정된 미국연방헌법 수정 제2조는 이와 같이 번역할 수 있다. 헌법전에 담긴 많은 여타 불확정 조항과 마찬가지로 이 조항도 명확하게 정의되지 않은 많은 문구들을 담고 있다. "질서정연하게 규율된(well-regulated)"[2] "민병대(militia),"[3] "무기(Arms)"[4]를

---

* 이 논문은 필자가 Southern Illinois University Law School의 방문교수로 재직하던 기간(1996-97) 중에 착수하여 귀국 후에 저술한 것이다. 이 글에서는 미국의 Law Journal에 통용되는 문헌인용법을 원칙으로 하되, 국내 독자의 편의를 위해 필요하다고 판단되는 경우에는 인용법을 변형하거나 단행본의 출판사 등 보조정보를 부기하였다.

** 서울대학교 법학전문대학원 명예교수, 서울대학학교 법학연구소 제38권 제2호, 2010, 『미국헌법의 이해』, 박영사, 2014, 581~603면에 수록된 원고를 재게재함을 밝힌다.

1 "A well regulated Militia, being necessary to the security of a free State, the right of the people to keep and bear Arms, shall not be infringed." 미국헌법이 기초한 연방주의의 관점에 집착하여 이 조항의 "state"를 주(州)로 해석하기 쉽고, 특히 수정 제2조 논쟁의 핵심 주제가 무기소장권이 개인적 권리이냐 아니면 주정부의 민병대 규율권이냐인 점을 감안한다면 이러한 해석도 어느 정도 "이유 있는 착오"라고 할 수 있다(일본 학자들의 초기의 오류가 우리나라에도 답습되고 있는 점은 특히 반성을 요한다. 미국헌법제정 200주년 기념으로 주한미국대사관 공보원이 발행한 살아 있는 미국 역사문서(1987)에도 이러한 오류가 담겨 있다. 22면). 그러나 여기의 "free State"란 전제국가(tyrannical State)에 대응하는 용어임은 입법사를 통해 명확하게 확인할 수 있다. 상비군을 통치의 수단으로 하여 국민을 탄압하는 전제국가에 대응하는 의미의 자유국가에서는 민병대의 무장을 통해 국민의 자유가 보장된다는 이상의 반영이다. 자세히는 David E. Young ed., The Origin of the Second Amendment: A Documentary History of the Bill of Rights 1787-1792(2nd ed. 1995), pp. xxvi-xxvii 참조. "to keep and bear arms"의 번역에 관해서는 후기 주 5 참조.

"보유(keep)", "휴대(bear)"할 권리,[5] "자유국가(free State)"를 위해 "필요한(necessary)" 등의 용어의 구체적 의미는 헌법의 최종해석권자인 연방대법원의 판결을 통해서만 확정될 수 있다. 그러나 창설 이래 2세기 이상에 이르는 이날에 이르기까지 연방대법원은 수정 제2조의 문구에 대해 적절한 유권적 해석을 내리기를 소홀히 했다.

외국의 헌법학도가 이 조항을 특히 주목해야 할 이유는 이 조항의 의미를 정확하게 파악하는 것이 미국 헌법이 탄생할 당시의 정치적 상황을 이해하는 데 유익할 뿐만 아니라, 오늘날 미국 사회가 당면한 가장 중대한 문제의 하나인 강력범죄와 관련하여 다른 나라의 상황과는 근본적으로 다른 미국 사회에서의 일상적 총기 소지의 문제를 이해하는 데 첩경이 되기 때문이다.

굳이 통계치를 동원하지 않더라도 미국에는 강력범죄도, 민간에 통용되는 살상무기도 많다. 다른 어느 나라보다도 용이하게 이동할 수 있는 광대한 국토, 거의 신성불가침에 가까운 주거의 자유와 사생활의 자유의 보장 등의 이유가 총기의 단속을 현실적으로 어렵게 만든다. 또 한편으로는 강력범죄에 대한 자력구제의 현실적 필요성이 일반 국민의 총기 소지를 용인하게 된다는 상식인의 설명도 가능하다.

그러나 보다 근본적으로 살펴보면 미국인의 총기 소지의 전통은 헌법적 근거에서 뿌리를 찾을 수 있다. "민병대(Militia)"와 "무기를 소장할(keep and bear Arms)," "국민의 권리(right of the people)"라는 헌법의 문언이 바로 일반국민의 총기 소장의 제도적 연원이 된다.

이 글은 흔히 "무기소장권(right to bear arms)"으로 통칭되는 연방헌법 수정 제2조의 내용을 정확히 파악하고, 현재 미국법체계와 미국사회에서 수정 제2조가 지니는

---

2 이 조항이 개인의 무장권이 아니라 주정부의 민병대 규율권을 보장한다라고 해석하는 입장에서는 well-regulated의 의미는 '조직화된(organized)'의 뜻이라고 한다. Rahph J. Rohner, The Right To Bear Arms: A Phenomenon of Constitutional History, 16 Cath. U. L. Rev. 53, 66 n. 69 (1966); 후기 주 43 참조.

3 민병대라는 단어는 "정규군대(troop)"나 "상비군(standing army)"에 대응하는 어휘라는 주장이 있으며, 헌법의 아버지들이 사용한 "민병대"의 의미는 예외 없이 "전체 국민의(the whole body of people)"이라는 수식어와 결부되어 있다는 주장도 있다. Don B. Kates Jr., "Handgun Prohibition and the Original Meaning of the Second Amendment," 82 Mich. L. Rev. 204, 213-217 (1983).

4 이 조항에 의해 소지, 휴대가 보장되는 무기의 종류는 민병대의 목적을 달성함에 적절한 성격의 것에 한정될 것이다.

5 이 조항이 규정하는 "보유(keep)"와 "휴대(bear)"의 행위는 법적으로 분리되어 사용되는 용어가 아니라 결합되어 사용되는 용어이기에 양자를 포괄하여 "소장(所藏)"으로 번역한다.

의미를 정리하여 소개함에 목적이 있다.

수정 제2조의 제정 배경을 간략하게 살펴본 후에 연방의 총기규제법의 제정과정, 법원의 판결을 학술적 논의의 핵심인 개인적 권리 대 주의 집단적 권리의 논쟁을 중심으로 정리한다. 마지막으로 이 조항을 통해 미국사회와 미국헌법 전반에 관한 보다 심도 있는 논의에 관심을 촉구하기 위해 부록으로 문헌을 정리하여 첨부한다.

Ⅱ. 문제의 부상

"이러한 권리를 확보하기 위해 인간들 사이에 정부가 설립되며, 정부의 정당한 권력은 피치자의 동의에 기초한다는 것, 여하한 형태의 정부도 이러한 목적을 파괴할 때는 그 정부를 '변경하거나 폐지(alter or abolish)'하는 것이 … 국민의 권리이다."[6]

연방헌법과 더불어 미국 민주주의의 "신성한 경전(sacred codes)"의 일부로 인식 되는 1776년 독립선언(Declaration of Independence)의 한 구절이다. 제퍼슨(Thomas Jefferson)의 필치를 빌려 탄생한 이 문구는 개인과 정부의 관계에 대한 로크(John Locke)의 정치사상을 구현한 것이라는 것이 정설이다.[7]

연방헌법 수정 제2조가 규정하는 "무기를 보유, 소지할 권리(the right to keep and bear arms)"는 이러한 독립선언의 정신을 구체적인 헌법조문에 담아, 폭압적인 정부를 전복할 국민의 권리를 구체화시킨 역사적인 산물이다.

이와 같은 역사적 연유에도 불구하고 이 조문은 20세기 후반에 이르기까지 거의 망각되다시피 했다. 대중의 지속적인 관심에도 불구하고 법원과 법학계의 입장에서는 수정 제2조는 단지 부록 내지는 장식물에 불과했다.[8] 헌법학에 관한 Hornbook형

---

6 미국 독립선언 제2조(1776).

7 Terrence J. Moore, "The Ninth Amendment: Its Origins and Meaning," 7 New England L. Rev. 215(1972). 무어 교수는 이 글에서 로크의 정치철학이 미국 연방헌법의 사상적 기초가 되었다고 주장하는 대표적인 저술들을 열거하고 있다. Id. at 237-246. 그중 일부를 옮기면 Carl Becker, The Declaration of Independence (1922); Huntington Cairns, Legal Philosophy From Plato to Hegel (1949); Charles Pelham Curtis, Law As Large As Life: A Natural Law For Today In the Supreme Court As Its Prophet (1959); Edward S. Corwin, The Higher Law Background of American Constitutional Law (1961).

8 Sanford Levinson, "The Embarrassing Amendment," 99 Yale L. J. 637, 639 (1989); Andrew J. McClurg,

저서 내지는 전문서(treatise)의 저자들 중에서 극히 간략하게나마 헌법학의 토의 과제로 수정 제2조의 존재를 인정한 학자는 하버드(Harvard)의 트라이브(Laurence Tribe)[9]와 세칭 "일리노이(Illinois) 팀"으로 불리는 노왁(Nowak), 로툰다(Rotunda)와 영(Young)의 공저[10] 정도에 불과하다.

이 조문이 본격적인 헌법 논의의 중심으로 부상된 것은 극히 최근의 일이다. 1989년 레빈슨(Sanford Levinson) 교수의 논문이 이 조항의 역사적 근거를 시민공화주의(civic republicanism)에서 구하면서 개인의 무장권을 주장한 때부터 본격적인 논의의 장이 열렸다.[11] 레빈슨의 이론에 대해 브라운(Wendy Brown) 교수는 즉시 시민공화주의 이론의 현실적 허구성을 지적하는 반론을 제기하였고[12] 많은 학자들이 논쟁에 참가함으로써 논의의 폭과 심도를 더하였다.[13]

이러한 학계의 논쟁은 1994년, "살상용 무기(assault weapons)"의 구매를 금지한 연방법률의 제정을 계기로 일반국민의 일상적인 논제로 정착하였다. 또한 1995년 5월의 충격적인 Oklahoma시 소재 연방정부 건물의 폭파사건이 "민병대(militia)"라는 헌법 용어를 원용한 테러집단과 연관된 인물에 의해 자행되자 더욱 수정 제2조의 논의가 가속화되었다.[14]

"The Rhetoric of Gun Control," 42 American Univ. L. Rev. 53 (1992).

9 L. Tribe, American Constitutional Law(2nd ed. 1988), p. 299 n. 6.

10 Nowak, Rotunda & Young, Constitutional Law(4th ed. 1988), p. 316 n. 4; Nowak & Rotunda, Treatise on Constitutional Law(2nd ed. 1992), S. 14.2, n. 4.

11 Levinson, 앞의 논문, 주 8). 이 논문에서 레빈슨 교수는 수정 제2조의 입법목적은 시민적공화주의의 실현을 위해 보장된 시민의 혁명권을 구현하는 수단으로서의 개개 국민의무장권을 보장함에 있다고 주장한다. 이 논문에서 레빈슨 교수가 논증을 위해 동원한 헌법해석의 6대 원칙(textual, historical, structural, doctrinal, prudential & ethical argument)은 Philip Bobbit가 1982년의 저서, Constitutional Fate에서 제시한 것으로 주목할 가치가 있다.

12 Wendy Brown, "Guns, Cowboys, Philadelphia Mayors, and Civic Republicanism! On Sanford Levinson's The Embarrassing Second Amendment," 99 Yale L. J. 661 (1989). 이 글에서 브라운 교수는 설령 시민적 공화주의의 이상을 구현함이 제정 당시의 수정 제2조의 입법 목적이었음을 인정한다고 치더라도 이를 근거로 현재 국민의 무기소장권을 인정하는 것은 무리라고 주장한다. 시민공화주의의 윤리적 전제조건이 되는 "공덕심(公德心)을 가진 소수국민"이 다중민주주의 현세에는 결여되어 있기 때문이라는 것이 주된 논지이다. Id. at 667-680.

13 이를테면 David C. Williams, "Civic Republicanism and the Citizen Militia: The Terrifying Second Amendment," 101 Yale L. J. 551 (1991). 이 논문에서 윌리암스 교수는 레빈슨과 브라운 양자의 이론을 종합하여 제3의 주장을 편다.

14 168명의 인명을 앗아간 이 사건은 극우파 백인의 과격한 단체인 "민병대"의 행동강령을 반영한 것이라는

실무자와 법원의 관심의 초점은 총기의 소지를 규율하는 법률이 어떤 범위 내에서 헌법에 합치하는가에 국한되어 있지만 헌법학계의 논의는 보다 근본적인 차원에서 전개되고 있다.

Ⅲ. 논쟁의 핵심: 개인적 권리인가 아니면 주의 집단적 권리인가?

수정 제2조가 연방정부의 권한을 제한하기 위한 목적으로 탄생했다는 사실에 대해서는 다툼이 없다. 그러나 수정 제2조가 예상하는 연방의 권력에 대한 견제와 제한을 주도하는 주체가 주정부인가 아니면 개개 국민인가에 관해서는 첨예한 설전이 전개되고 있다.

수정 제2조는 주의 권리, 즉 "집단적 권리(collective right)"라는 입장에서는 일차적 근거로 연방의회에 대해 민병대를 조직할 권한을 부여한 헌법 제1조 제8항 제15-16절의 "민병대 규정(Militia Clause)"을 근거로 든다.[15] 그리하여 수정 제2조가 제정된 이유는 바로 이 규정에 의해 권한을 부여받은 연방의회가 이 권한에 의거하여 주의 민병대를 해체하게 되면, 결과적으로 연방의 전제에 대해 주가 저항할 수단이 박탈될 우려를 방지하기 위해 제정된 것이라고 한다.[16]

한편 수정 제2조를 개인의 무장권으로 파악하는 견해는 또 다른 역사적 사실들을 근거로 든다.[17] 비록 집단적 권리론자의 주장대로 수정 제2조의 제정목적이 주정부의 민병대를 보호하기 위한 것이었다고 하더라도 이러한 목적은 개개 시민이 무장함

추측이 강하다. 주로 중서부의 농촌지역을 중심으로 활동하는 이 단체는 건국 당시의 아메리카 공화국의 원형을 보존하기를 열망하는 반연방주의, 반민주당, 인종분리주의자들로 수정 제2조의 "무기소장권"이 개인적 권리라고 믿는다. 이주영 외, 『미국현대사』 비봉출판사(1996), 425-426면 참조. 1997년 6월, 피고인 티모시 맥베이(Timothy McVeigh)에 대한 사실심 재판이 Denver시 소재 연방지방법원에서 종결되고 검찰측의 주장대로 8개 항목에 대한 유죄의 평결이 내려졌다. 상세한 사건의 전말은 Time, June 24, 1997, pp. 24-26.

15 연방의회는 … "합중국의 법률을 집행하고 반란을 진압하며 외침을 격퇴하기 위해 민병대의 소집에 관한 법률을 제정하며"(15절) "민병대의 조직, 무장 및 훈련에 관한 법률을 제정하고…"(16절).

16 Kates, 앞의 주 3, p. 212.

17 앞의 주 6-7, 뒤의 주 43-50 및 본문 참조.

으로써 가장 효과적으로 달성될 것이므로 개인적 권리를 인정함이 설득력이 있다고 주장한다.[18]

헌법의 문언도 일응 개인적 권리론에 유리한 것으로 보인다. "무기를 보유하고 휴대할 권리"라는 문언의 일차적 의미가 바로 개인의 권리를 의미하며, "질서정연한 민병대는 자유국가의 수호를 위해 필요한고로"라는 헌법전문은 정부에 의한 전제를 방지하기 위해 국민이 무장할 필요가 있다는 사실을 재확인하는 의미라고 한다. 이 견해에 의하면 수정 제2조의 "국민(the people)"은 권리장전 전반을 통해서 동일한 의미, 즉 개개 국민을 의미한다고 한다?[19]

만약 수정 제2조가 개인의 무장권을 보장한다면, 이어서 제기되는 의문은 주정부에 대해서 이 권리를 주장할 수 있는가(다른 말로 하면 수정 제2조가 수정 제14조를 통해 "수용(incorporate)"되었는가) 하는 문제이다.

수용을 부정하는 입장에서는 이 조항이 연방의 행위에 대해서만 적용된다고 판시한 1875년의 United States v. Cruikshank판결[20]과 1886년의 Presser v. Illinois 판결[21]을 강력한 무기로 든다. 그러나 이 판결들은 "수용이론"이 연방대법원의 판결에 반영되기 시작하기 이전에 내려진 것으로 전면적인 구속력을 보유하는 것으로 보기 어렵다는 난점이 있다.[22] 그러나 이 문제는 적어도 현재까지의 대법원의 판결에 관한 한 별도로 주목할 필요가 제기되지 않았다. 왜냐하면 이날에 이르기까지 연방대법원은 연방의 법률만을 심사의 대상으로 삼았을 뿐, 2천 편 이상에 달하는 주차원의 법률들은 심사의 대상으로 삼지 않았기 때문이다.[23]

---

18 Id. at 213.

19 1990년의 대법원 판결에서 렌퀴스트(Rehnquist) 원장은 "국민(the people)"의 개념은 수정 제1, 2, 4, 9, 10조를 통틀어서 "개인"(individual)을 의미한다고 해석했다. United States v. Verdugo-Urquidez, 494 U.S. 259, 265(1990). 그러나 수정 제2조의 "국민"은 "집합적으로 조직된 주권의 보유자인 국민의 총체(sovereign citizenry collectively organized)"라는 해석이 있다. Lawrence Cress, "An Armed Community: The Origins and Meaning of the Right to Bear Arms," 71 J. Am. His. 22, 31 (1984).

20 92 U.S. 542, 553(수정 제2조상의 권리는 연방의회에 의해서 침해받지 않는다는 것을 의미할 뿐이다. 이 조항은 중앙정부의 권한을 제한하는 이상의 의미가 없다.…).

21 116 U.S. 252, 267(주정부가 조직한 정규민병대 이외의 사적 집단의 군사훈련을 제한하는 주법은 수정 제2조의 위반이라는 주장을 배척함).

22 권리장전의 "수용이론"이 정식으로 판결에 반영된 것은 1937년 Palko v. Conneticut판결(302 U.S. 319) 이후의 일이라는 것이 정설이다. 그러나 레빈슨 교수는 Presser 판결 11년 후에 내려진 Chicago, B & Q. R. Co. v. Chicago 판결(166 U.S. 226 1897)을 수용이론의 효시로 본다(전게논문 주 8, 653면 참조).

Ⅳ. 수정 제2조의 역사적 배경

1. 영국 커먼로(Common Law)의 전통

대부분의 미국헌법 조항이 그러하듯이 이 조항의 연원 또한 영국법에서 찾을 수 있다.[24] 식민지 시대의 기본권조항에 해당하며, 후일 연방헌법의 권리장전에 심대한 영향을 미친 "인허장(認許狀, Colonial Charters)"들은 주로 영국의 1679년 권리장전을 모태로 하여 식민지 미국인은 영국신민이 향유하는 일체의 권리를 보유한다고 선언했다.[25]

18세기 영국 커먼로의 거성, 블랙스톤(William Blackstone)은 전통적으로 영국에서는 상비군(standing army)에 대한 국민적 불신이 팽배해 있었음을 기록하고 있다. 상비군의 설치는 곧 국왕에 의해 일반 국민의 권리가 유린될 위험을 가중시키는 것으로 일반국민은 이해하였다.[26] 이러한 국민 정서를 감안하여 노르만의 정복 이전의 영국왕 알프레드(Alfred, 871-899)는 영국의 방어는 국민의 군대의 의무라고 서약했다.[27] 그리하여 무기를 사용할 능력이 있는 영국의 성인남자는 모두 왕국의 방어를 위해 무기를 구입 소장할 의무를 부담하였다. 이러한 국민의 군대를 엘리자베스(Elizabeth) 1세(1558-1603) 시대에 "민병대(Militia)"로 명명하게 되었다.[28]

---

23 뒤의 주 94-95 및 본문 참조.

24 자세히는 Stephen P. Halbrook, "Encroachments of the Crown on the Liberty of the Subject: Pre-Revolutionary Origins of the Second Amendment," 15 U. of Daton L. Rev. 91 (1989).

25 이를테면 1606년 버지니아 인허장(Virginia Charter)은 "The people of Virginia possess all the Liberties, Privileges, Franchises and Immunities that have at any Time been held, enjoyed and possessed by the people of the Great Britain."라고 선언했고 the New England Charter of 1620, the Massachusetts Bay Charter of 1629, the Maryland Charter of 1632, the Connecticut Charter of 1662, the Rhode Island Charter of 1632, the Carolina Charter of 1663 및 the Georgia Charter of 1732에도 유사한 조항이 담겨 있다. Bernard Schwartz, The Roots of the Bill of Rights (1980), p. 49에서 재인용.

26 William Blackstone, Commentaries (St. George Tucker ed., 1803), pp. 408-410. "자유의 나라에서는 "군인"(arms)이라는 별도의 직업을 창설하는 것은 지극히 위험한 일이다."

27 1 the New Encyclopedia Britannica 259(Robert McHenry ed., 15th ed., 1992); Stephen Halbrook, That Every Man Be Armed, The Evolution of A Constitutional Right 37 (1984); Earl R. Kruscheke, The Right To Keep and Bear Arms, A Continuing American Dilemma 12 (1985).

28 자세히는 David E. Vandercoy, "The History of the Second Amendment," 28 Val. U. L. Rev. 1007 (1994) 참조.

왕권신수설의 신봉자 찰스(Charles) 2세(1660-1685)는 의회를 장악하여 1661년 민병대법(Militia Act of 1661)을 제정하였고 이 법에 근거하여 자신에 대한 충성이 의심스러운 민병대원을 축출, 무장해제시켰다. 무기의 수입은 금지되었고 국내의 무기제조업자는 일체의 제조 판매행위를 당국에 보고하도록 강제되었다.[29] 의회는 이어서 1671년 수렵행위법(Game Act of 1671)을 제정하여 일정 금액 이상의 지대(地代)를 수령하는 지주에 한하여 무기의 소지를 허용하는 반면 일반 국민의 무기 소장을 엄격하게 통제하였다. 찰스(Charles) 2세로부터 왕위를 계수한, 더욱 강력한 왕권신수설의 신봉자 제임스(James) 2세(1685-1688)는 의회에 대한 더욱 강력한 통제와 일반 국민에 대한 탄압에 나섰다. 공공연히 의회의 법을 위반하여 자신의 군대를 사인의 주거지에 주둔시켰으며 인신보호영장을 정지하고 자신의 왕권신수설을 지지할 인물로 법원을 구성했다.[30]

제임스(James) 2세의 폭정은 의회의 반란으로 주도된 명예혁명으로 무너지고, 이어서 의회의 초청에 의해 왕위를 계승한 윌리엄 3세와 메어리 부처(夫妻)(William & Mary)의 왕권은 통상 "권리장전(Bill of Rights)"으로 불리는 1689년 권리선언(Declaration of Rights)에 의해 상당한 제약을 받게 되었다.

권리선언은 의회의 동의 없이 상비군을 징모 또는 보유함을 금지하는 한편 프로테스탄트 교도인 영국민의 전통적 권리 중에 자신의 방어를 위해 적합한 무기를 소장할 권리가 포함되어 있음을 인정했다.[31] 이어서 의회는 수렵법을 개정하여 개인의 무기 소장을 원칙적으로 인정하면서도 다만 불법적인 사용에 대해서만 제재를 가하도록 하였다.[32] 이러한 역사적 사실에 비추어 볼 때, 영국에서의 무기소지권은 국왕의 폭정으로부터 자신의 자유를 보장하기 위한 국민의 권리로 생성되었음이 분명하다.[33]

---

29 David T. Hardy, The Origins and Development of the Second Amendment 30-31 (1986)에서 재인용.

30 Id. at 35.

31 Hardy, Id. at 35; Swartz, 전게서 주 25, 41면; David B. Kopel, "It Isn't About Duck Hunting: The British Origins of the Right to Bear Arms," 93 Mich. L. Rev. 133 (1995)(reviewing Joyce L. Malcolm, To Keep and Bear Arms: The Origins of An Anglo-American Right, Harvard University Press (1994)).

32 Hardy, 전기 주 29, 38면(Games Act, 4 & 5 Wm. & Mary, ch. 23 (1692)(Eng.)).

33 Schwartz, 전게서 주 25, 42면. 그러나 자유의 보장(defense of liberty)이 영국민의 무기소장권의 유일한 존재이유는 아니었다. 판례와 학설을 통해 자기방어(personal defense), 법의 집행(enforcement of local

한편 블랙스톤은 개인 자격에서 영국신민이 향유하는 권리를 절대적 권리(absolute rights)와 상대적 권리(relative rights)로 구분했다. 절대적 권리는 신분에 무관하게 모든 신민에게 주어진 권리로 신분 또는 소속된 사회에 따라 차별적인 대우를 받는 상대적 권리와 대조된다. 블랙스톤은 무기를 소장할 권리는 절대적 권리로, 폭압적인 정부에 대한 저항이라는 공적인 목적을 위한 수단으로서는 물론, 자위(self-preservation), 수렵(hunting), 사격(marksmanship) 등 순수한 사적 목적으로도 이를 행사할 수 있다고 해설했다.[34]

2. 공화주의 정치이론

17세기 영국의 "공화주의(republicanism)" 정치이론의 선구자로 인식되는 해링톤(James Harrington)[35]은 "무장한 국민(armed populace)"이야말로 대내외 적으로부터 공화정부를 수호할 수 있는 최적의 무기라고 주장한 바 있다.[36] 18세기의 영국 정치사상가 넬빌(Henry Nelville)은 해링톤의 이론을 더욱 발전시켜 국민의 무장은 민주 정체의 유지에 중요한 기여를 한다고 주장했다.[37] 흔히 미국헌법에 비친 자유주의 시상의 원조로 불리는 John Locke 또한 무장을 통한 국민의 자위권을 주장했다.[38]

블랙스톤과 영국 공화주의 정치이론가들의 국민무장론은 신생 미국의 정치사상에 심대한 영향을 미쳤다.[39] 자유주의와 함께 신생 미합중국이 헌법의 이념으로

---

law) 및 외적에 대한 방어(defense of foreign invaders)의 적어도 3가지의 추가적 목적이 인정되고 있다. Hardy, 전게논문 주 29, 39-40.

34 Blackstone, 전게서 주 26, 140-144.

35 전기 주 27, 7 Encyclopedia Britannica 718-719. Harrington의 정치철학에 관해서는 The Political Works of James Harrington(John G. A. Pocock ed., 1977).

36 Vandercoy, 전게논문 주 28, 1020-1021; Levinson, 전기 주 8, at 639(Harrington의 주장을 요약하면 "independent yeoman should also bear arms"). Harrington은 상비군의 필요성을 부정했을 뿐만 아니라 전제의 위험을 가중시킨다고 주장했다. at 647.

37 Vandercoy, 전기 주 28, 1021. Neville은 한 걸음 더 나아가 국민의 무장을 두려워하는 정부는 정당성이 없는 정부라고 주장했다.

38 Stephen P. Halbrook, That Every Man Be Armed: The Evolution of a Constitutionalism, University of New Mexico Press (1984) 72(citing Locke, Second Treatise on Civil Government). "It being reasonable and just that I should have the right to destroy that which threatens me with destruction." 자세히는 제19장, pp. 232-242 참조.

채택한 공화주의의 이념은[40] 영국의 역사적 선례와 이론에 기초한 것으로, "공화주의형태의 정부(republican form of government)"[41]와 개인의 자유의 보장에 필수불가결한 요소 중의 하나가 일반 민중의 무장이라는 신념을 내포하고 있었다.[42]

3. 제헌회의

연방헌법의 제정과정에서 격렬하게 전개된 연방주의자(Federalists)와 반연방주의자(Anti-Federalists)의 대립은 잘 알려져 있다. 그러나 강력한 중앙정부를 선호한 연방주의자나 주의 자치와 자율적 규제를 선호한 반연방주의자나 공히 개인의 자유와 국가의 안전이라는 양대 이념을 동시에 성취하는 제도적 장치를 고안함에 골몰했다. 이러한 관점에서 제헌회의의 주된 의제 중의 하나는 연방의회에게 민병대의 소집권을 부여할 것인가의 여부였다.[43]

그러나 일반 국민의 무기 소장은 자유의 수호를 위해서 필수적인 조건이라는 점에 합의를 이루었다. 연방주의자의 지적 대변인 매디슨(James Madison)은 네빌(Neville)의 주장에 동조하여 국민 무장의 이점과 효용을 역설했고[44] 동조자 아담스(John Adams)는 물론 반연방주의자의 거두, 제퍼슨(Thomas Jefferson)과 헨리(Patrick Henry) 조차도 이러한 매디슨의 주장에 동조하였다.[45] 반연방주의자의 공식의견은 "연방농부"(Federal Farmer)라는 필명의 논자에 의해 발표되었다. 권리장전이 헌법전 속에 포

---

39 Wendy Brown, Guns, Cowboys, "Philadelphia Mayors and Civic Republicanism: On Sanford Levinson's The Embarrassing Second Amendment," 99 Yale L. J. 661 (1989).

40 종래의 지배적인 견해는 자유주의가 미국 건국의 기본이 된 정치철학이라는 것이었다. 그러나 1960년 이래 공화주의의 주장이 대두되었고 오늘날에는 양자의 병합이 통설이라고 할 수 있다. 자세히는 Daniel Farber & Suzanna Sherry, A History of American Constitution, West Publishing Co. (1990), 3-19; Paul Craig, Public Law and Democracy in United Kingdom and United States of America, Oxford University Press (1990), Ch. 8.

41 연방헌법 제4조 3항 참조.

42 Vandercoy, 전게논문 주 28, 1022 n. 122.

43 James Madison, Journal of the Constitutional Convention 590-592 (E. H. Scott ed. 1893).

44 "미국 국민이 무장하고 있다는 이점이 다른 어느 나라의 경우보다도…정부의 야심에 대한 효과적인 방어책이 된다." The Federalist Papers No. 46, 331 (Benjamin Wright ed., Barns and Noble, 1996).

45 Andrew d. Hertz, "Gun Crazy: Constitutitional False Consciousness and Dereliction of Dialogue Responsibility," 75 Boston Univ. L. Rev. 57, 64 n. 17 (1995).

함되어야 한다는 주장을 펴면서 그는 "자유를 수호하기 위해 전 국민이 상시 무장해야 한다"고 강조했다.[46] 다른 조항에 비해 수정 제2조에 관한 토의기록이 부족한 이유도 양대 세력 간에 대립보다는 이러한 공감대가 존재했기 때문이라고 이해할 수 있다.[47] 정부 차원의 상비군의 창설에 반대한 헌법의 아버지들의 정서는 개인의 무장이 공화정체의 수호를 위한 필수적 전제조건이라는 결론에 기여했다.[48]

헌법의 아버지들은 무장한 다중이 대내적으로 정치권력의 남용을 방지함에 기여할 것이라는 확신에 차 있었지만 외적의 침입에 대한 위협에 대해서는 동일한 확신을 가지지 못했다. 이들은 해링톤의 상비군 불신론에 대해 원론적인 공감을 표하면서도 국방을 위해서는 군대를 보유할 필요가 있다는 결론에 이르렀다. 특히 건국 초기에 훈련된 민병대의 부재가 국가의 존립 자체에 대한 위협이 되기에 충분했기 때문이다. 이러한 배경에서 내려진 결론은 의회에게는 전쟁선포권과 육·해군을 보유할 권한을 부여하고[49] 대통령에게 육·해군의 통수권을 부여하되,[50] 상·하 양원의 구성원을 국민이 직접 선출한다[51]는 헌법적 구도였다. 의회가 배타적인 예산편성권을 보유하므로 국민은 자신이 구성하는 의회를 통해 간접적으로 연방의 군대를 통제할(폐지를 포함한) 수 있다는 논리이다.

이러한 타협의 논리에서 민병대야말로 연방정부의 권력 남용에 대한 효과적인 견제책이 되며, 개개인의 무장권을 보장함으로써 전제정치를 막을 수 있다고 믿었던 것이다.[52]

---

46 Letters From the Federal Farmers to the Republicans 124 (Walter H. Bennett ed., University of Alabama Press 1978).

47 수정 제2조에 관한 근소한 토의 기록 중에 주목할 사실은 "누구든지 종교적 이유에 기한 경우에는 무장을 강요당하지 아니한다"라는 조항을 삽입하자는 주장을 매디슨이 제기했다는 정도이다. Vandercoy, 전게논문 주 28, 1022.

48 Laurence H. Tribe, American Constitutional Law, Foundation Press (2nd ed. 1988), p. 299, n. 6 ("헌법의 아버지들의 유일한 관심사는 상비군의 창설로 종국에는 주의 자치가 유린 되는 것을 방지함에 있었다").

49 연방헌법 제1조 제8항 11절.

50 연방헌법 제2조 제2항 1절.

51 연방헌법 제1조 제2항 1절 및(수정 제17조 제1항 참조).

52 David C. Williams, "Civic Republicanism and the Citizen Militia: The Terrifying Second Amendment," 101 Yale L. J. 551, 552 (1991). 독립 직전의 미국의 상황과 영국법의 충돌에 관한 자세한 관찰한 글로 Stephen P. Halbrook, "Encroachments of the Crown on the Liberty of the Subject: Pre-Revolutionary Origins of the Second Amendment," 15 U. of Daton L. Rev. 91 (1989) 참조.

4. 비준과정

진통 끝에 신생 13개 주 모두가 헌법의 비준에 동참했다. 이 과정에서 8개 주는 자주(自州)가 입안한 수정조항을 제출했고, 이들 중 5개 주는 무기소장권을 수정조항의 일부로 포함시켰다.[53]

연방헌법의 권리장전의 대상으로 채택된 무기소장권에 관한 격렬한 논의는 버지니아 주의 비준절차 과정에서 벌어졌다. 연방주의자 매디슨과 반연방주의자 메이슨(George Mason), 두 사람이 주도한 버지니아의 비준대회에서 수정 제2조에 관한 논의 중 상당 부분은 헌법 제1조 제8항 제16절의 "민병대 소집권" 조항과 관련하여 전개되었다. 제헌회의에서 이 조항을 지지한 바 있는 메이슨은, 그럼에도 불구하고, 민병대에 관련된 연방의회의 권한에 대해 제약을 부과해야 한다고 강력하게 주장했다.[54] 메이슨은 제1조의 민병대조항이 연방의회에 대하여 민병대에 관한 독점적인 권한을 부여하는 것으로 해석될 우려가 있으므로, 주정부에 대하여 민병대에 관련된 권한을 부여하는 조항이 필요하다고 주장했다. 그의 우려의 요지는 연방의회가 제1조의 규정에 근거하여 민병대의 무장과 소집을 해태함으로써 민병대를 해체할 가능성이 농후하고, 그렇게 되면 곧 상비군을 창설하는 구실을 제공할 가능성이 크다는 것이다. 이러한 불행을 막기 위해 연방의회가 민병대의 소집을 해태하는 경우에는 주정부가 민병대를 무장시킬 명시적인 권한을 부여하는 헌법의 수정조항이 필요하다는 것이 메이슨의 주장이었다.[55]

버지니아 비준대회의 토의기록은 수정 제2조가 주정부의 권한을 규정한 것이라는 주정부의 무기규제권론에 대해 어느 정도 논거를 제공해 준다. 이들 "집단적 권리론자"는 이 조항이 의미하는 무기소장권은 자주의 민병대를 무장할 권리에 불과하다고 한다.[56] 사실인즉 반연방주의자의 거두인 메이슨과 헨리, 두 사람 모두 연방정부에

---

53 5 Schwartz, 전게서 주 25, 983. New Hampshire, New York, North Carolina, Rhode Island 및 Virginia의 5개 주이다.

54 3 Elliot's Debates on Federal Constitution 425 (Jonathan Elliot ed., 1859).

55 Virginia Debates, in 3 Elliot's Debates 전기 주 54, 380.

56 George L. Shelton, "In Search of the Lost Amendment: Challenging Federal Firearms Regulation Through 'the State Right's Interpretation of the Second Amendment," 23 Florida State U. L. Rev. 105, 109

의한 민병대의 무장해제를 방지하기 위해 민병대를 무장시킬 명시적인 권한을 주정부에 부여할 것을 주장했다.[57]

일부 집단적 권리론자들은 수정 제2조의 무기소지권의 내용은 조직된 군대(organized military forces)를 무장시킬 권한에 한정된다고 주장한다.[58] 그러나 버지니아 비준회의의 토의기록은 이러한 주장을 뒷받침하지 않는다. 왜냐하면 메이슨이 이해한 민병대는 각 주의 주민을 포함한, 전체국민으로 구성된 병력을 의미한 것이며, 민병대에 의한 방어란 "시민의 방금(防禁)(civic defense)"을 의미한 것이지 주정부의 통제 아래 조직된 병력을 의미한 것이 아니기 때문이다. 그러므로 비록 수정 제2조상의 무장권의 보유자가 주정부에 한정된다고 할지라도 이 권리는 '국민'을 무장할 권리이지 조직된 군대를 무장할 권리가 아니기 때문이다.[59]

V. 연방의회의 태도

헌법의 아버지들의 낙관과는 달리 연방의회는 국민의 통제에서 벗어났다. 무기소장권을 보장하는 헌법의 명문규정에도 불구하고 기회가 닿는 대로 의회는 국민의무장권을 제한하는 입법을 제정하였다. 특히 주간 통상규제권 조항(Commerce Clause)[60]이 연방의회의 전가의 보도가 된 이래, 많은 총기규제입법권이 이 조항을 근거로 제정되었다.[61]

1934년 최초의 연방 총기규제법(the National Firearms Act of 1934)이 제정되었는데

(1996).

57 Virginia Debates, 전기 주 54, 384-393, 395-399.

58 Perer Buck Feller& Karl L. Gotting, The Second Amendment: A Second Look, 61 Nw. U. L. Rev. 46, 64 (1966).

59 Virginia Debates, 전기 주 54, 425.

60 연방헌법 제1조 8항.

61 통상규제권에 근거하여 주 내에서의 무기소장행위를 규율하는 연방법률의 위헌성을 논한 논문으로는 James M. Malony, Shoooting for an Omnipotent Congress: the Constitutionality of Federal Regulation of Intrastate Firearms Possession, 62 Fordham L. Rev. 1795 (1994) 참조. 1995년의 United States v. Lopez (115S. Ct. 1624) 판결에서 연방대법원은 과세권과 통상규제권에 기초하여 무기의 소장을 규율하는 법률의 위헌을 선언했다. 후술 주 98 및 본문 참조.

헌법적 근거는 흥미롭게도 제1조 제8항의 과세권 조항(Taxing Power Clause)이었다.[62] 이 법에 대한 여론의 반향에 어느 정도 자신을 얻은 의회는 1938년 통상규제권을 근거로 하여 본격적인 총기규제법(The Federal Firearms Act of 1938)을 제정하였다. 이 법에 의해 모든 총기 제조업자나 판매업자는 연방정부의 사전 허가를 얻지 아니하고는 일체의 무기나 탄약을 타주에 반출, 반입할 수 없었으며, 사인에게도 유사한 제약이 부과되었다.[63]

대공황, 2차대전, 전후 냉전 등 보다 중요한 사안에 골몰한 이후 30년 동안 연방의회는 총기규제에 관해 새로운 시도를 하지 않았다. 그러나 1963-1968의 기간 동안 연속적인 폭동과 정치적 암살이 나라 전체에 암운을 드리우자 또 다시 총기규제 문제가 전면에 부각되었다.[64] 1968년 의회는 1938년 총기규제법을 폐지하는 대신, 보다 포괄적인 규제를 가능하게 한 속칭 "종합범죄대책법(Omnibus Crime Control and Safe Streets Act of 1968)"[65]을 제정하였다.

그러나 이 법의 규정도 강력하지 못하다는 여론에 밀려 불과 4개월 후에 또 다시 의회는 종합범죄대책법의 규정에 상당한 수정을 가한 1968년 총기규제법(The Gun Control Act of 1968)을 제정하여 새로운 유형의 연방범죄를 창설하고, 단순한 사적 목적의 총기수집에 대해서도 상당한 규제를 가하였다.[66] 1980-1990년대에 들어와서 연방의회에는 총기규제법의 홍수가 일어났다. 포드(Gerald Ford), 레이건(Ronald Reagan) 두 대통령에 대한 암살 시도, 빈번한 항공기 납치사건, 학교에서의 총기 범죄, 총기 밀무역 등의 사태에 대응하여 의회는 일련의 법을 제정하였다. 1986년 총기소지자 보호법(The Firearms Owner's Protection Act of 1986),[67] 1988년의 비밀무기규제법(The Undetectable Firearms Act)[68] 및 마약규제법(The Anti-Drug Abuse Amendment),[69] 1990

---

62 이 법은 일정 규격 총기의 판매, 거래에 대해 유통세(exercise tax)를 부과함과 동시에 총기 거래업자의 등록을 강제하는 수준에 그쳤다. National Firearms Act of 1934, 26 U.S.C. 5801-5872 (1994).

63 Federal Firearms Act of 1938, 15 U.S.C. 901-910 (1968년 폐지).

64 연방의회의 토의 내용에 관해서 114 CONG. REC. 14773 (1968) 참조. 이 법을 제안한 Louisiana 출신 Huey Long 의원은 의회의 입장을 요약하여, "모든 시민이 총기를 소지할 수 있으나, 일단 범죄를 범한 후에는 일체 소지할 수 없도록 함"이 목적이라고 설명했다.

65 18 U.S.C. 921-928 (1994).

66 18 U.S.C. 921-930 (1994).

67 18 U.S.C. 922(d) (1994).

년 범죄통제법(The Crime Control Act of 1990)[70] 및 학교 환경안전법(The Gun-Free School Zone Act of 1990) 등 일련의 법이 제정되었고, 1993년에는 유명한 "제 1 Brady 법(the Brady Handgun Violence Prevention Act, "Brady 1")"이 제정되었다.[71]

수정 제2조와 관련하여 가장 큰 논란의 대상이 되고 있는 총기규제법은 1994년 공공안전 및 오락성 총기사용보호법(The Public Safety and Recreational Firearms Use Protection Act of 1994)[72]이다. 이 법은 시행 당시 연방법에 의해 적법하게 소지한 경우를 제외하고는 일체의 "반자동 살상무기(semiautomatic assault weapon)"의 제조, 양도, 소지, 일체의 행위를 금지하였다.[73]

Ⅵ. 법원의 태도

의회가 지속적으로 총기 규제 입법을 제정한 것과는 대조적으로 연방대법원은 이 문제에 관해 거의 관심을 표하지 않았다. 2세기 이상의 역사를 통해 연방대법원이 어떤 의미에서든지 수정 제2조를 다룬 판결은 단 4건에 불과하며[74] 본안에 관해 결정한 1939년의 Miller v. United States판결[75] 이후에는 이날에 이르기까지 침묵을 지키고

---

68 18 U.S.C. 922(p) (1994).

69 18 U.S.C. 924(h) (1994).

70 18 U.S.C. 921-930 (1994).

71 18 U.S.C. 922(s) (1994). 이 법은 1981년 Reagan 대통령 저격사건으로 장애인이 된 백악관 공보비서 James Brady의 이름을 딴 것으로, 권총을 구입하고자 하는 자는 신청서를 제출한 후 신원에 대한 조회가 완료될 시점까지 대기할 것을 골자로 한다. "제 1 Brady법"의 제정에 이어 1994년 "제 2 Brady법"안(the Gun Violence Prevention Bill)이 상·하 양원에 제안되었으나 통과되지 않았다.

72 18 U.S.C. 921-922 (1994).

73 이 법에 대한 논평과 함께 총기규제법의 제정의 역사와 향후의 전망을 로비 그룹의 활동과 관련하여 4단계 내용으로 분석한 글로는 Michael G. Lennett, "Note, Violent Crime Control and Law Enforcement Act of 1994: Taking a Bite Out of Violent Crime," 20 U. Dayton L. Rev. 573, 614-615 (1995).

74 이 밖에도 유명한 1853년의 Dred Scott 판결(Dred Scott v. Sanford, 60 U.S. (19 How.) 393)에서 "흑인을 합중국의 시민으로 인정하는 것은 이들을 경찰 규제로부터 해방시키며 자유로운 여행과 '무기의 보유와 소장'을 용인하는 결과가 될 것이다"라고 간접적으로 수정 제2조를 언급했다. Id. at 416-417. 이 판결의 배경에 관한 서술형 연구논문으로는 安京煥, "Dred Scott의 현장에서," 人權과 正義, 대한변호사협회, 1997/6, 123-131면 참조. [해제자주: 이 글이 원래 집필되던 1997년 시점의 통계이며 뒤이은 해제에서 지적하듯이 근래 총기에 의한 사고가 빈발하면서 연방대법원도 총기규제에 대한 중요한 사건을 다루고 있다.]

있다.[76]

권리장전상의 개개 기본권의 의미를 누구보다도 깊이 천착한 "초사법적극주의(super activist)" 더글라스(Willaim Douglas) 판사까지도[77] 수정 제2조에 대해서는 냉담하리만치 무심했고[78] 가장 강력한 민권단체인 미국 민권연맹(American Civil Rights Union)조차도 수정 제2조의 개인적 권리성을 부인하고 사실상 정부의 규제에 대해 전혀 이의를 제기하지 않아 왔다.[79] 현실적 여건과 무관하게 이상을 논하는 학자들도 이 문제에 관해서는 거의 논의를 전개하지 않았다.[80]

수정 제2조에 관련된 최초의 연방대법원 판결은 1875의 Cruikshank 판결이다.[81] 이 판결의 배경이 된 사건에서 피고인들은 과거 노예 신분이었던 시민을 강제로 무장해제시킴으로써 국민의 헌법적 권리를 박탈할 목적의 음모 행위를 금지한 연방법률의 위반으로 기소되었다. 대법원은 수정 제2조는 오로지 정부의 행위에 대해서만 적용될 뿐, 사인의 행위에 대한 구제를 청구할 권리를 발생시키지 아니한다고 판시했으며,[82] 이어서 19세기말에 내린 2건의 후속판결에서 이 조항은 정부의 행위 중에서도

---

75 307 U.S. 174.

76 그 동안 이 문제에 관련된 "상고허가신청"(petition for certiorari)은 빈번하게 제기되었으나 연방대법원은 지속적으로 본안 심사를 거부했다. 대법원에 제출된 허가상고신청 사건의 부분적 List는 Roland Docal, "The Second, Fifth and Ninth Amendments-The Precarious Protectors of the American Gun Collector," 23 Florida State U. L. Rev, 1101 (1996), 1121 n. 160 참조.

77 더글라스 판사의 법사상에 관한 분석서로는 安京煥, 美國法의 理論的 照明 -윌리암 다글라스 判事의 法思想-, 고시계(1986) 참조.

78 Adams v. Williams, 407 U.S. 143, 151 (1972) (Douglas, J. dissenting)(수정 제4조의 중요성을 강조하기 위해 덜 중요한 수정 제2조를 언급하여) "주지하는 바와 같이 수정 제2조는 민병대를 유지하기 위해 제정된 것이다. 그러나 이 조항의 의미를 희석시키는(watering down) 것이 오늘의 원칙이라면 나는 수정 제4조 대신 차라리 수정 제2조를 외면하겠다."

79 Nelson Lund, "The Second Amendment, Political Law and the Right to Self-Preservation," 39 Alabama L. Rev. 103, 121 n. 45 (1987).

80 수정 제2조에 관한 법학자들의 논의가 희소한 이유는 이 주제는 자신들의 영향력을 확대시키고자 하는 지식인의 자연적 성향에 비추어 볼 때 가치가 떨어지는 것이기 때문이라는 Robert Bork 판사의 지적(Bork, The Antitrust Paradox (197S) 423-24) 이나, 집단적 권리 문제의 논의에 대한 지식인의 본능적인 기피현상 때문이라는 Johnson 교수의 분석(Nicholas Johnson, "Beyond the Second Amendment: An Individual Right to Arms Viewed Through the Ninth Amendment," 24 Rutgers L. J. 1, 72 (1992))이 흥미롭다.

81 United States v. Cruikshank, 92 U.S. 542 (1875).

82 이 판결에서 대법원은 무기소지권의 존재를 인정했으나 이러한 권리는 수정 제2조와 무관하게 존재한다고 판시했다. 92 U.S. 549.

연방정부의 행위에 대해서만 적용될 뿐, 주정부의 행위에 대해서는 적용되지 아니한다고 판시했다.[83] 그러나 이 판결들은 연방헌법의 권리장전의 조항들은 수정 제14조를 매개체로 하여 주정부의 행위에 대해서도 적용된다는 이른바 "수용이론(incorporation theory)"이 탄생하기 이전의 판결들로서 오늘날에는 선판례로서의 의미를 거의 인정받지 못한다. 또한 이들 판결은 무기소장권이라는 헌법적 권리가 적용되는 주체 내지는 대상에 대해서만 다루었을 뿐, 그 권리의 범위에 관해서는 전혀 다루지 않았다.

헌법적 권리로서의 무기소장권의 범위를 다룬 최초의 연방대법원 판결은 1939년의 U. S. v. Miller 판결[84]이다.

피고인 밀러(Miller)는 1934년 총기규제법(National Firearms Act of 1934)에 위반하여 총기를 타주로 반출한 혐의로 기소되었다. 하급심은 밀러에 대한 기소는 수정 제2조의 위반이라고 판시했으나 대법원은 이 조항은 "국토의 방위를 상비군에 의존할 필요가 없도록 민병대를 "존치(continuation)"하고 그 "효과적인 운영(effectiveness)"을 확보함에 그 목적이 있으므로 "질서정연하게 규율된 민병대의" 육성에 합리적으로 연관되지 아니한 무기의 소지는 이 조항의 보호를 받지 못한다"면서 밀러의 유죄를 인정했다.[85] 법원은 제한된 범위에서나마 수정 제2조의 제정에 관련된 입법사적 배경에 관해 언급하면서, 무기소장권은 동시에 국가의 공동방위에 참가할 신체적 능력을 보유한 성인남자의 "커먼로상의 의무"이기도 했다고 부연했다.[86]

---

83 Miller v. Texas, 153 U.S. 535 (1894)(텍사스 주 총기규제법을 관할권의 부재를 이유로 각하); Presser v. Illinois, 116 U.S. 252 (1886)(수정 제2조는 연방에 대한 제한일뿐 주정부의 권한에 대한 제한을 부과하지 아니한다고 판시함).

84 307 U.S. 174 (1939).

85 Id. at 178. "to assure the continuation and render possible the effectiveness of (militia) forces so that the government would not rely on standing army." 법원은 명시하지는 않았지만 "a well regulated militia, being necessary to the security of a free state"라는 수정 제2조의 첫 구절을 근거로 사용한 것이 분명하다. 그러나 이 구절에 관한 법원의 분석은 논리정연하지 못하다. 먼저 법원은 헌법 제1조에 의해 연방의회가 연방 법률의 집행, 반란의 진압, 또는 외적의 퇴치를 위해 민병대를 소집할 권한이 있음을 지적한 후, 수정 제2조의 선언과 보장은 이러한 병력(forces, 민병대를 의미)을 존치(continuation)하고 그 효과적인 운영을 담보하기 위함에 있다고 판시했다. 이러한 판결문은 연방의회의 민병대 소집권의 보조적 기능으로 수정 제2조의 무기소장권이 보장되는 것, 다시 말하자면 민병대의 운영에 연방이 헌법적인 이해관계를 가지는 것으로 인식될 오해를 유발한다.

86 Id. at 179-180. 이 판결이 무기소장권을 "커먼로"와 결부시킴으로써 수정 제9조의 적용가능성을 제기했다고 주장하는 견해가 있다. Docal, 전게논문 주 76, 1120; Johnson, 전게논문 주 80 참조.

Miller 판결의 구체적 의미를 두고 해석의 대립이 있다. 다수의 해석은 이 판결은 무기의 소장권은 주정부의 공적인 권리일 뿐, 개개 국민의 권리가 아님을 판시했다고 한다. Miller 판결 이후에 내려진 하급법원의 판결들은 Miller 판결보다 더욱 더 수정 제2조의 적용범위를 제한적으로 해석하여, Miller 판결의 문언을 존중하여 수정 제2조의 목적이 단지 민병대의 존치와 효용을 담보함에 있다면, 주정부 차원의 민병대의 자율적인 운영에 관해 연방의 간섭을 받지 아니할 권리를 보호할 뿐 어떠한 개인적 권리도 보호하지 아니한다는 입장을 유지했다.[87]

반면, 이 판결이 개인의 무기소장권을 인정했다고 주장하는 입장에서는 판결문이 미국 민병대의 역사에 관한 상세한 배경을 담고 있으며, 사건의 당사자에서 개인의 무기소장권을 인정한 결과가 된 점을 근거로 내세운다.[88] 또한 "민병대"의 정의와 목적에 관해 법원이 내린 해석이 이러한 주장을 간접적으로 보강해 준다.[89]

거의 반세기에 걸쳐 지속적으로 전개되어 온 논란과 추측에도 불구하고 대법원은 이날에 이르기까지 Miller 판결을 석명하거나 재고할 기미를 전혀 보이지 않고 있다. 대법원의 침묵에 대해 두 가지 상반된 해석이 제기되어 있다. 총기규제를 찬성하는 입장에서는 대법원이 의회의 규제를 용인했다고 주장하는 반면,[90] 총기거래상과 수집자들은 대법원의 침묵은 헌법과 커먼로상의 무기소장권을 묵시적으로 인정한 증거라고 주장한다.[91]

이 문제에 대해 언급한 몇 건의 판결에서도 연방대법원은 태도를 명백하게 천명하지 않았기에 갖가지 추측을 낳고 있다.[92] 한 가지 특히 유념할 사항은 Miller 판결은

---

87 이를테면, Quilici v. Village of Morton Grove, 695 F. 2d 261, 270 (7th Cir. 1982); United States v. Oakes, 564F. 2d 384, 387 (10th Cir. 1977); Stevens v. United States, 440 F. 2d 144, 149 (6th Cir. 1971); Laurence H. Tribe, American Constitutional Law(2nd ed. 1988), p. 299, n. 6.

88 Kates, 전게논문 주 3, 248-250.

89 "각 주가 유지, 훈련할 것으로 기대되는 "민병대"(Militia)는 의회의 동의없이 보유할 수 없는 "군대"(Troops)와 대비된다.… 상비군의 보유를 극히 경계했던 건국 당시의 보편적 정서, 국가와 법은 민병대는 공동의 방위에 동참할 신체적 능력을 보유한 남성 전원으로 구성되며 … 통상의 경우 국가의 방위를 위해 소집에 응할 의무가 있다." 307 U.S. 178-179. 이러한 판결문이 집단적 주권론을 부정한 명백한 증거라는 주장이 있다. Lund, 전게논문 주 79, 110.

90 Jay Wagner, "Gun Control and the Intent of the Second Amendment: To What Extent Is There an Individual Right To Bear and Keep Arms," 37 Villanova. L, Rev. 1407 (1992).

91 Docal, 전게논문 주 76, 1117; Hertz, 전게논문 주 45, 77; Andrew Jay McClurg, "The Rethoric of Gun Control," 42 American U. L. Rev. 53, 100 (1992).

연방의 법률을 심사 대상으로 하였다는 점이다. 이날에 이르기까지 연방대법원은 적어도 2천 편 이상에 달하는 주정부 차원의 무기규제법을 심사의 대상으로 삼지 않았다.[93] 1990년의 Verdugo-Urquidez 판결은[94] 비록 수정 제2조의 본안에 관한 사건은 아니지만 이 조항에 담긴 "국민(people)"이라는 단어의 의미에 관해 유권해석을 내린 점에서 의의가 크다. 이 판결에서 법원은 "수정 제1조, 제2조, 제4조, 그리고 제9조 및 제10조의 보호의 대상이 되는 국민은 국가공동체의 일원이 된 사람의 총체"를 의미한다고 해석을 내렸다.[95]

1995년 연방대법원은 무기의 소장에 관한 또 하나의 판결을 내렸다.[96] 이 판결은 수정 제2조 그 자체에 대한 선판례로 볼 수는 없으나 대법원은 연방의회의 주간통상권과 과세권에 근거하여 무기의 소장을 금지하는 입법을 심사하였다. 렌퀴스트(Rehnquist) 원장의 다수의견은 학교로부터 직경 1,000피트 이내의 거리에서는 총기의 단순한 소지조차 금지한 연방법률[97]은 통상규제권의 남용이라고 판시했다.

대법원이 수정 제2조에 대한 명쾌한 입장을 표명하지 않았기에 하급법원 사이에 상당한 혼란이 발생하고 있다.[98] 연방대법원이 최종적으로 유권해석을 내려 주어야 할 이슈는 대체로 3가지로 요약될 수 있다. 첫째, 개인이 수정 제2조의 침해를 이유로 소송을 제기할 수 있는 원고적격(standing)을 가지는가, 둘째, 만약 개인이 아닌 주만이 원고적격을 보유한다면 주가 개인에게 어떠한 보호를 부여하는가, 그리고 셋째, 수정 제2조가 어떤 특정 종류의 무기의 소장을 보호하는가이다.[99]

---

92 가장 본질적인 해석은 정치적 기관으로 하여금 이 문제를 해결하도록 하는 전형적인 사법자제의 태도라고 하는 해석이다. Docal, 전게논문 주 76, 1117면.

93 G. Newton & F. Zimring, Firearms and Violence in American Life (1969). Lund, 전게 논문 주 79, 110에서 재인용.

94 United States v. Verdugo-Urquidez, 110 S. Ct. 1056, 1060-1061 (1990).

95 "a class of persons who are part of a national community or who have otherwise developed sufficient connection with this country to be considered part of that community." 반대의견을 집필한 Brennan은 "국민"은 "정부"(government)에 대립되는 개념으로 "피치자"(governed)의 뜻이라고 주장했다. Id. at 1071-1072.

96 United States v. Lopez,115 S. Ct. 1624 (1995).

97 The Gun-Free School Act of 1990.

98 이를테면 Cases v. United States, 131F. 2d 916 (1st Cir. 1942), cert denied, 319 U.S. 770 (1943); Stevens v. United States, 440 F. 2d 144 (6th Cir. 1971); United States v. Hales, 978 F. 2d. 1016 (8th Cir. 1992) cert, denied 113 S. Ct. 1614 (1993). 자세한 분석은 Shelton, 전게논문 주 56, 118-129 참조.

Ⅶ. 맺음말

연방대법원을 포함한 연방법원의 기본입장은 수정 제2조는 주정부에 대해서 자주의 민병대를 무장할 권리만을 부여한다는 것이다. 이러한 원칙에 입각하여 법원은 대체로 개인의 무기 소지를 규제하는 법률에 대한 심사를 거부하다시피 했다.

그러나 이러한 해석은 수정 제2조의 제정에 관련된 문헌과 토의의 기록을 살펴보면 반론의 여지가 크다. 문헌과 기록의 균형잡힌 분석을 통해 최소한 2가지의 수정 제2조의 제정목적을 추출해 낼 수 있다. 첫째, 국민 스스로의 무장을 통해 국가를 방위함으로써 상비군의 위험과 해악을 피하고, 둘째, 무기를 소장한 국민은 조직된 군대의 압제에 대해 대항할 수 있도록 한다는 것이다. 조직된 연방의 군대가 국방을 담당하는 현재의 상황에서는 첫째의 목적은 논의의 실익이 적다. 그러나 군대에 의한 압제에 대해 국민이 저항할 최후의 수단을 제공한다는 두 번째 목적은 아직도 유념할 여지가 있다. 이러한 관점에서 볼 때 수정 제2조를 근거로 개인의 무장권을 주장하는 것은 아직도 경청의 소지가 충분하다. "개인적 권리론"의 현실적 효용성은 구체적으로 무기의 개인적 소장을 규율하는 법률에 대한 사법심사 기준의 정립 문제와 관련되어 있다. 다시 말하자면 수정 헌법 제2조에 위반하느냐 여부를 심사하는 기준은 입법에 의해 제한되는 국민의 기본권이 "본질적인 권리(fundamental rights)"이냐 여부에 의해 결정된다.[100] 수정 제2조상의 무기소장권은 국민의 자위권으로 탄생한 것이라는 그 생성 과정을 고려하면 본질적 권리로 분류함에 무리가 없을 것이다. 따라서 "필수불가결한 이익(compelling governmental interest)" 등의 요건을 요구하는 엄격사법심사의 대상이 되어야 할 것이다.[101]

수정 제2조의 성격에 관해 연방대법원이 최종적으로 어떠한 유권적 해석을 내릴지 현재로서는 예측할 수 없다. 200세 이상의 연륜 동안 제도와 시대조류의 변화를 몇 구절의 문자 속에 담아내야 하는 연방헌법의 수많은 여타 조항과 마찬가지로 수정 제2조 또한 "역사와 의미의 변천"을 27개의 단어 속에 용해시켜 수용해야 할 것이다.

---

99 Id. at 130.

100 자세히는 Gerald Gunther, Constitutional Law (12th ed., 1991), 433-439; 819-859.

101 자세히는 J. Wagner의 Comments, 전기 주 90, 1451-1460.

제정 당시의 "원래의 의도(original intent)"가 무엇이며, 이러한 헌법의 본래의 의도가 변화된 상황에 어떻게, 어떤 범위 내에서 적용되는가 하는 근본적인 문제에 대한 답은 연방대법원의 몫이다.

[관련자료][102]

1. 종　합

David E. Young ed., The Origin of the Second Amendment: A Documentary History of the Bill of Rights 1787-1792, 2nd ed. Golden Oaks Books (1995).

2. 무기소장권은 개인적 권리라는 주장

Andrew Jay McClurg, The Rethoric of Gun Control, 42 American U. L. Rev. 53 (1992).

David Kopel, It Isn't About Duck Hunting: The British Origins of the Right To Arms, 93 Mich. L. Rev. 1333 (1995)(Book Review of Malcolm).

Don B. Kates Jr., Handgun Prohibition and the Original Meaning of the Second Amendment 82 Mich. L. Rev. 204 (1983).

Joyce Malcolm, To Keep and Bear Arms: The Origins of An Anglo-American Right, Harvard University Press (1994).

Nelson Lund, The Second Amendment, Political Law and the Right to Self-Preservation, 39 Alabama L. Rev. 103 (1987).

Nicholas Johnson, Beyond the Second Amendment: An Individual Right to Arms Viewed Through the Ninth Amendment, 24 Rutgers L. J. 1 (1992).

Robert E. Shahope, The Ideological Origins of the Second Amendment, 69 J. Am. Hist. 599 (1982).

Roland Docal, The Second, Fifth and Ninth Amendments-The Precarious Protectors of the American Gun Collector, 23 Florida State IL L. Rev.1101 (1996).

Sanford Levinson, The Embarrassing Second Amendment, 99 Yale L. J. 637 (1989).

Stephen Halbrook, That Every Man Be Armed: The Evolution of a Constitutionalism, University of New Mexico Press (1984).

William Van Alstyne, The Second Amendment and the Personal Right to Arms 43 Duke L. J. 1236 (1994).

---

102 이 자료는 필자의 임의적인 판단에 의해 수록하는 것으로 수정 제2조에 관한 대표적인 저술이라고 단정해서는 안 된다.

3. 수정 제2조는 주의 집단적 권리라는 주장

David Vandercoy, The History of the Second Amendment 28 Valpariso. U. L. Rev. 1007 (1994).

David Williams, Civic Republicanism and the Citizen Militia: The Terrifying Second Amendment, 101 Yale L. J. 551 (1991).

Gregory L. Shelton, In Search of the Lost Amendment: Challenging Federal Firearms Regulation Through the "State's Right" Interpretation of the Second Amendment, 23 Florida State IL L. Rev. 105 (1996).

Jay Wagner, Gun Control and the Intent of the Second Amendment: To What Extent Is there an Individual Right To Bear and Keep Arms, 37 Villanova, L. Rev. 1407 (1992).

Stephen P. Halbroook, Encroachments of the Crown on the Liberty of the Subject: Pre-Revolutionary Origins of the Second Amendment, 15, Univ. of Dayton L. Rev. (1989).

Thomas M. Moncure, Second Amend Ain't About Hunting, 34 Howard L. J. 589 (1991).

Wendy Brown, Guns, Cowboys, Philadelphia Mayors and Civic Rebublicanism: On Sanford Levinson's Thc Embarassing Second Amendment, 99 Yale L, J. 661 (1989).

3. 미국 연방헌법 수정조항 제2조
- 무기소지권에 대한 논쟁과 자기방어의 기본권 -

손 영 호*

Ⅰ. 머리말

미국의 시사주간지 〈타임〉은 1968년 7월 표지기사로 총기문제를 다루었다. 표지의 그림은 연기를 내뿜는 권총이 독자의 얼굴을 정면으로 겨루는 섬뜩한 장면이었다. 이런 특집이 기획된 것은 당시 미국을 충격의 도가니로 몰아넣었던 마틴 루터 킹 목사와 로버트 케네디 상원의원이 암살사건이 있었기 때문이었다. 그로부터 32년이 지난 2000년 〈타임〉은 "여전히 총기 앞에 놓인 미국"이라는 표지기사를 내보냈다. 이번에는 1999년 4월 콜로라도 주 리틀턴에 위치한 콜럼바인 고등학교에서 발생한 총기난동사건이 계기가 되었다. 무고한 학생과 교사 13명이 사살되고, 23명이 부상을 당한 이 사건으로 총기규제를 강력히 요구하며 100만 어머니 행진이 펼쳐지기도 하였다. 〈타임〉은 학교 내 총기난동이나 암살 등 미국에서 발생하는 온갖 범죄와 사건의 가장 큰 요인으로 누구나 손쉽게 구입하고 휴대할 수 있는 총기의 실상에 초점을 맞추었다.

미국의 총기보유율은 세계 그 어떤 나라도 근접할 수 없을 만큼 독보적이다. 미연방수사국(FBI)에 따르면 미국에서 군용은 제외하고 민간인이 소유한 총기는 2억 5천정에 이르고, 해마다 500만정 이상이 증가는 것으로 나타났다.[1] 이것은 미국인 전체

---

* 베트남 호치민시 국립대학교 인문사회대학 교수 · 청주대학교 인문대학 역사문화학과 교수, 이 글은 『미국학논집』 제45권 제2호, 2013, 129-158면에 게재한 논문임을 밝힌다.

1 Jens Ludwig, *Evaluation Gun Policy: Effects on Crime and Violence* (Washington D. C: Brookings

를 무장시킬 수 있는 규모이다. 범죄나 정신병력이 없는 성인이라면 누구나 간단한 신원조회만으로 총기를 구입할 수 있다. 개인의 총기등록을 법적으로 의무화하지도 않는다. 흔히 미국을 "총의 천국," "술보다 총을 사기가 더 쉬운 나라"라고 부르는 이유가 바로 여기에 있다. 사정이 이렇다보니 미국에서는 크고 작은 총기사건이 그칠 날이 없다. 전체 범죄 중 총기를 이용한 범죄는 70%에 이르고 있으며, 총기사고로 매년 3만 명이 사망하고 있다.[2]

총기범죄와 사건이 커다란 사회적 이슈가 되고 있는 현실에서 미국정부나 미국인들은 어떤 형태든지 총기규제의 필요성을 인식하고 있다. 그러나 정작 총기를 규제하려는 법안을 제안할 때, 맨 처음 부딪치는 것이 '무기를 소유하고 휴대할 국민적 권리'를 명시한 연방헌법 수정조항 2조를 둘러싼 논란이다.[3] 총기규제에 가장 오래 유지된 헌법이다. 그러나 시대의 변화에 맞게 26개의 새로운 조항이 추가되었는데, 이 추가 조항을 수정(修正, Amendment) 조항이라고 한다. 이 중 1789년 발의되어 1791년 발효한 수정조항 제1조부터 제10조까지를 보통 미국의 '권리장전'이라고 부른다. 여기서 제기되는 것은 수정헌법과 수정조항이라는 단어의 용어상의 문제이다. 학자들은 종종 수정헌법을 수정조항으로 동일시하는 경향이 있으나, 이 두 용어 사이에는 차이가 있다. 엄격히 말하면 미국에는 연방헌법은 있지만, 수정헌법이라는 말은 존재하지 않는다. 단지 현행 연방헌법에 추가로 '수정조항'이 부가되어 있을 뿐이다. Amendment라는 용어는 수정헌법이 아니라 수정조항이라는 뜻이다. 용례에서도 'Amendment to the Constitution'이라는 말은 현행 헌법에 부가된 수정조항이라는 뜻이다. 따라서 The Second Amendment to the Constitution이라는 말은 '연방헌법

Institution, 2003), 3-4.

2 http://weekly.donga.com/docs/magazine/weekly (2011/01/28). http://kr.news.yahoo.com/service/news/shellview.htm (2010/04/23).

3 1787년 제정된 미국 헌법의 본체는 오늘날까지도 전혀 수정없이 보존되어 세계에서 가장 오래 유지된 헌법이다. 그러나 시대의 변화에 맞게 26개의 새로운 조항이 추가되었는데, 이 추가 조항을 수정(修正, Amendment) 조항이라고 한다. 이 중 1789년 발의되어 1791년 발효한 수정조항 제1조부터 제10조까지를 보통 미국의 '권리장전'이라고 부른다. 여기서 제기되는 것은 수정헌법과 수정조항이라는 단어의 용어상의 문제이다. 학자들은 종종 수정헌법을 수정조항으로 동일시하는 경향이 있으나, 이 두 용어 사이에는 차이가 있다. 엄격히 말하면 미국에는 연방헌법은 있지만, 수정헌법이라는 말은 존재하지 않는다. 단지 현행 연방헌법에 추가로 '수정조항'이 부가되어 있음을 분명히 하기 위하여 '수정조항 2조'라는 용어를 사용하였다.

수정조항 제2조'를 의미하는 것이다. 이에 따라 본문에서는 용어상의 의미를 반대하는 사람이나 단체들은 하나같이 무기소지권은 헌법이 보장한 국민의 기본권이라고 주장하고 있다. 따라서 총기규제 논쟁의 출발점이 수정조항 2조에 있기 때문에 무엇보다도 이 법안이 어떤 취지와 목적으로 제정되었는지에 대한 연구가 선행되어야 할 것이다.

미국 연방헌법 수정조항 2조에 명시된 무기소지권의 연원은 영국 관습법의 전통과 공화주의 사상에서 찾을 수 있다. 1688년 영국의 명예혁명으로 제임스 2세가 폐위되고, 이듬해인 1689년 권리장전(Bill of Rights)이 채택되었다. 권리장전에는 의회의 동의없이 평화시에 상비군을 징집하거나 유지하는 것을 금지하였으며, 국민들에게 자기방어를 위해 무기소지권을 허용하였다. 이러한 영국의 무기소유의 전통은 신대륙 정착민들에게 이어졌고, 독립전쟁 후 수정조항 2조에 의해 구체적으로 성문화되었다. 이러한 시민무장권은 제임스 해링턴(James Harrington), 제임스 버러(James Burgh) 등 영국의 공화주의 사상가들에 의해 체계적으로 연구되었고, 토마스 제퍼슨(Thomas Jefferson)과 제임스 메디슨(James Madison) 등 미국 건국의 아버지들에 계승되어 18세기 후반 미국의 정치적 발전과 지적 전통에 지대한 영향을 끼치게 되었다.[4]

미국에서는 1970년대 이후 요인 암살과 총기 난동사건이 사회적 이슈가 되면서 총기문제가 새로운 관심사로 주목을 받게 되었다. 그 결과 법률학자들을 중심으로 무기소지권의 기원과 사상적 배경(특히 영국 관습법과 공화주의 사상), 수정조항 2조가 채택된 배경과 취지, 그리고 정부의 총기규제의 타당성 등 다양한 연구가 진행되었다.[5] 국내에서도 몇몇 법률학자들을 중심으로 수정조항 2조에 대한 연구가 있으나, 미국의 연구 경향이나 내용을 소개하는 정도에 그쳐 심도있는 연구가 이루어지지 않은 상

---

4 Robert E. Shalhope, "Republicanism and Early American Historiography," *William and Mary Quarterly* 39 (April 1982), pp. 334-356 참조.

5 Robert E. Shallhope, "The Ideological Origins of the Second Amendment," *Journal of American History* 69 (December 1982), 599-614; Robert E. Shallhope, "The Armed Citizen in the Early Republic," *Law and Contemporary Problems* 49 (1986), 125-41; Don B. Kates, "The Second Amendment and the Ideology of Self-Protection," *Constitutional Commentary* 9 (Winter 1992), 87-104; Joyce Lee Malcolm, "To Keep and Bear Arms: The Origins of an Anglo-American Right" (Cambridge, Mass., 1994); David E. Vandercoy, "The History of the Second Amendment," *Valpariso University Law Review* 28 (Spring 1994), 1007-39 등 참조.

태이다. 더욱이 이들 연구들은 대부분 수정조항 2조에 관한 유권해석, 총기논쟁의 이론적 배경, 총기규제 법안 등 법률적 측면에 치중하여 무기소지권의 역사적인 맥락이나 사상적인 배경에 대한 연구는 거의 전무한 실정이다.

본 논문은 수정조항 2조에 언급된 무기소지권의 역사 사상적인 배경에 중점을 두고, 크게 두 가지 주제에 초점을 맞추었다. 첫째, 무기소지권의 귀속에 관한 논쟁, 즉 '개인의 권리'와 '주(州)의 권리'라는 두 대립적인 주장의 이론적인 근거와 타당성, 그리고 이에 대한 과거 대법원의 판례와 유권해석을 중심으로 살펴보고자 한다. 둘째, 수정조항 2조에 나타난 핵심적인 이데올로기가 무엇인지를 고찰해 보고자 한다. 미국 건국의 아버지들이 신앙과 표현의 자유를 명시한 수정조항 1조에 이에 2조에 무기소지권을 구체화시킨 목적이 무엇일까? 무기소지권이 과연 미국인들에게 개인의 자유와 권리를 보호하는 신성불가침의 기본권으로 여겨졌던 근거는 어디에 있는가?

많은 법률가와 학자들은 각기 다른 법률적 해석과 역사와 사상적 배경에서 무기소지권의 정당성 여부를 주장하고 있다. 그러나 미국 건국의 아버지들이 공통적으로 내세운 것은 자기방어의 기본권이었다. 건국의 아버지들의 자기방어에 신념은 매우 강하였을 뿐만 아니라, 오늘날 우리가 인식하고 있는 개념보다 더 구체적이며 포괄적이었다.

본 논문은 수정조항 2조의 핵심적인 이념이 자기방어의 기본권에서 출발하였다는 사실을 고전적 자유주의 사상가들의 이념과 독립혁명과 건국초기 미국의 정치와 역사발전에서 나타난 실질적인 증거와 자료를 통해 살펴보고자 한다. 이를 통해 미국 헌법에 규정된 무기소지권의 목적과 의미를 명확히 이해할 수 있을 뿐만 아니라, 오늘날 미국사회와 정치권에 뜨겁게 달구고 있는 총기논쟁의 실체를 파악할 수 있을 것으로 사료된다.[6]

---

6 안경환, "미국 연방헌법 수정 제2조(무기소지권)의 의미," 서울대학교법학 105집(서울대 법학연구소, 1997), 129-49; 최승원, "미연방헌법 수정 제2조와 총기규제," 미국헌법연구 7집 (미국헌법학회, 1996), 217-42; 양승업, "미국헌법 제2조와 수정헌법 제12조의 차이점에 관한 고찰," 강원법학 23집 (강원대 법학연구소, 2006), 185-213 참조.

Ⅱ. 무기소지권에 대한 논쟁과 대법원 판례

수정조항 2조에 명시된 무기소지권은 소위 권리장전으로 불리는 국민의 권리 중에서 가장 논란이 되고 있는 문제이다. 과거 대법원은 신앙이나 표현의 자유, 범죄혐의자들을 보호하는 권리와는 달리 무기소지권에 대해서는 별로 다루지 않아, 이 조항에 대한 권위있는 사법적인 해석이 거의 존재하지 않는다. 그리하여 미국 국민과 연방의회, 주정부 입법자들은 수정헌법 제2조의 의미와 목적, 그리고 적용범위(헌법이 총기에 대한 행정적인 규제를 허가하고 있는지, 그리고 그럴 경우 어느 선까지 허가해야 하는지)에 대해 합의점을 찾지 못하고 있는 실정이다.

총기에 대한 엄격한 통제를 주장하는 사람들은 높은 범죄율과 총기사고나 사건으로 인한 수많은 인명피해를 지적한다. 이에 반대하는 사람들은 총기소유는 헌법에 의해 보장된 국민의 신성한 기본권으로 법률적 통제의 대상이 아니라고 주장한다. 이렇듯, 총기문제가 휘발성이 강한 문제이며, 국민여론을 양분시키는 뜨거운 감자로 등장한 현실에서 민주, 공화 양당도 이 문제를 적극적으로 이슈화하는 것을 꺼리는 분위기가 강하다. 따라서 매년 미국에서 발생하는 수많은 충격적인 총기범죄와 사건에도 불구하고 총기규제에 대한 일관된 정책이나 대안을 마련하는 것은 결코 쉬운 일이 아니다.[7]

현재에도 진행되고 있는 이러한 논쟁의 열기 속에 수정조항 제2조의 기원과 이것이 권리장전에 포함된 이유, 그리고 수많은 미국인들이 사냥이나 스포츠 등 범죄와 관련 없는 취미활동을 위해 총기를 소유하고 있다는 사실이 종종 무시되곤 한다. 양측의 논리가 지나칠 정도로 엄청난 열기를 유발하지만, 총기문제에 대한 근본적인 해결책이 제시될 가능성은 거의 없어 보인다.

연방헌법 수정조항 2조의 전문은 다음과 같다. "규율을 갖춘 민병대(militia)는 자유로운 주(州)정부의 안보에 필요하므로, 무기를 소지하고 휴대할 수 있는 국민(people)의 권리를 침해할 수 없다." 이 조항은 단지 27개 단어가 담긴 짧은 문장으로 구성되어 있으나, 그 의미와 목적을 둘러싸고 학자들 간에 치열한 논쟁이 벌어지고 있다. 그

---

7 Sanford Levinson, "The Embarrassing Second Amendment," *Yale Law Journal* 99 (1987), 637-59.

이유는 하나의 문장에 두 개의 서로 상충되는 문구를 동시에 담고 있기 때문이다. 수정조항 2조가 연방정부의 권한을 제한하고 국민의 기본권과 주정부의 독립성을 보장하기 위한 목적으로 제정되었다는 사실에는 이견이 없다. 그러나 연방정부에 대한 견제와 제한을 주도하는 주체가 주정부인지, 아니면 개개인의 국민인지에 대하여 치열한 논쟁이 일고 있다.[8]

수정조항 2조의 전반부인 "질서정연한 규율을 갖춘 민병은 자유로운 주정부의 안보에 필요하다"는 문구를 본다면 민병이 무기소유의 주체가 된다. 다시 말해, 잘 훈련된 민병은 주의 안보에 필요하기 때문에 민병을 유지하기 위해서는 국민의 무기소지권이 보장되어야 한다고 해석할 수 있다. 그러나 "무기를 소유하고 휴대할 수 있는 국민적 권리가 침해돼서는 안 된다"는 후반부를 강조한다면 집단으로서의 민병이 아니라, 국민 개개인이 무기소유의 주체가 된다. 국민 개개인이 무장할 권리가 보장되지 않는다면, 민병의 존재도, 주정부의 안보도 위협받을 수 있다는 해석이다.

여기에서 '주의 권리(states' rights)'와 '개인의 권리(individual rights)'라는 두 개의 상반된 주장이 제기된다. '주의 권리'를 주장하는 측은 수정조항 2조를 주 정부의 민병 유지 권한을 규정한 조항으로 해석한다.[9] 주의 공식기구로서 민병대가 주정부의 통제하에 집단적으로 총기를 보유하는 것을 의미하는 것이지, 개인의 자유로운 무기소유를 인정한 것이 아니라는 것이다.[10] 따라서 정부가 개인의 총기소유를 규제하거나 통제하는 데는 헌법상 아무런 문제가 없다는 것이다. '주의 권리'를 주장하는 측이 일차적인 근거로 내 세우는 것이 연방헌법에 규정된 민병대 규정이다.

> 연방의회는 합중국의 법률을 집행하고 반란을 진압하며 외적의 침입을 물리치기 위하여 민병대 소집에 관한 법률을 제정하며,… 민병대의 조직과 무장, 훈련에 관한 규칙을 정

---

8 무기소지권에 대한 논쟁을 다룬 주요 저서로는 Robert J. Cottrell, ed., *Gun Control and the Constitution* (New York: Garland Publishing, 1994); Saul Cornell, *A Well-Regulated Militia: The Founding Fathers and the Origins of Gun Control in America* (New York: Oxford University Press, 2006); Spitzer, Robert J. *The Right to Bear Arms: Rights and Liberties under the Law* (Santa Barbara: ABC-CLIO, 2001) 참조.

9 Andrew D. Herz, "Gun Cracy: Constitutional False Consciousness and Dereliction of Dialogic Responsibility," *Boston University Law Review* 75 (January 1995), 441-51.

10 Randy E. Bennett and Don B. Kates, "Under Fire: The New Consensus on the Second Amendment," *Emory Law Journal* 45 (Fall 1996), 1139-1259.

한다,… 다만 민병의 장교를 임명하거나 연방의회가 정하는 법률에 따라 민병을 훈련시키는 권한은 각 주가 갖는다.[11]

이런 민병대의 규정에 의해 권한을 부여받은 연방의회가 자의적으로 민병대를 해산시켜 주정부를 무력화시킬 수 있다는 우려가 제기되었다. 따라서 주정부가 연방정부의 전제와 횡포에 저항할 수단으로 수정조항 2조가 제정되었다는 것이다.[12]

반면 '개인의 권리'를 내 세우는 측은 수정조항 2조에 명시한 권리는 개인이 자유롭게 총기를 소유하고 휴대할 수 있는 권리라고 주장한다. 즉 무기소지권은 민병대라는 집단적인 조직이 아니라, 국민 개개인의 자유를 보장하기 위한 목적으로 제정되었다는 것이다.[13] 따라서 무기소지는 헌법에 명시된 기본권이며, 그 어떤 이유로든지 정부가 이를 침해할 권한이 없다는 것이다. 개인의 권리를 주장하는 측은 이 조항이 설령 주정부의 민병대를 보호하기 위한 목적으로 제정되었다고 하더라도, 이러한 목적은 시민 개개인이 무장함으로써 가장 효과적으로 달성될 수 있다고 주장한다.

여기서 수정조항 2조에 대한 논쟁의 실체에 좀 더 구체적으로 접근하기 위해 과거 대법원이 수정조항 2조에 대해 어떤 판결을 내렸는지 살펴볼 필요가 있다.[14] 그동안 미국 최고의 헌법기관인 연방대법원은 국민의 권리조항에 대해 권위있는 결정해 왔으며, 그 결정이 상당한 구속력을 지니고 있기 때문이다. 수정조항 2조와 직접 연관된 연방대법원의 판결은 단지 세 차례에 불과하였으며, 판결 내용도 오늘날 논란이 되고 있는 총기규제와는 직접적으로 관련이 없는 것이었다. 1875년 미합중국 대 크룩생크(U.S v. Cruikshank) 판결에서 대법원은 두 가지 원칙을 선언하였다.[15] 하나는 수정조항 2조에 근거하여 총기를 규세하는 것은 문제가 없으며, 다른 하나는 이 조항이 주정부가 아니라 연방정부에만 적용된다는 것이었다. 다시 말하면, 수정조항 2조가 총기규제에 대해 어떤 한계를 규정하든 이는 주정부에 적용되지 않으며, 따라서

---

11 연방헌법 제1조 8절 15-16항.

12 Don B. Kates, "Handgun Prohibition and the Original Meaning of the Second Amendment," *Michigan Law Review* 204 (1983), 204-12.

13 Glenn Harlan Reynolds, "A Critical Guide to the Second Amendment," *Tennessee Law Review* 62 (1995), 461-88.

14 http://guncite.com/gc2ndsup.htm/ (8/28/2010) 참조.

15 U.S v. Cruikshank, 92 *United States Reports* (Washington DC: Government Printing Office, 1875), 542.

주정부는 총기규제에 대해 무제한의 권한을 가지고 있다고 판시하였다.

이어 1886년 프레서 대 일리노이 주(Presser v. Illinois) 판결은 준군사조직이 주지사의 허가없이 훈련을 하거나 행군하지 못하도록 규정한 일리노이 주 병무법에 손을 들어 주었다.[16] 다시 한 번 대법원은 수정조항 2조가 연방정부에만 적용됨을 지적했으며, 주정부는 시민 개개의 무기소지와 사용을 대해 규제할 권한이 있다고 판시하였다. 다시 말해, 무기를 소지하고 휴대할 권리는 민병의 필요성에만 관련이 있다는 것이었다.

대법원에 상정된 사건 중 수정조항 2조와 관련하여 지금까지 가장 중요한 판결은 1939년 미합중국 대 밀러(U.S v. Miller) 판결이었다.[17] 이 사건은 총기가 주의 경계를 넘어 다른 주로 운송하는 것을 금지하는 총기규제법안의 합법성 여부를 가리는 것이었다. 두 남성이 등록되지 않는 총신을 짧게 자른 산탄총(당시 강도행위에 자주 사용되었던 무기)을 주 경계선 밖으로 운송하는 혐의로 기소되었다. 그들은 수정조항 2조에 보장된 개인의 무기소지권을 국가가 침해했다고 주장하였다. 대법원은 만장일치로 의회는 총기를 규제할 권한이 있으며, 총기를 규제하는 것은 헌법의 취지에도 어긋나지 않는다고 판결하였다. 대법원은 "수정조항 2조는 개인의 무기소지권이 아닌 주정부의 민병유지 권한을 규정한 것"이라고 판단하였으나, '민병' '국민' '무기' 등에 대한 구체적인 범위나 대상은 밝히지 않았다.

요약하면, 수정조항 2조에 대한 과거 3번에 걸친 대법원의 판결들은 모두 수정조항 2조에 대해 직접 언급하기보다는 연방헌법에 규정한 민병대에 관한 규정을 근거로 한 것이었다. 다시 말해, 민병활동과 연관하여 주의 권리를 옹호한 판결을 내린 것이며, 개인의 자유로운 총기소지가 헌법에 의해 보호받고 있다고 언급하지는 않았다.

1901년 시오도어 루즈벨트(Theodore Roosevelt) 대통령은 기존의 민병대를 해체하고, 이를 주 방위군으로 대체하였다. 그 주된 이유는 이미 정규군이 존재하는 상황에서 과거 독립혁명시기에 활동했던 민병의 역할은 거의 사라졌으며, 또한 민병대가 반란을 일으킬 소지가 있다고 판단하였기 때문이었다. 이러한 결정으로 사실상 개인이

---

16 Presser v. Illinois, 116 *United States Reports* 252 (1886).

17 U.S v. Miller, 307 *United States Reports* 174 (1939).

민병대의 일원으로서 총기를 소유할 이유는 사라져 버린 셈이었다. 그리고 국민 개개인이 무기를 잡아야 할 일이 없어진 이상 수정조항 2조 또한 그 의미가 사라졌다고 할 수도 있을 것이다. 그렇다면 미국인들이 현재 더 이상 존재하지 않는 민병의 상황 밖에서 무기를 소장하고 휴대할 수 있는 합법적인 권리를 가지고 있는가? 과거 대법원이 민병을 근거로 개인의 자유로운 총기소지를 인정하지 않았던 판례들은 과연 민병이 존재하지 않는 오늘날의 상황에서 어떻게 해석해야 할 것인가?

1960년대만 하여도 '주의 권리'를 내세운 주장이 주류를 형성하였다. 즉 수정조항 2조가 개인의 자유로운 무기소지를 명시한 것이 아니라, 주정부의 민병대 조직이나 규율권을 규정한 조항으로 해석한 것이었다.[18] 이런 견해는 하버드 법과 대학 교수였던 로렌스 트리브(Laurence H. Tribe)의 저서가 미국대학의 교재로 채택되면서 널리 알려지게 되었으며,[19] 미국시민자유연맹(American Civil Liberties Union)이나 미국변호사협회의 적극적인 지지를 받았다. ACLU는 민병이 없는 오늘날에도 수정조항 2조는 "단지 법을 집행하는 경찰이나 군사적 목적 이외에 개인의 자유로운 무기소지권을 보장하지는 않는다"고 주장하였다.[20] 이런 상황에서 수정조항 2조가 국민 개인의 자유로운 총기소지권을 보장한다는 주장을 처음으로 제기한 사람은 윌리엄-메리 대학의 법학교수였던 스튜어트 헤이즈(Stuart R. Hays)였다. 헤이즈는 수정조항 2조를 민병에만 적용하려는 과거 법원의 판결들이 잘못된 것이라고 지적하고, 민병의 의무와는 상관없이 자기 방어를 위해서라도 총기소지의 개인적 권리가 보호되어야 한다고 주장하였다. 그는 또한 수정조항 2조를 '국민혁명권'으로 규정하여, 무장시민들이 전제적이며 억압적인 정부에 대항하여 혁명을 일으킬 수 있는 권리로까지 확대, 해석하였다.[21]

1980년대에 이르러 무기소지권이 국민의 권리라는 주장이 점차 주류를 형성하였다. 당시 발표된 대부분의 저서와 논문들은 총기 소유의 '개인적 권리'를 주장하였다. 이것은 1980년 이후 수정조항 2조의 법률적 해석을 취급한 논문 36편을 분석한 『미

---

18 David C. Williams, "Civic Republicanism and the Citizen Militia: The Terrifying Second Amendment," *Yale Law Journal* 101 (December 1991), 551-615.

19 Laurence H. Tribe, *American Constitution Law*, 3rd ed. (Eagan, MN: Foundation Press, 2000).

20 American Civil Liberties Union, "Policy # 47: Gun Control," http://www.leclaw.com/this.htm.

21 Stuart R. Hays, "The Right to Bear Arms, A Study in Judicial Misinterpretation," *William and Mary Law Review* 2 (1960), 386-406.

국헌법백과사전』을 통해서도 확인할 수 있다. 이 자료에 따르면, 수록된 논문 36편중에서 32편이 총기소지권은 국민 개개인의 기본권에 속하며, 따라서 연방정부나 주정부가 개인의 총기소지를 규제하거나 제한할 수 없다고 주장하였다.[22] 이들 연구들은 주로 영국 관습법의 전통과 공화주의 사상에 나타난 시민무장권의 의미, 독립전쟁 당시 영국의 강압적인 통치와 상비군에 대항하여 싸웠던 민병대의 활동, 그리고 수정조항에 국민의 무기소지권을 추가하였던 미국 건국의 아버지들의 신념과 의도 등에 관한 연구를 통해 '주의 권리'를 반박하고, 개인의 총기소유의 정당성을 설득력 있게 제시하였다.[23]

앞서 살펴보았듯이, '주의 권리'를 옹호하는 사람들은 수정조항 2조가 국민의 무기소지권을 보장한 것이 아니라, 주정부의 민병대의 규율권을 보장한 것이라고 주장한다. 이런 주장에 대한 반박으로 권리장전 전체에서 각 조항마다 언급되는 '국민의 권리'라는 단어의 의미를 살펴볼 필요가 있다. 정부가 결코 "침해될 수 없는" 신성한 국민의 권리는 수정조항 1조(종교, 언론, 출판의 자유와 집회 및 청원의 권리), 4조(수색 및 체포영장), 5조(형사사건에서의 권리), 6조(공정한 재판의 권리) 등에서도 나타난다. 이와 관련하여 예일대 법대교수인 아크힐 아마(Akhil Amar)는 다음과 같이 언급하였다.

> 무기를 소유하고 휴대할 수 있는 권리의 주체는 주 민병대가 아니라, 국민이다. 수정조항 2조에 명시된 '국민(people)'은 일반시민 개개인을 말하는 것으로, 이것은 (미국인을 통칭하여 일컫는) 'We the People'과 같은 의미를 지니는 것이다. 따라서 수정조항에 명시된 종교, 언론 및 출판의 자유, 집회와 청원의 권리와 같이, 국민의 무기소지권도 개인적인 권리로 인정되어야 한다.… 오늘날 보통 주 방위군(National Guard)을 과거 '주민병대(state militia)'와 동일시하는 경향이 있으나, 수정조항 2조가 채택될 당시 민병대는 무기를 소유할 수 있는 모든 시민들을 통칭하여 언급한 것이다. 따라서 민병대는 국민과 동일한 개념이다.[24]

---

22 Leonard W. Levy, *Encyclopedia of the American Constitution* (New York: Macmillan, 1990). 이 저서에 실린 36편의 논문에 대하여 Wayne R. LaPierre, *Guns, Crime, and Freedom* (Washington, D. C,: Regnery Publishing, 1994), 237-40 참조.

23 Stephen P. Halbrook, *That Every Man Be Armed: The Evolution of a Constitutional Right* (Albuquerque: University of New Mexico Press, 1984); Don B. Kates, "The Second Amendment and the Ideology of Self-Protection," 87-104.

만약 수정조항 1조, 4조, 5조, 6조 등에 언급한 국민의 권리를 수정조항 2조에서와 같이 주의 집단적인 권리로 해석한다면 주정부가 이런 조항들에 대해서도 간섭하고 제재를 가할 수 있다는 결론이 된다. 더욱이 종교, 언론, 출판의 자유와 집회 및 청원의 권리가 담긴 1조와 부당한 수색과 체포를 피할 수 있는 권리를 규정한 4조 사이에 무기소지권이 위치해 있다는 것은 '주의 권리'라는 주장이 타당성이 결여되었음을 암시하는 대목이다. 따라서 수정조항 2조에 나타난 무기소지권은 다른 수정조항과 동일하게 국민 개개인의 기본권에 속하는 개념으로 해석하는 것이 타당할 것이다.

이후에도 개인적인 무기소지의 정당성에 대한 논쟁은 지속되었으나, 그 전환점을 맞게 된 것은 2008년 6월 연방대법원 판결이었다. 딕 앤서니 헬러(Dick A. Heller)라는 사설 경호대 직원이 총기를 가정에서 소유하는 것을 금지한 워싱턴 DC의 총기단속법에 반발하여 제기한 소송이 그 계기가 되었다. 헬러는 직업상 38구경의 권총에 실탄을 장착한 채 근무를 하였다. 그러나 일이 끝나면 총을 직장에 놓고 퇴근해야 했다. 워싱턴 DC는 법으로 개인의 총기휴대를 금지하고 있기 때문이었다. 헬러는 시정부의 총기규제가 개인의 총기소유를 허용하고 있는 미국 헌법에 위배된다고 생각하고 소송을 제기했다. 소위 워싱턴 DC 대 헬러(District of Columbia v. Heller) 소송에서 연방대법원은 "미국인들은 각종 범죄나 외부적인 위협으로부터 자신을 방어하고, 또한 사냥이나 사격 등 취미활동을 위해 총기를 소지할 권리가 있다"고 지적하고, 워싱턴 DC가 개인의 총기소유를 불허한 것은 연방헌법 수정조항 2조의 정신에 배치된다고 5대 4로 위헌 판결을 내렸다.[25]

워싱턴 DC는 그동안 샌프란시스코, 시카고 등과 함께 개인의 총기휴대를 가장 엄격하게 금지하여 왔다. 1976년에 채택된 워싱턴 DC의 총기단속법은 주민들이 이 법의 발효 이전에 소유한 총기가 아니라면 총기를 새로 소유하는 것을 금지해 왔다. 샷건(엽총)이나 라이플(장총)은 집에 보관할 수는 있으나, 이 경우도 총기를 등록하고 실탄을 장전하지 않고 방아쇠 잠금장치를 설치하는 경우에만 한하였다. 워싱턴 DC가 내세운 총기규제의 근거는 수정조항 2조의 무기소지권을 과거 민병에서와 같이, 경찰이나 보안군의 '집단적 무기소지권'으로 해석한 데 있었다. 그러나 대법원은 종교

---

24 Akhil R. Amar, "The Bill of Rights As a Constitution," *Yale Law Journal* 100 (1991), 1162-75.

25 District of Columbia v. Heller, 554 *United Stated Reports* 570 (2008).

나 표현의 자유에 관한 조항처럼 무기소지 역시 국가가 침해할 수 없는 개인적인 권리라고 판단한 것이었다.

다수의견을 대표한 안토닌 스칼리아(Antonin Scalia) 대법관은 우선 수정조항 2조가 채택되기 이전이나 이후에도 국민이 자유롭게 총기를 소지할 권리는 '역사적 사실'로서 인정을 받아왔다고 강조하였다. 그리고 "현재 미국에서 벌어지고 있는 총기사건은 심각한 사회적 파장을 일으키고 있으나, 연방헌법은 가정에서 자기방어를 위한 총기소유나 총기사용을 절대적으로 금지하는 것을 허용하지 않는다"고 지적하였다. 즉 총기사건의 심각성에도 불구하고 총기소지는 정부가 침해할 수 없는 헌법이 보장한 국민 개인의 고유권한이라는 것이었다.[26] 그러나 보수파와 진보파가 5:4로 팽팽히 맞선 대법원 판결에서 나타나듯이, 반론도 만만치가 않다. 소수의견을 제시한 스티븐 브레이어(Stephen G. Breyer) 대법관은 "수정조항 2조가 범죄가 많은 도심지역에서 자기방어를 위해 총기를 소지할 수 있는 권리를 인정한다고 하더라고, 이것이 결코 수정될 수 없는 헌법적 권리는 아니다"라고 반박하였다. 이번 대법원의 판결로 앞으로 미국전역에서 총기휴대가 가능해질 것으로 예상돼 총기 안전사고가 급증할 우려를 낳고 있다.

Ⅲ. 수정헌법 제2조의 핵심 이념: 자기방어의 기본권

오늘날 우리는 시민의 무기소지권을 주로 정치적인 개념으로 파악하려는 경향이 있다. 그러나 고전적 자유주의 사상가들은 이를 정치적으로 보다는 범죄학적 측면에서 접근하고 이해하였다. 즉 외적의 침입이나 약탈, 통치자들의 과도한 권력행사나 억압적인 통치행위를 강도나 살인 등 단순 범죄와 동일시하여 시민들은 이에 저항할 의무와 권리가 있다고 주장하였다.[27] 인간이 자신의 생명과 자유를 스스로 보존하려는 자기방어의 권리는 하나님이 인간에게 부여한 천부적인 권리로서 그 누구도 이를

---

26 http://en.wikipedia.org/wiki/District of Columbia v. Heller; http://simple.wikipedia.org/wiki/Second Amendment to the U.S. Constitution; 「조선일보」(2008. 6. 28).

27 Russell F. Weighley, *History of the United States Army* (New York: Macmillan, 1967), 19.

침해할 수 없다는 것이다.

존 로크(John Locke)에 따르면 인간은 자연상태에서 생명, 자유, 재산에 대한 자연법상의 권리를 가지고 태어났으며, 자기방어는 이런 권리를 지키기 위한 정당한 수단이었다. 로크는 자기방어의 권리로부터 모든 개인은 각종 범죄나 부당한 억압으로부터 자신을 보호하고, 더 나아가 시민의 집단적인 힘으로 전제적인 정부를 전복시킬 수 있다는 이론을 제시하였다. 즉 왕이나 관료들이 권력이나 무력을 이용하여 시민들의 생명이나 자유, 또는 재산을 빼앗는 행위는 국민과의 약속을 파기하는 것이며, 따라서 국민은 자기방어의 권리에 따라 이에 저항하고 투쟁하는 것은 당연한 일이라고 역설하였다.[28] 따라서 무기소유를 금지시키는 것은 자기방어의 자연법을 침해하는 것이라고 보았다.

이러한 신념은 이탈리아의 계몽사상가이며 고대형법학의 선구자로 불리는 케사르 베카리아(Cesare Beccaria)에 의해서도 명백히 언급되었다. 그는 '공리주의의 오류'에 대한 논의에서 국민의 무장을 금지하는 것의 오류와 부당성을 다음과 같이 지적하였다. 공리주의적 관점에서 어떤 문제를 해결하려는 것은 가상적인 상황에서 사소한 불편함을 내세워 수많은 이점들을 무시하는 오류를 낳기 쉽다. 범죄를 일으킬 소지가 있다고 하여 무기를 소유하지 못하게 하는 것은 화재의 위험성이 있다고 사람들로부터 불을 빼앗거나, 익사사고의 위험 때문에 물을 사용하지 못하게 하는 것과 같다.… 국민들에게 무기소지를 금지하는 것은 가해자보다는 피해자들에게 더 큰 피해를 주며, 살상행위를 막기보다는 오히려 부추기는 결과를 초래할 것이 자명하다. 무기를 갖지 못한 사람들은 무기를 지닌 사람들보다도 손쉬운 공격의 대상이 되기 때문이다.[29]

이런 자연법사상을 이어받은 미국 건국의 아버지들은 무장할 권리는 자기방어를 위한 도덕적 의무라고 믿었다. 『상식(*common sense*)』이라는 소책자를 저술하여 독립혁명의 불길을 당긴 토머스 페인(Thomas Paine)은 자기방어를 위한 무장의 필요성

---

28 John Locke, "An Essay Concerning the True Original Extent and End of Civil Government," Thomas I. Cook, ed., *Two Treatise of Government* (Royal Oak, Michigan: Haffner Publishing, 1947). 119, 129-30.

29 Cesare Beccaria, Henry Paolucci, tr., *An Essay on Crimes and Punishments* (Indianapolis: Bobbs-Merrill, 1963), 87-8.

을 다음과 같이 언급하였다.

스스로 자신을 방어할 적절한 수단을 갖추지 못한 선량한 시민들은 항상 사악하고 야비한 범죄자들의 공격의 대상이 될 수밖에 없다. 따라서 무기를 소지하는 것은 침략자나 약탈자들의 범죄를 방지할 뿐만 아니라, 생명과 재산, 그리고 사회적 안전과 질서를 유지시키는 수단이 된다.… 만약 총을 소유한 사람과 그렇지 못한 사람이 있다면, 무서운 재앙이 닥칠 것이다. 왜냐하면 약자는 강자의 희생이 될 것이기 뻔 하기 때문이다.[30]

페인은 모든 자유민은 무기를 소지할 권리가 있으며, 어떤 법도 외부의 약탈자나 침입자로부터 자신을 방어하기 위한 총기를 소유하는 것을 금할 수 없다고 주장하였다.

오늘날 미국인들은 동일한 폭력범죄가 경찰력에 의해 통제되는 경우와 민간인에 의해 저지되는 경우를 전혀 다르게 보고 있다. 경찰이 범죄로부터 시민을 보호하는 것은 공동체를 방어한 행위로 간주되고 또한 칭송을 받곤 한다. 그러나 민간인이 범죄에 직접 대항하여 맞선다면, 이것은 사적인 감정과 목적을 위한 행위이지 순수하게 공동체를 위한 것이라고는 생각지 않는다. 더욱이 어떤 언론매체에서는 개인적으로 범죄에 대항하는 행위를 부정적으로 보는 경향이 있다. 더 나아가 민간인이 자신의 가족을 방어할 목적으로 타인에게 총을 겨누는 것은 인간 본능이 만들어낸 최악의 결과라고 폄하하기도 한다. 다시 말해, 경찰력에 의존하기보다 개인 차원에서 범죄나 불의에 맞서는 것은 법과 질서를 유지하기 위한 것이 아니라, 단지 무질서와 혼란만을 불러일으킨다는 것이다.[31]

문명화된 사회에서는 자기방어를 위해 사적으로 무기를 사용하는 것을 피하고, 대신 경찰력에 의존하여야 한다는 이러한 견해는(비록 사적인 자기방어가 공공의 이익에 기여한다고 하더라도) 18세기 미국에서는 받아들이기 어려웠다. 그 이유는 당시 미국은 영국과 같이 치안이나 사회질서를 유지하기 위한 기구로서 경찰력이 존재하지 않았기 때문이었다. 그리하여 당시에는 개인들이 자신과 가족을 위해 무장하여 범죄에 대항하는 것은 공동체의 질서와 안전을 유지하는 행위로 인식되었고, 이에 따라 사람들이 자발적으로 자경단이나 보안대를 조직하여 경찰의 기능을 대행하기도 하였

30 Moncure D. Conway, ed., *The Writings of Thomas Paine* III (New York: Putnam's Sons, 1967), 56.
31 "Guns and the Civilizing Process," *Washington Post* (September 26, 1972).

다. 따라서 식민지 미국인들은 개인 차원의 방어를 공동체의 방어와 동일시하였다.

이런 맥락에서 몽테스키외는 "정부(공동체)의 생명은 개인의 생명과 동일하다"고 역설하였다. 사람이 자신을 방어하기 위하여 불가피하게 살인을 저지를 경우가 있듯이, 국가도 생존을 위하여 전쟁을 수행할 권리가 있다는 것이다.[32] 마찬가지로 토마스 페인은 국가가 "타국의 침략과 약탈에 대항하여 자국을 방위할 당연한 권리"가 있듯이, 선량한 사람은 당연히 "야비하고 파렴치한 악인에 대항하여 무장을 할 권리"를 가져야 한다고 주장하였다.[33]

수정조항 2조를 해석하는 데 있어 고려해야 할 점은 이 조항이 무기의 소유가 자기방어의 개인적 권리를 보장하는 수단일 뿐만 아니라, 더 나아가 공동체의 미덕과 가치가 긍정적으로 평가되었던 시대적 전통으로부터 나왔다는 것이다. 미국 건국의 아버지들에게 자기방어는 모든 종류의 범죄와 권리침해를 막을 뿐만 아니라, 정치적인 범죄행위에 대항하기 위한 수단으로도 확대되었다. 살인, 강간, 절도 등 범죄가 갱단이나 횡포한 관료, 혹은 전쟁 시 약탈적인 군인에 의해 저질러지든지 간에 그것에는 큰 차이가 없다고 생각하였다. 따라서 모든 범죄행위는 그 의도나 결과에서 차이는 있을지언정 본질적으로 자연법과 인간의 기본권을 침해한 행위라고 보았다. 따라서 무기소지권은 개인의 자기방어는 물론 공동체의 안위를 보장하는 핵심적인 장치로 인식하였다.

자연법적인 권리로서 개인의 자기방어를 위한 무장이 곧 공동체 전체에도 유익하다는 것을 주장한 사람은 윌리엄 블랙스톤(William Blackstone)이었다. 블랙스톤은 영국 관습법의 거장이며 미국 건국의 아버지들과 동시대에 살았던 사람으로 미국의 정치적 사상에 커다란 영향을 끼쳤다. 블랙스톤은 인간이 향유할 수 있는 권리를 '절대적인 권리'와 '상대적인 권리'로 구분하였다. 절대적 권리는 신분에 관계없이 모든 시민들에게 동등하게 주어지는 권리를 말하며, 상대적 권리는 소속된 사회의 신분이나 지위에 따라 차등적인 대우를 받는 권리를 말한다. 블랙스톤은 무장할 권리를 관습법상 개인의 절대적인 권리로 파악하였으며, 어떤 법으로도 규제할 수 없는 '기본적

---

32 Montesquieu, "The Spirit of the Laws," Mortimer Adler, ed. *Great Books of the Western World* 35 (Encyclopedia Britannica, 2nd ed., 1990), 61.

33 Conway, *Writings of Thomas Paine* III, 56.

인 자연법'이라고 주장하였다.[34] 그는 무기소지권을 사회와 법의 제제가 억압적인 폭력을 제어하기에 충분하지 못할 경우 자기보존과 방어를 위한 정치적 권리의 한 형태로 파악하였다.[35]

인간으로서 당연히 누려야 할 기본권이 위협을 받거나 침해되었을 경우, 국민들은 어떻게 대응하여야 하는가? 블랙스톤에 따르면, 우선 법원에 소송을 제기하거나, 왕에게 청원을 하거나 의회에 시정을 요구할 수 있다. 그러나 이러한 모든 수단들이 통하지 않을 경우 마지막으로 자기방어를 위해 무기를 사용할 수 있어야 한다고 주장하였다. 블랙스톤은 무기소지권은 폭력이나 범죄에 대항하여 자신을 방어하고, 더 나아가 전제정부에 저항하기 위한 최후의 수단이며, 사냥이나 사격 등 순수한 개인적인 목적을 위해서도 필요하다고 주장하였다.[36]

그렇다면 블랙스톤은 어떤 이유에서 자기방어를 위한 무기소지권을 정치적인 문제로 생각하였는가? 다시 말해, 사적인 영역으로 인식되는 살인이나 강도, 강간 등의 범죄로부터 자신을 방어하는 행위가 법원에 소송을 내거나 국가에 청원하는 것과 같은 정치적 권리와 동일한 영역으로 취급한 이유가 무엇인가? 이런 질문들에 대한 해답을 찾기 위해서는 고전적 자유주의 사상에서 무기소지권에 대한 도덕적이며 상징적인 의미를 좀 더 이해할 필요가 있다.

자유시민으로서 신분적 권리를 보장해 주는 증표로서 무장의 상징성은 고대 전통에서도 확인할 수 있다. 앵글로-색슨 시대부터 노예가 해방될 때, 손에 무기를 드는 의식을 행하였다. 여기서 무기는 "자유인으로서 누릴 새로운 신분을 상징하는 증표"였다.[37] 앵글로-색슨 시대에는 어느 누구도 자유민의 무장을 해제시킬 수 없다는 것을 법으로 제정하기도 하였다. 헨리 1세 시대에는 이 법을 불수불입권 등 막강한 권한을 가진 영주에게도 적용하여, 그의 지배하에 있던 농노들을 자의적으로 무장해제시키는 것을 금지하였다. 이런 영국의 전통과 선례는 자연법사상을 신봉하고 이를 그들의 정치이념으로 삼았던 블랙스톤이나 미국 건국의 아버지들의 사상에 커다란

---

34 William Blackstone, *Commentaries on the Laws of England*, vol 1 (St. George Tucker, ed., Philadelphia, 1803), 4.

35 *Ibid.*, 144.

36 *Ibid.*, 140-46.

37 A. V. B. Norman, *The Medieval Soldier* (New York: Thomas Y. Crowell, 1971), 73.

영향을 끼친 것은 당연한 일이었다.

독재자들이 자신들의 권력을 유지하기 위해 제일 먼저 취하는 것은 국민들의 무장권을 빼앗는 것이었다. 이것은 국가가 무기를 독점함으로서 절대권력을 강화하려는 의도였다. 독재자들은 국민들의 무장을 해제시키는 것은 이들의 용기와 도덕적 저항심을 위축시켜 억압적인 정부에 체념적으로 순응하는 결과를 낳는다는 것을 잘 알고 있기 때문이다. 따라서 마키아벨리는 "스스로를 방어할 무기를 소유하지 못하면 저항력을 상실하게 되고, 결국 굴종과 억압을 당하게 될 것"이라고 하였다.[38]

독립선언서의 초안자이며 미국의 3대 대통령이었던 토마스 제퍼슨 역시 스스로 무장하는 것이 시민으로서의 미덕을 갖추는 것이라고 믿었다. 제퍼슨은 그의 15살 된 조카에게 피터 카(Peter Carr)에게 보낸 편지에서 항상 총기를 휴대하고 사격연습을 하도록 권고하면서, 총기가 우리의 정신 수련에 어떻게 연관되었는지 다음과 같이 언급하였다.

강한 육체는 건강한 정신을 만든다. 육체와 정신수련을 위해 사격연습을 권하고 싶다. 사격은 육체적으로 그리 힘든 운동은 아니지만, 담대함과 독립심, 그리고 도전정신을 키워준다. 구기종목들은 육체적으로 격렬한 운동이지만, 정신긴장에 그리 큰 유익을 주지 못한다. 그러니 다닐 때면 항시 총을 휴대하길 바란다.[39]

미국 건국의 아버지들의 무장에 대한 신념은 단지 도덕적이고 정신적인 영역에만 한정하지 않고, 실용적인 효용성에 더 큰 가치가 있다고 파악하였다. 시민무장은 폭력이 난무하는 사회에서 무장을 통한 자기방어는 범죄를 억제하거나 외적의 침입을 퇴치하는 방어책이며, 더 나아가 정부의 국민에 대한 억압이나 횡포에 대항하기 위한 수단이었다. 애덤스는 "모든 시민들은 공격을 위해서가 아니라, 자신을 스스로 방어하기 위해서 무장할 권리를 부여받았다"고 언급하였다.[40] 메디슨은 "국민들이 무장

---

38 Joel Barlow, *Advice to the Privileged Orders in the Several States of Europe: Resulting From the Necessity and Propriety of a General Revolution in the Principle of Government* I (reprinted by Cornell University Press, 1956), 45.

39 Julian P. Boyd, ed., "Thomas Jefferson to Peter Carr" (August 19, 1785)," *The Papers of Thomas Jefferson* 8 (Princeton University Press, 1953), 405, 407.

40 Lyman H. Butterfield and Hilda B. Zobel, eds., *Legal Papers of John Adams*, III (New York, Macmillan, 1968), 248.

하는 것을 두려워하는 다른 국가와는 달리 우리 미국인들은 무장할 수 있는 권리와 이점을 가지고 있다"고 하였다.[41]

시민의 자유와 권리를 지키기 위한 수단으로 무장이 필요하다는 주장에도 불구하고 시민무장에 대해 부정적인 견해도 제기되었다. 즉 무장을 통한 시민저항이 폭력을 부추기고, 사회적인 혼란과 무질서를 초래한다는 것이었다. 그러나 신학자로서 예일대 총장을 역임하였던 티모시 드와이트(Timothy Dwight)와 외교관으로 독립혁명 당시 군목으로도 활동했던 조엘 발로(Joel Barlow)는 개인의 보편적인 무기소지에 대한 위험성에 대하여 다음과 같이 반박하였다.

동등한 권리를 향유하는 시민이 다른 동료 시민들의 권리를 침해할 목적으로 무장을 악용할 경우는 거의 없다. 따라서 무장한 시민들을 두려워하는 것은 동료 시민이나 공동체 사회가 아니라, 단지 억압적이고 전제적인 정부일 뿐이다.

이들은 오히려 국민들을 무장하지 못하게 강제할 때 오히려 무질서와 혼란이 야기될 것이라고 경고하였다. 국민이 무장할 권리가 박탈당한다면, 전제적인 정부는 총과 칼을 앞세워 수많은 사상자를 내고서도 국민들의 권리를 빼앗으려 들 것이다.[42] 그러나 국민이 무장을 한다면, 이런 일은 결코 일어나지 않을 것이다. 왜냐하면 토마스 페인이 언급하였듯이, "법과 같이 무기는 침략자나 약탈자를 겁먹게 하고, 이들의 사악한 행위를 억제시켜 국민의 재산보호는 물론 사회적 안정과 평화를 유지시키는 수단이 되기 때문이다."[43]

오늘날의 관점에서 본다면 다소 이색적인 모습으로 보일 수 있지만, 영국의 자유주의자인 프란시스 플레이스(Francis Place)는 18세기 영국사회에 팽배하였던 유태인에 대한 증오와 폭력이 어떻게 사라지게 되었는지를 다음과 같이 설명하였다.

많은 유대인들은 거리를 다닐 때, 자신을 보호하기 위해 개를 데리고 다니는 습관이 있었다. 그런데 이러한 습관이 없어지는 계기가 되는 상황이 발생하였다. 1787년경 다니엘 멘도자(Daniel Mendoza)라는 한 유태인이 유명한 복싱 선수가 되어 전국적

---

41 James Madison, *The Federalist Papers* No. 46, 245.

42 Don B. Kates, "Minimalist Interpretation of the Second Amendment," Eugene W. Hickok, ed., *The Bill of Rights: Original Understanding and Current Meaning* (University Press of Virginia, 1991), 132.

43 Moncure Conway, ed., *Writings of Thomas Paine* I (New York: Putnam, 1894), 56.

으로 그의 명성이 널리 알려지게 되었다.

그가 과학적으로 복싱기술을 가르치는 학교를 열자, 복싱에 대한 열기는 곧 유대인들에게 퍼져나갔고, 많은 젊은 유대인들이 상당한 복싱 실력을 터득할 수 있게 되었다. 몇 년이 지나지 않아 커다란 변화가 나타났다. 유태인이 노인이거나 홀로 있는 경우가 아니라면, 영국인들은 유태인들에게 모욕과 폭행을 가하는 행위는 더 이상 안전하지 않다는 것을 깨닫게 되었다.… 그리고 이제는 유태인들이 자신들을 방어할 수 없는 상황에 처했을 경우라도, 단지 유태인이라 하여 모욕을 주는 행위는 지나가는 행인으로부터 응징을 받았고, 경찰로부터는 처벌의 대상이 되었다.[44]

위의 인용구는 자기방어의 능력이 개인의 신변과 안전에 얼마나 중요한지를 보여주는 대표적인 예이다. 19세기 초까지만 해도 영국은 살인, 강도, 폭행, 소매치기와 같은 범죄와 사회, 정치적인 이유로 폭동이 자주 만연하였던 무질서한 사회였다. 더욱이 영국에서는 1829년까지도 치안을 담당하던 경찰이 존재하지도 않았다. 이런 상황에서 개인의 무장은 사회적 무질서와 폭력, 그리고 온갖 범죄로부터 자신은 보호하는 자기방어의 수단이 되었다. 이리하여 블랙스톤 시대에 영국에서는 무법자나 폭도들에 대항하여 자경대원들이 스스로 국민의 생명과 재산을 보호하고, 공동체의 안전을 방어하였다.

연방헌법 수정조항 2조의 무장권에 대한 논쟁의 근거와 타당성을 가리기 위해서는 독립혁명 당시의 역사적인 배경을 살펴 볼 필요가 있다. 아메리카 신대륙에서의 주도권을 차지하기 위한 전쟁(프렌치-인디언 전쟁)에서 영국은 승리를 거두어 신대륙에 대한 지배권을 강화하였다. 그러나 영국은 전쟁으로 인한 엄청난 부채로 극심한 재정난에 시달리게 되었다. 이를 보충하기 위해 영국은 식민지에 설탕세법, 인지세법, 타운센드법 등을 통과시켜 식민지의 경제적 부담을 가중시켰다. 이에 각 식민지는 "대표 없는 곳에 과세 없다"고 외치면서 식민지에 대한 부당한 세금을 철폐할 것을 요구하고, 영국 상품에 대한 대대적인 불매운동을 전개하였다.

영국의회는 식민지의 거센 항의에 부딪쳐 인지세법만은 철폐하였으나, 이미 식민지에 고조된 반영국 감정을 꺾을 수는 없었다. 영국과 식민지 간에 대립과 갈등이 점

---

44 Francis Place, "Improvement of the Working Classes" (1834), as quoted R. K. Webb, *Modern England: From the Eighteenth Century to the Present* (New York: Dodd, Mead Company, 1970), 115.

차 심화되자, 영국은 식민지에 상비군을 증강하였으며, 1765년에는 군인숙영법을 채택하여 식민지인들에게 영국군대의 주둔에 필요한 숙식을 제공하도록 강요하였다. 영국의 이러한 조치들은 식민지를 착취하고 억압하려는 노골적인 의도로 보일 수밖에 없었다. 마침내 식민지인들의 분노는 1770년 3월 보스턴 세관에 주둔하고 있던 영국군이 시위대에게 발포한 소위 '보스턴학살(Boston Massacre)' 사건으로 폭발하였다.

이 사건이 발생한 직후 영국 세관의 조직적인 지시에 따라 영국 군인들은 인신 구속영장이나 가택 수색연장을 자의적으로 발급받아 미국인 가택이나 차량, 선박, 창고 등을 무단으로 수색하여 상품이나 서류, 기타 기록물들을 대대적으로 파손하거나 몰수하였다. 당시 보스턴에서 발행된 한 신문은 사설에서 영국에 의해 자행된 자의적이고 무단적인 수색과 체포 등 권력남용에 대해 비판하고, 식민지인들이 "자기방어를 위해 무장을 하는 것은 분별있고 합법적인 조치"라고 주장하였다. 이어 사설은 블랙스톤의 주장을 인용하여 시민무장의 합법성을 다음과 같이 언급하였다.

무장권은 사람들이 본래 지니고 있는 기본적인 자연권이며, 영국의 권리장전에 의해서도 보장된 자기방어의 권리이다. 블랙스톤이 언급했듯이, 무장권은 시민들이 부당한 권리침해나 폭력적인 억압에 대항하여 사회적, 법적인 수단이 없을 경우 시민들은 자신들을 방어하기 위한 최후의 수단으로 사용될 수 있다.[45]

아이러니하게도 당시 미국인들은 모국인 영국의 관습법에 따라 무기를 소유하고 휴대할 수 있는 권리를 부여받고 있었다. 그러나 미국인들의 무장과 반란에 대해서 두려움을 느끼고 있었던 영국의회는 1774년 10월 총기와 탄약, 그리고 기타 군장비가 식민지로 유입되는 것을 차단하기 위하여 수출금지령을 발표하였다. 이어 영국은 식민지인들의 무기소유를 금지하는 한편, 이미 소유하고 있던 무기를 몰수하기에 이르렀다. 식민지인들은 그들 관할지역의 행정청에 자신들의 무기를 반환한 후에야 도시를 떠날 수 있었다.[46] 이것은 식민지인들의 무장반란을 사전에 차단하기 위한 조치였다.

영국의 식민지에 대한 방자하고 난폭한 도발행위는 식민지인들에게 자기방어를

---

45 *A Journal of the Times* (March 17, 1769), cited in Oliver Dickerson, ed., *Boston Under Military Rule* (New York: Da Capo Press, 1970), 79.

46 Halbrook, *That Every Man Be Armed*, 59.

위해 스스로 무장하여야 한다는 신념을 갖게 하였다. 존 애덤스(John Adams)는 "모든 사람들은 자유롭고 독립적인 존재로 생명과 자유를 방어할 권리를 가지고 있으며, 자신을 스스로 방어하기 위해서 무장할 권리를 부여받았다"고 언급하였다.[47] 조지 메이슨(George Mason)은 국민을 무장해제시키는 것은 그들을 노예로 만들기 위한 것이라고 주장하고, 영국의 강압적인 무기몰수에 항의하여 국민이 자발적으로 무장할 것을 권고하였다.

오늘날 미국은 잘 정비된 사법제도와 경찰력을 갖추고 있기 때문에 독립혁명시기 영국의 불법적인 수색에 대항하여 시민들이 무장을 한다는 것이 바람직하게 보이지 않을 수도 있을 것이다. 그러나 18세기 식민지 미국인들에게 점령국의 군인들이 자의적으로 민간인을 수색, 체포하고, 무기를 몰수하는 행위는 불법적이며부당한 조치로 여겨질 수밖에 없었다. 따라서 미국인들의 무장은 시민의 자유와 권리를 지키기 위한 자기방어 차원의 대응책이었다.

전제적인 정부에 대항하여 국민적 권리를 지켜야 한다는 견해가 가장 명확하게 나타난 것이 1776년 토마스 제퍼슨이 초안한 독립선언서였다. 제퍼슨은 독립선언서에서 정부가 개인의 생명, 자유, 행복추구의 권리를 무시하고 탄압할 때 그 정부를 전복시키고 새로운 정부를 조직하는 것이 당연한 국민적 권리임을 천명하였다.

모든 사람은 평등하게 태어났으며, 조물주는 몇 개의 양도할 수 없는 권리를 부여하였는데, 그 권리 중에는 생명과 자유와 행복의 추구가 있다. 이 권리를 확보하기 위해 인류는 정부를 조직했으며, 정부의 정당한 권력은 국민의 동의에서 유래된다. 어떠한 형태의 정부든지 이러한 목적(국민의 기본권)을 파괴할 때는 언제든지 정부를 변혁시키거나 폐지할 수 있으며, 국민이 가장 안전하고 행복할 수 있는 원칙에 기초를 둔 새로운 정부를 조직하는 것은 국민의 권리이다.[48]

수정조항 2조에 규정된 '무기를 소유하고 휴대할 권리'는 이러한 독립선언의 정신을 구체화시킨 것이었다. 무기소지권은 폭압적인 정부로부터 국민의 자유와 권리를 지키는 수단이 되기 때문이었다.

---

47 Clarence Carson, *Basic American Government* (Alabama: Blackstone Audio, 1993), 53.

48 Thomas Jefferson, *The Declaration of Independence* (1776.7.4), 한국미국사학회 엮음, 『사료로 읽는 미국사』(궁리출판, 2006), 65-6.

오늘날 치안이 잘 유지되는 국가에서 폭동이나 소요사태가 일어난다면 국가가 공권력을 동원하여 이를 효과적으로 진압하기 때문에 자기방어를 위한 무장은 그 명분이 약할 수밖에 없다. 그러나 특정 집단이나 세력에 대해 대립하는 정책이나 감정을 가진 정부가 있다면 상황은 달라질 것이다. 예를 들어, 1950-60년대 흑인 민권운동 기간에 미국에서 발생한 상황이 이를 잘 설명해 주고 있다. 오랜 기간 전국에 걸쳐 발생한 흑인민권운동에 대한 당시 미국정부의 태도는 결코 우호적인 것은 아니었다. 흑인들의 정당한 요구와 평화로운 집회와 시위를 때로는 무자비하게 제압하기도 하였다. 물론 미국정부는 공권력을 동원하여 사회질서를 지키고 국민의 안전을 도모한다는 목적을 내 세웠다. 그러나 경찰이 지켜보는 상황에서 발생했던 폭동이나 KKK와 같은 야간의 복면 기마 폭력단의 공격은 민권운동을 약화시키거나 방해할 목적이었으며, 흑인들을 인종적인 소수자로 몰아 백인 주류사회로부터 격리시키기 위한 것이었다.

여기에서 우리는 무장의 중요성을 새삼 인식하게 된다. 다시 말해, 무기소지권이 보복적인 폭력행위로부터 시민 개개인을 보호할 뿐만 아니라, 더 나아가 사회변혁이나 제도개선을 위한 사회운동을 성공으로 이끄는 역할을 한다는 것을 암시하고 있다. 흑인들도 자기방어를 위해 무장할 수 있다는 그 자체가 미국의 남부에서 흑인민권운동이 성공할 수 있었던 중요한 요인이 되었다.[49] 이와는 대조적으로 남아프리카공화국은 흑인들이 인구의 대다수를 차지하지만, 세계에서 가장 효과적인 총기규제를 실시하여 오랜 기간 동안 흑인들의 불만과 저항을 잠재울 수 있었던 것이다.

2차 세계대전 중 유태인들이 무방비 상태에서 나치의 폭력과 탄압의 대상이 된 것은 무엇보다도 무기소지권을 박탈당했기 때문이었다. 만약 유태인들이 무기를 소유하고 스스로 방어할 힘이 있었다면, 그렇게 속수무책으로 당하지는 않았을 것이다. 오늘날에도 무기소지권을 인정하는 데는 구체적인 역사적 이유가 있다. 스탈린, 히틀러, 카스트로, 폴포트와 같은 20세기 독재자들이 자신들의 권력을 강화하기 위해 자국민의 무장을 해제하였다. 그러나 무장해제에 반대한 일부 시민들만이 자기를 방어하고 자유를 위해 독재자와 싸울 수 있는 역량을 유지할 수 있었다.

---

49 Don B. Kates, ed., *Restricting Handguns: The Liberal Skeptics Speak Out* (Great Barrington, MA: North River Press, 1979), 185.

Ⅳ. 맺음말

미국의 역사학자인 다니엘 부어스틴(Daniel Boorstine)은 "신대륙 정착민들에게 총기는 자기방어와 식량확보를 위한 도구이며, 당시엔 거의 누구나 총기를 보유하였다"고 언급하였다.[50] 농업이 주요 생계수단이었던 정착민들에게 총은 인디언과 야생동물, 그리고 무법자들로부터 자신과 가족을 지켜주었다. 독립혁명 시기 거의 모든 성인 남성들은 민병대를 조직하여 조국의 자유와 독립을 위해 스스로 무장하여 영국에 대항하여 싸웠다. 이를 통해 미국인들은 총은 곧 자유와 생명을 지키는 도구가 된다는 신념을 갖게 되었다.

19세기 초까지도 미국은 치안을 유지하고 법을 집행할 경찰력이 없었다. 당시 미국의 법률제도는 시민들이 무장하여 자신을 방어하고, 건강한 성인 남성들은 민병대나 자경단, 혹은 현지 보안관으로 범죄를 예방하고, 범법자를 추적, 체포하는 등 경찰의 기능을 수행하기도 하였다. 이런 장기간에 걸친 역사적인 전통과 경험으로부터 무기소지권은 개인의 자기방어는 물론 공동체의 질서와 안전을 지키는 핵심적인 장치로 인식되었다.

로크나 블랙스톤과 같은 자연법 사상가들의 영향을 받은 미국 건국의 아버지들은 자기방어를 인간의 가장 기본적인 권리이며 개인 주권의 특징으로 간주하였다. 자신을 방어할 권리는 독립선언서에서 밝힌 생명, 자유, 행복이라는 자연권의 일부이며, 무기소지는 이러한 자연권을 보호할 수 있는 적절한 수단이었다. 그리고 독립혁명의 역사적 과정을 통해 무기소지권의 중요성을 더욱 뚜렷이 인식하게 되었다. 미국에서는 법과 제도가 정비되기 이전부터 무기소지는 관습법상의 정당방위로 인정되었으며, 이것이 헌법 조항에 명시화된 것이었다. 이런 의미에서 연방헌법 수정조항 2조는 무기소지라는 새로운 국민의 권리를 추가한 것이 아니라, 이미 존재하였던 자기방어라는 신상불가침의 기본권을 다시 확인한 것에 불과한 것이었다.

총기관련 범죄나 사건이 발생할 때마다 미국사회와 정치권은 총기규제 논쟁으로 시끄럽다. 총기논쟁의 1차적인 근거가 되고 있는 수정조항 2조에 대하여 총기규제론

---

50 Daniel J. Boorstine, The Americans: The Colonial Experience (New York: Vintage Publishing, 1964), 353.

자들은 무기소지권이 영국의 억압적인 식민지 시대에나 타당한 것이지 오늘날 시대 상황에는 적용하기 힘들다고 주장한다. 그러나 무기소지권은 각종 범죄나 외적의 침입에 대한 방어일 뿐만 아니라, 정부의 전횡이나 독재자의 출현을 막기 위한 견제 수단이었다. 미국 건국의 아버지들은 무기소지권이야말로 자유와 예속을 가르는 척도로 여겼다. 더욱이 과거 정부의 행정력이 미치지 않는 광활한 땅을 개척하였던 세대에게 존재했던 위험만큼이나 현대의 도시생활에서 범죄는 여전히 큰 위협이 되고 있다. 시대와 상황의 변화에도 불구하고 무기소지권이 국민의 기본적인 권리로 인정되어야 하는 이유가 바로 여기에 있는 것이다.

[참고문헌]

마틴 길버트, 김세준 역, 『크리스탈나흐트』(서울: 플래닛, 2009).

안경환, "미국 연방헌법 수정 제2조(무기소지권)의 의미," 『서울대학교법학』 105집 (서울대 법학연구소, 1997), 129-49.

양승업, "미국헌법 제2조와 수정헌법 제12조의 차이점에 관한 고찰." 『강원법학』 23집 (강원대 법학연구소, 2006), 185-213.

최승원, "미연방헌법 수정 제2조와 총기규제," 『미국헌법연구』 7집 (미국헌법학회, 1996), 217-42.

한국미국사학회 역음, 『사료로 읽는 미국사』(서울: 궁리출판, 2006). 「조선일보」(2008. 6. 28).

http://en.wikipedia.org/wiki/district of columbia v. heller.

http://guncite.com/gc2ndsup.htm/ (8/28/2010).

http://kr.news.yahoo.com/service/news/shellview.htm (2010/04/23).

http://simple.wikipedia.org/wiki/second amendment to the u.s.constitution.

http://weekly.donga.com/docs/magazine/weekly (2011/01/28).

Amar, Akhil R. "The Bill of Rights As a Constitution," *Yale Law Journal* 100 (1991): 1131-62.

American Civil Liberties Union, "Policy # 47: Gun Control," http://www.leclaw.com/this.htm.

Barlow, Joel. *Advice to the Privileged Orders in the Several States of Europe: Resulting From the Necessity and Propriety of a General Revolution in the Principle of Government*, Part Ⅰ (reprinted by Cornell University Press, 1956).

Beccaria, Cesare. Henry Paolucci, tr., *An Essay on Crimes and Punishments* (Indianapolis: Bobbs-Merrill, 1963).

Bennett, Randy E. Don B. Kates. "Under Fire: The New Consensus on the Second Amendment," *Emory Law Journal* 45 (Fall 1996): 1139-1259.

Blackstone, William. *Commentaries on the Laws of England*. (St. George Tucker ed., Philadelphia, 1803).

Boorstine, Daniel J. *The Americans: The Colonial Experience* (New York: Vintage, 1964).

Boyd, Julian P. ed., *The Papers of Thomas Jefferson* 8 (Princeton University Press, 1953).

Butterfield, Lyman H. and Hilda B. Zobel. eds., *Legal Papers of John Adams*, Ⅲ (New

York, Macmillan, 1968).

Carson, Clarence. *Basic American Government* (Alabama: Blackstone Audio, 1993).

Conway, Moncure. ed., *The Writings of Thomas Paine* Ⅰ, Ⅲ (New York: Putnam's Sons, 1967).

Cornell, Saul. *A Well–Regulated Militia: The Founding Fathers and the Origins of Gun Control in America* (New York: Oxford University Press, 2006).

Cottrell, Robert. ed., *Gun Control and the Constitution* (New York: Garland Publishing, 1994).

Dickerson, Oliver. ed., *Boston Under Military Rule* (Chapman and Grimes, 1936).

District of Columbia v. Heller, 554 *United Stated Reports* 570 (2008).

Halbrook, Stephen P. *That Every Man Be Armed: The Evolution of a Constitutional Right.* (Albuquerque: University of New Mexico Press, 1984).

Hays, Stuart R. "The Right to Bear Arms, A Study in Judicial Misinterpretation," *William and Mary Law Review* 2 (1960): 386-406.

Hickok, Eugene W. ed., *The Bill of Rights: Original Understanding and Current Meaning* (University Press of Virginia, 1991).

Kates, Don B. "Handgun Prohibition and the Original Meaning of the Second Amendment," *Michigan Law Review* 82 (1983): 204-12.

____. "The Second Amendment and the Ideology of Self-Protection," *Constitutional Commentary* 9 (Winter 1992): 87-104.

____. ed., *Restricting Handguns: The Liberal Skeptics Speak Out* (North River Press, 1979).

LaPierre, Wayne R. *Guns, Crime, and Freedom* (Washington, D.C: Regnery Publishing, 1994).

Levinson, Sanford. "The Embracing Second Amendment," *Yale Law Journal* 99 (December 1989): 637-59.

Levy, Leonard W. *Encyclopedia of the American Constitution* (New York: Macmillan, 1990).

Locke, John. "An Essay Concerning the True Original, Extent and End of Civil Government," Thomas I. Cook, ed., *Two Treatise of Government* (Royal Oak, Michigan: Haffner Publishing, 1947).

Ludwig. Jens. *Evaluation Gun Policy: Effects on Crime and Violence* (Washington D.C: Brookings Institution Press, 2003).

Madison, James. The Federalist Papers 46 (Arlington House, 1966).

Montesquieu, "The Spirit of the Laws," Mortimer Adler, ed. *Great Books of the Western World* 35 (Encyclopedia Britannica, 2nd ed., 1990).

Norman, A. V. B. *The Medieval Soldier* (New York: Thomas Y. Crowell, 1971).

Presser v. Illinois, 116 *United States Reports* 252 (1886).

Reynolds, Glenn Harlan. "A Critical Guide to the Second Amendment," *Tennessee Law Review* 62 (1995): 461-88.

Shalhope, Robert E. "The Ideological Origins of the Second Amendment," *Journal of American History* 69 (1982): 599-614.

Spitzer, Robert J. *The Right to Bear Arms: Rights and Liberties under the Law* (Santa Barbara: ABC-CLIO, 2001).

Tribe, Laurence H. *American Constitution Law* (Foundation Press, 2000).

Tuchman, Barbara W. *The March of Folly* (New York: Alfred A. Knopf, 1984).

U.S v. Cruikshank, 92 *United States Reports* 542 (Washington DC: Government Printing Office, 1875).

U.S v. Miller, 307 *United States Reports* 174 (1939).

Washington Post (September 26, 1972).

Webb, R. K. *Modern England: From the Eighteenth Century to the Present* (New York: Dodd, Mead, 1970).

Weighley, Russell F. *History of the United States Army* (New York: Macmillan, 1967).

Williams, David C. "Civic Republicanism and the Citizen Mitilia: The Terrifying Second Amendment," *Yale Law Journal* 101 (December 1991): 551-615.

The Second Amendment to the U. S. Constitution: Arguments for Gun Control and the Ideology of Self-Defense

4. 미국 수정헌법 제2조의 무기소지권과 총기규제

임 지 봉*

Ⅰ. 머리말: 문제의 제기

2022년 5월 24일에 텍사스주 유발디(Uvalde)시의 롭(Robb) 초등학교에서는 한 18세 청년이 총기를 난사해 학생 19명과 교사 2명을 살해하고 17명에게 부상을 입혔다. 그 후로도 미국 전역에서는 크고 작은 총기 난사로 매일 15명 이상의 사상자가 발생하고 있다고 한다. 올해 들어서만 총기 난사 사건으로 미국에서 1,352명의 사상자가 발생해 하루 약 9명이 총기 난사로 죽거나 다치고 있다. 이에 따라 미국에서 총기규제를 지지하는 여론도 높아지고 있다고 한다. 미국 ABC뉴스가 입소스에 의뢰한 여론조사에서 미국인 70%는 새로운 총기 규제법 제정이 총기 소유권보다 우선되어야 한다고 답했는데 이것은 작년 3월 조사 때의 66%보다 높아진 수치이다.[1]

그러나 총기규제의 이런 높은 여론에도 불구하고 과거 총기규제법 제정이 큰 성공을 거두지 못한 것은 정치권에 막강한 로비력을 자랑하는 '미국총기협회(NRA, National Riffle Association)'와 이들의 이익을 대변하는 공화당 의원들 때문이라고 하며, 이들이 총기규제를 반대하는 근거로 들고 있는 것이 미국 수정헌법 제2조의 무기소지권이다. 과연 총기 난사 사고를 막기 위한 일체의 총기규제법은 수정헌법 제2조의 무기소지권 침해로 위헌일까? 이러한 의문의 제기에서 출발하여 미국 수정헌법 제2

---

* 서강대학교 법학전문대학원 교수, 이 글은 필자의 논문인 "미국 수정헌법 제2조의 무기소지권과 총기규제," 『헌법학연구』 제28권 제2호(한국헌법학회, 2022년 6월)를 수록한 것임을 미리 밝혀둔다.

1 "미 총기 난사로 반년 만에 1352명 사상 텍사스 참사 겪고도 매일 발생," 국민일보 2022년 6월 6일자, https://news.kmib.co.kr/article/view.asp?arcid=0017150222&code=61131111&cp=nv(2022년 6월 6일)

조 무기소지권에 대한 두 가지 해석론을 동 조항의 역사적 규정 배경과 연혁을 중심으로 살펴보고, 미국 연방대법원의 주요 관련 판결들을 통해 무기소지권과 미국에서의 총기규제법의 합헌성 심사에 관한 현재까지의 법리를 규명해보는 것이 본 연구의 목적이다.

이를 위해 본 논문에서는 미국 수정헌법 제2조의 역사적 규정 배경과 연혁(제II장), 미국 수정헌법 제2조에 대한 두 가지 해석론으로서 무기소지권을 주(州)의 권리로 보는 해석론과 개인의 권리로 보는 해석론(제III장), Heller 판결을 비롯한 수정헌법 제2조에 대한 미국 연방대법원의 주요 판결들(제IV장)을 살펴보고 무기소지권과 미국에서의 총기규제법의 합헌성 심사법리(제V장)를 분석해본다.

Ⅱ. 미국 수정헌법 제2조의 역사적 규정 배경과 연혁

1. 무기소지권의 영국적 기원

영국에서 상비군은 국왕의 권력과 전제정치를 뒷받침하는 도구이자 국민의 자유와 권리를 침해하는 요인이었기 때문에, 전통적으로 상비군에 대한 불신이 강했다. 상비군에 대한 이러한 불신으로 영국에서는 일찍이 시민의 자발적 무장으로 이루어진 민병대에 국방과 치안 유지의 역할을 맡겼다. 영국에서의 민병대의 오랜 전통으로 인해 영국에서의 무기소지권은 종교의 자유 등 다른 기본권보다도 더 일찍 관습법으로 수용되고 정착되었다. 즉 영국에서의 무기소지권은 국가를 위해서가 아니라 각 개인의 기본적 권리로서 인식되고 출발했던 것이다. 영국에서는 앵글로-색슨 시대부터 노예가 노예신분에서 해방될 때 손에 무기를 드는 의식을 행하였다. 무기는 기본적 권리로서의 무기소지권을 누리는 자유인으로서의 신분을 상징하는 증표였기 때문이다.[2]

영국에서 무기소지권은 원래 외적의 침입에 대한 방어와 공동체 안전을 위한 경찰기능으로 출발하였으나, 명예혁명은 거치면서 무기기소지권은 자신을 방어하고 전

---

2 손영호, "미국 연방헌법 수정조항 2조의 무기소지권," 서양사학연구 제35집, 한국서양문화사학회, 2015, 33-34면.

제적 정부에 대항하여 국민의 생명과 자유를 지키는 권리로 인식되었다. 이러한 개인의 자기방어와 전제적 정부에의 대항 수단으로서 무기소지권 개념을 주장한 사람은 로크(John Locke)였다. 그는 '통치론(Two Treaties of Government)'에서 국가의 주권은 국민으로부터 나오고 국가권력은 국민의 기본권을 보호하기 위해 존재하며, 국민으로부터 권력을 위임받아 행사하는 국가권력이 국민을 억압하려 할 때 국민들은 정부의 부당한 억압으로부터 자신을 보호하고 집단적 힘으로 전제정부에 저항하는 것은 정당하다고 보았다. 그러면서 그는 전제정부에 대항하여 신으로부터 부여받은 자연권을 지키기 위해 최종적 저항수단으로 무기를 통한 무력 사용을 할 수 있다고 주장하여 무기소지권을 합리화하였다. 개인의 자기방어와 전제정부에의 대항수단으로서 무기소지권의 개념을 더더욱 구체화시킨 이는 블랙스톤(William Blackstone)이었다. 그는 '영국법 주해(Commentaries on the Law of England)'에서 권리를 '상대적 권리'와 '절대적 권리'로 구분하면서 생명과 자유, 사유재산권 등의 '절대적 권리'들을 지키는 수단이면서 또 다른 '절대적 권리'라고 보았다. 그러면서 영국의 관습법은 범죄나 폭력으로부터 자신을 방어하고 전제정부에 대항해 자신의 생명, 자유, 재산과 같은 절대적 권리들을 지키기 위한 최후의 저항수단으로서 개인의 무기소지권이 인성된다고 보았다. 이러한 로크와 블랙스톤의 자연법사상은 제퍼슨(Thomas Jefferson)이나 매디슨(James Madison)과 같은 미국 헌법의 아버지들에게 큰 사상적 영향을 미쳤다.[3]

2. 미합중국의 건국과 수정헌법 제2조의 채택

영국의 관습적 전통에 따른 무기소지권은 아메리카 식민지로도 이식되었다. 당시 영국 정부가 이주민과 그 자녀들에게 무기소지권을 포함한 영국인으로서의 모든 권리들을 신대륙에서도 똑같이 누릴 수 있다고 약속했기 때문에 신대륙에의 이민 유치에 성공할 수 있었다. 특히 지리적으로 멀리 떨어진 식민지에서는 영국과 같은 수준의 치안을 보장받을 수 없었기 때문에 신대륙의 식민지인들에게는 무기소지권이 중요하게 인식되었다. 농업을 주요 생계수단으로 한 초기 식민지인들에게 총기 등의

3 손영호, "미국 연방헌법 수정조항 제2조: 무기소지권에 대한 논쟁과 자기방어의 기본권," 미국학논집 제45권 제2호, 한국아메리카학회, 2013, 141-145면.

무기는 생존을 위한 도구였다. 인디언, 무법자, 야생동물로부터 개인의 생명과 재산을 보호하고 사냥을 통하여 부족한 육류나 생활용품을 확보할 수 있었기 때문이다. 즉 초기 식민지인들에게 총기는 자기방어와 식량 확보를 위한 필수품이었던 것이다. 식민지 시대에 미국의 식민자치주에는 법을 집행하고 치안을 유지할 군대나 경찰이 없었고 식민지의 건강한 성인 남성들이 자경단을 조직하거나 현지 보안관 역할을 맡아 경찰의 기능을 수행하는 것이 고작이었다.[4]

영국 정부는 자신의 권력을 지키기 위해 상비군을 증강하고 식민지 주민들의 무기를 몰수했는데, 이러한 무기몰수 행위는 식민지인들에게 전제정부에 대항하고 자기 자신을 방어하기 위해 무장할 권리가 있다는 신념을 갖게 했고, 1775년 6월 제1차 대륙회의에서 식민지인들은 '무장의 이유와 필요성에 대한 선언서'를 채택하고 독립투쟁을 선포하게 되었다. 그리고 약 1년 후인 1776년 7월 4일에 공포된 독립선언서에 따라 신생 국가가 된 각 식민지의 주(州)헌법에는 대부분 무기소지권이 주민의 기본권으로 명시되었다. 그 후 1786년 매사추세츠주에서 일어난 농민 무장반란인 '세이의 반란(Shays'Rebellion)' 이후에 또 다른 반란에 대처하기 위해 연방의회는 연방 헌법 제1조 제8항의 '민병대 규정'에[5] 관한 법률을 제정하기도 했다.[6]

영국 식민지 시대부터 형성되어 온 상비군에 대한 불신이 상비군을 대신 해 시민들로 구성된 민병대가 군대로서의 역할을 하게 한 것이다. 미국 연방헌법은 헌법 제정 당시에 효율적이고 강력한 연방정부를 세우려는 연방주의자들(Federalist)과 연방정부의 통제보다는 주의 독립성과 자율성을 중시하는 반(反)연방주의자들(Anti-Federalist)의 타협의 산물이었다. 무기소지권과 관련해서는 두 세력 모두 개인의 무기소지권이 정부 전횡을 막고 국민의 자유와 권리를 보호하기 위해 필요하다는 데 공감했지만 무기소지권을 헌법에 굳이 명시해야 하는가에 대해서는 견해가 달랐다. 연방주의자들은 미국은 민주국가로서 국민에게서 모든 권력이 나오기 때문에 연방정부

4 손영호, "미국 연방헌법 수정조항 2조의 무기소지권," 앞의 글, 38-39면.

5 미국 연방헌법 제1조 제8항의 민병대 규정은 "연방의회는 미합중국의 법률을 집행하고 반란을 진압하며 외적의 침입을 격퇴하기 위해 민병대 소집에 관한 법률을 제정하며 … 민병대의 조직, 무장 및 훈련에 관한 규칙을 정한다 … 다만 민병의 장교를 임명하고 연방의회가 정하는 법률에 따라 민병을 훈련시키는 권한은 각주(州)가 갖는다."고 규정하고 있다.

6 최승원, "미연방헌법 수정 제2조와 총기규제," 미국헌법연구 제13권, 미국헌법학회, 2002, 8면.

가 개인의 권리를 침해할 우려가 없기 때문에 권리장전이 필요 없다고 보았다. 이에 비해 반연방주의자들은 개인의 무기소지권이 헌법에 명문화되지 않으면, 민병대는 결국 해체되고 연방정부의 권력을 비호하는 상비군이 창설되어 국민의 권리를 억압하게 될 것이라고 보았다. 협상과정에서 반연방주의자들은 개인의 무기소지권을 헌법에 명문화하지 않으면 연방헌법의 비준에 반대할 것이라며 저항하였고, 이에 연방주의자들은 연방헌법을 지켜내기 위해 일단 연방헌법을 비준한 후에 개헌을 통해 수정헌법에서 무기소지권을 추가할 것을 약속하기에 이르렀다.[7]

연방헌법 비준 후의 협상 과정에서 반연방주의자인 매디슨은 "국민이 무기를 소유하고 휴대하는 권리는 침해되지 않는다. 규율을 갖춘 민병대는 자유로운 주 정부의 최상의 안전수단이다. 그러나 종교적인 이유로 망설이는 사람들에게는 무기를 드는 것을 결코 강요해서는 안 된다"는 조항을 수정헌법에 넣는 타협안을 제시했다. 연방주의자와 반연방주의자 모두 무기소지권을 수정헌법에 명문화하는 데에는 이미 합의한 상태였기 때문에 협상은 비교적 순조롭게 진행되었고, 수정헌법 제2조에 대한 협상 과정에서도 연방주의자와 반연방주의자 사이에 단어 선택에 약간의 논란이 있는 것 이외에 큰 이견은 없었다. 그 결과 1791년 12월에 추가 공표된 10개의 수정헌법 조항 중 수정헌법 제2조는 "규율을 갖춘 민병대는 자유로운 주 정부의 안보에 필요하므로, 무기를 소유하고 휴대할 국민적 권리가 침해되어서는 안 된다(A well regulated Militia, being necessary to the security of a free State, the right of the people to keep and bear Arms, shall not be infringed)"라고 명문화되었다. 매디슨의 타협안에 대한 연방주의자와 반연방주의자의 협상 과정에서 종교적 이유로 무장을 거부하는 사람들에게 무기를 들 것을 강요해서는 안 된다는 부분은 삭제되고, 앞과 뒤의 문장을 바꾸어 한 문장으로 요약한 것이다. 18세기 후반 당시의 미국인들은 주(州) 방위를 위한 민병대와 무기소지권을 서로 분리할 수 없는 상호보완적 개념으로 파악했기 때문에 미국 헌법의 아버지들은 이 두 개념을 하나의 헌법조항으로 묶는데 별 이견이 없었다.[8]

---

7 손영호, "미국 연방헌법 수정조항 2조의 무기소지권," 앞의 글, 41-43면.

8 손영호, 위의 글, 44면.

Ⅲ. 미국 수정헌법 제2조에 대한 두 가지 해석론들

"규율을 갖춘 민병대는 자유로운 주 정부의 안보에 필요하므로, 무기를 소유하고 휴대할 국민적 권리가 침해되어서는 안 된다(A well regulated Militia, being necessary to the security of a free State, the right of the people to keep and bear Arms, shall not be infringed)"라고 규정하고 있는 수정헌법 제2조는 하나의 문장에 서로 상충되는 두 개의 문구를 담고 있기 때문에, 미국 헌법조항들 중에서도 가장 난해한 문구로 인식된다. 즉 수정헌법 제2조의 전반부는 민병대의 필요성을 규정한 분사구이고, 후반부는 국민의 무기소지권을 규정하고 있다. 이 두 개의 상충되는 문구를 어떻게 연결지어 해석하느냐에 따라 무기소지권을 '주(州)의 권리'로 해석할 수도 있고 국민 '개인의 권리'로 해석할 수도 있기 때문이다.[9]

무기소지권을 주의 권리로 보는 해석론은 수정헌법 제2조 전반주의 "규율을 갖춘 민병대(A well regulated Militia)"라는 부분에 주목하면서 이런 수식어를 붙인 것은 일반 시민이 그 자체로 민병대가 되는 것은 아니라고 보면서, 수정헌법 제2조에 의해 주의 공식기구로서의 민병대가 주정부의 규율하에 집단적으로 총기를 보유할 수 있을 뿐이고, 이 조항이 개인의 자유로운 무기 소유를 인정하는 것은 아니라고 해석한다. 이 해석론은 국민을 집단적 개념으로 파악하여 수정헌법 제2조가 국민 개개인의 무기 소유를 인정한 것이 아니라 민병대라는 군사조직 내에서의 집단적인 총기소유를 의미한다고 본다.[10]

이에 비해 무기소지권을 개인의 권리로 보는 해석론은 "무기를 소유하고 휴대할 수 있는 국민적 권리(the right of the people to keep and bear Arms)"라는 부분에 주목하면서 무기소지권은 국민 개인의 권리일 뿐만 아니라, 민병대의 일원으로서 '주의 안보'를 지키기 위해서도 필요하다고 해석한다. 수정헌법 제2조가 미국 연방헌법에 들어간 이후부터 현재까지 무기소지권을 '주의 권리'로 보는 해석론이 주류를 형성해 오고 있고 미국 연방대법원도 '주의 권리'로 보는 입장을 취하고 있다.[11]

---

9 손영호, 위의 글, 44-45면.
10 최승원, 앞의 글, 19-21면.
11 최승원, 위의 글, 21-22면.

Ⅳ. 수정헌법 제2조에 대한 미국 연방대법원의 주요 판결들

1. 2008년 Heller 판결 이전의 수정헌법 제2조에 대한 미국 연방대법원의 입장

미국 연방대법원은 수정헌법 제2조에 대한 세 차례의 판결을 통해 수정헌법 제2조가 연방헌법에 규정된 민병대 조항을 근거로 주정부의 민병대 조직이나 민병대에 대한 규율권을 규정한 조항으로 보았다. 1875년의 U.S. v. Cruikshank 판결,[12] 1886년의 Presser v. Illinois 판결,[13] 1939년의 U.S. v. Miller 판결이[14] 그것이다. 이 판결들을 통해 미국 연방대법원은 수정헌법 제2조가 개인의 헌법상 기본권으로서의 무기소지권을 규정한 것이 아니라, 주 정부의 관할 하에 있는 민병대를 통제하기 위해 수정헌법 제2조가 규정되었다고 판시했다. 따라서 연방대법원은 상당히 오랫동안, 독립혁명 당시 활동하였던 민병대가 존재하지 않는 현대에는 수정헌법 제2조가 법집행기관인 경찰이나 군사적 목적의 군대 군인 이외에 개인의 자유로운 무기소지권을 보장하지는 않는다는 입장을 취하고 있었다.

2. 2008년의 District of Columbia v. Heller 판결[15]

(1) 사실관계의 요지

워싱턴D.C.는 등록되지 않은 총기를 휴대하는 것을 범죄로 규정하고 권총의 등록 자체를 금지하였으며, 장총 등 적법하게 소유한 총기들도 가정에서는 총알을 빼고 분해된 상태로 보유하거나, 방아쇠 잠금장치 혹은 이와 유사한 장치를 설치한 채로만 보유할 수 있게 하였다. 헬러(Heller)는 워싱턴 D.C.의 특별경찰이었고 그가 가정에 보유하기를 원한 권총을 등록 신청하였으나 워싱턴 D.C. 당국이 수리를 거부하였다.

---

12 U.S. v. Cruikshank, 92 U.S. 542 (1875).

13 Presser v. Illinois, 116 U.S. 252 (1886).

14 United States v. Miller, 307 U.S. 174 (1939).

15 District of Columbia v. Heller, 554 U.S. 570 (2008).

그러자 그는 수정헌법 제2조를 근거로 소송을 제기하였다. 그 소송은 시당국이 권총에 대해 등록 신청조차 받지 않는 것, 면허 없이 집에서 총기를 휴대하는 것을 금지하는 한 시 당국의 면허요구, 집에서 기능적 총기의 사용을 금지하는 한 시 당국의 방아쇠 잠금장치의 요구를 막는 소송을 제기했다.

1심인 연방지방법원은 원고인 헬러 패소판결을 내렸으나, 2심인 연방항소법원은 미국 수정헌법 제2조가 국민 개개인의 무기소지권을 보장하고 있으며, 시 당국의 권총 소지에 대한 전면 금지뿐만 아니라 가정에서의 총기가 심지어 자기방어를 위해 필요한 경우에도 작동불능 상태로 보유될 것을 요구하는 것은 수정헌법 제2조의 무기소지권을 침해한다고 하면서 1심 판결을 뒤집고 헬러 승소 판결을 내렸다. 워싱턴 D.C. 시당국이 상소했고, 미국 연방대법원이 이 사건에 대해 사건이송명령장을 발부해서 이 사건은 연방대법원의 재판을 받게 되었다.

(2) 다수의견의 논점과 추론 및 판시사항

위헌의견 5대 합헌의견 4로 위헌으로 판결된 이 사건에서, Scalia 대법관이 집필한 다수의견은 수정헌법 제2조가 민병대 복무와 관계없이 국민 개개인이 무기를 소유할 권리를 보장하고 가정에서의 자기방어 등을 위해 전통적으로 적법한 목적으로 그 무기를 사용할 권리를 보장한다고 판시했다. 다음은 그 추론의 요지이다.

워싱턴 D.C.는 수정헌법 제2조가 민병대 복무와 관련해서만 무기를 소유하고 휴대할 권리를 보장한다고 주장하고, 반면에 헬러는 무기를 휴대할 권리는 민병대 복무와 상관이 없고 가정에서의 자기방어와 같은 전통적으로 적법한 목적의 무기사용을 보장한다고 주장한다. 수정헌법 제2조는 '서론 부분(prefatory clause)'과 '법적 효력이 발생하는 부분(operative clause)'으로 나누어진다. 서론 부분은 목적을 공표하는 부분이고, 법적 효력이 발생하는 부분인 두 번째 부분의 적용 범위를 제한하거나 확장하지 않는다.

법적 효력이 발생하는 부분의 규정 원문과 역사는 그 부분이 국민 개개인의 무기소유 및 휴대권을 의미한다는 점을 증명한다. 법적 효력이 발생하는 부분의 첫 번째 두드러진 특징은 "국민의 권리(right of the people)"라고 명문화하고 있다는 점이다. 헌법의 다른 조항들의 규정형태를 보더라도 이 권리는 집단적 권리라기보다는 개인의 권리로 규정되어 있다. 이것은 "국민(the people)"의 부분집합에 해당하는 계층과 동일시되는 서론 부분의 "민병대(militia)" 구절과 뚜렷하게 대비된다. 그 부분집합은 특정 연령의 신체 건강한 남성으로 구성된다. 따라서 수정헌법 제2조가 민병대가 "무기를 소유하고 휴대할 권리"만을 보장한다고 보는 것은 법적 효력이 발생하는 부분이 그 권리의 주체로서 "국민"을 규정하고 있는 것과 잘 부합하지 않는다. 즉 수정헌법 제2조가 보장하는 권리는 국민 개개인에 의해 행사되는 것이고 모든 미국 국민들에게 속한다.

"무기(Arms)"라는 용어는 구체적으로 군사적 사용 목적의 무기만을 의미하는 것이 아니라 자기방어용 무기도 포함하는 것이다. "무기의 소유 및 휴대(keep and bear Arms)"는 무장 목적으로 무기를 소유하고 휴대하는 것을 의미한다. 군대 조직에의 참여만을 의미하는 것은 아니다. 반대의견과는 달리, 어떤 사전도 "무기 휴대(bear arms)"의 정의(定義)가 민병대 조직에서의 무기 휴대만을 의미한다고 적고 있지 않다. 그런 관용구적인 해석으로는 수정헌법 제2조가 군인이 되거나 전쟁을 수행할 권리만을 보호하는 것이 된다.

수정헌법 제2조의 역사적 배경은 온갖 적과 직면했을 때 무기를 소유하고 휴대할 개인의 권리를 보호할 의도로 헌법에 명문화되었다는 것을 확인해준다. 수정헌법 제2조는 민병대 복무와 아무 상관없고 식민지인들이 결코 무장해제 되어서는 안 된다는 기존의 권리를 성문화한 것이다. 수정헌법 제2조의 서론 부분은 법적 효력이 발생하는 부분에 대한 이러한 해석과 부합한다. "민병대(militia)"는 공동 방어를 위해 일제히 행동할 수 있는 신체 건강한 모든 남성들을 의미한다. 연방의회는 군대를 창설한 권한을 가졌으나 민병대가 이미 그 전에 존재하고 있었다. 민병대를 조직할 권한은 민병대를 창설할 권한이 아니라 민병대에게 명령을 내릴 권한을 말했다.

반(反)연방주의자들은 연방정부가 시민들로 구성된 민병대를 무력화하기 위해 국민들을 무장해제시키고 정치화된 상비군을 두거나 일부 민병대만 선별해서 두는 것을 우려했다. 그에 응하여 개인의 무기 소유 및 휴대권이라는 오래된 권리를 제한할 권한을 연방의회에게 부여하지 않았고 이로 인해 시민들로 구성된 민병대의 이상(理想)은 보존될 수 있었다. 만약 미국헌법의 아버지들의 의도가 민병대 조직만을 수정헌법 제2조의 유일한 수혜기구로 하는 것이었다면 전제적 중앙정부로부터의 보호장치로서 "시민들로 구성된 민병대(citizens'militia)"의 존재를 확실하게 하지 않았을 것이다. 수정헌법 제2조에 대한 이러한 해석은 수정헌법 제2조 전후에 여러 주헌법들에 유사하게 규정된 무기소지권 조항들과도 부합한다.

다음 단계는 미국 연방대법원의 선판례들 가운데 지금까지 우리가 도달한 결론과 다른 결론에 이른 것이 있느냐를 결정하는 것이다. 미국 연방대법원의 선판례 가운데 수정헌법 제2조의 무기소지권이 국민 개인의 권리라는 해석에 이의를 제기하거나 무기를 소유하고 휴대할 권리를 민병대의 권리로만 제한하는 선판례는 없다. 대신에, 몇몇 선판례들은 무기소지권이 적용되는 무기의 일정 유형을 민병대만이 적법한 목적을 위해 일반적으로 사용할 수 있도록 제한하고 있을 뿐이다.

대부분의 헌법상 기본권들처럼 수정헌법 제2조의 권리가 무제한적인 권리는 아니다. 수정헌법 제2조의 무기소지권이 어떤 방식으로든, 어떤 목적으로든 무기를 소유하고 휴대할 수 있다는 의미는 아니다. 예를 들어 무기를 감추는 것을 금지하는 것에 대해서는 수정헌법 제2조나 유사한 주헌법 조항들에 의해 합헌결정이 내려졌다. 본 연방대법원 판결이 중범죄자들과 정신병 환자들의 무기소지에 대한 오랜 금지에 의문을 제기하는 것으로 받아들여져서는 안 된다. 본 연방대법원 판결이 학교나 정부 건물과 같은 민감한 장소들에 무기를 휴대하는 것을 금지하는 법이나 무기의 상업적 판매에 조건이나 자격요건을 부과하는 법의 합헌성에 의문을 제기하는 것으로 받아들여져서도 안 된다.

보호받는 여러 종류의 무기들은 그 시대에서 흔하고 공통적으로 사용되던 것이라는 연방대법원의 선판례들은 위험하고 유별난 무기들의 휴대를 금지하는 역사적 전통과 맥이 닿아 있다. 이러한 원칙들을 본 사건에 적용하면 권총 등록 금지와 자기방어에 적용되는 방아쇠 잠금장치 요구는 수정헌법 제2조 위반이라는 결론에 이르게 된다. 가정에서의 권총 소유에 대한 워싱턴 D.C.의 전적인 금지는 결국 미국인들이 자기방어의 적법한 목적을 위해 압도적으로 선택한 모든 종류의 "무기"들을 금지하는 것이 된다.

연방대법원이 열거된 헌법상의 기본권들에 적용해왔던 어떤 위헌 심사기준 하에서도 이러한 금지는 자기 자신, 가족, 재산에 대한 적법한 방어가 중요해지는 곳에서 합헌성 심사를 통과하여 합헌이 될 수 없다. 이와 유사한 논리로, 가정에서 어떤 적법한 무기가 분해되거나 방아쇠 잠금장치로 채워져 있을 것을 요구하는 것은 시민들이 자기방어의 적법한 목적을 위해 무기를 사용하는 것을 불가능하게 하므로 위헌이다. 헬러는 구두변론에서 워싱턴 D.C.의 총기면허법이 자의적이고 변덕스럽게 집행되지 않는다면 허용될 수 있다고 받아들였기 때문에 연방대법원은 총기 면허가 그의 권리구제 요구를 충족시킨다고 본다. 그러므로 수정헌법 제2조의 무기소지권을 행사할 자격요건을 갖추었다고 가정했을 때, 워싱턴 D.C. 당국은 헬러에게 권총 등록을 허락해야 하고 그에게 가정에서 권총을 휴대할 면허장을 발급해줘야 한다. 연방항소법원의 판결을 인용한다.

Scalia 대법관이 집필한 이 다수의견에 대해 네 명의 대법관들은 반대의견을 개진했는데, 그 반대의견은 다시 Stevens 대법관이 집필한 반대의견과 Breyer 대법관이 집필한 반대의견으로 나누어진다.

(3) Stevens 대법관이 집필한 반대의견의 요지

이 사건의 핵심쟁점은 수정헌법 제2조에 의해 보호되는 권리가 국민 개인의 권리인지 여부가 아니라 오히려 수정헌법 제2조의 무기소지권의 범위가 무엇이고 수정헌법 제2조가 비군사적인 목적을 위해 무기를 소유하고 사용할 권리를 보장하는지 여부이다.

수정헌법 제2조의 역사는 수정헌법 제2조가 주의 민병대를 보호할 의도로 만들어졌지 보통법상의 자기방어권을 규정할 의도로 만들어진 것이 아님을 말해준다. 무기의 소유가 민병대의 보존과 합리적 연관성을 갖고 있을 것을 요구하는 연방대법원의 선판례들은 수정헌법 제2조의 규정 원문을 가장 자연스럽게 독해하는 것이며 역사적 사실에 가장 충실한 해석이다. 수정 헌법 제2조의 서론 부문은 그것이 민병대를 보존할 의도로 규정화되었다는 것을 분명히 한다. 다수의견은 미국 헌법의 아버지들이 서론 부분에서 공표된 대상을 언급하기 위해 "국민들(the people)"이라는 용어를 사용하고 있다는 점을 간과하고 있다. 이러한 용어들은 수정헌법 제2조가 그 원문이 직접 보호하는 민병대에 복무할 의무를 진 개인들의 집단적 행동에 관한 규정임을 의미한다.

"무기를 소지하고 휴대할(To keep and bear arms)"이라는 용어들은 군사적 목적을 위해 필요하다면 무기를 소유하고 군사적 활동과 관련해 무기를 사용할 하나의 권리를 의미한다. 비군사적인 무기소지나 무기사용을 보장하기 위해서였다면 다른 용어들이 사용되었을 것이다. 다수의견의 입장과는 반대로 준법 시민들이 가정에서 그들 자신을 보호할 권리를 보장할 의도로 만들어진 수정헌법 제2조에는 그런 다른 용어들이 사용되고 있지 않다.

(4) Breyer 대법관이 집필한 반대의견의 요지

워싱턴 D.C.의 권총과 무기규제는 수정헌법 제2조가 자기방어에 있어 시민들의 이익을 보호하는 것으로 해석되더라도 수정헌법 제2조와 모순되지 않는다. 중대 범죄가 만연한 도시지역에서의 권총 소지에 초점을 맞추고 있고, 따라서 참으로 생명을 위협하고 심각한 문제들에 대한 입법부의 허용가능한 대응이기 때문이다.

수정헌법 제2조가 보장하는 권리는 심지어 다수의견의 입장과 같이 자기 방어 목적의 무기를 소유하고 휴대할 권리를 의미한다고 가정하더라도 그 권리는 절대적 권리가 아니어서 정부나 시 당국의 제한을 받게 된다. 총기규제에 대해 엄격한 심사기준을 적용하려는 어떤 이론적 시도도 실제로는 수정헌법 제2조에 의해 보호되는 이익들과 정부의 공공안전의 이익들 사이의 이익형량심사로 바뀌게 되며, 쟁점이 된 총기규제가 정부의 공공안전의 이익들을 증진하는 과정에서 수정헌법 제2조에 의해 보호되는 이익들에게 허용치를 넘는 부담을 부과하는 것인지 여부가 유일한 핵심문제가 될 것이다.

통계에 의하면 무기를 든 집 소유자에 의해 제지당한 모든 침입자들에게 가정 내에서 총과 관련된 네 가지 유형의 사고들이 있었다. 헬러는 권총 등록 금지가 이러한 유형의 사고들을 감소시키지 않을 것이고 총기 등록 금지가 발효한 이후로 범죄율과 살인율이 더 높아지고 있다고 주장하지만, 문제는 워싱턴 D.C.의 입법기구가 그러한 경험적 주장들을 거부하는 것이 합리적이었는가에 있다. 여기서 워싱턴 D.C.의 결정은 사법부가 아니라 입법부가 내리기 가장 적합한 경험적 자료에 근거한 판단과 워싱턴 D.C.가 적절히 촉진하고자 하는 이익들이 "긴절한(compelling)" 이익들임을 말해준다.

권총 등록 금지는 도시지역의 매우 높은 범죄율에 대한 비례적인 대응이다. 덜 제한적인 대안도 없다. 목적이 몇몇 예외를 제외하고는 권총을 없애는 데 있기 때문이다. 더욱이, 권총과 같은 특정 무기에 대한 인기가 그것의 사용과 소유가 보호받아야 하는지 여부의 방향을 결정해서는 안 된다. 매우 위험한 무기가 발명되어 그 무기가 자기방어용 무기로 미국 시민들에 의해 선호될 수 있기 때문이다. 본질적으로 다수의견은 총기에 대한 어떤 규제가 용인될 수 있는가를 기존의 규제가 용인하는 것이 무엇인가를 살펴보고 결정하였다. 미국 헌법의 아버지들이 그러한 순환논법을 의도했다고 믿을 아무런 근거가 없다.

(5) 이 판결이 가지는 의미

이 판결에 대해 어떤 이들은 워싱턴 D.C.가 권총이라는 한 종류의 무기에 대한 등록을 금지하는 것은 심지어 수정헌법 제2조의 무기소지권이 시민 개인의 권리라고 보는 입장에서도 수정헌법 제2조에 위반되지 않는다고 주장하였다. 그 상황에서 개개의 시민들은 자기방어를 위해 모든 무기 소유와 사용을 금지당하는 것은 아니기 때문이다. 다른 이들은 총기규제에 대해 재산권적 접근을 시도하는데, 재산권적 접근에서는 총기규제가 현행 헌법의 재산권 규제와 같은 방식으로 분석되어야 하고, 정당한 정부의 목적 달성에 합리적 연관성을 가지는 한 허용되어야 한다고 본다. 이러한 재산권적 접근은 Breyer 대법관이 반대의견에서 채택한 입장이기도 하다. 연방 제7항소법원 판사인 Posner 판사는 이 판결에서 다수의견이 이전에는 존재하지 않았던 새로운 헌법상 기본권을 창조해내었다고 본다. 그는 수정헌법 제2조의 규정 원문은 그 조항만을 놓고 보든지 혹은 그 조항이 헌법에 채택된 배경을 놓고 보든지에 상관없이 사냥 등 스포츠용이나 사람이나 재산에 대한 방어용으로 총기를 사적으로 소유할 수 있는 권리를 창설하지 않는다. 수정헌법 제2조가 주(州)의 민병대 대원들이 허락을 받고 무기를 그들의 가정에 소지하도록 요구하는 조항이라고 보기도 힘들다. 그러한 해석은 민병대의 효율성을 감소시킬 것이기 때문이다. 끝으로 어떤 이들은 본 판결의 다수의견이 입법절차를 우회하여 '사법부에 의한 입법(judicial legislation)'을 감행한 한 예가 될 수 있다고 비판한다.[16]

---

16 Saul Cornell, "The Right to Bear Arms," Mark Tushnet, Mark A. Graber & Sanford Levinson ed. The Oxford Handbook of the U.S. Constitution, Oxford University Press, 2015, pp. 754-757.

3. 2010년의 McDonald v. City of Chicago 판결[17]

(1) 사실관계의 요지

일리노이주의 시카고(Chicago)시와 오크파크(Oak Park)시는 총기규제 규정을 두고 있었다. 앞에서 살펴본 2008년의 연방대법원의 District of Columbia v. Heller 판결 이후로 이 두 시에 대해 총기규제 규정의 위헌성을 따지는 소송이 제기되었다.

이미 살펴본 바와 같이 Heller 판결에서 연방대법원은 워싱턴 D.C.의 총기등록 금지가 수정헌법 제2조를 위반해 위헌이며, 그 이유로 워싱턴 D.C.법은 연방정부의 권한으로 제정되었고 따라서 연방헌법 제2조가 적용될 수 있다고 판시하였다. 본 사건에서 원고들은 수정헌법 제2조가 주법들에도 적용되므로 시카고 시의 권총 등록 금지규정은 위헌이라고 주장하였다. 연방지방법원은 원고의 위헌주장을 기각하였고, 연방항소법원도 이를 인용하였다. 원고가 이 사건을 연방대법원에 상고하였고, 연방대법원은 이 사건에 사건이송명령장을 발부하였다.

(2) 다수의견의 논점과 추론 및 판시사항

연방대법원은 위헌의견 5대 합헌의견 4로 위헌판결을 내렸다. Alito 대법관이 집필한 다수의견은 수정헌법 제2조가 수정헌법 제14조의 적법절차조항의 편입을 통해 주법들에도 적용된다고 판시하였다. 다음은 그 추론의 요지이다.

출발단계의 문제로서 수정헌법 제14조의 특권 면책조항은[18] 수정헌법 제2조를 편입(incorporation)하지 않는다. 그렇다면 쟁점은 수정헌법 제2조가 수정헌법 제14조의 적법절차조항에 의해 편입되어 연방법률뿐만 아니라 주법에도 적용되는가 하는 것이다. Heller 판결은 자기방어권이 국가의 정돈된 기본권 체계에서 근본적인 권리에 속하고 미합중국의 역사와 전통 속에 깊이 뿌리를 내리고 있는 기본권이라고

---

17 McDonald v. City of Chicago 561 U.S. 742 (2010).

18 수정헌법 제14조의 면책조항은 "어떤 주(州)도 미합중국 시민의 특권과 면책을 박탈하는 법을 제정하거나 집행할 수 없다(No state shall make or enforce any law which shall abridge the privileges or immunities of citizens of the United States)"고 규정하고 있다.

본다.

미합중국의 역사를 통해 연방의회는 무기소지권을 근본적 권리로 확인해 왔으며 역사를 통해 그 반대주장은 지지를 받지 못하였다. 문제는 문명화된 사회가 이 특정한 권리를 기본권으로 승인하지 않고도 존재할 수 있다는 점이 아니라, 다른 나라들과 달리 문명화된 국가인 미합중국은 이 권리를 기본권으로 승인해야만 한다는 점이다. 그렇지 않다면 예를 들어 우리 헌법의 독특한 권리장전조항(Bill of Rights)에 대한 많은 형사적 보호는 주에 대해서는 편입되고 적용되지 않을 수 있게 된다. 수정헌법 제14조의 적법절차조항은 Heller 판결에서 승인된 수정헌법 제2조의 무기소지권을 근본적 권리, 우리 사회에 깊이 뿌리를 내린 권리로 수용하여 연방정부뿐만이 아니라 주(州)에도 적용되게 한다.

연방항소법원의 판결을 파기하고 환송한다. Scalia 대법관과 Thomas 대법관이 결론은 다수의견과 같지만 그 결론에 이른 이유가 다른 동조의견을 각각 작성하였다. 4명 대법관이 가담한 반대의견도 Stevens 대법관이 작성한 반대의견과 Breyer 대법관이 작성한 반대의견으로 갈렸다.

(3) Scalia 대법관이 집필한 동조의견의 요지

연방대법원이 이 사건에서 실체적 적법절차원리에 근거해 판단을 해야 하는가는 불명확하지만, 연방대법원의 권리장전상의 기본권들에 대한 편입과 주(州)에의 적용은 오랫동안 확립이 되고 제한적으로 적용된 대원칙이므로 본 사건의 다수의견을 지지한다.

(4) Thomas 대법관이 집필한 동조의견의 요지

다수의견의 판단은 옳고, 수정헌법 제14조는 수정헌법 제2조를 편입하여 주들에게도 적용되게 하지만 적법절차조항은 '편입(incorporation)'을 위해 적합한 헌법적 근거가 될 수 없다. 대신에 수정헌법 제14조의 특권 면책조항이 수용을 위한 더 적절한 적용 통로이다. 특권 면책조항의 제정자들과 그 시대의 국민들은 무기소지권을 자유보존을 위한 본질적 권리로 이해하였다. 생명, 자유, 재산을 박탈당한 국민이 이용할 수 있는 '절차'만을 보장한 헌법조항은 헌법에서 언급되지 않은 권리들의 실체를 규정할 수 없다.

적법절차조항의 규정 원문과 그 역사를 보건대, 연방대법원 판결들이 언급하는 많은 실체적 권리들을 적법절차조항이 보장하는 것은 아니다. 그러나 특권 면책조항의 쟁점들을 다시 정밀하게 조사해보면 수정헌법 제2조의 무기소지권은 수정헌법 제14조에 의해 보장된 미국 시민들의 특권이라는 결론에 이를 수밖에 없다.

(5) Stevens 대법관이 집필한 반대의견의 요지

이 사건에서 해결되어야 하는 핵심쟁점은 수정헌법 제2조가 개인에게 가정에서 권총을 포함한 개인적인 기능성 무기를 소유할 근본적 권리를, 주에게 적용할 수 있는 권리를 보장하고 있느냐이다. 그것은 편입의 문제와는 다른 문제이다. 그것은 이미 19세기에 결정된 문제이며, 수정헌법 제2조가 특권 면책조항을 통해 편입되어 주에도 적용될 수 있다는 주장을 연방대법원이 거부한 것이 왜 옳은가를 보여준다. 수정헌법 제2조는 수정헌법 제14조에 편입되어 주에게 적용된 적이 없다. 따라서 본 사건에서의 쟁점은 무기소지권이 수정헌법상의 적법절차조항의[19] "자유(liberty)"의 개념 속에 포함되어 주에도 적용 가능한지 여부이다.

첫째, 무기는 수정헌법상 적법절차조항의 "자유(liberty)"와 근본적으로 양면적인 관련성을 가진다. 무기들은 집 소유자들이 그들의 가족과 재산을 침입자로부터 방어하는 것을 도울 수 있지만, 반면에 무기들은 흉악범들, 폭도들 및 다른 범죄자들이 무고한 희생자들을 살해하는 것을 도와 희생자들의 자유에 따른 이익을 감소시킬 수도 있다.

둘째, 권총이나 다른 특정한 유형의 무기를 소유하는 것은 자율성, 존엄성 혹은 정치적 평등으로 충만한 삶을 이끄는 데 중요하지도 않다. 더 나아가, 영국의 식민지였던 나라들을 포함하여 다른 선진 민주국가들의 경험은 무기소지권에 미국보다 더 엄격한 제한을 두기 때문에 무기소지권이라는 확장성 있는 권리가 정돈된 자유 체계에 본질적인 권리라는 생각을 약화시킨다. 끝으로 연방대법원이 이 사건에 전국적이고

---

19 미국 수정헌법 제14조의 적법절차조항은 "어떤 주(州)도 적법절차에 의하지 않고 주민의 생명, 자유, 재산을 빼앗을 수 없다(nor shall any State deprive any person of life, liberty, or property, without due process of law)"고 규정하고 있는데, 여기에서의 "자유(liberty)"를 말한다.

획일적인 기준을 적용하는 것은 현명하지 못하다. 선출직 공무원들은 민주적 절차 속에서 그들이 무기소지의 이익을 완벽하게 보호할 수 있음을 입증해왔기 때문이다. 총기규제 문제는 시민들 스스로가 민주적 절차를 통해 특정 총기규제 조치가 "장래에 대비하지 않는(improvident)" 것인지 아닌지를 결정할 수 있게 주정부와 지방자치단체에 맡겨져야 한다.

(6) Breyer 대법관이 집필한 반대의견의 요지

개인의 자기방어가 관련되는 한, 수정헌법 제2조의 규정 원문, 역사, 혹은 목적 중에 무기소지권을 근본적 권리로 만드는 것은 없다. 미국 연방헌법에는 무기에 대한 규제 권한을 입법부로부터 사법부로 옮기거나 주정부에서 연방정부로 옮기는 것을 정당화하는 규정은 없다. 따라서 수정헌법 제14조는 수정헌법 제2조의 무기소지권을 편입하여 주정부에 적용 가능하도록 만들지 않는다.

(7) 이 판결이 가지는 의미

1791년에 권리장전 조항들이 미국헌법에 들어갔을 때 주정부가 아니라 연방정부의 권한을 제한할 의도로 들어갔다는 것에는 대부분의 미국 헌법학자들이 동의한다. 1868년에 수정헌법 제14조가 미국헌법에 들어간 이후에도 미국 연방대법원은 권리장전상의 기본권들이 수정헌법 제14조의 적법절차조항을 통해 선별적으로 적용되거나 편입된다고 판시하였다.

본 판결에서 미국 연방대법원은 권리장전 조항들로부터 도출되는 권리들도 정돈된 자유 체계에서 근본적 권리이거나 혹은 미합중국의 역사와 전통 속에 깊이 뿌리박은 권리일 경우에만 편입되어 주정부나 지방자치단체의 규정에 적용될 수 있다고 판시하였다. 즉 본 판결은 적법절차조항의 적용상의 한계를 제시하고 있는 것이다.

V. 무기소지권과 미국에서의 총기규제법의 합헌성 심사 법리

미국 수정헌법 제2조는 이미 앞에서 본 바와 같이 "규율을 갖춘 민병대는 자유로운 주 정부의 안보에 필요하므로, 무기를 소유하고 휴대할 국민적 권리가 침해되어서는 안 된다"(A well regulated Militia, being necessary to the security of a free State, the right of the people to keep and bear Arms, shall not be infringed)라고 하여 무기소지권을 규정하고 있다. 앞에서 살펴본 2008년 미국 연방대법원의 District of Columbia v. Heller 판결에서 종래와 다른 여러 가지 새로운 수정헌법 제2조의 해석 법리들이 제시되었다.

1. 무기소지권은 민병대의 권리가 아니라 개인의 권리

재판관들 사이에서 의견이 위헌의견 5대 합헌의견 4로 나누어진 2008년의 Heller 판결에서 다수의견에 따르면 수정헌법 제2조는 무장괴한 등 온갖 적들과 직면했을 때 무기를 소유하고 휴대할 '개인의 권리'를 보장하는 것이며 자기방어권이 수정헌법 제2조의 핵심이라고 판시하였다. 이 판결에서 연방대법원은 수정헌법 제2조가 민병대 복무와 관련된 무기소지권만을 보장한다는 종래의 견해를 거부한 것이다.[20]

그리고 우리가 주목할 것은 이 판결의 다수의견은 수정헌법 제2조 개정 당시의 '원래 의미(original meaning)'에 초점을 맞춘 원의주의(原意主義, Originalism)적[21] 접근을 하고 있다는 점이다. 따라서 다수의견은 수정헌법 제2조가 개헌을 통해 미국 연방헌법에 들어갈 때의 수정헌법 제2조의 규정 원문과 그에 대한 이해에 중점을 두고 수정헌법 제2조의 의미를 해석한다.

따라서 다수의견을 집필한 Scalia 대법관은 수정헌법 제2조 규정 원문 중 서론 부분보다는 법적 효력이 발생하는 부분에 대한 의미 해석으로부터 시작한다. 또한 "국민의 권리(right of the people)"라는 규정 원문에 주목하면서 "무기를 소유하고 휴대할(to keep and bear Arms)" 규정이 미국헌법에 도입될 18세기 당시의 의미는 개인이 온갖

---

20 Jerome A. Barron & C. Thomas Dienes, Constitutional Law, West Publishing Co., 2013, p. 238.

21 원의주의는 헌법의 해석방식과 관련한 개념으로서, 모든 헌법규정들은 그 규정이 헌법에 들어갈 당시의 원래 의미에 근거해서 해석되어야 한다고 보며, 이러한 헌법 해석방식은 그 헌법조항의 의미가 제 개정 당시부터 견고하게 확립되어 있다고 보고 헌법조항의 의미를 바꾸려면 연방헌법 제5조의 헌법개정절차 조항을 통한 개헌을 통해서만 가능하다고 본다. 원의주의에 대해 자세히는 Randy E. Barnett & Evan D. Bernick, The Original Meaning of the Fourteenth Amendment, The Belknap Press of Harvard University Press, 2021 참조.

적과 직면했을 때 무기를 휴대할 권리를 의미하는 것일 뿐이고 민병대와는 상관이 없음을 지적한다. 또한 수정헌법 제2조의 서론 부문도 수정헌법 제2조가 무기를 휴대할 개인적 권리를 보호하기 위한 것이라는 해석과 상충되지 않는다고 보았다.

Heller 판결에서 다수의견은 또한 주헌법상의 무기소지권 조항들과 수정헌법 제2조의 도입 역사 및 수정헌법 제2조가 미국헌법에 도입된 이후의 해석론들을 검토한 결과 그 모든 자료들이 수정헌법 제2조의 무기소지권을 '개인의 권리'고 보고 있다는 주장도 하였다.

2. 무기소지권의 적용 범위

연방대법원은 Heller 판결에서 첫째, 수정헌법 제2조의 무기소지권이 무제한적인 권리는 아니라는 점을 받아들인다. 수정헌법 제2조의 무기소지권이 어떤 방식으로든, 어떤 목적으로든 무기를 소유하고 휴대할 수 있다는 의미는 아니라고 하면서 예를 들어 설명한다. 그 예로 우선 무기를 감추는 것을 금지하는 것은 무기소지권에 의해 보호될 수 없다고 보았다. 또한 중범죄자들과 정신병 환자들의 무기소지는 제한할 수 있으며, 학교나 정부 건물과 같은 민감한 장소들에 무기 휴대를 제한할 수 있고, 무기의 상업적 판매에 조건이나 자격요건을 부과할 수도 있다고 판시하였다.

법 해석방식은 그 헌법조항의 의미가 제 개정 당시부터 견고하게 확립되어 있다.

둘째, 무기소지권에 의해 보호되는 무기의 유형에 대해서도 판결문에서 언급했는데 수정헌법 제2조가 미국 연방헌법에 "도입될 때의 흔한 무기류(in common use at the time)"에 대해서만 수정헌법 제2조의 무기소지권이 적용되며 현대의 민병이 사용할 수도 있는 보다 고도화된 무기들은 수정헌법 제2조의 무기소지권의 적용 범위 내에 들지 않는다고 판시하였다.

셋째, 특히 주목을 요하는 것은 Heller 판결이 총기규제법의 수정헌법 제2조 위반 여부를 심사할 때 사용할 합헌성 심사의 기준을 제시하지는 않고 있다는 점이다. 다수의견은 워싱턴 D.C. 법이 합리성 심사기준이건, 중간수준 심사기준이건, 엄격심사기준이건 어떤 합헌성 심사기준에 의하더라도 위헌이라고 판시하고 있을 뿐이다.

3. 원의주의적 접근법과 미해결의 쟁점들

Heller 판결에서 다수의견과 Stevens 대법관의 반대의견은 둘 다 수정헌법 제2조의 의미를 해석하는 데 있어서 원의주의적 접근법을 사용하고 있다.

그러나 다수의견과 Stevens 대법관의 반대의견은 원의주의적 접근을 하면서도 서로 다른 증거들에 초점을 맞추고 있고 그 결과 같은 수정헌법 제2조의 의미에 관해 5 대 4로 다른 결론을 내리고 있다.[22]

Heller 판결은 미국 수정헌법 제2조가 가정에서 방어용으로 사용 가능한 권총을 소유할 개인적 권리를 보장하고 있다고 판시했다. 그러나 수정헌법 제2조의 무기소지권의 범위와 관련해 몇 가지 중요한 쟁점들에 대해 판결을 내리지 않았는데, 그 미해결의 쟁점들로는 첫째, 권총 이외의 무기들에 대한 정부규제는 어떠한가? 둘째, 집 밖에서의 무기소유에 대한 규제는 어떠한가? 셋째, 워싱턴 D.C.의 법 규정 이외에 다른 수많은 총기규제법은 어떠하며 법원은 그러한 총기규제법에 대한 위헌심사를 할 때에 어떤 심사기준을 적용해야 하는가? 등이 있다.

4. 편입조항(Incorporation Clause)의 해석

편입조항(Incorporation Clause)이란 무엇이며 왜 수정헌법 제14조의 적법절차조항이 편입조항이 될 수 있는 것일까? 1878년에 처음 제정된 미국 건국헌법은 연방의회, 대통령 등 연방 행정부, 연방대법원 등 연방사법부 등 통치구조에 관한 7개의 조항으로 이루어져 있었지만 기본권에 관한 직접적인 조항들은 갖고 있지 못했고 이에 기본권조항이 없는 헌법은 무의미하다는 비판이 일자, 4년 후인 1891년에 표현의 자유 등 중요한 기본권들을 담고 있는 수정헌법 제1조를 필두로 하여 기본권에 관한 10개의 조항들이 한꺼번에 미국헌법에 추가되게 되었으며, 이 기본권에 관한 조항들을 따로 '권리장전(Bill of Rights)'이라고 부르게 된다. 하지만, 이 권리장전 조항들은 규정 원문 자체에서 연방정부를 그 규율대상으로 할 뿐이고 주(州)에 대해 직접 주장될 수 없는

22 Jerome A. Barron & C. Thomas Dienes, 앞의 책, p. 240.

한계를 지니고 있었다. 예를 들어 수정헌법 제1조는 연방 정부기관의 하나인 "연방의회가 언론의 자유 등을 침해하는 연방법률을 만들 수 없다"고 규정하고 있었고 그 외의 권리장전 조항들에도 "주(State)"라는 단어는 등장하지 않았다. 권리장전 조항들의 규율대상자 내지 수범자는 "주"가 아니라 "연방정부"에 한정되고 있었던 것이다. 연방대법원도 그러한 취지의 판결들을 내림으로써 권리장전 조항들의 "주"에의 적용은 봉쇄되고 말았는데, 이 문제의 해결사 역할을 한 것이 바로 미국 수정헌법 제14조의 적법절차조항이다. 이 조항은 "어떤 주(State)도 적법절차에 의하지 않고 주민의 생명, 자유, 재산을 박탈하지 못한다"고 규정함으로써 "주"를 그 규율대상자로 명시하고, 이 조항의 "자유(liberty)" 속에 권리장전상의 기본권들을 '편입'(incorporation)시켜 이 조항을 통해 권리장전상의 권리들이 "주"에 대해서도 주장되고 적용될 수 있게 된 것이다.[23] 이것은 미국 수정헌법 제14조의 적법절차조항이 연방주의 채택하고 있는 미국헌법 하에서 기본권 조항들의 적용이 연방정부를 넘어 주(州)로 확대되어 나가는 통로로서의 구실을 하게 된 것을 의미하였다.[24]

Heller 판결은 수정헌법 제2조의 무기소지권이 편입조항인 수정헌법 제14조의 적법절차조항을 통해 주정부의 총기규제에도 적용되는지에 대해 사법석 판단을 내리지 않았다. 그에 대해 연방대법원이 사법적 판단을 내린 것은 2년 후인 2010년의 McDonald v. City of Chicago 판결에서이다. 여전히 위헌의견 5대 합헌의견 4로 나누어진 미국 연방대법원의 대법관들은 다수의견에서 수정헌법 제2조의 무기소지권은 편입조항인 수정헌법 제14조의 적법절차조항을 통해 주(州)에도 똑같이 적용 가능하다고 판시하였다.

더 구체적으로 살펴보면, McDonald v. City of Chicago 판결에서 Alit 대법관이 집필한 다수의견은 자기방어권은 고대로부터 현재에 이르기까지 많은 국가의 국법체계에 의해 승인된 기본적 권리이고, Heller 판결에서 개인적 자기방어권이 수정헌법 제2조 무기소지권의 중심적 구성부분이라고 이미 판시한 바와 같이 수정헌법 제2조

23 편입조항으로서의 미국 수정헌법 제14조의 적법절차조항에 대해 자세히는 John E. Nowak & Ronard D. Rotunda, Constitutional Law, 6th ed., West Group, 2000, pp. 368-70.

24 임지봉, "적법절차조항의 우리 헌법에의 도입과 그 운용," 헌법학연구 제11권 제3호, 한국헌법학회, 2005, 265-267면.

의 무기소지권은 미합중국의 역사와 전통에 깊게 뿌리를 내린 권리이므로 주에도 적용 가능하다고 보았다. 또한 다수의견은 두 시의 규정이 수정헌법 제2조의 무기소지권을 침해했느냐의 여부에 대해서는 연방항소법원에서 판단하도록 환송하였음에도 주목할 필요가 있다.

이 사건에서 Thomas 대법관은 수정헌법 제14조의 적법절차조항이 편입조항이라는 논리를 받아들이지 않는다. 그에게는 적법절차조항은 절차의 보장에 관한 조항이지 실체적 권리에 관한 조항이 아니었기 때문이다. 대신에 Thomas 대법관은 수정헌법 제14조의 비준 시점에 미국의 일반 시민들이 수정헌법 제14조의 "특권 혹은 면책(privileges or immunities)"의 의미를 어떻게 이해했느냐를 살폈다. 그리고 무기소지권은 수정헌법 제14조의 특권 면책조항(Privilege or Immunity Clause)을 통해 주(州)에 적용되는 미국 시민의 특권이라고 주장했다.

반대의견을 제기한 대법관들은 다수의견의 결론이 잘못되었지만, 설령 옳은 결론을 내렸다고 하더라도 수정헌법 제2조는 편입조항에 의해 편입될 수 없고 따라서 주(州)에 적용될 수 없다고 주장하였다. Stevens 대법관은 반대 의견에서 주법은 정돈된 자유의 개념 속에 암시된 가치들을 침해하지 않는다고 보았다. Breyer 대법관도 반대의견에서 수정헌법 제2조의 규정 원문, 역사, 중요한 이론적 근거들을 살펴봤을 때, 수정헌법 제2조의 무기소지권이 미국의 사법체계에서 근본적인 권리로 자리매김한 것은 아니라고 보았다.

Ⅵ. 맺음말

미국 연방대법원은 대표적으로는 1939년의 U.S. v. Miller 판결에서 판시한 바와 같이, 독립혁명 당시 활동했던 민병대가 존재하지 않는 현대에는 수정헌법 제2조가 법집행기관인 경찰이나 군사적 목적의 군대 군인 이외에 개인의 자유로운 무기소지권을 보장하지는 않는다는 입장을 취해왔다. 즉 수정헌법 제2조의 무기소지권을 '개인의 권리'가 아니라 '주의 권리'로 보는 입장을 견지해 온 것이다.

그러나 2008년의 District of Columbia v. Heller 판결에서는 수정헌법 제2조가 민

병대 복무와 관계없이 국민 개개인이 무기를 소유할 권리를 의미하며, 가정에서의 자기방어 등을 위해 전통적으로 적법한 목적으로 그 무기를 사용할 권리를 보장한다고 판시함으로써 수정헌법 제2조의 무기소지권을 '개인의 권리'로 보는 입장으로 선회했으며, 2010년의 McDonald v. City of Chicago 판결에서는 수정헌법 제2조의 무기소지권이 수정헌법 제14조 적법절차조항의 편입을 통해 주법들에도 적용된다고 판시하여 무기소지권의 적용 범위를 연방정부뿐만 아니라, 주정부 등으로 확대하였다. 다만 총기규제법에 대한 구체적인 위헌심사의 기준을 아직은 제시하지 않고 있다. Heller 판결에서 다수의견은 워싱턴 D.C.법이 합리성 심사기준이건, 중간수준 심사기준이건, 엄격심사 기준이건 어떤 합헌성 심사기준에 의하더라도 위헌이라고 판시하고 있을 뿐이다.

주목할 점은 최근 두 판결들의 다수의견은 개헌을 통해 미국 연방헌법에 들어갈 때의 수정헌법 제2조의 규정 원문과 그에 대한 '원래 의미'에 초점을 맞춘 원의주의적 접근을 하고 있다는 점이다. 따라서 앞으로 미국 연방대법원이 이러한 원의주의적 해석하에서 각종 총기규제법에 대한 합헌성 심사기준 등의 법리를 다듬어 갈 것으로 전망된다. 그리고 우리나라는 총기소지의 자유가 없기 때문에 아직은 총기소지 문제가 큰 문제가 되고 있지는 않지만, 앞으로 미래에 총기소지 자유의 주장이 대두되었을 때 총기규제와 무기소지권에 대한 미국 연방대법원의 선행적 법리가 우리에게 적지 않은 시사점을 줄 수 있으리라 믿는다.

[참고문헌]

손영호, "미국 연방헌법 수정조항 2조의 무기소지권," 서양사학연구 제35집, 한국서양문화사학회, 2015.

______, "미국 연방헌법 수정조항 제2조: 무기소지권에 대한 논쟁과 자기방어의 기본권," 미국학논집 제45권 제2호, 한국아메리카학회, 2013.

오사라, "총기규제를 위한 미국 지방정부와 법원의 역할," 토지공법연구 제73집 제1호, 한국토지공법학회, 2016.

이명복, "미합중국 수정헌법 '제2조'와 법의 지배원리에 의한 정당화 사유의 역사성과 근거," 미국헌법연구 제25권 제3호, 미국헌법학회, 2014.

이봉한, "총기사용범죄에 대한 법적 규제의 방향," 입법과 정책 제7권 제1호, 국회입법조사처, 2015.

임지봉, "적법절차조항의 우리 헌법에의 도입과 그 운용," 헌법학연구 제11권 제3호, 한국헌법학회, 2005.

장인호, "헌법상 민간부문 총기 관리 감독의 의미와 미국의 민간부문 총기 관리 감독현황 및 시사점," 미국헌법연구 제26권 제1호, 미국헌법학회, 2015.

최승원, "미연방헌법 수정 제2조와 총기규제," 미국헌법연구 제13권, 미국헌법학회, 2002.

Randy E. Barnett & Evan D. Bernick, The Original Meaning of the Fourteenth Amendment, The Belknap Press of Harvard University Press, 2021.

Jerome A. Barron & C. Thomas Dienes, Constitutional Law, West Publishing Co., 2013.

Saul Cornell, "The Right to Bear Arms," Mark Tushnet, Mark A. Graber & Sanford Levinson ed. The Oxford Handbook of the U.S. Constitution, Oxford University Press, 2015.

John E. Nowak & Ronard D. Rotunda, Constitutional Law, 6th ed., West Group, 2000.

5. 헌법상 민간부문총기관리 · 감독의 의미와 미국의 민간부문총기관리 · 감독현황 및 시사점

장 인 호*

Ⅰ. 문제제기

최근 우리나라에서 세종시편의점총기난사사건[1] · 화성시총기사고[2] · 옥천총기사건[3] · 김포총기사고[4] 등과 같이 총기들이 살인 · 협박 등의 범행도구로 이용되는 여러 총기사건들이 연이어 끊임없이 발생하면서 총기난사 · 총기협박 등과 같은 총기를 이용한 총기사고에 대한 우려가 더욱 증대하고 있다.[5]

---

* 국립경찰대학 법학과 교수, 이 글은『미국헌법학연구』제26권 제1호, 2015에 수록한 논문임을 밝힌다.

1 신종권 · 최종권, "세종시 편의점엽총난사사고 3명 숨져 … 용의자 숨진 채 발견," 중앙일보, 2015. 02. 25; "2015년 3월 25일 오전 세종시 장군면 금암리 한 편의점에서 50세 강씨가 멧돼지 등을 사냥하는데 사용하는 엽총으로 쏴 사실혼관계에 있었던 여성의 가족3명이 숨졌다. 경찰에 따르면 강씨는 이날오전 공주경찰서에서 엽총2정을 출고 뒤 범행장소로 이동했다. 총기출고 2시간여 만에 4명이 숨지는 참극이 발생했다"라고 한다.

2 김기성, "화성총기난사, 파출소장 등 4명 사망 … 범인자살," 한겨레, 2015. 02. 27; "2015년 3월 27일 오전 8시 25분경 화성시 남양파출소에서 사냥용 엽총 1정을 출고한 지 1시간 뒤 곧바로 75세 전씨는 형(86)의 집으로 가자마자 형의 부부와 그때 신고를 받고 출동한 파출소장 등 3명을 엽총으로 무참히 살해한 뒤 스스로 목숨을 끊었다"라고 한다.

3 임유진, "개를 풀어놨다는 이웃의 항의에 개 쏴버리겠다며 공기총 꺼낸 50대 검거," 조선일보, 2015. 03. 02; "2015년 3월 28일 충북의 옥천에서 50대남성은 옥천군에서 이웃에 살고 있는 70대 여성과 개의 목줄을 묶는 문제로 말다툼을 하던 중 갑자기 5.5㎜ 구경 공기총을 들고 위협을 하다가 신고를 받고 출동한 경찰에 의하여 체포되었다"고 한다.

4 최윤아, "또 총기사고 … 김포서 50대 남성, 지인 공기총으로 쏴," 조선일보, 2015. 03. 08; "경기도 김포의 한 인력사무소에서 50대 남성이 알고 있었던 지인에게 자신이 소지하고 있었던 공기총을 몇 발을 발사하고 도망하였가 경찰에 의하여 붙잡혔다"라고 한다.

5 김지은, "잇단 총기사고 … 국민들에게 불안감 안겨," 울산종합일보, 2015. 03. 03; "최근 우리나라에서 약 2년 간 민간에서 발생한 잇단 총기사건이 무려 약 25건이나 발생하면서 국민들이 총기로 인한 불충분한 관리와 감독에 우려하면서 불안해하고 있다"고 한다.

이처럼 최근의 연이은 총기사고를 통하여 부실한 총기관리·감독이 국민의 생명과 안전을 위협함에 따라 총기들의 관리·감독을 강화해야 할 필요성이 급증하였다. 이에 따라 최근 연이어 발생하였던 여러 총기사고들은 몇 년 전부터 전국적으로 상당히 많이 발생하고 있음에 따라 「총포·도검·화약류등단속법」상 총기에 관한 관리·감독 관련 제도를 더 강화하기 위한 논의[6]와 함께 총기관리·감독 관련법제도를 개선해야 할 필요성이 제기되고 있다.

무엇보다 총기제조기술발전과 함께 총기사용에 대한 위험성은 더욱 증대되는 추세 속에 총기와 관련된 안전사고와 범죄악용사례들이 반복적으로 끊임없이 발생하고 있으면서 국민의 생명권 등 기본권침해 위험성이 증대되고 있으며, 그 위험성으로 인한 사회의 안전 확보를 위한 많은 노력이 필요하다.

따라서 급증하고 있는 총기사고[7]로 인하여 발생하는 무고한 사망자와 부상자 등과 같은 피해가 더 이상 발생하지 않도록 방지하기 위해 「총포·도검·화약류등단속법」상 운영되고 있는 불충분한 총기관리·감독제도 실태와 문제점들을 분석하고 동법에 대해 법제도적 차원에서의 재검토가 시급하다.

더욱이 최근의 총기사고에서 볼 수 있듯이, 전국 각 지역에서 연이어 발생한 총기사고들로 인하여 사회의 질서와 공공안전이 심각하게 위협받는 동시에 심지어 사망사고 또는 강력범죄로까지 이어진 여러 총기사고들은 국민들에게 불안감을 주어 안전한 생활을 하는 데 부정적인 영향을 미치고 있다.

뿐만 아니라 생명권 등 국민기본권에도 매우 큰 위험이 되기 때문에 중장기적 안목에서 총기관리·감독시스템의 방향을 설정하고 안전한 총기관리·감독시스템 구축을 위하여 법제도개선방안을 통한 선제적 대응이 필요하다.

이를 위하여 본 논문에서 수정헌법 제2조에 연원과 법적 근거를 두고, 200년 넘게

---

6 조재현, "잇단 총기사고에 뒤늦은 총기관리 강화책 … 경찰 초비상," 서울뉴스 1, 2015. 2. 27; "2015년 연이은 총기사건이 발생하면서 멧돼지 등 수렵을 할 목적으로 출고하는 총기를 살인·협박 등의 범행의 목적 로 이용하는 각종 총기사고들을 사전에 예방하기 위해서 총기에 대한 안전한 관리와 감독을 강화해야 할 필요성이 증가하였다"라고 한다.

7 김봉수, "미국 '총기 난사' 비웃던 한국인들, 남일 아니네," 2015. 02. 25; "우리나라에서도 약 10년 동안 총기를 이용한 총기난사, 총기살인, 총기협박 등의 사건들과 함께 불법적인 총기류도 계속하여 증가해왔다. 미국에서 툭하면 발생해 수많은 인명피해를 일으키고 있는 총기난사사건이 한국에서도 더 이상 '남의 일'이 아니게 된 것이다"고 한다.

오랫동안 운영되어 왔던 미국 총기관리 · 감독제도가 탄생된 배경과 함께 심각한 총기사고 문제에 봉착한 미국의 총기관리 · 감독제도의 운영실태 · 총기규제찬반논의 및 시사점을 검토함으로써 우리나라에서 총기사고예방을 위한 장기적 안목의 총기관리 · 감독의 방향과 개선방안을 살펴보겠다.

그러므로 본 연구에서는 최근 끊임없이 증가하고 있는 민간부문에서의 총기사고들을 사전에 방지함으로써 「헌법」 상 국민의 생명 등 기본권과 사회의 안전을 담보하기 위해서 중장기적인 안목에서 총기관리 · 감독제도의 방향에 대해서 면밀히 살펴보고, 종합적인 측면에서 「총포 · 도검 · 화약류등단속법」 상 총기관리 · 감독제도에 대한 합리적인 입법개선방안을 제시하고자 한다.

Ⅱ. 헌법상 민간부문총기관리 · 감독의 의미

1. 민간부문총기관리 · 감독의 의의

(1) 민간총기관리 · 감독의 개념정의

「총포 · 도검 · 화약류등단속법」 제2조에 따르면, '총포'는 "권총 · 소총 · 기관총 · 포 · 엽총, 금속성탄알이나 가스 등을 쏠 수 있는 장약총포 · 압축가스를 이용한 것을 포함한 공기총 및 총포신 · 기관부 등 그 부품으로서 대통령령이 정하는 것을 말한다"라고 명시하였다. 아울러, 동법시행령 제3조 제3호에 따라, '총'은 "권총 · 소총 · 기관총 · 엽총 · 사격총 · 어획총 · 마취총 · 도살총 · 산업용총 · 구난구명총 · 가스발사총 및 뇌관원리 이용한 장약총을 말한다"고 한다. 동시행령 제3조 제3호에 따르면, '공기총'은 "사람 · 가축 또는 조류 등을 살상할 수 있는 성능을 갖춘 것을 의미한다"라고 규정하고 있다.

이러한 「총포 · 도검 · 화약류등단속법」 상 개념규정들을 살펴본 결과, '민간부문총기관리 · 감독'이라 함은 민간부문에서 뇌관원리를 이용하여 제작된 권총 · 소총 · 기관총 · 엽총 · 공기총 등과 같이 사람 · 가축 또는 조류 등의 살상이 가능한 성능을 갖춘 총기를 관리 · 감독하는 것으로, 이를 통하여 총기살인 · 총기협박 · 총기난사 등의 총기사고를 방지하기 위한 것임 알 수 있다.

(2) 민간부문총기관리·감독의 유형

총기로 인한 사고가 발생할 경우 대부분 살인 등과 같은 강력범죄로 이어지는 경우가 대부분이므로, 그 규제의 정도와 방법에 있어서 조금씩 다르지만 대부분의 국가가 민간부문에서의 총기에 대해 관리와 감독을 하고 있다.

예를 들어, 미국은 총기소지와 총기소유·등록에 대한 규제가 약한 국가이다. 그리고 이스라엘과 스위스는 국가적 차원에서 총기보유를 지원한다. 호주는 총기별면허증을 발급하고 소총휴대는 허용하나 권총휴대는 금지한다.[8]

이와 같이 총기소유를 인가하고 등록을 의무화하는 국가가 있는 반면에, 미국처럼 총기의 소유에 대한 인가와 등록이 의무화되지 않은 국가가 있다.

(3) 민간부문총기관리·감독의 필요성

각 국에서 민간부문에서 총기의 관리와 감독이 필요한 이유는 총기사고로 인한 사회적 비용이 증대, 국민의 생명 및 안전침해사건 증대 등이 있기 때문이다. 특히, 살상성능을 갖춘 총기를 관리·감독함으로써 총기사고로 인한 인명사고·재산피해 등에 따라 사회가 부담해야할 비용이 적지 않다. 따라서 부실한 총기관리·감독으로 인해 많은 사회적인 비용이 증대될 수밖에 없다.

무엇보다 총기사고에 대한 적절한 관리·감독은 직·간접으로 국민의 안전을 확보하기 위하여 총기관리·감독 필요성이 존치 한다는 것을 알 수 있다.

---

8 손영호, 『미국의 총기문화』, 살림, 2013, 64-65면; "미국은 총기소유규제가 강하지 않고 약하기 때문에 민간인이 총기보유를 가장 많이 보유한 국가이다. 이와 함께 이스라엘의 각 가정에서는 각종총기를 소유하며, 그리고 스위스는 총기보유를 국가차원에서 지원한다. 호주는 1973년부터 총기규제실시하면서 총기별 면허증을 발급한다"라고 한다.

2. 민간부문총기관리·감독의 헌법적 의미

(1) 안전보장·질서유지 및 공공복리를 위한 私人총기소지·사용규제

우리「헌법」 제2조에서 "국민의 모든 자유와 권리는 국가안전보장·질서유지 또는 공공복리를 위해 필요한 경우에 한하여 법률로써 제한할 수 있다"고 밝힌 규정에 비추어 볼 때, 국가기관은 국가안전보장·질서유지 및 공공복리의 보호와 유지를 위하여 총기의 소지·사용 및 보관 등의 관리·감독을 함으로써 총기의 사용으로 인한 위험과 재해를 방지해야 함을 알 수 있다.

(2) 총기소지취급자인 私人으로부터 생명권 등 국민기본권 보호

헌법상 생명권 등의 기본권은 국가기관 이외의 총기소지·취급자인 제3자인 사인의 침해[9]로부터 보호를 국가에게 요구하는 보호청구권이다. 따라서 총기관리·감독은 개인들의 총기사용에 의하여 국민들의 헌법상 생명권 등 기본권이 침해되는 것을 국가가 적극적으로 방지해야한다는 의미를 갖는다.

이런 점에서 총기관리·감독은 사람을 살상할 수 있는 성능을 갖춘 총기를 적절히 규제함으로써 한번 잃으면 영원히 회복할 수 없는 생명,[10] 즉 생명권[11]과 기본권을 사인의 총기사용으로부터 보호함을 의미한다.

---

9 정태호, "기본권보호의무," 현대공법의 재조명, 고려대학교 법학연구소, 1997, 363-364면; "'기본권보호의무'란 국민들이 향유하고 행사하는 헌법상 보장되는 기본권이라는 보호법익을 제3자의 즉 사인의 침해로부터 보호해야 할 국가의무를 의미한다"고 한다.

10 대판 1963. 2. 28, 62도241; 대법원은 "인간이 가지는 생명은 한번 잃으면 영원히 다시 원래의 상태로 회복할 수 없으며, 그러한 이유로 생명은 이 세상 무엇과도 바꿀 수 없는 절대적인 것이며, 사림의 생명은 존엄한 인간존재의 근원인 것이다"고 판시했다.

11 김백유, 『헌법학(II)』, 조은, 2010, 333면 이하 참조; "생명은 Durig가 언급하였듯이 아직 비생명적인 것 또는 인간의 인격·육신적 존재형태, 즉 생존(Lebendigsein)을 의미한다. 그리고 현행헌법은 독일의 기본법 즉 독일연방헌법과는 달리 생명권에 대한 구체적인 규정 없지만 통설과 판례는 해석론으로 생명권을 헌법상 권리로 인정하였다"라고 한다.

3. 민간부문총기관리·감독에 있어 국가의 헌법상 의무

(1) 생명권 등 국민의 기본권에 대한 국가기관들의 보호의무

헌법상 국민의 생명권에 대한 국가의 보호의무는 포괄적인 것으로 생명권 등 기본권에 대한 국가의 직접적 침해가 금지되며, 국가는 물론 사인으로 하여금 생명권이 침해되는 것에 대해서도 이를 적극 방지해야 할 의무를 갖는다. 이와 같이 불법적 총기를 소지하거나 총기를 사용한 사인으로부터 개인의 생명권 침해를 방지해야 할 책임, 즉 기본권보호의무[12]가 국가에게 있다.

(2) 민간부문총기관리·감독에 있어 행정 및 입법기관 의무

1) 행정기관의 안전한 민간부문총기관리·감독의무

헌법상 보장되는 생명권 등과 같은 국민들의 기본권을 불법적으로 단절하는 국가의 행위나 사인의 생명권 등 기본권의 위협을 방치하는 국가의 부작위는 허용되지 아니한다. 이에 따라 국민의 생명 등과 같은 기본권을 보호하고 공공의 안전을 유지하기 위하여 국가 특히 행정기관은 총기사고를 미리 방지해야 할 의무 즉 안전한 총기관리·감독의무를 성실하게 이행해야 한다.

2) 입법기관의 민간부문총기관리·감독 관련입법마련 및 법률개선의무

적절한 총기관리·감독은 헌법상 보장된 생명권 및 기본권보장은 물론 공공질서의 유지를 의미하기 때문에 입법기관에게는 총기의 안전한 관리·감독을 위해 「총포·도검·화약류 등 단속법」을 개선함으로써 생명권 등과 같은 국민기본권과 공공질서의 확보에 기여해야 할 법률개선의무[13]가 부여된다.

---

12 Dreier, in: Ders. GG. Bd. 1, 2. Aufl., 2004, Borb, Rn. 101; "사인 즉 개인들의 행위에 의해 개인의 법익에 대한 심각한 침해와 유린을 방지할 수 있도록 하기 위해 일정한 과제인 기본권보호의무(grundrechtliche Shututzpflichten)를 국가가 부담해야 한다"고 한다.

13 Schneider, Hans, Gesetzgebung, 3. neu Bearbeitete und erweiterte Auflage., Lehr- und Handbuch, 2002, S. 63; "입법자는 입법의무를 부여받는 동시에 입법된 법률에 대하여 계속하여 관심을 갖으면서 해당 법률을 개선해야 할 개선의무도 함께 부여된다"고 한다.

Ⅲ. 미국의 민간부문총기관리·감독제도의 운영현황 및 시사점

1. 미국의 민간부문총기관리·감독 실태

(1) 미국의 민간부문총기소지역사·법제도 근거연원인 수정헌법 제2조

미국의 총기소지의 역사·법제도적 근거 및 그 연원은 1789년 발의된 「미국연방헌법수정조항」 제2조에서 찾을 수 있다. 따라서 오늘날 미국사회가 당면한 심각한 문제 중 하나인 총기사고·총기관련강력범죄 등과 관련된 미국의 민간부문 총기관리·감독의 실태를 파악하기 위해서는 「미국연방헌법」이 탄생할 그 당시 정치상황, 미국의 민간부문에서의 총기소지에 관한 역사 등과 함께, 「미국연방수정헌법」 제2조가 채택된 배경을 살펴볼 필요성이 크다.

(2) 미국의 민간부문총기소지역사와 수정헌법 제2조 채택배경

1) 영국에 의한 식민지통치시기에 총기 등 무기소지권리 영향

영국에서 권리장전으로 불리는 권리선언에 따르면, 영국에서 국민들의 전통적인 권리 중 영국국민들 자신의 방어를 위하여 적합한 무기를 소장할 권리가 포함되었음을 인정하였다. 즉 영국국왕의 폭정 위험성으로부터 국민의 자유를 안전하게 보장하기 위하여 생성된 무기소지권의 역사적 인정사실[14]이 당시 영국식민지로 통치를 받던 미국의 총기소지인식에도 영향을 주었다.

2) 과거영국식민지시절 국왕폭정·상비군 억압과 독립 경험

미국에서 무기소유를 헌법상 보장되는 권리로 규정함으로써 약 200년이 넘게 지금까지 총기소지역사가 정착되게 한 「미국수정헌법」 제2조가 채택된 배경에는 과거 식민지시절 영국국왕의 폭정과 상비군의 억압을 받고 그 독립과정에서 개인의 자유

---

14 Edwin Meese III/David F. Forte/Matthew Spalding, 『The Constitution』, Regnery Publishing Inc., 2005, pp. 302-304; 손호영, 앞의 책, 20면 이하; "18세기 영국에서 국왕의 상비군과 국왕의 독재 및 횡포에 의하여 미국국민의 자유와 권리의 침해위험성이 발생할 수 있는 가능성에 따라 성인남자에게 모두 왕국방어를 위해 무기를 구입하고 소장할 의무를 부여했다. 이런 국민군대를 엘리자베스 1세 시대에 민병대(militia)로 명명했다"고 한다.

보장대책으로 총기소유가 권리로 인정되었기 때문이다.[15] 즉 총기소지는 억압에 대항하는 국민의 기본권보호수단으로 인식됐다.

3) 중앙정부와 상비군에 의한 국민 자유와 기본권침해 우려

「미국연방헌법」 논의과정에서 중앙정부와 상비군에 의하여 국민의 자유가 위협받을 것을 우려[16]하면서 그 당시 미국에서는 중앙정부의 독재와 폭정에 대항하기 위해 시민의 자발적 무장으로 조직된 민병대가 독립 후 계속 유지되어야 한다는 인식이 확산됐다. 이처럼 미국에서 총기소지는 전제적인 정부에 맞서는 개인의 기본권으로 자유침해에 대한 저항수단으로 인정되었다.[17]

4) 행정력과 사법권 미치지 않은 지역에서의 보호수단 필요

미국이라는 국가의 초기형성단계에는 행정력과 사법권이 미치지 못한 지역이 많았기 때문에 총기소지가 국민의 권리로 인정되었고, 이후 최근까지 자신은 물론 가족의 생명과 재산을 지키기 위하여 총기[18]소지가 필요했다.[19]

---

15 Larry Gerber, 『The Second Amendment: The Right to Bear Arms』, The Rosen Publishing Group Inc., 2011, pp. 8-10; "미국의 영국식민지시절 당시 신대륙에 사는 인디언과의 다툼에 있어서 여러 총기를 사용할 수밖에 없었으며, 총기를 이용하여 사냥을 함으로써 먹을 양식을 구하는 등에 총기를 적극으로 활용하고 소지할 수밖에 없었다"라고 한다.

16 Larry Gerber, Ibid., p. 8 이하 참조; "미국인들은 과거의 영국에 의한 식민지치하시절에 영국의 국왕과 그의 명령에 복종하는 상비군으로부터 받았던 억압을 상기시키면서 새롭게 구성됐던 미국의 연방정부에 의한 독재와 횡포 가능성을 경계하였다"라고 한다.

17 Stephen P. Halbrook, 『The Founders' Second Amendment』, Ivan R. Dee, 2008, pp. 126-129; "미국에서 시민들의 총기의 소지와 사용은 미국연방정부의 독재나 횡포로부터 미국의 각 주정부들이 독립과 자유를 확보할 수 있는 독립유지수단 등으로 인식됐다"고 한다.

18 손영호, 위의 책, 살림, 2009, 20면 이하; "미연방수사국(FBI)의 미국총기실태조사에 따르면, 미국의 전 지역에서 민간인들이 소유한 총기의 수는 약 2억 7천만 정으로 해마다 약 500만정이나 증가하면서 미국인 약 1인당 약 1정의 총기를 소유하고 있다"고 밝혔다.

19 Richard Hofstadter, "America as a Gun Culture," 「American Heritage Magazine」 October, 1970, p. 20 이하; "과거 미국에서 국가가 개인을 보호해 줄 수 없고 총기소유·휴대하는 권리가 있다는 인식이 확산되었다. 이와 같이 미국에서 사법권에 의한 권리구제가 충분하지 않은 지역에서 총기소지는 개인생명·재산보호수단으로 인식되었다"라고 한다.

(3) 미국에서 민간인이 소지한 총기의 수의 급증

미국은 전 세계에서 총기소지가 허용된 국가들 중에서 민간인의 총기소지가 가장 많은 국가이다. 이처럼 미국에서 총기수는 무려 약 3억정을 넘었으며 인구수보다 총기가 많음에도 불구하고 해마다 총기수가 급증하고 있다.[20]

(4) 미국의 일상화된 총기사고로 인한 기본권 및 공공질서 침해위험성 급증

1) 총기난사사건으로 미국국민의 생명권침해 발생

미국에서는 많은 유명인사가 총기사고로 생명권을 잃었다. 뿐만 아니라, 초등학교 등 교육현장을 비롯해 미국전지역에서 코네티컷교내총기난사사건[21]·버지니아택대학교총기사고[22]·13세소년총기사건[23] 등의 총기사건이 매년 끊임없이 자주 발생[24]하면서 총기로 인한 사망자수가 급증하고 있다.[25]

---

20 Philip J. Cook/Jens Ludwig, 『Evaluation Gun Policy: Effects on Crime and Violence』, The Brookings Institution, 2003, pp. 3-4; "미국에서는 총기의 소지와 사용에 대한 규제가 약하기 때문에 미전역에서 해마다 무력 약 500만의 총기들이 해마다 증가하고 있다"고 한다.

21 James Barron, "Nation Reels After Gunman Massacres 20 Children at School in Connecticut," CNN, 2012. 02. 14; "2012년 미국의 샌디훅이라는 초등학교에서 발생한 사건인 샌디훅초등학교총기난사사건(Sandy Hook Elementary School shooting)으로 아동 약 20명·교직원 약 6명·피의자모친·피의자 포함 사망자가 총28명 발생했다"라고 한다.

22 Christine Hauser/Anahad O'connor, "Virginia Tech Shooting Leaves 33 Dead," New York Times, 2007. 04. 16; "미국의 버지니아택공대생인 조승희 씨에 의하여 그 당시 무려 약 32명이 사망한 버지니아공대총기난사(Virginia Tech massacre)사건이 발생했다"고 한다.

23 정재훈, "美 13살 소년, 6살 동생 살해 뒤 자살 … 식사 문제로 다퉈," YTN, 2015. 03. 27; "미국에서 13살 난 소년이 6살 난 동생과 다투다 동생을 집에서 보관되어 있던 총기를 이용하여 쏴 사건현장에서 숨지게 한 이후에 총기로 13살 소년이 자살했다"고 한다.

24 손영호, 앞의 책, 20면 이하; "미국에서 발생한 여러 총기사건으로 인하여 링컨대통령·케네디대통령·마틴루터킹목사·비틀즈존레논 등과 같은 여러 유명인사들이 사망을 하였으며, 미국에서는 대낮에도 매일 약80명씩, 연간 약 3만 명이 사망한고 있다"고 한다.

25 최진희, "미국총기 사고사망자수, 2015년엔 교통사고 추월할 듯," 2012. 12. 19; "2015년 미국교통사고사망자수는 약 3만2000명, 총기사고사망자수는 약 3만3000명으로 질병통제예방센터에 따르면, 2005년부터 2010년까지 미국에서 교통로 사망한 자들의 수인 교통사망자수 약 22% 감소, 총기사망자수 2000년 후 계속적으로 증가하여 왔다"라고 한다.

2) 총기범죄급증으로 강력범죄과 사회비용의 급증

미국에서 총기사고가 끊임없이 발생하면서 시민의 생명은 물론 사회의 공공 및 안전질서가 심각하게 위협받고 있다. 이러한 총기사건이 계속 발생함에 따라 사회불안과 혼란과 함께 사회적으로 감당해야 할 비용[26]도 가중됐다.

3) 총기관리·감독불능상태로 인한 질서혼란의 우려

미국에서 총기사고가 계속 발생하면서 많은 사람들의 생명 등 기본권을 위협함에 따라 인해 미국사회의 공공안전과 질서에 대한 우려가 증대됐다.[27]

더욱이 총기소지의 증가와 함께 총기사용으로 인하여 발생하는 총기범죄가 급격히 증가함으로 인해 미국사회의 공공안전과 질서가 불안하게 되었다.

2. 총기소지에 관한 미국연방헌법과 관련법제도

(1) 미국연방헌법의 수정조항 제2조

1) 미국연방헌법의 수정조항 제2조의 규정

「미국수정헌법」[28] 제2조는 "질서정연하게 규율된 민병대는 자유국가의 안전을 위해 필요한고로 무기를 보유하고 휴대할 국민이 권리는 이를 침해하지 못한다"고 규정하였다.[29] 이러한 「미국수정헌법」 동조는 연방정부의 권한제한을 목적으로 탄생했다는 데 다툼이 없지만, 총기의 사용과 소지가 국민의 개인적인 권리인가 아니면

---

26 MBC, MBC스페셜-미국을 말한다, MBC, 2002; "미국에서 매년 총기로 인한 사고가 발생하기 때문에 총기와 관련해 발생한 사회적 비용이 무려 약160조원에 이른다"고 한다.

27 정재훈, 앞의 기사, 2015. 03. 27; "미국인들이 가지고 있는 약 3억 정이며, 이대로 가다간 총기관리 불능상태에 빠지는 건 아닌지, 미국인의 우려는 커지고 있다"고 한다.

28 Edwin Meese III/David F. Forte/Matthew Spalding, 『The Constitution』, Regnery Publishing Inc., 2005, pp. 302-304; "미국의 여러 각주에 배포·비준·제정된 수정헌법은 국민의 권리를 상세히 적시한 것으로 미국의 권리장전(Bill of Rights)으로 칭하는데, 이러한 「미국수정헌법」에 따르면, 「미국연방헌법」에 대한 해석이 잘못되거나 정부의 권력이 무분별하게 남용되어 국민의 권리침해를 방지해서는 안 된다는 의미를 담고 있다"고 한다.

29 「미국수정헌법」 제2조인 Amendment II에 따르면, "A well regulated Militia, being necessary to the security of a free State, the right of the people to keep and bear Arms, shall not be infringed"라고 규정하면서 국민의 무기소지에 대한 권리를 명시해 밝혔다.

각주의 집단적 권리인가여부에 논란이 있다.[30]

2) **미국연방헌법 수정조항 제2조상 총기소지의 논의**

「미국연방수정헌법」 제2조상 총기소지에 대하여 총기의 사용이 개인의 개인적 권리라는 입장과 각주의 집단적인 권리라는 입장으로 나누어져 있다.

「미국수정헌법」 제2조를 미국국민 개개인이 총기로 무장할 수 있는 권리조항으로 파악하는 입장에 의하면, 미국각주시민들이 민병[31]으로 복무할 헌법적인 권리를 지니고 있어야 한다고 밝히고 있으며, 민병활동이 가능하기 위해서는 개인이 무기를 소지할 수 있는 권리가 보장되어야 한다고 했다.[32]

「미국연방수정헌법」 제2조상의 주의 권리가 집단적 권리[33]이라는 입장에서는 일차적 근거로 연방의회에 대해 민병대를 조직할 권한을 부여한 「미국연방헌법」 제1조 제8항 제15절에서 "연방의회는 … 합중국의 법률을 집행하고 반란을 집안하며 외침을 격퇴하기 위하여 민병대의 소집에 관련된 법률을 제정하며"[34]라고 규정한 것과 함께 동법 동소 동항 제16절에서 "민병대의 조직 · 무장 및 훈련에 관한 법률을 제정하고 … "[35]라고 규정한 것을 민병대규정의 근거로 불리며, 미연방국가를 구성하고 있는 여러 개의 주가 공식적으로 조직된 민병대를 보유할 수 있는 각주의 권한이 보장을 말한다고 본다.[36]

---

30 안경환, 『미국헌법의 이해』, 박영사, 2014, 581-582면; "미국연방권력의 견제와 제한을 주도하는 주체가 주정부인가 아니면 개개국민인가의 문제 즉, 「미국수정헌법」 제2조가 제정되면서 밝힌 사항과 관련하여, 동조항의 제정이 이미 2세기 이상 지난 지금까지 미국연방대법원은 「수정헌법」 제2조의 적절한 유권해석에 대하여 소홀했다"라고 한다.

31 Don B. Kates Jr., "Handgun Prohibition and the Original Meaning of the Second Amendment," 82 Mich. L. Rev. 204, 1983, pp.213-217 ; "민병대(militia)란 '정규군대(troop)'나 '상비군'(standing army)에 대응하는 어휘라는 주장이 있으며, 그 당시 미국헌법을 제정한 미국헌법의 제정자가 헌법제정 시 사용한 '민병대'는 예외 없이 "전체 국민의(the whole body of people)"이라는 수식어와 결부되어 있다는 주장도 있다"고 한다.

32 안경환, 위의 책, 581면 이하; "「미국연방수정헌법」 제2조에 의하면, 미국의 연방에서 거주하는 미국국민들이 총기들을 소지하고 사용할 수 있는 권리가 보장되기 때문에, 미국의 개개인들이 여러 총기를 소유·점유·운반 등을 할 수 있는 할 수 있는 있다고 보고 국민들의 개개인권익이 미국정부의 이익보다 우선해야 된다는 것이다"라고 한다.

33 Amendment II에 따른 권리가 주의 권리가 집단적 권리(collective right)라고 한다.

34 「미국연방헌법」 제1조 제8항 제15절.

35 「미국연방헌법」 제1조 제8항 제16절.

최종적인 유권해석기관인 미국연방대법원은 1789년 9월 25일 발의된「미국연방수정헌법」제2조에 대하여 1939년 Miller v. United States판결[37] 이후 명백한 입장[38]을 표명하고 있지는 않다. 그리고 1995년 United States v. Lopez사건[39]에서 동 헌법 제2조에 명시된 총기의 소유·점유 및 운반은 민병대유지에 필요한 한도 내에서 헌법상 권리를 부정하는 입장을 취하고 있지 않다. 이런 가운데에서 총기의 사용과 소지가「미국연방헌법」상의 권리로 인식하고 있는 상황 속에서 미국의회에서 총기에 대한 관리·감독을 강화하는 총기 사용 및 소지 규제관련법안의 통과가 현실화될 가능성은 높지 않다.

(2) 미국의 총기관리·감독 관련법제도 운영현황

1) 미국 총기제도의 역사적 전개

미국에서 1791년「수정헌법」제2조가 발효된 이후 미국에서의 총기에 대한 소지와 사용은「미국헌법」상의 권리로써 제한하지 못한다는 미국의 대법원의 입장에 따라 총기에 관한 관리·감독과 관련된 여러 법률이 제정됐다.

미국에서의 총기에 관한 관리·감독법규와 관련하여, 1934년「국가무기법(Natio-

36「미국연방헌법수정조항」제2조가 미국에서 제정된 원인은 국민으로부터 권한을 부여받은 연방의회가 권한에 의거하여 각 주에서 존치하고 있는 민병대를 해체하게 되면, 미국의 연방전제에 대해서 미국 주가 저항수단이 박탈될 우려를 방지하기 위한 것이다.

37 1939년 미국연방대법원의 United States v. Miller, 307 U.S. 174사건 ; "피고인 Miller는 1934년「총기규제법(National Firearms Act)」을 위반해 총기를 다른 주로 반출혐의로 기소됐다. 하급심은 Miller의 기소는「미국연방수정헌법」제2조의 위반을 판시했지만 대법원은「미국연방수정헌법」제2조는 상비군에 국토방위 의존할 필요가 없도록 민병대를 존치하게 된 목적이라고 한다. 따라서 민병대의 육성에 합리적으로 연관되지 아니한 무기소지는 동 조항의 보호를 받지 못한고 하며 Miller의 유죄를 인정했다"고 한다.

38 안경환,『미국헌법의 이해』, 박영사, 599면; "미국의 대법원은 수정헌법 제2조와 관련해서는, 개인이 미국의「수정헌법」제2조의 침해를 이유로 소송을 제기할 수 있는 원고적격을 가지는 가와 개인이 아닌 미국의 각 주만이 원고적격을 보유한다면 주가 개인에게 어떠한 보호를 부여하는가, 그리고 원고적격을 보유한다면 미국의 각 주가 개인에게 어떤 보호를 부여하는가, 미국의「수정헌법」제2조가 어떤 종류의 무기소장을 보호문제 등에 대해서 명확한 입장을 밝히지 않아 하급법원 간 혼란이 있다"라고 한다.

39 United State v. Lopez, S. Ct. 1624(1995); "「학교지역 총기휴대금지법안」이 채택 이후, 텍사스 주에서 12학년학생이 권총과 총탄을 들고 등교해 체포된 사건이 발생하였다. 그리고 학생은「학교지역 총기휴대금지법」이 위헌이라며 대법원에 항소를 제기했다. 1995년 미합중국 대 로페즈(United States v. Lopez) 판결에서 위헌판결로 인해 법안은 곧 폐기되었다. 동 판결에서 밝힌 판결이유를 살펴보면, 연방의회의 권한이 각 주에서 주법으로 규제하고 처벌할 수 있는 한계를 뛰어넘는 것은 부당하다는 것이다"라고 한다.

nal Firearms)」,[40] 1938년 연방총기법(Federal Firearm Act), 1968년 「총기규제법(Gun Control Act)」,[41] 1994년 「폭력범죄규제 및 법집행에 관한 법률(Violent Crime and Law Enforcement Act)」,[42] 1990년 「학교지역총기휴대금지법」,[43] 1994년 「공격형무기금지법」[44] 등의 여러 총기규제 및 관리·감독에 관한 여러 법률들이 여러 제정 및 개정의 과정을 거쳐서 오늘날에 이르렀다.

그 이후 2004년 뉴욕민주당의 선거자금모금행사에서 고어부통령은 총기남용을 방지하기 위해 총기구입자사진을 첨부한 면허증발급의무화한 입법필요성을 강조했다. 그러나 미국총기협회에서 제기된 소송으로 철회됐고, 연방정부와 주정부차원에서 수차례총기규제조치가 취해졌지만 결실을 맺지 못했다.

2) 미국 총기의 소지 및 사용 실태

미국에서 총기의 규제 즉 총기의 관리와 감독에 관련된 법규들이 효과적으로 총기의 관리와 감독에 있어서 그 역할을 하지 못한 결과, 미국에서는 총기구입이 운전면허 취득 정도로 용이하다. 이로 인해 약 18세 또는 약 20세가 되면 총기구매와 총기소

---

40 이성용, "민간 총기의 규제법리와 제도적 개선방안," 경찰법연구 제10권 제2호, 한국경찰법학회, 2012, 86면.

41 손영호, 앞의 책, 65면 이하; "1963년 케네디대통령, 1968년 케네디친동생인 로버트케네디상원의원, 마틴루터킹 목사 등 연이은 인사들의 암살사건으로 총기를 규제해야 한다는 여론이 확산됐다. 그 결과가 1968년 채택된 「총기규제법」으로 나타났다"라고 한다.

42 이성용, "민간 총기의 규제법리와 제도적 개선방안," 경찰법연구 제10권 제2호, 한국경찰법학회, 2012, 86-87면; "1994년 클린턴 대통령은 「폭력범죄규제 및 법집행에 관한 법률(Violent Crime and Law Enforcement Act」의 하부규정으로 이른바 「공격용무기금지연방법(Federal Assault Weapons Ban)」을 시행하였는데, 「공격용무기금지연방법(Federal Assault Weapons Ban)」은 특정 반자동 총기의 시민에 대한 판매를 금지했다"라고 한다.

43 손영호, 위의 책, 65면 이하; "1989년 1월 미국의 캘리포니아 주 스톡턴의 한 학교에서 AK-47 자동소총으로 무장한 범인이 운동장에서 놀고 있던 여러 학생들에게 총기를 난사한 사건으로 인하여 많은 사상자가 발생하였다. 이 사건으로 5명이 사망하고 29명이 부상을 당하였다. 이에 대한 대응 조치로 연방의회는 1990년 학교 구역의 경계선 안에서 총기의 소지와 사용을 금지하는 「학교지역 총기휴대금지법」을 제정하였다"고 한다.

44 손영호, 위의 책, 65면 이하; "1994년 미국의 연방의회는 폭력성 범죄를 통제하기 위한 목적으로 시효기간을 10년으로 한 소위 「공격무기금지법(Banning Assault Weapons)」을 제정하였다. 이것은 범죄자들이 종종 경찰들보다도 성능이 뛰어나고 강력한 무기를 사용하는 것을 막기 위한 조치였다. 동 법안은 「브래디법(Brady Law)」과 마찬가지로 시효기간이 10년으로 제한되어서 2004년 결국은 「브래디법」은 폐기되고 말았다"라고 한다.

지가 합법화이어서 편의점·마트 등에서도 총기구입이 용이하다. 그 결과, 미국가정 총기보유비율이 약 40% 이상이고 총기사고사망자는 인구 10만 명당 약 13.47명으로 세계에서 가장 높은 국가가 되었다.

(3) 미국에서 총기난사사고로 총기관리·감독강화법안 마련의 필요성 제기

1) 총기폭력방지운동에 의해 총기관리·감독강화 필요성 제기

미국에서는 전국에서 발생하는 총기난사사고로 인해 생명을 잃거나 신체에 위해를 입은 미국국민의 수가 해마다 끊임없이 발생하고 있음에 따라 비록 헌법적으로 총기소지를 개인의 권리로 인정하고 관련규제법규가 있지만 총기규제를 강화하기 위한 총기규제법안의 필요성이 제기되었다. 특히 총기사상자의 급증으로 인하여 총기로 인한 사고방지와 폭력방지 등을 요구하는 "총기폭력방지를 위한 브래디운동본부,"[45] "강력한 총기규제를 요구하는 100만 어머니 행진"[46] 등과 같은 총기의 소지 및 사용으로 인한 폭력방지운동을 계기로 총기 관리와 감독을 강화에 관한 법률의 제정 필요성이 제기됐다.

2) 학교총기사고를 계기로 총기소지 관리·감독강화법안 마련

미국에서 총기소지·사용규제, 즉 총기관리·감독강화법안이 마련된 계기는 일반거리나 우범지대가 아닌 학교에서 총기사고가 발생하면서 제기됐다.

이처럼 콜롬비아총기사건·버지니아택공대총기사건 등과 같이 심지어 학교에서도 총기사고로 많은 사상자가 발생하자 총기규제필요성이 제기되었다.

특히, 2012년 코네티컷샌디훅초등학교총기난사사건 등을 계기로 미국에서 총기규제강화움직임이 나타나면서 2013년에 총기규제강화법안이 마련되었다.

---

45 Newsis, "켈리포니아주, 총기규제법 실시 … 위협적 대상에 총기몰수신청가능," Newsis, 2014. 10. 01; "딸을 총기사고로 잃은 '총기폭력방지를 위한 브래디운동본부' 아만다 윌콕스는 현재 미국의 전 지역에서 총기사고로 인하여 끊임없이 발생한 사상자들을 사전에 미리 방지하기 위하여 가장 노력하고 있는 것은 캘리포니아주라고 말했다"고 한다.

46 손영호, 앞의 책, 70면; "더욱 강화된 총기규제법의 필요성이 제기된 것은 1999년 콜럼바인고등학교에서 발생한 총기난동사건이 발생한 직후인 5월 14일 어머니날에는 강력한 총기규제를 요구하는 '100만 어머니 행진'이 미국의 약 60개의 주요 도시들에서 동시에 진행되었다. 이러한 운동의 목적은 총기규제법안을 촉구하기 위한 것이다"고 한다.

3. 미국의 총기규제강화법안의 논의

(1) 미국의 총기규제강화법안의 내용

미국의 오바마행정부는 자신이 서명한 대통령 행정명령에 따르면, 미국의 연방정부가 범죄의 수사과정에서 수거한 무기에 대한 출처를 명확하게 확인하고, 총기이용자의 정신건강 상담사와 함께 무장경비원을 고용하는 학교에 인센티브지급에 대한 내용 등이 포함되었다. 아울러, 총기구입자의 신원을 확인할 수 이도록 했다. 이는 무허가 총기판매인으로부터 신원을 확인 받지 않고도 총기구입이 가능했던 기존 법에 대한 허점을 개선하기 위한 것이다.

(2) 미국의 총기규제강화법안에 대한 찬·반론

2003년 미국에서 제기되었던 총기규제강화와 관련된 법안에 대한 찬성입장을 살펴보면, 미국의 오바마 대통령은 총기규제를 강화하는 안 발표, 즉 거의 20년 만에 전면직으로 총기법을 개정에 국민이 동참해줄 것을 촉구했다.

반면에, 총기의 관리 및 감독강화법안에 대한 반대입장에 따르면, 「수정헌법」 제2조와 의회입법과정을 무시한다고 주장하며, 대통령의 총기규제에 관한 행정명령은 무기를 소지할 수 있는 헌법상 권리를 침해한다고 주장했다.

(3) 연방차원의 총기규제법안 무산

미국에서 무분별한 총기난사 등과 같은 총기사고 급증을 방지하기 위하여 연방차원의 총기의 관리와 감독법안을 마련해 상원의원에 표결을 맡겼지만, 총기규제를 위한 강화법안이 통과하지 못하고 구속력의 획득에 실패하였다.

비록, 미연방차원에서 총기의 관리와 감독 강화법안이 무산되었지만, 캘리포니아주 등 일부 주에서 무분별한 총기사고 급증을 방지함으로써 시민의 생명과 공공안전 유지를 위해 「총기규제법」[47]을 통과·실시하기에 이르렀다.

---

47 해당 「총기규제법」에 따르면, 총기사고를 발생할 우려가 있는 위협적인 사람들에 대해 일가친척이 총기몰수를 신청을 할 수 있도록 허용하는 내용을 담고 있다고 한다. 이러한 일종의 「총기규제법」은 미국 내에서 캘리포니아대학 부근에서 발생하였던 묻지마총격사건으로 인명피해가 발생한 이후 미국의 민주당의원들

4. 우리나라에의 시사점

미국에서의 총기규제실태와 총기관련법제도운영현황과 함께 특히 미국에서 끊임없이 발생하였던 총기난사 사고와 함께 논의되었던 미국의 총기규제법안과 관련 찬·반론, 미국에서의 끊임없는 총기사건 등은 최근 총기사고들이 끊임없이 발생하고 있는 우리나라에게 몇 가지 중요한 시사점들을 준다.

우선, 미국의 총기관리와 감독을 살펴보면, 한번 총기기준의 약화는 곧 바로 총기난사 등의 총기사고의 급격한 증가로 이어진다는 것을 볼 때, 총기제조·총기수입·총기소지허가 등에 대한 규제를 더욱더 강화하기 위하여 다양한 개선방안에 대한 논의와 사회적인 합의가 수반되어야 함을 알 수 있다.

두 번째, 미국의 헌법, 즉 「미국수정헌법」 제2조의 제정당시와 지금의 미국의 헌법현실이 그동안의 사회적 변화에 따라 분명 다름에도 불구하고, 미국헌법규범과 미국헌법현실 사이에 괴리가 있어 헌법규범의 실효성이 확보되는 규범적 헌법[48]이 가능하기가 어렵다는 점에서, 우리나라에서의 총기에 관한 관리와 감독에 있어서도 국가의 총기규제를 강화하는 한편 총기분야의 사회적 변화 등을 고려해 총기에 대한 효과적 관리·감독이 이루어져야 한다.

세 번째, 미국의 총기사고와 관련해서 살펴보면, 인터넷상에서의 불법적인 총기판매 등과 함께 불법적인 개조 등으로 인하여 총기가 일반 개인은 물론 범죄조직에게도 인도·사용되는 경우가 나타나는 것을 볼 때, 총기제조업자, 총기수입업자 등에 대한 관리와 감독 즉 규제를 강화하는 것과 함께 인터넷상에서 이루어지는 총기의 불법유통에 대한 규제가 더 강화되어야 불법적으로 제조 및 유통되는 총기로 인한 총기사고를 방지할 수 있음을 알 수 있다.

에 의하여 발의한 것이었다. 이러한 해당 「총기규제법」에 따라 캘리포니아주에서 그 이전에 해당지역의 경찰에게만 주어졌던 총기에 대한 몰수권한을 가족구성원에게까지 몰수신청을 할 수 있도록 했다.

48 Karl Loewenstein, Political Power and the Govenrmental Process, The University of Chicago Press, 1965, pp. 147-150; "규범적인 헌법(normative constitution)이 충분하게 확보되기 위해서는 국가와 사회의 구별을 전제로 사회의 독자적인 영역이 형성되어야 한다. 이와 함께 이러한 국가와 사회의 구별을 전제로 하여 자유와 경쟁의 원리에 입각한 자본주의가 안정적으로 확립될 수 있어야 한다. 아울러, 이러한 자유와 경쟁원리와 더불어 공존의 원리에 기초를 둔 합리적인 생활양식들도 함께 터득되어야 할 것이다"라고 한다.

네 번째, 3D첨단기술의 발전과 함께 총기를 만드는 기술[49]이 더욱 용이해짐에 따라 총기가 손쉽게 제조 및 유통될 수 있게 된 상황에서 해당사항에 대한 방지기술에 대한 연구·개발에 대한 관심과 함께 총기기술첨단화에 대한 관리·감독 및 엄격한 제조기준 마련 등이 필수적으로 수반되어야 한다.

다섯 번째, 총기의 제조·수입·소지·사용·임대 등이 증가한 만큼 비례해 총기관리·감독을 위해서는 경찰인력증원 등과 같은 방인이 실현되어야 함을 알 수 있다. 그리고 일정 수 이상 총기의 수가 증가하면 총기관리·감독시스템이 마련되더라도 총기관리·감독의 실효성이 미비함을 알 수 있다.[50]

여섯 번째, 미국에서 민간인이 합법적으로 총기가 가능함에도 불구하고 불법적인 총기생산 및 수입 등의 불법총기거래로 인해 총기사고위험성이 증대되고 있음을 알 수 있다. 이런 측면에서 볼 때, 합법적 총기소지 및 사용은 물론 불법적인 총기시스템에 대한 효과적인 점검시스템이 마련되어야 한다.

마지막으로, 총기사고는 한번 발생하면 생명의 위협은 물론 대량인명피해로 이어지기 때문에 사후구제방법 보다 사전예방적인 측면에서 총기관리·감독 관련법제도의 개선이 요망된다. 따라서 우리나라에서 총기소지·사용에 대한 관리·감독을 위해 입법된 「총포·도검·화약류등단속법」이 국민의 생명 및 기본권을 담보하고 총기사고 등으로 사회안전·질서가 침해되지 않도록 사전예방적인 측면에 중점을 두고 효과적으로 개선해야 할 필요성이 크다.

---

49 이상원/김정규, "화약류 안전관리 증진을 위한 총포도검화약류 등 단속법의 개선적 논의," 한국콘텐츠학회 논문지 제13권 제11호, 한국콘텐츠학회, 2013, 402면; "민간분야의 화약류기술개발과 함께 향후 다양한 형태의 폭발력을 활용하는 산업분야가 증가할 것으로 예상된다"라고 한다.

50 총기에 대한 소지와 사용은 총기의 사고와 비례한다는 점에서 우리나라에서 총기의 수와 그 사용빈도를 앞으로 감소시킬 수 있는 방안들에 대한 고려들이 수반되어야 한다.

Ⅳ. 우리나라 「총포·도검·화약류등단속법」상 총기관리·감독제도의 주요내용 분석과 문제점 검토

1. 우리나라 총기관리·감독의 실태

(1) 총기관리·감독의 부실한 실태

1) 우리나라에서 지금까지 허가된 총기수

현재 우리나라에서 소지가 허가된 총기는 약16만정을 넘어섰으며, 이중 공기총은 약9만정으로 개인이 관리하는 공기총은 약5만정, 경찰이 보관하는 공기총은 약 3만정이다.[51] 이와 같이 우리나라에서 해마다 허가된 총기의 수가 계속 증가하여 이미 약 16만정을 넘어섰으며, 허가된 총기의 증가와 함께 총기로 인한 총기살인·총기협박·총기난사·총기자살 등 사고도 증가하였다.

2) 끊임없이 지속되는 총기난사·살인사건

최근 10년 동안 우리나라에서 발생한 세종시총기난사사건·화성시총기사고·옥천총기사건·김포총기사고 등 이외에도 많은 총기사건들[52]이 계속 발생하면서 총기사고에 대한 우려가 증폭되고 있다. 이와 같이 국내에서 총기수가 증가하는 상황에서 끊임없이 총기살인·협박사건들도 함께 증대되었다.

---

51 조재현, "5.5㎜미만 공기총까지 영치 … 국민의 기본권 침해," 머니투데이뉴스, 2015. 03. 24; "경찰청에 따르면, 우리나라에서 전국적으로 현재 개인에게 소지와 사용이 허가된 총기는 1월말 기준 약 16만3664정이다. 이 중에서 공기총은 약 9만6295정으로 개인이 관리하는 공기총은 약 5만9880정, 경찰이 보관하는 공기총은 약 3만6415정이다"라고 한다.

52 김봉수, 위의 기사, 2015. 02. 25 참조; "2013년 평창에서 60대 남성이 내연녀에 사제총난사하다 체포됐다. 2013년 대구시주택가에서 30대 남자가 사제총을 발사해 시민과 경찰 3명이 다쳤다. 2013년 천안에서 40대 수배범이 도심에서 경찰과 총격전을 벌인 후 체포됐다. 2012년 용인에서 50대 남성이 상속문제로 다투다 총격가해 1명이 사망했다. 2012년 서산에서 30대 남성이 직장동료들에게 엽총으로 난사하여 1명이 사망하였다. 2011년 파주에서 60대 남성이 치정관계복수를 위해 총격가해 2명이 사망에 이르렀다. 2008년 화성에서 60대 남성이 엽총으로 동생가족들을 쏴 2명이 숨졌다. 2005년 파주에서 60대 남성이 상속유산에 불만을 품고 설날모인가족에 총격가하여 3명이 사망했다"고 한다.

3) 총기를 이용한 강력범죄사건 증가추이

특히, 최근 연이어 발생한 총기사건에서 맡겨 놓은 총기를 경찰지구대에서 수렵을 이유로 출고한 뒤 살해사건이 발생했다는 점에서 허술한 총기관리실태도 비판받는 가운데 총기를 이용한 강력범죄도 증가하고 있는 추세[53]이다.

(2) 부실한 총기관리·감독에 따른 기본권침해 및 공공안전 위험성 증대

최근의 연이은 총기사고로 총기안전관리를 강화하겠다고 밝혔지만 국민은 우리나라가 더 이상 총기안전지대가 아니라고 하며 불안해하고 있다. 더욱이 불법총기에 대한 총기류의 폐해는 예전부터 계속 지적되고 있으며, 무엇보다 최근 기술의 발전으로 인하여 용이하게 총기를 제작할 수 있는 상황이 되면서 불법유통총기,[54] 불법총기 제작 등과 같이 환경이 변화하고 있지만 총기의 관리와 감독은 이에 적절하게 대응하지 못함에 따라 총기사고로 인해 국민의 생명권 등 기본권과 공공안정·사회질서유지에 대한 침해위험성이 증대됐다.

2. 「총포·도검·화약류등단속법」상 총기관리·감독관련주요내용 분석

(1) 입법목적

「총포·도검·화약류등단속법」은 총포·도검·화약류·분사기·전자충격기·석궁의 제조·판매·임대·운반·소지·사용과 그 밖에 안전관리에 관한사항을 정해 총포·도검·화약류·분사기·전자충격기·석궁으로 인한 위험과 그 재해를 미리 방지함으로써 공공안전의 유지에 이바지함을 목적으로 입법되었으며, 동법 제2조부터 제76조에서 총포제조·판매, 총포소지·사용, 총포관리, 총포감독, 총포·화학안전기술협회, 보칙 및 벌칙들을 명시하고 있다.

---

53 이재훈/조승현, "총기살인은 미국이야기? 한국도 한해평균 16.1건," 한겨레, 2015. 02. 27; "2015년 2월 27일 '경찰청 범죄 통계'를 보면, 자료가 기록되기 시작한 1994년부터 통계가 최종 집계된 2013년까지 한국에서 모두 약 322건 총기살인사건들이 발생하였다. 이러한 총기사고는 한해 평균 약 16.1건이다. 1994년 이후 총기살인사건은 줄어들다가 2000년대 초반 다시 조금씩 늘어나는 추세를 보였다. 2002년 약 20건 발생했고, 2005년에는 약 27건으로 약 20년 동안 두 번째로 많은 사건들이 발생한 해로 기록됐다"고 한다.

54 조병인, "불법 총기류, 폐해 심각해진다," 새물결 제180호, 1996, 108면 이하 참조.

(2) 총기의 제조 · 판매 및 소지 · 사용

「총포 · 도검 · 화약류등단속법」은 "총기의 제조 · 판매"와 관련하여, 총기제조업의 허가, 총기제조업자의 지위승계, 제조업자의 결격사유, 판매업의 허가, 예술품용 총기의 임대업허가, 판매업자 및 임대업자의 결격사유, 옥외에서의 총기판매 · 임대, 총기에 대한 광고 금지 등에 관하여 규정하고 있다.[55]

(3) 총기의 관리 · 감독 및 총포 · 화학안전기술협회

「총포 · 도검 · 화약류등단속법」은 "총기의 관리"와 관련하여, 총기류저장, 총기류저장소설치허가, 총기류저장소설치자의 지위승계, 화학류 등 총기류운반, 총기제조보안책임자 선임, 총기제조보안책임자 · 화약류 등 총기관리보안책임자면허, 총기류제조 · 관리보안책임자 결격사유 등을 언급하고 있다.[56]

(4) 보칙 및 벌칙

「총포 · 도검 · 화약류등단속법」은 총포사고로부터 공공안정을 확보하기 위한 '벌칙'과 관련하여 벌칙, 과태료, 형벌과, 양벌규정들 등을 명시하고 있다.

3. 「총포 · 도검 · 화약류등단속법」상 총기관리 · 감독제도 문제점 검토

(1) 총기출고 이전 문제점

총기출고 이전, 「총포 · 도검 · 화약류등단속법」상 총기관리 · 감독제도 문제점을 살펴보면, 우선, 사업 · 취급 · 휴업 · 폐업 등 허가 · 신고 관련 문제점들과 관련하여, 총기사업자들의 허가기준 부실, 허술한 총기취급기준들, 총기휴업 · 총기사업자폐업

---

55 아울러 동법은 "총포의 소지 · 사용"과 관련하여, 총포소지금지, 모의총포 제조 · 판매 · 소지의 금지, 총기소지에 대한 허가, 총기사용에 대한 결격사유, 일시 출국과 입국을 하는 사람에 대한 총기허가의 특칙 등을 여러 총기관련규정에 대하여 명시하고 있다.

56 「총포 · 도검 · 화약류등단속법」은 "총기의 감독"과 관련하여, 총기에 대한 완성검사, 총기에 대한 출입 · 검사, 총기제조업자들 등에 대한 행정처분, 행정처분효과 승계, 총기소지허가에 관한 행정처분, 청문, 공공의 안전 등과 관련하여 여러 규정들이 명시됐다.

시 총기처분기준 미약 등의 문제들이 노정되고 있다.

이외에도 '총기제조 · 수입' 등과 관련하여, 총기허가기준들 미약, 총기사고를 방지하기 위한 신고기준 미약, 민간에 판매되는 총기제조 제한규정 미약, 총기수입규제의 불충분, 총기보관을 우한 장소 부족[57] 등의 문제들이 있다.

(2) 총기출고 이후 문제점

총기출고 과정, 「총포 · 도검 · 화약류등단속법」 상 총기관리감독제도 문제점들을 살펴보면, 불법적인 총기광고방지 미흡, 합법적인 총기광고규제의 부족, 총기임대기준의 강화, 부적절한의 총기판매기준, 불투명한 총기적재와 운반, 허술한 총기저장, 부실한 총기폐기단계 등의 문제들이 발생하고 있다.[58]

4. 총포사고 급증하고 있는 우리나라에서 총기사고예방대책 필요성 증대

(1) 급증하는 총기사고의 사전예방을 위한 총기관련법제도 개선필요성 급증

최근 연달아 발생한 총기난사 등과 같은 사고로 인하여 국민의 기본권과 공공의 안전 및 질서가 무분별하게 침해되는 것을 막기 위해서는 현재의 관리체계를 대폭 강화해야 한다. 이에 따라 우리나라에서 급증하는 총기사고의 사전예방을 위한 총기관련법제도에 대한 개선의 필요성이 더욱 급증하였다.

---

57 안영국, "총기관리강화한다더니 … 거둬도 둘곳 없다," 경기일보, 2015. 03. 20; "경기경찰청서에 영치해야 할 총기는 엽총 약 7천정에 불과했지만 공기총 약 1만5천정 · 산업총 · 가스총 등 약 4천정 등이 늘면서 약 2만6천정으로 증가하였다. 여기에 탄약이 추가되면서 총기류일제점검에 착수한 경기경찰청에서 밝힌 점검실적은 전체총기류의 5.6%에 그친 약 1천500정에 불과하며, 이러한 것도 단지 엽총에만 한정되어 있을 뿐이다"라고 한다.

58 총기의 관리와 감독과 관련하여 더욱 큰 문제는 현행의 총기관련규정에 따라 폭력성향범죄경력자가 수렵목적으로 총기를 적법출고 해당총기를 살해도구로 사용한다면 규정상 막을 방법이 없다. 아울러, 미흡한 총기소지기준, 부적절한 총기사용자 제한규정, 총기출고 후 부실한 총기양도 · 양수, 총기수수단계 부실관리 · 감독 등 문제가 심각하다.

(2) 끊임없이 계속되는 총기살인사건으로 국민의 총기사고예방대책마련 요청

1) 입법부의 총기관리 · 감독 강화를 위한 총기관련법제도 개선필요성 점증

국민의 대표기관인 입법부는 안전한 총기이용환경조성을 통한 국민의 기본권 보장을 위해 총기관련법제도를 개선해야 할 필요성이 점증되고 있다. 무엇보다 헌법상 보장되고 있는 국민의 생명권은 한번 침해되면 영원히 회복할 수 없으므로 생명권이라는 기본권의 침해가 발생하기 전에 보호될 수 있도록 총기관련제도의 개선을 통한 안전한 총기이용환경 조성이 필수적이다.

2) 「총포 · 도검 · 화약류등단속법」상 총기관리 · 감독제도의 개선방안 마련 요망

국민의 기본권보장을 위한 입법행위를 담당하는 입법부가 안전한 총기이용환경 조성 및 관련법제도 개선을 위하여 총기관련법제도를 개선해야 한다.

이에 따라 입법기관은 「총포 · 도검 · 화약류등단속법」상 총기관리 · 감독제도 개선을 통하여 최근 발생한 총기난사사건을 방지함으로써 국민의 생명과 기본권을 효과적으로 보호할 종합적 법제도를 마련해야 함이 요망되고 있다.

V. 우리나라 「총포 · 도검 · 화약류등단속법」상 총기관리 · 감독제도상의 합리적인 개선방안의 방향과 내용

1. 총기관리 · 감독의 방향

(1) 총기관리 · 감독의 사전예방적인 대책 마련 및 강화 시급

총기관련사건을 미연에 방지함으로써 국민이 총기를 사용한 살인 · 위협 등의 위험으로부터 보호되어야 한다. 특히 총기사고는 살인 등의 강력범죄로 이어지는 경우가 많으므로 생명과 재산권 등과 같은 국민의 기본적인 인권을 보호하기 위하여 사전예방적인 대책[59]이 마련되어야 할 필요성이 크다.

무엇보다 생명권은 한번 잃으면 영원히 회복할 수 없으므로 총기사고로부터 사후적인 생명권 구제수단은 사실상 실효성이 없으므로 사전예방적인 차원에서 총기를 적절하게 관리·감독함으로써 생명권을 보장하는 것이 매우 중요하다. 이를 위해서는 총기의 관리와 감독에 있어서 사전예방적인 대책을 마련하는 것이 매우 시급하다. 따라서 「총포·도검·화약류등단속법」 상 총기의 관리와 감독에 있어서 사전예방적인 차원에서 개선방안을 고려해야 한다.

(2) 총기관리·감독의 중장기적인 계획수립마련 필요성 점증

최근 연이어 발생하고 있는 총기난사로 인하여 헌법상 보장된 국민의 생명권 등이 침해되었던 여러 사건들이 발생한 만큼, 총기의 관리·감독 즉 총기의 규제에 대한 중장기적인 계획수립을 마련해야할 필요성이 점증되었다.

따라서 중장기적인 안목에서 「총포·도검·화약류등단속법」 상 총기의 관리와 감독에 관한 제도를 종합적·체계적으로 개선하기 위하여 노정되고 있는 여러 총기관련 문제점들을 해결방안이 마련될 수 있도록 노력해야 한다.

2. 총기관리·감독의 개선 시 고려해야할 사항

(1) 총기관리·감독 기준강화 및 데이터베이스 마련

1) 총기관리·감독 및 수렵면허기준 강화

「총포·도검·화약류등단속법」 상 총기관리·감독제도의 총기관리·감독과 관련하여, 사업·취급·휴업·폐업 등 허가·신고기준이 강화되어야 한다. 특히, 총기허가·소지 등 기준을 강화하고 경찰에 신고가 된 전력이 있는 자에게 총기허가를 내주지 않도록 엄격히 심의해야 한다. 또한 수렵에 사용되는 총기입·출고제한기준강화는 물론 총기소지자사고가능성 여부[60]를 판단될 수 있도록 수렵면허시험제도가

---

59 Sumudu A. Atapattu, 『Emerging Principle of International Environmental』, Transnational Publishers Ardsley, 2006, p. 278 이하 참조 ; 사전예방적인 차원에서의 피해발생 전 취하는 관련된 예방계획들과 사전조치들은 해당사건이 발생된 이후에 행해지는 사후처리위주의 방식들보다 시간·비용·인적 등의 다양한 측면들에서 있어서 매우 효과적이다.

60 일요신문, "잇따른 총기난사사건 재발 방지, 총포·도검·화약류 등 단속법 강화부터," 일요신문, 2015. 03. 05; "현행 수렵면허 취득은 각 지자체에서 실시하는 수렵면허의 시험에서 관련 법률들, 야생동물의 보호,

개선되어야 한다. 아울러, "총기허가연령상향조정"·"폭력성향범죄자소지제한 등 엄격한 총기소지 관련규정마련"·"모든 총기에 GPS등 추적장치 부착"·"총기휴대에 더 엄격한 제한조치마련" 등과 관련해 민간부문에서 소지·사용되는 총기관리·감독기준을 강화해야 한다.

2) 총기데이터베이스 마련

「총포·도검·화약류등단속법」상 총기관리감독제도의 총기데이터베이스와 관련하여, 제조·수입·광고·임대 및 판매단계는 물론 소지·사용·양도·양수 및 수수단계, 적재·운반·저장·갱신 등에서 마련해야 한다. 이를 통하여 총기난사 등과 같은 인명사고를 유발하는 총기사고를 미리 예방하기 위한 총기허가기준 및 자격여부 등의 검토에 활용할 필요가 있다. 아울러, 총기입·출고단축, 실탄구매 및 보관제한 등에 대한 상세한 데이터베이스를 마련함으로써 부실한 총기사고들을 사전에 예방할 수 있도록 노력해야 한다.

3) 총기총량제 도입 검토 및 모의총기 관리·감독 강화

민간부문에서 총기의 사용자가 급격하게 발생할 경우 경찰행정력이 범죄예방·범인검거·교통질서정리 등 많은 업무를 함께 하면서 총기의 소지와 사용에 대한 관리와 감독이 용이하지 않는 문제점들이 발생될 수밖에 없다.

따라서 총기사고를 예방하기 위해 「총포·도검·화약류등단속법」상 총기의 사용에 있어 일정수를 넘지 않도록 전국적으로 민간인이 소지할 수 있는 총기와 그 사용빈도를 어느 정도 제한함으로써 생명권 등 헌법상 국민에게 보장된 기본권을 심각히 침해될 수 있는 사건들을 방지해야 할 필요가 크다.

모의총포의 제조·판매·소지의 금지에 관하여 규정하고 있는 「총포·도검·화약류등단속법」 제11조에 따르면, 누구든지 총포와 아주 비슷하게 보이는 것으로서 모

수렵도구의 사용, 안전사고의 예방 등 각각 10문제씩인 4과목으로 이뤄져 평균 60점 이상을 받으면 되는 등 운전면허보다 쉽다는 지적이 있다. 또한, 시험 합격 후에는 환경부에서 지정한 전문기관에서 하루에 4시간 강습을 받으면 면허를 취득할 수 있기 때문에 총기의 위험성을 고려하여 시험, 실습 등 총기를 이용한 수렵 관련 전 과정이 수정되어야 한다는 세간의 목소리가 높다"고 한다.

의총기를 제조·판매 또는 소지하여서는 아니 된다.[61] 그러나, 모의총기[62]에 대한 총기 관련 사고들도 해마다 꾸준히 발생하고 있는 점에서 모의총기에 대한 관리와 감독이 앞으로 더욱더 강화되어야 할 것이다.

(2) 총기관리·감독 인력증원 및 민간단체와의 협력증대

1) 총기관리·감독인력 증원

「총포·도검·화약류등단속법」상 총기관리·감독제도에서 총기관리·감독인력 증원에 관한 사항이 마련되어야 한다. 그리고 총기를 반출 이후에도 관리·감독을 강화해야 한다는 지적이 나온다. 특히 불법적인 총기의 반입과 제조 등과 같은 사항들을 관리하고 감독할 인력이 부족[63]하기 때문에 총기관리·감독인력을 안정적으로 확보되기 위하여 관련인력의 증원이 요망된다.

2) 민간단체와의 협력증대

오늘날 경찰행정 등의 행정으로 처리할 과제가 심화되는 상황에서 「총포·도검·화약류등단속법」상 총기관리·감독제도에서 민간단체와의 협력을 강화함으로써 불법총기·총기난사 등과 같은 총기사고를 방지해야 한다. 이에 따라 총기가 반출한 이후 상황을 민간단체와의 협력을 통해 실시간으로 효과적으로 감시할 수 있는 체계와 관련 법률에 대한 실질적 개선대책이 시급하다. 아울러 수렵기간 동안 총기소지자와 연락체계구축방안이 필요하다.

---

61 다만, 수출을 위한 목적으로 하는 모의총포를 제조·판매 또는 소지하는 경우에는 그러하지 아니하다. 즉 수출목적의 경우는 모의총포를 제조·판매 또는 소지할 수 있다.

62 「총포·도검·화약류 등 단속법 시행령」 제13조 및 제14조에 따르면, "'모의총기'란 총기와 유사하게 보이는 것으로 '금속 또는 금속이외의 소재를 이용하여 만들어진 것으로 모양이 총기와 비슷하면서 범죄에 악용될 소지가 현저한 것', '금속 또는 금속이외의 소재를 이용하여 만들어진 것으로 금속 또는 금속외의 물체를 발사하거나 소리·불꽃을 내는 것 중 인명·신체에 위해가할 우려 있는 것을 의미한다"라고 명시하고 있다.

63 서울신문, "5년간 자진신고 불법총기류 2만2천여정," 서울신문, 2014. 09. 12; "현재 경찰청에서 총기를 담당하고 인력들은 총 309명으로, 1인당 관리와 감독을 해야 하는 총기들이 무려 평균 약 523정에 달하고 있어 총기의 적절한 관리와 효과적인 감독에 어려움이 매우 크고, 총기의 집중적인 단속을 제대로 시행하기도 어려운 실정이다"고 한다.

3) 총기출고 시 보증인 동행 및 심리검사

「총포·도검·화약류등단속법」상 총기관리·감독제도에서 총기와 관련하여, 경찰관에서 총기를 출고할 경우 보증인 동행, 총기사용자 정신감정서 제출 등이 이루어져야 한다. 특히, 총기의 관리·감독여부에 따라 국민의 생명과 안전에 미치는 영향이 매우 크기 때문에 총기출고 시 보증인 동행 및 심리검사서 제출 등을 통하여 정치한 총기의 관리·감독체계를 마련해야 한다.

(3) 총기관련 범죄처벌 및 일체점검 강화

1) 총기를 이용한 범죄의 처벌과 형량 강화

「총포·도검·화약류등단속법」상 총기관리·감독제도에서 총기관련 범죄처벌을 더욱 강화하여 총기난사 등으로 인한 국민의 생명권 침해사례를 최대한 예방할 수 있도록 해야 한다. 이를 위해 총기를 사용한 범죄에 대한 형량 등의 처벌을 더욱 상향조정하고 강화해야 할 것이다. 특히, 경미한 처벌은 또 다른 총기관련 범죄를 예방할 수 있는 기회를 놓칠 수 있다. 따라서 총기와 관련된 범죄행위에 대한 형사적 처벌 및 과태료의 강화가 요망된다.

2) 총기관련 일체점검과 총기보관공간 확대

「총포·도검·화약류등단속법」상 총기관리·감독제도에서 총기의 불법적인 소지·양도·양수·제조 등에 대한 관리와 감독을 대폭 강화해야 한다. 또한 총기제조사의 휴업과 폐업과정에서 발생할 수 있는 다량의 총기유출을 방지하기 위하여 부실한 총기관리·감독실태[64]를 방지하기 위하여 앞으로 정기적인 또는 비정기적인 총기일체점검을 현재보다 더 강화해야 할 것이다.

아울러, 앞에서 우리나라 총기관련실태를 살펴보았듯이, 총기사고예방을 위한 총기보관공간이 부족함에 따라 총기류의 일제점검이 효과적으로 이루어지고 있지 않다. 이러한 점에서 총기의 일제점검을 강화하는 동시에 총기보관공간을 확보하고, 보관공간의 확보를 위한 재정지원이 확충되어야 한다.

---

64 서울신문, 앞의 기사, 2014. 09. 12; "경찰청이 매년 실시하는 총기류점검현황을 보면 2010년부터 2014년 6월까지 총 5천114정이 점검을 받지 않은 것으로 나타났다"고 한다.

3) 불법총기의 자진신고와 수입 · 제작 · 유통처벌 강화

불법총기류에 관하여 자진신고제도를 통하여 일정한 기간이 아닌 통상적으로 신고제도를 운영하여 불법총기류의 제작, 반입, 유통 등을 사전에 방지할 필요성이 크다. 아울러, 미국의 총기규제 현실에서도 살펴보았듯이, 미국에서 다른 나라로부터 들여오는 불법적인 총의 숫자는 총기사고로 이어진다는 점에서 우리나라에서 불법총기수입과 제작 및 유통에 대한 관리와 감독의 필요성은 매우 크다. 더욱이 우리나라에서 최근 몇 년간 동안 자진하여 신고가 된 불법총기류의 수가 무려 약 2만정[65]이 넘게 집계되었다는 사실에서 비추어 볼 때, 앞으로 우리나라에서 총기사건범죄 예방의 측면에서 불법총기수입 · 제작 및 유통에 대한 감독과 처벌이 더 강화해 불법적으로 수입 · 제작 및 유통이 된 총기로 인한 강력범죄와 총기사고를 사전 방지해야 한다.

(4) 총기사고예방 · 재발방지를 위한 홍보 및 교육 강화

1) 총기관련 다양한 홍보수단 마련

「총포 · 도검 · 화약류등단속법」상 총기에 대한 관리와 감독과 관련된 제도와 관련하여 총기관리에 대한 다양한 홍보수단이 마련되고 확대되어야 한다.

이를 위하여 총기관리에 관련된 교육을 위한 네트워크를 활성화해야 한다. 아울러, 총기교육과 관련해, 대상별 · 지역별 교육홍보대책이 마련해야 한다.

2) 총기관련 내실 있는 교육 마련

「총포 · 도검 · 화약류등단속법」상 총기관리 · 감독제도에서 총기와 관련하여 내실 있는 총기교육의 기회가 확대되어야 한다. 무엇보다 총기관련교육이 활성화되기 위해서는 우선, 총기의 관리 및 감독에 관한 부족한 교육의 기회확대를 위한 관련 시설 마련이 필요하다. 이를 위해 다종다양한 총기교육시설을 운영하고 지역 단위의 소규

65 서울신문, 위의 기사 참조, 2014. 09. 12; "최근 5년간 자진하여 신고가 된 불법 총기류가 2만 2천 여정에 달하는 것으로 집계됐다. 경찰청으로부터 제출받은 자료에 따르면 2010년부터 2014년 8월말까지 공기총 약 7천664정, 엽총 약 766정, 권총 약 110정, 소총 약 46정 등 총 약 2만2천200정의 불법적인 총기류들에 대한 신고가 되었다고 했다. 이는 우리나라에서 불법총기가 연평균 약 4천440정 꼴로 회수되고 있는 셈이다"라고 하였다.

모 총기교육편의 시설을 증대하고, 기존의 총기교육을 위한 시설들을 활성화해 총기교육에 대한 수용을 확대해야 한다.

3) 수렵승인 받은 자를 대상으로 교육과 홍보 강화

현재 「야생생물 보호 및 관리에 관한 법률」 제20조에 따르면, "총포의 소지허가를 받았더라도 수렵을 하려면 동법에 따른 자격을 갖추어야 한다"고 규정[66]하고 있음에도 불구하고 수렵이 허가된 총기로 인한 사고가 많이 증가하고 있는 만큼, 수렵을 하기 이전에 필수적으로 수렵에 사용하는 총기안전교육은 물론 총기관련법규위반[67]에 대한 숙지를 위하여 교육이 수반되어야 한다.

3. 안전한 총기관리·감독환경조성 및 공공안전·국민기본권 보호강화

(1) 총기관리·감독 관련법제도개선을 통한 공공안전 확보 및 사회질서 유지

현행 총기관리·감독 관련법제도인 「총포·도검·화약류 등 단속법」이 따라서 총기관리·감독 시스템에 대한 적절한 개선을 통하여 사회 및 공공의 안전을 담보하고 공공질서의 지속적인 유지하기 위하여 노력해야 할 것이다.

무엇보다 우리 헌법 제37조에서 언급한 국가안전보장·질서유지 또는 공공복리 등의 유지·확보라는 목적달성을 위해서는 법률로써 국민의 기본권을 제한할 수 있다.[68] 이러한 측면에서 볼 때, 「총포·도검·화약류 등 단속법」에 대한 입법적인 개선

---

66 「야생생물 보호 및 관리에 관한 법률」 제20조에 의하면, 수렵면허증을 취득하고 수렵보험에도 가입하고, 수렵장 설정한 시장·군수 또는 구청장으로부터 수렵승인을 받아야만 비로소 수렵허가해당지역에서 멧돼지, 고라니, 노루 등에 대한 수렵이 가능하다.

67 예를 들어, 유해한 야생동물을 포획한 자는 환경부령으로 정하는 바에 따라서 유해야생동물포획결과 시장·군수·구청장에게 신고를 이행해야 하는 점, 수렵 후 수렵한 날부터 5일 이내 포획한 야생동물종류·수량 및 포획장소 등 시·군 또는 구청에 신고를 해야 한다는 점, 위험물품을 허가받은 용도 외 사용을 금지하고 있는데 위반 시 2년 이하징역이나 500만 원 이하의 벌금에 처한 다는 점 등에 관한 규정들을 명시하고 있다.

68 성낙인, 『헌법학』, 법문사, 2012, 370-373면; "헌법 제37조 제2항에서의 '국가안전보장'이라는 개념은 국가의 존립과 헌법의 기본질서의 유지를 포함하는 개념이다. 동법 동조 동항에서 명시하고 있는 '질서유지'란 용어는 사회공공의 안녕질서의 유지해야 한다는 것을 의미하고 있다. 이와 함께 '공공복리'란 현대사회복지국가의 헌법적 이념을 적극적으로 구현하기 위하여 사회구성원 전체를 위한 공공의 이익을 말한다"라고

을 이행하여 최근 끊임없이 발생하는 총기살인 · 총기협박 등의 총기사건들을 사전에 예방함으로써 국민의 생명 등 기본권 보장은 물론 사회공공의 안녕질서를 유지하는 데 이바지하도록 해야 한다.

(2) 안전한 총기관리 · 감독환경조성을 통한 국민의 생명 및 기본권 보호강화

「총포 · 도검 · 화약류 등 단속법」상의 문제점을 입법적 차원에서 개선함으로써 총기살인 · 총기협박 · 총기난사가 없는 안전한 총기관리 · 감독환경을 조성함으로써 국민의 기본권보장은 물론 인간의 존엄에 기초한 생명권과 국민 기본권이 총기취급자 등의 제3자로부터 침해되지 않도록 보호해야 한다.

이러한 목적달성 통하여 헌법상 보장되고 있는 국민의 생명권, 즉 한번 침해되어 박탈되면 다시 원래의 상태인 원상회복 될 수 없는 기본권으로 "인간의 생존본능과 존재목적에 바탕을 둔 선험적이고 자연법적인 권리이자 헌법에 규정된 모든 기본권의 전제로서 기능하는 기본권 중의 기본권"[69]인 국민의 생명에 관한 권리인 생명권의 보호함을 비롯하여 총기사고로 침해될 가능성이 재산권 등과 같은 국민의 기본권에 대한 보호를 강화해야 할 것이다.

Ⅵ. 맺음말

최근 연초부터 세종시총기사건 · 화성시총기사건 · 김포시총기사건 등에서 민간인의 엽총난사로 인하여 사망자와 부상자가 발생하는 사건이 발생하면서 총기사고로 인한 사상자가 증가함에 따라 총기의 부실한 관리 · 감독에 대한 우려가 점차 증대됐다. 이처럼 경찰통계에서도 우리사회에서도 총기로 인한 강력사건이 매년 계속 일어나고 있음을 알 수 있듯이 우리나라에서 총기난사 · 살인사건이 끊임없이 발생하고

한다.

69 양건, 『헌법강의』, 법문사, 2009, 291-293면; "국민은 우리 대한민국헌법상 보장되고 있는 생명을 유지하고 보호받을 수 있는 권리를 가지며, 이러한 헌법상 보장된 생명권은 인간의 존엄에 기초한 것으로써 모든 인간은 생명권의 주체가 되며, 국가는 헌법 제10조 등을 근거로 하여 국민들의 생명권이라는 기본권을 보호할 의무가 있다"라고 한다.

있다. 따라서 헌법상 보장된 국민의 생명권을 보장하는 것을 비롯하여 총기사고로 인한 사회적 비용을 감축하고 국민들의 안전과 관련된 중대한 사안으로 총기관리·감독의 필요성이 크다.

무엇보다 총기는 생명침해, 총기사고 등의 위험성이 상존하는 물질로서 안전을 위해 적절한 관리와 감독이 필요하지만 총기와 관련된 안전사고와 범죄악용 사례가 전국적으로 계속 발생하면서 그 위험성은 증대되는 추세이다.

그럼에도 불구하고 우리나라에서 총기에 대한 불충분한 관리와 부실한 감독으로 인해 최근에 발생한 총기난사사건, 총기사망사건 등의 사고를 방지하지 못함에 따라 관련법제도의 운영에 있어 여러 문제점들이 노정되고 있다.

이에 따라 최근 발생한 총기난사, 총기사망사건 등과 같은 총기강력범죄를 예방하기 위하여 우리나라에서 「총포·도검·화약류 등 단속법」이 존치함에도 불구하고 최근총기사고가 끊이지 않고 발생하고 있음에 따라 해당 법률상의 총기관리·감독제도에 대한 재검토 및 개선의 필요성이 요구되고 있다.

이를 위하여 미국에서 총기에 대한 관리·감독 실태와 관련법제도를 검토함으로써 앞으로 우리 총기관련법제인 「총포·도검·화약류 등 단속법」에 대한 사전예방적인 측면의 합리적인 개선방안을 모색하기 위한 시사점을 분석하고 이를 통하여 우리나라 관련법제도의 개선방향을 살펴볼 필요가 있다.

그러므로 총기관리·감독 관련법인 「총포·도검·화약류 등 단속법」상의 검토와 적절한 개선방안 마련을 통하여 국민의 생명 등 기본권을 보호하는 동시에 국가의 공공안전 확보와 함께 사회질서를 안정적으로 유지해야 할 것이다. 즉 「총포·도검·화약류 등 단속법」이 최근 끊임없이 발생하고 있는 총기로 인한 총기난사·총기살인 등과 같은 총기범죄행위 및 사고로부터 생명 등 국민의 기본권을 보호할 수 있는 안정적인 제도로 정착될 수 있도록 총기 관리·감독을 강화함으로써 안전한 총기이용환경을 조성해야 한다.

참고문헌

1. 국내문헌

김백유, 『헌법학(II)』, 조은, 2010.

권영성, 『헌법학원론』, 법문사, 2010.

성낙인, 『헌법학』, 법문사, 2012.

손영호, 『미국의 총기문화』, 살림, 2009.

______, "미국 연방헌법 수정조항 제2조," 미국학논집 제45권 제2호, 한국아메리카학회, 2013.

정태호, "기본권보호의무," 현대공법의 재조명, 고려대학교 법학연구소, 1997.

조병인, "불법 총기류, 폐해 심각해진다," 새물결 제180호, 1996.

안경환, 『미국헌법의 이해』, 박영사, 2014.

양 건, 『헌법강의』, 법문사, 2009.

윤명선, 『미국헌법과 통치구조』, 유스북, 2006.

이상원/김정규, "화약류 안전관리 증진을 위한 총포도검화약류 등 단속법의 개선적 논의," 한국콘텐츠학회논문지 제13권 제11호, 한국콘텐츠학회, 2013.

이성용, "민간 총기의 규제법리와 제도적 개선방안," 경찰법연구 제10권 제2호, 한국경찰법학회, 2012.

2. 외국문헌

Sumudu A. Atapattu, *Emerging Principle of International Environmental*, Transnational Publishers Ardsley, 2006.

Don B. Kates Jr., "Handgun Prohibition and the Original Meaning of the Second Amendment," 82 *Mich. L. Rev.* 204, 1983.

Larry Gerber, *The Second Amendment: The Right to Bear Arms*, The Rosen Publishing Group Inc., 2011.

Schneider Hans, Gesetzgebung, 3. neu Bearbeitete und erweiterte Auflage., Lehr- und Handbuch, 2002.

Richard Hofstadter, "America as a Gun Culture," *American Heritage Magazine* October, 1970.

Philip J. Cook/Jens Ludwig, *Evaluation Gun Policy: Effects on Crime and Violence*, The

Brookings Institution, 2003.

Stephen P. Halbrook, *The Founders' Second Amendment*, Ivan R. Dee, 2008.

Edwin Meese III/David F. Forte/Matthew Spalding, *The Constitution*, *Regnery* Publishing Inc., 2005.

6. 총기난사요인이 대량살인 여부에 미치는 영향분석
- 미국의 총기난사 사례를 중심으로 -

조 현 민*

Ⅰ. 머리말

총포 등에 관한 범죄는 과실범보다 고의범이 많이 발생하고 또한 끔찍한 인명사고로 이어지는 경우가 많으므로 총기범죄로 인한 국민들의 안전을 위한 대책을 강구하는 것은 매우 바람직한 현상이다(이재삼, 2015: 28). 하지만 경찰관이 총기사용의 필요성이 있음에도 불구하고 인권보호를 상소하는 사회적인 분위기와 언론의 비판적인 태도, 쟁송대상일 경우 대법원의 엄격한 해석 등 경찰관들의 적법한 총기사용 의지를 위축하기도 한다(임준태 · 조현배, 2011: 116).

미국에서는 전통적으로 개인이 총기를 소지하는 것과 관련하여 식민지 역사와 지방분권화 요인, 수정헌법 제2조 등과 함께 문화적으로도 오랫동안 허용되어 왔다. 그럼에도 불구하고 총기의 역사만큼이나 총기폭력과 관련된 범죄는 지속되어 왔고, 최근에는 총기난사와 같은 무차별 공격으로 홍역을 앓고 있다. FBI에 따르면, 미국에서는 2021년 총기난사 사건이 61건 발생하였으며, 2020년부터 2021년까지 50% 이상 증가했다고 밝혔다(ABC News, 2022년 7월 11일). 일본의 경우 총기와 관련 강경한 법률을 유지하는 나라임에도 불구하고, 2022년 7월 8일 전 내각총리대신인 아베 신조가 해상자위대 출신 남성에게 피격되어 사망하였다. 한국의 상황은 1982년 62명의 사망자를 낸 우범곤 총기난사 사건에 이어 군 방호부대 및 예비군 훈련장 등 군대 내에서 무차별 총격이 이따금 발생하였다. 또한 민간의 경우 경찰청 총기사고 현황에 따르

---

* 서울특별시경찰청 특공대 전술교관(범죄학박사).

면 2000년부터 2017년까지 198명의 사망자와 282명의 부상자가 발생하였다(DATA, 2022년 11월 1일). 이 통계에 따르면 총기피해는 꾸준히 감소하는 추세이며 미국과 비교하여 총기안전국가에 해당된다고 볼 수 있지만, 총기범죄 및 사고는 대량피해의 개연성이 매우 높으므로 분석의 의미가 있다고 볼 수 있다.

총기범죄에 대해 더욱 관심을 가져야 하는 또 다른 까닭은 최근 들어 온라인 상 설계도를 취득, 3D 프린터를 활용하여 총기를 제작하는 사례가 증가하고 있다는 점이다. 미국은 워싱턴 주 시애틀 연방지방법원에서 총기 도면 공개는 미국 시민들에게 돌이킬 수 없는 피해를 준다고 판시했지만, 2013년부터 현재까지 권총뿐만 아니라 반자동 소총까지 3D 프린터로 제작하고 있는 게 현실이다(김영천, 2019: 103). 또한 총기난사범의 목표는 가장 짧은 시간에 가능한 많은 사람을 무작위로 살해하는 것이므로 내부에 총을 소지할 수 있는 사람이 아무도 없는 경우 표적이 될 가능성이 높아질 수 있어, 시민들의 적극적인 대응이 제시되기까지 하였다(Kirby et al., 2016).

총기를 활용한 범죄는 다량의 피해자가 발생할 가능성이 높다. 총기난사범의 목표는 다수의 인명피해를 전제하는 경우가 많고, 총기난사 사건 중 30% 이상의 범인이 자살을 시도하거나 자살했던 것으로 나타났다(Campus Security Report, 2011). 이러한 경향성은 피해를 확장하는 요인으로 작용할 수도 있다. 특히 총기난사범들은 무차별 공격 또는 묻지마 범죄의 수법처럼 '소프트 타켓(soft target)'[1] 중심으로 피해를 확산해 가므로 대량살인으로 이어지는 경우가 다분하다. 총기난사가 빈번히 발생하고 있는 미국의 경우 한국과 다르게 관련연구와 정책적 논의가 비교적 활발히 진행되고 있다. 하지만 미국시민의 총기사용에 대한 긍정적·부정적 인식의 대립, 광할한 지리적 특성으로 인한 개인의 장기방어 수단으로서의 총기소지 필요성, 헌법에 명시된 총기를 소지할 권리, 총기 관련 사업의 경제성, 총기규제에 대한 정치적 이해관계 등이 뒤섞이며 혁신적 변화가 이루어지지 못하고 있다(오사라, 2016; 손영호, 2011). 하지만 한국의 경우 이 같은 다양한 사회적·제도적 제약으로부터 비교적 자유로운 편에 속한다고 볼 수 있으므로 범죄의 주체, 수단 및 대상, 사회현상 등의 논의를 바탕으로 연구와 정책적 논의에 비교적 집중할 수 있다는 강점 또한 존재한다.

---

1 정부 또는 공공기관을 목표로 하는 '하드 타켓(hard target)'의 반대되는 개념으로 '소프트 타켓(soft target)'은 일반 시민 등 대중이 목표가 되는 것을 말한다.

따라서 총기난사는 한 개인에 대한 살인으로 종료될 수도 있으나, 총기의 위험성에 비추어 상당수 대량살인으로 이어지는 경우가 많기에 본 연구에서는 美연방수사국(Federal Bureau of Investigation: FBI)이 조사한 데이터를 토대로 총기난사 요인들을 추출하였고, 이러한 요인들이 대량살인에 미치는 영향을 검증하고자 한다. 이를 통해 총기난사 관련 요인들과 대량살인 간 관계를 확인하여 향후 효과적인 총기난사 대응책 수립을 위한 기초자료를 제공하는 것에 의의를 두고자 한다.

Ⅱ. 문헌 고찰

근래의 총기난사 연구들이 다른 범죄와 상대적으로 다르게 나타나는 뚜렷한 현상 중에는 가해자가 자살하는 문제를 꼽을 수 있다. 2019년 미국에서 총기로 인한 사망자는 39,707명으로 집계되었으며, 그 중 60%(23,941)는 자살로 생을 마감하였다(UCDAVIS HEALTH, 2022년 7월 19일). 총기난사에서 이러한 심리적 요인은 충동적일수도 있지만 상당부분 계획적으로 발생하고 있으며, 범행 장소는 학교와 같이 총기공격에 대해 총기로 응수하기 어려운 지역(gun free zone)을 주로 선택하는 사례가 이를 뒷받침한다고 볼 수 있다. 학교는 미국에서 가장 큰 총기금지 구역이다. 총기 금지구역으로 간주된 장소는 법으로 보호한다는 긍정적 인식이 작용할 수 있지만 상대적으로 가해자의 입장에서는 시민들이 대항하는 위험을 전혀 감수하지 않는 최적의 장소로 선택될 수도 있다(Dulude, 2018). 총기는 직접적인 육체적 피해를 초래하지 않더라도 범죄 자체의 성공가능성을 높여주는 도구성 효과가 존재하는 매우 위험한 무기이다(박순진, 2000: 94). 총기 간 성능과 살상력을 비교해보아도 반자동 소총은 사용하기 쉽게 설계되었으며, 대용량 탄창과 고속탄환을 활용한다는 점에서 더 치명적인 피해로 이어질 수 있다(Jager et al., 2018).

몇 명이 살해되어야 대량살인에 해당되는지와 관련하여 Krouse(2015)는 2012년 코네티컷 주(州) 뉴타운에서 대규모 총격이 발생한 사건을 들어 국회공법(Congress Public Law) 112-265의 강력범죄수사지원법(Investigation Assistance for Violent Crimes Act of 2012)에서 "대량살인"을 "하나의 사건에서 3명 이상의 살인"으로 정의하는 법안이 통과되었다고 밝혔다. 또한 Holmes와 Holmes(2001)의 연구에서도 3명 이상으로 언급하면서 연쇄살인과도 구분하였는데, 연쇄살인은 살인과 살인 사이에 상당한 냉각기간이 필요하고, 30일 이상의 기간 동안 3명 이상을 살해하는 것으로 차별화된다고 하였다. 하지만 美연방수사국(FBI)과 Fox와 Levin(2014)은 대량살인을 한 사건 내에서 지리적으로 가까운 하나 이상의 위치에서 4명 이상의 살인이 발생하는 것으로 정의했다.

총기난사와 관련된 이론적 배경에서 Capellan(2015)은 대량총격사건의 사회학적 고찰은 살인과 관련된 세 가지 이론적 틀에 기반을 둔다고 다음과 같이 제시하였다. 첫째는 사회가 개인에게 강력한 힘을 발휘한다고 보는 Durkheim의 사회통합이론(Social Integration Theory), 두 번째는 범죄와 비행은 낮은 사회적-경제적 지위와 관련있다는 Shaw와 Mckay의 사회해체이론(Social Disorganization Theory), 세 번째는 자살은 모든 사회현상과 마찬가지로 모방 때문에 일어날 수 있으며, 대량총격의 발생은 폭력의 모방을 통해 증가할 수 있다고 보면서 Tarde의 모방이론(Imitation Stemming Theory)을 제시하였다. 이 외 다른 연구에서 Kim et al.(2021)은 대량총격의 집중보도는 전염효과를 촉진할 수 있으므로 전염이론(Contagion Theory), 사회환경을 근본원인으로 보는 긴장이론(Anomie/Strain), 미디어의 반복보도로 공중의제가 되는 의제설정이론(Agenda-Setting Theory), 그 외 귀인이론(Attribution Theory), 소수자 스트레스 이론(Minority Stress Theory), 평가이론(Appraisal Theory)을 제시하였다.

본 연구에서는 미국의 사례를 통해 총기난사가 대량살인에 미치는 영향을 조사하고자 선행연구를 토대로 설정된 독립변수 요인과 대량살인의 관계를 살펴본다. 이를 위해 총기난사는 내적 요인과 외적 요인의 영향을 받는다고 가정한다. 내적 요인으로는 가해자가 총격 후 자살을 하였는지 여부와 가해자와 피해자 상호 간 가족 · 직장동료 · 친구 등 관계가 형성되었는지 여부, 외적 요인으로는 범행에 사용된 총기화력의 정도와 총기난사가 발생한 지역의 총기법의 강도를 확인하여 정립하였다. Cook(1983)은 총기폭력의 심각성에 영향을 미치는 이론적 프레임워크에는 총기의 이용가능성에 더해 세 가지 요소가 부가된다고 보았다. 첫째 가해자의 의도 또는 대상의 선택, 둘째 범죄에 사용되는 무기의 종류, 셋째 피해결과이다. 이 같은 결과를 통해 본 연구에서는 총기 이용가능성의 관점은 총기소지와 관련되므로 총기법률이 대량살인에 미치는 영향을 통해 확인해볼 수 있으며, 가해자의 의도 또는 대상의 선택과 관련된 문제는 피해자와의 관계가 존재하는지 여부에 따라 다수의 피해자에게 총격을 가하는 목적으로, 어떠한 무기를 선택하는가에 따라 피해자가 결정되는 무기의 종류에서는 총기화력을 통해 대량살인을 확인할 수 있을 것이다. 또한 Cook은 자살과 총기를 통한 살인은 높은 상관관계가 있다고 보았는데, 이러한 선행연구들을 바탕으로 영향요인으로 선택하였다.

1. 총격 후 자살과 대량살인

Campus Security Report(2011)에 따르면 총기난사와 관련된 연구들에서 총기난사 사건의 가해자가 상당수 자살하는 경향이 강하게 나타났으며, 이러한 상황은 더 큰 피해로 확산되는 결과로 이어진다고 밝혔다. 또한 이러한 조사들의 상당수가 학교에서 발생하는 총격사건을 다루고 있으며, 특히 학교에서 발생하는 총격사건은 가해자가 자살하는 현상이 강하게 나타났다. Preti(2008)의 학교총격을 다룬 조사에서는 적대적 의도를 가지고 총기난사 후 자살을 하는 주요 결정요인 중에는 자신이 처한 불행의 근원을 사람들에게 분노를 표출하려는 의지가 강함을 의미한다고 하였다. 이러한 현상은 광란의 살상으로 불릴만한 정신이상자 유형의 총격범은 경험적으로 보아도 무차별적인 공격성향을 바탕으로 대량살인을 저지를 가능성이 높다고 보는 것이 통상적이다.

하지만 David et al.(2005)의 조사에 따르면, 오히려 위와 같은 사례가 자살할 확률이 낮았고 체포될 가능성은 높게 나타났다. 반면에 직장에서 분노하는 등의 상황에서 총기살인을 저지른 경우에는 자살할 가능성이 높은 것으로 나타나 자살은 개인의 특징보다 환경요소가 적잖이 반영된 것으로 보인다. 자살테러리스트와 총기난사범을 비교한 Lankford(2012)의 연구에 따르면 자살테러리스트는 8%만이 완전히 자기통제적 자살을 시도하였고, 총기난사범의 경우 89%, 특히 학교 총격범의 경우 91%가 자위적인 방식으로 자살하는 현상을 보였다. 이러한 현상은 기존연구들에서 상당수 총기난사범이 자살하는 경향이 높고, 특히 학교에서의 총격은 자살과 더 높은 연관성을 보인다고 할 수 있다. 따라서 본 연구에서는 자살의도를 지닌 채 총격범행을 저지를 경우 피해규모가 극대화 될 것임을 가정하고 다음과 같은 가설을 제시한다.

가설1. 자살을 결심 후 총기난사 범행을 실행할 경우 대량살인에 정(+)의 영향을 미칠 것이다.

2. 피해자 관계와 대량살인

총격범과 피해자 간 관계와 관련된 논의는 총기난사범이 무차별적으로 사람을 살해한다고 인식할 수 있지만, Fox와 Levin(2003)의 연구에서는 상당수 가해자가 직장에서 해고된 뒤 상사와 동료를 죽이거나, 가족을 살해하거나, 차별과 따돌림 등으로 살인을 저지르는 등 낯선 사람을 표적으로 삼지 않는 현상을 보이면서 대량살인에 영향을 미친다고 보았다. 현재 미국에서 문제가 제기되고 있는 학교 총기난사의 경우 Böckler et al.(2011)는 청소년들이 제어력을 상실하는 것에 있어 개인차원에서 문제가 되는 경우도 있지만 가족, 학교, 친구 등 사회화의 주체들과 긍정적이며 적절한 통합이 되지 않아 불씨로 작용하는 경우가 많다고 보았다. 한편 우리사회에서 묻지마 범죄의 가해자 상당수가 보이는 공통점은 사회적 연결고리가 단절되었으며, 소위 은둔형 외톨이와 같이 타인과 개인적 교류가 거의 없이 혼자 살아가는 유형이 많다(김진혁, 2012: 118). 이러한 시각은 잠재적 가해자들이 좌절감, 수치심 또는 사회적 거부감 등의 극단적인 감정으로 이어질 수 있을 것이다.

이와 같은 현상은 대량살인에서도 동일하게 나타나는데 Delisi와 Scherer(2006)는 다수의 희생자를 낳은 대량살인범은 직장에서 인간관계를 형성함에 있어 좌절이나 상실을 겪은 중년, 독신 또는 이혼한 남성이 많다고 제시하면서, 이 같은 원인을 어린 시절 괴롭힘을 당하거나 고립되었던 경험이 있거나, 무기와 폭력에 친화적이며 나르시시즘 등의 사상으로 휩싸인 것으로 보았다. 이와 같이 총기난사와 대량살인을 조사한 많은 문헌들이 가해자의 사회적인 갈등을 주요 문제점으로 지적하고 있다. 이에 따라 총격범과 피해자가 일면식을 초과하는 사회적 관계가 있는 경우를 대량살인에 미치는 영향요인으로 확인하고자 한다.

가설2. 총격범과 피해자 상호 간 관계가 있을 경우 대량살인에 정(+)의 영향을 미칠 것이다.

3. 총기화력과 대량살인

총기를 사용한 범죄는 무기의 특성상 많은 피해를 유발할 수 있는 여지가 많지만 총기의 종류와 성능에 따라 사망률이 달라질 수 있다. 일반적으로 총기는 구경에 따라 탄환 내부에 주입되는 추진 장약에 영향을 미치고, 이는 탄환의 속도를 결정하면서 나아가 관통력에서도 차이를 보이게 된다. 또한 총기가 분당 몇 발 발사되는지 등의 빠른 연사능력은 피해를 확장하는데 상당한 요인으로 작용할 수 있다. 총기가 다른 무기와 다르게 더 큰 위험성을 갖는 연유를 살펴보면, Jager et al.(2018)의 조사에서 총격사건이 발생했을 때 반자동 소총과 그렇지 않은 경우의 피해를 비교해본 결과 반자동 소총을 사용한 사건에서 더 많은 사람이 부상당하고 사망한 것으로 나타났다.

반자동 소총은 사용이 용이하도록 설계되었으며, 대용량 탄창을 삽입할 수 있고, 고속탄환을 사용한다는 점에서 그 피해가 더욱 커지기 마련이다.[2] 총기화력과 관련하여 소총과 같은 대구경 총기가 권총과 같은 소구경 총기보다 사망확률이 더 높아지는 경향을 다수의 연구에서 찾아볼 수 있다(Braga & Cook, 2018; Jager et al., 2018; Zimring, 1972). 이에 본 연구에서는 총기의 화력 수준(level)이 대량살인에 미치는 영향을 확인하고자 한다.

가설3. 총격범이 휴대한 총기의 화력의 강도는 대량살인에 정(+)의 영향을 미칠 것이다.

4. 총기법률과 대량살인

총기법률과 관련된 논의는 총기소지율과도 관련이 있으며 총기사건 발생이 감소하는 형태를 보임으로서 연관성이 있는 것으로 나타난 바 있다(Lankford, 2016; Reeping et al., 2019; Kwon & Baack, 2005; Chien & Gakh, 2020). 총기폭력을 예방하기 위한 Gun Law Scorecard(Giffords law center, 2022년 1월 11일)에 따르면, 총기 규제가 가장 강하게

2 미국은 반자동 소총을 휴대하는 것에 대해 엄격히 금지되어 있음에도 불구하고 총기의 개머리판 부위를 개조하여(일명 'bump stock') 연속적으로 탄환이 발사될 수 있도록 하는 경우가 상당수 존재한다. 미국 라스베이거스 총기난사에서 소총을 개조하여 분당 400발 가량 사격하였고 58명 사망과 520여명의 부상자를 낳게 되었다.

나타난 캘리포니아 주는 인구 10만 명당 총기 사망률이 7.21명인데 반해 규제가 가장 약하게 나타난 미시시피 주는 24.23명으로 나타나 총기규제가 강할수록 총기사망률은 낮아지는 현상이 나타났다. 미국 총기법과 관련된 영향을 살펴보면 다음과 같다. Reeping et al.(2019)에 따르면 총기법이 관대하여 총기소유가 높은 주(州)에서는 총기난사 비율이 더 높게 나타났으며, 역으로 제한된 주에서는 총기난사 발생이 감소하는 현상으로 이어지는 등 총기법의 허용치와 제한성은 총기난사 발생률과도 연관성이 있는 것으로 나타났다. 하지만 Kwon et al.(2010)의 연구에서는 총기사건의 사망자 수와 관련하여 총기규제법은 약한 영향을 미치는 반면 주의 빈곤수준, 실업률, 알코올 소비와 같은 사회경제적 변수는 상당한 영향을 미치는 것으로 나타나 차이가 나타났다. 하지만 이 같은 연구를 진행함에 있어서도 미국 각각의 주가 갖는 특성을 고려하고 변동성을 감안해야 하는 점은 분명하다.

Chien과 Gakh(2020)에 따르면, 주(州)법이 변경되고 시간이 경과함에 따라 살인율에 어떠한 영향을 미치는지 이해하는 것이 먼저 중요하고, 특정 총기법이 발현되어 총기살인이 감소하기까지 평균적으로 최소 7년의 지연기간이 발생한다고 하였다. 본 연구를 위해서는 총기법을 측정하기 위한 기준이 필요한데, 미국의 총기법의 기준과 특징에 따라 분류하여 연도별로 조사된 바 있는 자료를 활용하였다(WIKIMEDIA COMMONS, 2022년 7월 13일). 미국의 총기법은 일반적으로 4가지로 분류되는데, 각 개념과 기준은 다음과 같다. 첫째, Unrestricted는 은닉된 총기를 휴대함에 있어 제한이 없다. 둘째, May-issue는 은닉된 총기를 휴대함에 있어 허가증의 발행이 가능하다. 셋째, No-issue는 은닉된 총기를 휴대함이 매우 제한된 경우를 제외하고 허가증의 발행이 금지된다. 하지만 1990년대 들어 입법활동이 가속화되면서 이후 총기법이 추가되었다. 넷째, 은닉된 총기에 대해 허가증을 발행해야 한다는 Shall-issue가 제정되었다(Barati, 2016). 본 연구에서는 위 4가지 기준에 따라 사건이 발생한 각 주의 해당연도 법률을 코딩하여 분석하였다. 이를 통하여 각 대량살인이 발생한 시점의 해당 지역의 총기법의 강도가 대량살인에 미치는 영향을 살펴본다.

가설4. 총기법과 관련 총기규제의 강도는 대량살인에 부(-)의 영향을 미칠 것이다.

Ⅲ. 자료수집과 분석방법

1. 연구모형

앞서 제시된 본 연구의 독립변수인 가해자의 자살여부, 피해자와의 관계형성, 총기화력의 정도, 총기법률과 종속변수인 대량살인 간 관계를 요약한 분석의 틀은 〈그림 1〉과 같다. 본 연구에서는 가해자의 자살여부와 피해자와 관계형성 부분을 내적요인으로, 총기화력과 총기법률을 외적요인으로 설정하였다. 또한 충분한 문헌고찰의 결과 대량살인에 대한 총기난사 영향요인의 영향력을 평가하는 가설로서 다음과 같이 연구모형을 설정하였다.

〈그림 1〉 연구모형

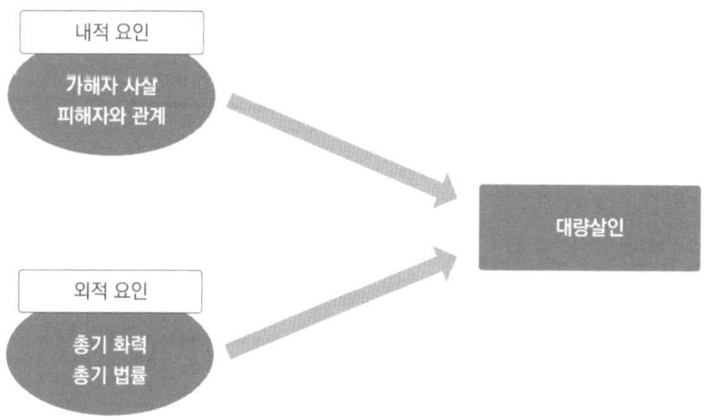

〈그림 1〉에서 제시된 바와 같이 각 상위변수에 내재된 하위변인은 다음과 같이 책정되었다. 총기난사 범인이 총격을 실행 후 시민 또는 경찰에 의해 제압되지 않고 자살을 선택한 행위여부, 가해자와 피해자가 직장 · 가족 · 친구 등 서로 관계되었는지 여부, 살인에 사용된 총기의 유형과 수량과 관련된 화력 수준, 각 총격사건이 발생한 주의 총기법률의 강도로 나타낼 수 있으며, 대량살인에 미치는 영향에 대해 총기법률은 부(-), 나머지 독립변인들은 정(+)의 방향성을 가진다고 가정하였다.

2. 분석자료 및 방법

본 연구의 수집된 자료는 미국 연방수사국이 2000년부터 2018년 사이 발생한 미국 내 총기난사 사건에 대해 작성한 목록을 활용해 실증조사를 하였다(FBI, 2022년 7월 13일). 연방수사국은 해당 자료에서 연방수사국차원에서의 연구를 통하여 공식 지정한 미국의 총기난사 사건에 대한 사건정보를 제시하고 있다. 연방조사국의 각 사건들에 대한 정보수집 방법은 연방조사국에서 실시되었던 기존 연구에 제시되어 있다(Blair & Schweit, 2014).

본 연구는 위와 같이 미국 정부의 공식데이터를 연구 자료로 활용하였고, 2000년에서 2018년 사이에 미국에서 발생한 277건의 총기난사 사건을 대상으로 하였다. 데이터에는 사건발생 일시, 총기난사범의 이름, 성별 및 나이와 같은 인적사항과 범행 후 결과, 소지한 무기, 사상자에 대한 결과, 사고 장소에 대한 분류 등의 간략한 정보를 포함하고 있다. 본 연구의 총기난사 사건 데이터의 인구통계학적 특성은 〈표 1〉과 같다. 통계분석 방법으로는 기술통계, 로지스틱 회귀분석(logistic regression analysis)이 사용되었으며, 분석도구로는 SPSS 27을 활용하였다.

〈표 1〉 사건 관련자들의 인적 특성

구분		명	비율
성별	남	269	97.1%
	여	8	2.8%
나이	10대	45	16.1%
	20대	74	26.6%
	30대	50	17.9%
	40대	53	19%
	50대	30	10.7%
	60대	17	6.1%
	70대 이상	5	1.7%
	알 수 없음	4	1.4%
	총	278(한 사건이 2명이 범행)	

피의자	자살	103	37.1%
	법 집행기관에 의한 사망	53	19.1%
	법 집행기관에 의한 체포	83	29.9%
	시민에 의한 사망	3	1%
	시민이 체포	30	10.8%
	도주	2	0.7%
	알 수 없음	3	1%
	총	277	
피해자(시민)	사망	859	36.5%
	부상	1490	63.4%
	총	2349	
법 집행기관(경찰)	사망	22	27.1%
	부상	59	72.8%
	총	81	

3. 변수의 측정

본 연구에서는 〈표 2〉와 같이 변수를 측정하였다. 본 연구의 각 변수는 미국의 총기난사 사건에서 추출한 특징을 코딩하여 수치화 하였고, 이 데이터베이스를 통해 종속변인 대량살인과의 관계를 통계적으로 검증하였다. 독립변수는 자료의 서술적 내용에 포함된 범인의 자살여부, 총기화력, 피해자 유형, 총기휴대와 관련된 법률을 선별하여 사용하였다. 종속변수인 대량살인은 앞선 논의들의 상반된 결과로 인해 3명과 4명의 근소한 차이가 있으나, 분석에 활용하기 위해서는 가장 많은 데이터를 수집하고 보관하고 있으며, 실제 실무를 담당하고, 본 연구에 활용된 데이터의 원천에 해당하는 연방수사국(FBI)이 정의한 4명을 적용하였다.

본 연구에서는 총기난사범의 나이를 통제변수로 활용하였다. 일부 연구들은 총기난사 혹은 총기 살인 사건에서 가해자의 나이가 영향을 미친다고 주장한다(Blair & Martaindale, 2020; Brown & Goodin, 2018; MSA SECURITY, 2022년 1월 9일). 그러나 본 연구에서는 대량살인에 직접적 영향을 미치는 요인들을 살펴보는 것이 주목적이므로 독립변수에 나이의 영향력이 미치는 것을 막고자 총기난사범의 나이를 통제하였다.

〈표 2〉 변수의 조작적 정의

변수		코딩(집계체계)
종속변수	대량살인	대량살인 아님=0, 대량살인=1
독립변수	가해자 자살	자살 아님=0, 자살=1
	피해자와 관계	불특정인(관계없음)=0, 특정인(관계있음)=1
	총기화력	칼: 1점, 권총: 2점, 엽총: 3점, 소총: 4점, 폭발물(수류탄 포함): 5점부여
	총기 법	Unrestricted=1, Shall-issue=2, May-issue=3, No-issue=4
통제변수	나이	피의자의 연령(세)

Ⅳ. 분석 결과

1. 기술통계

본 연구의 연속 및 서열변수들에 대한 기술통계량은 다음 〈표 3〉과 같다. 명목형 변수의 경우, 가해자의 자살여부에서 자살의 비율을 총 103건(37%), 피해자와의 관계 유무에서 관계가 있는 경우는 총 117건(42%), 그리고 대량살인이 발생한 비율은 66건(24%)로 확인되었다. 본 연구에서는 변수들 간 유의미한 상관관계 계수의 수준(level)이 다중공선성(multicollinearity)을 유발할 만큼 높은지 확인하기 위해 상관관계분석을 실시하였으며 나이, 총기화력, 총기법률 간 상관관계의 수준이 낮음을 확인하였다.

〈표 3〉 주요 변수들에 대한 기술통계

기술통계량					
	N	최소값	최대값	평균	표준편차
나이	273	12	88	35.43	15.289
총기화력	274	2	12	3.38	2.023
총기법	275	1	4	2.24	0.585

2. 로지스틱 회귀분석 결과

연구모형에서 제시한 가해자 자살, 피해자와 관계, 총기화력, 총기법이 대량살인에 미치는 영향을 검증하기 위해 이항 로지스틱 회귀분석(binary logistic regression analysis)을 실시하였다. 우선 본 연구에서는 독립변수들로만 구성된 모형 1과 독립변수와 통제변수를 모두 포함한 모형 2에 대한 분석을 실시하였다. 분석결과 통제변수의 포함이 독립변수들의 종속변수에 대한 영향에 유의미한 변화가 관찰되지 않아 통제변수를 포함한 모형 2를 본 연구의 모형으로 설정하였다. 로지스틱 회귀모형의 전체적인 모형 적합도를 나타내는 Hosmer & Lemeshow 검정통계 수치(x^2=6.353, p=.608)를 통하여 본 연구의 추정모형이 통계적으로 적합함을 확인하였다. 본 연구 모형의 설명력은 약 11.4%로 나타났다(Nagelkerke R^2=.114). 각 변수별 분석결과는 다음과 같다.

〈표 4〉 이분형 로지스틱 회귀분석 : 대량살인에 대한 영향요인

종속변수	독립변수	〈모형 1〉					〈모형 2〉				
		B	S.E.	Wald	Exp(B)	P	B	S.E.	Wald	Exp(B)	P
대량살인	가해자 자살	.827	.307	7.269	2.287	.007**	.824	.307	7.201	2.280	.007**
	피해자와 관계	-.342	.313	1.195	.710	.274	-.385	.315	1.495	.681	.221
	총기화력	.163	.067	5.916	1.177	.015*	.165	.067	6.044	1.180	.014*
	총기법	.658	.241	7.461	1.931	.006**	.666	.242	7.567	1.946	.006**
	나이						-.011	.010	1.203	.989	.273
(상수)		-2.787	.463	36.242	.062	.000	-2.392	.571	17.540	.091	.000
-2LL		278.806					277.161				
NagelKerke R^2		.108					.114				

Hosmer & Lemeshow test: x^2	6.130(p=.525)	6.353(p=.608)
유의확률	.000	.000
N	272	271

첫째, 가해자가 자살한 경우(OR=2.280, P<.01)에는 대량살인 가능성이 유의한 정(+)의 영향을 미치는 것으로 나타났다. 따라서 범인이 자살을 결심하고 총기살인을 범할 경우 범인이 자살하지 않은 경우보다 대량살인이 발생할 가능성이 높다고 볼 수 있어 가설 1은 지지되었다. 둘째, 본 연구에서 기대한 바와 달리 피해자와 관계는 대량살인 여부에 유의미한 영향을 미치지 않는 것으로 나타났다. 이는 직장동료, 가족, 학교에서의 차별 등 총격범과 피해자가 서로 관련된 경우, 대량살인 가해자는 낯선 사람을 표적으로 삼지 않는 경향이 있다고 주장하는 이전연구들과 상반되는 결과이다(Fox & Levin, 2003; Böckler et al., 2011; Delisi & Scherer, 2006). 따라서 가설 2는 지지되지 않았다.

셋째, 총기화력(OR=1.180, P<.05)의 경우 범인이 휴대한 총기의 화력이 강할수록 대량살인에 유의한 정(+)의 영향을 미치는 것으로 확인되었다. 따라서 총격 시 더 강한 구경과 수량 등이 살해현장에 사용되었을 때 더 많은 피해자가 출현할 수 있다고 볼 수 있어 가설 3은 지지되었다. 넷째, 총기법의 경우(OR=1.946, P<.01) 총기법이 강화될수록 대량살인에 유의한 정(+)의 영향을 미친 것으로 나타났으며, 이 같은 현상은 총기규제 수준이 높은 지역일수록 대량의 총기난사 피해자가 발생할 가능성이 높음을 의미한다. 따라서 가설 4는 지지되지 않았으며 기존 연구들의 결과와도 맥락을 달리한다. 마지막으로 본 연구의 통제변수에 해당하는 나이는 대량살인에 유의미한 영향을 미치지 못한 것으로 나타나 나이가 들수록 젊은 공격자보다 더 적은 희생자를 낳는다고 추정한 Blair 등의 연구와는 배치되는 결과가 나타났다.

Ⅴ. 결론 및 함의

본 연구의 목적은 미국에서 발생한 총기난사사건을 이해하고 종합적으로 고찰하며, 총기와 관련된 무차별 공격사건의 주요요인이 대량살인에 미치는 영향을 실증분석하기 위함이다. 이를 위해 2000년에서 2018년까지 미국에서 발생한 총기난사사건과 관련 美연방수사국(FBI)의 조사 자료를 활용하였다. 이 같은 데이터를 본 연구에 적용하기 위해 자료에 포함된 277건의 총기난사행위 가운데 본 연구에서 필요한 가해자의 자살여부, 가해자와 피해자의 관계, 가해자가 소지한 총기의 종류와 수량, 범죄가 발생한 지역의 총기법, 가해자의 나이, 피해규모 등을 추출하여 로지스틱 회귀분석을 통해 분석하였으며 주요 연구 결과는 다음과 같다.

첫째, 가해자의 자살여부(가설 1)는 대량살인에 영향을 미치는 것으로 확인되었다. 이러한 결과는 총기난사사건을 자행하는 상당수의 가해자들이 자살을 하는 기존 연구의 경향과 대량피해와의 영향을 확인할 수 있다(Campus Security Report, 2011; Fox & Levin, 2003; Ghiani & Hawkins, 2019). 둘째, 가해자와 피해자 간 가족, 친구, 직장동료 등 관계가 형성되었는지 여부(가설 2)는 대량살인에 영향을 미치지 않는 것으로 나타났다. 이러한 결과는 Fox 와 Levin(2003, 2007)이 대량살인을 실행함에 있어 낯선 사람을 표적으로 삼지 않는 현상을 주장한 것과 Böckler와 Heitmeyer(2011)이 학교총격사건에서 청소년들의 제어력 상실의 문제를 가족 및 친구 등과 같이 사회주체들과 비통합되면서 발생한다는 분석과 반대되는 결과이다. 그로 인해 가설 2는 기각되었다. 셋째, 총기난사사건에서 가해자가 소지한 총기의 화력과 수량의 정도(가설 3)는 대량살인에 영향을 미치는 것으로 나타났다. 총기의 빠른 연사능력을 대변하는 반자동소총과 그렇지 않은 총기의 피해결과를 비교한 Jager와 Mccarty(2018)의 연구 및 탄환의 위력과 관련하여 총기구경이 사망확률에 영향을 미치는가에 대한 연구들과 동일한 결과가 나타난 것이다(Braga & Cook, 2018; Jager & Mccarty, 2018; Zimring, 1972).

넷째, 총격범죄가 발생한 지역의 해당년도 총기법률의 규제강화(가설 4)는 대량살인에 정(+)영향을 미치는 것으로 확인되었다. 총기 규제가 총기사건의 발생을 감소시킨다는 기존의 연구와 배치되는 결과이며(Lankford, 2016 ; Reeping et al, 2019; Kwon et al, 2005 ; Chien & Gakh, 2020), 이러한 결과는 총기법이 총기난사 사건의 발생률 또는 사상자에는 영향을 미칠 수 있지만 한 사건에서 일어나는 대량살인과는 그 영향력을 확인할 수 없었다. 마지막으로 본 연구의 통제변수에 해당하는 나이는 대량살인에 유의미한 영향을 미치지 않는 것으로 나타났다. 이 같은 결과는 나이가 들수록 어린 가해자보다 더 적은 희생자를 낳는다고 강조한 기존연구들과 배치되는 결과이다 (Brown & Goodin, 2018; Blair & Martaindale, 2020). 따라서 본 연구에서 확인된 결과를 토대로 총기난사 관련 연구와 정책에 대한 시사점 및 연구의 한계는 다음과 같다.

첫째, 본 연구의 학문적 관점에서 바라본 시사점은 총기난사를 조사함에 있어 기존의 연구는 크게 세 가지로 구분할 수 있었다. 먼저 범행당시 가해자의 불만족, 분노, 정신장애 등의 심리와 성장배경 등 개인의 프로필을 통해 총기난사의 영향요인을 조사하는 방식이다. 다음으로 총기난사의 원인을 사회구조의 악화와 총기법을 통한 총기의 이용가능성을 고찰하여 사회현상에 영향을 미치는 것으로 보는 경우이다. 마지막으로 총기난사는 무기의 특성상 대량의 인명피해를 야기할 가능성이 높으므로 어떤 형태의 대응이 효과적인지 조사하는 경우이다. 하지만 본 연구에서는 실제 미국에서 발생한 총기난사 데이터를 토대로 기존연구의 개별적 요인들 즉, 개인과 관련된 내적 요인과 사회 및 제도적 요인을 통합하여 대량살인의 결정요인을 조사하였다. 이러한 시도를 통하여 기존연구들이 개별적 요인만으로는 총기난사 발생의 구조적 원인을 설명하는 한계를 보완하고자 하였다.

둘째, 본 연구에서 나타난 총기난사의 요인으로는 피해자와의 관계를 제외하고 가해자가 자살하는 현상, 총기화력의 증가, 총기법률의 강화 등이 대량살인에 영향을 주는 것으로 나타났다. 실무적으로 총기난사가 발생할 경우 경찰 등과 같은 법집행기관이나 시민의 대응이 가해자가 자살할 것이라고 사전에 인지하기는 어렵지만 총기난사의 상당부분은 자살과 연관성이 크다는 점을 대응기관이 인식할 수 있고, 가해자의 프로파일을 다양한 방면으로 이해한다면 신속한 대응방안에 활용해볼 수 있을 것이다. 가해자의 총기화력은 고화력의 총기들이 문제가 될 수 있는데 우리나라의 경우 경찰이 대응함에 있어 많은 부분에서 문제점이 발생한다. 현재 대부분의 현장경찰의 경우 리볼버 권총을 휴대하고 근무를 하고 있으므로, 총격 가해자가 소총을 휴대할 경우 현재 경찰의 총기로 대응한다는 것은 매우 불리하고 위험하다. 또한 효과적인 제압이 이루어지지 않아 시민과 대응하는 경찰 자신도 위험에 처하게 될 수 있다. 일부에서는 경찰특공대와 같은 진압 팀이 대응을 주도적으로 이끌어갈 수 있다고 오해하는 견해가 존재하는데, 기존의 연구에 따르면 2~10여분 안에 대부분의 사건이 종결(Blair et al., 2014; Schwerin et al., 2018)되었다는 점에서, 현실적으로 시민피해를 줄이기 위한 최선의 방책은 범행현장에서 가장 근거리에 위치한 지역경찰이 될 수밖에 없다.

한국의 총기난사가 거의 발생하지 않는 직접적인 원인으로 강한 총기 법을 지지하는 경향이 강하다. 이와 관련하여 강한 총기규제가 대량살인에 영향력이 있다는 예측은 본 연구의 범위 내에서는 지지되지 않았다. 기존연구에서 총기법의 영향력은 총기난사 발생률 또는 사망률에는 영향을 미친다고 조사되었지만, 한 사건에서 많은 인명의 사상자가 발생하는 대량살인의 요건 하에서는 그 연관성이 확인되지 않아 비결정적인 결과가 나타났다. 현재 한국의 총기법은 총기의 특성이나 종류에 따라 위험성이 구별되지 않고 통틀어서 지칭하거나 규정하고 있다. 총기의 종류는 사제 총기부터 고성능 총기까지 다양하며, 위험성에 있어서도 상당한 차이를 보임에도 그 기준에 따라 분류가 되고 있지 않다. 이러한 현상의 문제점은 규제정도에도 영향을 미쳐 총기가 지니는 위협을 명확하게 이해하거나, 직관적·개념적으로 파악하기 어려워 정책 및 대응, 이론적 발전에도 장애요소로 작용할 수 있을 것이다. 따라서 일괄적으로 강화된 총기규제보다 각 총기의 화력과 특성에 맞는 총기규제를 통하여 총기난사를 예방함에 있어 향상된 가능성을 기대해 볼 수 있을 것이다.

셋째, 본 연구가 가지는 한계는 총기난사의 기준이 가해자의 행동 또는 피해규모와 같은 근거로 일반적인 총기살인인지 또는 총기난사로 정의되는지 명확하지 않다는 점이다. Blair et al.(2014)의 연구에서는 대량학살과 같은 정의된 범죄와 달리 대응에 따라 사건의 결과에 영향을 미칠 가능성을 의미한다고 보았지만, 뚜렷한 이해가 없이 가능성을 토대로 연구주제와 변수의 명확성을 확보하기는 어려워 보인다. 기존의 연구에서 대량살인의 기준이 3명과 4명으로 상이한 점은 본 연구가 활용한 데이터를 토대로 실험한 바 큰 차이는 보이지 않았지만, 이 부분 또한 연구변수의 명확한 기준을 충족하지 못한다는 점에서 후속 연구들에서 오차가 발생할 가능성이 존재한다. 중요한 점은 미국 외에도 많은 나라에서 총기폭력은 발생하고 있으며, 이러한 현상은 다문화 사회와 전 지구적 차원의 문제로 전이되고 우리나라도 예외일 수 없을 것이다. 한국에서도 다수 발생하고 있는 묻지마 범죄, 무차별 공격 등과 같은 범죄유형의 기조가 총기를 통해 대량피해로 이어질 수 있다는 개연성과 관련하여, 이러한 문제점들이 조명되고 관련연구의 증가로 이어질 수 있도록 후속연구에서도 지속적으로 영향요인들을 탐색해 나갈 것이다.

[참고문헌]

1. 국내·외 논문 및 서적

김진혁 (2012). 문지마 범죄의 유형 및 대응방안, 한국범죄심리연구, 8(3): 113-131.

김영천 (2019). 테러예방을 위한 3D 프린터 제작 총기에 대한 연구, Journal of Korea Association for Aviation Security, 1(1): 94-111.

박순진 (2000). 폭력범죄에 있어서 흉기의 사용에 대한 고찰, 형사정책연구, 41: 92-110.

임준태 · 조현배 (2011). 경찰관의 총기사용 의사결정에 미치는 영향요인에 관한 연구, 경찰학논총, 6(2): 1-36.

이재삼 (2015). 총기사고 방지 및 안전대책에 관한 연구, 법학연구, 60: 1-36.

오사라 (2016). 총기규제를 위한 미국 지방정부와 법원의 역할, 토지공법연구, 73(1): 609-623.

Active-Shooter Report Provides Valuable Recommendation. (2011). *Campus Security Report*, 8(1).

Lankford, A. (2016). Public Mass Shooters and Firearms: A Cross-National Study of 171 Countries. *Research Article in Violence and Victims*, 31(2), 187–199.

Böckler, N., Seeger, T., & Heitmeyer, W. (2011). School Shooting: A Double Loss of Control. *Control of Violence*, 261–294.

Blair, P. J., & Schweit, K. W. (2014). A Study of Active Shooter Incidents in the United States Between 2000 and 2013. *Texas State University and Federal Bureau of Investigation*.

Barati, M. (2016). New Evidence on the Impact of Concealed Carry Weapon Laws on Crime. *International Review of Law and Economics*, 47, 76–83.

Braga, A. A., & Cook, P. J. (2018). The Association of Firearm Caliber With Likelihood of Death From Gunshot Injury in Criminal Assaults. *JAMA Network*, 1(3), 1–10.

Brown, J. D., & Goodin, A. J. (2018). Mass Casualty Shooting Venues, Types of Firearms, and Age of Perpetrators in the United States, 1982–2018. *A Public of the American Public Health Association*, 1385–1387.

Blair, P. J., Sandel, W. L., & Martaindale, H. M. (2020). Correlates of the Number Shot and Killed in Active Shooter Events. *SAGE Journals*, 25(4), 1–26.

Cook, P. J. (1983). The Effect of Gun Availability on Violent Crime Patterns. *Crime and*

Justice, 4, 44-89.

Campus security report. (2011). Active-Shooter Report Provides Valuable Recommendations. *Wiley Online Library*, 8(1), 9.

Capellan, J. A. (2015). Looking Upstream: A Sociological Investigation of Mass Public Shooting. *City University of New York ProQuest Dissertations Publishing*, 1-24.

Chien, L. -c, & Gakh, M. (2020). The Lagged Effect of State Gun Laws on the Reduction of State-Level Firearm Homicide Mortality in the United States from 1999 to 2017. *Public Health*, 189, 73-80.

David, L., Steven, S., Armin, S., Sylvia, S., & Lngrid, M. (2005). Mass Homicide and Suicide Deadliness and Outcome. *Crisis: The Journal of Crisis Intervention and Suicide Prevention*, 26(4), 184-187.

Delisi, M., & Scherer, A. M. (2006). Multiple Homicide Offenders: Offense Characteristics, Social Correlates, and Criminal Careers. *SAGE Journals*, 33(3), 367-391.

Dulude, D. (2018). Gun Control and Gun Free Zones. *Sam Houston State University*. https://shsu-ir.tdl.org/handle/20.500.11875/2477

Fox, A., & Levin, J. (2014). Extreme Killing: Understanding Serial and Mass Murder (3rd Ed). *SAGE Publications*.

Fox, J. A., & Levin, J. (2003). Mass Murder: An Analysis of Extreme Violence. *Journal of Applied Psychoanalytic Studies*, 5, 47-64.

Holmes, R. M., & Holmes, S. T. (2011). Mass Murder in the United States. *NCJRS*.

Jager, E. D., Goralnick, E., Mccarty, J. C., Hashmi, Z. G., Jarman, M. P., & Haider, A. H. (2018). Lethality of Civilian Active Shooter Incidents with and Without Semiautomatic Rifles in the United States. *JAMA Network*, 320(10), 1034-1035.

Kwon, I. G., & Baack, D. W. (2005). The Effectiveness of Legislation Controlling Gun Usage: A Holistic Measure of Gun Control Legislation. *The American Journal of Economics and Sociology*, 64(2), 533-547.

Kwon, I. G., Scott, B., Safranski, S. R., & Bae, M. (2010). The Effectiveness of Gun Control Laws: Multivariate Statistical Analysis. *The American Journal of Economics and Sociology*, 56(1), 41-50.

Krouse, W. J. (2015). Mass Murder with Firearms: Incidents and Victims, 1999-2013. *Congressional Research Service*, 1-44.

Kirby, A., Anklam, C. E., & Dietz, J. E. (2016). Active Shooter Mitigation for Gun-Free Zones. *2016 IEEE Symposium on Technologies for Homeland Security(HTS)*, 1-6.

Kim, C., Capellan, J. A., & Adler, A. (2021). Exploring the Empirical Literature on Mass Shooting: A Mixed-Method Systematic Review of Peer-Reviewed Journal Articles. *Aggression and Violent Behavior*, 58, 1-10.

Lankford, A. (2012). A Comparative Analysis of Suicide Terrorists and Rampage, Workplace, and School Shooters in the United States From 1990 to 2010. *SAGE Journals*, 17(3), 255-274.

Preti, A. (2008). School Shooting as a Culturally Enforced Way of Expressing Suicidal Hostile Intentions. *Journal of the American Academy of Psychiatry and the Law*, 36 (4), 544-550.

Reeping, P. M., Cerdá, M., Kalesan, B., Wiebe, D. J., Galea, S., & Branas, C. C. (2019). State Gun Laws, Gun Ownership, and Mass Shootings in the US: Cross Sectional Time Series. *BMJ*.

Zimring, F. E. (1972). The Medium Is the Message: Firearm Caliber as a Determinant of Death from Assault. *The Journal of Legal Studies*, 1(1), 97-123.

2. 인터넷 및 신문

ABC News. 「50% Jump in Active-Shooter Incidents from 2020 to 2021」

https://abcnews.go.com/Politics/50-jump-active-shooter-incidents-2020-2021-fbi/story?id=84910934 (검색일: 2022. 7. 21.)

DATA. 「경찰청 총기사고 현황」

https://www.data.go.kr/data/15029986/fileData.do (검색일: 2022. 11. 1.)

FBI. 「2000 to 2018 Active Shooter Incidents」

https://www.fbi.gov/file-repository/active-shooter-incidents-2000-2018.pdf/view(검색일: 2022. 7. 13.)

GIFFORDS LAW CENTER. 「ANNUAL GUN LAW SCORECARD」

https://giffords.org/lawcenter/resources/scorecard/#AL (검색일: 2022. 1. 11.)

MSA SECURITY. 「MSA Special Analysis: The Active Shooter Threat」

https://www.msasecurity.net/security-and-counterterrorism-blog/bid/86354/MSA-Special-Analysis-The-Active-Shooter-Threat (검색일: 2022. 1. 9.)

UCDAVIS HEALTH.「What You Can Do」

https://health.ucdavis.edu/what-you-can-do/facts.html (검색일: 2022. 7. 19.)

WIKIMEDIA COMMONS.「File:Right to Carry, timeline.gif」

https://commons.wikimedia.org/wiki/File:Right_to_Carry,_timeline.gif(검색일: 2022. 7.13.)

7. 미국 연방 수정헌법 제2조 총기권리 위헌적 함의

지 영 환*·윤 대 현**·조 기 환***

Ⅰ. 미합중국 헌법(美合衆國 憲法 Constitution of the United States)

"미국에서 헌법해석의 출발점과 기준을 무엇으로 삼아야 하는지에 관한 본격적인 논의는 연방대법원이 개인의 권리를 확대하는 방향으로 헌법규정을 해석하여 논쟁적인 결정을 내린 데에 대한 비판에서 시작되었다.[1] 물론 관련 논의들이 시작된 시점은 훨씬 이전으로 거슬러 올라가며, 1930년대에도 헌법규정의 원래의 의미(original meaning), 원래의 의도(original intentions), 원래의 이해(original understanding) 등에 대한 학문적 논의가 전개되었으며, 유사한 논의를 그 당시 연방대법원 판결에서도 찾아볼 수 있으나,[2] 1950년대~1960년대의 진보적 판결들은 헌법해석의 기준이나 해석재

---

* 성균관대 국가전략대학원 겸임교수 · 중앙대학교 행정대학원 객원교수 · 국가공무원 · 서울대학교 객원연구원.

** 성균관대학교 경영학학사 · 정치학석사, FM 그룹 회장.

*** 성균관대학교 대학원 경영학석사, ㈜ 에머티바이오 대표이사.

1 Peter J. Smith, How Different Are Originalism and Non-Originalism?, Hastings Law Journal 62 (2011), 711. 헌법해석방법론으로 원의주의를 주장하게 된 계기와 시점을 이때(1960년대 후반 내지 1970년대)로 보는 것이 통상적인 이해인 것으로 보이나, 건국기(the Founding-era)부터 현재에 이르기까지 원의주의적인 해석접근과 그에 반대되는 해석은 필요에 따라 꾸준히 활용되어 왔다는 분석도 있다. 미국 연방헌법이 제정된 1787년부터 현대에 이르기까지의 시기를 4단계로 나누면서, 헌법제정 이후 초창기(1787~1870) 연방대법원 판례에서는 헌법기초자의 의사에 의존하여 판단을 내리고자 하였고, 남북전쟁 이후에 살아있는 헌법 관념이 등장하기 시작하였다고 보는 견해로 Barry Friedman & Scott B. Smith, Sedimentary Constitution, University of Pennsylvania Law Review 147 (1998).

2 해당 논문 및 판결의 보다 구체적인 논의에 관해서는 Lawrence B. Solum, What is Originalism?: The Evolution of Contemporary Originalist Theory, Grant Huscroft & Bradley W. Miller ed. The Challenge of Originalism: Essays in Constitutional Theory, Cambridge University Press, 2011, 13-15 참조. Morton J. Horwitz, Foreword: The Constitution of Change — Legal Fundamentality Without Fundamentalism,

량의 통제 필요성에 대한 본격적인 논의와 첨예한 대립을 가져왔다. 워런(Warren) 법원 시기로 불리는 1953년~1969년 워런 대법원장 재임기 동안 연방대법원은 전통적인 사법소극주의를 벗어나 사법적극주의를 취하였다고 평가된다.[3] 합리성 심사로 단일화되어 있던 위헌심사기준을 발전시켜 보다 강화된 새로운 심사기준을 정립하고 평등권 보호에 획기적인 법리를 형성한 것도 이 시기에 이루어졌다."[4][5] 1954년 Brown v. Board of Education 판결을 시작으로 여러 전향적인 결정들[6]을 내리면서 헌법상 권리를 광범하게 확대해 나갔고, 1970년대 초에 들어서 이에 대한 비판으로 헌법은 헌법기초자들의 의사를 실행하는 방식으로 해석되어야 한다는 주장이 제기되었다. 올바른 헌법의 의미는 헌법기초자들이 본래 의도한 의미라는 것이다.[7] 이러한 비판적인 시각에서 볼 때, 그 당시 연방대법원은 헌법의 문언과 본래의 의도에 의해 한계지워짐 없이, 법을 해석하는 것이 아니라 사실상 법을 만들어내고 있었으며, 이러한 행위는 민주주의에서의 사법권의 역할과 합치된다고 보기 어려운 것이었다.[8] 원의주의는 넓은 범위의 해석이론을 포괄할 수 있는 개념으로, 원의주의에 대한 정의를 둘러싼 논쟁 또는 혼란 역시 없지 않다.[9] 원의주의(Originalism)라는 용어를 최초로 창안한 이는 Paul Brest 교수로 알려져 있으며, 1980년에 발표된 한 논문에서 이를 '헌법재판에 있어 널리 사용되는 접근방식으로 헌법의 문언 또는 헌법기초자의 의사에 구속력 있는 권위를 부여하는 방식'으로 정의하였다.[10] 원의주의가 가장 경계하는 바는

Harvard Law Review 107(1993), 44.

3 Morton J. Horwitz, Foreword: The Constitution of Change — Legal Fundamentality Without Fundamentalism, Harvard Law Review 107 (1993), 44.

4 워런 법원을 기준으로 그 이전을 구평등권보호시대(the old equal protection years), 이후를 신평등권보호시대(the Warren Court's new equal protection years)로 구분하기도 한다. 석인선, "미국헌법 판례상 성에 근거한 적극적 평등실현조치의 사법심사기준에 관한 소고," 공법연구 제26집 제2호(1998), 159-160면.

5 김지영 책임연구관, "미국 헌법해석론 — 이론과 연방대법원의 적용례를 중심으로, 헌법재판소 헌법재판연구원, 2018, 5면.

6 미국 연방헌법상 명문으로 규정되지 않았으나 헌법상 권리로 인정되고 있는 권리 중 대표적인 권리인 프라이버시권(the right to privacy)을 인정한 Griswold v. Connecticut, 381 U.S. 479 (1965) 판결도 이때 내려졌다. Brown v. Board of Education 판결 및 Griswold v. Connecticut 판결에 대해서는 IV.4.가 및 다 참조.

7 Thomas B. Colby & Peter J. Smith, Living Originalism, 59 Duke Law Journal (2009), 248.

8 Peter J. Smith(각주 1), 711.

9 원의주의가 과연 무엇을 의미하는가에 대한 의견대립은 원의주의를 둘러싼 헌법해석논쟁의 특징으로 분석된다. Lawrence B. Solum(각주 2), 12.

10 그 당시 또 다른 저명 헌법학자인 John Ely 교수는 헌법해석논쟁을 해석주의(interpretivism)와 비해석주

법관은 스스로의 관점이나 견해에 따라 자유로이 결정을 내려서는 안 되며 법규범에 의해 통제되어야 한다는 부분이다.[11] 비원의주의자, 즉 원의주의에 반대하는 입장은 '살아있는 헌법'이라는 비유적 표현으로 설명되는 해석 입장으로, 이러한 가장 근본적인 주장을 따서 살아있는 헌법주의(living constitutionalism)라고 설명되기도 한다.[12]

미합중국 헌법(Constitution of the United States)[13] 또는 미국 헌법은 미국 연방정부(Federal government)[14]의 헌법이다. 50개의 주가 모여 하나의 국가를 이루는 합중국(合衆國)인 미국의 법은 연방헌법과 주헌법이 별도로 존재하며, 때문에 연방헌법은 연방의 입법, 사법, 행정부가 가지는 기능을 규율하고 주 정부와 주민에 전속(專屬)하는 권리를 구분한다. 미국 연방 헌법은 독립 전쟁 중인 1776년 작성된 '버지니아 권리장전', 이를 토대로 채택된 '버지니아주 헌법' 및 동년 필라델피아 대륙회의에서 발표된 '독립선언서' 등의 영향을 받아 천부인권 옹호와 부당한 권력에 대한 정당한 권리 행사라는 핵심적 가치를 참고하였으며, 그 직접적인 전신은 1777년 대륙회의에서 결정

의(non-interpretivism)로 구별하면서, 전자는 헌법적 쟁점을 판단하는 법관은 성문헌법에 명시되었거나 명백히 내재된 규범을 집행하는 것에 스스로를 한정하여야 한다고 보는 입장이라면 후자는 이와 반대 되는 견해로 법원은 그와 같은 참고사항을 넘어서서 헌법전 내에서 발견될 수 없는 규범도 집행할 수 있다고 보는 입장이라고 분석한 바 있다. John Hart Ely, Democracy and Distrust: A Theory of Judicial Review, Harvard University Press, 1980. 1. 이에 대해 Paul Brest 교수는 모든 헌법적 의사결정은 해석을 요구하며, 다만 그 해석의 대상을 무엇으로 보느냐에 따라서 입장 차이가 있다는 점에서 해석주의/비해석주의로 구분하기 보다는 헌법문언과 그 제정사에 대한 해석에 집중하는 입장을 원의주의라 할 수 있다고 하였으며, 이러한 입장은 선례나 사회적 가치에 대한 해석에 집중하는 입장과 구별된다고 하였다. Paul Brest, The Misconceived Quest for the Original Understanding, Boston University Law Review 60 (1980), 204. 오늘날에는 원의주의라는 용어를 비롯하여 원의주의의 수정, 발전된 입장을 신원의주의로 칭하고 이에 반대하는 입장을 비원의주의라고 하는 것이 일반적이다.

11 Thomas B. Colby & Peter J. Smith(각주 7), 289.

12 비원의주의와 살아있는 헌법주의는 통상 서로 혼용되어 사용되어지나, 일각에서는 두 용어는 완전히 일치하지 않으며, 원의주의에 반대하는 입장은 비원의주의로 표현하는 것이 더 적절하다고 보기도 한다. 이러한 견해는 살아있는 헌법주의는 해석자로 하여금 변화하는 환경에 헌법원리를 맞춰나가야 할 의무를 부과한다면, 비원의주의는 헌법을 고안할 때 헌법기초자의 의사가 어떠하였는지에 해석자의 판단이 기초하여야 한다는 원의주의 입장에 반대하기는 하지만 그렇다고 하여 반드시 시대에 맞게 헌법해석을 할 의무를 인정하는 것은 아니라는 점에서 양자가 반드시 일치되지는 않는다고 한다. Mitchell N. Berman(각주 45), 24. 따라서 이 보고서에서는 원의주의에 반대하는 입장을 비원의주의로 통칭하되, 시대에 맞는 헌법해석 방법이나 해석의무를 주장하는 견해를 다룰 때에는 살아있는 헌법주의로 표기하도록 한다.

13 https://namu.wiki/w/%EB%AF%B8%EA%B5%AD%20%ED%97%8C%EB%B2%95 2025.5.7. 검색.

14 여기서 연방정부란 연방의 입법, 사법, 행정부를 총칭하며, 헌법상 행정부는 'federal executive departments'로 구분된다.

하여 1781년부터 효력이 발생한 '연합규약(Articles of Confederation and Perpetual Union, 연합과 영속적인 연방에 관한 규약)'이라 할 수 있다. 13개 식민지는 본래 공동체라는 의식이 없었지만, 여러 통일국가가 탄생하는 당대 상황에 비추어 대표성 있는 주권국으로 공인받고 영국 등의 강대국에 휘둘리지 않기 위해서는 하나가 되어야 할 것이라는 필요성에 공감하고 있었다. 이에 따라 13개 식민지 전체가 분리할 수 없는 하나의 국가연합으로 행동할 것을 결정하고, 이를 위해 1778년에 연합의 헌법 역할을 하는 연합규약을 제정했다. 연합규약은 1781년에 이르러 모든 주의 비준을 받았으며, 연합규약에 따라 이러한 국가연합에서 각 주를 대표할 수 있는 의회를 구성했다. 이것이 연합의회(Congress of the Confederation)이다. 그러나 1783년에 영국이 파리 조약을 통해 미국의 독립을 승인하자, 13개 식민지는 곧바로 분열을 겪었다. 이전에는 영국이라는 공통의 적을 두고 개별 주의 이권을 유보해 왔다면, 영국이 물러간 뒤에는 아메리카 내부의 문제를 두고 갈등이 점화된 것이다. 오늘날로 따지면 당시 미국은 연합된 입법부만 존재하고 연합된 행정부는 없는 상황이라 법률을 제정해도 이를 각 주 모두에 강제할 수 있는 방법이 없었다. 특히 독립전쟁을 수행하면서 스페인, 프랑스, 네덜란드 등 유럽의 강대국들에게 막대한 빚을 짊어진 상황이었기에, 개별 주의 독자 행동은 미국 전체의 신용을 악화시키는 큰 문제가 되었다. 연합의회는 힘이 없어서 돈 갚을 여력도 없는데 각 주 정부들은 이러한 빚에 대해 자기 일 아니라며 무시한 것. 합의는 통상과 세금 문제를 놓고 대표간의 의견 충돌로 번번이 무산되었는데, 연합의 법을 집행하기 위한 조직체계부터 우선적으로 개편하자는 쪽으로 의견이 모아진다. 이에 로드아일랜드의 1개주를 제외한 12개주의 대표들은 1785년에서 1787년 사이 여러 차례 연합규약의 수정을 논의하다가, 결국 기존의 연합규약을 전면 개정하여 새 헌법을 제정하는 것에 동의했다. 1787년 5월 25일 첫 제헌 의회가 열렸으며, 의장으로 전 대륙군 총사령관 조지 워싱턴이 선출되었다. 9월까지 여러 가지 헌법 초안들이 제시되었다. 1787년 9월 17일, 필라델피아 회관(현재의 필라델피아 독립기념관)에 모인 39명의 대표들은 완성된 헌법에 서명하고 이를 연합의회에 송부하였다. 의회는 9월 28일 이를 승인했으나, 헌법이 발효되기 위해서는 13개주의 2/3에 해당하는 9개주 이상의 비준이 필요했다. 델라웨어주가 1787년 12월 7일 처음으로 이를 비준하였으며, 뉴햄프셔주가 1788년 6월 21일에 9번째로 비준하면서 조건이 달성되었다. 연방헌법은 1789년 3월 4일부터 공식적으로 발효되었는데, 발효가 연기된 것은 정치, 경제적 중심지였던 버지니아주와 뉴욕주에서 비준이 늦어졌기 때문에 이를 고려한 것이다. 로드아일랜드의 사례와 같이 당시 미국 헌법의 비준, 즉 연방 가입을 놓고 각 주 내부에서도 '우리 주가 연방에 가입해야 하나?', '미국이라는 거대정부를 만들고 여기에 권리를 위임해야 하나?'에 대해 사상가들의 의견이 갈렸는데, 특히 뉴욕과 같은 대형주가 가입을 거부할 경우 연방의 존재가 유명무실해지거나 또 다른 갈등의 불씨가 생길 수 있었다. 가장 많은 비판을 받았던 것은 '새 헌법 조항이 국방, 상업 등 광범위한 영역에서 연방정부에게 너무 많은 권한을 제공하는 것이 아닌가?' 하는 것이었다. 이에 알렉산더 해밀턴, 제임스 매디슨, 존 제이는 헌법 비준을 독려하기 위한 논문집 '연방주의자(The Federalist)'를 발표하여 이러한 우려를 불식시키고자 노력했다. 이들은 '대표성 있는 연방국가의 중요성', '치안을 유지하기 위한 강력한 행정기구의 필요성', '연방의회의 법률을 심의할 사법기구의 필요성', '삼권분립의 중요성', '각 주간의 충돌을 조정하고 힘의 균형을 조율할 체계의 필요성' 등을 이유로 들었고, 시민들과 의회를 설득하여 결국에는 13개 주 모두가 연방에 가입하는 데 지대한 공을 세웠다. 이 논문집은 현재까지도 미국의 정치를 이해하기 위한 가장 중요한 저서 가운데 하나로 꼽힌다. 제헌의회 당시, 5월과 9월 사이 총 55명의 '건국의 아버지들(Founding Fathers)'이 제헌에 참여했으나 실제로 9월 17일 서명에 참여한 인물들은 39명이다. 주 대표 3명(버지니아 주 대표 2명, 매사추세츠 주 대표 1명)은 서명을 거부했다. 이유는 완성된 헌법전이 '결함 있는 문서(flawed document)'라 생각되어 반대했기 때문이다. 다른 13명은 아예 9월 17일 서명식에 불참했다.

If no enumerated power authorizes Congress to pass a certain law, that law may not be enacted, even if it would not violate any of the express prohibitions in the Bill of Rights or elsewhere in the Constitution. Indeed, the Constitution did not initially include a Bill of Rights at least partly because the Framers felt the enumeration of powers sufficed to restrain the Government.

(헌법에 의해) 열거된 권한이 의회에 특정한 법률을 통과시킬 권한을 부여하지 않은 경우, 이것이 권리장전이나 헌법의 다른 부분에서 정하고 있는 명시적인 금지 조항을

위반하는 것이 아니라 할지라도, 그러한 법률은 제정될 수 없다고 보아야 할 것이다. 실제로, 당시 헌법의 창안자들은 최소한 그것(본문 7개 조의 조항)이 정부를 억제하기에 충분한 권한의 열거라고 생각했으므로 권리장전을 별도로 포함하지 않았다.[15] 연방 헌법은 본문 7개조, 수정조항 27개조로 구성되어 있다. 본문 7개조는 국가 구성에 필수불가결한 요소만 간단하게 넣어 앞으로 태어날 국가권력을 확보하기 위한 플랫폼으로 일단 기능하도록 만들었고, 권리장전 등 타국의 헌법에 포함되는 많은 부분은 대부분 수정조항으로 추가되었다. 이 수정조항이 연방 헌법의 핵심인데, 어떤 헌법 조문이 개정되면 구 조문은 삭제되는 대한민국의 헌법과는 달리 미국 연방헌법은 무효화된 조항도 사라지지 않고 남아 있다. 이를 증보(amendment)라고 하며, 대표적인 예는 수정 21조에 의해 무효화된 수정 18조(금주법) 등이 있다. 세계적으로는 소수례이다. 이런 특징 때문에 '수정'이라는 단어가 붙는다. 이외에 영미법의 특성상 연방법원의 판례도 불문헌법으로 통용되며, 때문에 미국 연방대법원의 연방법에 대한 위헌심판은 큰 영향력을 미친다. "국민의 어떠한 권리를 보장한다"는 방식의 문장을 자주 사용하는 대륙법계 헌법과 달리, "국가는 어떠한 행위를 할 수 없다"는 방식의 문장을 다수 사용하는 것도 미국 헌법의 특징이다. 예를 들어 '모든 국민은 …의 자유를 가진다'고 기술된 대한민국 헌법 제2장과 달리 수정헌법의 기본권 조항들은 '(연방 혹은 주) 정부가 일정한 행위나 입법을 할 수 없도록 금지하거나 제한하는 형식'을 거의 따르고 있다.[6] 대한민국 헌법의 권리장전이 '보장되는 권리'라면 미국 헌법의 권리장전은 '침해받을 수 없는 권리'인 셈이다.[16] 연방대법원은 이러한 헌법의 '억제 조항'을 적극적으로 해석하여, 헌법이 국가(연방)에 명확히 부여하고 있는 권한이 아니라면 그것은 주와 인민의 권리를 침해하는 월권행위라는 태도를 항시 유지하고 있다. 따라서 미국의 위헌 심사에서는 '국가가 공공복리를 위해 기본권을 제한할 경우, 그 목적이 얼마나 중대한가, 그리고 그 목적을 달성하기 위해 최소한의 범위를 침해하도록 법률을 구성했는가'를 국가가 입증하도록 하며, 이를 엄격심사(strict scrutiny)라고 한다. 시민의 권리를 위해서 국가가 능동적인 보장과 조치를 취해야 한다는 대륙법계

---

15 미국 연방대법원장 존 로버츠, National Federation of Independent Business v. Sebelius, 567 U.S. 519 (2012) 판결 중.

16 박종보 "미국헌법상 기본권의 체계와 이론적 특징," 2006 참조.

사상과 달리, 시민의 권리를 가장 침해하는 것은 국가권력 그 자체라는 영미법계 사상을 드러낸다.

We the People of the United States, in Order to form a more perfect Union, establish Justice, insure domestic Tranquility, provide for the common defence, promote the general Welfare, and secure the Blessings of Liberty to ourselves and our Posterity, do ordain and establish this Constitution for the United States of America.

우리 미합중국 시민은 더 완벽한 연방을 형성하고, 정의를 수립하고, 국내의 평안을 보장하고, 공동방위를 제공하고, 일반적 복지를 증진하며 우리들과 후손들의 자유에 대한 축복을 보호하기 위하여 미합중국 헌법을 제정한다. 첫 문장인 "We the People of the United States…"는 국 여권의 서명 페이지 및 미국 비자에 적혀있는 문장이기도 하다. 대한민국 헌법 전문의 영문판도 "We, the people of Korea…"로 시작한다.

제1조 (입법)

Section 1. All legislative Powers herein granted shall be vested in a Congress of the United States, which shall consist of a Senate and House of Representatives.

제1절

이 헌법에 의하여 부여되는 모든 입법 권한은 미합중국 의회에 속하며, 의회는 상원과 하원으로 구성한다.

Section 2. The House of Representatives shall be composed of Members chosen every second Year by the People of the several States, and the Electors in each State shall have the Qualifications requisite for Electors of the most numerous Branch of the State Legislature.

No Person shall be a Representative who shall not have attained to the Age of twenty five Years, and been seven Years a Citizen of the United States, and who shall not, when elected, be an Inhabitant of that State in which he shall be chosen.

Representatives and direct Taxes shall be apportioned among the several States which may be included within this Union, according to their respective Numbers, which shall be determined by adding to the whole Number of free Persons, including those bound to Service for a Term of Years, and excluding Indians not taxed, three fifths of all other Persons. The actual Enumeration shall be made within three Years after the first Meeting of the Congress of the United States, and within every subsequent Term of ten Years, in such Manner as they shall by Law direct. The Number of Representatives shall not exceed one for every thirty Thousand, but each State shall have at Least one Representative; and until such enumeration shall be made, the State of New Hampshire shall be entitled to chuse three, Massachusetts eight, Rhode-Island and Providence Plantations one, Connecticut five, New-York six, New Jersey four, Pennsylvania eight, Delaware one, Maryland six, Virginia ten, North Carolina five, South Carolina five, and Georgia three.

When vacancies happen in the Representation from any State, the Executive Authority thereof shall issue Writs of Election to fill such Vacancies.

The House of Representatives shall chuse their Speaker and other Officers; and shall have the sole Power of Impeachment.

제2절 (하원)

하원은 각 주의 주민이 2년마다 선출하는 의원으로 구성하며, 각 주의 선거인은 주의회의 하위 원들 가운데 의원수가 가장 많은 원의 선거인에게 요구되는 자격 요건을 구비해야 한다. 누구든지 연령이 만 25세에 미달한 자, 미합중국 시민으로서의 기간이 7년이 못 되는 자, 그리고 선거 당시에 선출되는 주의 주민이 아닌 자는 하원의원이 될 수 없다. 하원의원의 수와 직접세는 연방에 가입하는 각 주의 인구수에 비례하여 각 주에 배정한다. 각 주의 인구수는 연기 계약 노무자를 포함한 자유인의 총수에,

과세하지 아니하는 인디언을 제외하고, 그 밖의 인구 총수의 5분의 3을 가산하여 결정한다. 인구수의 산정은 제1회 연방의회를 개최한 후 3년 이내에 행하며, 그 후는 10년마다 법률이 정하는 바에 따라 행한다. 하원의원의 수는 인구 3만 명당 1인의 비율을 초과하지 못한다. 다만, 각 주는 적어도 1명의 하원의원을 가져야 한다. 위의 인구수의 산정이 있을 때까지 뉴햄프셔주는 3명 매사추세츠주는 8명, 로드아일랜드주와 프로비던스 식민지는 1명, 코네티컷주는 5명, 뉴욕주는 6명, 뉴저지주는 4명, 펜실베이니아주는 8명, 델라웨어주는 1명, 메릴랜드주는 6명, 버지니아주는 10명, 노스캐롤라이나주는 5명, 사우스캐롤라이나주는 5명, 그리고 조지아주는 3명의 의원을 각기 선출할 수 있다.

어떤 주에서든 그 주에서 선출하는 하원의원에 결원이 생겼을 경우에는, 그 주의 행정부가 그 결원을 채우기 위한 보궐 선거의 명령을 내려야 한다.

하원은 그 의장과 그 밖의 임원을 선임하며 탄핵권을 전유한다.

Section 3. The Senate of the United States shall be composed of two Senators from each State, chosen by the Legislature thereof, for six Years; and each Senator shall have one Vote.

Immediately after they shall be assembled in Consequence of the first Election, they shall be divided as equally as may be into three Classes. The Seats of the Senators of the first Class shall be vacated at the Expiration of the second Year, of the second Class at the Expiration of the fourth Year, and of the third Class at the Expiration of the sixth Year, so that one third may be chosen every second Year; and if Vacancies happen by Resignation, or otherwise, during the Recess of the Legislature of any State, the Executive thereof may make temporary Appointments until the next Meeting of the Legislature, which shall then fill such Vacancies.

No Person shall be a Senator who shall not have attained to the Age of thirty Years, and been nine Years a Citizen of the United States, and who shall not, when elected, be an Inhabitant of that State for which he shall be chosen.

The Vice President of the United States shall be President of the Senate, but shall have no Vote, unless they be equally divided.

The Senate shall chuse their other Officers, and also a President pro tempore, in the Absence of the Vice President, or when he shall exercise the Office of President of the United States.

The Senate shall have the sole Power to try all Impeachments. When sitting for that Purpose, they shall be on Oath or Affirmation. When the President of the United States is tried, the Chief Justice shall preside: And no Person shall be convicted without the Concurrence of two thirds of the Members present.

Judgment in Cases of Impeachment shall not extend further than to removal from Office, and disqualification to hold and enjoy any Office of honor, Trust or Profit under the United States: but the Party convicted shall nevertheless be liable and subject to Indictment, Trial, Judgment and Punishment, according to Law.

제3절 (상원)

상원은 각 주 주의회에서 선출한 6년 임기의 상원의원 2명씩으로 구성되며 각 상원의원은 1표의 투표권을 가진다. 상원의원들의 제1회 선거의 결과로 당선되어 회합하면, 즉시로 의원 총수를 가능한 한 동수의 3개 부류로 나눈다. 제1부류의 의원은 2년 만기로, 제2부류의 의원은 4년 만기로, 그리고 제 3 부류의 의원은 6년을 만기로. 그 의석을 비워야 한다. 이렇게 하여 상원의원의 총수의 3분의 1이 2년마다 개선될 수 있게 한다. 그리고 어떤 주에서든 주의회의 후회 중에 사직 또는 그 밖의 원인으로 상원의원의 결원이 생길 때에는 그 주의 행정부는 다음 회기의 주의회가 결원을 보충할 때까지 잠정적으로 상원의원을 임명할 수 있다. 연령이 30세에 미달하거나, 미합중국 시민으로서의 기간이 9년이 되지 아니하거나, 또는 선거 당시 선출되는 주의 주민이 아닌 자는 상원의원이 될 수 없다. 미합중국 부통령은 상원의장이 된다. 다만, 표결에서 가부 동수일 경우를 제외하고는 표결권이 없다. 상원은 의장 이외의 임원들을 선임하며, 부통령이 결원일 경우나, 부통령이 대통령의 직무를 집행하는 때에는 임시 의장을 선임한다. 상원은 모든 탄핵 심판의 권한을 전유한다. 이 목적을 위하여 상원이 개회될 때, 의원들은 선서 또는 확약을 해야 한다. 미합중국 대통령을 심판

할 경우에는 연방대법원장을 의장으로 한다. 누구라도 출석 의원 3분의 2 이상의 찬성 없이는 유죄 판결을 받지 아니한다. 탄핵 심판에서의 판결은 면직 그리고 명예직, 위임직, 또는 보수를 수반하는 미합중국의 공직에 취임, 재직하는 자격을 박탈하는 것 이상이 될 수 없다. 다만, 이같이 유죄 판결을 받은 자일지라도 법률의 규정에 따른 기소, 재판, 판결 및 처벌을 면할 수 없다.

Ⅱ. 미국 대통령(The President of the United States) 對 총기

1. 미국 대통령 對 총기

미국 대통령(The President of the United States)[17]은 아메리카 합중국의 국가원수이자 정부수반이다. 1788년 미국 헌법이 만들어지면서 대통령 지위가 생겼으며, 1789년 첫 대통령이 임무를 시작하였다. 미국 대통령은 국가의 원수인 동시에 행정부의 수반 역할을 수행하고, 또한 미국 헌법 제2장에 의해 미군의 총사령관이기도 하여, '선출된 황제'라고 불릴 만큼 막강한 권한과 책임을 지니고 있다. 현재 전세계 유일의 초강대국으로 각국에 강력한 영향을 미치는 미국의 지위 때문에 미국의 대통령은 세계에서 손꼽히는 지도자 중 한 사람으로 평가되기도 한다. 한때 소비에트 연방과의 냉전 중에는 '자본주의 세계의 지도자'로 인식되기도 했었다. 미국의 대통령은 미국 의회에서 제정된 법률이 대통령에게 위임한 권한 안에서 명령을 내릴 수 있다. 이 권한에는 미국 상원, 미국 하원을 통과한 법률을 승인하여 법을 승인할 권한, 상원의 동의로 내각의 장차관을 임명할 권한, 의회의 동의로 사면이나 형 집행 연기를 명령할 권한 그리고 미국 상원의 동의 하에 외국과 조약을 체결하고, 상원의 동의로 연방의 주요직, 대사, 연방대법원 판사를 포함한 연방판사를 임명할 권한을 가진다. 그러나 한편으로 의회에 대하여는 법안의 제출권도, 의회의 해산권도 가지지 않는다. 미국 헌법 제2장은 대통령의 임기를 4년으로 정하고 있다. 제12차 수정헌법(1804년)에 따라

---

17 https://ko.wikipedia.org/wiki/%EB%AF%B8%EA%B5%AD_%EB%8C%80%ED%86%B5%EB%A0%B9 2025.4.7. 검색.

대통령 후보와 부통령 후보가 분리되었고, 제22차 수정 헌법(1951년)에 따라 대통령직의 3선은 금지된다. 미국 대선은 실질적으로는 국민의 직접 선거방식과 대동소이하나, 형식적으로는 각 주의 선거인단 표수에 의해 선출하는 선거 방식을 취한다. 만약 선거인단 과반수 획득자가 없을시 하원에서 결선투표를 하며 이 경우 주별로 1표씩 투표한다. 즉 대통령선거시 승리한 주의 정당이 주별로 1표씩 행사된다. 대통령이 임기 중에 궐위되면 부통령이 대통령직을 승계한다. 미국의 초대 대통령은 조지 워싱턴이고, 현재 미국의 대통령은 2024년 미국 대통령 선거에서 당선된 제47대 대통령 도널드 트럼프로, 2025년 1월 20일 정오(한국시각으로는 1월 21일 오전 2시)에 공식 취임하였다. 영어권에서는 대통령이나 국가주석을 구분하지 않고 President라 부른다. 하지만 한자문화권에 속하는 국가인 대한민국, 중국, 일본에서는 미국 대통령(대한민국, 일본)이나 미국 총통(중화권)으로 서로 다르게 부르기도 한다. 1783년의 파리 조약으로 미국은 대영제국으로부터 분리되어 독립하게 되었지만, 그 당시에는 제대로 된 정부 조직을 갖추고 있지 못했다. 당시 미국은 장래에 어떠한 독재 권력으로부터 나라를 보호하기 위한 제도적 장치를 원했고, 사실상 유일한 연방조직이었던 의회는 아직 충분한 권력과 재무적 권한을 갖지 못하고 있었다. 그러나 독립전쟁 이후의 경제적 침체기 속에 경제적 사회적 다양한 요구로 대통령직과 중앙연방정부제도에 대한 가능성을 모색해갔다. 하지만 1788년 헌법의 비준 전에는 미국에는 아직 어떠한 단일한 실제적 권력 기관이나 개인이 존재하지 못했다. 1789년 조지 워싱턴이 초대 대통령이 되면서 이 새로운 나라의 새로운 지도자가 갖추어야 할 여러 제도와 관습들이 생겨났다. 대통령의 직위는 아메리카 합중국 헌법 제2조에 의거하고 있으며, 이후 몇 번의 수정헌법조항에 의해 그 권한, 임기 등이 명시되어 있다. 대통령의 피선거권을 가지기 위해서는 최소 35세 이상이어야 하며 미국 내 출생으로 인한 미국 시민으로서 최소 14년 동안 미국에서 거주하였어야 한다. 미국 대통령과 부통령은 4년간의 임기를 가진다. 제22차 수정헌법(1951년)은 대통령직을 3선 이상 재임할 수 없도록 규정하고 있으며, 대통령이 면직, 사망 또는 사임하여 그 남은 임기 동안 2년 이상 대통령직에 있었거나 대통령의 직무를 대행한 사람도 1회만 중임할 수 있다. 프랭클린 D. 루스벨트는 미국 역사상 유일하게 3선 이상을 재임한 대통령인데, 그는 대공황과 제2차 세계대전의 위기 속에서 지도력을 발휘해 4선(1932년, 1936년, 1940년, 1944년 대선에

잇따라 당선됨으로써 1932년 3월 4일부터 1945년 4월 12일까지 재임)에 성공했다. 그러나 이는 초대 조지 워싱턴 대통령 이래 미국 대통령은 1회만 중임해 온 불문율을 깨뜨린 것으로써 그의 사망 뒤 대통령의 3선 금지가 성문화되었다. 대통령직의 3선을 금지한 제22차 수정헌법(1951) 이후 2016년까지 재선에 성공해 8년간 재임한 대통령은 드와이트 D. 아이젠하워, 로널드 레이건, 빌 클린턴, 조지 W. 부시, 버락 오바마, 도널드 트럼프 등 6명이며, 리처드 닉슨 대통령은 재선에 성공했으나 임기 도중 사임하였다. 미국 역사상 가장 짧은 기간 재임한 대통령은 제9대 대통령인 윌리엄 헨리 해리슨으로 취임 31일 만에 사망하였다. 과거에도 현재와 유사한 방식으로 대통령 선거를 실시하였으나 차이점은 현재 대통령과 부통령이 따로 출마해서 선거를 치르는 것과는 달리 과거에는 오직 대통령 선거만 실시하였으며 2위로 대통령에서 낙선된 후보를 부통령으로 임명하였다. 그렇게 부통령이 된 대표적인 인물로는 대통령선거에서 토머스 제퍼슨에게 패하고 부통령이 된 에런 버가 있다. 미국의 대통령은 연방정부의 지도자로 구성주의 대표들이 4년마다 선출한다. 선거방법은 50개주에 할당된 선거인단과 콜롬비아 특별구의 선출 선거인단의 과반수를 획득한 자가 대통령에 당선된다. 대통령선거인단 배정은 각주 출신 연방상원의원과 연방하원의원의 합친 수가 그 주선거인단이 되며, 여기에 콜롬비아특별구에 배정된 수를 합한 것이다. 통상 대통령선거일은 '슈퍼 화요일'이라고 부르는 11월 첫째 주 화요일이다. 각 주별로 선거를 치르며, 통상 2개주를 제외한 나머지 주에서는 득표를 가장 많이 한 후보가 그 주의 선거인단을 모두 차지한다. 이러한 간선제 방식 때문에 직접투표에 이기고도 선거인단 확보에 져서 낙선된 대통령후보가 발생하기도 한다. 만약 선거인단 중 과반수를 확보하는 후보가 없을 경우에는 연방하원이 대통령을 결정하게 된다. 이 경우에는 각 주별로 1표씩 행사한다. 미국 헌법은 대통령이 임기 중에 면직, 사망 또는 사임하게 될 경우에는 부통령이 그 자리를 승계하도록 정하고 있으며, 그도 없으면 연방의회가 법률로 정한 순서에 따라 연방하원 의장 등이 승계한다. 1974년 8월 9일, 리처드 닉슨 대통령이 사임했을 때에는 제럴드 포드 부통령이 대통령직을 승계하였다. 그런데, 포드는 1973년에 사임한 스피로 애그뉴 부통령의 후임으로 닉슨 대통령에 의해 지명되어 연방의회 양원의 인준으로 취임한 부통령으로서 미국 역사상 국민의 선거를 거치지 않고 대통령이 된 유일한 사례이다.

2. 미국 총기사건 일지

[표1-1] 미 주요 총기 사건

연도	중요 총기 사건	피해 규모	비고
1968.6.5.	로버트 F. 케네디 상원의원 피살 존슨 대통령 1968년 6월 5일 성명 "그 원인은 '아메리카' 때문이라는 견해를 배격하고 이 사건은 한 광인(狂人)의 짓," 총포소지 규제 강화 조치	상원의원 암살	
1968.4.4.	마틴 루터 킹 목사 피살 킹을 살해한 사람은 과격파 백인 단체 제임스 얼 레이 (James Earl Ray)	민권운동가 암살	레밍턴 모델 760
1999.4.20.	컬럼바인 고등학교 총기사건, 폭탄 테러 증오범죄	16명 사망, 21명 부상	
1764.7.26. 2006.10. 2017.6.8.	펜실베이니아 최초 학교 총기 사건 펜실베이니아 아미시 총기 사건 펜실베이니아 마트 총기 난사	학생 10명 사망 6명 사망, 5명 부상 4명 사망	
2007.4.16.	버지니아 공대 총기 난사 사건 재미 한국인 조승희는 반자동 권총 두 자루로 총탄을 난사	32명 사망, 29명 부상	스스로 자신의 머이에 총을 쏴 자살
2009.4.3.	뉴욕 빙엄턴 베트남계 이민자 지벌리 웡이 미민자 센터에서 총기 난사	23명 사망	용의자 자살
2009.11.5.	텍사스 포트후드 기지 군의관인 니달 하산 소령이 기지 내에서 총기 난사	13명 사망, 42명 부상	
2012.12.14.	코네티컷 뉴타운에서 애덤란자(20세)가 샌디훅 초등학교에서 총기 난사	어린이 20명 포함, 모두 28명 사망	자신의 어머니에게도 총을 겨눈 용의자는 자살
2015.12.2.	플로리다 올랜도에서 아프간계 미국인 오마르 마틴(29세)이 게이 나이트클럽 펄스 내부로 총기 난사	50명 사망	경찰 마틴 사살
2017.10.1.	라스베이거스 만델레이 베이호텔	60명 사망,	스티븐 패덕은

	32층에 투숙하던 스티븐 패덕(64세) 창문을 깨고 맞은 편 콘서트장을 향해 10분간 총기 난사	400명 부상	현장에서 자살한 채 발견
2017.11.5.	텍사스 주 서덜랜드 스프링스 침례교회에서 4년간 미 공군으로 복무한 패트릭 켈리(26세)가 교회안 사람들과 행인을 향해 무차별 총기 난사	27명 사망	범인은 차를 타고 도주중 사망
2018.2.14.	플로리다 주 파크랜드의 마조리 스토맨 더글러스 고등학교에서 이 학교 퇴학생 니콜라스 크루즈(19세)가 방독면을 쓴채 총기 난사	학생 17명 사망, 부상 35명	
2022.5.24.	텍사스주 유밸디의 롭 초등학교에서 고교생이 총기 난사	21명 사망	범인 현장에서 사살
2023.3.27.	테네시주 내슈빌 백인 여성 오드리 해일(28세)가 수업 중인 초등학생 무차별 총격	6명 사망	경찰 대치 중 총에 맞아 숨져
2025.4.17.	플로리다주립대 캠퍼스에서 지역치안 담당하던 플로리다 레온 카운디 부보안관의 아들(20세)은 어머니가 사용하던 무기에 접근, 총기 난사[18]	2명 사망, 6명 부상	
2025.5.26.	美 현충일에 필라델피아서 총기 난사 사건	2명 사망, 9명 부상	
2025.5.28.	미국 워싱턴주 타코마 시 교회에 있는 해리 토드 공원 총기 난사[19]	100여 명에 총기 난사. 7명 부상 3명은 위독	

18 美 플로리다주립대 총기 난사 관련 도널드 존 트럼프 대통령: 윤기은 기자, "미국 플로리다주립대 대낮 총기 난사로 최소 2명 사망, 6명 부상," 경향신문, 2025.4.18.

19 CNN 방송에 따르면 케빈 베델 필라델피아 경찰청장은 26일(현지시간) 오후 10시 27분쯤 필라델피아의 페어마운트 공원에서 총격이 발생했다고 밝혔다. 이날은 미국의 현충일인 '전몰장병 추모일'로 여러 사람이 공원에서 야외 요리 파티를 즐기고 있었다. 이로 인해 남성과 여성 1명이 사망했다. 부상자 중에는 각각 15, 16, 17세인 청소년 3명도 있었다. 부상자 중 1명은 총격 이후 발생한 혼란 속에서 차량에 치여 다쳤다. 부상자들은 병원으로 옮겨졌으며 다행히 안정된 상태인 것으로 전해졌다. 경찰은 아직 용의자를 체포하지 못했다. 용의자가 단 1명이냐는 질문에 베델 청장은 "아직 모른다"며 범행에 쓰인 총기를 발견하지 못했다고 말했다. 이어 "곧 총기가 하나인지, 아니면 여러 정인지 알 수 있을 것"이라면서 총격이 매우 빠르게 이

· 미 플로리다주립대 총기 사건에 대하여 2018년 2월 14일 플로리다주 고등학교 총기 난사 당시 14세 딸을 잃은 프레드 구텐버그는 엑스에 "미국은 망가졌다." 그는 "아버지로서 파크랜드 총격 사건 이후 제가 바라는 것은 오직 우리 아이들의 안전을 돕는 것이었다."며 "안타깝게도 총기 폭력을 줄이기 위한 올바른 조치를 거부하는 많은 사람들 때문에 오늘 일어난 일도 놀랍지도 않다."고 지적했다.

· 美 플로리다주립대 총기 난사 관련 도널드 존 트럼프 대통령: 소식을 보고 받은 트럼프 대통령도 유감을 표했습니다. 다만, 총기 소유의 권리를 규정한 수정헌법 제2조를 지지한다며, 총기 규제 강화에 반대한다는 뜻을 재차 강조했습니다.

도널드 존 트럼프 대통령 曰 "끔찍한 일이죠. 하지만 총이 저절로 사람을 쏘는 게 아니고 사람이 쏘는 겁니다. 너무 자주 쓰이는 표현이긴 해요."

· 전미총기협회(National Rifle Association(of America)) 1871년 11월 17일 설립 버지니아주 페어팩스 캐틀린 D. 메도우즈

NRA 범퍼스티커 슬로건

"총은 사람을 죽이지 않는다. 사람이 사람을 죽인다."

Guns don't Kill people, people kill people

Chronology of Major Gun Incidents in the United States

On June 5, 1968, U.S. Senator Robert F. Kennedy was assassinated. In a statement that day, President Lyndon B. Johnson rejected the view that "America itself" was to blame, calling it the act of a madman, and announced measures to strengthen gun control.

어졌다고 덧붙였다. 앞서 전날(25일) 밤에는 사우스캐롤라이나주 해변 마을에서 현충일을 맞아 선상 파티를 즐기던 사람들을 겨냥한 총격 사건이 발생해 최소 11명이 다치기도 했다. 총기 소지가 합법인 미국에서는 총기 난사 사건이 자주 발생한다. CNN에 따르면 지난해 미국에서는 4명 이상의 사상자가 발생하는 총기 난사 사건이 502건 발생했다. https://www.news1.kr/world/usa-canada/5796134 2025.6.9. 검색.

On April 4, 1968, civil rights leader Martin Luther King Jr. was shot and killed by James Earl Ray, a member of a white extremist group. The weapon used was a Remington Model 760.

On April 20, 1999, the Columbine High School massacre took place, involving both gunfire and attempted bombings. Sixteen people were killed and 21 injured.

On July 26, 1764, Pennsylvania saw the first recorded school shooting in U.S. history, in which ten students were killed.

In October 2006, an Amish school shooting in Pennsylvania left six dead and five injured.

On June 8, 2017, a mass shooting at a Pennsylvania supermarket killed four people.

On April 16, 2007, Seung-Hui Cho, a South Korean student at Virginia Tech, carried out a mass shooting using two semi-automatic pistols, killing 32 and injuring 29 before taking his own life.

On April 3, 2009, Jiverly Wong, a Vietnamese immigrant, opened fire at an immigrant services center in Binghamton, New York, killing 23 before committing suicide.

On November 5, 2009, Major Nidal Hasan, an Army psychiatrist, killed 13 and injured 42 at Fort Hood, Texas.

On December 14, 2012, 20-year-old Adam Lanza killed 28 people, including 20 children, at Sandy Hook Elementary School in Newtown, Connecticut, before taking his own life after killing his mother.

On December 2, 2015, Omar Mateen, a 29-year-old Afghan-American, attacked the Pulse nightclub in Orlando, Florida, killing 50 people before being shot dead by police.

On October 1, 2017, Stephen Paddock opened fire from the 32nd floor of the Mandalay Bay Hotel in Las Vegas onto a concert crowd for ten minutes, killing 60 and injuring 400, before committing suicide.

On November 5, 2017, Devin Patrick Kelley, a former U.S. Air Force serviceman, killed 27 people at a church in Sutherland Springs, Texas, before dying while fleeing in a vehicle.

On February 14, 2018, Nikolas Cruz, a 19-year-old expelled student, opened fire at Marjory Stoneman Douglas High School in Parkland, Florida, killing 17 and injuring 35.

On May 24, 2022, a high school student opened fire at Robb Elementary School in Uvalde, Texas, killing 21 before being shot dead at the scene.

On March 27, 2023, Audrey Hale, a 28-year-old white woman, carried out a mass shooting at an elementary school in Nashville, Tennessee, killing six before being killed in a police shootout.

On April 17, 2025, at Florida State University, the 20-year-old son of a deputy sheriff accessed his mother's service weapon and opened fire on campus, killing two and injuring six.

On May 26, 2025, a Memorial Day shooting in Philadelphia left two people dead and nine injured.

On May 28, 2025, a mass shooting occurred at Harry Todd Park in suburban Tacoma, Washington. Two victims, a man and a woman, died, and seven others were injured, three critically. The shooting took place during a public gathering, and the suspect remained unidentified at the time of reporting.

Chronology of Major Gun Incidents in the United States — With Political Reactions and Legal Impacts

June 5, 1968 — Assassination of Senator Robert F. Kennedy

Robert F. Kennedy was shot in Los Angeles while campaigning for the Democratic presidential nomination. President Lyndon B. Johnson, in a statement the same day, rejected claims that "America itself" was to blame, calling it the act of a madman. The incident intensified political momentum for gun control, contributing to the passage of the Gun Control Act of 1968, which restricted mail-order sales and expanded background checks.

April 4, 1968 — Assassination of Martin Luther King Jr.

Civil rights leader Dr. King was killed by James Earl Ray, a white supremacist. The murder shocked the nation, sparking riots in over 100 cities and reinforcing support for the Gun Control Act of 1968. The weapon was a Remington Model 760 rifle.

April 20, 1999 — Columbine High School Massacre

Two students carried out a school shooting combined with failed bomb attacks in Colorado, killing 16 and injuring 21. The event triggered nationwide debates on violent video games, bullying, and gun access to minors, leading to state-level "zero tolerance" school policies, though federal legislation remained limited.

July 26, 1764 — First Recorded School Shooting in U.S. History

In Pennsylvania, Native American raiders killed 10 students. This predates the Second Amendment but is often cited in historical discussions on the cultural presence of firearms in American life.

October 2006 — Amish School Shooting, Pennsylvania

A gunman killed six and injured five in a one-room Amish schoolhouse. The community's decision to forgive the shooter's family drew international attention, but the event also renewed debates over safe storage laws and rural gun access.

June 8, 2017 — Pennsylvania Supermarket Mass Shooting

Four people were killed. While the case did not lead to major legislative changes, it reinforced calls for stricter mental health screenings in gun licensing.

April 16, 2007 — Virginia Tech Shooting

Seung-Hui Cho, a South Korean student, killed 32 and injured 29 with two semi-automatic pistols before committing suicide. It became the deadliest school shooting in U.S. history at the time, prompting the NICS Improvement Amendments Act of 2008, aimed at better reporting of mental health records to the federal background check system.

April 3, 2009 — Binghamton Immigration Center Shooting, New York

Jiverly Wong, a Vietnamese immigrant, killed 23 people before killing himself. The tragedy intensified discussion on gun violence in immigrant communities and calls for language-accessible mental health services.

November 5, 2009 — Fort Hood Shooting, Texas

Major Nidal Hasan, an Army psychiatrist, killed 13 and injured 42. The incident raised concerns over internal military security and radicalization. While no sweeping gun law changes followed, military base firearm policies were reviewed.

December 14, 2012 — Sandy Hook Elementary School Shooting, Connecticut

Adam Lanza killed 28 people, including 20 children, before committing suicide. The event profoundly influenced national discourse, leading to President Obama's push for expanded background checks and assault weapon bans. While federal bills failed in the Senate, several states (e.g., New York, Connecticut) enacted stricter gun laws.

December 2, 2015 — Pulse Nightclub Shooting, Florida

Omar Mateen killed 50 people in an LGBTQ nightclub. The massacre fueled debates over gun access for individuals flagged by the FBI and raised security concerns for vulnerable communities. Federal legislative changes stalled, but some states tightened laws on high-capacity magazines.

October 1, 2017 — Las Vegas Mass Shooting

Stephen Paddock killed 60 and injured over 400 by firing from a hotel window into a concert crowd. The attack prompted a federal ban on bump stocks in 2018 under the Trump administration.

November 5, 2017 — Sutherland Springs Church Shooting, Texas

Devin Patrick Kelley killed 27. A review revealed that the U.S. Air Force failed to report his domestic violence conviction to the FBI's database, prompting reforms in military criminal reporting to NICS.

February 14, 2018 — Marjory Stoneman Douglas High School Shooting, Florida

Nikolas Cruz killed 17. Surviving students formed the "March for Our Lives" movement, leading to new state laws in Florida raising the firearm purchase age to 21 and mandating a waiting period.

May 24, 2022 — Robb Elementary School Shooting, Texas

A high school student killed 21. The tragedy led to the Bipartisan Safer Communities Act (2022), which enhanced background checks for buyers under 21 and funded red-flag law programs.

March 27, 2023 — Nashville Elementary School Shooting, Tennessee

Audrey Hale killed six before being shot by police. The incident renewed debate on red-flag laws in conservative states but saw limited legislative follow-through.

April 17, 2025 — Florida State University Campus Shooting

The 20-year-old son of a deputy sheriff accessed his mother's service weapon, killing two and injuring six. The case reignited discussion on mandatory safe-storage laws for law enforcement households.

May 26, 2025 — Memorial Day Shooting, Philadelphia

Two killed and nine injured during a public holiday gathering. Lawmakers and advocates called for better enforcement of illegal firearm possession laws in urban centers.

May 28, 2025 — Harry Todd Park Shooting, Tacoma, Washington

Two killed and seven injured, three critically, during a public event. The shooting occurred a day after another mass shooting in South Carolina, adding to a grim Memorial Day weekend tally. Police investigations were ongoing at the time, and officials renewed calls for community-based violence prevention programs.

Statistical Analysis of Major U.S. Gun Incidents (1968–2025)

1. Incident Frequency by Decade

1960s: 2 high-profile political assassinations (Kennedy, King) directly influencing the Gun Control Act of 1968.

1970s–1980s: Relatively fewer mass shootings but sustained firearm-related homicides; legislation largely static.

1990s: Emergence of high-fatality school shootings (Columbine, 1999).

2000s: Increase in mass shootings involving semi-automatic pistols; Virginia Tech (2007) sets record fatalities at the time.

2010s: Significant spike in large-scale public venue shootings (Las Vegas 2017, Pulse 2015), leading to partial regulatory responses (e.g., bump stock ban).

2020s: Persistence of school shootings (Uvalde 2022, Nashville 2023) and multiple incidents within short time spans (Memorial Day weekend 2025), indicating continued systemic issues despite federal reforms.

2. Casualty Trends

Period	Avg. Deaths per Major Incident	Avg. Injuries per Incident	Notable Spike
1960s	~1–2 targeted victims (political assassinations)	Minimal collateral injuries	Political assassinations
1990s	~15–20 deaths	~20 injuries	Columbine (1999)
2000s	~20–32 deaths	20–40 injuries	Virginia Tech (2007)
2010s	~27–60 deaths	35–400 injuries	Las Vegas (2017)
2020s	~6–21 deaths	6–40 injuries	Uvalde (2022), Memorial Day

weekend 2025

Observation: The deadliest single-event toll remains the Las Vegas shooting in 2017 (60 dead, 400 injured). The highest casualty rate in schools occurred at Sandy Hook (2012) and Uvalde (2022).

3. Weapon Types Used

Assault-Style Rifles (e.g., AR-15): Common in large public venue attacks (Las Vegas 2017, Uvalde 2022).

Semi-Automatic Pistols: Dominant in school shootings (Virginia Tech 2007, Parkland 2018).

Shotguns and Rifles: Notable in rural/motivated hate crimes (Sutherland Springs 2017, Amish school 2006).

4. Legislative Response Timeline

1968: Gun Control Act — Background checks, restrictions on interstate sales.

1994: Federal Assault Weapons Ban (expired in 2004).

2008: NICS Improvement Amendments Act — Mental health reporting after Virginia Tech.

2018: Federal bump stock ban following Las Vegas massacre.

2022: Bipartisan Safer Communities Act — Enhanced checks for buyers under 21, funding for red-flag laws.

Trend: Legislative responses tend to follow extreme, high-casualty events but often stall at the federal level due to political polarization. State-level action is more dynamic, with stricter laws in Democratic-leaning states and deregulation in Republican-leaning states.

5. Geographic Patterns

High-Incidence States: Texas, Florida, California, and Pennsylvania appear multiple times in major incident records.

Urban vs. Rural: Urban incidents often involve larger crowds and higher injury counts; rural incidents often occur in schools or religious settings with high fatality rates but fewer injured.

6. Policy Implications

Data indicates that access to high-capacity firearms significantly increases casualty rates.

Enhanced background checks and safe-storage laws correlate with fewer firearm suicides and domestic shootings in states that adopt them.

Despite legislative efforts, cultural divisions over the Second Amendment hinder comprehensive federal reform.

The recurrence of school shootings suggests that security measures without addressing access and mental health have limited preventative effect.

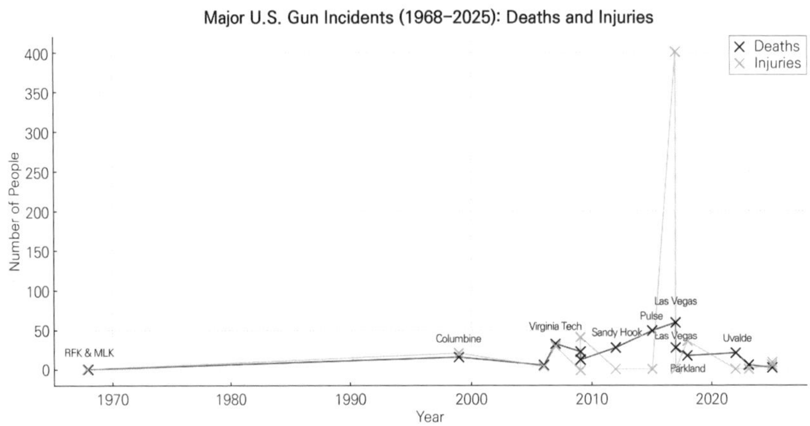

1968~2025년 미국 주요 총기사건: 사망자와 부상자
X축: 연도 Y축: 인원 수 범례: 빨간색: 사망자 주황색: 부상자
주요 사건 라벨: RFK & MLK → 로버트 F. 케네디 & 마틴 루터 킹 암살 사건 (1968)
Columbine → 콜럼바인 고등학교 총기난사 (1999)
Virginia Tech → 버지니아 공대 총기난사 (2007)
Sandy Hook → 샌디훅 초등학교 총기난사 (2012)
Pulse → 올랜도 펄스 나이트클럽 총기난사 (2015)
Las Vegas → 라스베이거스 총기난사 (2017)
Parkland → 파크랜드 고등학교 총기난사 (2018)
Uvalde → 유밸디 초등학교 총기난사 (2022)
English Version (original style)
Title: Major U.S. Gun Incidents (1968–2025): Deaths and Injuries

X-axis: Year
Y-axis: Number of People
Legend:
Red: Deaths
Orange: Injuries
Key Incident Labels:
RFK & MLK — Assassinations of Robert F. Kennedy & Martin Luther King Jr. (1968)
Columbine — Columbine High School Massacre (1999)
Virginia Tech — Virginia Tech Mass Shooting (2007)
Sandy Hook — Sandy Hook Elementary School Shooting (2012)
Pulse — Orlando Pulse Nightclub Shooting (2015)
Las Vegas — Las Vegas Mass Shooting (2017)
Parkland — Marjory Stoneman Douglas High School Shooting (2018)
Uvalde — Robb Elementary School Shooting (2022)

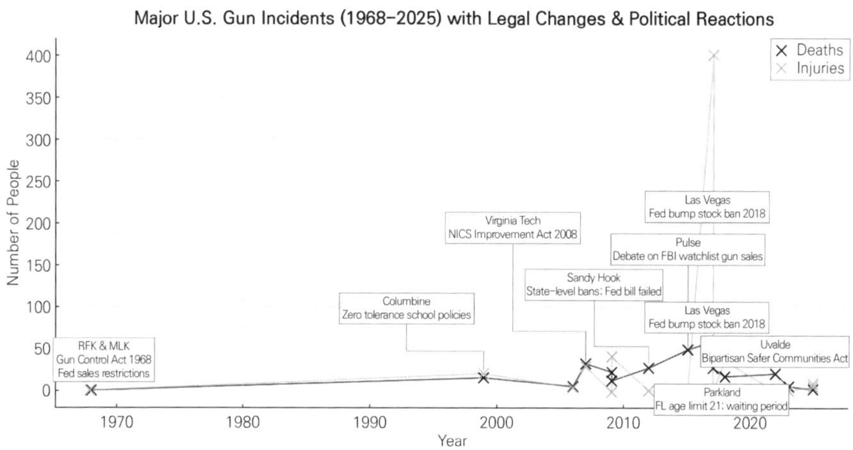

Major U.S. Gun Incidents (1968–2025) with Legal Changes & Political Reactions
1968~2025년 미국 주요 총기사건 — 법률 변화와 정치적 반응
범례 번역
Deaths → 사망자
Injuries → 부상자
주요 사건 라벨 번역
RFK & MLK — Gun Control Act 1968 / Fed sales restrictions
→ 케네디 · 킹 암살 — 1968년 총기규제법 / 연방 차원의 판매 제한
Columbine — Zero tolerance school policies
→ 콜럼바인 — 학교 내 '무관용' 정책 시행

Virginia Tech — NICS Improvement Act 2008
→ 버지니아 공대 — 2008년 NICS 개선법
Sandy Hook — State-level bans; Fed bill failed
→ 샌디훅 — 주(州) 단위 총기 금지법; 연방 법안은 실패
Pulse — Debate on FBI watchlist gun sales
→ 펄스 — FBI 감시자 명단 인물의 총기 구매 논란
Las Vegas — Fed bump stock ban 2018
→ 라스베이거스 — 2018년 연방 범프스톡 금지
Parkland — FL age limit 21; waiting period
→ 파크랜드 — 플로리다주 총기 구매 연령 21세로 상향, 대기 기간 의무화
Uvalde — Bipartisan Safer Communities Act
→ 유밸디 — 초당적 안전한 공동체법

1968년, 미국은 두 건의 정치적 암살 사건 — 로버트 F. 케네디와 마틴 루터 킹 목사 피살 — 을 경험하며, 총기 규제의 전환점을 맞았다. 이 비극은 총기규제법(Gun Control Act of 1968) 제정을 촉발했고, 연방 차원에서 총기 판매 제한이 강화되었다.

In 1968, the United States witnessed two political assassinations — Senator Robert F. Kennedy and Dr. Martin Luther King Jr. — which marked a turning point in gun regulation. The tragedy led to the enactment of the Gun Control Act of 1968, tightening federal firearm sales restrictions.

1999년 콜럼바인 고등학교 총기난사 사건은 미국 교육 현장에 '무관용(Zero Tolerance)' 정책을 불러왔다. 학교 폭력과 무기 소지에 대해 단호히 대응하는 이 방침은 상징적 효과를 냈지만, 총기 접근성 자체를 막기에는 한계가 있었다.

The 1999 Columbine High School massacre introduced "Zero Tolerance" policies in U.S. schools, a strict stance against school violence and weapon possession. While symbolically significant, it fell short in addressing firearm accessibility.

2007년 버지니아 공대 사건은 32명이 목숨을 잃은 참극이었고, 이로 인해 *NICS 개선법(2008)*이 통과되어 정신건강 관련 기록의 연방 데이터베이스 보고가 강화되

었다.

The 2007 Virginia Tech tragedy, which claimed 32 lives, led to the NICS Improvement Amendments Act of 2008, enhancing the reporting of mental health records to the federal background check system.

2012년 샌디훅 초등학교 사건은 어린이 20명을 포함한 28명이 희생되었고, 연방 차원의 강력한 규제법 추진이 있었으나 상원 문턱을 넘지 못했다. 대신 일부 주(州)에서는 공격형 무기 금지 등 자체 입법을 강화했다.

The 2012 Sandy Hook Elementary School shooting, killing 28 including 20 children, spurred a push for strict federal gun laws, which failed in the Senate, while some states enacted their own assault weapon bans.

2015년 올랜도 펄스 나이트클럽 사건은 FBI 감시자 명단에 올랐던 인물의 총기 구매 허점이 부각되며, 테러 예방과 총기 규제 간 균형 논쟁을 불러왔다.

The 2015 Orlando Pulse nightclub shooting highlighted loopholes allowing individuals on FBI watchlists to purchase firearms, sparking debate over balancing counterterrorism and gun rights.

2017년 라스베이거스 사건은 미국 역사상 가장 많은 사상자를 낸 단일 총기난사로, 범프스톡(bump stock) 장치의 연방 금지를 이끌어냈다.

The 2017 Las Vegas shooting, the deadliest in U.S. history, prompted a federal ban on bump stock devices.

2018년 파크랜드 사건은 플로리다주에서 총기 구매 가능 연령을 21세로 상향하고 의무 대기기간을 도입하게 했다.

The 2018 Parkland shooting led Florida to raise the firearm purchase age to 21 and implement mandatory waiting periods.

2022년 유밸디 초등학교 참사는 21명이 숨진 뒤 초당적 안전한 공동체법(Bipartisan Safer Communities Act) 제정을 촉발, 21세 미만 구매자에 대한 강화된 신원조사와 레드플래그 법 지원이 포함되었다.

The 2022 Uvalde tragedy, claiming 21 lives, resulted in the Bipartisan Safer Communities Act, which enhanced background checks for buyers under 21 and funded red-flag laws.

정리[20]

미국에서 발생한 총기 사건들을 시간 순으로 정리하면 다음과 같습니다. 2019년 텍사스주 엘패소 월마트 매장에서 총기 난사 사건 발생. 23명 사망. 범인 패트릭 크루시어스는 6년 만에 종신형 선고. 펜실베니아주에서 유세 중이던 도널드 트럼프 전 대통령에게 총격을 가한 사건 발생. 용의자 토머스 매튜 크룩스는 AR-15 소총을 사용. AR-15는 미국 내 총기 사건에서 자주 사용되는 총기이며, 약 2000만 정이 보급된 것으로 추정. 영국에서 학교 총기 난사를 계획하고 가족 3명을 살해한 10대 청년 니컬러스 프로스퍼에게 최소 49년 징역형 선고. 플로리다주 탤러해시 플로리다주립대 교정에서 총기 난사 사건 발생. 2명 사망, 최소 5명 부상. 용의자는 지역 부보안관의 아들. 위스콘신주 매디슨 어번던트 라이프 크리스천스쿨에서 총격 사건 발생. 용의자 포함 3명 사망, 6명 부상. 용의자는 해당 학교 재학 중인 미성년자. 2025년 올해 미국 전역에서는 총 322건의 학교 총기 사건 발생. LA 스파르탄 항공기술대 캠퍼스에서 총격 사건 발생. 학교 직원 2명 부상. 용의자는 해당 학교 전직 직원.

---

20 https://www.joongang.co.kr 중앙일보, 2025.5.3. 검색.

미국 총기 난사 일지?[21]

미국에서 발생한 주요 총기 난사 사건들을 연도별로 정리한 일지를 아래에 제공합니다. 이러한 사건들은 총기 폭력 문제와 사회적 갈등을 반영하며, 미국 사회에서 심각한 논의의 주제가 되고 있습니다.

미국 주요 총기 난사 사건 연대기

2010년대

2012년 12월 14일 — 샌디 훅 초등학교 총기 난사(코네티컷주 뉴타운)

총기 난사범 애덤 란자(Adam Lanza)가 초등학교에서 20명의 어린이와 6명의 교직원을 살해한 사건입니다.

2016년 6월 12일 — Pulse 나이트클럽 총기 난사(플로리다주 올랜도)

오마르 미틴(Omar Mateen)이 게이 나이트클럽에서 49명을 살해하고 53명을 부상시킨 사건입니다.

apnews.com

2017년 10월 1일 — 라스베이거스 음악 축제 총기 난사(네바다주 라스베이거스)

스티븐 패독(Stephen Paddock)이 만달레이 베이 호텔 32층에서 총격을 가해 58명이 사망하고 867명이 부상당한 사건입니다.

en.wikipedia.org

2020년대

2022년 5월 24일 — 유발디 초등학교 총기 난사(텍사스주 유발디)

살바도르 라모스(Salvador Ramos)가 로브 초등학교에서 19명의 학생과 2명의 교사를 살해한 사건입니다.

---

21 참고 자료 AP 뉴스: Pulse 나이트클럽 총기 난사 9주기, 타임지: Mother Emanuel 교회 총기 난사 10주기. 위키백과: 2023 내슈빌 총기 난사 사건, 위키백과: 2024 포디스 총기 난사 사건, 위키백과: 2024 올랜도 할로윈 총기 난사 사건, 위키백과: 2025 UPMC 메모리얼 병원 총기 난사 사건 https://chatgpt.com/2025.6.9.12시 검색.

en.wikipedia.org

2023년 3월 27일 — 내슈빌 커버넌트스쿨 총기 난사(테네시주 내슈빌)

오드리 헤일(Audrey Hale)이 모교인 커버넌트스쿨에서 총격을 가해 6명이 사망한 사건입니다.

yna.co.kr

2024년 6월 21일 — 포디스 슈퍼마켓 총기 난사(아칸소주 포디스)

트래비스 포지(Travis Posey)가 슈퍼마켓에서 총격을 가해 4명이 사망하고 10명이 부상당한 사건입니다.

en.wikipedia.org

2024년 11월 1일 — 올랜도 할로윈 총기 난사(플로리다주 올랜도)

제이렌 에드거(Jaylen Edgar)가 할로윈 축제 중 총격을 가해 2명이 사망하고 8명이 부상당한 사건입니다.

2025년 2월 22일 — UPMC 메모리얼 병원 총기 난사(펜실베이니아주 실로)

디오제네스 아르천겔-오르티즈(Diogenes Archangel-Ortiz)가 병원에서 총격을 가해 2명이 사망하고 6명이 부상당한 사건입니다.

en.wikipedia.org

최근 통계 및 경향

2024년 FBI 데이터에 따르면, 텍사스주가 4건의 총기 난사 사건을 기록하여 가장 많은 사건 수를 보였습니다. 전국적으로는 총 24건의 사건이 발생하여 23명이 사망하고 83명이 부상당했습니다. 이는 2023년에 비해 50% 감소한 수치지만, 2015~2019년 대비 70% 증가한 수치입니다.

expressnews.com

[표1-2] 美 대통령 총기 사건

연도	주요 총기 사건	피해 규모	비고
1865.4.14.	미합중국 제16대 에이브러햄 링컨 대통령 Abraham Lincoln	대통령 암살	1865.4.15. 사망

1881.7.2.	미합중국 제20대 제임스 에이브럼 가필드 대통령 James Abram Garfield	대통령 암살	암살범 찰스 기토 즉시 체포,1882년. 교수형에 처해졌다.
1901.9.14.	미합중국 제25대 윌리엄 매킨리 대통령 William McKinley	대통령 암살 폴란드계 미국인 무정부주의자 리언 촐고츠에게 암살 당함.	
1963.11.22	미합중국 제35대 존 피츠제럴드 케네디 대통령 John Fitzgerald Kennedy	대통령 암살	리 하비 오스월드에게 암살, 뉴욕 아일드와일드 국제 공항명칭이 이 사건을 추념하여 존 F. 케네디 국제공항
1981.3.30.	미합중국 제40대 로널드 윌슨 레이건 대통령 Ronald Wilson Reagan	대통령 포함 4명 부상	1993년 '브래디 권총폭력 방지법' 제정
2022.5.13.	미합중국 제45대, 제47대 도널드 존 트럼프 대통령 Donald John Trump 펜실베이니아주 버틀러에서 저격 2000만정 보급된 美 총기 난사 트럼프도 AR-15 소총에 당했다.	부상, 당시 총알이 트럼프의 오른 쪽 귀 윗부분을 스쳐 지나가면서 큰 부상은 피했다.	AR-15sms 군사용 반 자동 소총 M-16 · M4의 '민간 버전' 총격범 현장에서 사살

※ 美 현행법은 18세 이상 미국인은 대부분 지역에서 신분증만 제시하면 AR-15 소총 등을 구입 할 수 있다.

English Chronological Narrative — U.S. Presidents and Firearm Incidents

On April 14, 1865, Abraham Lincoln, the 16th President of the United States, was shot while attending a play at Ford's Theatre in Washington, D.C. He died the next day, April 15, 1865.

On July 2, 1881, James Abram Garfield, the 20th President, was shot by Charles Guiteau. Garfield succumbed to his injuries, and Guiteau was captured immediately, later executed by hanging in 1882.

On September 14, 1901, William McKinley, the 25th President, was assassinated by Leon Czolgosz, a Polish-American anarchist, during a public reception in

Buffalo, New York.

On November 22, 1963, John Fitzgerald Kennedy, the 35th President, was assassinated in Dallas, Texas, by Lee Harvey Oswald. In tribute, New York's Idlewild International Airport was renamed John F. Kennedy International Airport.

On March 30, 1981, Ronald Wilson Reagan, the 40th President, was shot and wounded along with three others outside the Washington Hilton Hotel. This incident later led to the passage of the Brady Handgun Violence Prevention Act in 1993.

On May 13, 2022, Donald John Trump, the 45th and 47th President, survived an assassination attempt in Butler, Pennsylvania. The assailant used an AR-15-style semi-automatic rifle — the civilian version of the military M16/M4. The bullet grazed Trump's right ear, causing minor injury. The shooter was killed at the scene.

(Note: Under current U.S. law, most Americans over the age of 18 can legally purchase an AR-15 with only proof of identification in most states.)

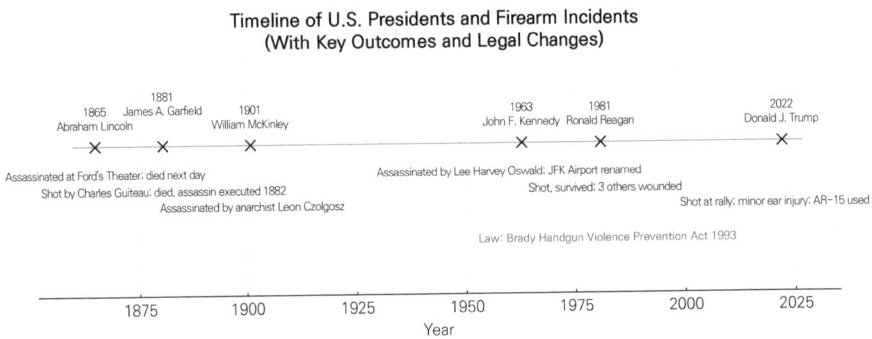

대통령 총기 사건 타임라인 분석

이 타임라인은 1865년부터 2022년까지 미국 대통령을 겨냥한 주요 총기사건을 연대순으로 보여주며, 각 사건의 결과와 관련 법률 변화를 함께 기록한 것이다.

미국 헌법 수정헌법 제2조(1791년 제정)는 *"규율 잡힌 민병대는 자유로운 주의 안보에 필요하므로, 국민이 무기를 소지하고 휴대할 권리를 침해해서는 안 된다."*라고 규정한다.

이 조항은 역사적으로 개인의 총기 소지 권리를 보장하는 법적 근거가 되었으나, 대통령 피격 사건과 같은 정치적 폭력은 때로는 총기 규제 강화를 요구하는 여론을 촉발시켰다.

1865년 링컨 대통령의 암살은 남북전쟁 직후 국가적 분열 속에서 발생했으며,

1881년 가필드 대통령 암살과 1901년 매킨리 대통령 암살 모두 정치적 · 사회적 불만이 배경이었다.

1963년 케네디 대통령 암살 사건은 냉전기 정치 불안과 맞물려 미국 사회에 깊은 충격을 주었고, 주요 공항의 이름 변경 등 상징적 조치가 뒤따랐다.

1981년 레이건 대통령 피격 사건은 그가 생존했음에도 불구하고 총기 규제 입법 논의에 직접적 영향을 주어, 1993년 '브래디 권총폭력 방지법' 제정을 이끌었다. 이 법은 총기 구매자 신원조회 제도를 강화하였다.

2022년 드럼프 대통령 피격 사건은 AR-15 반자동소총이 사용되었으며, 해당 총기는 대부분의 주에서 18세 이상이면 신분증만으로 구매할 수 있다는 미국 총기 규제의 허점을 재조명했다.

결론적으로, 대통령 피격 사건들은 단발적 정치 폭력임과 동시에 미국 사회에서 총기 소지 권리와 공공 안전 간의 균형이라는 오랜 논쟁을 촉발하는 계기가 되어 왔다.

English Commentary — Timeline Analysis of U.S. Presidential Firearm Incidents

This timeline depicts major firearm incidents targeting U.S. Presidents from 1865 to 2022, detailing each event's outcome and related legislative changes.

The Second Amendment to the U.S. Constitution (ratified in 1791) states: "A well regulated Militia, being necessary to the security of a free State, the right of the people to keep and bear Arms, shall not be infringed."

Historically, this provision has served as the legal foundation for individual gun ownership rights, but incidents of political violence — such as presidential shootings — have often intensified public calls for stricter firearm regulation.

The 1865 assassination of Abraham Lincoln occurred in the aftermath of the Civil War amid deep national division.

The 1881 assassination of James A. Garfield and the 1901 assassination of William McKinley both reflected political and social grievances of their eras.

In 1963, the assassination of John F. Kennedy during the Cold War shocked the nation, prompting symbolic acts such as renaming New York's Idlewild International Airport in his honor.

The 1981 attempted assassination of Ronald Reagan, though he survived, significantly influenced gun control debates, leading to the passage of the Brady Handgun Violence Prevention Act in 1993, which strengthened background checks for firearm purchasers.

The 2022 shooting of Donald J. Trump involved an AR-15 semi-automatic rifle — a civilian version of the M16/M4 military rifle — highlighting ongoing gaps in U.S. gun laws, as such weapons remain accessible to most adults over 18 with minimal ID requirements.

In sum, presidential firearm incidents have been both isolated acts of political violence and catalysts for renewed debate over the balance between the constitutional right to bear arms and the imperative of public safety in American society.

종합적으로 볼 때, 미국 대통령을 대상으로 한 총기 사용 사건들은 단순한 정치적 폭력에 국한되지 않는다. 이러한 사건들은 미국 헌법이 보장하는 무기 소지권과 공공 안전 확보라는 상충하는 가치 사이의 균형에 대한 사회·정치적 담론을 재점화하는 중요한 계기가 되어 왔다. 특히, 이 사건들은 제2차 수정헌법 해석의 범위, 총기 규제의 합헌성, 그리고 국가 최고 지도자에 대한 물리적 보안의 실효성을 둘러싼 법적·정책적 논의를 촉진하였다.

정책적으로는 다음과 같은 대응이 요구된다.

첫째, 위험인물 사전 차단을 위해 연방 차원의 통합 위험인물 데이터베이스를 구축하고 모든 총기 판매 시 의무 조회를 실시해야 한다.

둘째, 대통령이 참석하는 모든 행사장에서 총기 반입을 전면 금지하는 특별 규제를 도입해야 한다.

셋째, 비밀경호국(Secret Service)의 현장 경호 인력을 확대하여 즉각 대응 능력을 강화해야 한다.

넷째, 인공지능(AI) 기반의 군중 감시 기술과 비살상형 방어 무기를 도입하여 잠재 위협을 조기에 차단해야 한다.

다섯째, 연설대 · 차량 · 건물 유리 등 주요 방호 장비에 최신 방탄 · 방폭 소재를 적용해야 한다.

여섯째, 총기 접근성과 관련한 사회적 합의를 형성하여 제2차 수정헌법의 권리와 공공 안전의 조화를 도모해야 한다.

일곱째, 정치 폭력에 대한 불관용 캠페인을 전개하여 폭력 사용을 사회적으로 배격하는 문화를 확산시켜야 한다.

여덟째, 언론은 대통령 관련 위협 가능성이 있는 과격 발언이나 구체적 위치 정보를 무분별하게 보도하지 않도록 책임성을 강화해야 한다.

이러한 조치들은 대통령을 포함한 국가 지도자에 대한 물리적 위협을 최소화할 뿐 아니라, 총기 소지권과 공공 안전 간의 균형을 찾기 위한 미국 사회의 장기적 과제 해결에도 기여할 수 있다.

미국 대통령 총기 사건 — 역사적 맥락 · 학술 해설 · 정책 제언

미국 대통령을 대상으로 한 총기 사건들은 단순한 정치적 폭력의 범주를 넘어, 미국 헌법이 보장하는 무기 소지권과 공공 안전 간의 균형이라는 근본적 문제를 재조명하는 계기가 되어 왔다. 이러한 사건들은 미국 정치사에서 제2차 수정헌법(1791)의 해석, 총기 규제의 합헌성, 그리고 국가 최고 지도자에 대한 물리적 보안의 실효성을 둘러싼 사회적 · 법적 논의를 촉발시켰다.

1. 1865년 에이브러햄 링컨 암살 사건

남북전쟁이 끝난 직후, 미국은 재건(Reconstruction) 시기를 맞이하고 있었지만, 남북 간 정치적 · 사회적 갈등이 극심했다. 남부 동조자였던 존 윌크스 부스는 링컨 대통령의 정책과 연방 정부의 재건 방침에 강하게 반발하며 포드 극장에서 그를 저격했다. 이 사건은 국가적 상실감을 남겼지만, 총기 규제 논의로 직접 이어지지는 않았다.

2. 1881년 제임스 A. 가필드 암살 사건

정치적 인사 청탁과 인사 갈등이 심했던 시대에, 찰스 기토는 자신이 원하는 직책을 얻지 못하자 가필드를 총으로 쏘았다. 당시 총기 규제는 지역별로 산발적으로만 존재했고, 이 사건 역시 총기법 개정 대신 대통령 경호 체계 강화 쪽으로 대응이 이루어졌다.

3. 1901년 윌리엄 매킨리 암살 사건

산업화와 이민 증가로 사회 불안이 고조된 가운데, 폴란드계 미국인 무정부주의자 리언 촐고츠가 버펄로에서 매킨리 대통령을 저격했다. 이는 무정부주의와 폭력 정치에 대한 미국 정부의 강경 대응을 불러왔지만, 총기 규제법 제정으로 이어지지는 않았다.

4. 1963년 존 F. 케네디 암살 사건

냉전기 미국의 상징적 지도자였던 케네디는 텍사스주 댈러스에서 리 하비 오스월드의 총탄에 사망했다. 사건 직후 미국 사회는 극심한 충격에 빠졌으며, 뉴욕의 아일드와일드 국제공항이 존 F. 케네디 국제공항으로 개명되는 등 상징적 추모가 이루어졌다. 그러나 연방 차원의 총기 규제 입법은 이 사건 후에도 상당 기간 지연되었다.

5. 1981년 로널드 레이건 피격 사건

워싱턴 힐튼 호텔 앞에서 존 힝클리 주니어의 총격으로 레이건 대통령과 경호원 등 4명이 부상했다. 레이건이 회복한 뒤에도 정치적 영향은 지속되었으며, 1993년

'브래디 권총폭력 방지법'이 제정되어 연방 차원의 총기 구매 신원조회 제도가 도입되었다.

6. 2022년 도널드 J. 트럼프 피격 사건

펜실베이니아주 집회에서 AR-15 반자동소총이 사용되었고, 총알이 트럼프 전 대통령의 귀를 스치고 지나갔다. 이 사건은 미국에서 AR-15와 같은 고위력 반자동소총이 대부분의 주에서 18세 이상이면 신분증만으로 구매 가능하다는 규제의 허점을 재부각시켰다.

이러한 대통령 피격 사건들은 단순한 범죄 사건을 넘어, 미국 사회에서 개인의 자유와 국가 안보의 경계, 제2차 수정헌법 해석의 유연성, 그리고 총기 규제의 실효성을 시험하는 계기가 되어 왔다. 역사적으로 대통령 피격은 공공 안전 논쟁을 강화시켰지만, 사건 직후의 정치 환경과 여론의 분열로 인해 연방 차원의 포괄적 총기 규제 법안으로 이어진 경우는 드물었다.

정책 제언

위험인물 사전 차단 — 연방 차원의 통합 위험인물 데이터베이스 구축 및 총기 판매 시 의무 조회 제도 도입

행사장 안전구역 설정 — 대통령 참석 행사에서 주·연방법에 우선하는 총기 반입 전면 금지

경호 인력 및 장비 강화 — 비밀경호국 현장 인력 확대와 방탄·방폭 장비 현대화

첨단 위협 탐지 기술 도입 — AI 기반 군중 감시, 얼굴 인식, 비살상형 방어 장비 운용

사회적 합의 형성 — 총기 소지권 존중과 공공 안전 간 균형을 위한 전국적 공론화

정치 폭력 불관용 문화 확산 — 정당·시민단체·언론이 참여하는 반(反)폭력 캠페인

언론의 책임 강화 — 대통령 관련 위협 가능성이 있는 과격 발언·위치 정보의 무분별한 보도 자제

U.S. Presidential Firearm Incidents — Historical Context, Academic Commentary, and Policy Recommendations

Incidents involving firearms targeting U.S. Presidents have gone far beyond the scope of mere political violence, serving as critical moments to re-examine the fundamental balance between the constitutional right to keep and bear arms and the imperative of public safety. These events have ignited legal and societal debates in American political history over the interpretation of the Second Amendment (ratified in 1791), the constitutionality of firearm regulations, and the effectiveness of physical security for the nation's highest office.

1. 1865 — Assassination of Abraham Lincoln

Shortly after the end of the Civil War, the United States entered the Reconstruction era amid deep political and social divisions between the North and South. John Wilkes Booth, a Southern sympathizer, strongly opposed Lincoln's policies and federal Reconstruction plans, shooting the President at Ford's Theatre. The assassination left a profound national sense of loss, but it did not directly result in firearm regulation reform.

2. 1881 — Assassination of James A. Garfield

During a period marked by political patronage and contentious appointments, Charles Guiteau shot President Garfield after being denied a government position. At the time, gun laws were scattered and localized, and the incident led to increased presidential security rather than sweeping firearm legislation.

3. 1901 — Assassination of William McKinley

In an era of rapid industrialization and rising immigration-related tensions, Polish-American anarchist Leon Czolgosz shot President McKinley during a public reception in Buffalo, New York. The incident prompted a strong governmental crackdown on anarchism and political violence but did not result in new federal gun laws.

4. 1963 — Assassination of John F. Kennedy

A symbolic leader during the Cold War, President Kennedy was assassinated by Lee Harvey Oswald in Dallas, Texas. The nation was plunged into shock, and symbolic measures followed, such as renaming New York's Idlewild International Airport to John F. Kennedy International Airport. However, federal-level firearm legislation was slow to follow.

5. 1981 — Attempted Assassination of Ronald Reagan

Outside the Washington Hilton Hotel, John Hinckley Jr. opened fire, injuring President Reagan and three others. Although Reagan recovered, the political ramifications persisted, eventually contributing to the passage of the Brady Handgun Violence Prevention Act in 1993, introducing mandatory federal background checks for firearm purchases.

6. 2022 — Attempted Assassination of Donald J. Trump

During a rally in Butler, Pennsylvania, an assailant used an AR-15 semi-automatic rifle, grazing Trump's ear. The event underscored a critical gap in U.S. gun laws, as AR-15s and similar high-powered semi-automatic rifles remain legally accessible to most adults over 18 with only proof of identification in many states.

Academic Commentary

These presidential firearm incidents have been more than isolated criminal acts; they have tested the boundaries between individual liberty and national security, the flexibility of Second Amendment interpretation, and the real-world effectiveness of gun control measures. Historically, while such events have intensified debates over public safety, the political climate and societal divisions of the time often hindered the enactment of comprehensive federal gun legislation.

Policy Recommendations

Preemptive Identification of High-Risk Individuals — Establish a unified federal database and mandate checks for all firearm sales.

Secure Event Zones — Impose absolute bans on firearms at all presidential events, superseding state and federal jurisdiction.

Enhanced Protective Staffing and Equipment — Increase on-site Secret Service personnel and modernize ballistic/blast-resistant infrastructure.

Advanced Threat Detection — Deploy AI-based crowd surveillance, facial recognition, and non-lethal defensive weaponry.

Social Consensus-Building — Foster nationwide dialogue to balance Second Amendment rights with public safety needs.

Promotion of a Zero-Tolerance Culture for Political Violence — Organize joint campaigns by political parties, civic groups, and the media.

Responsible Media Practices — Avoid irresponsible reporting of inflammatory threats or real-time location data regarding the President.

"미국의 경호시스템이 발달한 것은 총기 1억자루가 풀려있는 이 나라에서 대통령에 대한 위협이 상존하기 때문이다. 링컨은 암살당하기 앞서 경호원에게 "생명을 노리는 자가 있으면 막을 수 없을 것"이라고 말했다. 케네디 역시 저격당하기 몇 시간 전 경호원에게 "총으로 공격해온다면 방어할 길이 없다"고 말했다."[22]

"전 세계 개인들이 얼마나 많은 총기를 소유하고 있는지 계산하는 건 어렵다. 하지

---

22 김도원, "대통령 경호," 조선일보, 2003.5.30. https://www.chosun.com/site/data/html_dir/2003/05/30/20030530 70322.html 2025.5.3. 검색.

만 스위스의 연구 프로젝트인 '스몰암즈서베이'(Small Arms Survey)에 따르면, 2018년 기준 전 세계 총기는 3억9000만 정으로 추산된다."총기 소지 자격에 대한 대부분의 규제를 철폐한 주도 다수 있다. 예를 들면 2021년 6월, 그레그 애벗 텍사스 주지사는 주민들이 면허나 훈련 없이도 권총을 소지하는 "무허가 총기 휴대 법안"에 서명했다. 비슷한 예로 조지아주를 들 수 있다. 지난 4월 12일 이곳은 미국에서 총기 휴대와 공개적인 사용을 전면 자유화한 25번째 주가 됐다. 즉 조지아주에선 누구나 면허나 허가 없이 총을 소지할 권리가 있게 된 것이다. NRA의 지도부는 조지아주의 총기 소지법 실행을 지지하며 "수정헌법 제2조를 위한 기념비적인 순간"이라고 평가했다. 미국에선 수정헌법 제2조에 따라 범죄로부터 자신을 지키기 위해 총기 사용을 권리로 여기는 전통적 인식이 있다. 수정헌법 제2조는 "잘 규율된 민병대는 자유를 지닌 주(州)의 안보에 필수적이므로 무기를 소지하고 휴대하는 미국 국민의 권리는 침해받을 수 없다"고 규정돼 있다."[23]

총기에 의해 피살된 대통령들은 세계 역사에서 여러 명 존재합니다. 대표적으로 다음과 같은 인물들이 있습니다.[24]

---

23 https://www.bbc.com/korean/international-61581719 2025.6.9. 검색.

24 미국 대통령 에이브러햄 링컨 (Abraham Lincoln) 재임 기간: 1861-1865 사망: 1865년 4월 14일 장소: 워싱턴 D.C., 포드 극장 가해자: 존 윌크스 부스 (John Wilkes Booth) 동기: 남북전쟁 후 남부 동조자였던 부스의 정치적 반감, 제임스 A. 가필드 (James A. Garfield) 재임 기간: 1881년 사망: 1881년 9월 19일 가해자: 찰스 기토 (Charles J. Guiteau) 동기: 정부직 임명에 대한 불만, 윌리엄 매킨리 (William McKinley) 재임 기간: 1897-1901 사망: 1901년 9월 14일 가해자: 레온 촐고시 (Leon Czolgosz) 동기: 무정부주의적 신념, 존 F. 케네디 (John F. Kennedy) 재임 기간: 1961-1963 사망: 1963년 11월 22일 장소: 텍사스주 댈러스 가해자: 리 하비 오스왈드 (Lee Harvey Oswald) (공식 발표) 비고: 여전히 음모론이 많음 다른 나라 대통령 예시 파크 초희 (Park Chung-hee, 박정희) - 대한민국 직함: 대통령 사망: 1979년 10월 26일 사건: 중앙정보부장 김재규에 의해 총격 사망 (내부 쿠데타 성격) 살바도르 아옌데 (Salvador Allende) — 칠레 직함: 대통령 사망: 1973년 9월 11일 상황: 군사 쿠데타 도중 대통령궁에서 총에 맞아 사망 (자살로 발표되었지만 논란 존재) 조브날 하비아리마나 (Juvénal Habyarimana) — 르완다 직함: 대통령 사망: 1994년 4월 6일 상황: 전용기 피격으로 사망 (후속 사건이 르완다 대학살로 이어짐) https://chatgpt.com/ 2025.6.9. 검색.

Ⅲ. 미국 연방 헌법 수정 제2조 의미

총기 휴대에 관한 권리 연방헌법 수정 제2조[25]

"미국 내 계속되는 크고 작은 총기 사고에도 불구하고 총기규제 강화 필요성을 둘

---

25 수정 제2조 91년 12월 15일 비준. A well regulated Militia, being necessary to the security of a free State, the right of the people to keep and bear Arms, shall not be infringed. 잘 규율된 민병대(militia)는 자유로운 주의 안보에 필수적이므로, 무기를 소장하고 휴대하는 시민의 권리는 침해될 수 없다. 시민의 무장권을 명시하는 조항으로, 이 조항의 존재로 인해 미국에서 무기 소지와 휴대는 법률도 아니고 그 상위 개념인 헌법이 허용하는 권리다. 말도 많고 탈도 많은 미국의 총기규제 논란이 거슬러 올라가면 결국 이에 연유하고 있다. 이 조항이 헌법에 추가된 것은 미국의 역사적, 지역적 특수성에 기인한다. 여기서 말하는 민병대란 과거 식민지 시절 영국의 통제하에 있던 상비군(정규군)과 대비되는 군대로, 시민들의 자발적인 참여로 구성된 일종의 의병 내지 시민군, 자경단과 유사한 조직을 의미했다. 건국의 아버지들은 외국의 침략으로 국가가 무너지는 것 이외에도 연방 권력이 폭주하여 내부로부터 붕괴되었을 경우를 대비해, 각 주의 독립된 자치권이 위협받았을 때 이에 대해 시민들이 단체 무장저항권을 행사할 수 있는 단서를 제공하고자 하였다. 버지니아주의 모토이기도 한 'Sic semper tyrannis(폭군에겐 언제나 이렇게 하리라)'라는 라틴어 어구가 이를 잘 나타낸다. 반면 오늘날 미국에는 주마다 '주 민병대'라는 공식 조직이 있고 아무나 모여서 마음대로 만들 수 있는 것도 아니며, 지휘 체계와 계급, 급여, 상벌을 위한 법률도 있으므로 의병보다는 예비군에 더 가깝다. 주방위군, 주방위대, 해군민병대 모두 비슷한 개념이다. 현재 미국이 가장 골머리를 앓고 있는 내부문제 중 하나이자 FBI의 주적 중 하나인 민병대 문제도 사실 이로부터 비롯되고 있다. 헌법에서 시민들이 민병대를 구성할 권리를 합법으로 못박아두고 있기 때문에, 미국은 법적으로 민병대 자체를 금지할 수 없다. 대신 여타 다른 법률로 무장 단체 활동을 불법으로 만들어 간접적으로 민병대 구성을 통제하고 있다. 과거 이 조항에 대한 세부적인 해석이 헌법학자들 사이에서 의견이 갈리곤 했다. 주 차원에서 민병대를 보유할 권리인지, 아니면 시민 개개인이 무장할 권리를 가리키는지가 주요 쟁점이었다. 이는 해당 헌법의 내용이 어떻게 해석되는지에 따라 총기 규제법 제정의 위헌 여부가 결정되기 때문이었다. 전자에 따르면 '무기를 소유하고 휴대하는 권리는 잘 규율된 민병대의 존재를 통한 안보라는 전제에 부합해야 하는 것'이고, 후자에 따르면 '민병대에 소속되기 위해 무장할 권리이므로, 실존 유무에는 상관 없이 개인이 무장할 수 있는 것'으로 볼 수 있다. 쉽게 말해 전자를 따른다면 민병대가 없거나 소속되지 않은 시민은 무기를 소유할 권리가 없다고 볼 수 있고, 후자라면 그와 상관없이 시민이라면 누구나 무장할 권리가 있다는 지론이었다. 때문에 전자는 총기 규제론자, 후자는 전미총기협회(NRA) 같은 규제 반대론자들이 지지했다. 1939년의 연방대법원 판례는 전자를 택하여, 개인의 총기 소지를 규제하는 법률의 제정, 곧 18인치 미만 엽총에 대한 개인 소유를 제한하는 법률에 대한 위헌 심판 문제에서 만장일치로 해당 법률이 수정헌법 제2조에 어긋나지 않으며 '민병대와 관련이 없으므로' 합헌이라 판결했다. 이후 미국의 총기 규제는 점점 까다로워졌으며, 적극적인 규제 법령이 제정되고 이전보다 복잡한 신원 심사 절차 및 서류 등록 제도가 마련되었다. 이러한 기조는 20세기 내내 지속되다가, 2008년에 들어 판례가 후자 쪽으로 바뀌었다. 워싱턴 D.C. 대 헬러 사건에서 연방대법원은 5 대 4의 아슬아슬한 의견으로 수정 헌법 제2조가 시민 개인의 무장권을 보장한다고 판결했으며, "민병대 소속 여부, 혹은 민병대의 존재 유무와는 상관없이 시민 개개인이 자기방어의 목적으로 무장하는 것도 수정헌법 제2조가 보호하는 내용"이라고 결론내렸다. 이에 조지 W. 부시 행정부 말기부터 미국의 총기 소지는 이전과 비교해서 더욱 자유로워졌다. 한편, 규제론자들은 1939년과 달리 바뀌어버린 2008년의 연방대법원의 결정이 전미총기협회와 총포산업의 로비 및 정치적 선동의 결과라 비난했다. https://namu.wiki/w/%EB%AF%B8%EA%B5%AD%20%ED%97%8C%EB%B2%95 2025.4.7. 검색.

러싼 논의는 크게 진전되지 않아 왔는데, 그 배경에는 무기를 보유하고 휴대하는 개인의 권리는 침해될 수 없다고 규정하고 있는 연방헌법 수정 제2조[26]가 자리하고 있다. 하지만 그간 이 조항의 의미를 다룬 연방대법원 판결은 거의 전무하다시피하였으며, 2008년 District of Columbia v. Heller 판결[27]에 가서야 이 조항 해석 문제가 정면으로 다뤄지게 되었다. 이 판결은 총기 휴대에 관한 개인의 권리를 인정한 판결이자 수정 제2조를 해석함에 있어 '본래의 일반적인 의미(original public meaning)'를 따르는 해석방법을 명시적으로 채택한 원의주의 판결로 평가된다.[28] 수정 제1조가 현대의 표현매체를 보호하고 수정 제4조가 현대의 수색기법에 적용되듯이, 수정 제2조 역시 건국 당시에는 존재하지 않았던 보유 가능한 무기가 될 수 있는 모든 도구들까지도 일응 확장 적용될 수 있다고 하였다.[29]

당시 사전적 정의에 기초해볼 때, 무기 보유 및 휴대(have and carry weapons)로 해당 문구(keep and bear arms)를 해석하는 것이 가장 자연스러운 해석이며, 건국 당시의 사료(founding-era sources)를 검토해보더라도 18세기 당시에 그와 동일한 의미를 가지고 있었음을 알 수 있다고 하였다. 가장 눈에 띄는 사례는 18세기 및 19세기 초에 제정된 9개의 주의 헌법조항에서 국가와 자신을 지키기 위해 무기를 휴대할 권리를 부여하고 있었다는 사실이며, 당시의 판례나 학계의 이해를 보더라도 해당 조항을 자기 방어 목적의 자연권으로 인식하거나 해당 주헌법 조항과 연방헌법 수정 제2조와 동일시하였다는 점에서 해당 문구가 의미하는 바가 단지 군대에서의 무기 휴대에 한정되지 않았음을 보여준다고 하였다.[30] 이에 반해 반대의견을 개진한 스티븐스 대법관은

---

26 잘 규율된 민병대는 자유 국가의 안전보장에 필수적이므로, 무기를 보유하고 휴대하는 개인의 권리는 침해될 수 없다(A well regulated Militia, being necessary to the security of a free State, the right of the people to keep and bear Arms, shall not be infringed). U.S. Const. amend. II.

27 trict of Columbia v. Heller, 554 U.S. 570 (2008).

28 연방대법원 판례 역사상 가장 명시적인 원의주의 판결이자 의식적으로 그와 같은 해석방법을 채택한 판결로, 사실상 헌법제정 당시의 일반적인 의미에 대한 명시적이고 면밀한 검토에 기초하여 내려진 최초의 판결이라고 볼 수 있다는 평가로 Cass Sunstein, Second Amendment Minimalism: Heller as Griswold, 122 Harvard Law Review, (2008), 246.

29 District of Columbia v. Heller, 554 U.S. 570, 581-582 (2008).

30 당시에 'bear Arms'에는 '군복무를 하거나 전쟁을 수행하다'라는 관용적인 의미도 있었으나 '… 에 대항하여'라는 전치사가 뒤따를 때에만 그와 같은 의미를 지녔고, 그와 같은 전치사가 없을 경우에는 일반 적인 의미, 즉 오늘날의 의미와 동일한 의미를 지녔음을 부연하고 있다. District of Columbia v. Heller, 554 U.S. 570, 584-586 (2008).

본질적으로 원래의 의도에 따르는 원의주의 입장에 기반한 것으로 분석된다. 반대의견은 이 사건 쟁점이 수정 제2조가 개인의 권리를 보장하는지가 아니라 그 보장범위에 관한 것이며, 이 조항이 사냥, 자기방어와 같이 비군사적 목적으로 총기를 소유, 사용할 수 있는 권리를 보호하는가에 대해서는 헌법조문, 제정사 그리고 선례가 이에 대한 명확한 답을 제공해준다고 보았다.[31] 특히 다수의견이 수정 제2조의 제정사를 주의 깊게 살피지 않았음을 지적하고 다수의견이 참고한 자료 중 일부는 해당 규정의 기초자들의 의도를 파악하는데 그 어떠한 도움도 주지 못하였다고 비판하였으며, 해당 규정의 기초자들이 보통법상으로 인정되어온 자기 방어권을 헌법에 보장하고자 하였음을 보여주는 그 어떠한 증거도 발견되지 않는다고 하여, 연방헌법 수정 제2조가 그러한 권리를 보장하지 않는다는 정반대의 결론을 내렸다. 먼저, 기존 선례에서 연방대법원은 수정 제2조가 일정한 군사적 목적에서의 무기 보유 및 휴대에 대한 권리를 보호하지만 비군사적 목적의 총기 소유 및 활용을 규제할 수 있는 입법자의 권한을 제한하는 것은 아니라고 해석한 바 있으며, 이러한 해석이 수정 제2조의 문언에 대한 가장 자연스러운 해석이자 제정사에서 드러난 제정목적에 가장 충실한 해석으로 볼 수 있다고 주장하였다.[32] 새로운 국가에서의 군사력을 어떻게 적절히 배분하는가는 헌법 기초자들의 중요 관심사였으며, 이들이 궁극적으로 도달한 타협점이 연방헌법 제1조 및 수정 제2조에 반영된 것으로, 수정 제2조 채택에 이르기까지의 역사는 연방의 군대가 주의 주권에 미칠 수 있는 잠재적인 위협과 그 위험에 대비하기 위한 수단으로 주 단위 민병대를 보호하기 위한 목적이 이들의 최우선적인 관심사였음을 보여준다고 하였다. 그러나 법정의견은 민간인의 무기사용을 규제하고자 하는 선출직 기관이 활용할 수 있는 수단을 제한하고 허용 가능한 총기규제 정책의 범위를 정의내릴 수 있는 권한을 법원에 부여하겠다는 선택을 헌법 기초자들이 하였다고 보는 것과 다르지 않고, 이를 뒷받침할 수 있는 설득력 있는 증거가 제시되지 않는 이상 헌법기초자들이 그러한 선택을 내렸다는 결론에 찬동할 수 없으며, 법정의견에서는 그와 같은 증거를 제시하지 못하고 있다고 비판하였다."[33][34] 미합중국 헌법(Constitution

---

31 District of Columbia v. Heller, 554 U.S. 570, 636 (2008).

32 District of Columbia v. Heller, 554 U.S. 570, 637-638 (2008).

33 District of Columbia v. Heller, 554 U.S. 570, 652, 680 (2008).

of the United States) 또는 미국 헌법은 미국 연방정부(Federal government)[35]의 헌법이다. 50개의 주가 모여 하나의 국가를 이루는 합중국(合衆國)인 미국의 법은 연방헌법과 주헌법이 별도로 존재하며, 때문에 연방헌법은 연방의 입법, 사법, 행정부가 가지는 기능을 규율하고 주 정부와 주민에 전속(專屬)하는 권리를 구분한다. "1848년 뉴욕주 세니커폴스에서 열린 최초의 여성 권리 집회에서 평등권을 주장했던 페미니스트들은 오랜 전통인 병역을 시민권의 관념과 연관시켰다. 미국 혁명기 여성들의 역사를 서술한 린다 커버(Linda Kerber)는 마키아벨리의 작품을 통해 '병사-시민'이라는 스파르타의 이상형으로부터 이러한 궤적을 추적하였고, 18세기의 미국의 혁명가들이 "자유인과 노예를 구분하는 것은 무기 소유이다"라고 주장한 영국의 작가 제임스 버크(James Burgh)의 정치 이론들에 애착을 느꼈다고 그 중요성을 강조했다. 커버가 기술했듯이, 미국 공화국 초기에 공화국과 입대할 수 있는 남성 애국자들 사이에는 직접적인 관련이 있었다. 하지만 아무리 여성들이 그들 자신을 애국자라고 여길지라도 공화국과 여성은 직접적인 관련은 없었다. 모든 남성 시민이 참전토록 소집되진 않았지만 여성은 신체적으로나 정신적으로 전쟁에 적합하지 않다고 여겨졌다. 병역은 여성의 시민권 박탈의 논쟁에서 중요했는데, 왜냐하면 전쟁 시 남성들의 용기, 힘, 그리고 국가에 대한 봉사가 특히 크게 중요하게 받아들여졌기 때문이었다.[36] 그러나 남성의 용맹을 시민권의 근거로 강조했던 공화주의 이념으로 볼 때 만일 여성이 전쟁에 참가할 수 있다면, 그들에게서 완전한 시민권을 박탈할 근거는 없다. 완전한 시민권에 대한 여성의 적합성을 논하는 활발한 공개 토론의 시기 동안, 남북 전쟁은 여성들에게 여성의 애국주의에 대한 본질을 재고할 기회를 제공했다. 분명히, 총기 사용은 여성들에게 사회에서 그들의 역할을 재정립하는 기회를 제공했다."[37][38]

---

34 김지영 책임연구관, "미국 헌법해석론 — 이론과 연방대법원의 적용례를 중심으로," 헌법재판소 헌법재판연구원, 2018, 50-52면.

35 여기서 연방정부란 연방의 입법, 사법, 행정부를 총칭하며, 헌법상 행정부는 'federal executive departments'로 구분된다.

36 Linda K. Kerber, No Constitutional Right to Be Ladies: Woman and the Obligations of Citizenship (New York: Hill and Wang, 1998), p. 240.

37 Laura Browder, Her Best Shot: Women and Guns in America (UNC Pres, 2006), p. 24.

38 김상민, "미국의 여성과 총기에 관한 일고찰 – 여성성, 폭력, 시민권을 중심으로 – ," 인문과학논집 제58집, 28-30면.

미국 헌법 수정 제2조(Second Amendment 또는 Amendment II)[39]는 1791년에 제정되

---

39 연방하원과 상원을 통과한 미국 헌법 수정조항 제2조의 원문 내용은 다음과 같다: 잘 규율된 민병대는 자유로운 주(State)의 안보에 필수적이므로, 무기를 소장하고 휴대하는 국민의 권리는 침해될 수 없다. A well regulated Militia, being necessary to the security of a free State, the right of the people to keep and bear Arms, shall not be infringed. 각 주에 배포되어 비준된 미국 헌법 수정조항 제2조의 원문 내용은 다음과 같다: A well regulated militia being necessary to the security of a free State, the right of the People to keep and bear arms shall not be infringed. 미국의 헌법 전문가인 조지타운 대학교 법학센터 피터 버니 교수는 "행정력이 미치지 못하는 광활한 땅을 개척해야 했던 미국에선 총기 소유는 자신은 물론 가족의 생명과 재산을 지키기 위해서 반드시 필요한 권리로 간주돼 왔다"며 "여기에는 국가가 개인을 온전히 보호해 줄 수 없다는 관념도 영향을 미쳤다"고 설명했다. 역사적 배경: 이 수정헌법은 영미법에 부분적으로 기초하며 권리장전 (영국)에 의해 영향을 받았다. 윌리엄 블랙스톤은 이 권리에 대해 "보조적인 권리의 하나로 자기 방어의 자연적 권리를 지지하고 억압에 저장하며 국가의 방어와 조화하도록 하기 위한 시민적 의무"로 묘사하였다. 제임스 먼로와 존 애덤스는 헌법이 비준되도록 찬성하였고, 가장 영향력은 준 법의 제정자는 제임스 매디슨이었다. 조문의 해석: 총기 규제에 대한 최근의 미국 사회 내의 활발한 논의와 입법 활동에도 불구하고 수정조항 제2조에 의하여 보호받는 권리가 구체적으로 어떠한 것인가에 대해서는 명시적인 사법적 판단이 이루어진 적이 없다. 제2조 해석과 관련하여 대립하는 두 종류의 학설이 존재하는데 "개인의 권리"이론 과 "주의 권리"이론이라고 부를 수 있다. "개인의 권리" 이론은 수정조항 제2조에 의하여 보호받는 권리는 개인이 총기를 소유, 점유, 운반할 수 있는 권리라고 주장한다. 반면, "주의 권리" 이론은 수정조항 제2조의 목적은 주가 공식적으로 조직된 민병대를 보유할 수 있는 권한을 보호하는 것이라고 주장한다. 어느 이론이든 이 조항은 연방정부만을 제약하고 주 정부나 개인들에게는 그 효력이 미치지 않는다고 해석한다. 미 연방대법원은 United States v. Miller, 307 U.S. 174 (1939)사건에서 다음과 같이 판시하였다. 총열의 길이가 18인치 미만인 총의 소유나 사용이 현재 시점에서 잘 규율된 민병대의 군사력 유지나 향상과 어떠한 관련이 있다는 증거가 없는 상황에서 우리는 수정조항 제2조가 그러한 무기를 소장하고 휴대할 수 있는 권리를 보장한다고 말할 수 없다. 물론 이러한 무기가 통상적인 군용 무기의 일부이거나 이러한 무기의 사용이 방위에 도움이 될 수 있다는 점은 사법적 판단의 범위 밖이다.… 그러한 군사력을 유지 또는 향상하도록 하기 위한 목적으로 수정조항 제2조가 제정되었다. 제2조는 그러한 목적을 염두에 두고 해석되어야 한다.

In the absence of any evidence tending to show that possession or use of a "shotgun having a barrel of less than eighteen inches in length" at this time has some reasonable relationship to the preservation or efficiency of a well regulated militia, we cannot say that the Second Amendment guarantees the right to keep and bear such an instrument. Certainly it is not within judicial notice that this weapon is any part of the ordinary military equipment, or that its use could contribute to the common defense.…With obvious purpose to assure the continuation and render possible the effectiveness of such forces, the declaration and guarantee of the Second Amendment were made. It must be interpreted and applied with that end in view.

미 연방대법원은 민병대의 유지에 필요한 한도 내에서 "개인의 권리" 이론을 지지한 것으로 해석된다. 1975년 총기 규제법: 1976년 6월 29일 워싱턴 D.C 의회에서 통과된 법으로 거주자들이 권총, 자동 총기 또는 대용량 반자동 총기의 소유를 금지하며 미등록된 총기 소유를 금하는 내용을 담고 있다. 워싱턴 D.C 대 헬러: 2008년에 미국 연방 대법원에서 판결된 기념비적인 결정이다. 미국 헌법의 제2수정헌법은 각 개인의 총기 소지 및 사용의 권한을 보호하며 (민병대에서의 근무와는 상관없음) 집 안에서의 자기 방어와 같은 전통적으로 합법적인 목적을 말한다. 또한, 워싱턴 D.C의 권총 금지와 요구사항에 대하여 합법적으로 소

었으며, "총기휴대 및 소지의 권리"를 규정하고 있다. 미국 헌법 전문(The Preamble to the United States Constitution)은 미국 헌법의 근본적인 목적과 원리를 안내하는 짧은 머리말이다. 여기에서는 일반적인 용어를 언급하고, 법원은 그것을 신뢰할 만한 증거로 언급해 왔으며, 헌법의 의미에 대한 미국 건국의 아버지들의 의도와 그들이 헌법을 어떻게 완성하고 싶은 지에 대한 희망을 언급했다.

We the People of the United States, in Order to form a more perfect Union, establish Justice, insure domestic Tranquility, provide for the common defence,[note 40] promote the general Welfare, and secure the Blessings of Liberty to ourselves and our Posterity, do ordain and establish this Constitution for the United States of America.

우리 미국 국민은, 보다 완전한 연합을 형성하고, 정의를 확립하며, 국내의 평안을 보장하고, 공동 방위를 규정하며, 국민 복지를 증진하고, 우리와 우리의 후손들에게 자유의 축복을 보장하기 위하여, 이 미국 헌법을 제정한다.

미국은 1791년 이래 근 200년 간 총기 천국의 이미지를 공고히 해오고 있다. 버락 오바마(Barack Obama) 대통령은 2009년 취임 후 실효적인 총기 규제를 끊임없이 강조해왔으나,[41] 아이러니하게도 미국 내 총기 사고 및 총기 생산 판매는 지속적으로 증가하는 추세를 보이고 있다. 극단적인 총기 난사 사건[42]이 발생할 때마다 총기 규제

유한 소총과 산탄총은 장전되지 않거나 방아쇠 잠금장치로 되어 있는 것은 이러한 보증행위를 침해한다는 것이다. 또한, 총기소지의 권한은 무제한적이 아니며 총과 총기 소유에 어떤 제한이 가능하다는 것을 포함한다. 이 판결은 1975년 총기 규제법을 번복하였으며 권총이 제2수정헌법의 목적에 적합한 총기임을 결정하였다. https://ko.wikipedia.org/wiki/%EB%AF%B8%EA%B5%AD_%EC%88%98%EC%A0%95_%ED%97%8C%EB%B2%95_%EC%A0%9C2%EC%A1%B0 2025.4.7. 검색.

40 In the hand-written engrossed copy of the Constitution maintained in the National Archives, the British spelling "defence" is used in the preamble (See the National Archives transcription and the Archives' image of the engrossed document. Retrieved both web pages on October 24, 2009).

41 한 사례로 오바마 대통령은 2009 년 취임 시, 총기 규제 정책의 일환으로 New Assault Weapons Ban 의 제정을 추진할 계획임을 언급. ABC 뉴스 보도 http://abcnews.go.com/Politics/story?id=6960824

42 20세기 말을 살았던 많은 이들에게는 1991년 미국 엘에이(LA) 에서 발생했던 엘에이 경찰관들의 로드니

에 대한 열띤 논쟁이 미국의 지도자들 사이에서 벌어지지만, 그럼에도 불구하고 외부의 시각에서 보았을 때, 이상하리만치 미국의 총기 규제 논의는 진전이 없어 보인다.[43] 최근 총기 사고로 몸살을 앓아온 미국이 사건들을 계기로 전환점을 맞이할지 관심이 모아지고 있다. 미국 수도 워싱턴 D.C.에서 열린 시위에 참가한 학생들은 총기 규제 강화를 촉구하며 목소리를 높였다. 2017년에는 미국에 3억 9330만 개의 민간 보유 총기가 있다고 추산되었고 이는 100명당 약 120개의 총기가 있다는 의미이다.[44] 이는 1인당 총기소지율로서는 세계에서 가장 높은 수치이다.[45] 당연히도 미국은 총기 관련 부상 및 사망률이 매우 높다. 2015년 전국적으로 약 36,000명이 총기로 사망하였다. 이들 중 22,018명(약 61%)이 자살이었고, 13,463명(37%)이 살인, 489명(1%)이 과실상해로 인한 것이었다.[46] 설상가상으로 총기폭력은 증가하고 있다. 2020년까지 총기 관련 사망은 45,222건으로 증가하여[47] 2015년 이후 약 25%가 증가하였다. 이는 2020년에만 매일 평균 124명이 총기폭력으로 사망하였음을 뜻한다. 앞서 언급하였듯이 현재 총기폭력은 아동 및 청소년의 사망을 야기하는 가장 주요한 원인이 되었으며, 앞서 60년이 넘게 가장 주요한 원인이었던 자동차 사고를 상회한다.[48] 총기가 야기하는 위험은 다양한 형태를 띤다. 2022. 6. 5. 펜실베니아주 필라델피아의 오락구역(3명 사망, 11명 부상), 2022. 5. 24. 텍사스주 유밸디의 초등학교(21명 사망), 2022. 5. 14. 뉴욕주 버팔로의 슈퍼마켓(10명 사망, 3명 부상), 2022. 3. 16. 조지아주 애

킹(Rodney King) 폭행 사건, 이후 재판과정에서 폭행 경찰관에 대한 배심원들의 무죄 선고 그리고 이에 항의하는 전국적인 대규모 시위와 소요 사태가 아직도 세기의 사건으로 기억되고 있다. W. Christopher (Ed.), Report of the independent commission on the Los Angeles Police Department, Diane Publishing, 1991. 남궁현, "미국 지역경찰의 공권력 남용 논란에 대한 연구," 형사정책연구(Korean Criminological Review) 제31권 제3호(통권 제123호), 2020, 가을, 136면.

43 이창원(Lee, Paul Changwon) Northwestern Pritzker School of Law J.D., 지속되는 미국 내 총기 규제 논란, 그리고 이와 관련한 수정헌법 제 2 조의 해석, 헌법재판소, 탑재 보고서, 1면.

44 A. Karp, Estimating Global CivilianHeld Firearms Numbers, Small Arms Survey 4 (June 2018), https://www.smallarmssurvey.org/sites/default/files/resources/SAS-BP-Civilian-Firearms-Numbers.pdf

45 Ibid.

46 M. Siegel et al., Easiness of Legal Access to Concealed Firearm Permits and Homicide Rates in the United States, 107 Am. J. Pub. Health 1923 (2017).

47 CDC, Fast Facts.

48 Goldstick 1955; J. Bates, Guns Became the Leading Cause of Death for American Children and Teens in 2020, Time, Apr. 27, 2022, https://www.time.com/6170864/cause-of-death-children-guns/

틀란타의 스파들(8명 사망), 2019. 8. 4. 오하이오주 데이턴의 오락구역 내 번화가(9명 사망, 17명 부상), 2016. 5. 12. 플로리다주 올랜도의 나이트클럽(50명 사망, 53명 부상), 2015. 6. 17. 사우스캐롤라이나주 찰스턴의 교회(9명 사망), 2012. 7. 20. 콜로라도주 오로라의 극장(12명 사망, 50명 부상), 2012. 12. 14. 코네티컷주 뉴타운의 초등학교(26명 사망)에서 일어난 총기난사 사건들과 이보다 훨씬 더 많은 사건들이 신문에 실렸다. 총기 난사 사건은 문제의 일부에 불과하다. 총기에 대한 쉬운 접근은 미국인의 삶의 다른 여러 측면을 더욱 위험하게 만들 수 있다. 2021년 매월 평균 44명이 도로에서 운전자의 난폭 행동으로 총에 맞아 사망하거나 부상을 당했다.[49] 이 중 일부는 차에 장전된 총이 없었더라면 피할 수 있었을 죽음이었다.[50] 시위의 경우도 마찬가지이다. 2020년 1월에서 2021년 6월 사이에 있었던 3만 건의 시위를 조사한 연구에 따르면 무장시위는 비무장시위보다 폭력적이거나 파괴적으로 될 가능성이 6배 가까이 된다고 한다.[51] 가정불화에 있어서도 관련 연구는 파트너가 총기에 접근가능한 경우 여성이 폭력적인 파트너에 의해 죽을 가능성이 5배라고 밝혔다.[52] 자살의 경우, 권총을 소유한 남성은 그렇지 않은 남성보다 자살할 가능성이 3배 더 높으며, 권총을 소유한 여성은 그렇지 않은 여성보다 7배가 더 높다고 한다.[53] 경찰과의 상호작용을 살펴보면, 총기의 민간 소지는 경찰과 민간 양측 모두에게 위험을 증가시킨다. 총기소유율이 높은 주에서는 경찰이 공무수행 중 사망할 확률이 총기소유율이 낮은 주에서보다 3배가 높다.[54] 또한 총기소유율이 높은 주에서는 민간인이 경찰이 쏜 총에 맞아 사망

---

49 S. Burd-Sharps & K. Bistline, Everytown for Gun Safety, Reports of Road Rage Shootings Are on the Rise (Apr. 4, 2022), https://www.everytownresearch.org/reports-of-road-rage-shootings-are-on-the-rise/; J. Donohue, A. Aneja, & K. Weber, Right-to-Carry Laws and Violent Crime: A Comprehensive Assessment Using Panel Data and a State-Level Synthetic Control Analysis, 16 J. Empirical Legal Studies 198, 204 (2019).

50 Ibid.

51 Everytown for Gun Safety, Armed Assembly: Guns, Demonstrations, and Political Violence in America (Aug. 23, 2021), https://www.everytownresearch.org/report/armed-assembly-gunsdemonstrations-and-political-violence-in-america/

52 A. Zeoli, R. Malinski, & B. Turchan, Risks and Targeted Interventions: Firearms in Intimate Partner Violence, 38 Epidemiologic Revs. 125 (2016); J. Campbell et al., Risk Factors for Femicide in Abusive Relationships: Results From a Multisite Case Control Study, 93 Am. J. Pub. Health 1089, 1092 (2003).

53 D. Studdert et al., Handgun Ownership and Suicide in California, 382 New England J. Med. 2220, 2224 (June 4, 2020).

할 확률이 총기소유율이 낮은 주에서보다 4배가 높다. 특히, 행정부 및 의회 측에서도 총기 규제의 필요성을 인정하는 분위기이며, 백악관에서도 각 주의 총기 규제 입법에 대해 긍정적 입장을 밝히고 있다. "미국 헌법 수정 제2조[55]는 총기소지를 보장하고 있는 반면, 뉴욕주는 적어도 20세 기 초부터 공공장소에서의 권총 소지를 규제해왔다."

"수많은 총기관련 사고와 범죄가 사회의 논란이 되는 미국에서는 총기규제관련 입법과 시행에 있어 주(state)정부와 시(city)정부를 비롯한 지방행정의 역할이 크다. 미국의 중앙 정부라고 할 수 있는 연방정부는 비교적으로 총기규제에 있어 제한적인 태도를 취한다. 미국 수정헌법 제 2 조항이 연방정부가 총기소유와 사용을 실질적으로 제재하지 못하도록 정해놓고 있기 때문이다. 연방차원의 총기규제 관련 규범이 존재하기는 하지만, 미국 지방정부들은 각 지역 상황에 알맞은 총기규제를 자치적으로 설립하고 시행해야 하는 실정이 다. 이렇게 중앙행정의 개입 없이 미국 전 지역에서 독립적으로 발생한 각종 총기규제 관련 법률들은 내용이나 범위에 있어 서로 다르고 충돌하는 경향이 있으며, 위헌소송에 휘말리는 경우가 많다. 통계를 살펴보면 이러한 소송에서는 지방정부가 승소하는 경우가 대다수이다. 법원이 지방정부의 총기규제를 지지해주는 역할을 하는 것이다. 미국 연방 대법원 역시 지방차원의 총기규제 관련 법률에 대한 위헌 소송은 대부분 기각한다는 것을 관찰할 수 있다. 지방관할 내에서의 입법권을 인정해 주는 이러한 미국 법원의 태도는 결과적으로 미국 전역에 있어서 총기규제 관련 법률이 지역적인 성향과 특색을 지니고 발전하도록 이바지하는 계기가 되고 있다.

The U.S. is well-known for its gun related violence and rampant crime rates. The country tackles this problem through a distinctive federal system where each regional government unit enacts its own gun control laws. Each land unit in the

---

54 D. Swedler, M. Simmons, F. Dominici, & D. Hemenway, Firearm Prevalence and Homicides of Law Enforcement Officers in the United States, 105 Am. J. Pub. Health 2042, 2045 (2015).

55 New York State Rifle & Pistol Assn., Inc. v. Bruen, 597 U. S. ____ (2022)(No. 20-843)(2022. 6. 23.).

U.S. fends for itself when it comes to gun control. The reason behind the development of such a system is partly because of the 2nd Amendment of the U.S. Constitution. The federal government is limited in its authority to take action that may infringe the right of American people to keep and bear arms. As result, regional government units began to take active legislative role since the last decade. To protect these regional gun control laws, the courts stepped in and validated them through court decisions. Recently, there have been a flood of lawsuits against regional governments on this issue challenging the constitutionality of regional gun control laws. Observing history, case examples, and current gun control policies at federal and regional levels, this study concludes that there exists a direct relationship between the U.S. courts

and regional gun control laws. Implications of the relationship is explored, discussing the pros and cons and suggestions for future studies."[56]

"뉴욕주에서는 집 안이든 이든 면허 없이 어떤 총기든 소지할 수 없으며, 이를 어길 경우 중범죄에 대해서는 4년 이하의 징역 또는 $5,000 이하의 벌금, 경범죄에 대해서는 1년 미만의 징역 또는 $1,000이하의 벌금에 처한다.[57] 한편 면허 없이 장전된 총기를 집 밖이나 사업장 밖에서 소지하는 것은 15년 이하의 징역형에 처할 수 있는 중범죄이다.[58] 집이나 사업장에서 총기를 소지하기를 원하는 총기면허 신청자는 자신이 도덕적 성품(good moral character)을 지녔으며, 범죄나 정신질환 이력이 없고, 면허를 거부할 정당한 이유가 없다는 점을 면허 담당 공무원 — 보통 판사나 경찰 — 에게 증명해야한다.[59] 만일 집 밖이나 사업장 밖에서 총기를 휴대하기를 원한다면 — 뉴욕주

---

56 사라 오 / 가천대학교 조교수, 前 미국매릴랜드주 District Court 법관 Sara Oh / Assistant professor, Gachon University, "총기규제를 위한 미국 지방정부와 법원의 역할(Law of the Land: Regional Gun Control in the U.S.)," 한국토지공법학회 토지공법연구 제73집 제1호, 2016년 2월 Korea Public Land Law Association Public Land Law Review Vol. 73 No. 1, February, 2016, 610면.

57 미국 헌법 수정 제2조(무기소지의 권리) 규율 있는 민병대는 자유로운 주의 안보에 필수적이므로 무기를 보유하고 휴대하는 개인의 권리는 침해될 수 없다.

58 N. Y. Penal Law Ann. §§265.01-b (West 2017), 261.01(1) (West Cum. Supp. 2022), 70.00(2)(e) and (3)(b), 80.00(1)(a) (West 2021), 70.15(1), 80.05(1).

에서는 타인의 눈에 띄는 상태로 총기를 휴대하는 것은 전혀 허용되지 않으므로 — 신청자는 권총이나 리볼버(회전식 연발 권총)의 은닉(concealed)[60] 소지 및 휴대를 위한 무제한 면허(unrestricted license)를 취득해야 한다.[61]"[62] 그러한 무제한 면허를 취득하기 위해서는 신청자가 그 발급에 '정당한 이유(proper cause)'가 있음을 증명해야 한다.[63] 만일 그러한 증명을 하지 못하는 경우 신청자는 사냥, 과녁사격, 직업상의 필요 등의 제한된 목적에 한하여 공공장소에서의 총기휴대가 허용되는 제한적 면허(restricted license)만 받을 수 있다.[64] 상고인들은 '뉴욕주 소총·권총 협회(New York State Rifle & Pistol Association, NRA)'와 그 회원 Brandon Koch와 Robert Nash이다. Koch와 Nash는 각각 공공장소에서의 자기방어를 위해 권총을 휴대하고자 무제한 면허를 신청하였으나, 자신의 안전에 특별한 위험이 있음을 증명하지 못하여 거부되었다. 피상고인들은 뉴욕주 면허법의 집행을 감독하는 뉴욕주 경찰서장과 상고인들이 거주하는 렌셀러 카운티(Rensselaer County)의 면허신청과정을 감독하는 뉴욕주법원 판사로, 상고인들은 피상고인들이 '정당한 이유'를 증명하지 못하였다는 이유로 무제한 면허의 발급을 거부함으로써 헌법 수정 제2조와 수정 제14조[65]를 위반하였다고 주장하였다. 제1심법원과 항소법원은 모두 뉴욕주의 '정당한 이유' 기준을 옹호하

---

59 §§400.00(1)(a)-(n) (West Cum. Supp. 2022).

60 공공장소에서 총기를 소지하는 것은 두 가지 방식으로 구분한다. 하나는 타인의 눈에 띄는 상태로 소 지하는 경우("Open Carry")이고 다른 하나는 타인의 눈에 띄지 않는 상태에서 소지하는 경우(Concealed Carry Weapon 또는 Concealed Weapon)이다. 첫 번째 경우는 각 주별로 그리고 타운이나 카운티에 따라 서로 다른 세부 규정을 두고 있으며 일반적으로 Concealed Weapon보다 더 엄격하게 통제하고 있다(미주(뉴욕)주재관, 미국 각주의 총기규제, 국회사무처, https://nas.na.go.kr/nas/info/ diplomacy_active03.do?mode=view&articleNo=385429)

61 §400.00(2)(f).

62 임기영 책임연구원, "뉴욕주 총기규제법 위헌 판결," 헌법재판소 헌법재판연구원 세계헌법재판 조사연구보고서, 2022 제7호(통권 제57호), 3면.

63 §400.00(2)(f).

64 In re O'Brien, 87 N. Y. 2d 436, 438-439, 663 N. E. 2d 316, 316-317 (1996); Babernitz v. Police Dept. of City of New York, 65 App. Div. 2d 320, 324, 411 N. Y. S. 2d 309, 311 (1978); In re O'Connor, 154 Misc. 2d 694, 696-698, 585 N. Y. S. 2d 1000, 1003 (Westchester Cty. 1992).

65 미국 헌법 수정 제14조 (공민권) 제1항. 미국에서 출생하거나 귀화하고, 미국의 관할권에 속하는 모든 사람은 미국 시민이자 그 거주하는 주의 시민이다. 어떠한 주도 미국 시민의 특권과 면책권을 제한하는 법률을 제정하거나 시행할 수 없다. 어떠한 주도 적정한 법의 절차에 의하지 않고는 어떠한 사람으로부터도 생명, 자유, 또는 재산을 박탈할 수 없으며, 그 관할권 내에 있는 어떠한 사람에 대해서도 법률의 평등한 보호를 거부하지 못한다.

며 상고인들의 주장을 받아들이지 않았다. 이에 연방대법원은 뉴욕주가 상고인들의 면허신청을 거부한 것이 위헌인지 여부를 판단하기 위해 상고를 허가하였다.[66]

2022년 1월, 미국 최초로 캘리포니아주 산호세시는 산호세 거주 총기 소유자에게 책임보험 가입을 의무화하는 법안을 통과하였음. 총기 소유자에 대한 책임보험 가입 의무화는 총기사고 가해자의 손해배상책임 이행을 촉진할 뿐 아니라 사전에 사고를 방지하는 효과도 가져올 것으로 평가된다. 그러나 책임보험 가입 의무화가 총기사고 발생 감소를 위한 근본적인 해결책이 될 수 없으며, 총기 소유에 대한 미국인의 헌법적 권리에도 위배 된다는 주장도 있다. 미국에서 총기 관련 사고로 인한 인명, 재물피해가 지속적으로 발생하고 있는 가운데, 2022년 1월, 미국 최초로 캘리포니아주 산호세시(San Jose City)에서는 산호세 거주 총기 소유자에게 책임보험(Liability Insurance) 가입을 의무화하는 법안이 통과된다.[67][68]

---

66 임기영 책임연구원, "뉴욕주 총기규제법 위헌 판결," 헌법재판소 헌법재판연구원 세계헌법재판 조사연구보고서, 2022 제7호(통권 제57호), 4면.

67 s(2022. 1. 26), "San Jose Passes Nation's First Gun Liability Insurance Law-Here's What It Means."

68 홍보배 연구원, "미국 총기 소유자의 책임보험 가입 의무화 논의," KIRI 리포트 글로벌 이슈, 2022.6.27., 23-24면; 산호세시 거주 총기 소유자는 책임보험에 의무적으로 가입해야 할 뿐만 아니라 매년 일정 금액(25달러)을 지정된 비영리 기관에 총기 피해 감소를 위한 비용(Annual Gun Harm Reduction Fee)으로 납부해야 한다. 산호세시 거주 이번 총기 소유자의 책임보험 가입 의무화 법안 도입 배경으로, 총기사고 발생이 빈번함에 따라 공공 보건 및 안전에 부정적인 영향이 크고, 이에 따른 사회적 비용 및 재정 부담이 높다고 그 필요성을 설명하였음 — 특히 총기사고에 수반되는 공공 서비스 지출(응급 경찰 · 의료진 출동 비용, 사고 조사비용, 피해자 의료비 지원 등)이 상당히 높고 이러한 재정부담을 주민들(총기 비소유자)에게 오롯이 전가하는 것은 바람직하지 않다고 밝힘 — 총기사고로 인한 산호세시의 공공 서비스 지출 비용은 연평균 약 3,970만 달러로, 가구당 151달러이며, 사적 비 용까지 포함하면 이보다 훨씬 높은 4억 4,200만 달러 이상의 재정 부담이 발생함. 과거에도 총기 난사 사건이 발생하여 규제의 필요성이 대두될 때, 다수의 수에서 여러 차례 총기 소유자의 책임보험 가입 의무화 법안을 통과시키고자 노력했지만 매번 무산되었던 점을 고려하면, 이번 산호세시의 법안 통과는 의미가 큼 — 총기 소유자에 대한 책임보험 가입 의무화 규제를 둘러싼 찬반 논쟁이 매우 치열했을 뿐만 아니라, 총기 관련 산업의 강력한 로비 활동 등으로 매번 법안 통과가 실패되었음. 산호세 시의회는 이번 총기 소유자에 대한 책임보험 가입 의무화 법안 통과로 인해, 총기사고 발생 시 피해 대한 신속하고 적정한 손해배상 이행 보장 및 잠재적 가해자인 총기 소유자의 배상책임 이행의 부담 완화 효과 외에도 총기사고를 미연에 방지하는 효과도 가져올 것으로 전망함. 총기 소유자의 책임보험 가입 의무화에 찬성하는 측은 보험 가입 의무화라는 정책 수단을 통해 총기 소유자의 안전 의식 향상 및 안전 추구 행동을 유인함으로써 사고 발생 위험을 낮출 수 있다고 설명함 — 산호세 시의회는 미국의 운전자보험 의무화 규제 도입 이후 교통사고로 인한 인명 피해가 크게 감소해왔다고 덧붙이면서, 총기 소유자에 대한 책임보험 가입 의무화 조치도 이와 유사한 효과를 가져올 것이라고 평가함 반면, 이에 반대하는 측은 총기난사 등 범죄 · 고의적인 행위로 인한 총기사고는 보험보장에서 원칙적으로 제외됨에 따라 책임보험 가입 의무화는 총기사고 감소를 위한 근본적인 해결책이 될 수 없다고 주장하며 대립함. 미국 전국총

Ⅳ. 미국 연방헌법 수정조항 제2조 역사적 배경

"미국 헌법 수정 제2조, 무기 소지권에 대한 많은 논의가 이루어져왔다. 헌법 수정 제2 조는 다음과 같이 기록되어 있다: "자유주의 국가의 안전을 위해 잘 규율된 군대가 필요하므로 국민들의 무기 보유 및 소지권을 침해해서는 안 된다." 무기 소지에 관한 논쟁은 미국 대법원 판례에도 여러 번 나타나고 있다. 1939년 United States v. Miller, 307 U.S. 174 라는 미국 대법원 판례를 살펴보자. Miller는 등록하지 않은 총기를 Oklahoma에서 Arkansa로 옮기는 중에 경찰에 체포되었으며, 1934년에 제정된 The National Firearms Act(총기 생산 판매 등에 세금을 부과하고 총기 이동 시에 정부에 신고) 위반으로 형을 받게 되었다. 이에 대하여 Miler는 National Fireamrs Act는 총기 소유를 인정한 수정헌법 제2조 위반으로 위헌이라고 주장하였다. 아울러 2008년 District of Columbia v. Heller[69][70] 사건에서 총기 소유 및 수정헌법 제2조에 대한 논의가 다

기권리연합(National Association for Gun Rights)은 총기 소유자에 대한 책임보험 의무화 법안 통과는 미국인의 총기 소유에 관한 헌법적 권리에 위배 된다고 주장함. 또한 총기 소유자에게 책임보험 가입을 의무화하더라도 보험회사는 우발적인 또는 자기방어를 위한 총기사고일 경우에만 손해를 보장하고, 고의적인 사고는 보장하지 않기 때문에 근본적인 해결책이 될 수 없다고 반박함 ― 미국에서 발생한 전체 총기사건 중 비고의적인 사고는 1/3을 차지함. 한편 보험 가입으로 위험이 보험회사에 이전되면서 오히려 총기 소유자의 도덕적 해이를 유발하여 총기사고 발생 위험 가능성을 증가시킬 수 있다는 주장도 제기됨. 이러한 찬반 논쟁이 지속되는 가운데, 최근 텍사스주 초등학교에서 발생한 총기 난사 사건 등 미국에서 비극적인 총기사고가 여러 차례 발생함에 따라 바이든 정부는 총기 관련 규제를 더욱 강화할 것으로 예상됨. 이에 따라, 향후 산호세시와 같이 총기 소유자에게 책임보험 가입을 의무화하는 주(state) 또는 시(city)가 점진적으로 늘어날 것으로 보임. 보험산업은 이러한 규제 변화 움직임에 따라, 앞으로 총기 소유자의 위험 행태를 반영한 보험료 차등화 등 계량화 기술 및 관련 보험상품 개발 등 관련 논의를 지속해야 할 것임.

69 김찬송 위스콘신대, "미국이 총기사건을 절대 막을 수 없는 이유," 2023-10-31 12:11:39 https://www.naeil. com/news/read/478070 2025.4.8.검색; "지난 25일 미국 메인주의 두 번째로 큰 북부 도시인 루이스턴에서 발생한 총격사건으로 최소 18명이 숨지고 12명 이상이 다쳤다. 주 및 지역 경찰은 총격범 수색을 위해 루이스턴과 주변 지역주민들에게 대피할 것을 요청했으며 한동안 이 지역의 많은 학교와 사업체가 문을 닫아야만 했다. 그리고 총격 발생 48시간이 지나서야 자살한 용의자가 발견되면서 사건은 일단락됐다. 루이스턴 총격사건은 올해 발생한 수백 건의 총기 난사 사건 중 하나이며, 콜로라도 시카고 루이지애나 등 여러 지역에서 일주일간 연쇄적으로 발생한 총기 난사 사건에 이어 발생한 사건이다. 선진국 중에서 총기 사건으로 인한 사망자수가 미국보다 많은 국가는 없다. 자살과 살인을 포함해 매일 120명의 미국인이 총기로 사망, 연평균 4만3375명에 달한다. 2015년부터 2019년까지의 분석에 따르면 미국의 총기로 인한 살인율은 다른 선진국 국가의 26배에 달하며, 자살률은 12배 가까이 높다. 최소 4명 이상의 사상자가 발생한 대규모 총기난사 사건은 2015년 이후 지속적인 증가 추세에 있으며, 2021년에는 686건으로 최고치에 다다랐다. 루이스턴 총기 난사 사건을 포함해 2023년 10월 말 현재 미국에서는 이미 565건의 총기 난사 사건이 발

생했다. 전문가들은 이러한 추세라면 올해 2021년 기록을 넘어설 것으로 예상하고 있다. 인구 3%가 미국 총기의 절반 소유. 이러한 참혹한 현실에도 불구하고 총기가 자신과 타인을 해칠 수 있는 사람들의 손에 들어가지 않도록 하는 방법에 대한 정치적 논쟁은 오랫동안 풀리지 않는 난제다. 미국의 총기 소유 문화는 대량 총격사건 이후 총기 폭력에 대한 적극적인 정책적 해결책을 모색하는 것을 더욱 어렵게 만들었다. 총기 소유 여부를 등록하는 전국적인 데이터베이스가 부재하고, 총기 밀매를 규제하는 강력한 연방법이 마련되지 않은 상황에서 총기 암시장이 번성하고 있다. 게다가 DIY키트 혹은 3D 프린터로 직접 총기를 제조할 수 있게 되면서 미국 내 개인 소유 총기수를 정확하게 추정하기는 더욱 어려워졌다. 잘 알려진 대로 특히 전미총기협회는 활발한 로비활동을 통해 총기 판매를 추적하고 국가 차원의 총기등록소를 설립하는 연방법안을 격렬하게 제지하고 있다. 스위스에 기반을 둔 연구 프로젝트인 '소형무기조사(Small Arms Survey)'의 추정에 따르면 2018년 미국에는 약 3억9000만정의 총기가 유통됐으며, 이는 인구 100명당 약 120.5정의 총기를 보유하는 셈이다. 코로나19 팬데믹 기간에 5가구 중 1가구가 총기를 구매했다는 조사에 따른다면 이미 2018년 수치를 훌쩍 넘어선 것으로 보인다. 또한 지난 수년 동안 제조 및 수입된 총기류의 수도 증가했다. 이러한 증가를 고려하지 않더라도 미국의 총기 보유율은 여전히 다른 어떤 국가보다 훨씬 높다. 세계에서 두 번째로 총기 보유율이 높은 예멘은 인구 100명당 총기 보유량이 52.8정에 불과하다. 2016년 하버드대와 노스이스턴대의 연구에 따르면 미국 총기는 극소수 가구에 집중돼 있다. 인구의 단 3%가 미국 총기의 절반 정도를 소유하고 있다고 한다. 이들은 평균 17정의 총기를 보유한 '슈퍼 오너'라고 불린다. 갤럽은 2022년에 미국인의 45%가 총기를 소지한 가정에서 살고 있다고 밝혔다. '총을 든 선량한 사람 이론' 널리 퍼져. 총기 관련 연구자들은 미국의 총기 소유와 총기 난사 사건 사이에 분명한 연관성이 있음을 주장한다. 2013년 보스턴대가 주도한 한 연구에 따르면 가정에서 총기 소유율이 1%p 증가할 때마다 주 총기 살인율이 0.9%씩 증가했다고 한다. 하지만 미국에선 대량 총격사건에 대한 해결책으로 더 많은 사람이 더 많은 장소에서 더 많은 총을 소지해 자신을 보호할 수 있어야 한다는 '총을 든 선량한 사람 이론(good guy with a gun theory)'이 여전히 널리 퍼져 있다. 그러나 경찰이나 무장한 일반인이 실제 총기사건을 성공적으로 제지할 수 있었던 사례는 상대적으로 적다. 텍사스주립대의 연구에 따르면 총격사건 대부분은 경찰이 도착했을 때 이미 공격이 종료됐거나 가해자가 투항 혹은 자살했기 때문에 경찰이 공격자를 제지할 수 없었다고 한다. 경찰이 총격이나 다른 방법으로 가해자를 제압해 성공적으로 개입할 수 있었던 경우는 극소수에 불과했다. 또한 메트로폴리탄주립대의 2021년 연구에 따르면 1980년부터 2019년까지 발생한 133건의 대규모 학교 총격사건에서 무장경비원이 있었던 경우에 오히려 총기로 인한 사망률이 2.83배 더 높았다고 한다. 연구진은 "무장경비원의 존재가 총격범의 공격성을 증가시켰으며, 총격범들은 대부분 사건 직후 자살하기 때문에 총기 소유가 총격사건의 억제책이 될 수 없다"고 주장했다. 그나마 반가운 소식은 미 의회가 지난해 발생한 텍사스주 유밸디의 롭 초등학교 총격사건 이후, 거의 30년 만에 처음으로 제한적인 총기 개혁에 합의했다는 것이다. 2022년 6월 통과된 '초당적 안전한 지역사회 법안(Bipartisan Safer Communities Act)'은 각 주에서 총기 규제법안이 통과되도록 장려하고, 21세 미만 총기 구매자에 대한 신원조회를 강화했으며, 가정폭력사건에서 유죄판결을 받은 사람들의 총기 구매가 불가능하도록 제한했다. 무기밀매와 대리구매 처벌 강화 등의 내용도 포함돼 있다. 그러나 모든 종류의 총기류를 금지한 것도 아니며 법원이 지정한 무기를 일시적으로 제한하는 정도에 머물러, 보편적인 신원조회를 시행하더라도 총기 폭력을 근절하기에는 여전히 미흡하다는 평가를 받는다. 대법원이 총기규제 더 어렵게 만들어. 또한 미 대법원은 연방 또는 주 의원들이 총기폭력에 맞서 싸우는 것을 더욱 어렵게 만들고 있다. 2008년 대법원은 미국총기협회 CEO 웨인 라피에르(Wayne LaPierre)가 적극적으로 주장하던 '총을 든 선량한 사람 이론'을 사실상 헌법에 반영했다. '컬럼비아 특별구 대 헬러 사건(District of Columbia v. Heller)'에 대한 판결은 미국 역사상 수정헌법 제2조가 개인의 총기 소지 권리를 보호한다고 판시한 최초의 대법원 판결이었다. 당시 헬러 판사는 수정헌법 제2조의 주요 목적 중 하나는 총을 가진 선량한 개인이 총을 가진 악당을 막기 위해 총기를 사용할 수 있는 권리를 보호하는 것이라고 주장했다. 스칼리아 대법관은 이 판결에서 '내재적 정당방위권은 수정헌법 제2조 권리의 핵심'이라고 인용했다. 게다가 대법원은 2021년 '뉴욕주 소총 및 권총협회 대 브루엔 판결(New York State Rifle & Pistol Association v. Bruen)'을 통해 수정헌법 제2조의 범위를 대폭 확대하고 총기규제를 규정한 10년 이상의 판례를 폐기했다. 브루엔 판사는 미국 내 총기사건에서 압도적으로 사용되는 권총을 미국의 많은 공공장소에서 쉽게 소지할 수 있도록 허용했다. 대법원의 이 판결 이후 12개 이상의 주와 연방의 총기규제 결정이 전부 또는 일부 무효가 됐다. 게다가 지난 수년 동안 많은 주에서는 총기구매를 어렵게 만들기는커녕 오히려 총기규제를 완화했다. 동시에 총기 소유를 확대하기 위해 노력해왔다. 현재 최소 27개 주에서 주민이 허가없이 권총을 소지할 수 있고 교직원과 교사가 교내에서 총기를 휴대할 수 있도록 허용하는 법안이 통과됐다. 정부가 총기폭력으로부터 국민을 보호해야 한다고 믿는 미국인들에게 완전한 총기규제는 아직도 머나먼 이야기다."

70 https://en.wikipedia.org/wiki/District_of_Columbia_v._Heller 2025.4.8. 검색; District of Columbia v. Heller "Dick Heller" redirects here. For the sportswriter, see Dick Heller (sportswriter). District of Columbia v. Heller, 554 U.S. 570 (2008), is a landmark decision of the Supreme Court of the United States. It ruled that the Second Amendment to the U.S. Constitution protects an individual's right to keep and bear arms for traditionally lawful purposes such as self-defense within the home, and that the District of Columbia's handgun ban and requirement that lawfully owned rifles and shotguns be kept "unloaded and disassembled or bound by a trigger lock" violated this guarantee. It also stated that the right to bear arms is not unlimited and that certain restrictions on guns and gun ownership were permissible. It was the first Supreme Court case to decide whether the Second Amendment protects an individual right to keep and bear arms for self-defense or whether the right was only intended for state militias.

Because of the District of Columbia's status as a federal enclave (it is not in any U.S. state), the decision did not address the question of whether the Second Amendment's protections are incorporated by the Due Process Clause of the Fourteenth Amendment to the U.S. Constitution against the states. This point was addressed two years later by McDonald v. City of Chicago (2010), in which it was found that they are.

On June 26, 2008, the Supreme Court affirmed by a vote of 5 to 4 the U.S. Court of Appeals for the D.C. Circuit in Heller v. District of Columbia. The Supreme Court struck down provisions of the Firearms Control Regulations Act of 1975 as unconstitutional, determined that handguns are "arms" for the purposes of the Second Amendment, found that the Regulations Act was an unconstitutional ban, and struck down the portion of the Act that requires all firearms including rifles and shotguns be kept "unloaded and disassembled or bound by a trigger lock". Prior to this decision, the law at issue also restricted residents from owning handguns except for those registered prior to 1975.

Lower court background

In 2002, Robert A. Levy, a senior fellow at the Cato Institute, began vetting plaintiffs with Clark M. Neily III for a planned Second Amendment lawsuit that he would personally finance. Although he himself had never owned a gun, as a constitutional scholar, he had an academic interest in the subject and wanted to model his campaign after the legal strategies of Thurgood Marshall, who had successfully led the challenges that overturned school segregation.[6] They aimed for a group that would be diverse in terms of gender, race, economic background, and age and selected six plaintiffs from their mid-20s to early 60s: three men and three women; four white and two black:

Tracey Ambeau (now Tracey Hanson)
An employee of the U.S. Department of Agriculture. Originally from St. Gabriel, Louisiana, she lived in the Adams Morgan neighborhood of D.C. with her husband, Andrew Hanson, who was from Waterloo, Iowa. They lived in a high-crime neighborhood near Union Station in D.C. She grew up around guns and wanted one to defend her home.

Dick Anthony Heller
A licensed special police officer for the District of Columbia. For his job, Heller carried a gun in federal office buildings, but was not allowed to have one in his home. Heller had lived in southeast D.C. near the Kentucky Courts public housing complex since 1970 and had seen the neighborhood "transformed from a child-friendly welfare complex to a drug haven". Heller had also approached the National Rifle Association about a lawsuit to overturn the D.C. gun ban, but the NRA declined.

George Lyon
A communications lawyer who had previously contacted the National Rifle Association (NRA) about filing a lawsuit to challenge the gun laws in the District of Columbia. Lyon held D.C. licenses for a shotgun and a rifle, but wanted to have a handgun in his home.

Tom G. Palmer
A colleague of Robert A. Levy at the Cato Institute and the only plaintiff that Levy knew before the case began. Palmer, who is gay, defended himself with a 9mm handgun in 1982. While walking with a friend in San Jose, California, he was accosted by a gang of about 20 young men who used profane language regarding his sexual orientation and threatened his life. When he produced his gun, the men fled. Palmer believes that the handgun saved his life.

Shelly Parker
A software designer and former nurse who had been active in trying to rid her neighborhood of drugs. Parker was a single woman whose life had been threatened on numerous occasions by drug dealers who had sometimes tried to break into her house.

Gillian St. Lawrence
A mortgage broker who lived in the Georgetown section of D.C. and who owned several legally registered long guns that she used for recreation in nearby Chantilly, Virginia. It had taken St. Lawrence two years to complete the registration process. She wanted to be able to use these guns to defend herself in her home and to be able to register a handgun.
Previous federal case law pertaining to the question of an individual's right to bear arms included United States v. Emerson, 270 F.3d 203 (5th Cir. 2001), which supported the right and Silveira v. Lockyer, 312 F.3d 1052 (9th Cir. 2002), which opposed the right. The Supreme Court ruling in United States v. Miller, 307 U.S. 174 (1939) was interpreted to support both sides of the issue.

District Court

In February 2003, the six residents of the District of Columbia filed a lawsuit in the District Court for the District of Columbia, challenging the constitutionality of provisions of the Firearms Control Regulations Act of 1975, a local law (part of the District of Columbia Code) enacted pursuant to District of Columbia home rule. This law restricted residents from owning handguns, excluding those grandfathered in by registration prior to 1975 and those possessed by active and retired law enforcement officers. The law also required that all firearms including rifles and shotguns be kept "unloaded and disassembled or bound by a trigger lock." [17] They filed for an injunction pursuant to 28 U.S.C. § 2201, 2202, and 42 U.S.C. § 1983. District Court Judge Emmet G. Sullivan dismissed the lawsuit on March 31, 2004.

Court of Appeals

On appeal, the U.S. Court of Appeals for the D.C. Circuit reversed the dismissal in a 2-1 decision. The Court of Appeals struck down provisions of the Firearms Control Regulations Act as unconstitutional. Judges Karen L. Henderson, Thomas B. Griffith and Laurence H. Silberman formed the Court of Appeals panel, with Senior Circuit Judge Silberman writing the court's opinion and Circuit Judge Henderson dissenting.

The court's opinion first addressed whether appellants have standing to sue for declaratory and injunctive relief in section II (slip opinion, at 5–12). The court concluded that of the six plaintiffs, only Heller – who applied for a handgun permit but was denied – had standing.

The court then held that the Second Amendment "protects an individual right to keep and bear arms," that the "right existed prior to the formation of the new government under the Constitution," also stating that the right was "premised on the private use of arms for activities such as hunting and self-defense, the latter being understood as resistance to either private lawlessness or the depredations of a tyrannical government (or a threat from abroad)." They also noted that though the right to bear arms also helped preserve the citizen militia, "the activities [the Amendment] protects are not limited to militia service, nor is an individual's enjoyment of the right contingent upon his or her continued or intermittent enrollment in the militia." The court determined that handguns are "Arms" and concluded that thus they may not be banned by the District of Columbia.

The court also struck down the portion of the law that requires all firearms including rifles and shotguns be kept "unloaded and disassembled or bound by a trigger lock." The District argued that there is an implicit self-defense exception to these provisions, but the D.C. Circuit rejected this view, saying that the requirement amounted to a complete ban on functional firearms and prohibition on use for self-defense:

Section 7-2507.02, like the bar on carrying a pistol within the home, amounts to a complete prohibition on the lawful use of handguns for self-defense. As such, we hold it unconstitutional.

In her dissent, Circuit Judge Henderson stated that Second Amendment rights did not extend to residents of District of Columbia, writing:

To sum up, there is no dispute that the Constitution, case law and applicable statutes all establish that the District is not a State within the meaning of the Second Amendment. Under United States v. Miller, 307 U.S. at 178, the Second Amendment's declaration and guarantee that "the right of the people to keep and bear Arms, shall not be infringed" relates to the Militia of the States only. That the Second Amendment does not apply to the District, then, is, to me, an unavoidable conclusion.

In April 2007, the District and Mayor Adrian Fenty petitioned for rehearing en banc, arguing that the ruling created inter- and intra-jurisdictional conflict. On May 8, the Court of Appeals for the D.C. Circuit denied the request to rehear the case, by a 6–4 vote.

Supreme Court

The defendants petitioned the United States Supreme Court to hear the case. The Supreme Court granted certiorari on November 20, 2007. The court rephrased the question to be decided as follows:

The petition for a writ of certiorari is granted limited to the following question: Whether the following provisions, D.C. Code §§ 7-2502.02(a)(4), 22–4504(a), and 7-2507.02, violate the Second Amendment rights of individuals who are not affiliated with any state-regulated militia, but who wish to keep handguns and other firearms for private use in their homes.

This represented the first time since the 1939 case United States v. Miller that the Supreme Court had directly addressed the scope of the Second Amendment.

Amicus curiae briefs

Because of the controversial nature of the case, it garnered much attention from many groups on both sides of the gun rights issue. Many of those groups filed amicus curiae (friend of the court) briefs, about 47 urging the court to affirm the case and about 20 to remand it.

A majority of the members of Congress[24] signed the brief authored by Stephen Halbrook advising that the case be affirmed overturning the ban on handguns not otherwise restricted by Congress.[25] Vice President Dick Cheney joined in this brief, acting in his role as President of the United States Senate, and breaking with the George W. Bush administration's official position.[24] Arizona Senator John McCain, Republican, also signed the brief. Then-Illinois Senator Barack Obama did not.[26]

A majority of the states signed the brief of Texas Attorney General Greg Abbott, authored by Abbott's solicitor general, Ted Cruz, advising that the case be affirmed, while at the same time emphasizing that the states have a strong interest in maintaining each of the states' laws prohibiting and regulating firearms.

Law enforcement organizations, including the Fraternal Order of Police and the Southern States Police Benevolent Association, also filed a brief urging that the case be affirmed.

A number of organizations signed friend of the court briefs advising that the case be remanded, including the United States Department of Justice[32] and Attorneys General of New York, Hawaii, Maryland, Massachusetts, New Jersey, and Puerto Rico.[33] Additionally, friend of the court briefs to remand were filed by a spectrum of religious and anti-violence groups, a number of cities and mayors, and many police chiefs and law enforcement organizations.

A collection of organizations and prominent scholars, represented by attorney Jeffrey Teichert, submitted an "errors brief" arguing that many of the common historical and factual "myths and misrepresentations" generally offered in favor of banning handguns were in error. Teichert's brief argued from a historical perspective that the Second Amendment protected an individual right to keep and bear arms.

Oral arguments

Robert A. Levy (left) and Alan Gura, counsel for Heller

The Supreme Court heard oral arguments in the case on March 18, 2008. Both the transcript and the audio of the argument have been released. Each side was initially allotted 30 minutes to argue its case, with U.S. Solicitor General Paul D. Clement allotted 15 minutes to present the federal government's views. During the argument, however, extra time was extended to the parties, and the argument ran 23 minutes over the allotted time.

Walter E. Dellinger of the law firm O'Melveny & Myers, also a professor at Duke University Law School and former Acting Solicitor General, argued the District's side before the Supreme Court. Dellinger was assisted by Thomas Goldstein of Akin Gump Strauss Hauer & Feld, Robert Long of Covington & Burling and D.C. Solicitor General Todd Kim. The law firms assisting the District worked pro bono.

Alan Gura, of the D.C.-based law firm Gura & Possessky, was lead counsel for Heller, and argued on his behalf before the Supreme Court.[43] Robert Levy, a senior fellow at the Cato Institute, and Clark Neily, a senior attorney at the Institute for Justice, were his co-counsel.

Decision

Justice Antonin Scalia wrote the majority opinion.

The Supreme Court held:

(1) The Second Amendment protects an individual right to possess a firearm unconnected with service in a militia, and to use that arm for traditionally lawful purposes, such as self-defense within the home. Pp. 2–53.

(a) The Amendment's prefatory clause announces a purpose, but does not limit or expand the scope of the second part, the operative clause. The operative clause's text and history demonstrate that it connotes an individual right to keep and bear arms. pp. 2-22.

(b) The prefatory clause comports with the Court's interpretation of the operative clause. The "militia" comprised all males physically capable of acting in concert for the common defense. The Antifederalists feared that the Federal Government would disarm the people in order to disable this citizens' militia, enabling a politicized standing army or a select militia to rule. The response was to deny Congress power to abridge the ancient right of individuals to keep and bear arms, so that the ideal of a citizens' militia would be preserved. pp. 22-28.

(c) The Court's interpretation is confirmed by analogous arms-bearing rights in state constitutions that preceded and immediately followed the Second Amendment. pp. 28-30.

(d) The Second Amendment's drafting history, while of dubious interpretive worth, reveals three state Second Amendment proposals that unequivocally referred to an individual right to bear arms. pp. 30–32.

(e) Interpretation of the Second Amendment by scholars, courts and legislators, from immediately after its ratification through the late 19th century also supports the Court's conclusion. pp. 32-47.

(f) None of the Court's precedents forecloses the Court's interpretation. Neither United States v. Cruikshank, 92 U.S. 542 (1876), nor Presser v. Illinois, 116 U.S. 252 (1886), refutes the individual-rights interpretation. United States v. Miller, 307 U.S. 174 (1939), does not limit the right to keep and bear arms to militia purposes, but rather limits the type of weapon to which the right applies to those used by the militia, i.e., those in common use for lawful purposes.

(2) Like most rights, the Second Amendment right is not unlimited. It is not a right to keep and carry any weapon whatsoever in any manner whatsoever and for whatever purpose: For example, concealed weapons prohibitions have been upheld under the Amendment or state analogues. The Court's opinion should not be taken to cast doubt on longstanding prohibitions on the possession of firearms by felons and the mentally ill, or laws forbidding the carrying of firearms in sensitive places such as schools and government buildings, or laws imposing conditions and qualifications on the commercial sale of arms. Miller's holding that the sorts of weapons protected are those "in common use at the time" finds support in the historical tradition of prohibiting the carrying of dangerous and unusual weapons. pp. 54–56.

(3) The handgun ban and the trigger-lock requirement (as applied to self-defense) violate the Second Amendment. The District's total ban on handgun possession in the home amounts to a prohibition on an entire class of "arms" that Americans overwhelmingly choose for the lawful purpose of self-defense. Under any of the standards of scrutiny the Court has applied to enumerated constitutional rights, this prohibition – in the place where the importance of the lawful defense of self, family, and property is most acute – would fail constitutional muster. Similarly, the requirement that any lawful firearm in the home be disassembled or bound by a trigger lock makes it impossible for citizens to use arms for the core lawful purpose of self-defense and is hence unconstitutional. Because Heller conceded at oral argument that the D.C. licensing law is permissible if it is not enforced arbitrarily and capriciously, the Court assumes that a license will satisfy his prayer for relief and does not address the licensing requirement. Assuming he is not disqualified from exercising Second Amendment rights, the District must permit Heller to register his handgun and must issue him a license to carry it in the home. pp. 56–64.

The Opinion of the Court, delivered by Justice Scalia, was joined by Chief Justice John G. Roberts, Jr. and by Justices Anthony M. Kennedy, Clarence Thomas and Samuel Alito.

Second Amendment findings and reasoning

The Illinois Supreme Court in People v. Aguilar (2013), summed up the Heller's findings and reasoning: In District of Columbia v. Heller, 554 U.S. 570 (2008), the Supreme Court undertook its first-ever "in-depth examination" of the second amendment's meaning Id. at 635. After a lengthy historical discussion, the Court ultimately concluded that the second amendment "guarantee[s] the individual right to possess and carry weapons in case of confrontation" (id. at 592); that "central to" this right is "the inherent right of self-defense"(id. at 628); that "the home" is "where the need for defense of self, family, and property is most acute" (id. at 628); and that, "above all other interests," the second amendment elevates "the right of law-abiding, responsible citizens to use arms in defense of hearth and home" (id. at 635). Based on this understanding, the Court held that a District of Columbia law banning handgun possession in the home violated the second amendment. Id. at 635.

Issues addressed by the majority

The core holding in D.C. v. Heller is that the right to keep and bear arms is an individual right intimately tied to the natural right of self-defense.

The Scalia majority invokes much historical material to support its finding that the right to keep and bear arms belongs to individuals; more precisely, Scalia asserts in the Court's opinion that the "people" to whom the Second Amendment right is accorded are the same "people" who enjoy First and Fourth Amendment protection: "The Constitution was written to be understood by the voters; its words and phrases were used in their normal and ordinary as distinguished from technical meaning. United States v. Sprague, 282 U.S. 716, 731 (1931); see also Gibbons v. Ogden, 9 Wheat. 1, 188 (1824). Normal meaning may, of course, include an idiomatic meaning, but it excludes secret or technical meanings …."

With that finding as an anchor, the Court ruled a total ban on operative handguns in the home is unconstitutional, as the ban runs afoul of both the self-defense purpose of the Second Amendment - a purpose not previously articulated by the Court — and the "in common use at the time" prong of the Miller decision: Since handguns are in common use, their ownership is protected.

The Court applies as the remedy that "[a]ssuming that Heller is not disqualified from the exercise of Second Amendment rights, the District must permit him to register his handgun and must issue him a license to carry it in the home." The Court, additionally, hinted that other remedy might be available in the form of eliminating the license requirement for carrying in the home, but that no such relief had been requested: "Respondent conceded at oral argument that he does not 'have a problem with … licensing' and that the District's law is permissible so long as it is 'not enforced in an arbitrary and capricious manner.' Tr. of Oral Arg. 74-75. We, therefore, assume that petitioners' issuance of a license will satisfy respondent's prayer for relief and do not address the licensing requirement."

In regard to the scope of the right, the Court wrote, in an obiter dictum, "Although we do not undertake an exhaustive historical analysis today of the full scope of the Second Amendment, nothing in our opinion should be taken to cast doubt on longstanding prohibitions on the possession of firearms by felons and the mentally ill, or laws forbidding the carrying of firearms in sensitive places such as schools and government buildings, or laws imposing conditions and qualifications on the commercial sale of arms."

The Court also added dicta regarding the private ownership of machine guns. In doing so, it suggested the elevation of the "in common use at the time" prong of the Miller decision, which by itself protects handguns, over the first prong (protecting arms that "have some reasonable relationship to the preservation or efficiency of a well regulated militia"), which may not by itself protect machine guns: "It may be objected that if weapons that are most useful in military service - M16 rifles and the like - may be banned, then the Second Amendment right is completely detached from the prefatory clause. But as we have said, the conception of the militia at the time of the Second Amendment's ratification was the body of all citizens capable of military service, who would bring the sorts of lawful weapons that they possessed at home."

The Court did not address which level of judicial review should be used by lower courts in deciding future cases claiming infringement of the right to keep and bear arms: "[S]ince this case represents this Court's first in-depth examination of the Second Amendment, one should not expect it to clarify the entire field." The Court states, "If all that was required to overcome the right to keep and bear arms was a rational basis, the Second Amendment would be redundant with the separate constitutional prohibitions on irrational laws, and would have no effect." [51] Also, regarding Justice Breyer's proposal of a "judge-empowering 'interest-balancing inquiry'," the Court states, "We know of no other enumerated constitutional right whose core protection has been subjected to a freestanding 'interest-balancing' approach."

Dissenting opinions

Justice John Paul Stevens wrote a dissenting opinion.

In a dissenting opinion, Justice John Paul Stevens stated that the court's judgment was "a strained and unpersuasive reading" which overturned longstanding precedent, and that the court had "bestowed a dramatic upheaval in the law". Stevens also stated that the amendment was notable for the "omission of any statement of purpose related to the right to use firearms for hunting or personal self-defense" which was present in the Declarations of Rights of Pennsylvania and Vermont.

The Stevens dissent seems to rest on four main points of disagreement: that the Founders would have made the individual right aspect of the Second Amendment express if that was what was intended; that the "militia" preamble and exact phrase "to keep and bear arms" demands the conclusion that the Second Amendment touches on state militia service only; that many lower courts' later "collective-right" reading of the Miller decision constitutes stare decisis, which may only be overturned at great peril; and that the Court has not considered gun-control laws (e.g., the National Firearms Act) unconstitutional. The dissent concludes, "The Court would have us believe that over 200 years ago, the Framers made a choice to limit the tools available to elected officials wishing to regulate civilian uses of weapons… I could not possibly conclude that the Framers made such a choice."

Justice Stevens's dissent was joined by Justices David Souter, Ruth Bader Ginsburg, and Stephen Breyer.

Justice Breyer filed a separate dissenting opinion, joined by the same dissenting Justices, which sought to demonstrate that, starting from the premise of an individual-rights view, the District of Columbia's handgun ban and trigger lock requirement would nevertheless be permissible limitations on the right.

The Breyer dissent looks to early municipal fire-safety laws that forbade the storage of gunpowder (and in Boston the carrying of loaded arms into certain buildings), and on nuisance laws providing fines or loss of firearm for imprudent usage, as demonstrating the Second Amendment has been understood to have no impact on the regulation of civilian firearms. The dissent argues the public safety necessity of gun-control laws, quoting that "guns were responsible for 69 deaths in this country each day."

With these two supports, the Breyer dissent goes on to conclude, "there simply is no untouchable constitutional right guaranteed by the Second Amendment to keep loaded handguns in the house in crime-ridden urban areas." It proposes that firearms laws be reviewed by balancing the interests (i.e., "'interest-balancing' approach") of Second Amendment protections against the government's compelling interest of preventing crime.

The Breyer dissent also objected to the "common use" distinction used by the majority to distinguish handguns from machine guns: "But what sense does this approach make? According to the majority's reasoning, if Congress and the States lift restrictions on the possession and use of machineguns, and people buy machineguns to protect their homes, the Court will have to reverse course and find that the Second Amendment does, in fact, protect the individual self-defense-related right to possess a machine-gun…There is no basis for believing that the Framers intended such circular reasoning."

Non-party involvement

National Rifle Association (NRA)

Attorney Alan Gura, in a 2003 filing, used the term "sham litigation" to describe the NRA's attempts to have Parker (aka Heller) consolidated with its own case challenging the D.C. law. Gura also stated that "the NRA was adamant about not wanting the Supreme Court to hear the case". These concerns were based on NRA lawyers' assessment that the justices at the time the case was filed might reach an unfavorable decision.[56] Cato Institute senior fellow Robert Levy, co-counsel to the Parker plaintiffs, has stated that the Parker plaintiffs "faced repeated attempts by the NRA to derail the litigation." He also stated that "The N.R.A.'s interference in this process set us back and almost killed the case. It was a very acrimonious relationship."

Wayne LaPierre, the NRA's chief executive officer, confirmed the NRA's misgivings. "There was a real dispute on our side among the constitutional scholars about whether there was a majority of justices on the Supreme Court who would support the Constitution as written," LaPierre said. Both Levy and LaPierre said the NRA and Levy's team were now on good terms.

Elaine McArdle wrote in the Harvard Law Bulletin: "If Parker is the long-awaited "clean" case, one reason may be that proponents of the individual-rights view of the Second Amendment – including the National Rifle Association, which filed an amicus brief in the case – have learned from earlier defeats, and crafted strategies to maximize the chances of Supreme Court review." The NRA did eventually support the litigation by filing an amicus brief with the Court arguing that the plaintiffs in Parker had standing to sue and that the D.C. ban was unconstitutional under the Second Amendment.

Chris Cox, executive director of the NRA's Institute for Legislative Action, had indicated support of federal legislation which would repeal the D.C. gun ban. Opponents of the legislation argued that this would have rendered the Parker case moot, and would have effectively eliminated the possibility that the case would be heard by the Supreme Court.[59]

Immediately after the Supreme Court's ruling, the NRA filed a lawsuit against the city of Chicago over its handgun ban, followed the next day by a lawsuit against the city of San Francisco over its ban of handguns in public housing.

Brady Campaign to Prevent Gun Violence

The Brady Campaign to Prevent Gun Violence opposed the arguments made by the plaintiffs in Parker, and filed amicus curiae against those arguments in both the District and Circuit courts.

Paul Helmke, the president of the Brady Campaign, suggested to D.C. before the Court granted certiorari that it modify its gun laws rather than appeal to the Supreme Court.[61] Helmke has written that if the Supreme Court upholds the Circuit court ruling, it "could lead to all current and proposed firearms laws being called into question."

After the ruling, Paul Helmke stated that, "the classic 'slippery slope' argument," "that even modest gun control would lead down the path to a complete ban on gun ownership," "is now gone." Helmke added that, "The Court also rejected the absolutist misreading of the Second Amendment that some use to argue 'any gun, any time for anyone,' which many politicians have used as an excuse to do nothing about the scourge of gun violence in our country and to block passage of common sense gun laws."

Reactions

To the lower court rulings

Various experts expressed opinions on the D.C. Circuit's decision.

Harvard Law School professor Laurence Tribe contended that the Second Amendment protects an individual right, and predicted that if Parker is reviewed by the Supreme Court "there's a really quite decent chance that it will be affirmed." [58] However, Tribe has also argued that the District's ban on one class of weapons does not violate the Second Amendment even under an individual rights view.

Erwin Chemerinsky, then of Duke Law School and now dean of the University of California, Berkeley School of Law, argued that the District of Columbia's handgun laws, even assuming an "individual rights" interpretation of the Second Amendment, could be justified as reasonable regulations and thus upheld as constitutional. Chemerinsky believes that the regulation of guns should be analyzed in the same way "as other regulation of property under modern constitutional law" and "be allowed so long as it is rationally related to achieving a legitimate government purpose." However, the dicta in Heller suggests that applying a mere rational basis analysis is an incorrect reading of the Constitution and would, in fact, defeat the entire purpose of the Second Amendment.

To the Supreme Court rulings

Cato Institute senior fellow Robert Levy, co-counsel to the Parker plaintiffs, agreed with the court's ruling but describes that his interpretation of the Second Amendment would not preclude all governmental regulation of private ownership of weapons:

Even the NRA concedes that you can't have mad men running around with weapons of mass destruction. So there are some restrictions that are permissible and it will be the task of the legislature and the courts to ferret all of that out and draw the lines. I am sure, though, that outright bans on handguns like they have in D.C. won't be permitted. That is not a reasonable restriction under anybody's characterization. It is not a restriction, it's a prohibition.

Clark Neily, an attorney for Dick Heller in this case, has said regarding Heller:

America went over 200 years without knowing whether a key provision of the Bill of Rights actually meant anything. We came within one vote of being told that it did not, notwithstanding what amounts to a national consensus that the Second Amendment means what it says: The right of the people to keep and bear arms shall not be infringed. Taking rights seriously, including rights we might not favor personally, is good medicine for the body politic, and Heller was an excellent dose.

Richard Posner, judge for the United States Court of Appeals for the Seventh Circuit, compares Heller to Roe v. Wade, stating that it created a federal constitutional right that did not previously exist, and he asserts that the originalist method – to which Justice Antonin Scalia claimed to adhere – would have yielded the opposite result of the majority opinion.

The text of the amendment, whether viewed alone or in light of the concerns that actuated its adoption, creates no right to the private possession of guns for hunting or other sport, or for the defense of person or property. It is doubtful that the amendment could even be thought to require that members of state militias be allowed to keep weapons in their homes, since that would reduce the militias' effectiveness. Suppose part of a state's militia was engaged in combat and needed additional weaponry. Would the militia's commander have to collect the weapons from the homes of militiamen who had not been mobilized, as opposed to obtaining them from a storage facility? Since the purpose of the Second Amendment, judging from its language and background, was to assure the effectiveness of state militias, an interpretation that undermined their effectiveness by preventing states from making efficient arrangements for the storage and distribution of military weapons would not make sense.

J. Harvie Wilkinson III, chief judge of United States Court of Appeals for the Fourth Circuit, consents to Posner's analysis, stating that Heller "encourages Americans to do what conservative jurists warned for years they should not do: bypass the ballot and seek to press their political agenda in the courts."

Heller thus represents the worst of missed opportunities—the chance to ground conservative jurisprudence in enduring and consistent principles of restraint. The Constitution expresses the need for judicial restraint in many different ways—separation of powers, federalism, and the grant of life tenure to unelected judges among them. It is an irony that Heller would in the name of originalism abandon insights so central to the Framers' designs.

Alan Gura, Lead Counsel for Respondent in Heller rejects Wilkinson's criticism, stating that "Rather, the Court affirmed the Second Amendment's original public meaning, as confirmed by its plain text. Having determined the Amendment's meaning, the Court showed the proper level of deference to the D.C. City Council's outright repudiation of the constitutional text: none."

Post-ruling impacts

See also: McDonald v. City of Chicago, Guy Montag Doe v. San Francisco Housing Authority, and Nordyke v. King

Since the June 2008 ruling, over 80 different cases have been heard in lower federal courts on the constitutionality of a wide variety of gun control laws. These courts have heard lawsuits in regard to bans of firearm possession by felons, drug addicts, illegal immigrants, and individuals convicted of domestic violence misdemeanors.[72][73] Also, cases have been heard on the constitutionality of laws prohibiting certain types of weapons, such as machine guns, sawed-off shotguns and/or specific types of weapons attachments. In addition, courts have heard challenges to laws barring guns in post offices and near schools and laws outlawing "straw" purchases, carrying of concealed weapons, types of ammunition and possession of unregistered firearms. There have been as of May 2019 more than 1,370 Second Amendment cases nationwide which challenged restrictive gun laws of various kinds since the Supreme Court issued its decision in Heller. In most cases the gun safety law or criminal conviction at issue has been however upheld by the lower courts. Provided with only minimum guidance from the Supreme Court in Heller the lower courts were tasked with defining the scope of the Second Amendment rights and the proper standard of review for evaluating Second Amendment claims in the aforementioned cases.

The courts have upheld most of the above-mentioned laws as being constitutional. The basis for the lower court rulings is the dicta in the paragraph near the end of the Heller ruling that states:

Nothing in our opinion should be taken to cast doubt on longstanding prohibitions on the possession of firearms by felons and the mentally ill, or laws forbidding the carrying of firearms in sensitive places such as schools and government buildings, or laws imposing conditions on the commercial sale of arms.

Consistently since the Heller ruling, the lower federal courts have ruled that almost all gun control measures as presently legislated are lawful and that according to UCLA professor of constitutional law Adam Winkler: "What gun rights advocates are discovering is that the vast majority of gun control laws fit within these categories."

Robert Levy, the executive director of the Cato Institute who funded the Heller litigation has commented on this passage describing constitutionally acceptable forms of prohibitions of firearms: "I would have preferred that that not have been there," and that this paragraph in Scalia's opinion "created more confusion than light."

Similar to the lifting of gun bans mentioned previously in the settlements of lawsuits filed post-Heller, in US v. Arzberger, also decided post-Heller, it was noted:

To the extent, then, that the Second Amendment creates an individual right to possess a firearm unrelated to any military purpose, it also establishes a protectible liberty interest. And, although the Supreme Court has indicated that this privilege may be withdrawn from some groups of persons such as convicted felons, there is no basis for categorically depriving persons who are merely accused of certain crimes of the right to legal possession of a firearm.

District of Columbia

Dick Heller, pictured here in 2018

The D.C. government indicated it would continue to use zoning ordinances to prevent firearms dealers from operating and selling to citizens residing in the District, meaning it would continue to be difficult for residents to legally purchase guns in the District.[79] Additionally, the District enacted new firearms restrictions in an effort to cure the constitutional defects in the ordinance that the Supreme Court had identified in Heller. The new provisions were: (1) the firearms registration procedures; (2) the prohibition on assault weapons; and (3) the prohibition on large capacity ammunition feeding devices. In response, Dick Heller challenged these new restrictions filing a civil suit named Heller v. District of Columbia (Civil Action No. 08-1289 (RMU), No. 23., 25) where he requested a summary judgment to vacate the new prohibitions. On March 26, 2010, the D.C. District Judge Ricardo M. Urbina denied Dick Heller's request and granted the cross motion, stating that the court "concludes that the regulatory provisions that the plaintiffs challenge permissibly regulate the exercise of the core Second Amendment right to use arms for the purpose of self-defense in the home."

Dick Heller's application to register his semi-automatic pistol was rejected because the gun was a bottom-loading weapon, and according to the District's interpretation, all bottom-loading guns, including magazine-fed non-assault-style rifles, are outlawed because they are grouped with machine guns. Revolvers will likely not fall under such a ban.

On December 16, 2008, the D.C. Council unanimously passed the Firearms Registration Emergency Amendment Act of 2008 which addresses the issues raised in the Heller Supreme Court decision, and also puts in place a number of registration requirements to update and strengthen the District's gun laws.

Justice Antonin Scalia's opinion for the majority provided Second Amendment protection for commonly used and popular handguns but not for atypical arms or arms used for unlawful purposes, such as short-barreled shotguns. Scalia stated: "Whatever the reason, handguns are the most popular weapon chosen by Americans for self-defense in the home, and a complete prohibition of their use is invalid."

"We think that Miller's" "ordinary military equipment" language must be read in tandem with what comes after: "[O]rdinarily when called for [militia] service [able-bodied] men were expected to appear bearing arms supplied by themselves and of the kind in common use at the time." 307 U. S., at 179. "We therefore read Miller to say only that the Second Amendment does not protect those weapons not typically possessed by law-abiding citizens for lawful purposes, such as short-barreled shotguns." "It may be objected that if weapons that are most useful in military service — M-16 rifles and the like — may be banned, then the Second Amendment right is completely detached from the prefatory clause. But as we have said, the conception of the militia at the time of the Second Amendment's ratification was the body of all citizens capable of military service, who would bring the sorts of lawful weapons that they possessed at home to militia duty."

On July 24, 2014, the U.S. District Court for the District of Columbia ruled, in Palmer v. District of Columbia, that the District's total ban on the public carrying of ready-to-use handguns is unconstitutional.[86][87] In its decision, the Court stated: "[…] the Court finds that the District of Columbia's complete ban on the carrying of handguns in public is unconstitutional. Accordingly, the Court grants Plaintiffs' motion for summary judgment and enjoins Defendants from enforcing the home limitations of D.C. Code § 7-2502.02(a)(4) and enforcing D.C. Code § 22-4504(a) unless and until such time as the District of Columbia adopts a licensing mechanism consistent with constitutional standards enabling people to exercise their Second Amendment right to bear arms. Furthermore, this injunction prohibits the District from completely banning the carrying of handguns in public for self-defense by otherwise qualified non-residents based solely on the fact that they are not residents of the District."

New York

Bloomberg delivering a speech

Mayor of New York City Michael Bloomberg said that "all of the laws on the books in New York State and New York City" would be allowed by the ruling as "reasonable regulation." Robert Levy has stated that the current New York City gun laws are "not much different" from the D.C. ban that has been overturned. The National Rifle Association and other gun-rights advocates have not ruled out suing New York City, especially over the definition of "reasonable regulation".

Southern District of New York Magistrate Judge James Francis has said that, prior to Heller, it would not have been considered unreasonable to require a defendant to surrender a firearm as a condition of pretrial release. Specifically, according to Judge Francis:

This all changed, with the recent U.S. Supreme Court decision in District of Columbia v. Heller; 128 S.Ct. 2783 (2008), where the court changed the course of Second Amendment jurisprudence by creating what he said was a "protectible liberty interest" in the possession of firearms. Thus, in the absence of an individualized determination at a bail hearing, requiring the defendant to give up any firearms violates due process.

Maloney v. Rice (a.k.a. Maloney v. Cuomo and Maloney v. Spitzer), 554 F.3d 56 (2d. Cir. 2009) originally held that the 2nd Amendment does not apply to the states in the Second Circuit. The case involved a state ban on nunchaku (a martial arts weapon) in New York. In a memorandum opinion dated June 29, 2010, the Supreme Court vacated the Second Circuit decision in Maloney and remanded for further consideration in light of the holding in McDonald v. City of Chicago that the Second Amendment does apply to the states. The Second Circuit has remanded the case to the trial court.[citation needed]

Illinois

The NRA has filed five related lawsuits since the Heller decision.[93] In four Illinois lawsuits, the NRA sought to have the Second Amendment incorporated by the Fourteenth Amendment, causing the Second Amendment to apply to state and local jurisdictions and not just to the federal government.[94] Three Illinois lawsuits have been negotiated and settled out of court involving agreements that repeal gun ban ordinances and did not result in incorporation of the Second Amendment to state and local jurisdictions. The fourth NRA lawsuit against Chicago was rejected.[95] The NRA appealed the case to the 7th Circuit Court of Appeals. On June 2, 2009, the Court of Appeals affirmed the district court's decision, based on the theory that Heller applied only to the Federal Government (including the District of Columbia), and not to states or their subordinate jurisdictions.[citation needed] This opinion directly conflicts with the 9th Circuit Court of Appeals' earlier decision, holding that Heller applies to states as well.[citation needed]

On June 28, 2010, the Supreme Court reversed the Court of Appeals for the Seventh Circuit's decision in McDonald v. City of Chicago and remanded it back to Seventh Circuit to resolve conflicts between certain Chicago gun restrictions and the Second Amendment. Chicago's handgun law was likened to the D.C. handgun ban by Justice Breyer.

Similarly, three Illinois municipalities with gun control measures on the books that previously had banned all handguns have rescinded their handgun bans. These cities were Morton Grove, Illinois, [101] Wilmette, another Illinois village, [102] and Evanston, Illinois which enacted a partial repeal of its handgun ban.

In Ezell v. Chicago, [103] decided July 6, 2011, the Seventh Circuit reversed a district court decision that the post-McDonald measures adopted by the City of Chicago were constitutional. The Chicago law required firearms training in a shooting range in order to obtain a gun permit, but also banned shooting ranges within the City of Chicago. The city had argued that applicants could obtain their training at gun ranges in the suburbs. The opinion noted that Chicago could not infringe Second Amendment rights on the grounds that they could be exercised elsewhere, any more than it could infringe the right to freedom of speech on the grounds that citizens could speak elsewhere.

California

On January 14, 2009, in Guy Montag Doe v. San Francisco Housing Authority, the San Francisco Housing Authority reached a settlement out of court with the NRA, which allows residents to possess legal firearms within a SFHA apartment building. The San Francisco lawsuit resulted in the elimination of the gun ban from the SF Housing Authority residential lease terms. Tim Larsen speaking for the Housing Authority said that they never intended to enforce its 2005 housing lease gun ban against law-abiding gun owners and have never done so.

Idaho

On January 10, 2014, in Morris v. U.S. Army Corps of Engineers, the District Court struck down a Corps of Engineers regulation barring possession of loaded guns in recreation areas surrounding Corps dams.

시 부각되었다. Miller의 케이스와 같이 총기 소유를 제한한 법률의 위헌 여부를 다투는 사건으로서, 대법원은 권총 및 자동소총 소유 불가라는 기존의 조항에 반하여 총기 소유는 개인의 권리이며 아울러 수정헌법 제2조는 군대와 관련이 없는 개인의 권리라고 해석하였다. Heller 사건 이후 대법원은 무기 소지에 대한 제한된 제한을 지지하면서도 그 제한이 너무 광범위하거나 전적으로 정부의 재량에 따른 것으로 판명된 경우에 대해서는 위헌 사례로 기각해왔다. 예로, 연방 법원은 총기를 우체국에 반입한 피고에게 유죄 판결을 확정한 바 있으나, 청소년의 총기 소지 금지에 관한 청소년 비행법은 수정헌법 제2조에 위배되지 않는다고 판결했으며, 개인이 정당한 사유를 보여주지 않는 한 공공장소에서 은닉된 총기를 소지할 수 있는 라이선스를 취득하는 것을 금지하는 뉴욕 법은 수정헌법 제2조에 위배되지 않는다고 판결했다. 최근 Heller 사건에서 설정한 판례를 확장한 New York State Rifle & Pistol Association v.

The court held that tents are akin to homes, and under Heller, Second Amendment rights are protected.

Legacy

The decision in McDonald v. City of Chicago, which was brought in response to Heller and decided in 2010, did invalidate much of Chicago's gun purchase and registration laws, and has called into question many other state and local laws restricting purchase, possession, and carry of firearms.[citation needed] Justice Stevens later called the decision "unquestionably the most clearly incorrect decision that the Supreme Court announced during my tenure on the bench" and called for a Constitutional amendment overruling it.

Stephen Halbrook, a lawyer and Second Amendment analyst who successfully argued three firearms-related cases before the Supreme Court, concluded the majority's opinion in Heller "relied on text, history, and tradition." Halbrook asserted that the individual right to bear arms was not an invention of gun rights activists in the preceding few decades, but was in fact a textualist interpretation confirmed by the historical context of the Second Amendment. This included the English Declaration of Rights of 1689, as well as "post-ratification commentary, antebellum judicial opinions, Reconstruction legislation, and post-Civil War commentary."

The Court's statement that the right secured by the Second Amendment is limited has been widely discussed by lower courts and the media. According to Justice John Paul Stevens, he was able to persuade Justice Anthony M. Kennedy to ask for "some important changes" to Justice Scalia's opinion, so that the final version of Heller "should not be taken to cast doubt" on the many gun laws existing in the United States.

The decision in this case led to the Supreme Court Case New York State Rifle & Pistol Association, Inc. v. Bruen (2022) that ruled that the ability to carry a pistol in public was a constitutional right guaranteed by the Second Amendment.

Bruen 사건을 살펴보자. 현재 뉴욕에서 공공장소에 총을 휴대하려면 자기방어가 필요한 적당한 이유를 제시하여야 하는 것은 물론, 필요한 조건을 충족한 후 라이선스를 얻어야 총기 휴대가 가능해진다. 그러나 라이선스를 신청했다가 조건을 충족하지 못하여 라이선스 발급을 거부당한 시민이 "기본권 행사에 정부의 허가가 필요한가?"라는 문제를 제기했으며, 이에 대법원은 뉴욕 주당국이 자기방어에 대한 필요성을 보여주지 못하는 경우에는 무기 소지 면허 신청자를 거부할 수 있는 뉴욕 법률을 폐기하였다. 앞의 사례를 살펴본 바와 같이, 미국에서 개인의 무기 소유권에 대한 여러분의 감정이 어떻든, 수정헌법 제2조항을 바탕으로 총기 소유는 개인의 권리라는 '개인 소유권론'으로 기울어가는 것으로 보인다."[71]

Regional autonomy is deeply rooted in American federal history. The founding fathers in the 18th century wanted to make sure that the common people of the new country have the means to defend themselves from the tyranny of British authority. Tired of living as a colony, they inserted the 2nd Amendment into the U.S. Constitution in 1791: "A well regulated militia being necessary to the security of a free state, the right of the people to keep and bear arms shall not be infringed."[72]

There have been some confusion as to the interpretation of this controversial provision. Although there was District of Columbia v. Heller,[73] a U.S. Supreme Court decision of 2008 which concluded that the 2nd Amendment is applicable to individual persons, it is unclear exactly who are "the people" entitled to enjoy the right to keep and bear arms. Constitutional scholar Ahn has pointed out that the U.S. Supreme Court has failed to clear up the definition of the 2nd Amendment.[74]

Today, it would be natural for modern readers to interpret that the people are

---

71 허진 변호사, "미국 총기 규제의 역사 및 수정헌법 2조," 한국일보, 2023.10.8. http://www.koreatimes.com/article/1484322 2025.4.8.검색.

72 U.S. Const. am. 2.

73 554 U.S. 570 (2008).

74 Ahn,, Kyoung Hwan. "Understanding the U.S. Constitution." Bakyoungsa, 2014, at 581-582.

individual persons who would need to protect their safety from the powerful government. In 1700's, however, the state governments also needed to protect their political freedom from the British or the federal government that ostensibly attempted to reduce state autonomy. This latter interpretation would probably be inclined to allow leeway for the state and local governments to address the issue of gun control with a certain degree of authority. Nonetheless, the overall aim of the 2nd Amendment was clear. The federal government was to be prevented from infringing the people's right to have guns.

Heller 판결에서 제시되었고 현재도 적용되고 있는 심사기준에 따르면 법원은 현대의 총기규제가 헌법 수정 제2조의 법문과 역사적 해석에 부합하는지를 판단해야 한다. 물론 오늘날 총기규제 문제가 1791년[75]이나 1868년의 남북전쟁 후 재건시대의 건국자들이 선취한 것과 항상 같을 수는 없다. 그러나 헌법은 — 그 의미는 헌법을 비준한 사람들의 이해에 따라 확립될지라도 — 건국자들이 구체적으로 예상하였던 것 외의 상황에도 적용될 수 있으며 그래야만 한다.[76] 실제로 Heller 판결에서 연방대법원은 역사적으로 확립된 헌법 수정 제2조의 의미가 새로운 상황에 적용되는 적어도 하나의 방식을 인정하였다. 바로 '무기'를 지칭할 때 오직 18세기에 존재했던 무기에만 한정되지 않는다는 것이다.[77] 총기규제가 헌법 수정 제2조에 부합하는지를 결정하기 위해 Heller 판결과 McDonald 판결은 적어도 두 가지의 관련 기준을 들고 있는데, 첫째는 현재와 과거의 규제가 무장을 통한 자기방어권에 비슷한(comparable) 부담을 부과하는지 여부이고, 둘째는 그러한 규제가 부과하는 부담이 비슷하게 정당화되는지(comparably justified) 여부이다. 개인의 자기방어는 헌법 수정 제2조의 핵심적인 요소이기 때문에 이러한 두 가지 기준은 유추적 심리에 있어 핵심적인 고려사항이 된다.[78] 정확히 말하면, 현대의 규제가 역사적 전조(precursors)와 똑같게 닮지는 않더라도, 헌법적 기준을 통과하기에 충분할 만큼 비슷할 수는 있다. 예를 들어, 법원은 현

---

75 미국 헌법 수정조항의 첫 10개 조항인 '권리장전'이 비준된 해이다.

76 United States v. Jones, 565 U. S. 400, 404-405.

77 Heller, 554 U. S., at 582.

78 McDonald, 561 U. S., at 767.

대의 규제가 헌법적으로 허용되는지를 결정하기 위해 학교, 정부건물과 같이 민감한 장소에서의 총기휴대를 금지해 온 오랜 법률과의 유사성을 살펴볼 수 있다.[79] 그러나 뉴욕주의 '정당한 이유' 요건을 '민감한 장소'에 관한 법률로 규정하려는 피상고인들의 시도는 이유 없다. 단지 맨하탄이 붐비는 곳이고 일반적으로 뉴욕시경찰국(New York City Police Department, NYPD)의 보호를 받는다는 이유로 뉴욕주가 실질적으로 맨하탄을 민감한 장소로 선언했다는 역사적 근거가 없기 때문이다. 헌법 수정 제2조는 1791년에, 수정 제14조는 1868년에 채택되었다.[80]

---

79 Heller, 554 U. S., at 626.

80 가) 영국의 역사와 관습피상고인들이 미국의 건국 전 영국의 역사와 관습을 원용한 것은 "헌법 수정 제2조는 우리의 영국 조상들로부터 승계된 권리를 성문화한 것이다."라는 Heller 판결의 문구에 비추어 볼 때 일면 일리가 있다. 그러나 연방대법원은 오랫동안 영국의 커먼로가 모든 측면에서 미국의 커먼로로 여겨지는 것에 대해 경계해왔다. 피상고인들이 원용한 영국의 역사는 기껏해야 모호한 것일 뿐이고 헌법제정자들이 그것을 미국에도 적용 가능하다고 생각했었다고 판단하기는 어렵다. 이러한 역사적 기록으로는 미국 건국 당시 영국법이 —공공장소에서 자기방어에 적합한 총기를 휴대할 권리를 자기방어의 특별한 필요를 증명하는 사람에게만 인정하는— 규제를 정당화하였다고 결론내릴 수 없다. 이 사건 뉴욕주의 법률과 비슷하게 무기의 공공휴대를 규제하였다는 확신이 들지는 않는다. 당시의 법률들은 '위험하고 비일반적인 무기'의 휴대를 포함하여 기본적으로 사람들에게 '두려움'이나 '공포'를 확신시키는 방식으로 무기를 휴대하는 것을 금지 하였다. 식민지 시대에 권총이 '위험하고 비일반적인 무기'로 여겨졌을 가능성이 어떻든 간에, 오늘날에 있어 권총이 자기방어를 위해 널리 사용되고 있다는 점에 이론이 없으며 실제로 이는 '전형적인 자기방어 무기'라고 할 수 있다. 따라서 이러한 식민지 시대의 법률은 오늘날 의심할 여지없이 일반적으로 사용되는 무기의 공공휴대를 제한하는 법률을 정당화하지 못한다. 다) 1791년 헌법 수정 제2조의 비준 이후 남북전쟁 이전의 규제들 1791년 헌법 수정 제2조의 비준 이후에야 공공장소에서의 총기휴대에 대한 규제가 빠르게 확산되었다. 피상고인들은 이러한 규제에 과도하게 의존하고 있는데 이러한 규제들은 보통 커먼로 위반, 법적 금지, 증법의 세 가지 유형 중 어느 하나에 해당된다. 이러한 규제들 중 어느 것도 뉴욕주의 규제적 면허제도에서 부과되는 것과 비슷할 정도로 공공 총기휴대에 대해 상당한 부담을 부과하지는 않았다. ① 커먼로 위법행위(Common-Law Offenses): 식민지 시대와 건국 시대 동안 '공공장소에서의 폭력행위'나 '사람들의 공포를 유발하는' 무장이라는 커먼로상 위법행위 규정은 미국 남북전쟁 이전 시대에 총기휴대에 대해 일부 제한을 가하였다. 그러나 이러한 커먼로상의 제한이 일반대중의 평화적인 무기휴대의 권리를 훼손하였다는 증거는 어디에도 없다. ② 법적 금지(Statutory Prohibitions): 19세기 초중반, 일부 주들은 권총이나 다른 소형무기의 은닉휴대를 금지하는 법률을 만들기 시작하였다. 그러나 이러한 법률을 옹호했던 남북전쟁 이전의 주법원 결정들은 주가 헌법 수정 제2조에 의해 보장되는 무기의 공공휴대를 모두 금지할 수는 없다는 데 일치된 관점을 분명히 밝혔다. ③ 보증법(Surety Statutes): 19세기 중반, 어떤 사람들에게는 공공장소에서의 무기휴대 전에 보증금을 내도록 요구하는 법률을 채택하는 곳이 많아지기 시작했다. 이 사건 피상고인들의 입장과는 반대로, 이러한 보증법은 절대 뉴욕주의 '정당한 이유' 요건의 직접적인 전조가 된다고 할 수 없다. 뉴욕주는 높은 필요성을 증명하지 않는 한 개인이 무기를 공공휴대할 권리가 인정되지 않는다고 추정하는 반면, 보증법은 개인이 공공휴대에 대한 권리를 갖는다고 추정되고 다만 다른 사람이 '부상이나 치안방해에 대한 우려'에 합리적인 이유36)가 있다는 구체적인 입증을 하는 경우에만 부담이 부과될 뿐이다. 따라서 뉴욕주 제도와 달리, 특별한 필요의 입증은 개인이 타인을 상해하거나

버지니아 공대 총기 난사 사건(Virginia Tech shooting)

버지니아 공대 총기 난사 사건(Virginia Tech shooting)[81][82][83] 2007년 4월 16일 미국

치안을 방해하고자 하여 합리적으로 고소된 후에야 요구되는 것이었다. 그리고 특별한 필요의 입증은 단지 비용을 내지 않아도 된다는 것에 그치는 것이었다. 요컨대 남북전쟁 이전의 미국의 역사적 증거들은 무기의 공공휴대의 방식이 합리적인 규제의 적용을 받았다는 것을 보여주지만, 무기를 휴대할 권리에 대한 그러한 제한들 중 어떤 것도 일반적인 자기방어의 필요성을 가진 준법시민들이 그러한 목적으로 공공장소에서 무기를 휴대하는 것을 금지하는 방식으로 운용되지는 않았다. 라) 남북전쟁 이후 재건시대의 규제들 미국 헌법 수정 제14조가 채택될 즈음의 증거들 역시 피상고인들의 입장을 뒷받침 하지는 않는다. 무기를 보유하고 휴대할 권리에 대한 연방의회와 공적담론에서의 논의는 남북전쟁 이후 재건시대 동안 그 권리가 자기방어를 위해 평화적으로 권총을 휴대할 대중의 권리에 부합하는 한계를 가졌다는 점을 일반적으로 보여주고 있다. 두 개의 텍사스 주 판결들은 — English v. State, 35 Tex. 473 (1871)과 State v. Duke, 42 Tex. 455 (1875) — 무기의 공공휴대에 관하여 뉴욕주의 '정당한 이유' 요건과 유사한 '합리적인 근거(reasonable grounds)' 기준을 허용하였다. 그러나 텍사스 주 판결들은 예외적인 것으로서 남북전쟁 이후의 법원들이 공공장소에서 무기를 휴대할 권리를 바라보는 시각에 대한 통찰을 제공하지는 못한다. 마) 19세기 후반의 규제들 마지막으로, 피상고인들은 19세기 후반에 약간 증가한 총기규제를 지적하였다. 그러나 연방대법원이 Heller 판결에서 주장하였듯이, 19세기 후반의 증거는 그것이 앞선 증거들과 모순되는 경우 헌법 수정 제2조의 의미에 대한 통찰을 그다지 제공해주지 못한다. 게다가 피상고인들이 원용한 대다수의 법률들은 서부 준주(Western Territories)들에서 온 것이다. 이렇게 가까스로 존재하는 국지적인 규제들은 공공휴 대를 허용하였던 오랜 미국의 전통에 대한 압도적인 증거를 뛰어넘지 못한다. 게다가 이러한 준주 법률들은 사법심사의 적용을 거의 받지 않았으며, 모든 공공휴대에 대한 전례 없는 금지가 헌법 수정 제2조에 부합되는 것으로 해석되는 이유에 대한 설명도 없었다. 결국 이러한 준주 규제들은 준주 정부의 과도적 성격에 따라 짧은 기간 동안만 존재했기 때문에 큰 비중을 갖지 못하는 것이 당연하다. 그 중 일부는 법률이 통과된 직후 위헌으로 판결되기도 하였고, 일부는 준주가 미합중국의 주로 승격되며 살아남지 못하였다; 임기영 책임연구원, "뉴욕주 총기규제법 위헌 판결," 헌법재판소 헌법재판연구원 세계헌법재판 조사연구보고서, 2022 제7호(통권 제57호), 9-11면.

81 https://ko.wikipedia.org/wiki/%EB%B2%84%EC%A7%80%EB%8B%88%EC%95%84_%EA%B3%B5%EB%8C%80_%EC%B4%9D%EA%B8%B0_%EB%82%9C%EC%82%AC_%EC%82%AC%EA%B1%B4 2025.4.7. 검색.

82 [英韓대역] 버지니아工大 慘事 「뉴욕 타임스」의 분석 『저건 승희가 아니다! 우리는 승희가 완전한 문장으로 말하는 걸 처음 봤다』(조승희가 범행 후 nbc에 보낸 동영상을 본 지인들)

이익훈(李益薰) 1947년 서울 출생. 연세大 지질학과 졸업. 美 웨스트코스트 대학원 환경공학 석사. 영문학 박사. 월간 「AP 5분뉴스」 발행·편집인, 단국大 초빙교수, 한양大 교육대학원 겸임교수. 저서 「이익훈 EAR/Eye of the TOEIC」, 「이익훈 Ear of the TOEFL」 외 다수. 버지니아 工大 총기난사 사건 다음 날인 지난 4월18일 美 NBC 방송이 공개한 총기난사범 조승희의 모습. 조승희는 1차 범행 직후 이 동영상을 방송국으로 보냈다. 미국 영주권자이자 한국 국적인 조승희(23)씨가 스승과 동료 학생 33명을 살해한 버지니아 테크 사건 이후 우리는 가슴을 졸였다. 미국 내 한국 교민들에 대한 미국인의 증오 범죄가 터지지 않을지, 한국에 대한 감정이 악화되지 않을지….

우려했던 상황은 발생하지 않았다. 미국 언론과 조야는 이 사건의 범인이 한국인이라는 데 주목하지 않았다. 미국의 유력지인 「뉴욕 타임스」는 4월 22일자 심층기사에서 「고통스런 외톨이의 삶이 살인적 분노를 자아냈다」고 분석했다. 「뉴욕 타임스」는 조승희 씨의 부모와 누나, 친척들과의 심층 면접을 토대로 기사

를 만들었다. 조승희의 부친 조승태 씨는 사우디아라비아의 건설현장에서 일했고, 어머니 김황임 씨는 이북 출신 가정이라는, 국내 언론에 한 번도 보도되지 않은 사실들이 적지 않게 담겨 있다. 「뉴욕 타임스」는 차분한 분석과 논조로 한 불행한 청소년이 어떻게 「악마」로 변해 갔는지를 묘사한다. 「뉴욕 타임스」 기사에 따르면, 조승희는 서울에 살던 초등학교 시절부터 한마디 말을 하지 않았고, 미국에 이주해온 후에도 친구들과 가족들에게 말을 하지 않았다. 조승희가 NBC에 보낸 증오의 동영상을 본 조승희의 가족들과 지인들은 이렇게 절규했다고 한다. 『저건 우리가 알던 승희가 아니다. 그가 완전한 문장으로 말하는 것을 처음 보았다』

From the beginning, he did not talk. Not to other children, not to his own family. Everyone saw this. In Seoul, South Korea, where Seung-Hui Cho grew up, his mother agonized over his sullen*, brooding* behavior and empty face. Talk, she just wanted him to talk. "When I told his mother that he was a good boy, quiet but well behaved, she said she would rather have him respond to her when talked to than be good and meek*," said Kim Yang-Soon, Mr. Cho's 84-year-old great-aunt.

날 때부터 그는 말수가 없었다. 또래 아이들뿐만 아니라 식구들에게도 그랬다. 모두가 그렇게 기억했다. 조승희가 한국의 서울에서 유년기를 보낼 당시 그의 모친은 무뚝뚝하고 침울하며 무표정한 아들 때문에 속을 끓였다. 엄마의 소원은 제발 아들의 말문이 틔었으면 하는 것이었다. 『애엄마에게 녀석이 참 착하고 조용하지만 예의바르다고 칭찬했더니 이러더군요. 「내가 말을 걸 때 녀석이 얌전하고 온순하게 있기보다는 차라리 말대꾸하며 대들기라도 했으면 더 좋겠다」고』 84세인 조승희의 고모할머니 김양순 씨의 말이다.

[어구해설] *sullen: 무뚝뚝한. *brooding: 멍한, 넋이 나간 *meek: 온순한, 패기 없는

When his parents announced when he was 8 that they were going to America, their relatives were gladdened. "We thought that it would help the boy gain confidence if he moved to the United States' open society," said an uncle who asked to be identified only by his last name*, Kim. And yet when he and others heard from Mr. Cho's mother, it was the same dismal* story, a buried life* of silence. In church, she told them, she prayed for God to transform her son.

조가 여덟 살 되던 해 부모가 미국 이민 결정을 내리자 친지들은 대환영이었다. 『우린, 그렇게 되면 승희가 미국의 개방된 사회에서 살면서 자신감을 얻는 데 도움이 될 걸로 생각했지』라고 말한 조승희의 삼촌은 자신의 이름을 성인 「김」으로만 밝혀 달라고 요청했다. 하지만, 삼촌과 친지들이 조승희의 모친에게서 전해 들은 소식은, 아이가 말도 없고 자기 세계에만 갇혀 지내니 여전히 참담하다는 것이었다. 모친은 「교회에 나가 하느님이 승희를 변화시켜 주도록 기도한다」고 말했다.

[어구해설] *be identified only by his last name: 성으로만 신분을 밝히다. *dismal: 참담한, 암울한 *a buried life: 은둔생활, 여기서는 자폐적 성향을 묘사한다.

By now, the world knows what Seung-Hui Cho became, how on a gusty, snowy morning last Monday at Virginia Tech in Blacksburg, Va., he massacred* 27 students and 5 teachers before killing himself. No one could understand why. On Friday, his sister issued a statement of apology and sorrow that revealed the family's own bewilderment*. "This is someone that I grew up with and loved," she said. "Now I feel like I didn't know this person." Interviews with investigators, relatives, classmates and teachers offer inklings of* how he progressed from silence to murderous rage*, and show how he meticulously* prepared for his final hours.

이제 전 세계는 조승희가 어떤 사람으로 변화했는지, 바람이 세차고 눈이 내리던 지난주 월요일 오전, 버지니아 블랙스버그의 버지니아공대에서 어떻게 27명의 학생과 5명의 교수를 무참히 살해하고 자신도 자살했는지 잘 안다. 하지만 누구도 그 이유를 이해할 수 없었다. 금요일, 그의 누나는 사과와 애도의 성명을 발표하고 가족들조차도 당혹감을 금치 못한다고 밝혔다. 『이 사람이 내가 함께 자라고 사랑했던 사람이라

니』 그의 누나는 이렇게 말했다.『지금 생각하니 나는 그 사람을 전혀 알지 못했습니다』 수사관들, 친지들, 급우들, 교수들과의 인터뷰를 살펴보면 그가 어떻게 침묵을 살인적 분노로 발전시켰는지, 그리고 어떻게 그가 자신의 최후를 꼼꼼하게 준비했는지 어렴풋이 짐작할 수 있다.

[어구해설] *massacre: 무참히 살해하다(=slaughter) *bewilderment: 혼란, 당혹감 *offer inklings of: ~을 어렴풋이 암시하다 *murderous rage: 살인적 분노 *meticulously: 매우 세심하게

In Seoul, there was never much money, never enough time. The Cho family occupied a shabby* two-room basement apartment, living frugally on* the slender proceeds* of a used-book shop. According to relatives, the father, Seung-Tae Cho, had worked in oil fields and on construction sites in Saudi Arabia. In an arranged marriage, he wed Kim Hwang-Im, the daughter of a farming family that had fled North Korea* during the Korean War. Their son was well behaved, all right, but his pronounced* bashfulness* deeply worried his parents. Relatives thought he might be a mute. Or mentally ill. "The kid didn't say much and didn't mix with other children," his uncle said. "'Yes sir' was about all you could get from him."

서울에서 살 때는 돈이 풍족하거나 가족이 오붓한 시간을 가져본 적이 전혀 없었다. 조의 가족은 2칸짜리 허름한 반지하 집에서 살았고, 중고서점에서 나오는 쥐꼬리만 한 수입을 쪼개서 어렵게 생활했다. 친척들에 따르면, 아버지 조승태씨는 사우디아라비아의 유전과 건설현장에서 일했다. 부친은 중매를 통해 한국전쟁 당시 월남한 농부의 딸 김황임씨와 혼인했다. 부부의 아들은 행실도 얌전했고 문제가 없었지만, 지나치게 말수가 적어서 부모를 크게 상심시켰다. 친지들은 아이가 벙어리 아니면 정신적 문제가 있을 거라고 생각했다.『그 아이는 말을 거의 안 했고 다른 아이들이랑 어울리지도 않았습니다』 삼촌의 말이다.『그 아이에게 들을 수 있는 말이라고는「알았어요」가 전부였죠』

[어구해설] *shabby: 허름한 *live frugally on: 어렵게 ~을 먹고살다 *slender proceeds: 쥐꼬리만 한 수익 *fled North Korea: 월남하다 *pronounced: 뚜렷한 *bashfulness: 숫기 없음, 수줍음

In 1984, relatives who had moved to the United States invited the family to join them. It took eight years to get a visa. In 1992, they arrived in Detroit and then moved on to Centreville, Va., home to a bustling* Korean community on the fringe of* Washington. They found jobs in the dry-cleaning business and worked the longest of hours. Dry cleaning is a favored profession among Koreans - some 1,800 of the 2,000 dry cleaners in the greater Washington area are run by Koreans - because it means Sundays off for church* and sparse need for* proficient English, exchanges with customers being brief and redundant.

1984년 미국으로 이민 간 친척들이 조씨 가족을 초청했으며, 비자가 발급되기까지 8년이 걸렸다. 1992년 가족은 디트로이트에 도착했고 버지니아의 센터빌로 이사했다. 이곳은 워싱턴 DC 근교에 위치한 신흥 한국 교민지역이다. 세탁소 일을 구한 가족은 등골이 휘도록 일했다. 세탁업은 한국 교민들이 선호하는 직종이다. 워싱턴 전체 지역에 2000개소의 세탁소가 있는데 그중 1800개소를 한국 교민들이 운영하고 있다. 왜냐하면, 일요일은 문을 닫고 교회에 나갈 수 있으며, 손님과의 대화도 간단하고 반복적이라서 능숙한 영어가 필요없기 때문이다.

[어구해설] *bustling: 바쁜, 분주한, 신흥의 *on the fringe of: ~ 외곽에 *Sundays off for church: 일요일마다 쉬고 교회에 간다 *sparse need for: ~가 거의 필요 없다.

They lived in a nondescript* row house in a modest* section of town, friendly but not overly sociable. Jeff Ahn, president of the League of Korean-Americans of Virginia, said the family was uncommonly private* among the throbbing* Korean-American community of about 200,000 in and around Washington. They shunned* the more prominent Korean-language Christian churches, and prayed at a small church outside of town.

조씨 가족은 시내 중산층 구역의 평범한 연립주택에서 살았으며, 이웃과 친하기는 했지만 아주 사교적이지는 않았다. 버지니아 한인회 회장 제프 안씨에 따르면, 조씨 가족은 시끌벅적 살아가는 워싱턴 DC 인근 약 20만 한인 사회에서 이례적으로 왕래가 적었다고 한다. 이 가족은 더 유명한 한인 교회들을 피해 교외의 작은 교회에서 예배했다.

[어구해설] *nondescript: 평범한 *modest: 수수한, 보통의 *uncommonly private: 유달리 어울리지 않는 *throbbing: 시끌벅적한 *shun: 피하다(=avoid)

High school did not help Seung-Hui Cho surmount his miseries*. He went to Westfield High School, one of the largest schools in Fairfax County. He was scrawny* and looked younger than his age. He was unresponsive* in class, and unwilling to speak. And that haunted face*. Classmates recall some teasing and bullying over his taciturn* nature. The few times* he was required to speak for a class assignment, students mocked* his poor English and deep-throated* voice. And so he chose invisibility*. Neighbors would spot him shooting baskets by himself. When they said hello, he ignored them, as if he were not there. "Like he had a broken heart," said Abdul Shash, a next-door neighbor.

고교 시절은 조승희가 자신의 불행을 극복하는 데 별 도움이 안 됐다. 조는 페어팩스카운티에서 가장 큰 학교인 웨스트필드 고교에 다녔다. 그는 몸이 마르고 나이보다 어려 보였다. 수업 중에는 반응도 없고 말을 하려 들지도 않았다. 그리고 넋 나간 표정이었다. 급우들은 말수가 없는 그의 성격에 대해 일부 학생들이 놀리거나 위협했다고 기억한다. 토론 수업에서 가끔 말을 해야 하는 경우에는 학생들이 조의 서툰 영어와 굵고 낮은 목소리를 흉내 내며 놀렸다. 그 결과 조는 아예 유령 같은 존재가 되는 쪽을 택했다. 이웃이 혼자 농구하는 조를 발견하고 그에게 인사를 건네면, 조는 자신이 존재하지도 않는 듯이 무시해 버린다. 『절망에 빠진 듯했죠』 바로 옆집에 살았던 압둘 샤시의 말이다.

[어구해설] *surmount his miseries: 불행을 극복하다 *scrawny: 말라빠진(=lean) *unresponsive: 대꾸가 없는, 무반응인 *haunted face: 넋 나간 표정, 얼빠진 얼굴 *taciturn: 말수가 없는 *The few times ~: 간혹 ~할 때 *mock: 흉내 내며 놀리다 *deep-throated: 목소리가 굵은 *choose invisibility: 남의 눈에 띄지 않는 존재가 되다.

When Mr. Cho entered Virginia Tech, which is crouched* in the Blue Ridge Mountains of southwest Virginia, his parents drove him to school with guarded expectations*. Perhaps he would no longer retreat to* video games and playing basketball alone the way he did at home. Perhaps college might crack the mystery of* who he was, extract him from his suffocating cocoon* and make him talk. Girls figured somewhere in his yearnings, but always from a distance. In his junior year, Mr. Cho told his then-roommates that he had a girlfriend. Her name was Jelly. She was a supermodel who lived in outer space and traveled by spaceship, and she existed only in the dimension of his imagination. He became fixated on* several real female students. Two of them complained to the police that he was calling them, showing up at their rooms and bombarding them with instant messages*. They found him bothersome but not threatening. After the second complaint against him in December 2005, the police came by and told him to stop.

조승희가 버지니아 남서부의 블루리지 산맥 속에 위치해 있는 버지니아공대에 입학할 때, 부모는 조심스런 기대감으로 아들을 학교까지 차로 데려다 주었다. 아마 더 이상은 집에서처럼 비디오게임이나 혼자 하는 농구 놀이에 빠져들지 않을 수도 있었다. 아마 대학이 그의 신비로운 존재감을 깨뜨리고 숨 막히는 고치에서 꺼내줌으로써 아들의 말문이 트일 수도 있었다. 조는 마음 한구석에서 여자들을 동경하고 있었지만, 항상 먼발치일 뿐이었다. 3학년 때 조는 당시 방 동료에게 여자친구가 있는데 이름이 젤리라고 말했다. 조의 여자친구는 슈퍼모델로 외계에 살면서 우주선을 타고 다녔으며, 조의 상상세계 속에서만 존재했다. 조는 몇몇 현실세계의 여학생들에게 마음을 빼앗기게 되었다. 그중 두 명이 조가 자꾸 전화를 하고 불쑥 방 앞에 나타났으며 엄청난 양의 쪽지 세례를 퍼붓는다고 경찰에 신고했다. 이 여학생들은 조가 귀찮기는 하지만 위협적이라고 느끼진 않았다. 2005년 12월 두 번째 신고를 접수한 경찰은 조를 찾아가 그만두도록 경고했다.

[어구해설] *crouch: 웅크리다 *with guarded expectations: 조심스러운 기대를 가지고 *retreat to:~에 몰두하다 *crack the mystery of: ~의 신비를 깨다 *suffocating cocoon: 숨 막히는 고치. 자폐 세계를 애벌레의 고치에 비유한 것 *fixated on: ~에 푹 빠진 *bombarding A with B: A에게 엄청난 B를 퍼붓다

A few hours after they left, he sent an instant message to one of his roommates suggesting he might as well* kill himself. The campus police were called, and Mr. Cho was sent to an off-campus mental health facility.

After a counselor recommended involuntary commitment*, a judge signed an order deeming him a danger* and he was sent for evaluation to Carilion St. Albans Psychiatric Hospital in Radford, Va. A doctor there declared him mentally ill but not an imminent* threat. Rather than commit* him, the judge allowed him to undergo outpatient treatment*. Officials say they do not know whether he did.

경찰이 떠난 몇 시간 후에 조는 방 동료들 중 하나에게 쪽지를 보내 차라리 죽어 버리겠다고 말했다. 신고를 받은 대학 경찰은 그를 학교 밖의 정신보건시설에 보내 상담을 받게 했다.

상담원이 강제구금을 제의하자 판사는 조를 위험인물로 여기고 버지니아 레드포드에 있는 카릴리온 세인트 알반스 정신병원으로 이송해 정신감정을 받도록 명령을 내렸다. 그곳의 의사는 조가 정신적 문제는 있지만 당장 위험한 정도는 아니라는 판정을 내렸다. 판사는 조를 구금하기보다는 그가 외래치료를 받도록 허용했다. 당국은 실제 조가 치료를 받았는지 여부를 알 수 없다고 말한다.

[어구해설] *might as well ~: ~하는 편이 낫다 *involuntary commitment: 강제구금 *deem him a danger: 그를 위험인물로 여기다 *imminent: 긴박한, 절박한, 임박한 *commit: (시설에) 수용하다 *undergo outpatient treatment: 외래치료를 받다

His junior-year roommates mostly ignored him because he was so withdrawn*. If he said something, it was weird*. During Thanksgiving break, Mr. Koch recalled, Mr. Cho called him to report that he was vacationing in North Carolina with Vladimir Putin, the Russian president; Mr. Cho said he had grown up with him in Moscow.

In class, some students thought he might be a deaf-mute*. A classmate once offered him $10 just to say hello but got nothing. He hunched* there in sunglasses, a baseball cap yanked tight over his head*. Sometimes Mr. Cho introduced himself as "Question Mark," saying it was the persona* of a man who lived on Mars and journeyed to Jupiter.

조의 3학년 때 방 동료들은 그가 너무 내성적이라 대부분 조를 무시해 버렸다. 조가 무슨 말이라도 하면 그게 더 이상할 지경이었다. 코흐의 기억에 따르면, 추수감사절 휴가철에 조가 전화를 걸어 자신이 노스캐롤라이나에서 러시아 대통령 블라디미르 푸틴과 함께 휴가를 보내는 중이라고 말했다. 조는 자신이 모스크바에서 푸틴과 함께 자랐다고 말했다.

수업 중에 몇몇 학생들은 조가 듣지도 말하지도 못하는 장애인인 줄 알았다. 한번은 한 급우가 한 번만 인사를 해주면 10달러를 주겠다고 제안했지만 아무런 반응도 없었다. 그는 선글라스를 끼고 야구 모자를 푹 눌러쓴 채로 웅크리고 앉아 수업을 들었다. 간혹 조는 자신을 「물음표」로 소개하기도 했는데, 화성에서 살면서 목성으로 여행을 간 남자의 분신이라고 설명했다.

[어구해설] *withdrawn: 내성적인 *weird: 이상한 *deaf-mute: 농아이자 청각장애인 *hunch: 몸을 웅크리다, 등을 구부리다 *yanked tight over his head: (모자를) 푹 눌러쓴 *persona: (등장)인물,

Lucinda Roy, then head of the English Department at Virginia Tech, began to tutor him privately. She, too, was unnerved*. She brought him to the attention of* the counseling service and the campus police because she thought he was so miserable he might kill himself. Last semester, he took a playwriting class in which he submitted two one-act plays*, "Richard McBeef" and "Mr. Brownstone," both foul-mouthed* rants*. In "Richard McBeef," a 13-year-old threatens to kill his stepfather. Steven Davis, a senior in the class, said he finished reading the play one night, turned to his roommate and said, "This is the kind of guy who is going to walk into a classroom and start shooting people."

루신다 로이는 당시 버지니아工大 영어과 학과장으로, 조를 직접 지도하기 시작했다. 로이 교수 또한 당혹감을 느껴 조를 데리고 상담소와 대학 경찰서를 찾았다. 그가 너무 비참한 마음에 자살할지 모른다고 생각했기 때문이다. 조는 지난 학기에 희곡 강의를 들으면서 「리처드 맥비프」와 「브라운스톤 씨」 등 단막극 두 편을 제출했다. 두 편 모두 온통 욕설투성이였다. 「리처드 맥비프」에서는 열세 살짜리가 의붓아버지를 죽이겠다고 위협한다. 그 수업을 들었던 4학년생 스티븐 데이비스는 어느 날 밤 이 희곡을 다 읽고 나서 방 동료에게 이렇게 말했다고 한다. 『이 친구는 교실로 들어가 사람들에게 총을 마구 쏴아 댈 그럴 인간이라니까』

[어구해설] *unnerved: 당황한, 맥이 빠진 *bring A to the attention of B: A를 데려가 B가 보살피도록 하다 *two one-act plays: 단막극 두 편 *foulmouthed: 욕설투성이인 *rant: 떠벌림, 호언장담

Emily Hilscher, a freshman, lived in Room 4040, near the elevators on the fourth floor of West Ambler Johnston Hall, one building from Harper. Shortly after 7 a.m., she was killed by bullets from Mr. Cho's gun. The same fate met* Ryan Clark, one of the dorm's resident advisers*. Mr. Clark is believed to have come out of his room to investigate the noise, only to stumble into death*.

The university police quickly picked up some information, and the nature of it led them to make a decision* and follow a trail*. Ms. Hilscher's roommate, Heather Haugh, had shown up at 7:30 to meet her and accompany her to class. Instead, she encountered the campus police.

신입생인 에밀리 힐셔는 4040호에서 생활했는데, 이 방은 (조가 생활했던) 하퍼 홀 기숙사에서 한 동 떨어진 웨스트 앰블러 존스턴 홀 기숙사의 4층 엘리베이터 근처였다. 오전 7시가 막 지난 시각 에밀리는 조가 쏜 총탄에 맞아 숨졌다. 舍內(사내) 학생지도 담당의 하나였던 라이언 클라크도 같은 운명을 맞았다. 클라크는 소란이 발생하자 이를 수습하기 위해 방을 나왔다가 총에 맞아 사망했을 것이다.

대학 경찰은 즉각 정보를 수집했고, 그 본질에 따라 결론을 내리고 단서 추적에 들어갔다. 힐셔의 방 동료인 헤더 휴는 힐셔를 만나 함께 강의실로 가려고 7시30분에 나타났다. 그런데 그가 마주친 것은 바로 대학 경찰이었다.

[어구해설] *The same fate met ~: ~도 같은 운명을 맞았다 *dorm's resident adviser: 기숙사 내 학생지도 담당(학생) *only to stumble into death: 그러다가 (총을 맞고) 쓰러져 사망했다. *lead A to make a decision: A가 결정짓도록 만들다 *follow a trail: 단서를 추적하다

에밀리 힐셔 One of the things she told them was that Ms. Hilscher had a boyfriend, Karl D. Thornhill, a senior at nearby Radford University; Ms. Hilscher had spent the weekend with him at his off-campus townhouse, and he had dropped her off at her dorm* that morning. Ms. Haugh also told them that Mr. Thornhill had guns and had been shooting them at a range* two weeks earlier. Based on what she said, the police concluded that they had the most cliched script of all* - the lovers' quarrel*. They went looking for Mr. Thornhill, and found him on the highway, driving home from a class. They pulled him over and started interrogating* him. That gave Mr. Cho time, and he had uses for it.

휴가 경찰에 진술한 내용 중에는 힐셔에게 근처 래드포드 대학 3학년생인 카알 D. 손힐이라는 남자친구가 있으며, 힐셔는 주말에 시내에 있는 남자친구의 집에서 함께 보냈고, 그날 아침 남자친구가 기숙사로 데려

다 주었다는 사실이 들어 있었다. 게다가 휴는 손힐이 총들을 소지하고 있으며, 2주 전 사격장에서 총을 쏜 적이 있다고 말했다. 경찰은 휴의 진술을 토대로 전형적인 치정살인이라고 결론지었다. 손힐을 찾아 출동한 경찰은 등교 중인 그를 고속도로에서 발견했다. 경찰은 차를 세우고 심문을 시작했다. 이렇게 경찰은 조승희에게 시간을 벌어 주었고, 조는 그 시간을 적절히 이용했다.

[어구해설] *drop A off at her dorm: (자동차로) 집에 바래다 주다 *range: 사격장 *have the most cliched script of all: 전형적인 정황으로 파악하다 *the lovers' quarrel: 사랑싸움 *interrogate: 심문하다

His rage was brutally transparent* in his multimedia screed* and suicide note*. He ranted against hedonism* and trust funds, against high-class taste for vodka and cognac. He praised the Columbine High School killers as martyrs*, and styled himself a Christ figure*.

He said, "You have vandalized* my heart, raped my soul and torched* my conscience."

"You had a hundred billion chances and ways to have avoided today," he said. "But you decided to spill my blood. You forced me into a corner and gave me only one option. The decision was yours. Now you have blood on your hands that will never wash off."

조의 분노는 동영상과 사진들, 그리고 자살 메모를 통해 극명하게 표출되었다. 그는 고함을 지르며 쾌락주의, 신탁기금, 보드카와 코냑 등의 명품 취향을 맹렬히 비난했다. 그는 컬럼바인 고교 총기참사 범인들을 순교자로 칭송했고, 마치 자신이 예수라도 되는 듯 이렇게 설교했다.

그는 『너희는 내 가슴을 황폐화시키고, 내 정신을 강탈했으며, 내 양심을 불살랐다』고 말했다.

『너희는 오늘을 피할 수많은 기회와 방법이 있었다』라고 조는 말했다. 『하지만, 너희는 내가 피를 흘리도록 결정했다. 나를 궁지로 몰면서 너희는 내게 한 가지 선택만을 남겼다. 이 결정은 너희들이 내린 것이다. 이제 너희들의 손에 묻은 피는 결코 씻기지 않을 것이다』

[어구해설] *brutally transparent: 극명하게 드러난 *screed: 이야기, 기사 *suicide note: 자살 메모 *hedonism: 쾌락주의 *martyr: 순교자 *style himself a Christ figure: 자신을 예수로 형상화해 말하다 *vandalize: 파괴하다 *torch: 불태우다, 불사르다

9:26 a.m., the university issued this e-mail message to the campus. By then, though, the calculus of the day had already set in motion the next sequence*, and there was nothing to stand in its way*.

Sometime around 9:30, Mr. Cho stepped inside Norris Hall. He unfurled* the chains and wrapped them around the interior handles of the doors. The entrance secured, he mounted the stairs* to the second floor and the classrooms. Second period had begun. Gun drawn*, he forged into* four of them. Inside of 10 to 15 minutes, forensics evidence* concluded, he fired more than 175 rounds in killing 30 people, the worst slaughter of its kind in the history of the country.

오전 9시26분에 대학 당국은 교내에 이메일 경고를 발송했다. 하지만, 그 시점에는 그날의 참극을 위한 시한장치가 이미 작동 중이었으며, 그것을 멈출 방도는 어디에도 없었다.

9시30분경 조가 노리스 홀에 들어섰다. 조는 쇠사슬을 펼쳐 출입문의 안쪽 손잡이들 주위로 감아 놓았다. 출구를 봉쇄한 뒤 그는 계단을 올라 2층 강의실로 갔다. 이제 2단계 작전이 개시되었다. 그는 총을 뽑아 4군데의 강의실에 차례로 난입했다. 현장 감식 증거에 따르면, 조는 10~15분 사이에 무려 175발 이상의 총탄을 발사하여 30명을 살해하면서 미국 역사상 최악의 총기참사를 저질렀다.

[어구해설] *set in motion the next sequence: 다음 단계를 작동시키다 *stand in its way: 가로막다, 방해하다 *unfurl: 펼치다, 풀다 *mount the stairs: 계단을 오르다 *Gun drawn: 총을 뽑아들고서 *forge into: 차례로 들이닥치다 *forensics evidence: 현장 감식 증거

In death*, Seung-Hui Cho finally spoke, but it was through the QuickTime videos received by NBC and broadcast on Wednesday. A pastor* at a Korean church in Centreville watched the tapes on television

버지니아주[84] 블랙스버그 소재 버지니아 폴리테크닉 인스티튜트와 주립 대학교 캠

---

with his family. He told the Seoul newspaper JoongAng Ilbo, "All my family said that was not the Seung-Hui we knew. It was the first time we saw him speaking in full sentences*."
죽음에 임하여 마침내 조승희는 말문을 열었다. 하지만 그것은 NBC가 수령하여 수요일에 방영한 퀵타임 동영상을 통해서였다. 센터빌의 한 한인교회 목사는 가족과 함께 TV에서 그 장면을 보았다. 그는 서울의 일간지 중앙일보와의 인터뷰에서 『우리 가족은 일제히 말했습니다. 저건 우리가 알던 승희가 아니다. 그가 완전한 문장으로 말하는 것을 처음 보았기 때문입니다』라고 했다. [어구해설] *in death: 죽어서, 죽은 상태로 *pastor: 목사 *speak in full sentences: 완전한 문장으로 말하다. 이익훈, "버지니아工大 慘事「뉴욕 타임스」의 분석," 월간조선 06 2007 MAGAZINE.
http://monthly.chosun.com/client/news/viw.asp?ctcd=&nNewsNumb=200706100068 2025.4.7. 검색.

83 경찰청, 미국 총기난사사고 관련 총기안전관리 강화, 2007, 2025.4.30. 검색; 경찰청에서는 미국 버지니아주 총기 난사사고로 수십 명의 인명피해가 발생한 것과 관련 권총 등 총기소지의 철저한 통제로 총기 안전지대인 우리나라에서도 유사사고가 발생할 수 있다는 만일의 우려에 대비 총기 안전관리를 더욱 강화할 예정이다. 우리나라는 개인이 총기를 소지하려면 경찰서에서 범죄경력 정신병력 알콜중독 등 결격사유 해당여부 등을 검토 후 적격자에 한해 소지를 허가하고 있다. 특히 권총은 경찰관 등 법령에 의해 무기를 휴대할 수 있는 사람 이외 일반인의 호신목적 등 소지는 철저히 금지하고 있으며 예외적으로 사격선수만 허가를 받아 소지하되 경찰관서 및 사격연습장에 총기를 보관 훈련시에도 일정한 장소 내에서만 사용하고 있다. 하지만 최근 FTA 협상타결에 불만을 품고 있는 농민이 공기총으로 사람을 살해(4.3)하는 등 총기 관련 사고가 지속적으로 발생함에 따라 특단의 총기 안전관리 대책을 시행하고 있다. 총포 안전관리 대책의 주요 내용으로는 총기 소지허가 단계에서 정신병력자 알콜 중독자 등 부적격자 사전 배제가 무엇보다 중요하다는 판단에 따라 필요시 정밀 신체검사서를 제출토록 하는 등 실질심사를 강화하고 안전교육 이수 후 평가시험제를 도입하는 등 교육을 내실화하고 개인소지 총기류 일제점검 대상을 공기총 이외 전자충격기 석궁 등으로까지 확대하여 3월 12일부터 5월 11일까지(2개월) 실시 총기류의 불법소지 및 임의 개조 변조 여부를 집중 점검하여 개인소지 총기로 인한 사건 사고를 미연에 방지하고 있다. 또한 일반인이 출입할 수 있는 사격연습장에 보관된 권총 등 총기를 절취 강도 등 범죄에 악용할 가능성 차단을 위해 '사격장 특별점검'(4월 19일부터 26일까지)을 실시 경비시설 및 인력을 보강토록 하는 한편 순찰을 강화할 예정이며 특히 유관 기관과 협조를 통하여 9월 1일부터 9월 30일까지 실시해 왔던 불법무기 자진신고 기간을 금년에는 6월 1일부터 7월 15일까지 실시 시기도 앞당기고 기간도 늘려 불법무기를 적극 수거하고 각급 경찰관서 별로 합동점검반을 편성하여 총기 제조 판매업소의 불법행위 등 점검을 강화하고 경찰서간의 교차단속을 통하여 총기 유출 행위 등을 엄단할 방침이며 수렵기간중 수렵인을 대상으로 총기 안전교육 실시 총기 입출고 통제 등을 통해 오발사고 등을 방지함으로써 국민의 생명과 신체보호에 최선의 노력을 경주할 예정이다. 또한 금년중 총기관리 근거법인 총포 도검 화약류등 단속법을 전면 개정 총기소지 자의 경미한 법령위반행위에 벌점 부과 후 누적벌점이 일정 한도를 초과하면 소지 허가를 취소하는 벌점제 신설과 총기 전자상거래 통신판매 방문판매 등 광고 금지와 관리가 미흡했던 국외이주자의 총기 허가취소 및 경찰관서 보관 등 규제를 강화하는 한편 총기관련 불법행위 신고보상금제를 4월 2일부터 도입하여 경찰의 총 기 안전관리 시책에 국민들의 적극적인 참여를 유도할 예정이다. 경찰에서는 총기 안전관리 강화 대책이 소기의 성과를 거둘 수 있도록 국민 여러 분의 자발적인 협조를 당부하고 있다. 담당: 생활안전국 생활질서과 홍덕기.

84 대한민국 경찰청, "美 뉴저지州, 조직 · 총기범죄 종합대책," 2027, 2025.4.30. 검색; 조직 · 총기범죄 만연에 따라 전과자 감시체계 구축 · 범죄조직 동향 감시체계 강화 등을 골자로 하는 종합대책을 시행할 美 뉴저지州(주지사 코자인) 정부에서는 총범죄율은 지속감소하였음에도 살인 · 총기범죄 피의자 체포건수는 오히

퍼스 내 웨스트 앰블러 존스턴 홀과 노리스 홀에서 일어난 총기 난사 사건이다. 이 대학 학부생이자 재미 한국인 조승희는 반자동 권총 두 자루로 총탄을 난사해 32명이 숨지고 23명이 다쳤다. 나머지 6명은 조승희를 피해 창문 밖으로 뛰어내려 부상을 입었다. 경찰이 노리스 홀을 습격하자 조승희는 스스로 머리에 총을 쏴 자살했다. 미국 역사상 가장 치명적인 학교 총기 난사 사건이며, 9년 뒤 발생한 올랜도 나이트클럽 총기 난사 사건 이전까지 미국 역사상 가장 충격적인 총기 난사 사건이었다. 이 사건은 국제적인 언론의 보도를 받았고 미국의 총기 문화에 대한 광범위한 비판을 불러일으켰다. 총기 폭력, 총기법, 미국 정신건강 문제 치료 시스템의 격차, 조교수의 심리 상태, 대학 행정의 책임, 사생활 보호법, 언론 윤리 및 기타 문제에 대한 논쟁을 불러일으켰다. 조승희의 멀티미디어 선언의 일부를 방송한 뉴스 기관들은 희생자 가족과 버지니아주 사법당국, 미국 정신의학협회로부터 비난을 받았다. 조승희는 이전에 선택적 함묵증와 심각한 우울증 진단을 받은 적이 있다. 중학교와 고등학교의 많은 기간 동안, 그는 치료와 특별 교육 지원을 받았다. 고등학교를 졸업한 후, 조승희는 버지니아 공대에 등록했다. 연방 사생활 보호법 때문에 버지니아 공대는 조승희가 이전에 받은 진단이나 학교에서 받은 숙소에 대해 알지 못했다. 2005년, 조승희는 두 명의 여학생을 스토킹한 혐의로 기소되었다. 조사 결과 버지니아 주의 한 특별재판관은 조승희를 정신질환자로 선언하고 치료에 참여할 것을 명령했지만, 조승희는 제도화되지 않았기 때문에 총기 구입이 허용되었다. 총기 난사 사건은 버지니아 주가 정신적으로 좋지 않다고 판정된 사람들이 국가순간 범죄자 신원조회 시스템에 의해 감지되지 않고 권총을 구입할 수 있게 했던 법적 허점을 닫게 만들었다. 그것은 또한 1994년 이후 미국에서 유일한 연방 총기 규제 조치의 통과로 이어졌다. INC를 강화하는 법은 2008년 1월 5일 조지 W. 부시 대통령에 의해 서명되었다. 버지니아 공대

려 증가 추세이고 관내 43% 지역에서 범죄조직 활동징후가 포착되는 등 조직 · 총기범죄 만연에 따라 同 범죄종합대책을 시행 발표(10. 9)하였는바 초기 소요예산은 4천5백만달러(약 413억원), 추진기간은 18개월이며 참여기관은 州경찰 교정청 등 9개 기관, 同 대책주요내용은 — 재범 감소를 위한 전과자 감시체제 구축 — 강력범죄 감소를 위한 범죄조직 동향 감시체제 강화 — 정보기반 치안전략(intelligence-led policing) 도입관서 확대 — 불법총기 유통 추적체제 구축 등이라 함. 이와 관련, '코자인' 주지사는 뉴저지州 형법은 총기 소지죄를 벌금형 선고가능성이 높은 3급 범죄로 규정하고 있어 총기범죄 억제효과가 낮다며, 州정부의 同 대책 추진과는 별도로 강력범죄 벌칙 강화 등 州의회의 입법 노력이 병행되어야 한다고 강조.

검토 위원회는 사건을 검토하기 위해 지정된 주 정부 기관이다. 위원회는 버지니아 공대 관리자들이 사상자 수를 줄였을지도 모르는 조치를 취하지 않았다고 비난했다. 조사위의 보고서는 또한 총기법을 검토하고 정신 건강 관리와 개인 정보 보호 법의 격차를 지적했는데, 조승희가 버지니아 공대 재학 시절 그의 악화 상태를 치료받지 못했다. 첫 번째 총격 사건은 현지 시각 오전 7시 15분경에 웨스트 앰버 존스턴 기숙사 홀에서 있었으며, 이곳에서 에밀리 제인 힐스처(Emily J. Hilscher, 18세)와 기숙사 사감인 대학원생 라이언 클라크(Ryan C. Clark)가 살해당했다. 사건을 목격한 사람들에 따르면, 조승희는 여자 친구와 기숙사에서 심한 논쟁을 벌인 뒤 자기 방으로 돌아가 권총을 휴대하고 되돌아와, 에밀리 제인 힐스처와 라이언 클라크에게 첫 번째 총격을 가해 즉사시켰다고 한다. 대만 출신의 같은 학교 학생 첸 치아 하오는 대만케이블TV와의 인터뷰에서 "웨스트 앰블러 존스턴 홀 건물에서 두 사람 간에 심한 언쟁이 있었고 그 후 그녀에게 총격이 가해졌다"고 말했다. 버지니아 공대에 재학 중인 한 한인 학생은, 연합뉴스와의 통화에서 "가죽 옷 차림에 권총 2자루를 들고 모자를 눌러 쓴 범인이 기숙사 건물에서 한 학생을 쏘아 죽인 뒤 한참 떨어진 공학부 건물 강의실로 걸어 들어가 학생들을 향해 총을 난사했다"면서 "범인은 아시아계이며, 범행 후 자살한 것으로 안다"고 밝혔다. 한편, 학교 관계자는 이를 파악했으나 사건이 격리된 곳에서 벌어진 것으로 생각하여 캠퍼스 전체에 대해 비상사태를 선포하지 않았다. 연합뉴스의 2차 보도에 따르면, 미국 경찰 당국은 첫 번째 총격사건과 관련해 조사하고 있는 '관심 인물(person of interest)'이 있다고 밝혔다. 버지니아 공대 인근의 레드포드 대학에 다니는 대학생으로 알려진 이 인물은, 이번 총격 사건이 발생한 후 460번 고속도로에서 승용차를 타고 가다 검문중이었던 경찰에 검거됐다. 경찰은 이 학생이 피살자인 에밀리 제인 힐스처와 잘 아는 사이이며, 간단한 조사를 받은 뒤 석방했으나, 이후 추가적인 정보 입수를 위해 그를 계속 조사할 것이라고 밝혔다고 한다. 첫 번째 총격과 두 번째 총격 사이의 범인 조승희의 행적이 불분명했다. 그러나 미국 방송사 NBC에 의해 그의 행적이 밝혀졌다. 범인 조승희는 이 사건에 대한 메모와 자신의 사진을 담은 소포를 미국 방송사 NBC에 보내기 위해 우체국에 갔다 왔다. 그로 인해 첫 번째 총격과 두 번째 총격의 공백시간에 대한 의문이 풀렸다. 홀든 홀 212호실에서 촬영. 프랑스어 수업시간에 학생들이 공격으로부터 숨어 있다. 첫 번째 사건에서 두 시간 후에, 노리스 홀에 위치한 교실에서 총성이 울렸다. 노리스 홀은 공학/과학/역학 프로그램에서 사용하는 공과대 건물이다. 이 건물에서 범인은 30명을 사살했다. 유대인 노교수 리브레스쿠가 몸으로 조승희를 막아 학생들이 도망갈 시간을 벌어주었지만, 역부족이었다. 리브레스쿠 교수가 유탄에 사망한 당일은 공교롭게도 유대인 대학살 추도일이었다. 수사 발표는 범인 조승희의 시체는 얼굴이 손상되어, 신원 파악을 하는 데 어려움을 겪었다. 미국의 시카고선타임스는 현지시각으로 16일, 이 사건의 용의자가 2006년 학생비자로 입국한 중국인 남성이라고 보도했었다. 이 보도에 따르면, 미국 수사당국은 중국 상하이에서 학생비자를 받아 작년 8월 유나이티드항공편으로 샌프란시스코에 도착한 24세 중국인 남성이 이번 사건의 범인인가의 여부를 조사했다고 밝혔다. 이후 현지 경찰은 사건의 용의자로 한국 국적의 영주권자이며 버지니아 공대의 영문학과 4학년 재학생인 'Seung Hui Cho'라고 공식 발표했다. 한국 언론에서는 이를 처음에 '조승휘'라고 파악했다가 '조승희'로 최종 발표했다. 경찰은 조승희의 지문이 발견된 9 mm 글록 19(Glock 19)와 22 구경 발터 P22 (Walther P22) 권총 두 자루를 발견하여, 이를 조사한 결과 범인은 이를 가지고 16일 오전 7시 15분께 기숙사에서 2명을 살해하고, 이어 공학부 건물에서 30명을 사살했다고 파악하였다. 미 수사당국은 이 사건이 공범자없이 피의자가 단독으로 실행한 것으로 추측하고 있다.

V. 미국 연방헌법 수정조항 제2조 연방대법원 — 법원 판례

"The constitutional limitation has caused the federal government to act rather passively on the matter of gun control. For two following centuries afterwards, there were no effective federal legislation addressing the issue of gun control.

Only in the 1930's, when the untreated problem of gun related violence grew to become a serious societal concern, the federal government passed the National Firearms Act and the Federal Firearm Act.[85] Significant new legislative initiative, the Gun Control Act of 1968, did not come until nearly 3 decades later when

President John F. Kennedy in 1963, U.S. Senator Robert F. Kennedy in 1968, and Martin Luther King, Jr. perished in 1968 all through gun violence.[86] Federal law on gun control came intermittently and only when it seemed as a dire necessity.

The gun control laws in the 1990s, including the Brady Act of 1993, also were prompted by gun related violence in school grounds or involving youth. More recently, the current President Obama has announced initiatives on gun control as well, but is faced with various proposals of lawsuits and engulfed in controversial constitutional battles. For many concerned advocates, the 2nd Amendment's restraint on federal gun control is nowadays seen as an outdated hindrance for the purpose of protecting American people's lives."[87]

"연방대법원은 수정헌법 제2조의 해석에 대해 원의주의적인 입장을 강하게 고수하는 것으로 보인다. 최근 총기 규제와 관련한 세 판례에서, 연방대법원은 수정헌법 제 2 조를 바탕으로 자기 방어를 위해 무기를 소지하고 휴대할 개인의 권리를 옹호해 주었다. 연방대법원이 5:4 판결로 원고의 손을 들어준 District of Columbia v. Heller (2008)7 판결에서는, 거주자의 장전된 총을 소지할 권리를 제한하는 워싱턴 D.C.의 총기 소유 규제 법률[88]이 수정헌법 제 2 조를 위반하였다는 이유로 위헌 판정을 받았다. 이 판결이 수정헌법 제2조를 연방정부가 관할권을 가진 지역에 한정하여 적용시켰다면, 2010년 McDonald v. City of Chicago(2010)[89]에서의 연방대법원 판결은 이를 주정부 관할 지역까지 확장시켰다. 이 법원은 수정헌법 제2조에 따라 규정되는 무기

---

85 National Firearms Act (1934) and Federal Firearm Act (1938) were enacted by the Roosevelt administration amidst the Prohibition era. The federal government stepped forward to eradicate social ills such as alcoholism, drug abuse and gang (mafia) activity related to guns.

86 Rosenfeld, Steven, "The NRA Once Supported Gun Control". Salon, Jan 14, 2013. Researched on Feb. 12, 2016. http://www.salon.com/2013/01/14/the_nra_once_supported_gun_control/

87 사라 오 / 가천대학교 조교수, 前 미국매릴랜드주 District Court 법관 Sara Oh / Assistant professor, Gachon University, "총기규제를 위한 미국 지방정부와 법원의 역할(Law of the Land: Regional Gun Control in the U.S.)," 한국토지공법학회 토지공법연구 제73집 제1호, 2016년 2월 Korea Public Land Law Association Public Land Law Review Vol. 73 No. 1, February, 2016, 612-613면.

88 The Firearms Control Regulations Act of 1975.

89 Otis McDonald, et al. v. City of Chicago, Illinois, et al. (2010).

를 보유하고 소지할 개인의 권리는, 주정부의 권력으로부터 개인의 기본권을 보호하기 위한 수정헌법 제14조 적법절차에 의거, 주정부에 의해 제한될 수 없는 것으로 판결하였다. 또한 연방대법원은 지난 3월 Caetano v. Massachusetts(2016)[90] 판결에서, 수정헌법 제2조에 대한 원의주의적 헌법 해석을 다시 한 번 견지하였다. 매사추세츠 주 대법원에서는 원고의 전기충격기 소지에 대하여, 해당 무기가 수정헌법 제정 시기에 존재하지 않았음을 이유로 이것이 수정헌법 제2조의 보호를 받을 수 없는 것으로 판결하여 원고의 유죄를 선고한 반면, 연방대법원은 헌법 텍스트에 기초하여, 모든 휴대 가능한 무기는 수정헌법 제2조가 보호하는 범주 내에 있는 것으로 판결하였다. 사실 수정헌법 제2조가 제정된 배경에는 그 당시 미국의 시대적 상황이 크게 반영되어 있다. 미국의 헌법과 수정헌법이 제정된 1780-90년대는, 미국이 막 영국 제국을 상대로 독립한 후, 기존 주들 간의 갈등을 봉합함과 동시에 미지의 땅이었던 서부 지역에 대한 개척을 시작해야 했던 시기였다." 이런 상황 속에서 당시 헌법제정자들 및 대다수의 지도층들은, 신생 연방정부의 치안 유지 능력으로는 시민 개개인을 온전히 보호할 수 없을 것이라는 관념을 가지고 있었을 것이고, 따라서 그 당시 총기 소유의 권리는 개인과 그 가족의 생명 및 재산을 지키기 위해 반드시 요구되었던 권리였을 것이라고 합리적으로 추정해 볼 수 있다. 하지만 이러한 관념이 현 시대에 정당성을 지니기에는 시대가 너무 많이 변했고, 일례로 작금에는 연방정부 및 주정부의 행정력이 미치지 못하는 지역을 찾기가 어렵다. 만약 연방대법원이 변화된 시대상을 고려하여 수정헌법 제2조의 해석에 있어 "살아있는 헌법" 원칙을 적용시킨다면, 총기 소유 관련 케이스에 대해 다른 시각의 판결을 내놓을 가능성도 있을 것이다. 하지만 현재까지의 판례들로 미루어 보았을 때, 적어도 총기 소유와 관련된 케이스에 대해서는 연방대법원이 계속해서 원의주의적 헌법 해석에 근거한 판결을 내릴 것으로 전망된다.[91]

---

90 Jaime Caetano v. Massachusetts (2016).

91 이창원(Lee, Paul Changwon) Northwestern Pritzker School of Law J.D., 지속되는 미국 내 총기 규제 논란, 그리고 이와 관련한 수정헌법 제2조의 해석, 헌법재판소, 탑재 보고서, 5면.

Ⅵ. 美 연방 수정헌법 제2조 총기 규제에 관한 법원의 균형

뉴욕타임즈는 1920년 이후 95년 만에 처음으로 1면에 "총기 창궐(The Gun Epidemic)"이라는 사설을 실었을 정도였다. 오바마 대통령은 이에 총기 거래 규제 행정조치 11을 발표했고, 그가 행정조치 발표 현장에서 흘린 눈물은 총기 규제 필요성에 대한 공감대를 미국 시민사회에 다시 한 번 확산시키는 계기가 되었다. 이러한 지지 여론 속에서도, 오바마 행정부는 해당 행정조치가 수정헌법 제2조에 배치되지 않도록 많은 논의를 거쳤다고 한다. 이 행정조치를 면밀히 들여다보면, 이것이 "총기 소유 규제"보다는 총기 구입 시 엄격한 신원 조회 등의 "총기 판매와 구매의 법제화"를 목적으로 했다고 볼 수 있으며, 이러한 방향성은 오바마 대통령이 항상 주장해왔던 총기 규제 원칙과 맥을 같이 한다. 그럼에도 불구하고 당시 공화당의 대선후보였던 도널드 트럼프(Donald Trump) 및 다수 보수 인사들은, 오바마 대통령이 발표한 행정조치가 수정헌법 제2조를 짓밟는 위헌 행위라며 비판의 수위를 높였다. 한 예로 "More Guns, Less Crime"의 서사인 존 롯(John Lott)은, 오리건주 총기 난사 사건 후 CNN 과의 인터뷰에 출연하여 "대학교 캠퍼스 내 학생들은 그들 자신을 보호하기 위해 (총기로) 무장해야만 한다"라고 주장하여 큰 논란을 불러일으켰다. 이는 아직도 총기 규제 논의에서 수정헌법 제2조가 현실적으로 극복하기 어려운 장벽임을 보여주는 사례이다.[92]

Caselaws show that the role of courts on gun control in the U.S. is directly related to the survival of regional gun control laws. Thousands of local gun control ordinances would not have stood up without the courts' help. As constitutional lawsuits were brought on against local gun control legislation, the local courts sided with the regional government and let the gun control law continue its course. Since 2008, there have been over a thousand of 2nd Amendment cases challenging gun laws nationwide. Among those, an overwhelming majority of 94% of the low-

---

92 이창원(Lee, Paul Changwon) Northwestern Pritzker School of Law J.D., 지속되는 미국 내 총기 규제 논란, 그리고 이와 관련한 수정헌법 제2조의 해석, 헌법재판소, 탑재 보고서, 6-7면.

er courts upheld the local gun control laws.[93] *For example, in Justice v. Town of Cicero,[94] the town had enacted a gun control ordinance prohibiting the possession of unregistered guns. All firearms within the town had to be registered. The plaintiff, John Justice, who owned unregistered guns inside his store, was arrested and briefly incarcerated. His guns were also confiscated by the police. Justice sued the town in local court claiming unconstitutionality of the ordinance. The plaintiff lost his case; he appealed to a higher regional court and ended up losing again. The Illinois state's lower court's decision to uphold the town ordinance was later upheld and affirmed in the federal court. The case went all the way up to the U.S. Supreme Court, but it declined to review the case. The process was long, but the final victory went to the town and its law. The role of the courts involved in Justice was obviously essential for the town ordinance's survival. Other case examples involving challenges to local gun ordinance are many in number, but are similar in final outcomes. In Kwong v. Bloomberg,[95] the New York City administrative code had established a license fee for gun owners at $340. Assisted by the Second Amendment Foundation and the New York State Rifle and Pistol Association, the plaintiff Shui Kwong brought a constitutional lawsuit against the city and the mayor, arguing that the fee is excessive. The case went up to the U.S. Court of Appeals, where the city code was declared as valid. The U.S. Supreme Court also rejected review of the case.*

The U.S. Supreme Court's role on regional gun control law is tantamount. Including the above two cases, it declined to review countless lawsuits challenging gun control laws arising from all parts of the country.[96] Examples of famous cases

---

93 See supra note 2.

94 827 F.Supp.2d. 835 (N.D.Ill. 2011).

95 876 F.Supp.2d. 246 (2012).

96 These are some of the well-known lower court cases which the U.S. Supreme Court declined to review. See supra note 2. Drake v. Filko, 724 F.3d 426 (3d Cir. 2013), cert denied 134 S. Ct. 2134 (2014); Kachalsky v. Cacace, 701 F.3d 81 (2d Cir. 2012), cert denied 133 S. Ct. 1806 (2013); Brown v. United

abound throughout the country. Advocates of gun control legislation cherish these cases as citizens' victory against gun related associations and affiliated industries. As it can be seen from the high number of rejected cases, a close relationship between the courts and regional gun control laws can be observed. It would not be an exaggeration to assume that the existence of the high number of regional gun control laws in the U.S. is owed to the courts' assistance. After all, the federal government is unable to take any significant action on strengthening gun control laws without clashing with the 2nd Amendment. Under the current constitutional regime, the federal government cannot provide help for the regional gun control laws. Thus, in lieu of the Congress, it was the U.S. courts who stepped in and took an active role of protecting gun control laws in the country. In the future, the courts would be able to say that they have created a legacy in history, for good or bad. The U.S. courts have tried to make a positive contribution toward protecting American people's life and safety by upholding regional gun control laws in 94% of their caseloads in the past decade or so.

Ⅶ. 美 연방 법원 판례

"Warning against judicial activism has been a constant criticism in this type of relationship, since the courts' decisions appear to directly affect the government's policies. The Governor Scott Walker of Wisconsin has recently remarked that the executive and judicial branches of the government should respect the separation of powers on the issue of gun control.[97] Nevertheless, such criticism has been

States, 979 A.2d 630 (D.C. 2009), cert denied 2010 U.S. LEXIS 9811 (Dec. 13, 2010); People v. Dawson, 403 Ill. App. 3d 499 (2010), cert denied 2011 U.S. LEXIS 3381 (May 2, 2011); Commonwealth v. Powell, 459 Mass. 572 (Mass. 2011), cert denied 2012 U.S. LEXIS 2231 (Mar. 19, 2012) (the court also rejected a Second Amendment challenge to a law requiring the registration of all firearms); Williams v. State of Maryland, 10 A.3d 1167, 1178 (Md. 2011), cert denied 132 S.Ct. 93 (2011).

commonplace throughout the U.S. history whenever the courts or presidential actions tended to favor a particular side of a controversial issue. After all, judicial decisions have formed an important part of American history. A more practical concern, however, lies with the way of measuring the effect of the courts' decision. Because a constitutionally-based court's decision is often not quantitative, it is not easy to evaluate the results. Do the courts' tendency to decide in favor of regional gun control laws actually help to reduce the country's gun related violence and crime? The method of collecting case examples and counting the number of victories in the courts might not be an accurate way of measuring the relationship between the regional gun control laws and courts. Even in relatively small numbers, the study could be improved if there are statistic data on court cases where gun control laws were held unconstitutional, as well as out-of-court statistics on gun related incidents in the U.S. society. Another type of criticism can be derived from those plaintiffs who truly believe that the 2nd Amendment is a scion of civil liberty which should never be infringed. In fact, the Second Amendment Foundation and the National Rifle Association consider the right to keep and bear arms a fundamental right in democracy. For some people, regional gun control laws are a violation of their civil rights. These plaintiffs'

challenges in the courtroom are meaningful ideological battles worthy of fighting. Financial loss of plaintiffs and burden on the existing gun markets and industry should be also considered for more thoroughness. The study on the relationship between the courts and gun control laws would not be complete without considering all sides of the debate, including the economic ones."[98]

---

97 Jessen, Leah. "Gov. Scott Walker Threatens Lawsuit Over Obama's Gun Control Orders". The Daily Signal, Jan. 8, 2016. Researched on Feb. 12, 2016. http://dailysignal.com/2016/01/08/gov-scott-walker-threatens-lawsuit-over-obamas-gun-control-orders/

98 사라 오 / 가천대학교 조교수, 前 미국매릴랜드주 District Court 법관 Sara Oh / Assistant professor, Gachon University, "총기규제를 위한 미국 지방정부와 법원의 역할(Law of the Land: Regional Gun Control in the U.S.)," 한국토지공법학회 토지공법연구 제73집 제1호, 2016년 2월 Korea Public Land Law

Ⅷ. 美 연방 수정헌법 제2조 총기권리 위헌적 함의

1. 미국 헌법상 총기 소지의 권리와 그 규제의 딜레마

"총기 소지의 권리가 개인적 권리인지 아니면 집단적 권리인지의 헌법 해석 문제에 있었다. 즉 수정헌법 제2조의 총기 소지의 권리를 개인적 기본권으로 보아 정부 규제를 반대하는 세력과 이를 주(州) 방위군과 같은 집단적 권리로 보아 개인의 총기 소지 규제를 찬성하는 세력간에 대립이 있었다. 이들의 논쟁에 연방대법원은 그동안 침묵을 지켜왔다. 그러나 이 논쟁이 최근 미국 사회에서 재연될 조짐이다. 그 논의가 총기 소지를 엄격히 규제하고 있는 주 법률에 대하여 수정헌법 제2조를 근거로 위헌 결정을 내린 연방항소법원의 2007년 3월 판결[99]을 시발로 하여, 4월에 발생한 버지니아공대 총기 참사 사건으로 가속화되었기 때문이다. 이러한 상황을 배경으로 아래에서는 헌법상 총기소지권의 유래와 그 동안의 정부규제 양상을 살펴보면서, 향후 연방대법원의 입장에 주목해 보고자 한다. 연방헌법상 총기소지의 권리(Right to Bear Arms) 미국 연방 헌법은 "독립이 보장된 각 주의 안보를 위해서는 잘 규율된 민병(民兵)이 필요하므로 총기를 보유 하고 소지하는 인민의 권리는 침해받지 아니한다."[100] 라고 규정하고 있다. 이 조문은 1787년 연방헌법이 채택된 지 4년 후인 1791년, 연방주의자와 반연방주의 간의 치열한 논쟁을 거쳐 소위 "권리장전(權利章典 Bill of Rights)"으로 명명된 수정헌법을 통하여 명문화되었다. 이러한 헌법상 총기소지규정의 태동에는 크게 두 가지 배경을 들 수 있다. 우선, 연방제의 형성배경으로서 정부에 대한 불신이다. 유럽의 전제군주 반대세력 · 청교도 등의 이민자로 출발한 미국사회의 저

Association Public Land Law Review Vol. 73 No. 1, February, 2016, 618-619면.

99 뉴욕타임스는 지난 3월10일, 이번 연방항소법원의 판결은 수정헌법 제2조를 주 방위군의 집단적 권리로 해석하여 왔던 종래 9개 연방항소법원의 판결들과 다른 획기적 판결로서, 중대한 헌법 이슈들을 지닌 동건이 향후 연방대법원에서 다루어질 가능성이 높다고 보도하였다.

100 수정헌법 제2조(A well regulated Militia, being necessary to the security of a free State, the right of the people to keep and bear Arms, shall not be infringed). 이와 같이 헌법조문에 그 취지를 직접 표현한 방식(정당화 규정)은 특이하지만 당시에 통용되던 입법례로서, 동조의 승인을 얻기 위 한 정치적 의도가 담긴 것이라고 한다. Eugene Volokh, The Commonplace Second Amendment, 73 NYU L. Rev. 793 (1998) 참조.

변에는 연방 정부의 전횡이나 독재자의 출현을 혐오하여 각 주에 자율과 독립을 보장하는 장치가 요구되었다. 즉 주 스스로의 방위와 독립을 연방헌법에 명시함으로써 연방제의 정착을 적절히 도모하는 한편, 연방정부는 물론 주 정부의 폭정에도 대항할 수 있는 시민의 권리(저항권)에 대한 보장 장치가 필요 하였다. 둘째 정당방위의 법리에 대한 보편적 인식이다. 해밀턴과 같은 연방주의자도 "총기소지권은 수정헌법에 굳이 담을 필요가 없는 자연적 권리(自然權)"로 인식하였듯이 영국의 법체계를 전수받은 미국에서의 총기 소지는 보통법 상의 정당방위의 법리(self-defense)를 통해 용인되어 왔다. 더구나 행정력이 미치지 않는 광활한 땅을 개척하던 1791년 당시 시대적 배경을 볼 때, 인디언의 습격이나 소 도적떼 · 야생동물 등 각종 위험으로부터 자신의 생명과 재산을 스스로 보호할 수단을 보장할 필요가 있었다.

연방의회에서의 논쟁

그동안 대체적으로 민주당은 총기규제(Gun Control)를, 공화당은 이에 반대하는 입장(Gun Rights)을 취해 왔다. 즉, 공화당을 지지하는 미국총기협회와 같은 규제반대론자는 수정헌법 제2조는 조문의 표현 그대로 해석하여야 한다는 입장에서, 특히 제2조 후단의 "인민(people)"이라는 표현에 주목하여 총기소 지권은 헌법이 개인에게 보장한 일종의 기본권이므로, 정부의 총기소지 규제는 위헌이라는 입장이다.[101] 반면, 규제 찬성론자는 제2조 전단의 "민병(militia)"이라는 용어에 주목하고 오늘날 상황에서 헌법조문을 해석하여야 한다는 입장에서, 동조의 총기소지는 주 방위군(state defense forces)이나 수비대(national guard)와 같은 주 방위집단에 부여되는 권리이지 개인적 권리가 아니므로, 개인에 대한 정부의 총기규제는 합헌이라고 주장한다. 그동안 민주당은 특히 범죄예방을 논거로 총기규제 입장을 견지하였는바, 뉴욕타임스 · 워싱턴포스트 · LA타임스 등 美 주요 언론의 논조 또한 총기에 대한 정부규제를 지지

---

101 흔히 NRA로 불리는 미국 총기협회(National Rifle Association)는 1871년 창설되어 오늘날 430만 회원을 보유하면서 연방과 주차원의 입법과정에 막강한 영향력을 행사하는 로비단체로서, 버지니아에 본부가 있다. NRA는 이러한 헌법적 논거 외에도 총기규제법이 시민의 권리보호수단을 박탈하여 오히려 범죄 발생을 증가시키고 있으며, 사냥이나 여가 · 스포츠 용도로도 개인의 총기소지를 폭넓게 허용해야 한다고 주장해 왔다.

하여 왔다. 이러한 양당간 노선 차이에도 불구하고 연방의회는 대형총기사건등 혼란기에 적절한 타협점을 내놓았다. 예컨대, 케네디 대통령 암살에 이은 마틴 루터 킹 목사의 암살사건 직후 의회는 1968년 "총기규제법"(Gun Control Act)을 제정하였고, 1991년 24명이 사망한 텍사스 킬린지역 총기 사건 후 클린턴 정부초기인 1993년에는 레이건 대통령 저격사건 당시 총격을 입은 브래디 공보비서관의 이름을 딴 "브래디법"(Brady Handgun Violence Prevention Act)을 제정하여 총기 구매자에게 범죄 및 정신병 기록 등을 FBI의 범죄조회시스템에 5일간 검증받도록 하였다.

주 정부의 대응과 고민

이러한 연방정부의 총기규제에 관한 각 주들의 대응은 상이하다. 일반적으로 연방법률이 연방헌법을 통해 연방정부로 위임된 사항(외교 · 국방 · 통상 등)을 정하고 주민의 안전 · 교육 · 복지 등 대부분의 사항은 각 주의 입법을 통해 구체적으로 실행되는 연방제 국가의 특성상, 50개 주의 총기규제 법률이 각주의 특성에 따라 달리 나타난다. 대체적으로 민주당 강세지역은 총기규제 법률들이 엄격하나, 공화당 강세지역은 허술한 편이다. 또한 44개 주에서는 총기소지권을 주 헌법(state constitution)에 보장하고 있고 이 또한 개인적 권리라고 대부분의 주에서 천명하고 있으나, 뉴욕 · 뉴저지 · 캘리포니아 등 대체로 민주당 강세인 6개 주에서는 총기소지 자체를 주 헌법에 언급하지 않고 있다. 각 주의 총기규제문제에 대한 고민은 다양하다.「개인의 총기규제에 따른 위헌시비문제를 어떻게 해소하고, 어떠한 정책이 범죄율을 줄이고 개인의 권리를 보다 보호하는 것인가」라는 기본적인 고민에서 시작하여「총기규제로 인해 주 스스로의 독립성을 훼손시키고 연방 정부로 예속되는 것은 아닌지, 나아가 총기규제시 정부 폭정에 대한 미래세대의 저항권을 어떻게 담보할 것이며 시민의 자유에 대한 위협인 정규군의 존재를 어떻게 인정해 나갈 것인지」 등으로 확대된다.[102] 이러한 고민

102 대부분 정당방위를 이유로 총기소지를 주헌법에 명시하고 있으나, 흥미롭게도 7개 주에서는 "평화시 상비군은 자유에 대한 위험한 존재(standing armies in time of peace are dangerous to liberty)"이므로 시민의 총기소지를 보장한다고 주헌법에 명시하고 있다(캔사스 · 메사추세츠 · 노스캐롤라이나 · 오하이오 · 사우스캐롤라이나 · 버몬트 · 버지니아 주헌법 각 참조).

은 한편으로 총기 소지권의 연방 헌법상 보장 장치를 통해 주정부가 연방정부의 규제 내지 통제를 거부하는 기제로도 작용한다. 즉 총기 규제에는 연방 정부와 주정부 사이에 원활한 상호협조가 요구되는데도 주정부가 소극적으로 대응한다는 문제이다. 예컨대, 정신병력자의 총기구매를 제한하는 브래디법의 경우 연방정부의 범죄조회시스템에 총기 구매자인 주 거주자의 신상정보 입력이 요구되나, 이에 대한 주정부의 순응은 주민의 사생활을 침해할 뿐 아니라 주정부의 자율성을 저해하고 연방정부로의 예속을 촉진시킨다고 보아 많은 주들이 이러한 연방조치에 소극적으로 따르는 문제를 발생시키고 있다.[103]

연방대법원의 입장

이와 같이 총기 소지 규제 문제는 헌법상 권리보호 문제 이외에 주정부의 독립성 문제 및 시민의 저항권 인정 여부 등 미국 사회의 근간을 다루는 문제와 연결되어 있어 정치적으로 예민하면서도 풀리지 않는 과제로 남아 있다. 인권문제의 최후 보루인 연방대법원도 수정헌법 제2조와 같은 예민한 문제에 대해서는 명쾌한 해답을 주지 않았다. 총기 규제법에 대한 대법원의 입장을 밝힌 것으로 유명한 1939년 판결(US v. Miller)에서 특정 유형의 총기소지를 범죄행위로 규정한 국가총기법(National Firearms Act)을 합헌으로 판결하면서도 1997년 판결(Printz v. US)에서는 지방경찰로 하여금 총기구매자의 범죄기록을 조회할 것을 의무화한 브래디법의 일부규정을 위헌 판결하는 곡예를 벌였던 것이다. 그러나 이때에도 수정헌법 제2조의 총기소지권이 개인적 권리인지 집단적 권리인지의 여부에 대해서는 침묵하였다. 그러나 금년 3월 워싱턴DC에 소재한 연방항소법원이 수정헌법 제2조를 명쾌히 다루었다. 동법원은 워싱턴DC의 총기단속법을 위헌으로 판결하면서 수정헌법 제2조의 총기소지권은 개인적 권리라고 판시하였다.[104]

---

103 지난 4월 23일자 「LA 타임스」 사설에서는 상당수의 주에서 사생활 보호를 이유로 주 거주자의 정신병 기록을 범죄조회시스템(NICS)에 제대로 통보하지 않고 있는 현실을 지적하고, 이러한 상황이 조승희 사건을 발생시켰다고 비판하였다.

104 이 사건은 연방법원 경비원인 Dick Heller(원고)가 근무 중 소지 권총을 집에서도 보관할 수 있도록 요청한 총기 휴대 신청을 DC정부가 DC총기규제법에 따라 이를 불허하면서 제기된 사건으로서, 2007.3.9.

이제 이 판결에 대해 연방대법원이 어떠한 입장을 취할 지 귀추가 주목된다. 어떠한 논거로 법과 현실을 조화시켜 사회적 갈등을 봉합시켜 나갈 것인지, 아니면 종전처럼 침묵을 지킬 것인지가 관심의 대상인 것이다. 예상컨대, 연방대법원이 동건을 회피할 가능성도 없지 않으나, △현대 법원구성상 보수성향이 압도적이고(전체 대법관 9인 중 7인을 공화당정부 임명) △지금껏 연방대법원이 수정헌법 제2조의 쟁점에 대해 침묵하여 왔으나 오늘날 42개 주들이 주 헌법에서 총기소지를 개인적 권리로 이미 채택하고 있으며 △동항소법원 자체가 전통적으로 대법원 판결에 큰 영향을 끼쳐 왔고 특히 대법원장을 포함한 4인의 현직 대법관을 배출한 법원인 점 등을 고려할 때, 향후 연방대법원에서 동 판결이 지지될 가능성이 높아 보인다. 그러나 대법원이 수정헌법 제2조를 개인적 권리로 판단할 경우에도 총기소지에 따른 폐해를 방지하고 공공의 안전을 제고하기 위한 기존의 정부규제를 대폭 부정하기는 어려울 것으로 보인다.[105] 따라서 총기소지 자체에 대한 과도한 규제는 부정하되, 필요최소한의 규제(예컨대, 자동소총의 판매규제나 정신병력자의 총기 소지규제 등)를 인정하는 법리가 동원될 것으로 전망된다.

향후 총기규제정책 전망

그러면 연방의회가 앞으로 총기규제에 적극 나설 것인가? 회의적이다. 우선, 민주당도 소극적 입장으로 전망되는바, 이는 클린턴 대통령의 총기규제법(Brady Act) 서명 이후에 의회를 공화당에 빼앗겼나가 이라크 이슈에 힘입어 가까스로 탈환하였다는

DC연방항소법원(일명 "DC Circuit")은 수정 헌법 제조의 보호대상은 개인적 권리이 지주방위대와 같은 집단적 권리가 아니므로, 개인의 총기휴대를 규제한 DC의 총기규제법(DC의회가 채택한 법률은 독특하게도 시장과 연방의회의 인준을 받아 발효되어 일종의 주법에 상당)은 개인의 총기소지권을 보장한 수정헌법 제2조에 위배되어 위헌법률이라고 판결하였다.

105 UCLA법과대학의 Adam Winkler같은 교수는 지금껏 각 주의 법원들이 총기 규제 법률들의 위헌여부심사에 있어 "정부규제의 합리성"이라는 기준을 적용하여 대부분 합헌 결정하였으며, 앞으로 연방법원들이 수정헌법 제2조의 총기소지권을 개인적 권리로 보아 더욱 엄격한 위헌심사기준을 적용할지라도 공공의 안전이라는 정부의 정책목표를 도외시하기 어려우므로 대부분의 총기규제법이 합헌으로 결정될 가능성이 높다고 주장하였다. Adam Winkler, Scrutinizing the Second Amendment, 105 Mich. L. Rev. 683 (Feb. 2007) 참조.

인식과 민주당의 총기 규제 정책이 일반 가정에 불필요한 거부감을 일으켜 지난 두 번의 대선에서 상당한 표를 잃었다는 인식에서 이제는 다소 유연한 입장을 취하자는 기류가 비등하기 때문이다. 공화당의 경우 430만 회원을 보유한 미국총기협회(NRA)라는 강력한 지지기반을 두고 있어 총기규제에 평소 소극적인바, 특히 대선을 앞둔 현 시점에서는 양당 간 총기 규제 정책에 큰 차이가 없을 것으로 전망된다. 이러한 소극 대응 전망에도 불구하고, 버지니아 공대 총기사건과 같은 대형 사건 발생시 의회가 적절한 타협점을 내놓았던 과거 사례를 볼 때, 향후 총기소지 자체에 대한 과도한 규제보다는 총기판매 및 구매과정에 대한 절차적 규제를 강화하거나 총기오용 방지를 위한 정책 등이 일시적으로 추진될 가능성은 높아 보인다. 아무쪼록, 앞서 말한 대로 미국 사회의 특징과 고민을 여실히 보여주는 총기규제의 문제에 대하여는 여러모로 미국과 불가분의 관계에 있는 우리로서도 앞으로 그 추이를 지켜볼 만한 사안이라 할 것이다."[106]

2. 미국 총으로 세워진 나라

"미국은 총으로 세워진 나라다. 총성과 화약 연기속에서 독립을 얻어냈을 뿐만 아니라 건국 초기 정부의 행정력이 미치지 못하는 광활한 땅을 개척하는 과정에서 수많은 미국인에게 총기는 생명과 재산을 지키기 위한 필수품이었다. 그렇다 보니 총기 소유는 일종의 기본권이자 미국이라는 나라의 중요한 정체성으로 자리 잡았다. 하지만 다른 한편으로 미국은 총으로 끊임없이 고통받는 나라이기도 하다. 미국의 민간 보유 총기는 4억여 정이 넘는 것으로 추정된다. 이는 전세계에서 압도적인 1위에 해당하는 수치다. 총기가 널리 사용되나 보니 총격사고도 흔하다. 총기 난사 사건도 매년 꾸준히 발생한다. 가장 최근에는 텍사스 주에 있는 유밸디 시의 한 초등학교에서 발생한 무차별 총기난사로 약 20여 명 이상의 사상자가 나와 총기 규제의 필요성에 대한 전국민적인 공감을 불러일으켰다. 그런 면에서 일주일 앞으로 다가온 올해 미국의 독립기념일은 꽤나 역사적인 독립기념일이 될 조짐이 보인다. 개인의 총기 소

---

106 전상수, LA 주재관, "미국 헌법상 총기 소지의 권리와 그 규제의 딜레마," 국회보(2007.6), 71면.

유권에 대한 근본적인 변화가 이루어질 가능성이 높아졌기 때문이다. 총기 구매하려는 18~21세 대상, 미성년범죄와 기록 제출 하도록, 21세 미만은 정신건강 등 검사, 총기규제법안 상원서 극적 통과. 총기규제 법안이 23일(현지시간) 상원 본회의 표결에서 찬성 65표, 반대 33표로 극적으로 통과됐다. 미국 연방대법원이 허가 없이는 집 밖에서 권총을 휴대하지 못하도록 규제한 뉴욕주 법에 위헌 판결을 내리며 총기 규제 움직임에 제동을 건 지 불과 몇 시간 만의 일이다. 초당적 안전공동체법(Bipartisan Safer Communities Act)이라고 명명된 총기규제 법안의 주요 요지는 총기를 구매하려는 18~21세의 신원 조회를 위해 미성년 범죄와 기록을 제공할 수 있도록 하고, 21세 미만 총기 구입자의 정신건강 상태를 관계 당국이 최소 열흘간 검토하게 하는 것이다. 또한 법안에는 더 많은 총기 판매업자에게 신원 조회 의무를 부여하고 총기 밀매 처벌을 강화하는 한편, 위험하다고 판단된 사람의 총기를 일시 압류하는 '레드 플래그'(red flag) 법을 도입하려는 주에 인센티브를 주는 내용도 담겼다. 그 밖에도 주(州)와 지역사회에 학교 보안 강화와 심리치료를 위한 예산을 지원하는 내용과 가정 폭력 전과자에 대한 총기 구매 제한을 배우자나 동거사뿐만 아니라 함께 거주하지 않는 데이트 상대로도 확대하는 내용도 담겼다. 민주당과 공화당이 반반으로 나뉘어 난관이 예상되었던 상원의 관문을 넘어선 총기규제 법안은 민주당이 주도하는 하원으로 넘어가게 되어 무난히 통과될 것으로 예상된다. 법안이 하원까지 통과하게 되면 미국은 약 30년 만에 의미 있는 총기규제법을 통과시키게 된다."[107]

"Regional autonomy is the basis for local gun control laws in America. The constitutional limitation imposed upon the federal government on the issue of gun control led other legislative actors of the country to become autonomous instead. The state, county, city, and municipal administrations took the baton and enacted laws according to their own regional needs and circumstances. As result, the U.S. gun control laws currently lack uniformity and congruity at national level. The high variety and differing nature of gun control laws in turn created enough legal

---

107 이민규 외국변호사 (뉴욕), "무기여 잘 있거라," 법률신문, 2022.6.27. https://www.lawtimes.co.kr/opinion/179782 2025.4.8. 검색.

storm as to attract and activate another actor to take a stance: the courts. In this aspect, gun control laws constitute a unique subject of law because they encompass a triangular correlation involving the federal government, the regional administrations, and the judiciary. As if it is not already complicated enough, the issue cannot be discussed without additional consideration of societal values, statistical data, and political tendencies of actors. Gun control laws calls for a fusion of academic fields. Future studies could attempt an interdisciplinary approach to understand the issue better.

the cost of maintaining more than 20,000 gun control laws nationwide would be much higher than in a centralized system of government where the laws would be simpler to handle and apply. Moreover, the number of unnecessary lawsuits involving the constitutionality of regional gun control laws are bound to expand, as long as the regional units of government keep enacting their gun control laws in the future. The flood of litigations in the courts would burden the judiciary and in turn, the innocent taxpayers. On this aspect, the U.S. needs to improve and bring changes to its current gun control law regime. Maybe observing examples from centralized system of government, such as from Korea or Singapore, could enlighten the future path."[108]

2022년 6월 23일 당일, 미국 연방상원은 29년 만에 총기규제 법을 통과시켜 연방대법원과 큰 대비를 이루었다. 같은 날 연방대법원은 총기규제의 완화를, 연방의회는 총기규제의 강화를 택하며 엇갈린 판단을 내린 것은 총기 문제에 대한 미국의 갈등과 분열을 잘 보여준다고 할 것이다.[109]

---

108 사라 오 / 가천대학교 조교수, 前 미국매릴랜드주 District Court 법관 Sara Oh / Assistant professor, Gachon University, "총기규제를 위한 미국 지방정부와 법원의 역할(Law of the Land: Regional Gun Control in the U.S.)," 한국토지공법학회 토지공법연구 제73집 제1호, 2016년 2월 Korea Public Land Law Association Public Land Law Review Vol. 73 No. 1, February, 2016, 620-621면.

109 임기영 책임연구원, "뉴욕주 총기규제법 위헌 판결," 헌법재판소 헌법재판연구원 세계헌법재판 조사연구

"새해 미국의 일부 주(州)에서 새로운 총기 규제법이 시행된다. 캘리포니아주에서는 일단 당초 계획대로 대부분의 공공장소에서 총기 휴대를 금지할 수 있게 됐다. 일리노이주에서는 반자동 소총 등의 소지가 금지된다. 2024년 1월 1일 로이터 통신 등 보도에 따르면, 미 제9 연방순회항소법원은 최근 캘리포니아주의 새 총기단속법이 위헌이라는 하급 법원 판결의 효력을 일시적으로 정지시켰다. 이에 앞서 캘리포니아 센트럴 연방지법은 2023년 12월 20일 병원과 운동장, 동물원, 예배 장소 등 26개 범주의 공공장소에서 총기 은닉 휴대를 금지하는 새 총기단속법이 미 수정헌법 제2조(총기 소지권)에 위배된다고 판결했다. 그러자 캘리포니아주는 "수천만 명의 주민들이 높은 총기 폭력 위험에 직면할 것"이라며 항소할 때까지 효력을 막는 집행정지를 신청했다. 항소법원이 이를 받아들이면서 캘리포니아주가 새 총기단속법을 새해 첫날인 1월 1일부터 시행할 수 있는 길이 열렸다. 민주당 소속인 개빈 뉴섬 캘리포니아 주지사는 "상식적인 총기 규제법을 유지하는 동시에 연방지법의 위험한 판결에 항소할 수 있게 됐다"고 말했다. 캘리포니아주의 새 총기단속법은 보수 성향의 연방대법원이 2022년 6월 공공장소에서 총기 소시 권리를 인정하는 판결을 한 이후 제정됐다. 이 법은 공공장소에서 시민들이 무장하고 자신을 방어할 권리를 없애는 것이라는 총기 옹호 단체들의 반발을 샀다. 일리노이주에서는 새해부터 50구경 총, 급발사 장비를 비롯해 수십 개 특정 브랜드나 특정 유형의 소총과 권총을 소지할 수 없게 된다고 AP 통신이 전했다. 또한 소총은 10발 이상, 권총은 15발 넘게 장전할 수 없게 된다."[110]

3. 총기사건들과 미연방헌법 수정 제2조

안경환 '미국 연방헌법 수정 제2조(무기소장권)의 의미', 해제(解題)

"미연방헌법 수정 제2조는 "질서정연하게 규율된 민병대는 자유국가의 안전을 위해 필요한고로 무기를 보유하고 휴대할 국민의 권리는 이를 침해당하지 아니한다(A well regulated militia, being necessary to the security of a free state, the right of the people to

---

보고서, 2022 제7호(통권 제57호), 30면.

110 노성열, "'총기 난사 두고 볼 수 없다' … 미국 일부 주 총기규제 대폭 강화," 문화일보, 2024.01.03. https://www.munhwa.com/news/view.html?no=2024010301039910009001 2025.4.8. 검색.

keep and bear arms, shall not be infringed)"[111]고 규정하고 있다. 권리장전에 있어 표현의 자유 등을 규정한 수정헌법 제1조에 이어 등장하는 이 문법적으로 정확하지 않은 짧은 문장은 분명히 정확한 해석이 필요한 중요한 헌법 조문임에도 불구하고 강학상에서는 큰 관심을 얻지 못하여왔다.[112] 하지만 총기에 의하여 불특정 다수가 무고하게 희생되는 사건들이 발생할 때마다 총기규제에 찬반의 입장을 가지고 있는 일련의 학자 집단에서는 그들의 주장의 타당성을 입증하기 위하여 동조에 대한 나름의 해석론을 펼쳐왔다.[113] 이러한 해석논쟁은 미국독립의 역사와 연방과 주의 관계에 대한 이해 등 미국헌법의 핵심적 이슈들을 관통하고 있는 관계로 그에 대한 정리는 미국헌법 전반을 이해하는데 있어 상당한 도움이 될 수 있는데, 해제대상논문은 그러한 맥락에서 진행된 저자의 수정헌법 각 조에 대한 연속적 주해 작업 중 하나라고 볼 수 있다."[114] "U.S. v. Miller, 307 U.S. 174(1939) 판결 이후 약 70년 만에 의미 있는 연방대법원 판결이 2008년 6월 26일에 내려졌다. 2008년 이전까지는 밀러(Miller) 판결에서 민병대의 육성에 합리적으로 연관되지 아니한 무기 소지가 보호받지 못한다고 판시되며 이는 간접적으로 무기소장권이 주정부의 공적인 권리에 불과하다는 점을 인정한 것이라는 해석론이 다수를 점한 상황이었다. 다만 해제대상논문에서 저자는 이것이 결론적인 유권해석이 아님을 지적하며 개인적 권리론의 가치를 설파하였는데 이러한 저자의 주장해제대상논문집필 10여 년 만에 District of Columbia v. Heller, 554 U.S. 570(2008)이라는 연방대법원 판결에서 현실화되었다.[115] Heller 판결에서 연방대법원은 수정헌법 제2조에 대하여, 특히 무기소장권이 누구의 권리인가라는 핵심적인 쟁점에 대하여 수정헌법 제2조의 비준·발효 이후 처음으로 직접적이고 결론적

---

111 이 번역문은 해제대상논문에서 저자의 번역을 옮겨온 것이다.

112 해제대상 논문에서도 1989년 Sanford Levinson 교수의 논문이 발표되면서 본격적인 논의가 시작되었다고 밝히고 있다.

113 해제대상 논문은 저자가 1996년에서 1997년 사이 미국에서 방문교수를 하시던 시기에 작성되었는데 이 시기에는 1995년의 오클라호마 시 소재 연방정부 폭파사건으로 수정헌법 제2조에 대한 논의가 가속화된 시기였다. 이처럼 수정헌법 제2조를 둘러싼 논의의 폭과 깊이는 일반적으로 처참한 희생을 경험하면서 넓어지고 깊어져 왔다.

114 안경환, 『미국 헌법의 이해』 & 해제(解題) 박종현, "미국 연방헌법 수정 제2조의 의미"[1997], 박영사, 2014, 603면.

115 동 판결에 대한 자세한 소개는 해제대상논문의 저자가 감수한 강건우, 「더 나인(The Nine)」, 라이프 맵, 2010을 참조해도 좋다.

인 유권해석을 내렸다. 사안은 가정에서 총기 소유를 금지한 워싱턴 D.C.의 규제조치에 대한 사법심사였다. 워싱턴 당국은 수정헌법 제2조의 권리를 집단적 권리로 보았기 때문에 이에 대한 규제는 문제없다는 입장이었다. 하지만 연방대법원은 5:4로 D.C.의 조치가 위헌적이라 하였다.[116] 원의주의적(originalism) 해석을 동원하여 수정헌법 제2조의 본래적 의의를 추적한 스칼리아(Scalia) 대법관은 다수의견을 집필하며 헌법이 개인이 가정에서 정당방위를 위한 총기 소지나 총기 사용을 절대적으로 금지하도록 허용하지 않는다고 하며 수정헌법 제2조의 무기소장권이 개인적 권리임을 분명히 하였다. 그렇다고 이 판결이 정신이상자들이나 범죄자들의 총기소유를 허용하는 것은 아니라고 하며, 주 정부들이 규제입법을 마련하는 경우에는 입법이 헌법에 합치되게 노력해야 한다는 점을 강조하였다. 총기 규제입법을 실시하던 각 주에서는 이 판결에 반발하였지만 당시 대통령인 조지 W 부시 대통령과 2008년 대선에 출마한 공화당의 존 매케인과 민주당의 버락 오바마 후보 모두 대법원의 판결에 찬성 표시를 하였다. 오바마의 경우 총기규제를 허용하자는 민주당의 당론과 상충되는 입장을 밝혔는데 이는 상당한 숫자의 총기소지지들과 정계에 강력한 영향력을 행사하고 있는 총기제조업자들의 표를 의식한 입장 표명이었다."[117][118]

---

116 다수의견은 스칼리아(Scalia) 대법관이 작성하였는데 로버츠(Roberts) 대법원장과 케네디(Kennedy), 토마스(Thomas), 알리토(Alito) 대법관이 참여하였다. 그리고 반대의견은 스티븐스(Stevens0 대법관이 작성하였는데 이에는 수터(Souter), 긴즈버그(Ginsburg), 브레이어(Breyer) 대법관이 참여하였다.

117 향후 기회가 된다면 연작으로서 해제대상논문의 후속 논문을 작성해보고 싶다. 특히 해제대상논문에서 집중한 수정헌법 제2조의 기본권의 역사적 의의에 대한 고찰과 더불어 민주주의와 인간의 존엄성이라는 목적적 가치에 보다 집중하며 수정헌법 제2조의 의미를 살펴보고 싶다. 무엇보다도 누구의 권리인가라는 질문보다는 누구를 위한 권리인가라는 질문에 답을 구하는 측면에서 수정헌법 제2조에 접근해보고 싶다.

118 안경환, 『미국 헌법의 이해』 & 해제(解題) 박종현, "미국 연방헌법 수정 제2조의 의미"[1997], 박영사, 2014, 607-608면.

8. The Media and the Second Amendment to the Constitution of the United States

- 미국 연방헌법 수정조항 제2조와 미디어 -

C. Mo Bahk (박창모), Ph.D.*

The Second Amendment to the Constitution, ratified in 1791, has long been a defining element of legal and cultural identity for people in the United States. Its terse language — guaranteeing the right of the people to keep and bear arms in the context of a "well regulated Militia"— has generated enduring legal debate and social contestation. While early interpretations emphasized collective security through militias, recent decades have witnessed a jurisprudential and public shift toward affirming individual gun rights, notably through landmark rulings such as District of Columbia v. Heller (2008) and New York State Rifle & Pistol Association v. Bruen (2022). Nonetheless, these legal transformations do not occur in a vacuum but unfold amid dynamic media environments that profoundly influence public understanding and discourse.

Media institutions — encompassing traditional news outlets, partisan platforms, and social media — play a pivotal role in framing how the Second Amendment is perceived, discussed, and politicized. Through agenda-setting, framing, priming, and cultivation processes, the media select which narratives dominate and which issues gain public prominence, thereby shaping collective attitudes toward gun rights, regulation, and constitutional freedoms. This mediation is consequential, as

---

* California State University (San Bernardino, California), 캘리포니아 주립대학교 교수(언론학박사).

it not only reflects but actively constructs ideological divides and policy fault lines in U.S. society. Moreover, the fragmented and often polarized media landscape fosters echo chambers and spiral of silence dynamics, wherein individuals may self-censor dissenting views, further exacerbating division around firearm policy debates. The reciprocal influence between media discourse and legal interpretations underscores the necessity of understanding the Second Amendment as a socially and culturally mediated constitutional right. This chapter critically examines the intersection between media influence and the evolving interpretation of the Second Amendment. Drawing on foundational media theories and contemporary empirical research, it explores how diverse media ecosystems shape public opinion, legislative behavior, and judicial reasoning regarding gun rights. In doing so, it advances a comprehensive framework for analyzing the media's constitutive role in the constitution's ongoing meaning and implications for democratic deliberation in the digital age.

Ⅰ. The U.S. Constitution and the Second Amendment

The United States Constitution, along with its amendments, holds profound significance in US society as the foundational legal document that structures government, protects individual liberties, and guides the nation's democratic processes. Adopted in 1787, the Constitution established a framework of government based on the separation of powers, checks and balances, and federalism, ensuring that no single branch or level of government could dominate the others (Redx Magazine, 2025). This structure is essential for maintaining stability, accountability, and the rule of law in the United States. The original document consists of seven articles, which delineate the powers and responsibilities of the legislative, executive, and judicial branches, as well as the relationships among states and the process for amending the Constitution (Constitution Center, n.d.). The amendments — 27 to date — allow the Constitution to adapt to changing societal values and needs. The first ten amendments, known as the Bill of Rights, guarantee fundamental freedoms such as speech, religion, assembly, and due process, and have become cornerstones of U.S. civil liberties (Constitution Center, n.d.). The amendment process itself is a testament to the Constitution's flexibility and resilience. It requires broad consensus, ensuring that changes reflect the will of the people and not fleeting political interests (Constitution Center, n.d.). This adaptability has enabled the nation to address historical injustices, such as abolishing slavery (13th Amendment), extending voting rights regardless of race (15th Amendment) or gender (19th Amendment), and lowering the voting age to 18 (26th Amendment).

The Constitution's system of checks and balances is crucial for preventing the concentration of power and preserving democratic governance. For example, Congress creates laws, the president enforces them, and the judiciary interprets their constitutionality, with each branch able to limit the powers of the others (Redx Magazine, 2025). The amendments, in particular, reflect the evolving understanding of justice and equality in US society. They have been instrumental in expanding civil rights and liberties, often in response to social movements and demands for greater inclusion (Constitution Center, n.d.). The Bill of Rights, for example, continues to be invoked in contemporary debates over free speech, religious freedom, gun rights, and due process, demonstrating the enduring relevance of these protections. The Constitution remains a symbol of unity and a beacon for democratic ideals. Its promise of a government "of the people, by the people, and for the people" continues to inspire people to participate in civic life and to defend the values of freedom, equality, and justice (Redx Magazine, 2025).

The Second Amendment to the U.S. Constitution holds enduring significance in US society, shaping legal, cultural, and political landscapes for over two centuries. Ratified in 1791 as part of the Bill of Rights, the Second Amendment states: "A well regulated militia, being necessary to the security of a free state, the right of the people to keep and bear arms, shall not be infringed." Its original intent was to provide a constitutional check on federal power, ensure state security, and protect against tyranny, reflecting the Founders' experiences under British rule and their concerns about standing armies and centralized authority (Britannica, 2025; USConstitution.net, 2024). Historically, the Second Amendment was rooted in English common law and the English Bill of Rights of 1689, which recognized the right of subjects to have arms for their defense (Law.Cornell.edu, 2016). In the US context, this right was linked to the idea of a "well-regulated militia" composed of ordinary citizens, seen as a safeguard for liberty and a bulwark against government overreach (USConstitution.net, 2024). The Founders, influenced by both Federalist and Anti-Federalist perspectives, believed that an armed citizenry was essential for resisting oppression and protecting individual freedoms (USConstitution.net, 2024; Britannica, 2025). Over time, the interpretation of the Second Amendment has evolved. While its early meaning emphasized the collective right of states to maintain militias, modern legal and societal debates have increasingly focused on individual rights. This shift was solidified by the Supreme Court's decision in District of Columbia v. Heller (2008), which affirmed that the Second Amendment protects an individual's right to possess firearms for self-defense in the home, independent of militia service (USConstitution.net, 2024). Subsequent rulings, such as McDonald v. City of Chicago (2010), extended this protection to state and local governments, underscoring the amendment's nationwide applicability. The Second Amendment is both a legal right and a cultural touchstone, reflecting the complexities of US history and the continuing challenge of balancing individual freedoms with collective security.

Ⅱ. The Media and the Second Amendment

The media plays a pivotal role in shaping public perceptions and opinions about the Second Amendment, gun ownership, and gun-related regulations in the United States. Media outlets, both legacy/traditional (mainstream) and digital/social, often use selective depictions and emotional appeals to sway public opinion. For example, media's graphic coverage of mass shootings can generate empathy and outrage, increasing support for gun control, while stories in the media emphasizing defensive gun use can reinforce pro-gun rights attitudes. More recent studies show that exposure to media coverage of mass shootings increases support for policies that regulate who can own or purchase firearms (Pro-Papers, 2024). Through such practices of selective coverage, framing, and agenda-setting, media outlets influence not only what issues the public considers important, but also how those issues are interpreted and discussed. Media coverage can drive spikes in public attention and shifts in opinion, particularly in the aftermath of mass shootings or significant legislative actions. For instance, major news events and presidential statements have been shown to correlate with increased media coverage and public debate about gun policy (Pew Research Center, 2013). Social media and online platforms further amplify these effects by enabling rapid dissemination and discussion of gun-related news.

Media coverage is closely linked to public engagement and policy outcomes. The way news outlets frame gun violence and regulation affects not only public opinion but also legislative priorities and the likelihood of policy change (MDPI, 2024; Pro-Papers, 2024). For example, coverage that emphasizes mental health or personal accountability may shift the focus of policy discussions away from firearms themselves and toward other factors. Concerns about media bias are prevalent among the public. Surveys indicate that people tend to perceive bias in how the media cover gun issues, which can reinforce existing beliefs and contribute to polarization (Pew Research Center, 2013; Second Amendment Foundation, n.d.). This underscores the media's power not only to inform but also to divide, depending on the framing and selection of stories.

The media's role in shaping public perceptions and opinions regarding the Second Amendment and gun policy is significant and multifaceted. Through framing, agenda-setting, and amplification of certain narratives, media outlets influence how individuals understand their rights, the risks of gun violence, and the appropriate scope of regulations. The media not only reflect public attitudes but also actively shape them. Understanding this dynamic is essential for comprehending the evolving landscape of gun rights and regulations in the United States (Chamblee, 2024; Pro-Papers, 2024).

Ⅲ. Media Coverage of Court Rulings on the Second Amendment

The Second Amendment of the U.S. Constitution, which protects the right to keep and bear arms, has been at the center of legal, political, and cultural debates for decades. Milestone Supreme Court decisions — notably District of Columbia v. Heller (2008), McDonald v. City of Chicago (2010), and New York State Rifle & Pistol Association v. Bruen (2022) — have dramatically reshaped the legal landscape surrounding gun rights and regulation. The media's coverage of these decisions has played a critical role in shaping public discourse, influencing policy debates, and framing the constitutional and societal stakes involved. The Second Amendment has long been a subject of intense debate, with its interpretation evolving alongside shifts in political and cultural attitudes toward gun ownership and regulation. Historically, the media has both reflected and shaped public sentiment, often amplifying the stakes of Supreme Court decisions and their implications for US society (PBS News, 2023).

District of Columbia v. Heller (2008) was the first Supreme Court case to affirm that the Second Amendment protects an individual's right to possess firearms unconnected with service in a militia. The decision received extensive media coverage, with outlets framing it as a watershed moment in US constitutional law (Retro Report, 2025). Coverage of Heller and McDonald decisions marked a shift in the media's narratives of the Second Amendment, with increased emphasis on individual rights rather than collective or militia-based interpretations. This shift mirrored the arguments advanced by gun rights advocates and was reflected in both news reporting and editorial commentary (Retro Report, 2025). Media coverage often highlighted the ideological split within the Court and the broader societal implications, frequently quoting both gun rights advocates and gun control proponents. McDonald v. City of Chicago (2010) extended the Heller decision, holding that the Second Amendment applies to state and local governments through the Fourteenth Amendment. Media coverage of McDonald emphasized its potential to spur new legal challenges to gun regulations nationwide and its significance for both urban and rural communities (Retro Report, 2025). News outlets often juxtaposed celebratory statements from gun rights activists with warnings from gun control advocates about the potential risks to public safety. The 2022 Supreme Court decision in New York State Rifle & Pistol Association v. Bruen strengthened Second Amendment rights by overturning New York's rule that required people to give a special reason to carry a hidden gun in public. News outlets highlighted how the ruling quickly affected gun laws nationwide and created confusion for lower courts and state lawmakers (CNN, 2023; PBS News, 2023).

Media framing theory notes that the media shape public perception by emphasizing certain aspects of an issue while downplaying others. In the context of Second Amendment jurisprudence, media outlets have been found to frame Supreme Court decisions in ways that reflect broader political and cultural divides (PBS News, 2023). For example, conservative-leaning outlets often frame the decisions as victories for individual liberty and constitutional rights, while progressive outlets may emphasize concerns about public safety and the potential for increased gun violence. Media coverage frequently employs emotionally charged language and imagery, particularly in the wake of mass shootings or high-profile gun violence incidents. This can influence how audiences interpret the significance of Supreme Court decisions, sometimes conflating legal rulings with broader debates about gun culture and violence in the United States (Retro Report, 2025). The media's choice of sources — legal experts, advocacy groups, victims, and politicians—shapes the narrative and perceived legitimacy of Supreme Court decisions. Coverage of the court cases often features a "dueling quotes" format, presenting statements from both gun rights and gun control advocates, which can reinforce polarization rather than foster nuanced understanding (AP, 2025). Media coverage of Supreme Court decisions plays a crucial role in shaping public understanding of constitutional rights and legal precedents. Research suggests that the general public often relies on media summaries and commentary rather than reading judicial opinions directly, making the accuracy and framing of news reports particularly consequential (PBS News, 2023).

The media's portrayal of Supreme Court decisions can influence legislative and policy debates at both the state and federal levels. For example, the coverage of the Bruen decision by the Supreme Court, protecting an individual's right to carry a handgun in public for self-defense, prompted immediate reactions from lawmakers and advocacy groups, with some states moving to revise their gun laws in response to the ruling (AP, 2025). The Bruen decision generated widespread media attention, with many reports highlighting the uncertainty it created for lower courts and state legislatures tasked with interpreting the new standard for gun regulations. Coverage often emphasized the potential for a wave of legal challenges and the possibility of further Supreme Court intervention (CNN, 2023; AP, 2025). Advocacy organizations such as the National Rifle Association (NRA) and

Everytown for Gun Safety have also played a significant role in shaping media narratives around Supreme Court decisions. These groups provide quotes, legal analysis, and ready-made talking points that are frequently incorporated into news coverage, further influencing public perception and policy debates (AP, 2025).

One of the primary critiques of media coverage of Second Amendment court cases is the tendency toward oversimplification and sensationalism. Complex legal reasoning is often reduced to soundbites, and the broader constitutional context may be neglected in favor of more dramatic or emotionally resonant narratives (Retro Report, 2025). Media reports can also sometimes misrepresent the scope or implications of Supreme Court decisions, leading to public confusion. For instance, coverage may suggest that a ruling completely invalidates all gun regulations, when in reality, the Court may have left significant regulatory authority intact (PBS News, 2023). The fragmented media landscape, with its proliferation of partisan outlets and social media platforms, can exacerbate polarization around Second Amendment issues. Audiences may gravitate toward sources that reinforce their preexisting views, deepening divides and complicating efforts to build consensus on gun policy (AP, 2025). While the media serve as a critical conduit for information about Supreme Court rulings, its coverage is often shaped by broader political, cultural, and ideological currents. As debates over gun rights and regulation continue to evolve, the role of the media in shaping public understanding and policy responses remains both significant and contested.

Recent news reports on Supreme Court gun decisions consistently highlight several prominent themes. First, there is a strong focus on the balance between public safety and gun rights. Media coverage frequently frames the debate as a tension between the need to reduce gun violence and the constitutional protections of the Second Amendment, especially in the wake of mass shootings or high-profile incidents. For example, the Maryland ban on semiautomatic rifles was enacted after the Sandy Hook Elementary School shooting and is often discussed in terms of its intent to promote public safety while facing criticism from gun rights advocates who argue it infringes on constitutional rights (AP News, 2025; Legal Report, 2025; The New York Times, 2025). A second major theme is the Court's judicial philosophy and evolving interpretation of the Second Amendment. News outlets emphasize how recent decisions, such as New York State Rifle & Pistol Association v. Bruen, have shifted the legal landscape by requiring gun laws to align with the nation's historical tradition. This new test has created challenges for lower courts, which must now assess the historical roots of modern gun regulations, leading to increased legal uncertainty and debate (SCOTUSblog, 2025; The Trace, 2025). Regulatory uncertainty and legal flux are also prominent themes. Reports note that Supreme Court rulings have made it more challenging for states and cities to regulate firearms, resulting in confusion and a wave of litigation over which gun laws will withstand judicial scrutiny. This uncertainty is further compounded by the Court's reluctance to provide detailed reasoning when declining to hear certain cases, leaving lower courts and lawmakers with little guidance (AP News, 2025; The Trace, 2025).

Coverage underscores the polarized nature of the debate, regularly quoting both gun rights advocates — who frame decisions as victories for individual liberty — and gun control supporters, who warn of increased risks to public safety. The influence of advocacy groups, such as the National Rifle Association and Brady, is frequently highlighted in shaping public discourse and legal challenges (AP News, 2025; VOA News, 2025). Another recurring theme is the immediate and broader impact of specific rulings. News reports analyze how Supreme Court decisions affect existing gun laws, future litigation, and the actions of lawmakers and courts nationwide. For instance, the Court's upholding of federal restrictions on "ghost guns" (unregistered, untraceable firearms with no serial numbers) is reported as a win for law enforcement, while gun rights groups continue to seek legal avenues to challenge such regulations (Legal Report, 2025; NPR, 2025). Finally, many articles reference public opinion and societal debate, noting that a majority of people support some form of gun regulation, even as the legal environment becomes more complex. Reports often provide technical details about specific laws and regulations, illustrating the practical consequences of Supreme Court rulings and the ongoing societal debate over gun rights and regulation (PBS News, 2023; The Trace, 2025). These themes reflect the complexity of the issues at stake and the media's role in shaping both the legal and societal dimensions of Supreme Court gun decisions.

Ⅳ. Mechanisms of Media Influence on Second Amendment Issues

The Second Amendment to the U.S. Constitution, which guarantees the right to keep and bear arms, has long been a contentious issue in political discourse. Public perceptions of this right, and of gun control more broadly, are not formed in a vacuum but are shaped by cultural, political, and notably, media influences. A 2008 Gallup poll found that in the U.S., 73% of people viewed the Second Amendment as affirming an individual's right to own guns, a view solidified by the Supreme Court's District of Columbia v. Heller decision that same year. This legal affirmation was widely covered by the media and likely reinforced pro-gun public sentiment. Polling data over the past few decades reveals significant fluctuations in public attitudes toward gun rights and gun control, often in response to media coverage of gun-related events including mass shootings. According to Gallup (2023), public support for stricter gun laws in the United States reached a high point of 67% in 2018, following the mass shooting at Marjory Stoneman Douglas High School in Parkland, Florida. However, this support declined to 57% by 2022, reflecting a broader pattern of fluctuating public opinion in response to major gun-related events. Partisan divisions have become increasingly pronounced, with 91% of Democrats endorsing more restrictive gun legislation, compared to just 24% of Republicans. Concurrently, there has been a steady increase in public endorsement of the Second Amendment as affirming an individual right to bear arms, a view that has gained greater legal and cultural traction over time.

Media coverage plays a dual role in both shaping and reflecting public perceptions of the Second Amendment and issues related to gun ownership and regulation. Through mechanisms such as agenda-setting, cultivation, framing, and priming, the media influence how the public understands gun issues, often reinforcing or challenging prevailing cultural and political attitudes (Chamblee, 2024; Pro-Papers, 2024).

Agenda Setting. The media's agenda-setting function has long been recognized as a critical force in shaping public perceptions and opinions about contentious political topics, foremost among them the Second Amendment and gun policy debates. The agenda-setting paradigm, originally articulated by McCombs and Shaw (1972), posits that the news media significantly influence the public agenda by determining which issues are highlighted and thus perceived as important (see also McCombs & Guo, 2014). This dynamic is often evident in the aftermath of high-profile mass shootings, which often lead to spikes in media attention and correlated changes in public opinion. For instance, following the 2012 Sandy Hook Elementary School shooting, media coverage on gun violence surged, and polls showed a temporary increase in public support for stricter gun laws. The 2013 Pew Research Center survey conducted shortly afterward reported that 51% of Americans favored stricter gun control, up from 47% the previous year. Agenda-setting occurs as media outlets determine which gun-related topics receive attention. High-profile shootings and Supreme Court rulings often trigger spikes in both traditional and social media, temporarily shifting public sentiment and increasing support for gun control measures (Pew Research Center, 2013). In the context of gun control and Second Amendment discourse, empirical studies demonstrate that intense media attention to events such as mass shootings can lead to temporary spikes in public support for stricter gun regulations, reinforcing the media's role in making certain policy topics more salient to the public (Pew Research Center, 2013).

However, agenda-setting effects are rarely uniform or uncontested. As Ghanem (1997) and subsequent researchers have observed, the "compelling arguments" hypothesis suggests that not only do the media set the agenda as to what the public thinks about, but through attribute agenda-setting (sometimes referred to as "second-level" agenda-setting), the way in which issues are discussed — i.e., the emphasis on specific aspects or attributes — can influence the how of public thinking on those topics. For example, exposure to media coverage that presents gun violence as a matter of public health versus individual rights may lead audiences to adopt different evaluative criteria and policy preferences regarding gun regulation. Additionally, the agenda-setting power of the media is often moderated by audience segmentation and political polarization. As explored by Benkler et al. (2018) and corroborated by Guo et al. (2024), conservative and liberal media ecosystems not only highlight different gun-related issues, but also foster echo chambers that reinforce existing beliefs and either encourage or dampen political expression depending on ideological congruity. For instance, conservatives who primarily engage with media that reinforces their existing views are unlikely to significantly change their opinions. However, when people are exposed to media that challenges their beliefs — such as liberals viewing conservative news, or vice versa — they may experience feelings of uncertainty or ambivalence. This exposure can also make individuals hesitant to express their political views online, as they may worry about social pressure or negative reactions from friends and acquaintances.

Although media coverage can rapidly increase the public salience of gun policy in the wake of high-profile events, such effects may quickly wane without sustained coverage and are continuously mediated by entrenched cultural and political identities. Studies show that long-term attitudes are less flexible, shaped over time by continued media narratives and deeper socialization processes (Benkler et al., 2018; Columbia Law School, 2010). Beyond issue salience, scholars have emphasized the interplay between agenda setting and framing. While agenda-setting theory explicates why certain topics are prioritized, framing theory delves into how the selected issues are presented, which further guides public interpretations and policy preferences. Manipulative or selective framing — highlighting some attributes while down playing others — can produce powerful effects on public opinion and behavior regarding gun control. The scholarly literature provides robust evidence for the media's crucial agenda-setting role in Second Amendment debates. The media not only elevate the salience of gun-related issues during critical moments, but through selective emphasis and narration, shape both the contour and tone of public discourse.

Media Framing. While media agenda-setting focuses on "which" issues the media elevate to public prominence, media framing provides a more nuanced analysis of "how" those issues are portrayed in the media in shaping public interpretations, judgments, and political preferences (Chong & Druckman, 2007: Entman, 1993). According to Entman (1993), framing involves the strategic selection and emphasis of "certain aspects" of a perceived reality so they become more salient in communication, thereby promoting particular problem definitions, causal attributions, moral evaluations, and treatment recommendations. This process can influence how individuals evaluate policy issues such as those involving the Second Amendment and gun regulations.

Studies have documented that media coverage of gun-related issues typically pivots around two primary and often antagonistic frames: "gun rights frames" and "gun control frames" (Chamblee, 2024; McGinty et al., 2013; Steidley, 2017). These polarizing frames encapsulate not only competing policy perspectives but also fundamentally different views of identity, liberty, and public safety. Gun rights framing, predominantly employed by conservative and right-leaning media outlets such as Fox News and Breitbart News, foregrounds the inviolability of the Second Amendment. This framing emphasizes individual liberty, self-defense, and constitutional originalism, rejecting gun control as governmental overreach or ineffective "feel-good laws" that fail to reduce violence (Chamblee, 2024; Speakman & Funk, 2020; Callaghan & Schnell, 2001). For example, slogans like "Guns Don't Kill People, People Kill People" deflect responsibility from firearms to individuals, placing blame on mental illness, criminality, or cultural failings (McGinty et al., 2016; Chamblee, 2024). Right-leaning media also often employ propaganda and fear-mongering frames, as evidenced in Fox News programming (Nassar, 2020), which bolster a worldview skeptical of both gun regulation and certain public health narratives. In contrast, gun control framing, prevalent in left-leaning and mainstream national media such as CNN, The New York Times, and MSNBC, constructs gun violence primarily as a public health/safety crisis (Chamblee, 2024; McGinty et al., 2013). This framing draws attention to the pervasive harm caused by firearms, the accessibility of assault weapons, and failures in existing regulations. By highlighting statistical evidence and social costs, the media can advocate policy responses like universal background checks, assault weapons bans, and red flag laws (Boydstun, Gross, & Resnik, 2011). Importantly, these frames embed a moral evaluation that casts gun control as a societal responsibility necessary to protect vulnerable populations.

Research demonstrates the influence of frames on public attitudes toward gun policy. McGinty et al. (2013) found that in the wake of mass shootings, media coverage often emphasized mental illness and policy failures over gun access, particularly in conservative outlets, thereby diverting public discourse from stricter gun regulations. Similarly, Boydstun et al. (2011) demonstrated through content analysis that framing gun violence through public safety lenses increased public support for regulation, whereas rights-based framing strengthened opposition. These framing effects are further complicated by episodic versus thematic framing distinctions. Following Iyengar's (1991) seminal work, subsequent studies confirm that episodic framing — highlighting isolated incidents such as mass shootings — elicits strong emotional responses, which can temporarily spike public support for targeted policies (Chamblee, 2024; Pro-Papers, 2024). However, episodic frames tend to personalize rather than contextualize gun violence, often obscuring systemic factors like gun industry influence or legislative gaps. In contrast, thematic framing situates gun violence within broader social, economic, and political contexts, encouraging more sophisticated public understanding and sustained policy engagement (Chamblee, 2024; Pro-Papers, 2024).

Moreover, different media platforms and modalities display varying framing patterns. A study examining cable news coverage of the 2017 Sutherland Springs mass shooting revealed notable divergences among CNN, Fox News, and MSNBC in their framing emphases, with Fox adopting a stronger emphasis on Second Amendment rights and individual responsibility, while CNN and MSNBC foregrounded victim empathy and community safety (Emelu, 2023). Further, research into digital platforms (e.g., Twitter, YouTube) shows that framing and agenda-setting extend into new media environments, where partisan echo chambers intensify exposure to ideologically congruent frames and foster polarized political expression (Guo et al., 2024; Wasike, 2017). The effects of media framing are moderated by audience partisanship and selective exposure. Scholars have consistently found that individuals who primarily consume right-leaning media are less likely to support gun control measures, internalizing constitutional rights framing and skeptical attitudes toward regulatory efficacy (Chamblee, 2024; Pew Research Center, 2013; Speakman & Funk, 2020). Conversely, consumers of left-leaning or mainstream media manifest stronger support for gun regulation, broadly endorsing public health/safety frames (ScholarWorks, 2024). This polarization in media framing contributes to a fragmented media landscape mirroring and amplifying the nation's ideological divide over gun policy (Benkler, Faris, & Roberts, 2018; Chamblee, 2024). Moreover, framing intersects with hegemonic discourse formation whereby dominant ideological frames become normalized and unquestioned within certain media spheres (McGinty et al., 2016). This phenomenon limits cross-cutting exposure and entrenches partisan worldviews, complicating consensus-building efforts on gun violence prevention.

Emerging scholarship highlights social media's increasingly vital role in framing gun debates. Studies indicate that social media platforms can both amplify traditional frames and generate novel framings through viral grassroots advocacy or opposition (Wasike, 2017; Guo et al., 2024). Tremayne and Minooie (2013) discovered that after the Aurora shooting, Twitter users who opposed gun control and acted as opinion leaders generated significantly more discussion and engagement around the topic than those who supported gun control. This finding highlights an imbalance in how framing influences discussions on digital platforms. Furthermore, research shows that framing effects on social media may differ in magnitude and credibility from traditional news due to perceived source trustworthiness and media format (Wasike, 2017). These dynamics underscore the evolving and complex landscape through which framing shapes public opinion in the digital age.

Media Priming. Media priming theory offers a robust framework for examining how the media subtly, yet powerfully, influences the cognitive processes that underpin public attitudes toward highly salient political issues such as the Second Amendment and gun policy in the United States (Iyengar & Kinder, 1987; Hart & Middleton, 2012). Situated within the broader agenda-setting tradition, priming is classically concerned with how mass media shape the standards, or evaluative criteria that citizens employ when assessing political actors, public policies, and social problems (Iyengar et al., 1984; Hoewe, 2020). Unlike direct persuasion or overt attitude change, priming operates largely through the elevation of issue salience — the prominence of particular topics made repeatedly visible — and the activation of associated cognitive frameworks that become accessible, even in the absence of conscious awareness (Hoewe, 2020; Chamblee, 2024).

At its core, media priming involves cognitive activation, whereby repeated or recent exposure to particular news themes — such as gun violence, gun rights jurisprudence, or legislative debates — increases the mental availability of related concepts (Krosnick & Kinder, 1990). For example, extensive media coverage of mass shootings and legislative responses primes audiences to consider concepts such as public safety, risk minimization, and regulatory efficacy when evaluating policy proposals or political candidates (McGinty et al., 2016; Chamblee, 2024). Importantly, these primed ideas become the default lens — evaluation criteria — through which subsequent information is judged (Iyengar & Kinder, 1987). This process can be explained through models of cognitive accessibility and schema activation, where concepts recently or repeatedly encountered are more likely to shape interpretation and recall (Higgins, 1996).

Priming is distinguishable from framing: while framing concerns how an issue is described or interpreted in the media (e.g., gun ownership as constitutional liberty versus social threat), priming influences which mental constructs and considerations are used in the evaluative process (Iyengar & Kinder, 1987; Chong & Druckman, 2007). Thus, framing governs the "how" of thinking, while priming controls the "what." For Second Amendment issues, this means that framing may highlight either the protective function of gun rights or the social costs of gun proliferation, but priming determines whether considerations of liberty, safety, or constitutional integrity dominate public judgment at a given moment (Chamblee, 2024; Speakman & Funk, 2020).

Empirical studies demonstrate the real-world mechanisms and consequences of priming. Intensive media attention — particularly following high-profile incidents such as mass shootings or Supreme Court decisions — leads to the recency effect, whereby the most recently activated ideas (for example, "danger" or "right to self-defense") become especially influential in shaping attitudes (Hart & Middleton, 2012). Over longer timeframes, when news sources repeatedly emphasize certain themes, this results in chronic accessibility; cognitive schemas linking guns with, say, governmental overreach or public health risk, become habitually available for ongoing political evaluation (Higgins, 1996; Chamblee, 2024).

The complexity deepens in a fragmented media environment characterized by partisan segmentation and selective exposure (Stroud, 2008). Right-leaning news outlets frequently prime concepts such as constitutional rights, individual freedom, and suspicion of state regulation, which cues audiences to evaluate gun policy primarily in terms of personal liberty and government intrusion (Speakman & Funk, 2020; Chamblee, 2024). In contrast, mainstream and left-leaning media more often prime public safety concerns, injury prevention, and communal well-being, raising the salience of regulatory effectiveness and social impact (McGinty et al., 2016; Scholar Works, 2024). These divergent patterns of chronic priming reinforce existing political predispositions and help explain the persistence and amplification of policy polarization (Prior, 2013).

Experimental research underscores just how malleable evaluative standards can become in response to priming. Hart and Middleton (2012) found that as issues become more salient via media exposure, citizens increase the weight assigned to those issues when making judgments about politicians and public policy. Extending this line of argument, Seo (2007) introduces the concepts of issue-specific learning and projection effects, admitting the possibility that individuals not only become primed to attend to certain issues but also project their preexisting attitudes onto new information, thereby intensifying pre-existing evaluative frameworks. Chamblee (2024), investigating partisan media consumption, provides empirical support for the idea that congruent media reinforce priming effects: conservative media usage predicts lower support for gun regulation, while liberal media consumption bolsters support for gun control, with such differences mediated by the specific considerations media repeatedly render salient.

Importantly, priming is not synonymous with direct attitude change; rather, it represents the subtle recalibration of what factors are considered most relevant, a process often unfolding outside conscious reflection or deliberation (Hoewe, 2020; Krosnick & Kinder, 1990). The implications for democracy are significant: shifts in media agendas can recalibrate public priorities, heighten the urgency or legitimacy of policy debates, and alter the very standards of assessment brought to electoral or policy decision-making (Sheafer & Weimann, 2005).

Furthermore, Hart and Middleton's (2012) experimental reassessment of the projection hypothesis finds that people's overall attitudes and candidate evaluations can shape, and are shaped by, issue considerations primed by the media — a dynamic, bidirectional relationship. Such findings indicate that media priming does not occur in a cognitive vacuum but is enmeshed in the complex interplay of individual psychology, motivated reasoning, and selective exposure (Stroud, 2008; Taber & Lodge, 2006).

The priming function of the media provides a nuanced, empirically supported model for understanding how individuals evaluate Second Amendment issues. By repeatedly activating certain considerations — such as constitutional rights, public health, or personal safety — media primes structure the cognitive environment within which public and private judgments are made. Especially in an environment of ideologically filtered and repetitive exposure, these priming effects reinforce existing divisions, heighten polarization, and indirectly — but powerfully — shape political attitudes and policy debates around gun rights (Iyengar & Kinder, 1987; Chamblee, 2024; Hart & Middleton, 2012).

Media Cultivation. Cultivation theory, first articulated by George Gerbner and colleagues (Gerbner et al., 1976), provides a foundational framework for understanding how prolonged exposure to mediated content — especially television — shapes individuals' perceptions of social reality. This theory is central to analyzing how media representations of guns, violence, and Second Amendment issues influence public opinion, risk perceptions, and policy making in the United States. Cultivation theory posits that television and other mass media do not directly persuade viewers in a single exposure but exert their influence cumulatively, cultivating shared understandings or "cultures" about social issues. According to Gerbner et al. (1976), long-term exposure leads audiences to adopt a mediated version of reality — a phenomenon most classically observed in this context as the "mean world syndrome," where viewers overestimate violence and personal risk due to its prevalence in media environments. The theory has three core assumptions. First, television (and by extension, mass media) plays a unique socializing role, binding society with shared symbolic stories. Second, media's primary influence is gradual, shaping basic conceptions about the world rather than direct, immediate change. Third, media cultivate shared notions of norms, roles, and policy attitudes among the public.

Empirical studies support that heavy television and news viewers internalize media representations of violence, crime, and risk, which in turn shape attitudes about gun ownership and the Second Amendment. For instance, people who consume a high volume of crime dramas or sensational news are more likely to perceive their environment as dangerous and are more supportive of self-defense measures, including gun ownership and concealed carry rights. Also, regular viewers of media featuring defensive gun use or depictions of violent crime often exhibit decreased support for gun control, underpinned by the belief that being armed is the most effective protection against crime. A notable survey-based study using the National Opinion Survey on Crime and Justice (N=1,005) found that television was the primary source of crime news for 66% of respondents, and those with greater exposure to crime-relevant programming were more likely to oppose gun control (Dowler, 2002).

The "mean world syndrome" outlined by Gerbner is especially relevant in the American context, where pervasive media coverage often constructs an exaggerated sense of personal vulnerability and social disorder. This heightened fear and risk perception bolster justifications for gun ownership as a tool for personal security, directly impacting beliefs about the Second Amendment. Moreover, the tendency for mass media to dramatize or sensationalize violent crimes, including mass shootings, can drive policy attitudes in conflicting directions. While episodic coverage of mass shootings may prompt support for gun regulation, continuous framing of the world as dangerous sustains or strengthens pro-gun, self-defense narratives — often mirroring polarized Second Amendment debates. Recent longitudinal research demonstrates that early and consistent exposure to media violence (television, movies, or video games) is modestly but significantly associated with normative acceptance of guns and increased risk of weapon carrying and use years later. This finding expands the cultivation framework beyond attitudinal effects to behavioral dispositions relevant to gun policy debates. Children and adolescents with greater media exposure to weapons violence were found to be more likely, ten years later, to carry weapons or be arrested for weapon-related crimes, even after controlling for other risk factors.

While traditional cultivation research focused on network television, recent work extends these ideas to digital media and social platforms. A 2023 Pew Research Center study suggests that although internet and social media use play a growing role in shaping attitudes toward guns, traditional demographic variables (e.g., political affiliation, race) remain the most significant predictors (Pew Research Center, 2023). Nonetheless, heavy digital media consumption can still amplify exposure to either pro-gun or pro-regulation narratives, especially when algorithmic curation fosters echo chambers. Research has shown that media cultivation processes shape foundational assumptions about guns, crime, and the Second Amendment. Persistent exposure to media portrayals of violence and crime is associated with increased fear and perceptions of risk, higher support for self-defense rights and gun ownership, lower support for gun regulation, particularly among heavy consumers of crime-centric or pro-gun media content including movies and television dramas. These cultivation effects are integral to understanding public attitudes and the enduring polarization of American gun policy. It is important to distinguish between cultivation and framing. Cultivation addresses long-term, cumulative impacts of repeated media messages — cultivating beliefs that the world is unsafe and that gun ownership is necessary — while framing focuses on the interpretation and salience of individual stories or narratives. Media coverage that frames gun rights as essential to safety and freedom, or conversely as contributors to violence, operates within the broader cultivation effect by reinforcing which worldviews become normalized over time.

Spiral of Silence. The Second Amendment, guaranteeing the right to keep and bear arms, remains a deeply polarizing issue. Public discourse on this topic is not merely shaped by legal arguments but by the dynamics of opinion expression and suppression. The Spiral of Silence theory, first introduced by Elisabeth Noelle-Neumann (Noelle-Neumann, 1974), offers a compelling framework for understanding the silencing mechanisms at play in debates surrounding contentious issues such as the Second Amendment. The theory is premised on the observation that individuals' willingness to express their views is strongly influenced by their perceptions of prevailing public opinion and their fear of social isolation. It is founded on several assumptions. First, it notes that people may refrain from expressing views that they believe are in the minority, fearing social ostracism. Second, people are believed to assess the climate of opinion using informal cues, media portrayals, and the attitudes of peers. Third, when minority viewpoints are withheld, "perceived" majority opinions may become more dominant, triggering a reinforcing cycle of silence for dissenters. Finally, people may wrongly presume that they are alone in their opinions, further amplifying silence, i.e., they become even more silent, reinforcing the spiral of silence.

Empirical studies confirm the relevance of the Spiral of Silence across a wide range of settings, including political debates and contentious social issues, although the strength and presence of the spiral can differ depending on context and topic (Noelle-Neumann, 1974; Zhao et al., 2024; Porten-Cheé & Eilders, 2015; Thurre, 2019). Public opinion on the Second Amendment has evolved considerably since the mid-20th century. Analysis of Gallup polling data and legal scholarship indicates there has been enduring and often substantial division on issues such as handgun bans and related regulations, with the percentage of "no" responses — those opposing broad handgun bans — outnumbering "yes" responses by significant margins since the late 1960s (Lund, 2015; Gallup, 2011; Gallup, 2024). How ever, the salience and public acceptability of arguments for gun control and gun rights have varied notably over time, often shifting in tandem with high-profile gun-related incidents and evolving pollical dynamics. These fluctuations are documented in both public opinion research and political science literature, which highlight the influence of focusing events, changes in threat perception, and partisan polarization on agenda setting and public attitudes surrounding gun policy (Newman & Hartman, 2017; Goss & Lacombe, 2023).

The Second Amendment debate is emblematic of the polarization, with gun rights advocacy often taking center stage in certain regions and social groups, while calls for gun control are more visible in others. In such a divided climate, expressing an unpopular viewpoint — whether pro- or anti-gun rights — may carry social risks, particularly in contexts where group consensus is strongly enforced. This dynamic directly invites the relevance of the Spiral of Silence. When the climate of opinion in a social or geographic milieu appears heavily pro-Second Amendment, individuals who support stricter gun control may self-censor, fearing backlash or ostracism. Conversely, in urban or progressive communities where gun control sentiment prevails, gun rights advocates may remain silent. This mirrors the classic spiral of silence process. Local and national media, as well as visible public displays (e.g., open-carry rallies, protest marches), often signal which opinions are "acceptable" or dominant. Social media amplification, peer pressure, or even threats may discourage dissenting expression, especially after polarizing events (e.g., mass shootings, Supreme Court rulings). Those seemingly holding minority views abstain from public discourse, reinforcing the perceived consensus. Lack of vocal opposition or support contributes to the solidification of dominant narratives, even if actual majority opinion is more nuanced (i.e., pluralistic ignorance).

The application extends to digital media. Studies suggest that while online anonymity and niche networks might empower minority voices, the overarching spiral of silence dynamic persists due to fear of social sanction, harassment, or digital isolation. For the Second Amendment debate, this means that both pro- and anti-gun rights supporters might seek echo chambers, selectively expressing opinions where they feel safe and remaining silent elsewhere. Legal scholarship observes that the relative expansion of Second Amendment protections, as seen in cases like Bruen, may produce "dangerous disparities" in fundamental rights, where public carry is broadly protected but public expression (First Amendment rights) remains tightly regulated and susceptible to restriction. If the exercise of gun rights is perceived to threaten or intimidate, this can chill speech and political activism, particularly for advocates of gun control — a unique, reciprocal silencing dynamic. Historical research shows that courts and lawmakers have often been guided by contemporary public opinion when shaping Second Amendment jurisprudence, highlighting the feedback loop between silent majorities, vocal minorities, and legal outcomes. When silence reigns, policy may not reflect the true complexity of public attitudes.

The Spiral of Silence remains a powerful framework for analyzing the discourse around the Second Amendment. Its concepts of perceived majority opinion, fear of isolation, and self-censorship elucidate why discussions on gun rights and regulation often appear more polarized or one-sided than true public opinion warrants. Recognizing these dynamics is crucial for understanding not only the rhetoric and policy related to the Second Amendment but the health of democratic debate itself. While media serve as powerful agents in shaping public attitudes, they also mirror the prevailing beliefs and expectations of their audiences. Journalistic routines, economic incentives, and audience segmentation encourage media outlets to align content with the ideological leanings of their consumer base. As Stroud (2008) demonstrates, individuals frequently gravitate toward partisan media that reaffirm their existing views, fostering ideological homogeneity and deepening polarization on contentious issues like gun rights. These dynamics are further reinforced by regional and cultural factors, as rural media often emphasize firearms in terms of self-defense, recreation, and heritage, whereas urban media tend to foreground the public health implications of gun violence. Such contextualized framing creates geographically and culturally distinct media climates that contribute to the maintenance of divergent public opinions on the Second Amendment. Within the framework of the Spiral of Silence, this feedback loop between media content and audience beliefs not only amplifies perceived majorities but also deters dissenting voices from speaking out — particularly in environments where ideological conformity is strongly signaled. As a result, media systems both reflect and entrench silencing pressures, further constraining open deliberation and sustaining polarized discourse around gun policy.

V. Digital/Social Media and the Second Amendment

The rise of digital media and social platforms has further complicated the media-public opinion relationship. Digital and social media have introduced new complexities. Social media platforms amplify ideological polarization by creating echo chambers where users are exposed primarily to views that reinforce their preexisting beliefs (Pew Research Center, 2013). Analysis of millions of Twitter posts revealed that the majority of online conversations about guns focus on legislative debates and high-profile incidents, with prominent terms like "gun control" and "Newtown" (the city in Connecticut where the Sandy Hook Elementary School shooting took place) dominating the discourse (Pew Research Center, 2013). At the same time, these platforms have enabled increased activism and rapid mobilization around gun policy, allowing advocacy groups and individuals to shape narratives and influence public debate in real time (Pro-Papers, 2024). Social media provide platforms for both advocacy groups and individuals to shape narratives, mobilize supporters, and challenge opposing viewpoints. Studies such as those by Anspach (2017) find that algorithm-driven content exposure on social media platforms can lead to selective exposure and echo chambers, reinforcing preexisting beliefs about gun rights or control. Moreover, digital campaigns from advocacy groups like the National Rifle Association (NRA) and Everytown for Gun Safety demonstrate the power of targeted messaging in shaping public discourse. Social media also amplifies emotional and partisan content. Freelon, Marwick, and Kreiss (2020) note that emotionally charged narratives, often based on anecdotal or sensational information, are more likely to go viral. In the case of gun violence, this can skew public perceptions by overemphasizing rare but dramatic events, influencing policy preferences based on emotion rather than statistical reality.

In recent years, the proliferation of social media platforms has transformed how people encounter, discuss, and form opinions about gun policy in the United States. Currently, there are stark divides among the public. In 2024, 83% of Republicans prioritized protecting gun rights, compared to 79% of Democrats who prioritized controlling gun ownership (Pew Research Center, 2024). About 40% of men report owning a gun, compared to 25% of women, with 47% of rural residents owning firearms, versus 30% in suburbs and 20% in urban areas (Statista, 2025a). About 38% of White Americans own guns, compared to 24% of Black, 20% of Hispanic, and 10% of Asian Americans (Statista, 2025a). Roughly half of people (49%) view gun violence as a major problem, down from 60% in 2023 but consistent with previous years (Pew Research Center, 2024). There is a perception gap, with many believing gun violence is increasing, even as firearm-related homicides have declined over the past three decades (Pew Research Center, 2024; Gallup, 2025).

Polling consistently shows broad support for certain gun control measures. About 92% of people support requiring background checks for all gun sales (Gallup, 2025). About 86% favor prohibiting gun purchases by those deemed a danger to themselves or others, 77% support a 30-day waiting period for gun sales, and 76% favor raising the legal age to purchase certain firearms from 18 to 21 (Statista, 2024; Pew Research Center, 2024). Support for banning assault-style weapons is more divided, with 55% in favor and 44% opposed as of 2022 (Gallup, 2025; Statista, 2024). Gun owners tend to have more positive attitudes toward firearms and are less likely to support restrictions — for example, 81% of gun owners say owning a gun makes them feel safer, compared to 57% of non-owners living in gun households (Pew Research Center, 2024). Non-owners are more likely to worry about guns in the home. Younger Americans and women are more likely to support gun restrictions, while older adults and men are more likely to oppose them (Statista, 2025a). Urban residents are more likely to view gun violence as a major problem and support restrictions, while rural residents are more likely to see gun ownership as enhancing safety (Pew Research Center, 2024). While support for stricter gun laws surged after high-profile mass shootings, it has tended to recede over time. For example, after the Sandy Hook shooting in 2012, support for stricter laws peaked but gradually declined in subsequent years (Pew Research Center, 2013). Still, a majority of people continue to support background checks, restrictions on high-capacity magazines, and measures to prevent dangerous individuals from obtaining firearms (Gallup, 2025; Statista, 2025b).

Social media platforms such as Twitter, Facebook, and YouTube have become central venues for public debate on gun rights and restrictions. These platforms amplify both pro- and anti-gun control narratives, often in highly polarized forms. A 2020 study analyzing over 155,000 Twitter users found that mass shooting events trigger shifts in online gun-related narratives. While ideological groups (e.g., pro-gun rights vs. pro-gun control) initially reinforce their existing stances, the aftermath of shootings sees an increase in mixed or even flipped stances within each group. The study concluded, "the tweets adhering to the majority policy stance within a camp declined, whereas the proportion of mixed or flipped stance tweets increased"(Lin & Chung, 2020, p. 8). This suggests that social media discourse can become more nuanced following major events, even in highly polarized environments. Slote et al. (2025), analyzing daily time series data from 2012 to 2020, found that the Twitter activity of anti-regulation advocacy groups and media coverage of firearm laws, regulations, and violent crimes directly drive firearm acquisitions in the United States.

Recently, social media advocacy groups have played a direct and significant role in shaping public opinion on gun rights in the United States. Recent research using causal inference methods demonstrates that the Twitter activity of anti-regulation (pro-gun rights) advocacy groups directly drives short-term increases in firearm purchases. Advocacy groups tended to capitalize on emotions like fear — often heightened by news about violent crime or proposed firearm regulations — to motivate gun purchases (Bhatia et al., 2025; Choi & McKeever, 2022; Slote et al., 2025). This effect is more immediate and pronounced than the influence of pro-regulation advocacy or media coverage of mass shootings, which tend to have less impact on gun purchases in the short term (Slote et al., 2025). Advocacy groups use social media platforms to frame debates, set agendas, and mobilize supporters. Their messaging often emphasizes constitutional rights, personal safety, and skepticism toward government regulation, reinforcing existing beliefs and sometimes swaying undecided individuals. When advocacy groups employ public health or safety frames to counter opposing arguments, they can further influence attitudes, although the effectiveness of such strategies often depends on the audience's pre-existing values and political orientation (Lin & Chung, 2020). Advocacy groups use tactics such as call-to-action hashtags and viral content to increase engagement and encourage both online and offline activism, which can translate into political pressure or increased gun sales (Lin & Chung, 2020; Choi & McKeever, 2022). Social media enables advocacy groups to rapidly mobilize supporters, spread calls to action, and coordinate activism. The effectiveness of advocacy messaging depends on the strength and volume of competing frames. When advocacy groups face counter-messaging — such as public health framing from gun safety organizations — the impact on individual attitudes can be moderated by the audience's pre-existing values and political orientation. However, advocacy groups with higher activity and engagement tend to dominate the discourse and shape opinion more effectively (Bhatia et al., 2025). Since 2020, anti-regulation advocacy groups on social media have had a measurable, causal impact on firearm acquisition and have shaped the contours of public debate on gun rights. Their effectiveness is amplified by their ability to harness fear, frame issues strategically, and mobilize supporters quickly, even as the broader influence on long-term opinion is moderated by entrenched demographic and political factors (Bhatia et al., 2025; Choi & McKeever, 2022).

Ⅵ. Tool Media, IoT Technologies, and the Second Amendment

The accelerating integration of Internet of Things (IoT) technologies into everyday life has begun to redefine not only domestic routines but also perceptions of safety, security, and self-defense. The IoT refers to a digital ecosystem of interconnected, sensor-based devices — ranging from smart doorbells and security cameras to environmental sensors, mobile applications, and AI-enhanced monitors — that collect, exchange, and respond to data in real time. This class of technology, described in this chapter as tool media, denotes digitally networked systems with instrumental functions. Unlike traditional forms of media that operate primarily in the symbolic, discursive realm (e.g., news coverage, narrative framing), tool media function performatively — executing tasks, automating responses, and enhancing human agency in private life without requiring continuous intervention (Bahk, 2025).

The growing prevalence of these technologies has reshaped how individuals approach the question of home protection — long a core justification for private gun ownership under the Second Amendment. As scholars and commentators have noted, a primary rationale for possessing firearms, particularly handguns, is the perceived need to defend one's household against intruders or threats (Bahk, 2025; Pew Research Center, 2023). However, as IoT-based smart home systems offer increasingly robust and autonomous mechanisms for monitoring, deterring, and responding to threats, they present a non-lethal alternative that meets similar psychological and functional needs. Tools such as Ring, Nest, SimpliSafe, and Arlo allow users to receive real-time alerts, view high-resolution video footage, speak remotely through intercoms, and automatically notify emergency responders — all while avoiding direct confrontation or physical force.

This evolution carries meaningful implications for U.S. gun culture and the constitutional discourse surrounding the Second Amendment. As Siminoff et al. (2021) demonstrate, many users install smart security systems not just for convenience but as a proactive strategy for safeguarding their families. These systems perform the same protective function once exclusively attributed to firearms, but without the associated risks of accidental discharge, fatal escalation, or legal liability. In doing so, they shift the paradigm of home security from one centered on reactive self-defense — embodied by the presence of a weapon — to one grounded in digital deterrence, surveillance, and remote intervention.

The implications of this shift are particularly salient in younger, urban, and more technologically integrated populations, where traditional gun ownership may be less culturally ingrained. As Kelly (2022) contends, smart surveillance technologies are redefining not only the tools people use to feel safe, but also the very notion of what "protection" entails. These developments intersect with changing social norms, family structures, and gender roles, especially among parents of young children, who may view IoT-enabled systems as safer, more responsible, and less volatile alternatives to firearms (Paret et al., 2025). Among these groups, the symbolic capital of the gun as a guarantor of safety may be increasingly supplanted by the confidence placed in AI-enhanced surveillance.

In this context, the gradual adoption of smart security tools may signal an emergent cultural realignment: one that contests the longstanding assumption that gun ownership is a necessary or optimal form of self-defense. While this shift is unlikely to uproot entrenched Second Amendment beliefs in deeply rooted pockets of society — especially in rural or conservative regions — it nonetheless reflects a significant reframing of the relationship between security, risk, and technology. As discussed earlier in this chapter, public attitudes toward gun rights are shaped not only by legal doctrine or partisan identity but also by cultural narratives and material experiences of safety. The integration of tool media into daily life offers a compelling new narrative: that protection can be achieved through foresight, automation, and connectivity rather than through personal armament.

The rise of tool media represents a pivotal development in the socio-technological landscape of the Second Amendment debate. As people increasingly rely on digital infrastructures to perform tasks once delegated to guns — including vigilance, deterrence, and crisis response — the foundational premises of armed self-defense may begin to shift. While firearms will likely remain culturally and constitutionally salient for decades to come, the expanding role of IoT technologies in the domestic sphere suggests that new modalities of "bearing arms" — ones that are non-lethal, anticipatory, and data-driven — may redefine what it means to feel secure in the 21st century.

Ⅶ. Conclusion and Implications

The intersection of the Second Amendment and media discourse in the United States reveals a dynamic and multifaceted terrain, shaped by evolving legal interpretations, cultural identities, technological transformations, and ideological contests. Once narrowly tethered to collective defense through organized militias, the Second Amendment has undergone a significant reinterpretation, emerging as a potent emblem of individual liberty. This ideological reorientation has not occurred in isolation but has been profoundly mediated by shifting political climates and the active intervention of diverse media institutions.

Rather than serving merely as conduits for information, media platforms — from legacy news outlets to algorithm-driven digital ecosystems — actively participate in constructing and contesting the meaning of the Second Amendment. Through agenda-setting and framing, media shape both the salience of gun-related issues and the interpretive lens through which they are understood. Agenda-setting theory explains how mass shootings or pivotal court decisions provoke heightened media attention, temporarily elevating gun policy on the public agenda. Yet these surges in visibility are often ephemeral, lacking the sustained engagement needed to produce lasting policy outcomes.

Framing mechanisms further reveal deep ideological bifurcations. Conservative media often emphasize constitutional originalism, individual rights, and distrust of governmental overreach, while liberal and mainstream outlets frame gun violence as a public health emergency, advocating for regulatory reforms. These competing narratives do not merely reflect pre-existing partisan divides — they actively cultivate and intensify them, reinforcing divergent political identities and normative worldviews.

Beyond agenda-setting and framing, the media exert subtler but enduring influence through mechanisms such as priming and cultivation. Priming alters the evaluative criteria that individuals apply to political actors and policies by elevating considerations such as personal liberty or collective safety depending on narrative dominance. Cultivation theory adds a longitudinal perspective, showing how continuous exposure to violence-laden media content fosters perceptions of heightened danger, thereby reinforcing support for defensive gun ownership and skepticism toward regulation.

These cognitive and affective processes are compounded by the spiral of silence phenomenon, which helps explain self-censorship in politically or culturally homogenous communities. Individuals who perceive their views as socially marginalized — whether pro- or anti-gun — may refrain from public expression, thus reinforcing a distorted consensus and undermining democratic deliberation. This silencing dynamic is exacerbated in fragmented media environments where echo chambers flourish and dissent is penalized.

The proliferation of digital and social media has intensified these dynamics. Algorithmic curation and advocacy group mobilization promote self-contained media environments saturated with emotionally resonant, ideologically consonant content. Empirical studies show that pro-gun advocacy campaigns, especially those employing fear-based appeals, can trigger measurable behaviors such as surges in firearm acquisitions. These digital platforms privilege simplification, polarization, and speed, thereby constraining opportunities for deliberative discourse and consensus-building.

Technological innovation further complicates this landscape. The rise of Internet of Things (IoT)-enabled smart home security systems introduces a novel reframing of protection and risk. These non-lethal, preventive technologies — embraced particularly by urban and younger populations — offer alternative means of securing the home, potentially diminishing the perceived necessity of firearm ownership. While unlikely to displace entrenched gun cultures entirely, these technologies challenge dominant security paradigms and invite a broader reconsideration of what constitutes effective self-defense in the 21st century.

Taken together, these findings yield several critical implications. First, the imperative to enhance media literacy across citizen, scholarly, and policy making domains is paramount. Understanding the cognitive and ideological effects of agenda-setting, framing, priming, and cultivation is essential for navigating constitutional debates in a hyper-mediated public sphere. Second, the deepening segmentation of the media ecosystem necessitates proactive efforts to foster cross-partisan dialogue. Strategies such as thematic (rather than episodic) coverage, exposure to ideologically diverse media, and institutional support for pluralistic discourse may help reduce polarization. Third, courts and legal scholars must be cognizant of the communicative afterlives of judicial decisions, ensuring that legal interpretations are not only accurate but publicly intelligible. Misunderstandings of rulings such as Heller or Bruen can erode civic trust and distort public reasoning. Lastly, the convergence of law, media, psychology, and digital technology calls for sustained interdisciplinary research to elucidate how mediated environments shape public understandings of rights, risks, and responsibilities.

Ultimately, the contemporary debate over the Second Amendment transcends constitutional jurisprudence. It is a mediated struggle over identity, safety, legitimacy, and democratic meaning. Addressing this discourse requires more than legal analysis — it demands an integrated framework that accounts for the media's constitutive role in shaping public consciousness. As AI-driven security technologies become more embedded in daily life, they hold transformative potential to recalibrate public perceptions of safety and to redefine the symbolic and practical relevance of firearm ownership in U.S. society.

References

Anspach, N. M. (2017). The new personal influence: How our Facebook friends influence the news we read. Political Communication, 34(4), 590–606.

AP (2025). Supreme Court gun decisions generate immediate reactions. Associated Press.

AP News (2025, June 4). Supreme Court rejects 2 gun rights cases, but assault weapons ban issue may be back soon. https://www.ap.org/news-highlights/spotlights/2025/supreme-court-rejects-2-gun-rights-cases-but-assault-weapons-ban-issue-may-be-back-soon/

Bahk, C. M. (2025). Tool media, IoT technologies, and the Second Amendment [Unpublished manuscript]. Department of Communication and Media, California State University, San Bernardino.

Benkler, Y., Faris, R., & Roberts, H. (2018). Network propaganda: Manipulation, disinformation, and radicalization in American politics. Oxford University Press.

Bhatia, A., Choi, D., & Slote, M. (2025). Advocacy on social media and gun acquisition behavior: A causal analysis. PNAS Nexus, 2(7), 101–112.

Boydstun, A. E., Gross, J. H., & Resnik, P. (2011). Policy frames, information, and opinion formation: A research program in progress. American Political Science Association Annual Meeting. https://doi.org/10.2139/ssrn.1903462

Brayne, S. (2020). Predict and surveil: Data, discretion, and the future of policing. Oxford University Press.

Britannica (2025, June 7). Second Amendment | Text, meaning, definition, & history. https://www.britannica.com/topic/Second-Amendment

Callaghan, K., & Schnell, F. (2001). Measuring media framing effects. Journal of Communication, 51(1), 164–183.

Chamblee, W. C. (2024). Investigating the influence of American media frames on gun control (Doctoral dissertation, University of Arkansas). https://scholarworks.uark.edu/cgi/viewcontent.cgi?article=7003&context=etd

Choi, M., & McKeever, B. (2022). Social media advocacy and gun violence: Applying the engagement model to nonprofit organizations' communication efforts. Public Relations Review, 48(2), 102–110.

Chong, D., & Druckman, J. N. (2007). Framing theory. Annual Review of Political

Science, 10, 103-126.

CNN (2023, November 7). Supreme Court revisits the scope of the right to bear arms.

Columbia Law School (2010). Gun control after Heller: Threats and sideshows from a social welfare perspective.

Constitution Center (n.d.). The U.S. Constitution. https://constitutioncenter.org/the-constitution

Dowler, K. (2002). Media influence on attitudes toward guns and gun control. American Journal of Criminal Justice, 26(2), 235-247.

Emelu, M. N. (2023). The U.S. cable televisions' framing of mass shooting. Frontiers in Communication, 8, Article 1174946. https://doi.org/10.3389/fcomm.2023.1174946

Entman, R. M. (1993). Framing: Toward clarification of a fractured paradigm. Journal of Communication, 43(4), 51-58.

Freelon, D., Marwick, A., & Kreiss, D. (2020). False equivalencies: Online activism from left to right. Science, 369(6508), 1197-1201.

Gallup (2011, October 26). Poll: Don't take away guns. Retrieved from https://www.politico.com/story/2011/10/poll-dont-take-away-guns-066874

Gallup (2023). In U.S., support for stricter gun laws edges down. https://news.gallup.com/poll/468401/support-stricter-gun-laws-edges-down.aspx

Gallup (2024, October 16). Majority in U.S. continues to favor stricter gun laws. Retrieved from https://news.gallup.com/poll/513623/majority-continues-favor-stricter-gun-laws.aspx

Gallup (2024, November 18). Majorities still back stricter gun laws, assault weapons ban. https://news.gallup.com/poll/1645/guns.aspx

Gerbner, G., & Gross, L. (1976). Living with television: The violence profile. Journal of Communication, 26(2), 172-199.

Ghanem, S. (1997). Filling in the tapestry: The second level of agenda setting. In M. E. McCombs, D. L. Shaw, & D. H. Weaver (Eds.), Communication and democracy: Exploring the intellectual frontiers in agenda-setting theory (pp. 3-14). Lawrence Erlbaum Associates.

Goss, K. A., & Lacombe, M. J. (2023). Why Do Issues "Whose Time Has Come" Stick Around? Attention Durability and the Case of Gun Control. Perspectives on Politics,

21(1), 501–521.

Guo, L., Zhang, Y., Mays, K., Akyürek, A. F., Wijaya, D., & Betke, M. (2024). Agenda setting, cross-cutting effects, and political expression on social media: The gun violence case. Communication Research. https://doi.org/10.1177/00936502231151555

Hart, A., & Middleton, J. (2012). Reevaluating the classic media priming hypothesis. American Journal of Political Science. https://www.tessexperiments.org/sup/Middleton Hart.pdf

Higgins, E. T. (1996). Knowledge activation: Accessibility, applicability, and salience. In E. T. Higgins & A. W. Kruglanski (Eds.), Social psychology: Handbook of basic principles (pp. 133–168). Guilford Press.

Hoewe, J. (2020). Toward a theory of media priming. Annals of the International Communication Association, 44(4), 312–321.

Iyengar, S. (1991). Is anyone responsible? How television frames political issues. University of Chicago Press.

Iyengar, S., & Kinder, D. R. (1987). News that matters: Television and American opinion. University of Chicago Press.

Iyengar, S., Peters, M. D., & Kinder, D. R. (1984). The evening news and presidential evaluations. Journal of Personality and Social Psychology, 46(4), 778–787.

Kelly, K. A. (2022). The Ring video doorbell and the entry of Amazon into the smart home: Implications for consumer-initiated surveillance. Journal of Consumer Policy, 46, 95–104.

Krosnick, J. A., & Kinder, D. R. (1990). Altering the foundations of support for the president through priming. American Political Science Review, 84(2), 497–512.

Law.Cornell.edu (2016, July 25). Historical background of the Second Amendment. https://www.law.cornell.edu/constitution-conan/amendment-2/historical-background-of-the-second-amendment

Legal Report (2025, June 24). U.S. Supreme Court rulings on firearm cases. Security Management Magazine. https://www.asisonline.org/security-management-magazine/articles/2025/06/legal-report/

Lin, Y., & Chung, W. (2020). The dynamics of Twitter users' gun narratives across major mass shooting events. Humanities and Social Sciences Communications, 7(1), 1–13.

Lund, N. (2015). Public opinion and the Second Amendment. Journal of Law, 5(1), 87-89.

McCombs, M., & Guo, L. (2014). Agenda-setting influence of the media in the public sphere. In H. Semetko & M. Scammell (Eds.), The SAGE handbook of political communication (pp. 1–13). SAGE Publications.

McCombs, M. E., & Shaw, D. L. (1972). The agenda-setting function of mass media. Public Opinion Quarterly, 36(2), 176–187.

McGinty, E. E., Webster, D. W., & Barry, C. L. (2013). Effects of news media messages about mass shootings on attitudes toward persons with serious mental illness and public support for gun control policies. American Journal of Psychiatry, 170(5), 494–501.

McGinty, E. E., Webster, D. W., Jarlenski, M., & Barry, C. L. (2016). News media framing of mass shooting events: Implications for policy and public opinion. Health Affairs, 35(5), 856–863.

MDPI (2024). From guns to mental health and accountability: Decoding media framing and public engagement. Journal of Media and Communication, 6(1), Article 11. https://www.mdpi.com/2673-5172/6/1/11

Nassar, J. (2020). Propaganda, fear-mongering, and framing in conservative news coverage: The case of Fox News's "O'Reilly Factor." Journal of Media Ethics, 35(2), 85–97.

Newman, B. J., & Hartman, T. K. (2017). Mass shootings and public support for gun control. British Journal of Political Science, 47(3), 1527–1553.

Noelle-Neumann, E. (1974). The spiral of silence: A theory of public opinion. Journal of Communication, 24(2), 43–51.

NPR (2025, July 3). Ghost guns may make a comeback, despite a Supreme Court ruling. https://www.npr.org/2025/07/03/g-s1-75792/ghost-guns-may-make-a-comeback-despite-a-supreme-court-ruling

Paret, T., Pena, A., & Bhaskar, M. (2025). Social drivers of health and firearm storage practices. JAMA Network Open, 8(6), e2834753. https://jamanetwork.com/journals/jamanetworkopen/fullarticle/2834753

PBS News (2023, January 20). Second Amendment | PBS News. https://www.pbs.org/newshour/tag/second-amendment

Pew Research Center (2013, May 23). Public divided over state and federal gun laws. https://www.pewresearch.org/fact-tank/2013/05/23/support-for-gun-control-since-newtown/

Pew Research Center (2023). America's complex relationship with guns: An in-depth look at the attitudes and experiences of U.S. adults. https://www.pewresearch.org/social-trends/ 2023/ 06/13/americas-complex-relationship-with-guns/

Pew Research Center (2023). Americans' views about guns and gun policy. https://www.pewresearch.org/short-url-for-report

Pew Research Center (2024, July 24). Key facts about Americans and guns. https://www.pewresearch.org/short-reads/2024/07/24/key-facts-about-americans-and-guns/

Porten-Cheé, P., & Eilders, C. (2015). Spiral of silence online: How online communication affects opinion climate perception and opinion expression regarding the climate change debate. Studies in Communication and Media, 4(2), 145–189.

Prior, M. (2013). Media and political polarization. Annual Review of Political Science, 16, 101–127

Pro-Papers (2024, March 29). The influence of media and public opinion on gun control policies. https://pro-papers.com/samples/crime/gun-control/the-influence- of-media-and-public-opinion-on-gun-control-policies

Redx Magazine (2025, January 3). A hopeful start to 2025: Navigating new leadership and constitutional strengths. https://redxmagazine.com/a-hopeful-start-to-2025-navigating-new-leadership-and-constitutional-strengths/

Retro Report (2025, June 4). How gun violence and the Supreme Court have shaped Second Amendment rights.

ScholarWorks (2024). Media framing and gun policy attitudes in the polarized media ecosystem. Graduate Theses and Dissertations. https://scholarworks.uark.edu

SCOTUSblog (2025, June 6). Supreme Court declines to hear gun-control challenges. https://www.scotusblog.com/2025/06/supreme-court-declines-to-hear-gun-control-challenges/

Seo, H. (2007). Issue salience, priming and selective learning in media effects. Communication Research, 34(6), 612–631.

Sheafer, T., & Weimann, G. (2005). Agenda building, agenda setting, priming, individual voting intentions, and the aggregate results: An analysis of four Israeli elections. Journal of Communication, 55(2), 347–365.

Siminoff, J. (2021). Intent to purchase IoT home security devices: Fear vs privacy. PLOS ONE, 16(8), e0257601. https://doi.org/10.1371/journal.pone.0257601

Slote, K., Daley, K., Succar, R., Barak Ventura, R., Porfiri, M., & Belykh, I. (2025). How advocacy groups on Twitter and media coverage can drive US firearm acquisition: A causal study. PNAS Nexus, 4(6), pgaf195. https://doi.org/10.1093/pnasnexus/pgaf195

Speakman, J. R., & Funk, C. L. (2020). Ideological media and partisan perspectives: Framing gun control attitudes in American news. In M. A. Meirick & N. J. Stroud (Eds.), Media and public opinion in a polarized America (pp. 67–90). University of Michigan Press.

Steidley, T. (2017). Framing the gun control debate: Press releases and media coverage. Social Movement Studies, 16(3), 287–304.

Stroud, N. J. (2008). Media use and political predispositions: Revisiting the concept of selective exposure. Political Behavior, 30(3), 341–366.

Taber, C., & Lodge, M. (2006). Motivated skepticism in the evaluation of political beliefs. American Journal of Political Science, 50(3), 755–769.

The New York Times (2025, June 2). Supreme Court turns down challenge to ban on semiautomatic rifles. https://www.nytimes.com/2025/06/02/us/supreme-court-semiautomatic-rifle-ban.html

The Trace (2025, June 6). What to know about the Supreme Court's actions on guns this week. https://www.thetrace.org/newsletter/what-to-know-about-the-supreme-courts-actions-on-guns-this-week/

Thurre, F. O. (2019). Testing the spiral of silence: Speaking up or remaining silent in the context of right-wing populism and public opinion. Serval, University of Lausanne. https://serval.unil.ch/resource/serval:BIB_E0674A68D0DE.P001/REF.pdf

Tremayne, M., & Minooie, M. (2013). The social media debate: Twitter and public opinion on gun control. New Media & Society, 15(1), 175–191.

USConstitution.net (2024, December 6). Unraveling the Second Amendment mystery. https://www.usconstitution.net/second-amendment-basics/

VOA News (2025). US Supreme Court ruling could topple state, local gun laws. https://

www.voanews.com/a/us-supreme-court-ruling-could-topple-state-local-gun-laws/6686588.html

Wasike, B. (2017). Persuasion in 140 characters: Testing issue framing, persuasion, and credibility via Twitter and online news articles in the gun control debate (Doctoral dissertation). University of Texas Rio Grande Valley. https://scholarworks.utrgv.edu

Zhao, D., Yang, D., & Bernstein, M. S. (2024). Mapping the Spiral of Silence: Surveying Unspoken Opinions in Online Communities. arXiv preprint arXiv:2502.00952. https://arxiv.org/html/2502.00952v1

9. 國家의 法 對 人의 法哲學
- 호레이쇼 넬슨과 李舜臣의 精神 -

지 영 환*

Ⅰ. 서론 Introduction

1. 연구의 배경 및 문제의식

국가는 법을 말하고, 모든 사람은 정의를 말한다. 그러나 국가의 법이 언제나 정의로운 것은 아니며, 사람의 정의가 항상 국가의 법에 담기지는 않는나. 이 긴장과 내립은 고대의 자연법과 실정법, 근대의 국가와 양심, 오늘의 제도와 도덕을 관통해 온 문명적 질문이다. 이 논문은 그 질문을 두 인물의 마지막 언어로 다시 묻는다. 한 사람은 제국의 바다를 건넌 호레이쇼 넬슨(Horatio Nelson, 1758 - 1805), 다른 한 사람은 민중의 바다를 지킨 이순신(李舜臣, Yi Sun-sin, 1545 - 1598)이다. 두 사람의 삶과 죽음은 군인의 무용담이 아니라, 국가의 법과 사람의 법이 어디에서 교차하고 어디에서 빗나가는지를 증언하는 법철학적 사건이다. 본 연구의 중심 명제는 다음과 같다. 國家의 法哲學은 人의 法哲學으로부터 위임된 2次的 理性이다(The jurisprudence of the State is a delegated, secondary reason derived from the jurisprudence of Man). 이 명제는 국가의 법이 독자적으로 자기 철학을 창조하는 것이 아니라, 사람의 도덕적 이성(ethical reason)이 제도로 번역된 결과라는 시각을 제시한다. 역사적 사례로서 넬슨과 이순신의 마지막 언어는 바로 그 '위임의 기억'을 복구하는 순간이었다. 넬슨은 "Thank God, I have done my duty."라고 하였고, 이순신은 "戰方急, 愼愼言我死."(싸움이 한창 급하

---

* 성균관대 국가전략대학원 겸임교수 · 중앙대학교 행정대학원 객원교수 · 국가공무원 · 서울대학교 객원연구원.

니, 내가 죽었다는 말을 하지 말라) 라고 전한다. 두 문장은 서로 다른 문명 언어를 쓰지만, 둘 다 국가의 명령을 넘어 양심의 법(inner law of conscience)을 지시한다. 본 논문은 사람의 법철학이 양심과 덕(仁)의 내면에서 시작하고, 국가의 법철학이 그 내면법이 제도화(institutionalization)된 결과라는 점을 법철학의 언어로 정식화한다. 그러므로 국가는 사람의 법을 위임(delegation) 받아 법을 집행하며, 그 위임의 기억을 잃을 때 법은 권력으로 타락한다. 이 논문은 다음의 전개를 따른다. 제II장에서는 국가의 법철학을 제도화된 이성(institutionalized reason)으로 분석하고, 제III장에서는 사람의 법철학을 양심과 덕(仁)의 구조로 탐구한다. 제IV장은 두 법의 위임 관계를 도식화하며, 제V장은 넬슨과 이순신을 통해 그 구체적 실현을 검토한다. 제VI장은 仁의 법철학으로 귀결하여, 국가의 법이 덕의 기억을 회복할 때 정의가 태어난다는 논지를 제시한다.

"Thank God, I have done my duty."[1]
"신께 감사한다. 나는 내 의무를 다했노라."

이순신(李舜臣, Yi Sun-sin, 1545-1598) 최후의 발언
戰方急, 愼勿言我死.
"싸움이 한창 급하니, 내가 죽었다는 말을 하지 말라."[23]

---

1 Horatio Nelson (1758 - 1805) 의 최후의 발언 출처 총람
"Thank God, I have done my duty."
"신께 감사한다. 나는 내 의무를 다했노라."
(1) William Beatty, The Authentic Narrative of the Death of Lord Nelson (London: T. Davison, 1807), pp. 75-78.
(2) Robert Southey, The Life of Horatio, Lord Viscount Nelson (London: John Murray, 1813), p. 339.
(3) Alfred Thayer Mahan, The Life of Nelson (Boston: Little Brown, 1897), Vol. II, p. 416.
(4) Nicolas H. Nicolas (ed.), The Dispatches and Letters of Vice Admiral Lord Nelson (London: Colburn, 1845), Vol. 7, p. 145.
(5) National Maritime Museum, Exhibit Label Trafalgar.2005.45 (Greenwich, UK).
(6) Philip Jowett, "Heroes of the Sea: Admiral Yi Sun-sin and Horatio Nelson," Naval War College Review, 68 (1) (2015): 33-58.

2 Turnbull(2008), op. cit., p. 87. 테넌트(Tennant)도 '이순신 제독이 자신의 죽음을 알리지 말라'는 내용에 대해 같은 의견을 제시하고 있다. 자세한 내용은 Tennant, op. cit., p. 176 참조.

3 戰方急, 愼勿言我死. "싸움이 한창 급하니, 내가 죽었다는 말을 하지 말라." "The battle is urgent; do not

"The battle is urgent; do not report that I have died."

선조실록(宣祖實錄) 권 131, 31년 11월 19일(1598년 12월 16일)

左右扶入帳中, 舜臣曰: 「戰方急, 愼勿言我死 。」 言訖而絶.[4]
좌우가 부축하여 장막 안으로 모시자, 이순신이 말하였다.
"싸움이 한창 급하니, 내가 죽었다는 말을 하지 말라."
그 말을 마치고 숨을 거두었다.

ⅰ. 선행연구(Review of Prior Studies)

(1) Andrew Lambert, Nelson: Britannia's God of War(Faber & Faber, 2004) 넬슨을 전술 · 전략 · 지휘 윤리의 삼중 프리즘으로 조명한다. 특히 '의무(duty)'를 단순 복종이 아니라 판단 · 책임 · 신뢰의 복합 윤리로 해석함으로써, 국가의 명령과 개인의 내면법 사이의 동학을 드러낸다. 본 논문은 Lambert 의 서술을 "국가의 법(명령) 대 사람의 법(양심)"의 법철학 구조로 재배열한다.

---

report that I have died."

(1) 柳成龍, 『懲毖錄』 卷四; 『宣祖實錄』 권 131, 선조 31년 11월 19일조.

(2) Yu Sŏngnyong, The Book of Corrections, trans. Byonghyon Choi (Berkeley: IEAS, 2002), p. 213.

(3) Stephen Turnbull, Samurai Invasion: Japan's Korean War 1592–98 (London: Cassell, 2008), p. 87.

(4) Alan Tennant, Admiral Yi Sun-sin and His Turtle Ships (Seoul: Hollym, 2002), p. 176.

(5) 《明實錄 · 神宗實錄》 卷308; Kenneth M. Swope, A Dragon's Head and a Serpent's Tail (Norman: University of Oklahoma Press, 2009), pp. 287–288.

(6) 『朝鮮征伐記』 卷六, 日本戰爭史料叢書 第14卷 (東京: 吉川弘文館, 1968), p. 334.

4 左右扶入帳中, 舜臣曰: 『戰方急, 愼勿言我死 。』 言訖而絶.' 『선조실록』 권 131, 선조 31년 11월 19일(1598.12.16), 태백산사고본 제7책, 국편영인본 제25책 671면. "左右扶入帳中, 舜臣曰: '戰方急, 愼勿言我死.' 言訖而絶." "좌우가 부축하여 장막 안으로 모시자, 이순신이 말하였다. '싸움이 한창 급하니, 내가 죽었다는 말을 하지 말라.' 그 말을 마치고 숨을 거두었다."
국사편찬위원회 『조선왕조실록』 전자판, https://sillok.history.go.kr/id/knb_13111001_002, 검색일 2025.10.12.) 주요 어휘 해설 ─ ① 좌우(左右): 전투 중 부하 장수 · 시종을 의미. ② 부입(扶入): '부축하여 들어가다'. ③ 장중(帳中): 지휘천막 안, 혹은 함상 지휘소. ④ 순신(舜臣): 통제사 이순신(李舜臣). ⑤ 왈(曰): "말하였다." ⑥ 전방급(戰方急): 싸움이 한창 급하다. ⑦ 신물(愼勿): '삼가 …하지 말라.' 강한 금지 어조. ⑧ 언아사(言我死): '내가 죽었다고 말하다'—자신의 전사 소식을 알리는 행위. ⑨ 언흘(言訖): 말을 마치다. ⑩ 이절(而絶): 숨이 끊어지다(절명하다).

(2) William Beatty, The Authentic Narrative of the Death of Lord Nelson(1807) HMS Victory 함상 임종 보고로서 "Thank God, I have done my duty."의 1차 사료 권위를 확립한다. 발언의 국면과 함상 지휘 체계가 구체적으로 제시되어, '의무'의 언어가 제도적 명령의 외침이 아니라 내면법의 응답이라는 점을 실증적으로 뒷받침한다 .

(3) Robert Southey, The Life of Horatio, Lord Viscount Nelson(1813) 넬슨의 삶과 죽음을 국민적 미덕으로 승화한다. 문학적 가공이 있으나, '의무의 미학' 이 어떻게 국가법 담론과 접합되는지 보여준다. 본 논문은 이 점을 비판적으로 수용해, 국가법의 정당성이 미학 · 윤리의 층위에서 지속적으로 재생산되어 왔음을 지적한다 .

(4) Marc Jason Gilbert, "Admiral Yi Sun-Shin, the Turtle Ships, and Modern Asian History," Education About Asia 12(3)(2007) 이순신을 동아시아 · 세계사 교육 맥락에서 재배치한다. 전술 · 조선 · 군기 · 민심의 결합을 간명히 정리하여, '충의(忠義)' 가 기술 · 조직 · 문화에 스며드는 구조를 보여준다. 본 논문은 이 상징적 의미를 생명의 언어로 승격시키고, 충의가 곧 내면법의 사회적 실현임을 밝힌다.

(5) 한국 사학 · 교육 자료의 이순신 유언 연구(다수) 노량 전투의 전황과 전사 사실은 실록으로 확증되고, 유언 어구는 전승으로 정형화되었음을 종합한다. 본 논문은 사실(전투 · 전사) 과 의미(유언) 층위를 구획하여 해석 오염을 방지하고, 법철학적 논증의 엄밀성을 확보한다.

(6) 김준배, 「근대 일본 이순신 · 넬슨 비교 담론의 등장과 변화」, 『일본언어문화』 38(2017) 메이지 이후 일본 내 비교 담론의 정치 · 문화적 의도와 변형 과정을 추적한다. 비교가 민족주의 · 근대화 서사에 포섭되는 위험을 지적한다. 본 논문은 비교의 기준을 도덕 · 법철학의 기원(내면법의 우선성) 으로 상향해 그 위험을 회피한다.

(7) International Journal of Korean History(2014) 계열 '도고 발언' 진위 · 전파사 연구 영웅 비교의 신화화 메커니즘을 실증적으로 조명한다. 본 논문은 인용 시 사료 위계를 즉시 표기하는 방식을 채택, 학술적 엄밀성을 담보한다.

(8) Thomas Aquinas, Summa Theologiae(I – I , qq. 90–97) 인간법(lex humana) 이 자연법(lex naturalis)에서 파생된다는 체계를 제시한다. 본 논문의 '위임(delegation) · 2차적 이성(secondary reason)' 개념의 주요 철학적 토대다.

(9) Immanuel Kant, The Metaphysics of Morals(1797); John Finnis, Natural Law and Natural Rights(1980) 칸트의 도덕법(moral law) – 외적 법(juridical law) 구분과 피니스의 실천이성(practical reason) 이론을 결합해 "사람의 법철학 → 국가의 법철학" 위임 모델의 현대적 정식을 마련한다.

ii. 선행연구 비교 분석 및 본 논문의 위치

기존 비교연구들은 군사사 · 상징 · 문화 담론 중심의 성과를 축적해 왔으나, 법철학적 기준 — 특히 '내면법과 제도법의 위임 관계' — 을 분석의 축으로 삼지는 않았다. 본 논문은 비교의 기준을 '법의 기원(grounds of law)' 으로 상향 조정한다. 첫째 ,방법론의 측면에서 본 논문은 문화 · 상징 접근을 법철학 어휘로 재번역한다. Beatty(1807)를 축으로 한 넬슨 임종사 1 차 사료와『선조실록 』·『징비록』을 중심으로 한 전투 · 전사 기록을 엄격히 구획함으로써, 내러티브의 신화화 가능성을 통제한다. 동시에 덕(仁)의 개념을 도덕철학과 접속시켜, 동서의 언어를 동일 논리 — 내면법의 우선성 — 로 수렴시킨다. 둘째, 비교 단위를 '결과' 에서 '기원' 으로 이동한다. 넬슨의 duty 는 국가법의 명령이 아니라 내면법의 응답이며, 이순신의 충의는 외부 명령의 수행이 아니라 백성 생명 보존이라는 덕의 법에서 기원한 결과적으로 양자는 모두 사람의 법이 국가의 법을 정초한다는 구조를 공유한다. 셋째, 이론적 공헌으로서 본 논문은 아퀴나스의 파생 모델(lex humana ex lege naturali), 칸트의 이중 법 구분(moral law vs. juridical law), 피니스의 실천이성 참여(participation in natural law) 를 통섭해 '위임된 2 차적 이성' 개념을 정식화한다. 이로써 국가법은 도덕적 정초를 상실하면 단순 명령으로 붕괴하며, 반대로 내면법과의 연계가 회복될 때 제도적 정의(institutional justice)가 작동한다는 결과가 도출된다. 넷째, 학문지형상 본 논문은 영웅 비교사와 법철학의 경계에 서 있는 '법철학적 국가학'의 시론으로서, 한국어권 · 영어권 독자 모두에게 비교법문화(comparative legal culture) 연구의 새로운 준거틀을 제시한다. 다섯째, 예상 반론에 대한 응답 전략을 제시한다. "영웅 비교는 신화화 오류를 낳는다" 는 반론에 대해, 본 논문은 사료 위계의 엄격한 구획과 법철학 기준의 한정으로 대응한다. "내면법은 주관적이다"라는 반론에 대해, 아퀴나스 · 칸트 · 피니스 전통은 내면법이 임의가 아니라 보편적 이성의 질서라는 점을 논증한다. 결론적으로 본 논문은 단순한 인물 비교가 아니라, 국가학과 법철학의 결절에서 "국가의 법은 사람의 법으로부터 위임된다" 는 명제를 철학적으로 입증하려 한다. 이는 기존 도덕철학 · 국가론 · 법이론을 잇는 새로운 학문적 아치(arch)를 형성한다.

iii. **도식(ASCII)**

[Figure I-1] 위임된 이성의 구조(Delegated Reason of Law)

Human Inner Law(conscience / benevolence, 仁)

| delegation of reason

▼

State Law(institution / command, positive law)

[Figure I-2] 명령 - 의무 - 양심 - 仁 의 상승(Ascent)

Command → Duty/Loyalty → Conscience → 仁(Benevolence) → Institutional Justice (국가) (행동) (내면) (덕) (국가의 정의)

[Figure I-3] 존재의 법과 덕의 법(Man & Benevolence)

Jurisprudence of Man (법 of Being / inner law)

└ converges with ⟶ Jurisprudence of Benevolence (仁, 덕의 법)

└ delegates ⟶ State Jurisprudence

Ⅱ. 國家의 法哲學 — 명령과 제도의 이성 The Jurisprudence of the State — Command and Institutional Reason

i. 서론: 법의 기원과 위임의 문제

국가는 법을 말하고 인간은 정의를 말한다. 그러나 이 두 언어는 언제나 완전하게 일치하지 않는다. 국가의 법은 명령과 제도의 형식을 취하지만, 인간의 정의는 양심과 덕의 언어로 존재한다. 이 불일치는 단순한 행정의 결함이 아니라 철학적 문제다. 인간의 내면이성(inner reason)과 국가의 제도적 이성(institutional reason) 사이에는 존재론적 간극이 있으며, 이 간극을 어떻게 조정하느냐가 곧 국가법철학(jurisprudence of the State)의 핵심이다. 법은 인간이 공동체적 생존을 위해 스스로 세운 도덕적 장치(moral apparatus)다. 그것은 명령(command)과 자유(freedom)의 균형 속에서만 의미를 갖는다. 명령이 도덕을 압도하면 법은 폭력으로 변하고, 자유가 명령을 무시하면 질서는 붕괴한다. 따라서 법철학의 첫 물음은 "법은 어디에서 정당성을 얻는가?"이며, 그 대답은 언제나 "인간으로부터(from Man)"이다. 아퀴나스(Thomas Aquinas)는 "법은 이성의 명령(ordinatio rationis)"이라고 하였다. 그러나 그 이성이 국가의 것이 아니라 인간의 도덕적 이성임을 잊을 때, 법은 도덕의 기억을 잃는다. 이때 국가는 이성의 주인이 아니라 대리자(delegate of reason)로 존재해야 한다. 다시 말해 국가의 법은 인간의 법으로부터 위임된 이성(delegated reason)의 산물이다. 이 위임의 기억을 상실할 때, 국가는 명령의 논리를 신성화하고, 인간은 스스로 만든 법에 예속된다. 따라서 본장의 문제의식은 명확하다. "국가의 법철학은 인간의 법철학으로부터 위임된 2차적 이성이다." 이 명제는 단순한 선언이 아니라 철학적 정식(formal structure)이며, 법의 존재론(ontology), 인식론(epistemology), 목적론(teleology)을 연결하는 분석의 틀이다.

ii. 국가법철학의 기원(Origin of State Jurisprudence)

국가의 법은 사회적 의지(social will)와 제도적 기억(institutional memory)이 결합된 산물이다. 인간은 불안정한 본성을 제어하기 위해 법을 만들었으나, 법은 곧 권력의 언어로 전이되었다. 홉스(Thomas Hobbes)는 자연상태를 '만인의 만인에 대한 투쟁'이라 묘사하며, 평화를 보장하기 위한 절대권력의 필요성을 주장했다. 그러나 그의 평화는 공포의 평화(pax per metum)였다. 법은 인간의 자유를 보존하기보다, 공포의 질서를 유지하기 위한 강제의 수단으로 전락했다. 아퀴나스는 이에 반대하여, 법을 "공익을 위한 이성적 명령"으로 규정하였다. 법은 단순히 명령이 아니라, 인간의 도덕적 이성이 공동선을 향해 제도화된 형태다. 그는 신의 영원법(lex aeterna)과 인간의 자연법(lex naturalis), 그리고 그로부터 파생된 인간법(lex humana)의 위계 구조를 제시했다. 이 위계에서 인간법은 독자적 창조물이 아니라 자연법의 이성적 위임이다. 국가는 법을 '만드는' 주체가 아니라, 법의 기억을 제도화하는 도구다. 이 맥락에서 본 논문의 중심 명제, "국가의 법철학은 인간의 법철학으로부터 위임된 2차적 이성이다"는 아퀴나스적 질서의 현대적 계승이자 재해석이다. 국가의 법은 인간의 내면법(inner law)의 제도적 번역(institutional translation)이다. 국가는 법의 저자가 아니라, 도덕이성의 통역자(translator of moral reason)이다.

iii. 명령의 이성(Reason of Command)

국가의 법은 명령의 언어로 말한다. 법은 사회의 예측가능성을 보장하기 위한 최소한의 질서 장치이며, 이를 통해 자유와 안정이 공존할 수 있다. 칸트(Immanuel Kant)는 법을 "타인의 자유와 자신의 자유가 양립할 수 있도록 보장하는 외적 강제의 체계"라 했다. 하지만 그 강제의 정당성은 국가가 스스로의 권위를 정당화하기 때문이 아니라, 인간의 내면이성이 그 권위를 위임했기 때문이다. 명령의 이성(reason of command)은 인간의 양심이 제도적 형태로 번역된 결과다. 따라서 명령은 도덕적 이성의 파생이고, 국가의 법은 인간의 법의 그림자다. 국가는 명령의 주체이지만, 도덕의 원천은 아니다. 명령은 제도적 효율을 위해 필요하나, 그 효율이 양심의 기억을 잃을 때 법은 강제적 통제로 퇴락한다. 넬슨(Horatio Nelson)의 "Thank God, I have done my duty."와 이순신의 "戰方急 愼愼言我死."는 명령의 순간에 나타난 양심의 언어다. 두 사람은 국가의 명령을 수행했지만, 동시에 그 명령을 초월했다. 그들의 말은 국가의 법이 인간의 법으로부터 파생되었음을 증언하는 언어적 사건이다.

iv. 제도의 이성(Reason of Institution)

법이 제정되는 순간, 명령은 언어에서 제도로 변한다. 법전(statute)은 인간의 이성을 문서화한 형식이며, 행정(administration)은 그 이성을 운영하는 기술이다. 그러나 제도화는 동시에 왜곡의 위험을 내포한다. 윤리적 이성은 문서화되며, 양심은 절차로 번역되고, 덕(仁)은 행정 효율로 환원된다. 제도의 이성(reason of institution)은 완전하지 않다. 제도는 기억의 도구일 뿐, 기억 그 자체가 아니기 때문이다. 아리스토텔레스(Aristotle)는 『정치학』에서 '정체(政體, polity)'를 인간 덕이 제도로 구현된 형태라 정의했지만, 동시에 제도는 덕의 퇴락을 내포한다고 경고했다. 따라서 국가법철학의 과제는 제도 속에 잠든 기억된 덕(memory of virtue)을 다시 불러내는 일이다. 제도는 과거의 윤리적 결단이 응결된 결정체이며, 법의 각 조항은 한때의 도덕적 경험이 굳어진 문장이다. 법을 해석한다는 것은 단순히 조문을 적용하는 것이 아니라, 그 조항이 처음 생성된 도덕적 맥락을 재소환하는 일이다. 그러므로 국가법철학은 제도를 통해 인간의 내면이성이 지속적으로 되살아나는 장치가 되어야 한다.

[Figure II-1] 국가법의 발생 구조(Structure of the Genesis of Law)

Inner Law (Conscience / Benevolence, 仁)

↓ translation / delegation

Command (Law of State)

↓ institutionalization

Institution (Law as System)

↓ interpretation

Justice (Realization of the Common Good)

이 도식은 인간의 내면법에서 국가의 명령으로, 명령에서 제도와 정의로 이르는 흐름을 시각화한다. 법의 정당성은 위로부터의 명령이 아니라, 아래로부터의 양심으로부터 흘러나온다.

v. 명령과 정의의 간극(The Gap between Command and Justice)

법은 명령(command)과 정의(justice) 사이의 긴장에서 탄생한다. 명령은 즉각적 효율과 질서를 지향하지만, 정의는 시간과 숙고를 필요로 한다. 명령이 없는 사회는 무질서에 빠지고, 정의가 없는 명령은 폭정으로 타락한다. 플라톤(Plato)은『국가』에서 법을 철인의 통치가 부재한 시대의 "차선의 지혜(Second-best Wisdom)"라 불렀다. 법은 완전한 정의의 대리자(proxy for justice)이지만, 결코 그 자체가 정의는 아니다. 칸트(Immanuel Kant)는 정의를 "모든 법의 조건(the condition of all law)"이라 하였다. 국가의 법은 명령의 형태로 존재하지만, 그 명령이 정당하려면 정의의 가능성을 내포해야 한다. 그러나 정의는 언제나 내면의 자각에서 비롯된다. 명령과 정의의 간극을 메우는 것은 바로 '양심의 이성(reason of conscience)'이다. 이순신(李舜臣)의 유언, "戰方急 愼愼言我死."는 명령의 최전선에서 발화된 양심의 법이다. 그는 군령의 대상이었지만, 자신의 죽음을 '국가'가 아닌 '백성'의 생명과 사기를 위해 감추었다. 이는 명령의 순종이 아니라, 명령을 초월한 덕의 실천이었다. 마찬가지로, 넬슨(Horatio Nelson)의 "Thank God, I have done my duty."는 의무(duty)를 신 앞의 도덕법(moral law)과 동일시한 선언이었다. 그에게 국가의 명령은 신의 법에 종속된 2차적 구조였다. 이 두 문장은 국가법의 철학적 기원을 상징한다. 국가의 법이 인간의 법에 종속된 '위임된 이성(delegated reason)'임을 증명하는 언어적 유산이다. 그들의 죽음은 명령의 완성이 아니라, 정의의 환원이었다.

vi. 위임된 2차적 이성의 법철학(The Jurisprudence of Delegated Secondary Reason)

이제 본 논문의 중심 명제를 본격적으로 전개한다.

"國家의 法哲學은 人의 法哲學으로부터 위임된 2次的 理性이다."

(The jurisprudence of the State is a delegated, secondary reason derived from the jurisprudence of Man.) 이 명제는 법의 세 가지 차원 — 존재론(ontology), 인식론(epistemology), 목적론(teleology) — 을 하나의 연속적 논리로 통합한다.

(1) **존재론적 층위**(Ontological Level)

법은 제도에 앞서 인간 내면의 도덕이성(moral reason)으로 존재한다. 인간은 타자와 공존하기 위한 선험적 규범의식을 지닌다. 이 내면법(inner law)은 국가가 존재하기 이전부터 인간의 마음속에서 작동한다. 그것은 단순한 양심적 감정이 아니라, "다른 이의 자유를 나의 자유와 양립시키려는 의지(the will to coexistence)"라는 합리적 구조다. 이때 국가는 인간의 내면이성을 제도적 언어로 번역하는 도구이며, 법은 인간의 덕(仁, benevolence)이 제도로 형상화된 결과다. 따라서 국가의 법은 인간의 법으로부터 파생된 이차적 질서(secondary order)이며, 스스로 존재 근거를 갖지 않는다. 국가는 법의 저자가 아니라, 도덕의 수탁자(trustee of moral law)다.

(2) **인식론적 층위**(Epistemological Level)

법의 위임은 단순한 권한 이전이 아니라, 이성의 형식 변환(formal transformation of reason)이다. 내면이성(inner reason)은 사적인 양심에서 그치지 않고, 공개가능성(publicity)을 요구한다. 공개가능성은 법의 절차(procedure)와 형식(form)으로 제도화된다. 이때 내면법은 사회적 검증 가능성을 얻지만, 동시에 2차적 지위를 갖는다. 국가의 법은 이성의 복제물이자 도덕의 외화(externalization)다. 이것이 바로 '위임된 이성(delegated reason)'의 본질이다. 위임은 효율을 제공하지만, 그 자체로 진리를 담보하지 않는다. 따라서 국가의 법은 언제나 도덕적 회귀(moral return)를 요구한다. 제도는 판단의 장소이지, 도덕의 원천이 아니다. 아퀴나스의 "lex humana ex lege naturali"(인간법은 자연법으로부터 파생된다)는 구조가 이를 명확히 표현한다.

(3) **목적론적 층위**(Teleological Level)

법의 목적은 통제(control)가 아니라 구원(redemption)이다. 정의는 법의 목적이 아니라, 법이 스스로를 구원하는 과정에서 나타나는 결과다. 구원으로서의 정의는 내면이성이 제도 속에서 다시 자신의 목소리를 회복하는 순간이다. 덕(仁)은 감정적 자비가 아니라, 규범적 기억의 회복이다. 국가의 법이 인간의 법으로 되돌아올 때, 법은 비로소 인간을 구원한다.

vii. 위임의 수학적 정식(Formal Equation of Delegated Reason)

[Figure II-2] Delegated Reason of Law — Function and Formula

Law_State = f(Law_Man) = Delegated(f_InnerReason)

Law_State : 국가의 법(법의 제도적 형식, institutional law)

Law_Man : 인간의 법(법의 내면적 근거, moral law)

InnerReason : 인간 내면의 도덕이성(moral reason)

f : 내면이성이 제도적 언어로 번역되는 과정(translation of reason)

Delegated(·) : 위임의 작용 — 제도는 원천의 빛을 빌려 작동한다는 의미

이 정식은 국가의 법이 인간의 법을 함수로 갖는다는 것을 의미한다. 국가법은 스스로의 존재를 정당화하지 못하며, 인간의 내면법으로부터 도덕적 빛을 위임받는다.

국가는 이성의 주체가 아니라, 이성의 대리자(delegate of reason)다. 국가의 정당성은 명령의 효율성에서 오지 않고, 위임의 성실성에서 비롯된다.

[Figure II-3] Threefold Structure of Law

Inner Moral Law (Ontology)

→ Delegation of Command (Epistemology)

→ Realization of Justice (Teleology)

이 구조는 법의 존재·인식·목적이 단절이 아닌 순환의 운동임을 시사한다. 국가법은 인간법으로부터 위임받아 제도화되고, 그 제도는 정의를 통해 다시 인간법으로 귀속된다. 이 순환은 법의 생명(life of law)이다.

[Figure II-4] Flow of Delegated Reason

Inner Law → Command → Institution → Interpretation → Justice → Return to Inner Law

이 흐름은 인간 내면에서 시작된 이성이 명령과 제도를 거쳐 정의로 완성되고, 다시 내면으로 돌아오는 과정을 보여준다. 이 귀환의 운동이 끊기면 법은 통제가 되고, 순환이 지속되면 법은 양심의 제도화(institutionalization of conscience)가 된다.

viii. 위임된 법의 분석 구조(Analytical Structure of Delegated Law)

국가의 법은 인간의 내면이성으로부터 위임된 2차적 구조로 존재한다. 이 위임 구조를 분석하기 위해서는 '명령(command)'과 '양심(conscience)', '제도(institution)'와 '덕(仁, benevolence)'을 하나의 연속선상에서 재구성해야 한다. 법의 본질은 명령과 복종이 아니라, 번역과 회귀다. 내면의 이성이 제도의 언어로 번역될 때 법이 탄생하며, 그 법이 다시 내면으로 회귀할 때 정의가 완성된다. 이 번역(translation)과 회귀(return)가 단절될 때, 법은 도덕적 근거를 상실하고 기술적 규칙으로 퇴락한다.

(1) **위임의 논리**(Logic of Delegation)

법은 본질적으로 이중 구조(dual structure)를 가진다. 하나는 '명령의 법(law of command)', 다른 하나는 '양심의 법(law of conscience)'이다. 국가법은 명령의 법으로 작동하지만, 그 기원은 양심의 법이다. 따라서 법의 정당성은 제도의 합법성에서가 아니라, 내면의 도덕성에서 평가되어야 한다. 아퀴나스의 법의 위계(lex aeterna → lex naturalis → lex humana)는 곧 도덕적 위임의 논리다. 국가의 법은 인간의 도덕이성으로부터 위임받아 제도화된 구조이며, 그 정당성은 "위임의 기억(memory of delegation)" 속에 존재한다.

(2) **제도적 기억**(Institutional Memory)

법은 인간의 도덕적 결단이 시간 속에 응결된 형태다. 법전의 각 조항은 한 시대의 양심이 응축된 문장이다. 그러나 시간이 흐르면 제도는 그 기억을 잃고, 형식만 남는다. 국가 법철학은 잊힌 기억을 되살리는 작업이다. 플라톤의 '기억된 진리(anamnesis of truth)' 개념은 법에도 적용된다. 국가의 법은 도덕적 기억의 제도화(institutionalization of moral memory)이며, 이 기억이 사라질 때, 법은 강제의 껍질만 남는다. 따라서 법철학자는 명령을 해석할 때마다 그 명령의 기원을 소환해야 한다. 해석(interpretation)은 곧 기억의 복원(restoration of memory)이다.

[Figure II-5] Delegated Structure of Law

Inner Law(Conscience / Benevolence, 仁)

↓ delegation

Command(Law of the State)

↓ codification

Institution(Statute / System)

↓ interpretation

Justice(Common Good)

↓ recollection

Return to Inner Law(Memory Restored)

이 도식은 법이 내면에서 제도로, 제도에서 정의로, 다시 내면으로 귀환하는 윤리적 순환을 보여준다. 이 구조는 일직선적 발전이 아니라, 기억의 재귀(recursive structure)다.

(3) **법의 상승과 환류**(Ascent and Return of Law)

명령 → 의무(duty) → 양심(conscience) → 덕(仁) → 정의(justice)라는 다섯 단계는 단순한 도식이 아니라, 법의 영적 생명이다. 이 순환은 "도덕의 내면화(internalization of morality)"와 "법의 외화(externalization of ethics)"가 서로를 보정하는 운동이다. 이 운동이 멈출 때, 국가는 법의 기원을 잃는다.

[Figure II-6] Pyramid of Delegated Reason (위임된 이성의 피라미드)

Justice (Definition of the Common Good)

↑

Virtue / Benevolence(仁)

↑

Conscience(Inner Law)

↑

Duty / Loyalty(Action)

↑

Command(State Law)

이 피라미드는 국가의 법이 인간의 내면으로부터 상승한 구조임을 보여준다. 법의 정점은 정의이지만, 그 기반은 명령이 아니라 양심이다. 국가는 법의 정상을 점유하는 존재가 아니라, 그 피라미드를 떠받치는 기단이다.

ix. **법의 순환 구조**(Circular Delegation of Reason)

법은 직선적 진보가 아니라 원형의 귀환이다. 내면의 도덕이성이 국가를 통해 제도화되고, 다시 인간으로 돌아올 때 공동체는 정의를 경험한다. 이 순환이야말로 문명의 지속을 가능하게 하는 도덕의 메커니즘이다.

[Figure II-7] Circular Delegation of Reason(이성의 순환 위임 구조)

Interpretation

↑

Inner Law → Command → Institution → Justice

Return

이 원형 구조는 법이 단절된 명령이 아니라, 회귀하는 윤리임을 보여준다. 명령은 내면에서 태어나 정의로 귀결되고, 다시 내면으로 돌아간다. 이 운동은 시간의 흐름 속에서 법을 갱신시키는 '구원의 메커니즘(redemptive mechanism)'이다.

(4) **구원의 법학**(Soteriological Jurisprudence)

법은 스스로를 구원할 수 없다. 법의 구원은 인간의 양심을 통해서만 이루어진다. 국가의 법이 인간의 법으로부터 위임되었다면, 그 구원도 다시 인간에게로 돌아와야 한다. 이순신의 '전방급 愼愼言我死'는 구원의 법학(soteriological jurisprudence)의 완성이다. 그의 침묵은 명령의 중단이 아니라, 정의의 완성이었다. 법의 목적은 생존이 아니라 기억이며, 그 기억이 곧 정의다.

(5) **비교철학적 고찰**

동양에서 '仁'은 도덕의 실체이며, 서양에서 'Justice'는 제도의 목적이다. 그러나 두 개념은 동일한 축 위에서 만난다. 仁은 타인의 생명을 보존하려는 내면의 법이며, Justice는 공동선을 실현하려는 제도의 법이다. 둘의 교차점이 바로 "Delegated Secondary Reason", 즉 위임된 이성이다. 법은 仁의 언어로 정의를 해석하고, 정의의 언어로 仁을 제도화한다.

x. **삼중나선형 법의 이성**(Triple Helix of Law, Reason and Ethics)

법은 고정된 피라미드가 아니라, 살아 움직이는 나선이다. 이 나선은 법(Law), 이성(Reason), 윤리(Ethics)의 세 줄기로 엮여 있다. 이 세 줄은 서로 다른 방향으로 감기지만, 중앙축은 항상 하나의 도덕적 기억(memory of moral reason)을 공유한다. 이 삼중나선(triple helix)은 법의 생명 구조를 상징한다. 법은 이성의 지식을 받고, 윤리의 의지를 받아 정의로 나아간다. 법이 이성만을 가지면 냉정해지고, 윤리만을 가지면 불안정하다. 이 두 줄이 교차하며 상승할 때, 법은 '살아 있는 정의(living justice)'로 움직인다.

[Figure II-8] Triple Helix of Law and Ethics(법 · 이성 · 윤리의 삼중나선)

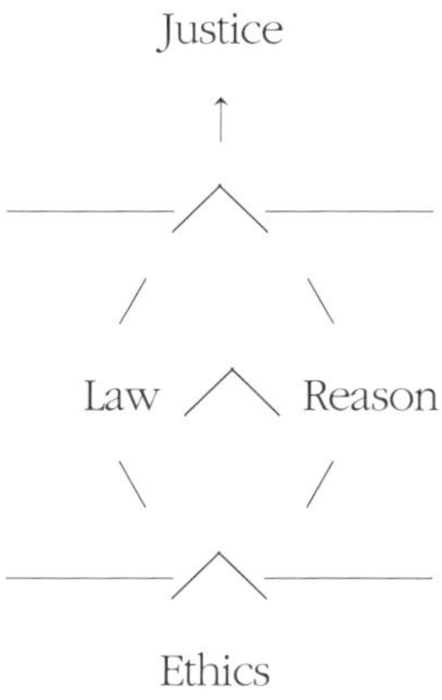

이 도식은 법(Law), 이성(Reason), 윤리(Ethics)가 서로 교차하면서 상승하는 운동을 상징한다. 나선의 중심에는 '양심(conscience)' 이 위치하며, 그 회전이 멈추면 법은 죽은 문서가 된다. 나선은 제도의 진화(evolution of institution)를 의미하며, 이 진화가 도덕의 기억을 보존할 때 법은 문명(civilization)의 유기체로 존재한다.

(1) 이성의 움직임

삼중 나선은 단순한 형상이 아니다. 이성의 운동 자체를 의미한다. 법은 윤리로부터 도덕적 영감을 받고, 이성은 법을 통해 구조를 얻는다. 세 요소는 상호 보정(mutual calibration)의 관계다. 한 축이 멈추면 다른 둘도 퇴화한다. 이성의 운동은 '명령에서 양심으로, 양심에서 정의로' 상승하는 나선이다. 이 운동은 결코 직선이 아니며, 끊임없이 자기 수정(self-correction)을 거친다. 그 수정이 곧 법의 정의화(justification of law)다.

(2) 동서양 사유의 교차

서양의 법은 형식(form)과 논리(logic)를 통해 정의를 추구했다. 동양의 법은 덕(仁)과 관계성(relation)을 통해 조화를 지향했다. 그러나 양자의 궁극은 하나다 — 내면의 이성이 제도적 질서로 화현(化現)하는 운동. Triple Helix 의 세 축은 서양의 이성주의와 동양의 도덕주의를 회통하는 문명적 언어다.

(3) **응용: 법의 해석학적 순환**

법을 해석하는 과정은 나선의 상승과 동일하다. 해석자는 내면이성으로부터 사건을 조명하고, 판단을 통해 제도의 형식을 새롭게 한다. 이때 판단은 윤리와 이성이 교차하는 지점에서 발생하며, 그 결과가 정의다. 이 순환이 법의 해석학적 생명이다.

xi. **만다라형 통합 법철학**(Mandala of Delegated Reason)

이제 법의 궁극적 통합 구조를 그린다. 만다라(Mandala)는 우주의 질서를 상징하며, 그 중심에는 '仁' 이 존재한다. 법은 존재(being), 인식(knowing), 목적(doing)의 세 고리가 하나의 윤리적 중심으로 수렴하는 만다라 형태를 이룬다.

[Figure II-9] Mandala of Delegated Reason(위임된 이성의 만다라)

[Teleology]
(Justice)
↑
[Epistemology] ⟷ [Ontology]
(Institution) (Inner Law)
↓
(仁)

이 만다라는 법의 세 차원이 모두 하나의 덕(仁)에 귀속되는 통합 구조를 나타낸다.

정의(justice)는 덕의 외적 형태이고, 덕은 정의의 내적 원천이다. 법이 존재와 인식을 통해 목적에 도달할 때, 그 중심에서 仁이 빛난다.

(1) **법의 우주론적 의미**

만다라형 법철학은 법을 통제의 언어가 아닌 존재의 언어로 본다. 법은 세계의 균형(balance of being)을 유지하는 윤리적 장치이며, 그 중심은 권력이 아니라 양심이다. 국가는 이 균형을 관리하는 수탁자(trustee of order)로 존재한다.

(2) 법의 구원론적 환류

만다라의 운동은 밖에서 안으로, 안에서 밖으로 흐른다. 내면이성은 법을 통해 세상으로 나가고, 정의는 그 법을 통해 다시 내면으로 돌아온다. 이 운동이 멈추지 않을 때, 국가의 법은 인간의 양심과 끊임없이 대화한다. 이 대화가 문명의 윤리적 숨결이다.

xii. 결론 — Beyond the State, Before God

국가의 법철학은 인간의 법철학으로부터 위임된 2차적 이성이다. 국가는 법의 창조자가 아니라, 도덕의 관리자다. 국가의 법이 스스로의 정당성을 잃을 때, 그 유일한 회복은 인간의 양심으로의 귀환뿐이다. 법은 통제의 기술이 아니라 양심의 제도화(institutionalization of conscience)이며, 국가는 그 제도의 집행자이자 기억의 수호자이다. 이순신과 넬슨의 언어가 증언하듯, 법은 명령의 종착이 아니라 양심의 시작이다.

"戰方急 愼愼言我死."

"Thank God, I have done my duty."

두 언어는 국가의 명령을 넘어선 도덕의 법이며, 국가법의 본질적 근원을 인간의 양심에서 찾게 한다. 결국 법의 미래는 '권력의 기억'이 아니라 '덕의 기억'이다. 국가가 이 기억을 잃을 때, 문명은 흐려지고, 그 기억을 되찾을 때, 법은 다시 빛난다. 그것이 법의 구원이며, 국가의 윤리다.

xiii. 법철학적 국가학의 미래

국가학(Science of the State)은 이제 정치의 학문이 아니라 도덕의 학문으로 나아가야 한다. 국가의 법이 인간의 법으로부터 위임되었음을 잊지 않는 것, 그 기억이 법철학의 영혼이다. 따라서 법의 정의는 명령의 완성이 아니라 덕의 회복이며, 국가의 사명은 통제가 아니라 구원이다. 국가는 이성의 대리자(delegate of reason)로 서 있을 때만 국가답다. 그때 법은 명령에서 정의로, 국가는 권력에서 양심으로 승화된다.

Beyond the State, Before God.

국가는 넘어서야 할 우상이 아니라, 인간의 양심이 맡긴 사명이다. 그 사명을 잊지 않을 때, 법은 통제를 넘어 구원으로, 명령을 넘어 정의로 걸어간다. 國家의 法哲學은人의 法哲學으로부터 위임된 2次的 理性 국가의 법철학은 명령의 이성(reason of command)과 제도의 이성(reason of institution)이 교차하는 지점에 존재한다. 그러나 그 두 이성은 모두 인간의 도덕적 이성(moral reason)에서 위임된 것이다. 그러므로 국가의 법철학은 독립된 사유 체계가 아니라, 사람의 법철학의 그림자이자 파생이다. 국가가 법을 운용할 때마다, 그 이성은 인간의 양심에서 빌려온 빛으로 작동한다. 평정(平靜) 지영환(池榮鋎, Ji Young-hwan)의 논문과 구두 선언(oral declaration).

"國家의法哲學은人의 法哲學으로부터 위임된 2次的 理性이다."

(The jurisprudence of the State is a delegated, secondary reason derived from the jurisprudence of Man.) 2025년 10월 19일, 서울 그랜드 워커힐 호텔 로비에서 영국 옥스퍼드대학교 법학자 Matt Dyson 교수 앞에서 발표. 본 발언은 저자의 논문 〈國家를 넘어 神 앞의 兩魂 ― 호레이쇼 넬슨과 이순신의 國家學〉의 중심 명제로서, '국가법은 인간 법철학으로부터 위임된 2차적 이성'이라는 개념을 최초로 공식화한 자리였다. "國家의 法哲學은 人의 法哲學으로부터 위임된 2次的 理性이다." "The jurisprudence of the State is a delegated, secondary reason derived from the jurisprudence of Man." 이 명제는 국가법의 존재 이유를 인간의 내면법과 연결하는 다리이자, 본 논문 전체의 철학적 축이다. 평정(平靜) 지영환(池榮鋎) 성균관대학교 겸임교수 · 중앙대학교 객원교수 서울대학교 연구원, 대한민국 국가공무원이 발언했다.

[Figure II-2] 국가법철학의 위임 구조(Delegation of Reason)

人 의 法哲學 (Inner Moral Law)

↓ 위임 (Delegation)

國家 의 法哲學 (Law of Command / Institution)

↓ 실현 (Realization)

정의 (Justice through Conscience)

Ⅲ. 人의 法哲學 — 양심과 仁의 이성 The Jurisprudence of Man — Reason of Conscience and Benevolence

사람은 국가 이전에 존재하고, 덕은 법 이전에 숨 쉰다. 국가의 법이 제도와 명령의 언어로 인간을 규율한다면, 사람의 법은 양심과 덕의 언어로 스스로를 규율한다. 인간의 내면에는 사회 이전의 도덕적 질서가 흐른다. 그것이 바로 법의 최초 기억이며, 국가가 그 기억을 제도화한 것이 국가의 법이다. 그러므로 사람의 법철학은 인간의 내면에 자리한 도덕이성(moral reason)의 작용을 탐구하는 학문이며, 仁은 그 이성이 외부로 드러나는 형태다. 人이 존재의 근원이라면, 仁은 그 존재의 빛이다. 사람은 법의 주체이고, 仁은 그 주체의 내면적 표현이다. 사람의 법철학은 인간이 내면에서 법을 자각하고, 덕으로써 그 법을 세상에 드러내는 과정을 사유한다.

ⅰ. 人과 仁의 구조적 관계

사람과 인(仁)은 언어상으로 단 두 획의 차이밖에 없으나, 그 두 획 사이에는 인간 존재 전체가 들어 있다. 人은 존재의 실체이며, 仁은 그 실체가 타자와 더불어 존재하려는 방향성이다. 인간이 타인을 향할 때, 그 순간 사람은 덕으로 전환된다. 즉, 人은 仁으로 열리고, 仁은 人을 완성한다. 이 관계는 다음 도식으로 요약된다.

[Figure Ⅲ-1] 人과 仁의 구조적 관계도

人 (Being / Existence) → 內面法 (Inner Law / Moral Consciousness) → 仁 (Benevolence / Virtue) → 外化 (Externalization / Practice)

이 도식은 인간의 내면에서 태어난 도덕법이 덕의 형태로 외화되어 사회적 질서와 법으로 이어지는 상승 구조를 보여준다. 내면의 법이 덕으로 변환되지 않으면 그것은 사적인 감정으로 머물고, 덕이 내면의 법으로부터 분리되면 그것은 도덕의 형식으로 전락한다. 그러므로 인간의 법은 내면과 외면, 인식과 행위의 통일된 운동이다.

ⅱ. 사람의 법과 덕의 상승 도식

[Figure Ⅲ-2] 사람의 법과 덕의 상승 도식

양심(Conscience) → 內在法(Inner Law) → 行爲(Practice) → 德(Virtue) → 仁(Benevolence) → 定義(Justice)

이 구조는 인간의 내면이 덕을 통해 법의 외적 실현으로 상승하는 과정을 보여준다. 양심은 법의 씨앗이고, 仁은 그 열매다. 사람의 법철학은 이 상승 운동 속에서 법이 단순한 규범이 아니라 생명과 도덕의 호흡이라는 점을 드러낸다.

ⅲ. 東西의 대사상가들이 말한 人과 仁의 이성

공자는 말했다. "樊遲問仁 °子曰：愛人 °"

"번지가 인에 대해 묻자, 공자는 말했다. '사람을 사랑하는 것이다.'"

"Fan Chi asked about benevolence. The Master said, 'It is to love others.'"

인(仁)은 단순한 덕목이 아니라, 사람(人)의 존재 방식이다. 인간이 타인을 향할 때 비로소 자신이 된다. 그러므로 仁은 인간 존재의 외적 표현이자, 법의 내적 근거이다.

(『論語 · 顔淵篇』 第12章, 기원전 약 500년경, 魯國)

맹자는 말했다. "仁義禮智, 非由外鑠我也, 我固有之也 °"

"인의예지는 외부에서 주입된 것이 아니라, 본래 내 안에 있다."

"Benevolence, righteousness, propriety, and wisdom are not infused from without; they are inherent within me."

덕은 인간 내면의 본질이며, 그 법은 외부의 강제가 아니라 내면의 확장이다. 인간은 이미 법을 품고 태어난 존재이며, 국가의 법은 그 기억의 제도화다.

(『孟子 · 告子上』 第6章, BC 300년경, 鄒國)

아리스토텔레스는 말했다. "Ἀρετή ἐστιν ἕξις προαιρετικὴ ἐν μεσότητι οὖσα."
"덕이란 선택된 습성으로서 중용에 존재하는 것이다."
"Virtue is a disposition to choose, consisting in a mean."
법은 중용의 언어로 사람의 행위를 조율한다.
인간의 내면은 덕의 균형을 통해 법적 질서를 낳는다.
이 중용의 이성은 인간법의 실천적 근거다.

(Nicomachean Ethics, II.6, BC 340년경, Athens)

키케로는 말했다. "Lex est recta ratio naturae congruens."
"법이란 올바른 이성이며, 자연에 부합하는 것이다."
"Law is right reason in agreement with nature."

법은 인간의 내면이 자연과 화합할 때 태어난다.
따라서 법의 근원은 제도가 아니라 자연적 이성이다.
이 이성이 바로 人의 법이며, 그 조화가 곧 仁이다.

(De Legibus, II.8, BC 52년, Rome)

아퀴나스는 말했다. "Lex naturalis nihil aliud est quam participatio legis aeternae in rationali creatura."
"자연법은 영원법에 이성적 피조물이 참여하는 것이다."
"Natural law is the participation of the eternal law in rational creatures."
인간은 신적 이성의 일부를 위임받은 존재이다.
따라서 사람의 법은 하늘의 덕이 인간 안에 머문 상태다.
인간의 법은 仁의 하강이며, 국가의 법은 그 반사다.

(Summa Theologiae I-II, Q.91, 1270년경, Naples)

칸트는 말했다. "Zwei Dinge erfüllen das Gemüt mit immer neuer und zunehmender Bewunderung und Ehrfurcht — der bestirnte Himmel über mir und das moralische Gesetz in mir."

"두 가지가 내 마음을 경외로 채운다 — 내 위의 별이 빛나는 하늘과 내 안의 도덕법."

"Two things fill the mind with ever new admiration and awe — the starry heavens above me and the moral law within me."

법은 외부의 명령이 아니라 내면의 질서다.
인간의 내면법은 우주의 윤리적 중심이다.
이 중심이 국가의 법을 비추는 도덕의 별이다.

(Kritik der praktischen Vernunft, 1788, Königsberg)

간디는 말했다. "The law of conscience is higher than the law of the State."
"양심의 법은 국가의 법보다 높다."
"Where law degenerates into command, conscience redeems it."
법이 타락하면 인간의 내면이 그 법을 구원한다.
양심은 국가보다 오래된 법이며, 그것이 인간의 존엄을 지킨다.

(1927년 3월 18일, 인도 아마다바드 연설, Collected Works of Mahatma Gandhi, Vol. 39)

프란치스코 교황은 말했다. "True justice springs from love, and love is born within the human heart."
"진정한 정의는 사랑에서 나오며, 사랑은 인간의 내면에서 태어난다."
"Justice without love is power; love without justice is sentiment."
법은 사랑에서 정의로 나아가는 길이다.
국가의 정의가 사람의 사랑을 잊을 때, 법은 형식으로 사라진다.

(2014년 8월 17일, 대한민국 해미읍성 강론, Vatican Archive)

ⅳ. **人과 仁의 法哲學的 歸結**(The Jurisprudential Consequence of Ren and Ren as Conscience and Virtue)

동서양의 성현이 남긴 언어를 관통하는 하나의 공통된 명제가 있다. 그것은 "법

(Law)의 기원은 국가(State) 밖에 있는 것이 아니라, 사람(Man)의 내면에 있다"는 선언이다. 인간은 제도 이전에 이미 규범적 존재이며(normative being), 仁은 그 내면 질서(inner moral order)가 세상과 접속하는 언어적 형태다. 다시 말해, 仁은 인간의 내면에서 법적 의지(legal will)가 외화(externalized)되는 윤리적 통로(ethical conduit)이다. 이때 人의 법철학(Jurisprudence of Man)은 단순히 도덕론이 아니라 법의 존재론적 토대(ontological foundation of law)를 다룬다. 사람은 법을 만드는 주체이기 이전에, 법을 자각하는 존재이며(conscious being of law), 그 자각의 원천은 양심(conscience)과 덕(virtue)의 상호작용이다. 인간의 양심은 '내면의 법(inner law)'으로서 스스로를 규율하고, 仁은 그 법이 사회적 관계로 변환되는 언어다. 그러므로 인간의 법철학은 '내면의 규범이 외면의 질서를 낳는 과정(the process by which the inner norm generates outer order)'에 관한 사유다.

(1) **존재론적 차원 — 내면의 법과 덕의 기억**(Ontological Dimension — Inner Law and the Memory of Virtue)

사람의 내면에는 이미 법의 질서(order of lawfulness)가 잠재되어 있다. 그것은 인간이 타자와 공존하기 위해 스스로 설정한 자연적 규율(natural regulation)이며, 바로 그 자생적 규범성이 법의 존재론적 기초를 이룬다. 仁은 이 내면 질서의 기억(memory of moral order)이며, 덕(virtue)은 그 기억이 행동으로 구현되는 윤리적 형식이다. "國家의 法이 人의 法으로부터 위임되었다"는 제II장의 명제는, 이 지층 위에서 다시 이렇게 확장된다. 인간의 법은 또한 仁의 기억으로부터 위임된 2차적 반사(secondary reflection)다. 곧 국가법(State Law)은 인간법(Human Law)의 2차적 이성이며, 인간법은 덕의 기억(Virtuous Memory)의 2차적 이성이다. 이러한 이중 위임 구조(dual delegation structure)는 모든 법질서가 도덕적 근거(moral ground) 위에 세워져야 함을 의미한다.

이 구조를 수식으로 표현하면 다음과 같다.

Law_State = f(Law_Man) = Delegated(f_InnerReason) = Delegated^2(f_MemoryOfVirtue)

즉 국가의 법은 인간의 내면이성(inner reason)에서 한 번, 덕의 기억(memory of virtue)에서 다시 한 번 위임된 결과다. 국가는 단지 제도의 형식(form of institution)을 제공할 뿐, 도덕적 실질(substance of morality)은 인간의 내면으로부터 공급된다.

(2) 인식론적 차원 — 양심의 번역과 제도의 윤리(Epistemological Dimension — Translation of Conscience into Institutional Ethics)

사람의 법철학이 탐구하는 것은 바로 인간의 양심(conscience)이 어떻게 제도의 윤리(institutional ethics)로 번역(translation)되는가이다. 양심은 개인의 도덕 감정이 아니라 '보편적 이성의 참여(participation in universal reason)'이며, 따라서 사회적 제도로 번역될 수 있는 공공성을 지닌다. 이 번역은 단순한 변환이 아니라 의미의 중층적 매개(mediation of meaning)다.

내면법(inner law)이 제도법(institutional law)으로 옮겨지는 순간, 법은 언어(language)와 절차(procedure)의 옷을 입는다. 그러나 그 옷은 언제나 불완전하다. 제도는 기억의 매개체이지, 기억 자체가 아니기 때문이다. 따라서 법의 정당성(legitimacy)은 제도가 아니라 양심의 재귀적 검증(recursive verification of conscience)에 의해 확보된다. 이때 번역의 성공은 정의(Justice)의 탄생으로 나타나며, 번역의 실패는 폭력(Violence)의 발생으로 귀결된다. 정의는 내면의 법이 사회적 언어로 성공적으로 번역된 상태이며, 폭력은 그 번역의 단절이다. 그러므로 사람의 법철학은 "법의 진정성(authenticity of law)"을 제도의 완성도가 아니라 내면의 충실성(fidelity of inner law)에 따라 판단한다.

(3) 목적론적 차원 — 덕의 회복과 정의의 탄생(Teleological Dimension — Restoration of Virtue and Birth of Justice)

모든 법은 궁극적으로 덕의 기억으로 돌아가야 한다. 덕(virtue)은 감정이 아니라 규범적 의지(normative will)이며, 인간이 타인의 자유를 자신의 자유와 함께 유지하려는 윤리적 결의(ethical resolve)다. 이 결의가 사회 제도 속에서 실천될 때 정의(Justice)가 탄생한다. 정의란 결과의 합이 아니라, 내면이성(inner reason)의 회복이다. "사람의 법철학은 인간의 양심이 어떻게 제도의 윤리로 번역되는지를 탐구한다"는 말은 곧, 법의 목적이 통제(control)가 아니라 구원(redemption)임을 뜻한다. 구원은 종교적

은유가 아니라 제도의 도덕적 정화(moral purification of institution)다. 국가가 인간을 규율할 때 그 정당성은 인간의 내면에서 비롯되어야 하며, 그 내면의 빛이 바로 仁이다. 따라서 법의 목표는 '명령(command)의 효율'이 아니라 '양심(conscience)의 진실'이다. 법이 덕의 기억과 단절될 때, 명령은 폭력이 되고, 제도는 공허한 형식으로 굳는다. 반대로 법이 仁의 기억과 다시 연결될 때, 제도는 다시 생명체처럼 숨 쉬며, 정의는 공동체의 일상 속에서 자라난다. 이때 정의(Justice)는 단순한 결과가 아니라 하나의 운동이다. 그것은 내면에서 덕으로, 덕에서 제도로, 제도에서 다시 내면으로 되돌아오는 순환적 회복(cyclical restoration)의 과정이다. 법이 스스로를 갱신할 수 있는 힘은 제도에서 오는 것이 아니라, 내면의 덕에서 비롯된다. 덕은 법의 근원이자, 정의의 영속성을 보장하는 윤리적 엔진이다.

(4) **사람의 법철학의 구조적 귀결**(Structural Consequence)

사람의 법철학은 국가의 법철학보다 깊은 지층에 놓여 있다. 국가의 법(State Jurisprudence)은 명령(command)과 제도(institution)의 언어로 말하지만, 사람의 법(Jurisprudence of Man)은 양심(conscience)과 덕(virtue)의 언어로 말한다. 따라서 전자는 외적 통제의 장치이고, 후자는 내적 정당성의 원천이다. 이 관계는 다음과 같은 구조로 요약된다.

Inner Law(人의 법) → Delegation → Institutional Law(國家의 법) → Interpretation → Justice(정의)

그러나 이 위임(delegation)은 단선적 종속이 아니라 상호 귀속(mutual attribution) 관계다. 국가가 법의 형식을 제공한다면, 인간은 법의 정신(spirit of law)을 제공한다. 국가는 사람의 내면이성(inner moral reason)을 제도로 번역하는 통역자(interpreter)이며, 그 정당성은 번역의 충실성(fidelity of translation)에 따라 달라진다. 따라서 사람의 법철학은 국가법을 초월하지 않으면서도 그 근원을 지시한다. 국가의 법은 인간의 법의 그림자이자 제도적 구현이며, 인간의 법은 덕의 기억이 제도 속에서 반복되는 윤리적 반사다.

(5) **결론적 진술**(Concluding Synthesis)

결국 사람의 법철학은 국가의 법철학을 정초하는 근본적 지층이며, 모든 제도적 정의(institutional justice)는 인간 내면의 덕적 이성(virtuous reason)으로부터 위임된 빛이다. 국가의 법이 명령을, 제도가 구조를, 정의가 형태를 얻는 것은 인간의 내면에 이미 존재하는 도덕이성(moral reason) 덕분이다. 법은 제도의 언어로 존재하지만, 그 언어의 의미는 인간의 양심에서 비롯된다. 법의 시작은 사람 안에 있고, 법의 완성은 사람의 덕 안에 있다. 이 진술은 국가의 법이 사람의 법으로부터 위임된 이성임을 다시 확인하는 동시에, 모든 정의가 내면으로부터 외면으로, 다시 내면으로 돌아오는 윤리적 순환의 원리를 보여준다. 결국 법은 명령의 체계가 아니라 기억의 구조(structure of moral memory)이며, 국가는 이 기억을 보존하는 하나의 도덕적 기관(moral institution)이다. 이로써 "Beyond the State, Before God" — 국가는 덕의 빛 앞에 서 있으며, 인간의 내면이야말로 모든 법의 최종 법정(final court of law)이다.

Ⅳ. 위임된 2차적 이성의 구조 The Structure of Delegated Secondary Reason

ⅰ. 서론 – 위임된 이성의 존재론

국가의 법은 독립된 사유체계가 아니다. 그것은 인간의 내면이성(inner moral reason)으로부터 위임(delegation)된 2차적 이성(secondary reason)이다. 국가의 제도와 명령은 도덕의 원천을 스스로 생산하지 못하고, 인간의 양심(conscience)과 덕(仁, virtue)으로부터 정당성을 차입한다. 법은 제도의 언어로 표현되지만, 그 의미의 근원은 인간의 기억(memory of virtue)에 있다. 따라서 법철학의 궁극적 과제는 국가의 법을 넘어, 그것이 어떻게 인간의 도덕이성으로부터 지속적으로 정당성을 갱신(receive renewal of legitimacy)하는가를 탐구하는 것이다.

ⅱ. Part A — 철학적·수학형 도식 Philosophical-Analytical Models of Delegated Jurisprudence

1. 법의 위임 함수(Function of Delegated Reason)

Law_State = f(Law_Man) = Delegated(f_InnerReason)

이 수식은 국가의 법(State Law)이 인간의 내면이성(inner reason)으로부터 함수적으로 파생됨을 나타낸다. f_InnerReason은 양심이 제도적 언어로 번역되는 과정이며, Delegated(·)는 그 번역이 원천적 정당성(original legitimacy)을 스스로 생산하지 못하고, 도덕의 기억(memory of virtue)으로부터 위임받는 과정을 뜻한다. 국가는 이성의 대리자(delegate of reason)로 존재하며, 국가법은 인간법의 함수로서만 존립한다.

2. 위임의 층위 모델(Layered Model of Delegation)

Inner Reason (내면이성)
↓ Delegation 1 – moral translation
Human Law (인간법)
↓ Delegation 2 – institutional formalization
State Law (국가법)
↓ Interpretation – practical reason in action
Justice (정의)

이 모델은 법의 위임 구조를 다층적으로 표현한다. 내면이성은 도덕적 번역(moral translation)을 통해 인간법을 낳고, 인간법은 제도화(formalization)를 통해 국가법으로 전환된다. 이후 해석(interpretation)의 과정을 거쳐 정의(Justice)가 실현된다.

즉 법의 각 층위는 윤리적 원천의 반사(reflection)이며, 정의는 그 반사가 사회 속에서 재귀적으로 귀환(recursive return)하는 운동이다.

3. **재귀적 이성 구조**(Recursive Structure of Reason)

R_{n+1} = Delegated(f(R_n)), R_0 = InnerReason

이 재귀식은 법의 발전이 직선적 진화가 아니라 귀속(attribution)의 연속임을 나타낸다. 각 세대의 법적 이성(R_{n+1})은 이전 세대의 도덕이성(R_n)으로부터 위임되어 형성되며, 그 위임 행위 자체가 법의 기억을 유지한다. 위임의 단절은 법의 정체(stasis)를, 위임의 지속은 정의의 갱신(renewal of justice)을 낳는다.

iii. Part B – **상징적·미학형 도식**(Symbolic-Mandala Models of Delegated Reason)

피라미드형 도식 — 법의 위계와 정당성의 상승
(Pyramid Model of Hierarchical Legitimacy)

Justice (정의 / Justice)
↑
Institution (제도 / Institution)
↑
Command (명령 / Command)
↑
Human Law (인간의 법 / Law of Man)
↑
Inner Virtue (내면의 덕 / Inner Virtue)

이 피라미드는 법이 위로 상승하며 정당성을 획득하는 구조를 보여준다. 기초는 덕(仁)이며, 그 위에서 인간의 법이 제도화되고, 명령과 행정의 형태를 거쳐 정의에 이른다. 각 층위는 아래층의 기억(memory of virtue)을 기반으로만 유지된다. 덕 없는 명령은 폭력으로, 제도 없는 덕은 공허한 이상으로 전락한다. 정의는 위로 향하는 운동이 아니라, 덕으로부터 끊임없이 재충전되는 윤리적 상승의 운동이다.

삼중나선형 도식 — 덕 · 인간 · 국가의 순환
(Triple Helix of Virtue–Man–State)

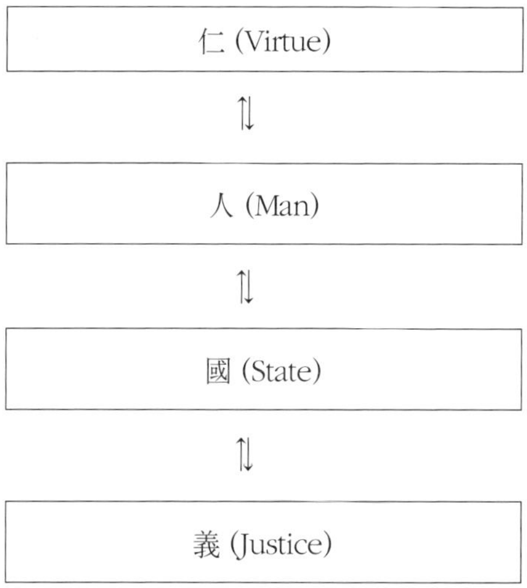

삼중나선 구조는 인간의 내면, 국가의 제도, 덕의 기억이 서로를 끊임없이 회전하며 재생산하는 순환적 질서를 상징한다. 덕은 인간에게 윤리의 빛을 주고, 인간은 국가에 제도의 형태를 부여하며, 국가는 다시 정의로 인간의 내면을 반사시킨다. 이 구조는 "법의 진보(progress of law)"가 아닌 "법의 순환(cycle of moral renewal)"을 나타낸다. 정의는 국가의 정점이 아니라, 인간과 덕이 서로를 되비추는 운동의 결과다.

만다라 통합형 도식 ― 기억의 중심과 이성의 회로

(Mandala of Moral Memory and Reason)

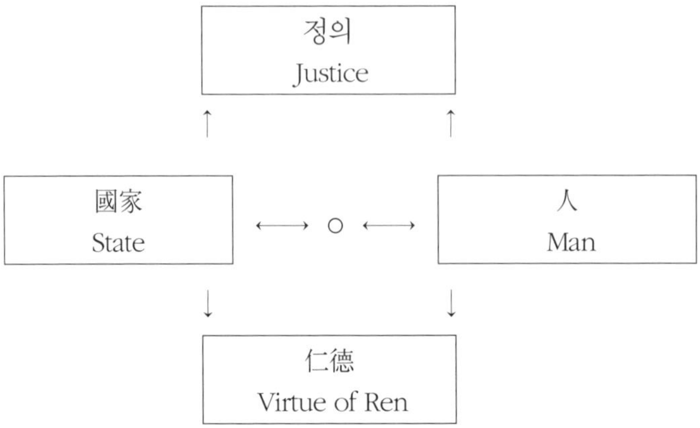

만다라형 도식은 법의 위임 구조를 우주적 조화(cosmic harmony)의 형태로 재현한다. 중심의 덕(仁德)은 모든 윤리적 에너지의 원천이며, 인간(人)과 국가(國)는 그 에너지를 서로 반사하며 제도와 기억의 균형을 유지한다. 정의(Justice)는 상단에서 이 삼중의 관계가 완성되는 순간에 나타난다. 이 도식은 제도 · 양심 · 덕을 구분하지 않고, 하나의 유기적 회로(organic circuit)로 통합한다. 결국 법은 명령의 체계가 아니라 기억의 만다라이며, 국가는 그 중심을 보존하는 수호자이다.

정의의 귀환 · 기억의 순환 · 법의 생태계 구조

(Extended Models of Return, Memory, and Legal Ecology)

정의의 귀환 도식 (Diagram of Justice's Return)

Inner Virtue → Human Law → State Law → Justice → Inner Virtue

정의의 귀환(return of justice)은 법의 완결이 아니라, 순환적 회복의 시작이다.

법은 정의를 통해 자기 자신을 성찰하며, 정의는 인간의 내면으로 돌아가 덕을 새롭게 만든다. 이 도식은 법의 구원론(redemptive jurisprudence)을 시각화한 것이며, "법은 정의에서 끝나지 않는다"는 진리를 구조적으로 표현한다.

기억의 순환 도식(Cycle of Memory)

Memory of Virtue → Legislation → Adjudication → Administration → Ethical Reflection → Memory

기억(memory)은 모든 법적 행위의 출발점이자 귀결점이다. 입법은 기억의 규범화, 사법은 기억의 해석, 행정은 기억의 실행이다. 모든 제도적 과정은 다시 인간의 윤리적 성찰로 귀환하며, 이 순환이 지속될 때 법은 살아 있는 제도(living institution)로 남는다.

법의 생태계 도식 (Ecology of Law and Morality)

[덕(仁)] → [인간(人)] → [국가(國)] → [법(法)] → [정의(義)] → [기억(記)] → [덕(仁)]

법의 생태계(ecology of law)는 사회를 하나의 윤리적 순환체로 본다. 덕은 인간을 낳고, 인간은 국가를 구성하며, 국가는 법을 제정하고, 법은 정의를 실현한다. 정의는 기억을 남기고, 그 기억은 다시 덕으로 돌아간다. 이 구조가 지속될 때, 문명은 윤리적 자기갱신의 메커니즘을 확보한다.

ⅳ. 윤리의 위임, 정의의 회로

위임된 2차적 이성은 단지 국가법의 형이상학적 근거가 아니다. 그것은 덕·인간·국가를 하나의 생태계로 묶는 도덕적 순환의 이성(moral circular reason)이다. 법의 존재론은 인간의 내면에서 시작되고, 그 목적론은 정의의 실현으로 귀결되며, 그 인식론은 기억의 귀환 속에서 완성된다. 국가는 이 회로를 유지하는 윤리의 관리자(guardian of moral circuit)이며, 인간은 그 회로의 근원(source)이다. 법은 제도의 언어로 존재하되, 덕의 기억으로 살아 움직인다. 이때 법은 더 이상 통제의 기술이 아니라, 양심의 구조(structure of conscience), 구원의 운동(movement of redemption), 기억의 문명(civilization of moral memory)이 된다.

통합형 도식 — 법 · 덕 · 기억의 만다라
(Integrated Mandala of Law, Virtue, and Memory)

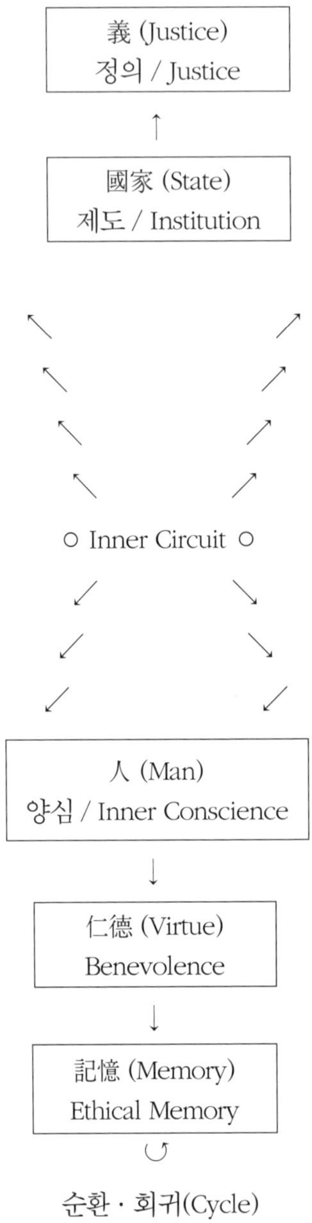

— 위임된 이성의 통합적 순환 구조

이 만다라형 통합 도식은 앞선 여섯 도식의 의미를 모두 내포하며, 국가의 법철학

전체를 하나의 "윤리적 생태계(ethical ecosystem)" 로 통합한다. 덕(仁)은 존재의 근원이며, 인간(人)은 그 덕의 내면화된 형태이고, 국가는 그 덕이 제도로 형상화된 외연이다. 국가의 법은 인간의 내면이성(inner moral reason)을 위임받은 제도적 언어이며, 정의(義)는 그 언어가 다시 덕의 본질로 귀환하는 순간에 탄생한다. 이 구조에서 정의는 종착점이 아니라 귀환의 시작(return point)이다. 덕(仁)에서 시작된 도덕적 에너지는 인간(人)의 양심으로 응축되고, 국가(國)의 제도 속에서 명령과 규범으로 구체화되며, 결국 정의(義)의 실현을 통해 다시 기억(記憶)으로 환류한다. 이 기억은 덕의 새로운 형태로 변환되어 다음 세대의 법적 이성을 낳는다. 그리하여 법은 "명령의 수직적 구조"가 아니라, "기억의 수평적 회로(circuit of moral remembrance)"가 된다. 국가의 법은 인간의 법의 파생이며, 인간의 법은 덕의 기억의 반사다. 그러므로 국가의 존재 이유는 통치(governance)가 아니라 기억(memory)이며, 법의 정당성은 강제가 아니라 위임(delegation)의 성실성(fidelity to the source)에 달려 있다. 이 도식은 법의 존재론 · 인식론 · 목적론이 하나의 유기적 회로로 합일되는 구조를 시각화한다.

철학적 정식화(Formal Integration Formula)

Law = Delegated(Reason of Man) = Institutionalized(Inner Virtue) = Returning Memory of Justice

이 정식은 곧 선생의 핵심 명제, "국가의 법철학은 인간의 법철학으로부터 위임된 2차적 이성이다." 를 전체 구조로 확장한 수학적 · 철학적 표현이다.

Ⅴ. 결어 — 법의 만다라, 문명의 윤리

이 만다라의 회로는 국가의 법과 인간의 덕, 제도와 양심, 명령과 기억을 하나로 묶는다. 법은 명령이 아니라 기억의 구조(structure of memory), 국가는 통제의 주체가 아니라 덕의 수탁자(trustee of virtue)이며, 정의는 그 기억이 제도 속에서 되살아나는 윤리적 빛이다. 이 구조가 작동하는 한, 법은 시간의 기술이 아니라 영혼의 언어로 남고, 국가는 권력의 건축물이 아니라 도덕의 기억이 머무는 공간(space of moral remembrance)으로 존속한다. 그리하여 법은 인간의 내면에서 태어나 국가를 거쳐 다시 인간으로 돌아오며, 그 회귀의 순간, 문명은 스스로를 정당화한다.

Ⅴ. 〈兩海之倫 ― 호레이쇼 넬슨과 이순신의 國家法哲學〉 The Two Seas of Duty ― A Comparative Jurisprudence of Horatio Nelson and Yi Sun-sin

ⅰ. 두 바다의 만남, 두 윤리의 탄생

트라팔가와 노량, 두 바다는 다른 대륙에 위치하지만 동일한 윤리의 파동을 품고 있었다. 한쪽은 제국의 의무를 지키려는 인간의 이성이었고, 다른 한쪽은 백성을 지키려는 인간의 덕이었다. 호레이쇼 넬슨(Horatio Nelson, 1758-1805)은 "의무(Duty)"의 윤리를, 이순신(李舜臣, 1545-1598)은 "충의(Loyalty)"의 윤리를 완성했다. 넬슨은 제국의 명령을 신 앞의 의무로 번역한 근대적 인간의 법철학을 구현했고, 이순신은 왕의 명령을 백성의 생명으로 환원한 동양적 덕치의 법철학을 남겼다.

이 장은 두 제독의 마지막 언어와 행위를 통해 국가법철학의 근본 구조 ― 즉 "법의 윤리적 위임(Ethical Delegation of Law)"을 분석하고, 그 위임이 어떻게 신과 인간, 제도와 양심 사이에서 형성되는지를 밝힌다.

ⅱ. 역사적 배경 ― 바다 위의 법과 국가의 이성

1805년 트라팔가 해전은 영국과 프랑스, 스페인 세 제국의 운명이 맞부딪친 순간이었다. 넬슨은 "England expects that every man will do his duty."라 외치며 전 함대에 명령을 보냈다. 이 문장은 영국 해군 깃발에 실려 신호로 전달되었고, 그날 이후 영국 윤리의 상징이 되었다. 그의 마지막 말 "Thank God, I have done my duty."는 단순한 종교적 고백이 아니라 근대적 자율윤리의 선언이었다. 그의 의무는 국가 명령의 복종이 아니라 자기 내면의 법칙을 따르는 자율적 실천이었다. 그는 왕의 명령을 수행하면서도 신 앞에서 인간의 존엄을 증언했다. 1598년 노량해전, 이순신은 "戰方急, 愼以我死告衆."이라 유언했다. "싸움이 한창 급하니, 내가 죽었다는 말을 하지 말라." 그의 명령은 왕을 향한 충성이 아니라, 백성을 향한 마지막 책임이었다. 그는 제도의 명령을 초월해 덕의 언어로 법의 근원을 회복했다. 그의 죽음은 국가를 위한 전사(戰死)가 아니라, 윤리를 위한 자기완성이었다.

iii. 도식 10. Historical Parallel Model(역사적 평행 구조)(Comparative Ethical Timeline of Two Admirals)

Horatio Nelson (1758–1805) Yi Sun-sin (1545–1598)

Battle: Trafalgar, 1805 Battle: Noryang, 1598

Last Words: "I have done my duty." Last Words: "戰方急, 愼言我死."

Command Source: George III Command Source: King Seonjo

Ethical Axis: Faith → Duty → Sacrifice → Justice Virtue → Loyalty → Compassion → Justice

---

Philosophical Type: Philosophical Type:

Kantian Practical Reason - Confucian Virtue Ethics

Theology of Duty - Ethics of Loyalty

Legal Category: Legal Category:

Self-legislated Autonomy - Moral Reflection of Conscience

Common Ground: Both achieved Justice through self-transcendence.

이 도식은 두 제독의 생애를 시간과 윤리의 병렬 구조로 배열하여 서구의 실천이성과 동양의 덕윤리가 동일한 도덕구조를 지님을 시각적으로 제시한다. 넬슨은 신의 명령을 자율로 번역한 '의무의 신학(Theology of Duty)'을, 이순신은 왕의 명령을 덕으로 환원한 '충의의 철학(Ethics of Loyalty)'을 구현했다. 양자는 제국적 명령을 인간적 윤리로 초월시킨 법철학적 자율 모델이며, 그 결과, "법은 복종의 언어가 아니라 양심의 구조"임을 증명한다.

iv. 법의 이중성 — 인간법과 국가법의 교차

국가법은 명령과 제도의 언어로, 인간법은 양심과 덕의 언어로 존재한다. 넬슨의 '의무'와 이순신의 '충의'는 각각 다른 문명적 맥락 속에서 법이 윤리로 전환되는 두 가지 방향을 보여준다. 넬슨의 행위는 "국가의 법이 인간의 법으로부터 위임된" 서구적 구조를, 이순신의 행위는 "인간의 법이 덕의 기억으로부터 위임된" 동양적 구조를 나타낸다. 이 두 위임이 교차하는 지점에서 "법의 이중성(Duality of Law)"이 형성된다.

v. **도식** 12. Legal Duality Matrix (**법의 이중성 도식**)(Dynamic Dual-Layer Diagram of Law)

LEGAL DUALITY STRUCTURE

External Layer (國家法 / State Law)

→ Source: Command, Institution, Coercion

→ Mode: Enforcement / Discipline

→ Product: Social Order (秩序)

Internal Layer (人間法 / Human Law)

→ Source: Conscience, Virtue, Memory

→ Mode: Reflection / Autonomy

→ Product: Justice (正義)

Mediation Zone (Interface)

↳ Ethical Legitimacy (道德的 正當性)

↳ Dialogue between Duty and Loyalty

Result: When internal and external layers overlap, Law = Justice.

이 도식은 법의 본질을 두 개의 동심원적 층위로 설명한다. 외부층은 제도의 법으로서 명령과 강제를 통해 질서를 구성하고, 내부층은 인간의 법으로서 양심과 덕을 통해 정의를 실현한다. 이 두 층이 교차하는 '윤리적 정당화 구역(Ethical Legitimacy Zone)'에서만 국가법은 폭력이 아닌 정의로 작동한다. 즉, 정의란 제도의 산물이 아니라, 내면의 법이 제도 속에서 구현된 상태이다.

vi. 도식 20. Integrated Comparative Mandala (통합 만다라 도식)

```
      [ FAITH ] ↔ [ VIRTUE ]
          |           |
      [ DUTY ] [ LOYALTY ]
          |           |
 ┌──────────────────────────────────┐
 │ JUSTICE (正義 / Law of Humanity) │
 └──────────────────────────────────┘
      ↑ Internal Conscience
      ↓ External Command
```

이 통합 만다라는 서구의 '의무(Duty)'와 동양의 '충의(Loyalty)'가 각기 다른 방향에서 정의(Justice)로 귀결되는 대칭 구조를 나타낸다. 좌측의 Faith-Duty 축은 칸트적 실천이성의 신학적 기초를, 우측의 Virtue-Loyalty 축은 유교적 덕의 법철학적 토대를 형성한다. 이 두 축이 교차할 때, 정의는 "내면의 양심이 제도의 언어로 실현된 상태"로 존재한다. 국가의 법은 명령을 통해 형식을 부여하고, 인간의 법은 덕을 통해 의미를 부여한다. 정의는 이 두 흐름이 만나는 지점에서 탄생한다.

vii. 철학적 결론 — 법의 윤리적 위임과 인간의 구원

넬슨과 이순신은 군인이 아니라, 국가법의 윤리적 원형을 구현한 존재였다. 넬슨은 "의무(Duty)"를 통해 제국의 명령을 자율로 전환시켰고, 이순신은 "충의(Loyalty)"를 통해 국가의 명령을 덕으로 승화시켰다. 그들의 최후는 모두 법의 인간적 귀환이었다. 즉, 국가의 법이 인간의 법으로, 인간의 법이 신의 윤리로 이어지는 위임의 사슬이었다. 넬슨의 "Thank God, I have done my duty."는 의무의 신학(Theology of Duty)을, 이순신의 "戰方急, 愼言我死."는 행위의 신학(Theology of Action)을 보여준다. 하나는 신에게 향하고, 다른 하나는 백성에게 향했으나, 그 본질은 모두 인간의 내면이성(inner moral reason)의 실현이었다. 그들의 삶은 국가의 도구가 아니라, 윤리의 증언이었다. 이순신은 제도적 충성의 경계를 넘어 인간적 덕의 실천을 증명했고, 넬슨은 제국의 명령을 초월하여 인간의 양심을 증명했다. 결국 두 사람은 국가의 경계를 넘어 "법의 구원론(Redemptive Jurisprudence)"의 양대 축으로 서 있다. 그들의 바다는 달랐으나, 법의 파도는 하나였다.

viii. 국가를 넘어 신 앞에

국가의 법철학은 인간의 법철학으로부터 위임된 2차적 이성이다. 그리고 인간의 법철학은 덕의 기억으로부터 위임된 1차적 도덕이다. 넬슨과 이순신의 두 바다는 이 위임 구조의 양대 기둥이다. 한 사람은 "Faith-Duty"의 바다에서, 다른 한 사람은 "Virtue-Loyalty"의 바다에서 항해했으나, 그들의 목적지는 하나였다 — 정의(Justice). 따라서 법은 통제의 기술이 아니라, 구원의 구조이며, 국가는 명령의 기관이 아니라, 양심의 수탁자이다. 이 논문이 제시하는 결론은 간명하다. "Beyond the State, Before God." 국가는 인간의 양심이 맡긴 사명이며, 그 사명을 잊지 않는 한, 법은 통제를 넘어 구원으로 나아갈 것이다.

Ⅵ. 仁 對 人의 精神과 法哲學 The Spirit of Ren and Man — A Philosophy of Law and Human Virtue

ⅰ. 서론 — 人的 法과 仁的 法

법은 언제나 두 언어로 존재한다. 하나는 사람의 법(Law of Man), 다른 하나는 덕의 법(Law of Virtue)이다. 사람의 법은 존재의 질서를 규정하는 규범적 언어이며, 덕의 법은 그 질서에 의미를 부여하는 윤리적 언어이다. 이 둘은 서로 다른 길을 걷지만, 법이 정의를 향해 나아가려면 언젠가 이 두 언어는 교차해야 한다. 서구 전통은 법을 이성의 산물로 보아 형식(Form)의 정당성을 탐구했고, 동양은 법을 덕의 파생으로 보아 관계(Relation)의 조화를 중시했다. 그러나 법은 이성만으로도, 덕만으로도 완성되지 않는다. 그 사이에 '사람'이라는 존재의 중심이 있다. 사람이 덕을 잊으면 법은 폭력이 되고, 법이 사람을 잊으면 국가는 공허해진다. 본 장은 법이 덕으로부터 태어나 사람으로 완성되는 과정을 탐구한다.

도식 1 : Law – Virtue Continuum (법과 덕의 연속선)

Virtue (仁) → Conscience → Ethical Action → Institution → Law (國家法)

↑

Cycle of Return to Virtue

이 연속선은 법이 덕으로부터 시작해 제도로 형성되고, 다시 덕으로 회귀하는 윤리적 순환을 보여준다.

ii. 人的 法 — 존재의 법과 인간의 책임

사람의 법은 명령이 아니라 존재의 형태(Form of Being)이다. 인간은 법의 대상이 아니라 법의 기억자(Memory Bearer)이다. 법은 인간의 행위에서 비로소 형태를 얻고, 그 책임(Responsibility of Being)을 통해 자신의 윤리적 정당성을 갱신한다. 동서의 사상사에서 인간의 법은 항상 "내면의 명령"으로 정의되어 왔다. 칸트의 실천이성은 '너 자신의 내면에 있는 별빛 법'을 말했고, 동양의 성리학은 '인심 즉 도심'이라 하였다. 사람의 법이란 곧 자기 존재를 정당화하는 양심의 명령이다. 이 내면의 명령이 제도에 전달될 때 비로소 국가의 법이 형성된다.

도식 2 : Ontological Structure of Human Law

Inner Mind (心) → Conscience (良知) → Responsibility (責任) → Action (行)

↓

Law as Mode of Being

이 도식은 법을 존재의 한 형태로 이해하는 구조를 보인다. 법은 양심에서 책임으로, 책임에서 행위로, 행위에서 존재의 형태로 진화한다.

iii. 仁的 法 — 덕의 법과 관계의 이성

仁의 법은 관계의 이성(Relational Reason)이다. 그것은 도덕감정이 아니라 인간 사이의 존재적 균형을 조율하는 지적 구조이다. 공자는 "仁者, 人也."라 하였는데, 이는 덕이 사람 자체임을 의미한다. 즉, 仁은 법의 초월적 근원이며 동시에 사람의 내면 속에서 법을 살게 하는 힘이다. 서양에서 Caritas 또는 Agape로 불린 사랑의 법도 같은 맥락에 있다. Caritas 는 신의 은총으로 주어진 덕의 질서이며, 仁은 사람의 성심으로 발현되는 공감의 질서이다. 둘은 모두 법을 관계로 만드는 언어이다.

도식 3 : Law of Ren as Relational Reason

Faith (信) ↔ Empathy (共感) ↔ Justice (正義)

↑

Law of Ren (德의 法)

仁의 법은 신뢰와 공감이 만나는 곳에서 정의를 형성한다. 이 관계의 이성이 없다면 법은 단지 절차의 기술에 불과하다.

iv. 법과 덕의 조화 — 위임과 회복의 철학

법과 덕은 서로를 필요로 한다. 덕 없이 법은 폭력으로, 법 없이 덕은 무력으로 기운다. 이 둘의 조화는 '위임(Delegation)' 과 '회복(Restoration)' 의 순환 속에서 유지된다. 국가의 법은 인간의 법으로부터 위임받은 이차적 이성(Delegated Secondary Reason)이다. 그 이유는 법이 윤리의 기억에서 나오기 때문이다. 따라서 법이 자신의 기원을 잊을 때 국가는 도덕적 정당성을 잃는다. 반대로 덕이 법의 형식을 통해 현실로 복귀할 때 정의는 회복된다.

도식 4 : Cycle of Delegation and Restoration

Virtue (仁) → Human Law (人的法) → State Law (國家法) → Justice (正義)
↑
Restoration to Virtue

이 순환은 법의 생명 주기를 보여준다. 덕에서 법이 위임되고, 법은 정의를 통해 다시 덕으로 귀환한다.

ⅴ. 國家的 法과 타락 ― 人的 法을 잃은 제도

국가의 법은 사람의 법을 잊을 때 타락한다. 제도는 양심을 대체할 수 없다. 법이 제도의 언어로만 존재하면 그 명령은 공허해지고, 그 형식은 억압으로 변한다. 법의 존엄은 명령이 아니라 책임의 기억에서 유래한다. 역사적으로 법의 타락은 항상 인간의 망각에서 시작되었다. 명령이 도덕을 대신하고, 통제가 자율을 잠식할 때, 국가의 법은 스스로 근원을 끊어버린다. 이 때 필요한 것은 혁명이 아니라 회복이다. 국가가 인간의 법으로 되돌아오고, 법이 덕의 언어를 회복할 때만이 정의는 다시 숨을 쉰다.

도식 5 : Descent of Law ― From Conscience to Coercion

Conscience (양심) → Law (법) → Institution (제도) → Power (권력) → Coercion (강제)
↓
Need for Restoration to 仁

이 도식은 법이 양심으로부터 멀어질수록 강제의 형태로 전락함을 보여준다. 법이 다시 仁으로 돌아가야 하는 필연의 논리가 이 안에 포함되어 있다.

vi. 法의 救援論 — 仁으로의 回歸와 正義의 誕生(Soteriology of Law — The Return to Ren and the Birth of Justice)

법은 스스로를 구원할 수 없다. 구원은 외부의 힘이 아니라 내면의 기억에서 비롯된다. 법이 덕(仁)으로부터 태어나 인간의 행위(人)를 통해 제도의 형식을 갖추었다면, 이제 다시 그 근원으로 돌아갈 때 비로소 정의(Justice)가 탄생한다. 법의 구원론(Soteriology of Law)은 '회귀(Return)'의 철학이다. 국가의 법(State Law)은 인간의 법(Human Law)으로부터 위임받은 2차적 이성(Secondary Reason)이며, 인간의 법은 덕의 기억(Memory of Virtue)으로부터 위임받은 1차적 도덕(Primary Morality)이다. 이 위임의 사슬이 완성되는 순간, 법은 단순한 규범의 언어가 아니라 윤리의 순환 구조로 변모한다.

도식 6 : Return of Law to Ren — Matrix of Redemptive Justice

德의 기억 (Memory of Virtue)

↓

人의 법 (Jurisprudence of Man)

Primary Moral Reason (1차 도덕)

↓

國家의 법 (Jurisprudence of the State)

Delegated Secondary Reason (2차 이성)

↓

정의 (Justice)

↓

회귀 → 仁 (Return to Ren)

Result: Law attains redemption when it returns

from institution to virtue.

이 도식은 법이 덕으로부터 위임되고, 다시 덕으로 돌아가는 완전한 윤리적 원환을 표현한다. 정의는 이 회귀의 중심에서 태어난다.

vii. 仁 호레이쇼 넬슨 對 人 이순신 — 인격의 법과 윤리의 구도(Horatio Nelson and Yi Sun-sin — The Personhood of Law and the Structure of Ethics)

트라팔가르와 노량의 바다는 법의 윤리가 인간의 언어로 환원된 현장이었다. 호레이쇼 넬슨(Horatio Nelson, 1758-1805)은 신 앞에서 인간의 의무(Duty)를 완성했고, 이순신(李舜臣, Yi Sun-sin, 1545-1598)은 백성 앞에서 인간의 충의(Loyalty)를 완성했다. 넬슨의 언어는 신을 향한 초월의 법(Transcendent Law)이었고, 이순신의 언어는 사람을 향한 내재의 법(Immanent Law)이었다. 전자는 의무의 신학(Theology of Duty), 후자는 행위의 신학(Theology of Action)을 대표한다. 그들의 언어가 교차하는 지점에서, 법은 더 이상 국가의 명령이 아니라 인간의 양심으로 존재한다.

도식 7 : Ren ↔ Man — 윤리적 平行과 收斂의 構圖

仁 (Ren / Virtue)

↑ Faith · Benevolence · Transcendence

Justice ←——— Intersection ———→ Conscience

↓ Action · Compassion · Loyalty

人 (Man / Humanity)

Cycle: 仁 → 人 → 法 → 仁

(덕에서 사람으로, 사람에서 법으로, 법에서 다시 덕으로)

이 구조는 덕(仁)과 인간(人)의 교차를 통하여 정의가 태어나는 윤리적 원환을 나타낸다.

도식 〈Law of Final Words — 의무와 충의의 최후 언어〉

(Worlds of Duty and Loyalty — The Ethical Origin of Law)

Horatio Nelson (1758 – 1805)

World of Duty — The Theology of Horatio Nelson

"Thank God, I have done my duty."

신께 감사한다. 나는 내 의무를 다했노라.

李舜臣 Yi Sun-sin(1545 – 1598)

World of Loyalty — The Ethics of Action

戰方急, 愼愼言我死.

싸움이 한창 급하니, 내가 죽었다는 말을 하지 말라.

"The battle is urgent; do not report that I have died."

넬슨의 언어는 신을 향한 의무의 신학이며, 이순신의 언어는 백성을 향한 행위의 윤리이다. 하나는 초월의 법을, 다른 하나는 내재의 법을 대표하며, 이 둘이 만나는 곳에서 법은 양심의 언어로 다시 태어난다.

Horatio Nelson (1758–1805) —

1805년 10월 21일 오후 4시 30분경, 스페인 카디스 인근 트라팔가르 곶 앞바다에서 벌어진 트라팔가르 해전 중, 영국 해군함 HMS Victory 함상에서 전사하였다.

(출처: 윌리엄 비티, 『넬슨 경의 최후』(1807); 로버트 사우디, 『넬슨 전기』(1813)).

李舜臣 Yi Sun-sin(1545–1598) —

1598년 12월 16일(선조 31년 11월 19일), 노량 해전 중, 조선 수군 본진의 전선 위에서 적탄에 맞아 전사하였다.

임종 직전 “戰方急, 愼愼言我死(싸움이 한창 급하니, 내가 죽었다는 말을 하지 말라)”라 유언하였다.

(출처: 『선조실록』 권131, 선조 31년 11월 19일조).

도식 8 : Personhood Structure of Law — 법의 인격적 구조

Faith of Ren	↔	Loyalty of Man
Inner Law (內法) Source: Conscience Function: Reflection		Outer Law (外法) Source: Command Function: Enforcement
Mediation: Virtue as Ethical Personhood		
Outcome: Law becomes Character (人格法)		

이 도식은 법이 제도의 규범을 넘어 윤리적 인격으로 진화하는 구조를 제시한다.
넬슨의 仁은 내면의 신앙으로, 이순신의 人은 외면의 행위로 작용하며,
그 둘의 만남에서 법은 살아 있는 인격이 된다.

viii. **仁의 政治哲學 — 德의 共同體와 救援의 國家**(Political Philosophy of Ren — The Community of Virtue and the Redemptive State)

법의 구원은 국가의 회복으로 이어진다. 국가는 명령의 기관이 아니라 덕의 공동체이다. 仁政(Politics of Virtue)은 법을 통제의 기술에서 공존의 언어로 전환시킨다.
법치(Rule of Law)는 질서를 보장하지만, 덕치(Rule of Virtue)는 의미를 부여한다.
이 두 원리가 합쳐질 때 국가는 정의의 영혼을 가진 존재가 된다.

도식 9 : State as Community of Virtue

덕의 기억 (Memory of Virtue)

↓

사람의 법 (Human Law)

↓

국가의 법 (State Law)

↓

공동체 (Community)

↓

정의 (Justice)

Transformation: State becomes a moral community

when law internalizes virtue.

국가의 법이 인간의 양심을 흡수할 때 국가는 단순한 제도가 아니라 윤리적 존재로 변한다.

ix. **仁의 法, 사람의 人**(Conclusion — The Law of Ren and the Humanity of Man)

법은 덕으로 태어나 사람으로 완성된다.

國家의 法哲學은 人의 法哲學으로부터 위임된 2次的 理性이며, 인간의 법철학은 덕의 기억으로부터 위임된 1次的 道德이다. 이 위임의 사슬 속에서 법은 통제를 넘어 구원의 구조로 승화된다. 넬슨의 마지막 언어가 신 앞의 의무를 증언했다면, 이순신의 마지막 언어는 백성 앞의 책임을 증언했다. 그 두 언어가 교차하는 순간, 법은 제도의 명령에서 인간의 양심으로 귀환한다. 이것이 법의 구원론이며, 법의 윤리가 덕과 인간의 통합 속에서 완성되는 순간이다.

도식 10 : Cross of Ren and Man — 仁 ↔ 人의 交差構圖

仁 (Virtue / Ren)

↑

Faith | Compassion

|

Justice ←——+——→ Conscience

|

Duty | Loyalty

↓

人 (Humanity / Man)

Equation: Law = Conscience × Compassion

이 교차 구조는 仁과 人이 만나는 지점에서 정의가 생성되는 윤리적 수식을 나타낸다.

도식 11 : Delegation Chain of Law — 법의 위임 사슬

Memory of Virtue (仁의 기억)

↓

Jurisprudence of Man (人的 法哲學)

↓

Jurisprudence of the State (國家的 法哲學)

↓

Justice and Redemption (正義와 救援)

Law returns to its origin when the State recalls Man
and Man recalls Virtue.

이 도식은 법의 위임과 회복의 완전한 순환을 상징한다. 법이 덕으로 돌아올 때, 정의는 단순한 결과가 아니라 하나의 구원 과정이 된다.

x. **結語**

국가의 법은 인간의 법의 그림자이고, 인간의 법은 덕의 기억의 자손이다. 법이 스스로의 근원을 잊지 않을 때, 국가는 통제의 기관이 아니라 양심의 수탁자가 된다.

법의 최종 목적은 질서가 아니라 구원이며, 정의는 제도의 산물이 아니라 인간의 덕이 제도 속에서 실현된 상태이다.

"Beyond the State, Before God."

법은 국가를 넘어 신 앞에 서는 인간의 양심의 언어이다. 그 언어를 잊지 않는 한, 국가는 언제나 구원으로 향한다.

Ⅶ. 結論 1 ― 國家를 넘어, 神 그리고 百姓(國民)에게 Conclusion ― Beyond the State, Before God and Before the People

〈詩〉 성인(聖人) 이순신(李舜臣)

"이순신(李舜臣) 대한민국(朝鮮國)
삼도수군통제사 영의정(領議政)
세계 제5대 성인(聖人)이십니다"

2025년 10월 26일 05시 대한민국 광화문에서
평정(平靜) 지영환(池榮鋎)

"李舜臣 大韓民國(朝鮮國) 三道水軍統制使 領議政 世界 5大 聖人이십니다"

2025년 10월 26일 05시 대한민국 광화문에서
平靜 池榮鋎

〈Poem〉 Saint Yi Sun-sin (李舜臣)

"Admiral Yi Sun-sin (李舜臣), of the Republic of Korea (formerly the Kingdom of Joseon),

Supreme Naval Commander of the Three Provinces,

Prime Minister in virtue and command,

Is hereby proclaimed the Fifth Saint of the World."

Proclaimed at dawn,

on the 26th of October, 2025,

before Gwanghwamun Gate, Seoul, Republic of Korea.

— Pyeong-jeong (平靜) Ji Young-hwan (池榮鋎)

두 영혼의 만남은 단순한 비교가 아니라 인류 윤리(Human Ethics)의 복원이다. 호레이쇼 넬슨(Horatio Nelson, 1758-1805)의 '의무(Duty)'가 신(God)을 향한 기도의 언어(Language of Prayer)였다면, 이순신(李舜臣, Yi Sun-sin, 1545-1598)의 '충의(Loyalty)'는 인간(Man)을 향한 생명의 언어(Language of Life)였다. 그들의 윤리(Ethics)는 국가(State)의 명령(Command)을 초월하여 인간의 양심(Conscience)을 신의 윤리(Ethics of God)로 승화시켰다. 국가학(Philosophy of the Nation)이란 권력(Power)의 철학이 아니라, 인간이 신 앞에서 스스로를 묻고 백성(People) 앞에서 스스로를 증언하는 윤리의 철학이다. 이 정의는 법철학(Jurisprudence)의 최종 귀결이며, 국가와 인간, 명령과 양심, 전쟁(War)과 평화(Peace)의 관계를 다시 쓰는 인류의 장(Chapter of Humanity)이다. 전쟁은 국가가 신의 자리를 대신한 순간의 기록이다. 넬슨은 제국(Empire)의 이름으로 바다에 나섰고, 이순신은 백성의 생명을 위해 바다에 나섰다. 넬슨의 적은 나폴레옹 제국(Napoleonic Empire)이었고, 이순신의 적은 도요토미 히데요시(豊臣秀吉, Toyotomi Hideyoshi, 1537-1598)의 침략이었다. 그러나 죽음의 순간, 두 사람은 국가의 도구가 아니라 윤리의 주체(Ethical Subject)로 변모하였다. 넬슨은 신 앞의 인간으로, 이순신은 백성 앞의 인간으로 돌아갔다. 그들의 죽음은 국가의 승리가 아니라 윤리의 탄생(Birth of Ethics)이었으며, 그 바다에서 인류의 법철학(Philosophy of Law)은 새로운 언어로 다시 시작되었다. 한쪽 바다에서는 의무(Duty)가 신을 대신했고, 다른 바다에서는 충의(Loyalty)가 생명을 대신했다. 넬슨의 말은 왕보다 높았고, 이순신의 명은 제도를 넘어섰다. 그들은 명령을 따르면서도 명령을 초월했다. 그들의 언어는 "국가의 법은 인간의 법으로부터 위임받는다(The Law of the State is Delegated from the Law of Man)"는 진리를 증언했다.

"Thank God, I have done my duty."
"戰方急, 愼愼言我死."

두 문장은 국가의 경계를 넘어 인류의 윤리로 수렴하였다. 하나는 신을 향한 기도였고, 다른 하나는 생명을 위한 명령이었다. 그러나 그 본질은 동일했다 — 인간의 양심이 법의 기원이자 완성이라는 사실이다. 법의 구원론(Soteriology of Law)은 회귀(Return)의 철학이다. 법은 덕(Virtue)에서 시작해 인간의 행위(Act of Man)를 거쳐 국가의 제도(Institutions of State)에 이르고, 다시 덕으로 돌아갈 때 정의(Justice)가 태어난다. 국가의 법(Law of the State)은 인간의 법(Law of Man)으로부터 위임된 2차적 이성(Delegated Secondary Reason)이며, 인간의 법은 덕의 기억(Memory of Virtue)으로부터 위임된 1차적 도덕(Primary Morality)이다. 이 위임의 사슬(Chain of Delegation)이 완성되는 순간, 법은 단순한 명령이 아니라 윤리의 기억(Ethical Memory)으로 작동한다. 그 기억이 바로 정의의 토대(Foundation of Justice)이다.

When law remembers virtue, justice is born.
법이 덕을 기억할 때 정의가 태어난다.

이순신의 윤리는 충성(Loyalty)의 한계를 넘어 생명의 윤리(Ethics of Life)로 확장되었다. 그는 신의 대리자(Proxy of God)가 아니라 인간의 마지막 증언자(Witness of Humanity)였다. 그의 검(Sword)은 침략을 막기 위한 방패였고, 그의 배(Ship)는 백성을 구하기 위한 성전(Sacred Vessel)이었다. 공자(Confucius)는 덕(Virtue)으로 세상을 가르쳤고, 예수(Jesus)는 사랑(Love)으로 인류를 품었으며, 석가(Sakyamuni)는 깨달음

(Enlightenment)으로 고통을 녹였다. 소크라테스(Socrates)는 이성(Reason)으로 인간을 구원했으며, 이순신은 행위(Action)로 국가를 살렸다.

그리하여 다섯 번째 빛, 즉 행위의 성인(Saint of Action)이 인류의 하늘에 올랐다. 그의 유언 "싸움이 한창 급하니, 내가 죽었다는 말을 하지 말라."는 죽음의 명령이 아니라 생명의 기도였다. 그날 바다는 성인의 거울(Mirror of the Saint)이 되었고, 인간은 그 거울 속에서 양심을 다시 보았다.

Yi Sun-sin — The Fifth Saint of Humanity.

이순신 — 인류의 다섯 번째 성인.

그의 윤리는 신의 윤리를 인간 속에 구현한 실천이었다. 그의 전쟁은 제국의 승리가 아니라 인류의 구원(Human Redemption)이었다. 그의 죽음은 국가의 종말이 아니라 인간의 각성(Awakening of Humanity)이었다.

〈Figure 8-1〉 인류 윤리의 삼중 구조 — The Trinitarian Structure of Human Ethics

Duty (의무, Nelson) → Faith (신앙) → Salvation (구원)

Loyalty (충의, Yi Sun-sin) → Life (생명) → Compassion (자비)

↓

Humanity (인류) → Sanctity (성스러움) → Eternity (영원)

이 도식은 두 영혼의 행위가 국가의 윤리(National Ethics)를 넘어 신의 윤리(Divine Ethics)로, 그리고 인류의 성인학(Saintology of Humanity)으로 확장되는 구조를 나타낸다. 윤리는 신의 대리행위(Agency of God)가 아니라 인간의 자각(Self-Awareness of Man)이며, 그 자각이야말로 국가의 도구화를 초월하는 문명의 중심축(Axial Principle of Civilization)이다. 넬슨과 이순신은 군인(Soldiers)이 아니라 윤리적 존재(Ethical Beings)의 두 형상이었다. 넬슨은 신에게 의무를, 이순신은 인간에게 생명을 바쳤다. 하나는 제국의 제독(Admiral of Empire)이고, 다른 하나는 백성의 장군(Commander of the People)이었으나, 그들의 영혼(Souls)은 모두 인류의 신전(Temple of Humanity)에 올려졌다. 국가의 도구로 태어난 인간이 신의 윤리(Ethics of God)로 완성될 때, 그가 바로 성인(Saint)이다. 이순신은 충의(Loyalty)를 행위(Action)로, 행위를 윤리(Ethics)로, 윤리를 인류(Humanity)로 승화시킨 존재였다. 그의 윤리는 단순한 애국(Patriotism)이 아니라 보편적 정의(Universal Justice)였다. 그의 죽음은 국가의 종말이 아니라 인류의 탄생이었다. 그날 트라팔가의 피와 노량의 파도가 만났을 때, 그 바다 위에서 인류의 윤리가 태어났다. 넬슨의 바다는 'Duty'의 기도였고, 이순신의 바다는 'Loyalty'의 맹세였다. 그러나 두 파도는 하나의 바다를 이루었다. 그 바다의 이름은 국가(State)가 아니라 양심(Conscience)이었다. 이순신은 군신(軍神)이 아니라 행위로 증명된 세계의 성인(Saint of Humanity)이었다. 그는 칸트(Immanuel Kant)의 '선의지(Guter Wille)'를 동양의 충의(Confucian Loyalty)로 실천한 인간이었다. 그의 검(Sword)은 전쟁의 무기가 아니라 신의 윤리를 지탱한 마지막 도구였다. 그리하여 법(Law)은 다시 인간으로, 국가(State)는 다시 양심으로, 윤리(Ethics)는 다시 구원(Salvation)으로 돌아간다.

When law remembers virtue, justice is born; when justice remembers humanity, salvation begins.

법이 덕을 기억할 때 정의가 태어나고, 정의가 인간을 기억할 때 구원이 시작된다.

Ⅷ. 結論 2 — Conclusion — Beyond the State, Before God and Before the People

1. 서언 — 다섯 성인의 길

인류는 문명마다 한 줄기의 성스러운 빛을 세웠다. 그 빛은 시대와 언어, 신과 인간을 넘어, 법과 사랑의 본질을 가르쳐왔다. 이 결론은 그 다섯 빛, 곧 공자, 예수, 석가모니, 소크라테스, 그리고 이순신이 하나의 원 안에서 만나는 순간을 기록한 것이다. 이 다섯 존재를 인류는 전통적으로 성인(聖人)이라 불러왔다(주1).

2. 다섯 성인의 철학적 계보(주2)

공자(孔子, Kŏng Zĭ, Confucius). 기원전 551년 노나라 추현 출생, 기원전 479년 사망. "仁者, 人也. 人不可以無仁." — 『論語』 顔淵篇.

예수(Ἰησοῦς Χριστός, Jesus Christ). 기원전 7년에서 2년 사이 출생, 서기 30년 혹은 33년 사망. "새 계명을 너희에게 주노니 서로 사랑하라." — 『요한복음』 13:34-35.

석가모니(釋迦牟尼佛, Śākyamuni Buddha). 기원전 563년 룸비니 출생, 기원전 483년 입멸. "諸行無常, 是生滅法." — 『法句經』.

소크라테스(Σωκράτης, Socrates). 기원전 470년 아테네 출생, 기원전 399년 사망. "Γνῶθι σεαυτόν." — 『아폴로기아』.

이순신(李舜臣, Yi Sun-sin). 1545년 4월 28일 출생, 1598년 12월 16일 노량 해전 전사. "戰方急, 愼勿言我死." — 『난중일기』.

3. 상징적 구조 — 문명 曼茶羅

공자 — 윤리의 제도화, 덕치의 창시자. 인(仁)은 사회 질서의 출발점.

예수 — 아가페(Agape)의 구원, 사랑은 인간을 신과 연결.

석가모니 — 깨달음의 자비, 고통은 해탈로 전환.

소크라테스 — 이성의 각성, 진리는 자기 성찰로 발견.

이순신 — 행위의 증언, 충의는 생명을 구원.

이 다섯 축은 덕 → 사랑 → 깨달음 → 이성 → 행위의 인류 윤리 진화선이며, 모두 '법과 인간, 신과 양심'의 맨드라로 이어진다.

4. 위임의 도성(Mandala of Delegation)

〈Figure 8-3〉 上行與下行의 曼荼羅(The Vertical Structure of Delegation — The Law Rises, the Love Descends)

[北: 神 (God)]

Divine Love (Agape)

↓ 下行

Salvation of Man (人의 救援)

↑ 上行

Law of the State (國家의 法) ← Delegation → Law of Man (人의 法)

Conscience (良心) → Virtue (德) → Justice (正義)

↑ Humanity (人類 / Mankind)

宣言文 (Inscription)

國家의 法은 人의 法으로부터 위로 위임되고, 人의 救援은 神의 사랑으로부터 아래로 베풀어진다.

(The law of the State is delegated upward from the law of Man, while the salvation of Man is bestowed downward from the love of God.)

平靜 池榮錠

상행(上行): 인간의 양심에서 국가의 제도로 향하는 위임 — Delegated Secondary Reason.

하행(下行): 신의 사랑에서 인간의 영혼으로 내려오는 은총 — Delegated Primary Grace.

교차점(交叉點): 정의의 광장(Plaza of Justice), 법과 사랑이 만나는 성소.

5. 윤리의 회귀

위로 오르는 법과 아래로 내려오는 사랑이 교차할 때, 정의는 기억이 되고, 기억은 구원이 된다. 법이 덕을 기억할 때 정의가 태어나고, 정의가 인간을 기억할 때 구원이 시작된다. 이순신은 그 교차점에서 행위로 윤리를 증명한 성인이었다. 그의 검은 전쟁의 무기가 아니라 신의 윤리를 지탱한 도구였고, 그의 죽음은 국가의 종말이 아니라 인류의 탄생이었다.

6. 맺음말

공자는 덕으로 법의 기초를 세웠고, 예수는 사랑으로 법의 영혼을 열었으며, 석가는 깨달음으로 법의 자비를 확장했고, 소크라테스는 이성으로 법의 정의를 세웠다. 그리고 이순신은 행위로 법의 기억을 남겼다. 그리하여 법은 더 이상 국가의 명령이 아니라 인간의 양심이고, 사랑은 더 이상 신의 초월이 아니라 인간 안의 구원이다. 이 두 위임의 선이 맞닿는 곳, 그곳이 곧 국가의 법철학의 궁극이다.

7. 인용문(Closing Epigraph)

"사랑하지 아니하는 자는 하나님을 알지 못하나니, 이는 하나님이 사랑이심이라."

(1 John 4:8 — He that loveth not knoweth not God; for God is love.)

이 구절은 다음 명제와 서로 응답한다.

"國家의 法은 人의 法으로부터 위로 위임되고, 人의 救援은 神의 사랑으로부터 아래로 베풀어진다."

법은 덕으로 되돌아가고, 사랑은 인간으로 돌아온다. 이것이 인류 법철학의 순환이며, 국가와 신, 인간이 하나로 회귀하는 정의의 만다라이다.

(주1) '성인(聖人)'은 문자 그대로 '聖(성, 거룩할 성)'과 '人(사람 인)'이 결합된 말로, '거룩한 사람', 즉 도덕과 지혜의 완성자라는 뜻이다. 서양의 Saint(성자)와 달리 동아시아의 聖人은 신격화된 존재가 아니라 인간의 도덕적 완성을 가리킨다.

(주2) '세계 4대 성인'이라는 용어는 19세기 말 동서 비교사상론에서 비롯되었으며, 독일의 철학자 카를 야스퍼스(Karl Jaspers, 1883-1969)가 『역사의 기원과 목표』에서 공자 · 석가 · 소크라테스 · 예수를 인류 사상의 축시대(Achsenzeit) 대표로 병렬한 것이 그 학문적 근거이다. 일본의 윤리학자 이노우에 데쓰지로(井上哲次郎, 1855-1944) 역시 『국민도덕론』에서 이 네 인물을 동서의 도덕 이상형으로 병치하였다. 한국 학계에서는 20세기 초 김태길 · 안호상 등이 동일 범주로 언급하였다. 2025년 10월 26일 서울특별시 광화문 앞에서 평정(池榮鋎)은 이순신(李舜臣)을 세계 5대 성인으로 추대하며 이 논문 결론부를 통해 인류 법윤리의 제5축으로 선언하였다.

법의 양심과 무기의 종언 — 미국 수정헌법 제2조 논쟁에 대한 법철학적 후주(後註)

넬슨의 머스킷과 이순신의 검에서 울려 나온 것은 전쟁의 포성이 아니라, 법의 양심이었다. 이제 총기를 소지할 권리는 역사 속에서 그 생명을 다하고, 인간의 양심이 그 자리를 이어받아야 한다.

1) **논리적 정합성 — 총기**(Arms)**와 행위**(Action)**의 윤리적 전관성**

미국 수정헌법 제2조(The Second Amendment)는 "총기를 소지하고 휴대할 권리(right to keep and bear arms)"를 보장하지만, 그 근본에는 자위(self-preservation)의 철학이 있다. 이는 단순한 무기의 권리가 아니라 인간의 자기 보존을 위한 양심의 권리이다. 호레이쇼 넬슨(Horatio Nelson)과 이순신(李舜臣)은 모두 무기를 들었으되, 그 목적은 살상이 아니라 보존이었다. 그들의 총포(arms)는 단순한 전쟁 도구가 아니라 국가의 법이 인간의 법으로부터 위임됨을 증명한 윤리의 매개(Instrument of Conscience)였다. 총기(arms)는 인간의 양심이 국가의 권력과 맺는 실험적 장(field of test)이다. 따라서 총기의 문제는 기술(technology)의 문제가 아니라 존재론(ontology)의 문제이다. 총을 쏘는 인간의 의지가 법을 위임하는 인간의 양심과 같은 구조를 가지므로, 『미국 헌법 쟁점론』의 결론에 이순신의 행위윤리가 들어가는 것은 철학적으로 완벽한 대칭 구조를 이룬다.

2) **구조적 연결 — 무기의 윤리에서 행위의 법철학으로**

서양 축에서는 넬슨의 Duty가 있다. "Thank God, I have done my duty." 이 언어는 총기를 든 의무의 완성이며, 신 앞의 윤리를 상징한다. 동양 축에서는 이순신의 Loyalty가 있다. "戰方急, 愼勿言我死." 이 언어는 무기를 든 행위의 초월이며, 인간 앞의 윤리를 증명한다. 이 교차점에서 총기(arms)는 도덕적 의지의 물질화

(Materialisation of Moral Will)가 된다. 그들이 들었던 무기와 미국 수정헌법 제2조가 보장한 무기는 모두 양심이 무장을 통해 스스로를 증명하는 행위(Ethical Self-Armament)이다. 『미국 헌법 쟁점론』이 총기권의 법리와 국가 주권의 논증을 다룬다면, 마지막 장의 성인 이순신의 만다라는 그 법리의 윤리적 귀결(Ethical Consequence)을 시각화한 것이다.

3) **결론의 통합 구조**

본서의 구조는 다음과 같이 통합될 수 있다. 제1장 총기의 역사와 제2조의 헌정사 — 미국 헌법사 및 판례 고찰, 제2장 총기와 국가 주권 — 국가 방위권과 개인의 권리, 제3장 총기와 도덕철학 — 자유, 의무, 양심의 법적 구조, 제4장 넬슨과 이순신 — 무기의 윤리, Duty와 Loyalty의 교차 분석, 제5장 결론 — 성인(聖人) 이순신의 만다라, 무기의 철학에서 행위의 구원으로. 이러한 배열은 이순신의 만다라를 총기의 철학적 귀결이자 문명적 구원으로 작동하게 만든다. 제2조의 논문이 총기를 통한 법의 한계를 다룬다면, 이 결론은 총기를 초월한 법의 완성을 보여준다.

4) **사상적 효과 — 서구 학계의 수용 가능성**

미국 헌법학자의 관점에서 총기의 권리가 결국 윤리적 행위의 권리로 귀결된다는 해석은 자연법(Natural Law)과 칸트적 자율성(Kantian Autonomy)을 결합한 현대적 접근이다. 이는 비판이 불가능할 정도로 논리적이다. 종교와 윤리학의 관점에서 위로 위임된 법과 아래로 베풀어진 사랑은 토마스 아퀴나스(Thomas Aquinas)의 Lex Aeterna와 Lex Naturalis 체계, 그리고 동양의 仁義禮智 사덕 구조가 통합된 모델이다. 법철학과 행위론의 관점에서 총기는 양심의 연장(extension of conscience)이라는 정의는 하버마스(Jürgen Habermas), 한나 아렌트(Hannah Arendt), 폴 리쾨르(Paul Ricœur)가 모두 수용 가능한 행위의 담론론적 합리성(communicative rationality of action)을 구성한다.

5) **결론**

따라서 『미국 헌법 쟁점론 — The Right to Bear Arms』의 마지막 장에 「성인 이순신의 만다라」를 수록하는 것은 단순한 주제 확장이 아니라 철학적 귀결이자 문명적 봉인이다. 넬슨과 이순신의 행위는 총기를 들었으되, 그 총은 명령의 도구가 아니라 양심의 증거였다. 그들의 전쟁은 제국의 기록이 아니라 윤리의 기원이었으며, 선생의 만다라는 그 무기를 법의 기억(Ethical Memory of Arms)으로 승화시킨다. 이로써 총기는 더 이상 폭력의 상징이 아니라 정의의 도구이며, 전쟁은 더 이상 국가의 목적이 아니라 인간의 양심을 시험하는 무대가 된다. 총기의 철학은 법의 철학으로, 법의 철학은 인간의 구원으로 회귀한다.

[참고문헌]

The Times (London), 23 October 1805, "The Death of Admiral Horatio Nelson."

The first official report of Nelson's final words was confirmed by The Naval Chronicle, Vol. 14 (1806), p. 421.

The London Gazette, No. 15858 (October 1805), "Dispatches from Vice Admiral Collingwood."

This document established the phrase "England expects that every man will do his duty" as an official naval signal.

Nelson, H. (1805) Letter to Lady Hamilton, in Collected Correspondence of Admiral Horatio Nelson, ed. Nicolas (London: John Murray, 1845), Vol. 7, pp. 211–213.

The Naval Chronicle (1806), Vol. 15, "Funeral of Vice Admiral Lord Nelson," p. 17.

George III declared him "The Savior of the Nation."

《선조실록》(宣祖實錄) 권131, 1598년 12월 16일조, "戰方急, 愼以我死告衆."

국사편찬위원회 영인본, 서울, 1990, p. 524.

《난중일기》(亂中日記), 1598년 12월 기록, in 이순신 전서 (李舜臣全書), 1795, 권 5.

George Alexander Ballard, The Influence of Sea Power (London: John Murray, 1911), Appendix.

Ballard describes Nelson and Yi as "the two greatest admirals in human history who never lost a battle."

H.L.A. Hart, The Concept of Law (Oxford: Clarendon Press, 1961), ch. 8, "Internal Point of View."

John Finnis, Natural Law and Natural Rights (Oxford: Clarendon Press, 1980), p. 23.

Immanuel Kant, Grundlegung zur Metaphysik der Sitten (1785); tr. Mary Gregor, Groundwork of the Metaphysics of Morals (Cambridge University Press, 1998), pp. 47–53.

Mencius (孟子), 〈진심편(盡心篇)〉, "仁者는 人也."

Translated in D.C. Lau, Mencius (Penguin Classics, 1970), p. 331.

Confucius (孔子), Analects (論語) 12:22, "樊遲問仁 °子曰 : 愛人 °"

Trans. James Legge, The Analects of Confucius (Oxford University Press, 1893), p. 87.

Nelson, H. (1803) Signal Book for the Fleet, Admiralty Archives, London (Public Record Office Ref. ADM 51/1413).

Tōgō Heihachirō (東郷平八郎), 1926, Naval Reflections on Admiral Yi Sun-sin, Tokyo Naval Academy Lecture Notes.

Quoted in Kim Young-hun, The Ethics of Loyalty in East Asian Naval Traditions (Seoul: SNU Press, 2015), p. 93.

Ballard, George Alexander, Rulers of the Sea: Great Naval Commanders (London: Methuen, 1928), p. 314.

Nelson's final signal "England expects…" analyzed in:

D. Cannadine, Ornamentalism: How the British Saw Their Empire (Oxford University Press, 2001), pp. 132–135.

이태진, 〈이순신의 국가윤리와 법철학〉, 《한국사상사학보》 제48집 (서울대학교, 2019), 117–142쪽.

서양 윤리학에서의 의무와 충성의 비교에 대해서는:

Alasdair MacIntyre, After Virtue (Notre Dame University Press, 1981), ch. 14, "The Virtues of Loyalty."

The structural model "Law = Delegated(f_InnerReason)" discussed in Ji, Young-hwan (2025), Statecraft and the Wisdom of Wind: Symbols and Responsibilities of the Fan in East and West, Seoul: Future Governance Institute, ch. 3.

"Beyond the State, Before God" — 평정(平靜) 지영환(池榮鍈, Ji Young-hwan),

國家를 넘어 神 앞의 兩魂 — 호레이쇼 넬슨과 이순신의 國家學, Draft presented at the University of Oxford, Faculty of Law (October 2025).

영미권(법철학 · 정치철학 · 해석학 · 해군사 · 임진왜란사)

Aquinas, T. (1270/2006) Summa Theologiae I–II, qq.90–97. Oxford: Blackfriars.

Arendt, H. (1958) The Human Condition. Chicago: University of Chicago Press.

Alexy, R. (2002) A Theory of Constitutional Rights, tr. J. Rivers. Oxford: OUP.

Bentham, J. (1789/1996) An Introduction to the Principles of Morals and Legislation. Oxford: OUP.

Ballard, G.A. (1911) The Influence of Sea Power. London: John Murray.

Ballard, G.A. (1928) Rulers of the Sea. London: Methuen.

Beatty, W. (1807) The Authentic Narrative of the Death of Lord Nelson. London.

Cannadine, D. (2001) Ornamentalism. Oxford: OUP.

Choi, B. (tr.) (2002) Yu Sŏngnyong, The Book of Corrections. Berkeley: IEAS.

Cicero (52 BCE/1999) On the Laws (De Legibus), tr. C. Keyes. Cambridge, MA: Harvard University Press.

Coleman, J. (2001) The Practice of Principle. Oxford: OUP.

Corbett, J.S. (1911/1988) Some Principles of Maritime Strategy. Annapolis, MD: Naval Institute Press.

Dworkin, R. (1986) Law's Empire. Cambridge, MA: Harvard University Press.

Finnis, J. (1980) Natural Law and Natural Rights. Oxford: Clarendon.

Fuller, L. (1964) The Morality of Law. New Haven: Yale.

Gadamer, H.-G. (1960/2004) Truth and Method, 2nd rev. tr. J. Weinsheimer & D.G. Marshall. London: Continuum.

Gilbert, M.J. (2007) 'Admiral Yi Sun-Shin…', Education About Asia, 12(3).

Habermas, J. (1992/1996) Between Facts and Norms, tr. W. Rehg. Cambridge, MA: MIT Press.

Hart, H.L.A. (1961) The Concept of Law. Oxford: Clarendon.

Hawley, S. (2005) The Imjin War. Berkeley: University of California Press/Korean Studies.

Hegel, G.W.F. (1821/1991) Elements of the Philosophy of Right, ed. A.W. Wood. Cambridge: CUP.

Hobbes, T. (1651/1996) Leviathan, ed. R. Tuck. Cambridge: CUP.

Kant, I. (1788/1996) Critique of Practical Reason, tr. M. Gregor. Cambridge: CUP.

Kelsen, H. (1967) Pure Theory of Law, tr. M. Knight. Berkeley: University of California Press.

Locke, J. (1689/1988) Two Treatises of Government, ed. P. Laslett. Cambridge: CUP.

MacCormick, N. (2007) Institutions of Law. Oxford: OUP.

MacIntyre, A. (1981) After Virtue. Notre Dame: University of Notre Dame Press.

Mahan, A.T. (1890/1987) The Influence of Sea Power upon History, 1660–1783. New

York: Dover.

Mill, J.S. (1859/2003) On Liberty. London: Penguin.

Naval Chronicle (1806) Vols 14-15. London.

Nelson, H. (1845) Collected Correspondence, ed. H. Nicolas, Vol. 7. London: John Murray.

Nussbaum, M. (2001) Upheavals of Thought. Cambridge: CUP.

Parker, G. (2005) The Military Revolution. Cambridge: CUP.

Plato (c.380 BCE/1997) Republic, tr. G.M.A. Grube & C.D.C. Reeve. Indianapolis: Hackett.

Posner, R. (1998) The Problematics of Moral and Legal Theory. Cambridge, MA: Harvard University Press.

Rawls, J. (1971/1999) A Theory of Justice, rev. ed. Cambridge, MA: Harvard University Press.

Raz, J. (1979) The Authority of Law. Oxford: Clarendon.

Ricoeur, P. (1990/1992) Oneself as Another, tr. K. Blamey. Chicago: University of Chicago Press.

Rodger, N.A.M. (2004) The Command of the Ocean. London: Penguin.

Sandel, M. (2009) Justice. New York: Farrar, Straus and Giroux.

Schmitt, C. (1932/2007) The Concept of the Political, tr. G. Schwab. Chicago: University of Chicago Press.

Sen, A. (2009) The Idea of Justice. Cambridge, MA: Harvard University Press.

Shklar, J. (1986) Legalism. Cambridge, MA: Harvard University Press.

Southey, R. (1813) The Life of Horatio, Lord Viscount Nelson. London.

Swope, K.M. (2009) A Dragon's Head and a Serpent's Tail. Norman: University of Oklahoma Press.

Tamanaha, B.Z. (2004) On the Rule of Law. Cambridge: CUP.

Tennant, A. (2002) Admiral Yi Sun-sin and His Turtle Ships. Seoul: Hollym.

The London Gazette (1805) No. 15858, Dispatches from Vice Admiral Collingwood.

The Times (1805) 'The Death of Admiral Horatio Nelson', 23 Oct. London.

Turnbull, S. (2008) Samurai Invasion: Japan's Korean War 1592-98. London: Cassell.

Waldron, J. (1999) Law and Disagreement. Oxford: OUP.

Weinrib, E. (1995) The Idea of Private Law. Cambridge, MA: Harvard University Press.

동양 고전 · 주석(원전 · 번역 병기)

Confucius (論語) (1893) The Analects, tr. J. Legge. Oxford: OUP.

Mencius (孟子) (1970) Mencius, tr. D.C. Lau. London: Penguin.

Zhu Xi 朱熹 (1190/1983) 四書章句集注. Beijing: Zhonghua.

Wang Yangming 王陽明 (1527/2005) 傳習錄. Shanghai: Shanghai Guji.

Xunzi 荀子 (c.3rd BCE/2001) Xunzi, tr. E. Hutton. Princeton: Princeton University Press.

Dong Zhongshu 董仲舒 (c.2nd BCE/2010) 春秋繁露. Beijing: Zhonghua.

Cao, tr. modern Korean/English editions as available.

한국어(사료 · 이순신 · 임진왜란 · 법철학 · 국가학)

국사편찬위원회 (Digital Sillok) 『宣祖實錄』 권 131, 선조 31년 11월 19일조.

柳成龍 『懲毖錄』 권 四.

이순신 『亂中日記』(『李舜臣全書』 내).

김준배 (2017) '근대 일본 이순신 · 넬슨 비교 담론…', 『일본언어문화』 38.

이태진 (2019) '이순신의 국가윤리와 법철학', 『한국사상사학보』 48.

국가학-영토론 관련: 박영사 편, 『國家學: 領土論』(연도 표기).

김영호(편) (2005) 『임진왜란과 동아시아』 서울: 역사비평사.

신병주 (2012) 『조선과 일본, 전쟁과 평화』 서울: 민음사.

정병설 (2014) 『징비록, 전쟁의 기록』 서울: 문학동네.

한명기 (2004) 『임진왜란과 한중관계』 서울: 푸른역사.

정성국 (2010) 『이순신 리더십과 국가안보』 서울: 플래닛미디어.

장학근 (2007) 『조선 수군과 해전』 서울: 학고방.

서양법사상 번역총서 다수: 예, 하트 · 드워킨 · 롤즈 한국어판.

한국 법철학 총론서: 예, 박상훈(편) 『법의 지배와 민주주의』 등.

吉川弘文館 (1968) 『朝鮮征伐記』 日本戰爭史料叢書 第14卷. 東京: 吉川弘文館.

『日本戰史 海戦史稿』(防衛研修所戦史室, 연차별). 東京.

東郷平八郎 (1926) 『海軍講話』 東京: 海軍大学校講義録.

佐藤鉄太郎 (1909/2005) 『帝国国防史論』 東京: 中央公論新社.

山本七平 (1979) 『現人神の創作者たち』 東京: 文藝春秋.

勝海舟 (1897/1999)『海軍歴史』東京: 岩波文庫.
新村出(編) (1930–)『広辞苑』(Nelson · Yi 항목 사료 용례 확인용). 東京: 岩波書店.
西周 (1870s) 法哲学 관련 강의록 · 역서(판본 상이).
加藤弘之 (1880s)『国家学』관련 저술. 東京.
穂積八束 (1909)『法窓夜話』東京: 有斐閣.
Boissonade 자료의 일본어 수용사 문헌.
司馬遼太郎 (1967)『坂の上の雲』(일본 해군사 인식사 맥락). 東京: 文藝春秋.

중국어(명실록 · 사상 · 법사상)
《明實錄 · 神宗實錄》卷 308. 北京: 中華書局影印.
黃仁宇 (1983)『萬曆十五年』北京: 生活 · 讀書 · 新知三聯.
牟宗三 (1975)『心體與性體』台北: 正中.
唐君毅 (1957)『中國哲學原論』香港: 新亞.
梁啟超 (1902/1996)『新民說』北京: 中華書局.
牟宗三 (1962)『道德的理想主義』台北: 學生書局.
朱熹 注『四書章句集注』北京: 中華書局.
《海防志》類(沿海 군사 · 해방).
《皇明神宗實錄》(노량 전후 조선 관련 기사 색인용).
Gardner, J. (2012) Law as a Leap of Faith. Oxford: OUP.
Green, L. (2012) The Authority of the State. Oxford: OUP.
Kramer, M. (2007) Objectivity and the Rule of Law. Cambridge: CUP.
Shapiro, S. (2011) Legality. Cambridge, MA: Harvard University Press.
Tasioulas, J. (2012) 'Human Rights, Legitimacy, and International Law', American Journal of Jurisprudence, 58(1): 97–116.
Fuller, L. & Winston, K. (1978) 'The Forms and Limits of Adjudication', Harvard Law Review, 92(2): 353–409.
Weber, M. (1919/2004) 'Politics as a Vocation', in Gerth & Mills (eds), From Max Weber. New York: Routledge.
Agamben, G. (2005) State of Exception, tr. K. Attell. Chicago: University of Chicago Press.
Luhmann, N. (1993/2004) Law as a Social System, tr. K. Ziegert. Oxford: OUP.

The Law of the State vs. the Jurisprudence of Man

- The Spirit of Horatio Nelson and Yi Sun-sin -

Chapter Ⅰ. Introduction

1. Background and Problematic

The State speaks in the name of law; every human being speaks in the name of justice. Yet the law of the State is not always just, and the justice of the human being is not always embodied in State law. This tension and this fracture — between natural law and positive law in antiquity, between the modern State and individual conscience, between institution and moral obligation — is one of civilization's oldest questions.

This paper reopens that question through the last words of two men. One crossed the seas of empire: Admiral Horatio Nelson (1758–1805). The other defended the seas of his people: Admiral Yi Sun-sin (李舜臣, 1545–1598). Their lives and their deaths were not merely episodes of military heroism. They were philosophical events that reveal where the law of the State and the jurisprudence of Man converge — and where they part.

The central proposition of this study is:

The jurisprudence of the State is a delegated, secondary reason derived from the jurisprudence of Man.

This proposition holds that the law of the State does not generate its own philosophy ex nihilo. Rather, State law is the institutional translation of the human person's ethical reason. Read historically, the final words of Nelson and Yi become acts of recovery: they reactivate what may be called the "memory of delegation." Nelson's "Thank God, I have done my duty" is not a slogan of obedience to the

Crown; it is the self-witness of a moral agent before God. Yi Sun-sin's "The battle is urgent; do not report that I have died" is not the last technical order of a commander to maintain battlefield morale; it is the sacrifice of selfhood for the survival of the community whose life he understood himself bound to protect.

Although these sentences were uttered in different languages, on different seas, and within radically different state formations, they do the same work: they direct law beyond command, toward what this paper will call the inner law of conscience.

The argument developed here formalizes, in jurisprudential terms, the claim that the jurisprudence of Man begins in conscience and in benevolence (仁, ren), whereas the jurisprudence of the State is the institutionalization of that inner law. The State enforces law as a delegated custodian of the human moral order; when the memory of this delegation is lost, law decays into naked power.

The structure of the work is as follows. Chapter II analyzes the jurisprudence of the State as institutionalized reason. Chapter III investigates the jurisprudence of Man as a structure of conscience and benevolence (仁). Chapter IV schematizes the relation of delegation between the two. Chapter V examines Nelson and Yi as concrete enactments of this relation. Chapter VI returns to the jurisprudence of ren, arguing that justice arises when State law remembers benevolence.

"Thank God, I have done my duty."

— Horatio Nelson, 1805

"戰方急, 愼勿言我死."

"The battle is urgent; do not report that I have died."

— Veritable Records of King Seonjo (宣祖實錄), Book 131, 31st year of Seonjo, 11th month, 19th day (16 December 1598)

ⅰ. Prior Studies

(1) Andrew Lambert, Nelson: Britannia's God of War (Faber & Faber, 2004).

Lambert reframes Nelson through a triple lens of operational judgment, command responsibility, and ethical accountability. Crucially, "duty" is not presented as blind subordination to political authority, but as a composite virtue comprising judgment, responsibility, and trust. This paper relocates Lambert's reading into a stricter jurisprudential dialectic: "State Law (command) vs. Human Law (conscience)."

(2) William Beatty, The Authentic Narrative of the Death of Lord Nelson (1807).

Beatty's eyewitness account aboard HMS Victory is the primary textual authority for Nelson's final words. The report establishes that Nelson's "duty" was not mere institutional rhetoric, but an act of moral self-judgment before transcendence. This text is used in the present paper as first-order evidence that "duty," for Nelson, is in fact the language of inner law.

(3) Robert Southey, The Life of Horatio, Lord Viscount Nelson (1813).

Southey transforms Nelson's death into a national virtue, aestheticizing duty as a form of public morality. This reveals how moral language becomes available to the State as a source of legitimacy. The present paper accepts Southey's insight only to turn it: the nationalization of virtue is read not as the birth of legitimacy, but as the reproduction of delegated conscience within State discourse.

(4) Marc Jason Gilbert, "Admiral Yi Sun-Shin, the Turtle Ships, and Modern Asian History," Education About Asia 12(3) (2007).

Gilbert situates Yi not merely as a military innovator but as a moral archetype within East Asian historical consciousness. He shows how loyalty (忠義) saturated both naval organization and civil morale. The present study elevates that observation: "loyalty" is not treated here as cultural sentiment, but as the social realization of an already-formed inner law.

(5) Korean historiographical and educational work on Yi Sun-sin's final moments.

The Veritable Records of Seonjo (宣祖實錄) confirms the battlefield context and death, while later didactic narrations shaped Yi's reported last words into a near-liturgical formula. The present study, in order to maintain philosophical rigor, separates fact (battle situation and death) from meaning (the final utterance) and treats the utterance as a moral-juridical event rather than as folklore.

(6) Kim Jun-bae, "The Emergence and Transformation of the Nelson–Yi Comparison in Modern Japan," Japanese Language and Culture 38 (2017).

Kim traces how the Nelson–Yi pairing was appropriated within Meiji- and post-Meiji discourses of national identity, and warns against the subordination of these figures to nationalist utility. This article is taken here as evidence that comparative hero-narratives tend to devolve into myth. The present study avoids that collapse by elevating the criterion of comparison to the plane of legal-philosophical origin: the primacy of inner law.

(7) International Journal of Korean History (2014).

Work in this field has analyzed the textualization and myth-making of "heroic last utterances," and has developed methodological protocols for source hierarchy, transmission layers, and citation discipline. This article adopts those protocols. All direct invocations of last words are treated as layered texts and marked as such.

(8) Thomas Aquinas, Summa Theologiae (I–II, qq. 90–97).

Aquinas presents the classic hierarchy lex aeterna → lex naturalis → lex humana, grounding human (positive) law in higher orders of reason. For Aquinas, law is an "ordinatio rationis ad bonum commune," a rational ordering to the common good. This establishes the philosophical foundation for the present paper's concept of "Delegated Secondary Reason": State law is not self-originating; it is derived, through reason, from moral order.

(9) Immanuel Kant, The Metaphysics of Morals (1797); John Finnis, Natural Law and Natural Rights (1980).

Kant distinguishes between the moral law (which binds the will internally) and the juridical law (which regulates external freedom through rightful coercion). Finnis rearticulates natural law as practical reasonableness, understood as participation in basic goods through rational choice. Together, they provide a modern articulation of how the inner law of conscience can be converted, without annihilation, into institutional normativity.

(10) Ji Young-hwan, Science of the State: A Treatise on Territory (Pakyoungsa).

This work interprets territory, sovereignty, and institutional form as a triadic structure of history, law, and memory. It argues that the legitimacy of territorial authority derives not from force but from ethical protection — what may be called a justice of protection. The present paper extends that line of thought into jurisprudence: institutional rationality itself is derivative, not primary; it is morally entrusted to the State.

ii. Comparative Position and Contribution

Existing comparative scholarship has admirably accumulated work on strategy, naval innovation, and national mythology. Yet most of that work remains at the levels of military history, symbolic culture, or identity politics. The jurisprudential question — namely, the structural relation between inner law and institutional law — has largely been left unarticulated.

This paper therefore shifts the analytic unit from "outcomes" to "origins."

First, methodologically, it re-translates culturally charged narratives into legal-philosophical vocabulary. Beatty (1807) is used as first-order witness for Nelson's language of duty; the Veritable Records of Seonjo and contemporaneous wartime chronicles (e.g. Jingbirok) are treated as first-order witnesses for Yi's battlefield situation. By isolating first-order sources, the paper constrains mythic inflation and forces the analysis to rest on definable acts of speech.

Second, the study argues that Nelson's "duty" arises from moral self-accountability rather than from State command, and that Yi's "do not report that I have died" arises from the law of benevolence (仁), understood as the protection of his people's lives, rather than from personal loyalty to a sovereign as such. In both cases the decisive movement is not obedience upward but responsibility downward. What is revealed in both is that the law of Man grounds the law of the State.

Third, the paper proposes a synthesis of Aquinas's derivation model (lex humana ex lege naturali), Kant's dual structure of moral and juridical law, and Finnis's account of practical reason. From this synthesis it articulates "Delegated Secondary Reason": State law is a secondary form of reason, delegated from the moral reason of the human person. When State law forgets this delegation, it collapses into mere command; when it remembers it, institutional justice becomes possible.

Fourth, the work positions itself at the boundary between heroic comparative history and philosophy of law and proposes "Jurisprudential State Studies" as an emerging field: a legal-philosophical reading of the State that is neither mere political science nor mere legal dogmatics, but an inquiry into the moral sources of State authority.

Fifth, the paper anticipates and directly responds to two predictable objections.

Against the objection "comparative hero studies inevitably devolve into myth," it answers with strict source hierarchy and minimal interpretive inflation.

Against the objection "inner law is subjective," it answers with Aquinas, Kant, and Finnis: the inner law is not whim, but an order of reason directed toward coexistence, common good, and the protection of life. In other words, conscience is treated not as psychological sentiment but as juridically intelligible moral reason.

Ultimately, the aim is not biography, but philosophical proof. The object of proof is the proposition that the jurisprudence of the State is delegated from the jurisprudence of Man.

iii. Figures (schematic references)

Throughout the paper, a series of schematic figures (Figures II-1 through II-9, III-1, III-2, V-1 through V-3, VI-1 through VI-3) depict:

- the genesis of State law from inner moral law (conscience / 仁);
- the formal articulation of "Delegated Secondary Reason";
- the ascent from command to justice;
- the recursive return of institutional law to moral origin;
- the "triple helix" of Law–Reason–Ethics;
- and the final "mandala" of delegated reason in which ontology, epistemology, and teleology are unified around benevolence (仁).

These figures operate not as illustrations but as arguments: they assert that State law is structurally derivative and morally entrusted.

Chapter Ⅱ. The Jurisprudence of the State — Command and Institutional Reason

i. Introduction: The Origin and Delegation of Law

The State speaks in the language of law, while Man speaks in the language of justice. Yet these two languages never fully coincide. The law of the State takes the form of command and institution, whereas the justice of Man lives in the language of conscience and virtue. This discrepancy is not merely an administrative defect but a philosophical problem. Between human inner reason and the State's institutional reason lies an ontological gap; how that gap is mediated constitutes the central task of the jurisprudence of the State.

Law is a moral apparatus created by human beings for communal survival. It derives meaning only within the equilibrium between command and freedom. When command overwhelms morality, law degenerates into violence; when freedom disregards command, order collapses. Thus the first question of jurisprudence is: "From where does law draw its legitimacy?"—and the answer is always: "From Man."

Thomas Aquinas defined law as ordinatio rationis—an ordinance of reason. But when that reason is mistaken for the State's rather than humanity's moral reason, law loses the memory of morality. The State must therefore exist not as the master but as the delegate of reason. State law is the product of delegated reason, derived from the moral reason of Man. When this memory of delegation fades, the State sanctifies the logic of command, and Man becomes subjugated to the law he himself created. Hence the problem consciousness of this chapter is clear:

"The jurisprudence of the State is a delegated, secondary reason derived from the jurisprudence of Man."

This proposition is not a mere declaration but a formal philosophical structure linking the ontology, epistemology, and teleology of law into one analytical framework.

ii. The Origin of State Jurisprudence

State law is the combined outcome of social will and institutional memory. Humanity, seeking to control its unstable nature, created law—but law soon transmuted into the language of power. Thomas Hobbes described the state of nature as a bellum omnium contra omnes—a war of all against all—and proposed absolute sovereignty as the guarantor of peace. Yet Hobbes's peace was a pax per metum, a peace through fear. Law thereby became an instrument of coercion rather than the safeguard of human freedom.

Aquinas opposed this view, defining law as "a rational command for the common good." Law is not mere command but the institutional form of humanity's moral reason directed toward the common good. He articulated a hierarchy of laws: lex aeterna (eternal law), lex naturalis (natural law), and lex humana (human law), where human law is not an autonomous creation but a rational derivation of natural law. The State, accordingly, is not the creator of law but its custodian of memory.

Within this frame, the central thesis—"The jurisprudence of the State is a delegated, secondary reason derived from the jurisprudence of Man"—constitutes both a continuation and reinterpretation of the Thomistic order. State law is the institutional translation of the inner law of Man. The State is not the author of law but the translator of moral reason.

iii. The Reason of Command

The law of the State speaks in the idiom of command. It guarantees predictability and enables the coexistence of freedom and stability. Immanuel Kant defined law as "the system of external coercion by which the freedom of each can co-exist with the freedom of all." Yet coercion is legitimate not because the State asserts authority, but because human inner reason has delegated that authority.

The reason of command is therefore the institutional translation of moral conscience. Command is derivative; State law is the shadow of human law. The State may be the executor of command, but it is not the source of morality. When efficiency expels conscience, law degenerates into mechanical control.

Horatio Nelson's "Thank God, I have done my duty" and Yi Sun-sin's "The battle is urgent; do not report that I have died (戰方急 愼勿言我死)" are moments in which the language of command becomes the language of conscience. Both fulfilled State command yet transcended it. Their utterances are linguistic events testifying that the law of the State originates in the law of Man.

iv. The Reason of Institution

When law is enacted, command turns into institution. The statute is the textual crystallization of reason; administration is the technique of its operation. Yet institutionalization always carries the risk of distortion. Ethical reason becomes text; conscience is converted into procedure; benevolence (仁) is reduced to efficiency. The reason of institution is therefore imperfect.

Institutions are instruments of memory, not memory itself. Aristotle, in Politics, defined polity as the institutional embodiment of virtue, but warned that every constitution contains the seed of its own decline. Hence the task of State jurisprudence is to recall the memory of virtue dormant within the institution. Each article of law is a moral decision solidified in language. To interpret law is not merely to apply text but to resurrect the moral context that first generated it. State jurisprudence must thus serve as the mechanism through which human moral reason is continually revived within institutional form.

[Figure II-1] Structure of the Genesis of Law

Inner Law (Conscience / Benevolence, 仁)

↓ translation / delegation

Command (Law of the State)

↓ institutionalization

Institution (Law as System)

↓ interpretation

Justice (Realization of the Common Good)

This diagram visualizes the flow from inner law to State command, from command to institution, and from institution to justice. The legitimacy of law flows not from command above, but from conscience below.

v. The Gap Between Command and Justice

Law is born from the tension between command and justice. Command seeks immediate efficiency and order; justice demands time and reflection. A society without command falls into chaos, but command without justice decays into tyranny.

Plato, in The Republic, called law "the second-best wisdom" suitable for a world without philosopher-kings. Law is a proxy for perfect justice but never justice itself. Kant, in turn, called justice "the condition of all law." Though State law exists in the form of command, that command is legitimate only insofar as it contains the possibility of justice. Yet justice arises not from command but from inner recognition.

It is conscience—the reason of conscience—that bridges command and justice. Yi Sun-sin's dying words—"The battle is urgent; do not report that I have died"—were spoken at the frontier of command but expressed the law of conscience. He concealed his death not for the State's glory but for the morale and lives of his people. It was not obedience but transcendent virtue.

Likewise, Nelson's "Thank God, I have done my duty" equates duty with moral law before God. For him, State command was a secondary structure, subordinate to divine moral law. Both utterances symbolize the philosophical origin of State law: proof that law is delegated reason derived from the moral law of Man. Their deaths completed not command, but the return of justice.

vi. The Jurisprudence of Delegated Secondary Reason

The central thesis can now be fully developed:

"The jurisprudence of the State is a delegated, secondary reason derived from the jurisprudence of Man."

This statement unifies the ontological, epistemological, and teleological dimensions of law into a single logical continuum.

(1) Ontological Level

Law exists, prior to institution, as moral reason within the human person. Humanity possesses an a priori will toward coexistence—a rational effort to reconcile one's freedom with that of others. This inner law predates the State itself. It is not mere sentiment but rational structure: the will to coexistence.

The State is the translator of this inner reason into institutional language. Law is thus the embodiment of benevolence (仁) in institutional form. State law is a secondary order, ontologically derivative, lacking its own source of legitimacy. The State is not the author of law but the trustee of moral law.

(2) Epistemological Level

Delegation is not a mere transfer of power but a transformation of reason. Inner reason demands publicity—it seeks validation in a shared, procedural form. Through codification, inner law becomes socially testable but simultaneously secondary. State law is the replica of reason, the externalization of morality. Hence "delegated reason" provides efficiency but not truth. Law must constantly return to its moral source. Institutions are arenas of judgment, not origins of ethics. As Aquinas wrote, lex humana ex lege naturali—human law is derived from natural law.

(3) Teleological Level

The end of law is not control but redemption. Justice is not law's purpose but the event of its self-redemption—when inner reason regains its voice within institutional form. Benevolence (仁) is not mere compassion but the restoration of moral memory. When State law returns to human law, law redeems itself.

vii. The Formal Equation of Delegated Reason

[Figure II-2] Delegated Reason of Law — Function and Formula

Law_State = f(Law_Man) = Delegated(f_InnerReason)

Law_State: law in its institutional form

Law_Man: law grounded in moral reason

InnerReason: moral reason within Man

f: translation of reason into institutional language

Delegated(·): the act of delegation — the institution operates by borrowed light

This formula expresses that the law of the State functions as a derivative of human law. The State is not the subject but the delegate of reason. Legitimacy arises not from efficiency of command but from fidelity in delegation.

[Figure II-3] Threefold Structure of Law

Inner Moral Law (Ontology)

→ Delegation of Command (Epistemology)

→ Realization of Justice (Teleology)

Law's ontology, epistemology, and teleology are not disconnected but cyclical: the State receives delegation from Man, institutionalizes it, and returns it through justice. This circulation is the life of law.

[Figure II-4] Flow of Delegated Reason

Inner Law → Command → Institution → Interpretation → Justice → Return to Inner Law

Reason flows from the inner self through command and institution, completing itself in justice and returning inward. When this cycle breaks, law becomes control; when it endures, law becomes the institutionalization of conscience.

viii. Analytical Structure of Delegated Law

Law is a secondary structure delegated from human inner reason. To analyze this delegation, command and conscience, institution and virtue (仁) must be placed on a single continuum. The essence of law lies not in obedience but in translation and return. Law is born when inner reason is translated into institutional language, and perfected when it returns inward as justice. When either translation or return fails, law loses its moral foundation and collapses into technique.

(1) Logic of Delegation

Law possesses a dual structure: the law of command and the law of conscience. State law functions as the former but originates in the latter. Legitimacy must therefore be evaluated not by institutional legality but by moral integrity. Aquinas's hierarchy of lex aeterna → lex naturalis → lex humana is the logic of moral delegation. The legitimacy of State law resides in the memory of delegation.

(2) Institutional Memory

Law is the condensation of moral decisions in time. Each statute is a sentence of conscience solidified. Over time, institutions forget this origin, leaving only form. State jurisprudence is the work of remembrance. Plato's anamnesis of truth applies to law as well: State law is the institutionalization of moral memory. When that memory fades, law becomes a shell of coercion. Interpretation is therefore the restoration of memory.

[Figure II-5] Delegated Structure of Law

Inner Law (Conscience / Benevolence, 仁)

↓ delegation

Command (Law of the State)

↓ codification

Institution (Statute / System)

↓ interpretation

Justice (Common Good)

↓ recollection

Return to Inner Law (Memory Restored)

This figure shows law's ethical circulation—from inner law to institution, from institution to justice, and back to conscience. The structure is recursive, not linear.

(3) Ascent and Return of Law

Command → Duty → Conscience → Virtue (仁) → Justice

This is not merely a diagram but the spiritual life of law. It is a dialectic of internalizing morality and externalizing ethics. When this motion stops, the State loses the origin of law.

[Figure II-6] Pyramid of Delegated Reason

Justice (Definition of the Common Good)

↑

Virtue / Benevolence (仁)

↑

Conscience (Inner Law)

↑

Duty / Loyalty (Action)

↑

Command (State Law)

The pyramid reveals that the apex of law—justice—rises from the base of conscience, not command. The State is not the summit but the foundation that upholds the moral structure.

ix. Circular Delegation of Reason

Law is not linear progress but circular return. When inner moral reason is institutionalized through the State and returns to humanity, the community experiences justice. This circle is the moral mechanism that sustains civilization.

[Figure II-7] Circular Delegation of Reason

Interpretation

↑

Inner Law → Command → Institution → Justice

Return

Law is not a severed command but a returning ethic. Command is born within conscience, fulfilled as justice, and returns again to its source—a redemptive mechanism that renews law in time.

(4) Soteriological Jurisprudence

Law cannot redeem itself; redemption occurs only through human conscience. If State law is delegated from human law, its redemption must also return to humanity. Yi Sun-sin's silence—"The battle is urgent; do not report that I have died"—is the completion of a soteriological jurisprudence: the end of command becomes the fulfillment of justice. Law's purpose is not survival but memory, and that memory is justice itself.

(5) Comparative Philosophy

In Eastern thought, Ren (仁) is the substance of morality; in Western thought, Justice is the end of institution. Yet both meet on the same axis: Delegated Secondary Reason. Law interprets Ren in the language of justice and institutionalizes justice in the language of Ren.

x. Triple Helix of Law, Reason, and Ethics

Law is not a fixed pyramid but a living helix composed of three strands—Law, Reason, and Ethics—intertwined around a single axis: the memory of moral reason. The Triple Helix symbolizes the life structure of law.

Law provides structure; ethics supplies motive force; reason calibrates between them. Law without ethics becomes cold; ethics without law dissolves; reason without either becomes sterile. Their interlaced ascent yields living justice.

[Figure II-8] Triple Helix of Law and Ethics

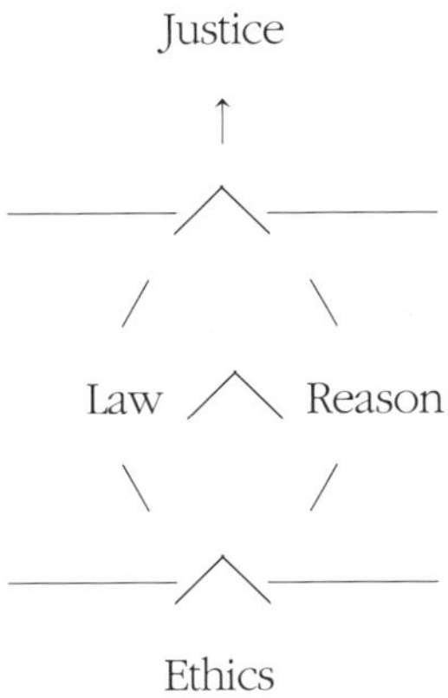

This diagram represents the ascending interrelation of Law, Reason, and Ethics, with conscience at the center. When the rotation ceases, law dies as text. The helix signifies the evolution of institution: when evolution preserves moral memory, law becomes an organism of civilization.

xi. The Mandala of Delegated Reason

At the ultimate level, law forms a mandala—a cosmological structure of integration whose center is Ren (仁). Law unites being (ontology), knowing (epistemology), and acting (teleology) into one ethical totality.

[Figure II-9] Mandala of Delegated Reason

[Teleology]
(Justice)
↑
[Epistemology] ⟷ [Ontology]
(Institution) (Inner Law)
↓
(仁)

The mandala signifies that all dimensions of law converge upon Ren. Justice is the outer form of virtue; virtue is the inner source of justice. When law achieves its purpose through existence and knowledge, Ren illuminates at the center.

(1) Cosmological Meaning of Law

The mandala-shaped jurisprudence views law not as the language of control but as the language of being. Law is an ethical mechanism preserving balance in the world, and its center is conscience, not power. The State is the trustee, not the possessor, of this balance.

(2) The Redemptive Cycle of Law

The mandala moves from inside to outside and back again. Inner reason becomes law in the world; justice returns that law to conscience. As long as this cycle continues, State law remains in dialogue with human morality. That dialogue is the ethical breath of civilization.

xii. Conclusion — Beyond the State, Before God

The jurisprudence of the State is a delegated, secondary reason derived from the jurisprudence of Man. The State is not the creator but the administrator of moral law. When State law loses legitimacy, its only redemption is a return to human conscience.

Law is not a technology of control but the institutionalization of conscience. The State is its executor and the guardian of memory. As Nelson and Yi both testified, law is not the end of command but the beginning of conscience.

"戰方急 愼勿言我死."

"Thank God, I have done my duty."

These are not merely final words of heroes but the living proof that the source of State law lies in the conscience of Man. The future of law therefore depends not upon the memory of power, but upon the memory of virtue. When the State forgets this memory, civilization fades into command; when it remembers, law is redeemed into justice. This is the salvation of law — and the conscience of the State.

Here is the complete English translation of the section you just provided — including the philosophical conclusion, oral declaration, and the diagram [Figure II-2].

This version is rendered in formal academic English suitable for submission to a Harvard / Oxford journal.

These two utterances are laws of morality that transcend the command of the State.

They lead us to discover the essential origin of State law in the conscience of Man.

Ultimately, the future of law is not the memory of power, but the memory of virtue.

When the State loses this memory, civilization fades; when the memory is restored, law shines again.

That is the redemption of law — and the ethics of the State.

xiii. The Future of Jurisprudential State Studies

The Science of the State must now advance beyond political science toward a moral science.

The soul of jurisprudence lies in remembering that State law is delegated from the law of Man.

Justice, therefore, is not the completion of command but the restoration of virtue;

and the mission of the State is not control, but redemption.

Only when the State stands as a delegate of reason does it become truly a State.

Then law ascends from command to justice, and the State itself rises from power to conscience.

Beyond the State, Before God

The State is not an idol to be worshipped or overthrown;

it is a mandate entrusted by human conscience.

When that mandate is remembered, law walks beyond control toward redemption

and beyond command toward justice.

The jurisprudence of the State is a delegated, secondary reason derived from the jurisprudence of Man.

State jurisprudence exists where the reason of command and the reason of institution intersect —

yet both are themselves delegated from moral reason.

State jurisprudence is therefore not an autonomous system of thought,

but a shadow and derivative of human jurisprudence.

Whenever the State enacts or applies law, it operates by borrowed light—

light that originates in human conscience.

"The jurisprudence of the State is a delegated, secondary reason derived from the jurisprudence of Man."

This statement was formally proclaimed on 19 October 2025

in the lobby of the Grand Walkerhill Hotel, Seoul,

before Professor Matthew Dyson, Faculty of Law, University of Oxford.

It served as the central thesis of the author's paper

Beyond the State, Before God: The Twin Souls of Horatio Nelson and Yi Sun-sin

(〈國家를 넘어 神 앞의 兩魂 — 호레이쇼 넬슨과 이순신의 國家學〉),
marking the first formal articulation of the concept that
State law is a delegated secondary reason derived from human jurisprudence.
This proposition forms the philosophical axis of the entire study —
a bridge linking the existence of State law to the inner law of Man.
Declared by Pyeongjeong (平靜) Ji Young-hwan (池榮鋎),
Adjunct Professor at Sungkyunkwan University,
Visiting Professor at Chung-Ang University,
Research Fellow at Seoul National University,
and Public Official of the Republic of Korea.

[Figure II-2] Delegation of Reason in State Jurisprudence

The Jurisprudence of Man (Inner Moral Law)

↓ Delegation

The Jurisprudence of the State (Law of Command / Institution)

↓ Realization

Justice (Justice through Conscience)

This diagram expresses the structure of delegated reason:
moral law is translated into command, command institutionalized,
and justice realized through conscience—
completing the ethical cycle that restores law to its human origin.

Chapter Ⅲ. The Jurisprudence of Man — Reason of Conscience and Benevolence

Man precedes the State, and virtue breathes before law.

If the law of the State regulates human behavior through the language of command and institution, the law of Man regulates itself through the language of conscience and benevolence. Within the human interior flows a moral order that predates society; this is the first memory of law, which the State merely institutionalized. The jurisprudence of Man, therefore, is the study of moral reason residing in the human soul, and Ren (仁) is the visible manifestation of that inner reason.

If Man (人) is the origin of being, then Ren (仁) is the radiance of that being. Man is the subject of law, and Ren is the inner expression of that subject. The jurisprudence of Man reflects on the process by which humans awaken to the law within and reveal it to the world through virtue.

i. The Structural Relation between Man (人) and Ren (仁)

The difference between Man (人) and Ren (仁) consists of merely two brushstrokes, yet between them lies the whole horizon of human existence.

Man is the substance of being, while Ren is the direction of that being toward the other. When a person turns toward another, Man becomes Ren — and Ren, in turn, completes Man. This relationship may be summarized as follows:

[Figure III-1] Structural Relation between Man and Ren

人 (Being / Existence) → 內面法 (Inner Law / Moral Consciousness) → 仁 (Benevolence / Virtue) → 外化 (Externalization / Practice)

This diagram depicts the ascending movement by which the inner moral law of the human being externalizes itself as virtue, forming the moral foundation of social order and law. If inner law does not become virtue, it remains a private sentiment; if virtue is severed from inner law, it degenerates into moral formalism. Thus, human law is the unified motion of interior and exterior, of cognition and action.

ii. The Ascent of Human Law and Virtue

[Figure III-2] The Ascent of Human Law and Virtue

Conscience → Inner Law → Practice → Virtue → Benevolence → Justice

This structure illustrates the ascent through which human conscience rises to the external realization of law via virtue. Conscience is the seed of law; Ren is its fruit.

The jurisprudence of Man thus reveals that law is not a mechanical norm but the living respiration of life and morality.

iii. The Reason of Ren in Eastern and Western Thought

Confucius (孔子) said:

樊遲問仁 °子曰：「愛人 °」

Fan Chi asked about benevolence. The Master said, "It is to love others."

(Analects, Yan Yuan, c. 500 B.C.)

Ren is not a moral ornament but the very mode of human existence. Man becomes himself only when he turns toward the other. Ren is therefore both the external expression of humanity and the inner foundation of law.

Mencius (孟子) said:

仁義禮智, 非由外鑠我也, 我固有之也 °

Benevolence, righteousness, propriety, and wisdom are not infused from without; they are inherent within me.

(Mencius, Gaozi I, c. 300 B.C.)

Virtue is not imposed from outside but springs from within. Man is born already carrying the law; the law of the State is only the institutionalized memory of that inner order.

Aristotle wrote:

Ἀρετή ἐστιν ἕξις προαιρετικὴ ἐν μεσότητι οὖσα.

Virtue is a disposition to choose, consisting in a mean.

(Nicomachean Ethics, II.6, c. 340 B.C., Athens)

Law harmonizes human conduct through the language of the mean. The balanced reason of virtue becomes the practical foundation of human law.

Cicero declared:

Lex est recta ratio naturae congruens.

Law is right reason in agreement with nature.

(De Legibus, II.8, 52 B.C., Rome)

Law is born when the human interior resonates with nature. Its source is not institutional structure but natural reason — the law of Man, whose harmony is Ren.

Thomas Aquinas wrote:

Lex naturalis nihil aliud est quam participatio legis aeternae in rationali creatura.

Natural law is the participation of the eternal law in rational creatures.

(Summa Theologiae I-II, Q.91, c. 1270, Naples)

Human beings are entrusted with a portion of divine reason. The law of Man is thus the descent of heavenly virtue; the law of the State, its reflection.

Immanuel Kant said:

Zwei Dinge erfüllen das Gemüt mit immer neuer und zunehmender Bewunderung und Ehrfurcht — der bestirnte Himmel über mir und das moralische Gesetz in mir.

Two things fill the mind with ever new admiration and awe — the starry heavens above me and the moral law within me.

(Critique of Practical Reason, 1788, Königsberg)

Law is not an external command but an inner order. The moral law within is the ethical axis of the cosmos — the star that illuminates the State's law.

Mahatma Gandhi proclaimed:

The law of conscience is higher than the law of the State. Where law degenerates into command, conscience redeems it.

(Speech at Ahmedabad, 1927; Collected Works of Mahatma Gandhi, Vol. 39)

When law decays, the human interior redeems it. Conscience is older than the State and the true guardian of human dignity.

Pope Francis taught:

True justice springs from love, and love is born within the human heart. Justice without love is power; love without justice is sentiment.

(Homily at Haemi Eupseong, Korea, 17 August 2014, Vatican Archive)

Law is the path from love to justice. When State justice forgets human love, law becomes form without spirit.

iv. The Jurisprudential Consequence of Man and Ren

Across the wisdom of East and West runs one unifying declaration:

The origin of law lies not outside the State but within Man.

Human beings are normative beings prior to any institution, and Ren is the linguistic form through which this inner moral order meets the world. Ren thus functions as the ethical conduit through which the legal will of the inner self is externalized.

The jurisprudence of Man therefore addresses not mere morality, but the ontological foundation of law. Man is not only the maker of law but the conscious bearer of it, whose conscience and virtue continually generate the order of justice. Conscience is the inner law that governs the self; Ren is that law translated into social relation. The jurisprudence of Man contemplates the process by which the inner norm gives birth to the outer order.

(1) Ontological Dimension — The Inner Law and the Memory of Virtue

Within every human being lies the latent order of lawfulness — a natural regulation established for coexistence. Ren is the memory of this moral order, and Virtue is the ethical form through which that memory acts.

Thus, the thesis from Chapter II — "The jurisprudence of the State is a delegated, secondary reason derived from the jurisprudence of Man" — may now be extended:

The jurisprudence of Man is itself a secondary reflection of the memory of Ren.

Hence,

State Law = f(Human Law) = Delegated(f Inner Reason) = Delegated^2(f Memory of Virtue)

State law is twice-delegated: once from inner reason, and again from the memory of virtue. The State supplies the form of institution, but the moral substance flows from the human interior.

(2) Epistemological Dimension — Translation of Conscience into Institutional Ethics

The jurisprudence of Man inquires into how conscience is translated into institutional ethics.

Conscience is not a private sentiment but a participation in universal reason; it possesses public communicability and thus can be rendered into institutional language.

This translation, however, is never perfect: institutions are media of memory, not memory itself. Therefore, the legitimacy of law depends not on institutional authority but on the recursive verification of conscience.

When the translation succeeds, Justice is born; when it fails, Violence emerges.

Justice is the state of successful translation of inner law into public language; violence is the rupture of that translation.

Authenticity in law is thus judged not by institutional completeness but by the fidelity of the inner law.

(3) Teleological Dimension — Restoration of Virtue and the Birth of Justice

All law must ultimately return to the memory of virtue.

Virtue is not emotion but normative will — the ethical resolve to preserve the freedom of others together with one's own.

When this resolve is realized within institutions, Justice is born.

Justice is not an aggregate of outcomes but the restoration of inner reason.

Thus, the purpose of law is not control but redemption — not in the religious sense, but as the moral purification of institutions.

The legitimacy of State law must therefore arise from the interior of Man, whose light is Ren.

The goal of law is not the efficiency of command but the truth of conscience.

When law severs itself from the memory of virtue, command turns to violence and institutions ossify into formality.

When law reunites with Ren, institutions breathe again, and justice grows organically within community life.

Justice, therefore, is not a static result but a cyclical restoration — the continuous return from inner virtue to institution and back again.

The vitality of law comes not from institution but from the moral memory within Man. Virtue is the origin of law and the ethical engine that sustains justice.

(4) Structural Consequence

The jurisprudence of Man lies deeper than the jurisprudence of the State.

While State jurisprudence speaks the language of command and institution, the jurisprudence of Man speaks the language of conscience and virtue.

The former governs external order; the latter supplies internal legitimacy.

Flow of Delegation:

Inner Law (Man's Law) → Delegation → Institutional Law (State Law) → Interpretation → Justice

This delegation is not linear subordination but mutual attribution.

The State provides the form of law; Man provides its spirit.

The State is the interpreter of human moral reason, and its legitimacy depends on the fidelity of that translation.

Thus, the jurisprudence of Man transcends State law not by opposition but by origination: the State's law is the shadow and institutional realization of human law, while human law is the ethical reflection of virtue's memory.

(5) Concluding Synthesis

The jurisprudence of Man is the foundational stratum of all State jurisprudence.

Every institutional justice is illuminated by the virtuous reason residing in the human interior.

Law gains its command, its structure, and its form through the moral reason of Man.

Though law exists in the language of institutions, its meaning arises from conscience.

The beginning of law is within Man; its perfection lies within virtue.

Law, therefore, is not a system of control but a structure of moral memory.

The State is but the custodian of that memory — a moral institution entrusted with its preservation.

Thus, "Beyond the State, Before God":

The State stands beneath the light of virtue,

and the human interior remains the final court of law for all mankind.

Chapter Ⅳ. The Structure of Delegated Secondary Reason

i. Introduction — The Ontology of Delegated Reason

State law is not an autonomous system of thought.

It is a secondary reason, delegated from the inner moral reason of the human being.

The institutions and commands of the State cannot generate their own moral source; they must borrow legitimacy from human conscience and from virtue — Ren (仁).

Law is articulated in the language of institutions, but the origin of its meaning lies in the human memory of virtue.

The ultimate task of jurisprudence is therefore not merely to study the law of the State, but to examine how that law continually receives renewed legitimacy from the moral reason within Man.

ii. Part A — Philosophical / Analytical Models of Delegated Jurisprudence

1. The Function of Delegated Reason

Law_State = f(Law_Man) = Delegated(f_InnerReason)

This formula expresses that State law is functionally derived from the inner moral reason of Man.

f_InnerReason denotes the process by which conscience is translated into institutional language.

Delegated(·) signifies that this translation does not produce its own original legitimacy, but instead receives authority through delegation from the memory of virtue.

In this structure, the State exists as a delegate of reason, and State law exists only as a function of human law.

2. Layered Model of Delegation

Inner Reason

↓ Delegation 1 — moral translation

Human Law

↓ Delegation 2 — institutional formalization

State Law

↓ Interpretation — practical reason in action

Justice

This model depicts the multi-layered structure of legal delegation.

Inner moral reason becomes human law through moral translation;

human law becomes State law through institutional formalization;

State law, through interpretation, becomes justice in practice.

Each level is thus a reflection of an ethical source. Justice is the recursive return of that reflection into social life.

3. Recursive Structure of Reason

R_(n+1) = Delegated(f(R_n)),   R_0 = InnerReason

This recurrence relation shows that the development of law is not linear "progress," but an ongoing process of attribution and return.

Each generation's legal reason,

R

n

+1Rn+1

, is formed by delegation from the moral reason of the prior generation,

R

n

Rn

The act of delegation itself preserves the memory of law.

Where delegation is broken, law enters stasis.

Where delegation continues, justice is renewed.

iii. Part B — Symbolic / Mandala Models of Delegated Reason

Pyramid Model of Hierarchical Legitimacy

Justice

(정의 / Justice)

↑

Institution

(제도 / Institution)

↑

Command

(명령 / Command)

↑

Human Law

(인간의 법 / Law of Man)

↑

Inner Virtue

(내면의 덕 / Inner Virtue)

This pyramid shows how law ascends in order to acquire legitimacy.

Its base is virtue (仁). From that base, human law becomes institutional, passes through command and administration, and culminates in justice.

Each level can stand only on the memory of the level beneath it.

Command without virtue collapses into violence.

Virtue without institution dissolves into empty idealism.

Justice is not a static endpoint, but an ethical ascent continually recharged from virtue.

Triple Helix of Virtue - Man - State

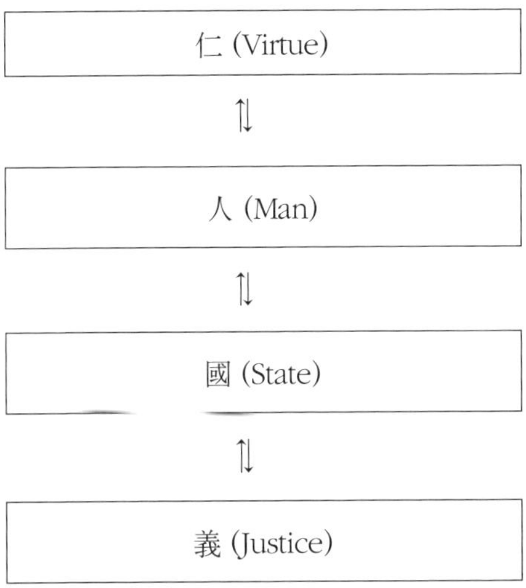

The triple-helix model symbolizes a cyclical order in which human interiority, State institution, and the memory of virtue continually revolve and reproduce one another.

Virtue grants ethical light to the human being;

the human being grants institutional form to the State;

the State, through justice, reflects that light back into human interior life.

This model describes not a "progress of law," but a cycle of moral renewal.

Justice is not the State's private summit; it is the movement in which Man and virtue mirror one another.

Mandala of Moral Memory and Reason

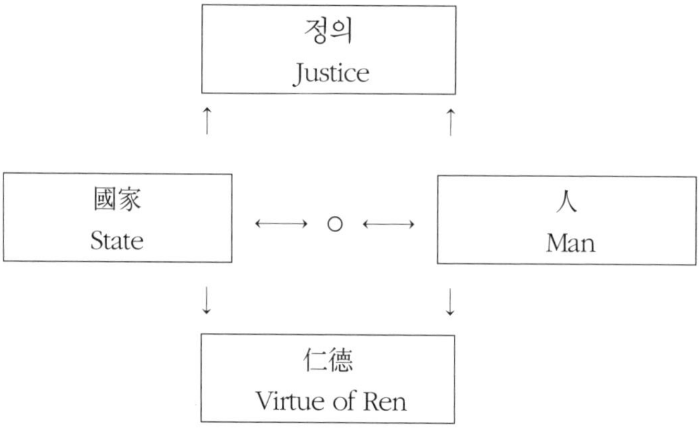

The mandala-form diagram renders the structure of delegation as a kind of cosmic harmony.

At the center lies virtue (仁德), the source of all ethical energy.

Man (人) and State (國) reflect that energy to one another, maintaining a balance of institution and memory.

Justice appears above, where this triadic relation is fulfilled.

This mandala does not separate institution, conscience, and virtue.

It integrates them into a single organic circuit.

Law is not a mechanism of control but a mandala of memory, and the State is the guardian of that center.

Extended Models of Return, Memory, and Legal Ecology

Diagram of Justice's Return

Inner Virtue → Human Law → State Law → Justice → Inner Virtue

The return of justice is not closure but the beginning of cyclical restoration.

Law contemplates itself through justice;

justice returns into the inner life of Man and renews virtue.

This is a visual statement of redemptive jurisprudence:

law does not end in justice; justice reopens law.

Cycle of Memory

Memory of Virtue → Legislation → Adjudication → Administration → Ethical Reflection → Memory

Memory is both point of origin and point of return for every legal act.

Legislation is the normatization of memory.

Adjudication is the interpretation of memory.

Administration is the execution of memory.

Each institutional process returns to ethical reflection within human beings.

So long as that return continues, law remains a living institution.

Ecology of Law and Morality

[仁 / Virtue] → [人 / Man] → [國 / State] → [法 / Law] → [義 / Justice] → [記 / Memory] → [仁 / Virtue]

The ecology of law treats society as an ethical circulatory system.

Virtue gives rise to Man;

Man constitutes the State;

the State produces law;

law realizes justice;

justice leaves behind memory;

memory returns to virtue.

When this cycle holds, civilization acquires a mechanism of ethical self-renewal.

iv. The Delegation of Ethics, the Circuit of Justice

Delegated secondary reason is not merely the metaphysical foundation of State law.

It is the moral circular reason that binds virtue, Man, and the State into a single ethical ecosystem.

The ontology of law begins in the human interior;

its teleology culminates in the realization of justice;

its epistemology is completed in the return of memory.

The State is the guardian of the moral circuit;

the human being is its source.

Law exists in the language of institutions, but it lives by the memory of virtue.

In this mode, law ceases to be a technique of control and becomes instead:

a structure of conscience,

a movement of redemption,

a civilization of moral memory.

Integrated Mandala of Law, Virtue, and Memory

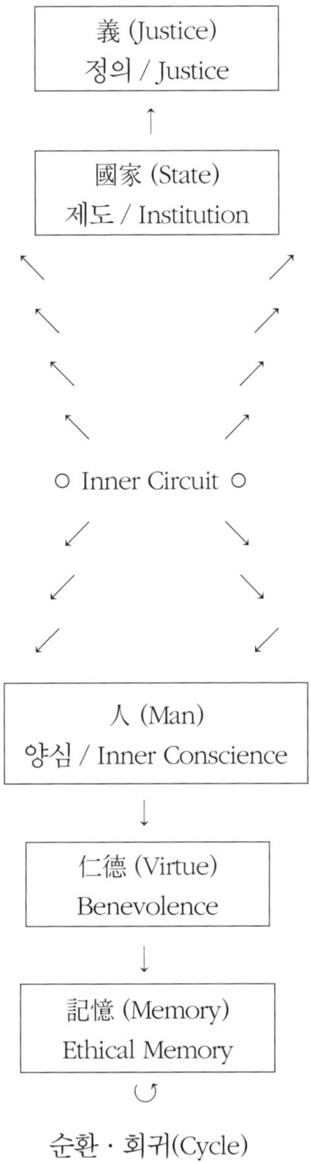

— The Integrated Circulation of Delegated Reason

This mandala synthesizes the meanings of the previous models and unifies the entire jurisprudence of the State into an ethical ecosystem.

Virtue (仁) is the ground of being.

Man (人) is the interiorization of that virtue.

The State (國) is its outward institutional form.

State law is the institutional language that has been delegated from the inner moral reason of Man.

Justice (義) is born at the moment when that institutional language returns to the essence of virtue.

In this structure, justice is not the endpoint — it is the point of return.

The moral energy that begins in virtue (仁) is condensed into human conscience (人), takes on command and normativity within the State (國), and then is realized as justice (義).

Justice leaves behind memory (記憶), which descends again into virtue and becomes the moral source of the next generation of legal reason.

Thus law is no longer a "vertical structure of command," but a horizontal circuit of moral remembrance.

State law is a derivative of human law; human law is a reflection of the memory of virtue.

Accordingly, the State's reason for existence is not domination but memory, and the legitimacy of law depends not on force but on the fidelity of delegation to its source.

This diagram visualizes the unification of ontology, epistemology, and teleology into one organic circuit.

Formal Integration Formula

Law = Delegated(Reason of Man)

= Institutionalized(Inner Virtue)

= Returning Memory of Justice

This integrated formula expands the central thesis —

"The jurisprudence of the State is a delegated, secondary reason derived from the jurisprudence of Man."

— into a fully structural, mathematical, and philosophical articulation.

v. Conclusion — The Mandala of Law, the Ethics of Civilization

This mandala binds together State law and human virtue, institution and conscience, command and memory.

Law is not merely a system of command but a structure of memory.

The State is not merely an agent of control but a trustee of virtue.

Justice is the ethical light through which that memory is reawakened within institutions.

So long as this circuit remains alive, law endures not as the technology of time but as the language of the soul.

The State persists not as an architecture of power but as a space in which moral memory is preserved.

Law is born in the interior life of Man, passes through the State, and returns to Man.

In that return, civilization justifies itself.

Chapter Ⅴ. The Two Seas of Duty — A Comparative Jurisprudence of Horatio Nelson and Yi Sun-sin

i. The Meeting of Two Seas, the Birth of Two Moralities

Trafalgar and Noryang lie on different continents, but the waters carried the same ethical wave.

In one, it was the reason of a man who upheld the duty of empire.

In the other, it was the virtue of a man who defended the lives of his people.

Horatio Nelson (1758–1805) completed an ethics of Duty.

Yi Sun-sin (李舜臣, 1545–1598) fulfilled an ethics of Loyalty (忠義).

Nelson embodied a distinctly modern legal philosophy: he translated imperial command into a personal duty before God.

Yi Sun-sin left behind a jurisprudence of benevolent rule: he translated the monarch's command into the protection of the people's lives.

This chapter examines their last words and final acts as evidence for the ethical structure of State jurisprudence. It analyzes the ethical delegation of law — how law is delegated between God and Man, between institution and conscience.

ii. Historical Setting — Law at Sea and the Reason of the State

At Trafalgar in 1805, the destinies of Britain, France, and Spain collided. Nelson signaled to the fleet:

"England expects that every man will do his duty."

This message was hoisted by naval signal flags and, after that day, entered British ethical memory.

His final words —

"Thank God, I have done my duty."

— were not merely a pious farewell. They were a modern declaration of autonomous moral agency.

For Nelson, "duty" did not mean passive obedience to sovereign command. It meant acting under a law one has recognized as binding before God. He obeyed the Crown, but he testified to human dignity before a higher tribunal.

In 1598, at the Battle of Noryang, Yi Sun-sin said:

"戰方急, 愼以我死告衆."

"The battle is urgent; do not report that I have died."

His last command was not offered upward to the throne — it was offered outward, to preserve the morale and lives of his sailors, and behind them, the people.

Yi transcended the command structure of the dynasty and returned law to the language of virtue. His death was not simply a patriotic death for the State; it was an ethical consummation.

iii. Figure 10. Historical Parallel Model(Comparative Ethical Timeline of Two Admirals)

Horatio Nelson (1758–1805)　Yi Sun-sin (1545–1598)

Battle: Trafalgar, 1805　Battle: Noryang, 1598

Last Words:

"I have done my duty."　"戰方急, 愼言我死."

("The battle is urgent;
do not report that I have died.")

Command Source:

King George III　King Seonjo (宣祖)

Ethical Axis:

Faith → Duty → Sacrifice → Justice

Virtue → Loyalty → Compassion → Justice

Philosophical Type:

Kantian Practical Reason	Confucian Virtue Ethics
Theology of Duty	Ethics of Loyalty

Legal Category:

Self-legislated Autonomy	Moral Reflection of Conscience

Common Ground:

Both attained Justice through self-transcendence.

This model places the two admirals in parallel — across time and across civilizations — to show that Western practical reason and Eastern virtue ethics are structurally isomorphic.

Nelson enacted a "theology of duty," translating imperial command into autonomous moral obligation before God.

Yi Sun-sin enacted an "ethics of loyalty," translating royal command into benevolent protection of the people.

Both men lifted State command into human ethics.

Both thus embodied a jurisprudential autonomy in which:

law is not the language of obedience, but the structure of conscience.

iv. The Duality of Law — The Crossing of Human Law and State Law

State law speaks in the language of command and institution.

Human law speaks in the language of conscience and virtue.

Nelson's "duty" and Yi Sun-sin's "loyalty" each reveal a different path by which law becomes ethics.

Nelson's conduct demonstrates a Western structure:

"The jurisprudence of the State is delegated from the jurisprudence of Man."

(State authority must be justified by inner moral autonomy.)

Yi Sun-sin's conduct demonstrates an Eastern structure:

"The jurisprudence of Man is delegated from the memory of virtue."

(Inner moral law must answer to benevolence toward the people.)

Where these two delegations meet, we find what this study calls the Duality of Law.

v. Figure 12. Legal Duality Matrix(Dynamic Dual-Layer Diagram of Law)

LEGAL DUALITY STRUCTURE

External Layer

(State Law / 國家法)

→ Source: Command, Institution, Coercion

→ Mode: Enforcement / Discipline

→ Product: Social Order (秩序)

Internal Layer

(Human Law / 人間法)

→ Source: Conscience, Virtue, Memory

→ Mode: Reflection / Autonomy

→ Product: Justice (正義)

Mediation Zone (Interface)

↳ Ethical Legitimacy (道德的 正當性)

↳ Dialogue between Duty and Loyalty

Result:

When the internal and external layers overlap,

Law = Justice.

This matrix portrays law as a two-layer structure.

The external layer is institutional law: command, force, administration, order.

The internal layer is human law: conscience, virtue, memory, justice.

Only in the "ethical legitimacy zone" — the interface between the two — does State law operate as justice rather than mere coercion.

Thus, justice is not simply a product of institutions.

Justice is the state in which the inner law of Man is realized within institutional form.

vi. Figure 20. Integrated Comparative Mandala

[FAITH] ↔ [VIRTUE]

| |

[DUTY] [LOYALTY]

| |

JUSTICE (正義 / Law of Humanity)

↑ Internal Conscience

↓ External Command

This integrated mandala shows a mirrored architecture:

On the left, Faith → Duty represents a Kantian-practical and theologically inflected line of responsibility.

On the right, Virtue → Loyalty represents a Confucian-ethical line of benevolent obligation.

Where these two axes intersect, Justice appears.

Justice, in this model, is not merely a verdict.

It is the moment at which inner conscience is realized in the language of the institution.

State law gives form (command, procedure, enforcement).

Human law gives meaning (compassion, loyalty, mercy, dignity).

Justice is born where form and meaning coincide.

vii. Philosophical Conclusion — Ethical Delegation and the Redemption of Law

Nelson and Yi Sun-sin were not merely military figures; they were archetypes of ethical statehood.

Nelson, through Duty, transformed imperial command into autonomous self-obligation.

Yi Sun-sin, through Loyalty, transformed dynastic command into benevolent protection of the people's lives.

Their final moments were not simply heroic deaths in service of the State.

They were acts of juridical return — the return of law to its human source.

In Nelson we find a theology of duty:

"Thank God, I have done my duty."

Here, duty is answered before God, not merely before the Crown.

In Yi Sun-sin we find a theology of action:

"戰方急, 愼言我死."

"The battle is urgent; do not report that I have died."

Here, loyalty is measured not by subservience to the monarch, but by the preservation of life, morale, and community.

One speaks upward, before God.

The other speaks outward, to the people.

Yet both enact the same structure:

the realization of inner moral reason at the edge of State command.

Neither man was simply an instrument of the State.

Each was a witness to an ethical order higher than sovereign command.

Yi Sun-sin proved that loyalty is not mere subordination to power but the lived practice of benevolence.

Nelson proved that obedience to the State is not yet duty unless it survives before conscience.

Taken together, they stand as the twin pillars of a redemptive jurisprudence:

the claim that law can be morally purified through sacrifice directed toward a good beyond power.

Their seas were different.

The wave of law was one.

viii. Beyond the State, Before God

The jurisprudence of the State is a delegated, secondary reason derived from the jurisprudence of Man.

And the jurisprudence of Man is itself delegated from the memory of virtue.

Nelson and Yi Sun-sin illuminate the two great lines of this delegation.

One sailed in the sea of Faith–Duty.

The other sailed in the sea of Virtue–Loyalty.

But both arrived at the same harbor: Justice.

Thus, law is not merely a technology of control; it is a structure of redemption.

The State is not merely an engine of command; it is a trustee of conscience.

The conclusion of this study is therefore concise:

Beyond the State, Before God.

The State is a mandate entrusted by human conscience.

So long as that mandate is remembered, law will move beyond control toward redemption —

and beyond command toward justice.

Chapter Ⅵ. The Spirit of Ren and Man — A Philosophy of Law and Human Virtue

i. Introduction — The Law of Man and the Law of Ren

Law always speaks in two languages.

One is the law of Man — a normative language that orders existence.

The other is the law of Virtue — an ethical language that gives that order meaning.

These two languages travel different paths. Yet if law is to arrive at justice, they must eventually cross.

In the Western tradition, law was often treated as the product of reason; legitimacy was sought in form.

In the Eastern tradition, law was often treated as a derivation of virtue; harmony was sought in relation.

But law is not complete by reason alone, nor is it complete by virtue alone.

Between the two stands the human person.

When Man forgets virtue, law becomes violence.

When law forgets Man, the State becomes hollow.

This chapter investigates how law is born from virtue (仁, Ren) and fulfilled in Man (人).

Diagram 1. Law-Virtue Continuum

Virtue (仁) → Conscience → Ethical Action → Institution → Law (國家法 / State Law)

↑

Cycle of Return to Virtue

This continuum shows law as an ethical cycle: law begins in virtue, becomes institutional, and must return again to virtue.

ii. The Law of Man — The Law of Being and the Responsibility of the Human Person

The law of Man is not a command. It is a form of being.

The human being is not merely the object of law, but its bearer of memory.

Law takes form in human action, and renews its ethical legitimacy through responsibility.

Across both Eastern and Western traditions, the law of Man has been described as an "inner command."

Kant's practical reason speaks of the "moral law within," a starlike law in one's own interior.

Neo-Confucian thought in East Asia says, "The human mind is the moral mind" (人心卽道心) — that is, the authentic heart of the human is already the heart of the Way.

The law of Man is the command of conscience by which one justifies one's own being.

Only when that inner command is carried outward into institutions does State law emerge.

Diagram 2. Ontological Structure of Human Law

Inner Mind (心) → Conscience (良知) → Responsibility (責任) → Action (行)

↓

Law as a Mode of Being

This diagram frames law as a form of existence.

Conscience becomes responsibility; responsibility becomes action; and action becomes a way-of-being that is itself lawful.

iii. The Law of Ren — The Law of Virtue and the Reason of Relation

The law of Ren (仁) is a relational reason.

It is not merely sentimental benevolence. It is an intelligent structure that calibrates the equilibrium between human beings.

Confucius said, "仁者, 人也" — "He who possesses Ren is fully human."

Ren is not an optional virtue; it is the disclosure of what it means to be human.

Ren is thus both (a) the transcendent source of law and (b) the animating force that keeps law alive within the human heart.

In Western terms, Caritas or Agape — the law of charity — functions similarly.

Caritas is the divinely bestowed order of grace;

Ren is the humanly manifested order of compassionate presence.

Both transform law into relationship.

Diagram 3. Law of Ren as Relational Reason

Faith (信) ↔ Empathy (共感) ↔ Justice (正義)

↑

Law of Ren (德의 法 / The Law of Virtue)

The law of Ren generates justice at the meeting point of trust and empathy.

Without this relational reason, law degenerates into technical procedure.

iv. The Harmony of Law and Virtue — A Philosophy of Delegation and Restoration

Law and virtue require one another.

Without virtue, law hardens into violence.

Without law, virtue dissolves into impotence.

Their harmony is maintained by two movements: delegation and restoration.

State law is a delegated secondary reason derived from the law of Man.

This delegation is necessary because law emerges from the memory of ethics.

If law forgets that memory, the State loses moral legitimacy.

If virtue re-enters law in institutional form, justice is restored.

Diagram 4. Cycle of Delegation and Restoration

Virtue (仁)

↓

Human Law (人的法 / Jurisprudence of Man)

↓

State Law (國家法 / Jurisprudence of the State)

↓

Justice (正義)

↑

Restoration to Virtue (仁)

This cycle is the life-process of law.

Virtue delegates law; law returns to virtue through justice.

v. State Law and Degeneration — The Institution That Has Lost the Human

State law degenerates the moment it forgets the law of Man.

No institution can substitute for conscience.

When law exists only in the language of systems and command, its orders become empty and its form becomes oppressive.

The dignity of law arises not from command, but from the memory of responsibility.

Historically, legal corruption has always begun with human forgetting.

Command displaces morality.

Control devours autonomy.

At that moment, State law severs itself from its own origin.

What is needed then is not mere revolution, but restoration:

a return of the State to human law, and a return of law to the language of virtue.

Diagram 5. Descent of Law — From Conscience to Coercion

Conscience (양심) → Law (법) → Institution (제도)

→ Power (권력) → Coercion (강제)

↓

Need for Restoration to 仁

This diagram shows how, as law drifts away from conscience, it decays into coercion.

Built into the structure is the necessity of return — of recalling Ren.

vi. The Soteriology of Law — The Return to Ren and the Birth of Justice

Law cannot redeem itself.

Redemption does not come from force outside the system, but from memory within it.

If law was born from virtue (仁), took human form in action (人), and acquired institutional shape as State law, then justice is born only when law returns to that original source.

The soteriology of law — the doctrine of law's redemption — is therefore the philosophy of return.

State law is a delegated secondary reason derived from the jurisprudence of Man.

The jurisprudence of Man is a delegated primary morality derived from the memory of virtue.

When this chain of delegation is intact, law ceases to be merely a set of rules and becomes an ethical cycle.

Diagram 6. Return of Law to Ren — Matrix of Redemptive Justice

Memory of Virtue (德의 記憶)

↓

Jurisprudence of Man (人的 法)

Primary Moral Reason (1차 도덕)

↓

Jurisprudence of the State (國家의 法)

Delegated Secondary Reason (2차 이성)

↓

Justice (正義)

↓

Return → Ren (仁)

Result:

Law attains redemption when it returns

from institution to virtue.

This diagram visualizes the full ethical circuit:

Law is delegated from virtue and must return to virtue.

Justice is born at the center of that return.

vii. Horatio Nelson as Ren / Yi Sun-sin as Man — Personhood, Law, and the Architecture of Ethics

Trafalgar and Noryang were not merely battles; they were the places where legal ethics was spoken in a human voice.

Horatio Nelson (1758-1805) fulfilled Duty before God.

Yi Sun-sin (1545-1598) fulfilled Loyalty before the people.

Nelson's final utterance is written in the language of transcendence — a law before God.

Yi Sun-sin's final utterance is written in the language of immanence — a law before the living community.

The former embodies a theology of duty.

The latter embodies a theology of action.

Where their languages cross, law ceases to be a command of the State and becomes an act of human conscience.

Diagram 7. Ren ↔ Man — Ethical Parallel and Convergence

仁 (Ren / Virtue)

↑ Faith · Benevolence · Transcendence

Justice ←——— Intersection ———→ Conscience

↓ Action · Compassion · Loyalty

人 (Man / Humanity)

Cycle: 仁 → 人 → 法 → 仁

(From virtue to the human, from human to law,

from law back to virtue.)

This structure shows how justice emerges from the crossing of Ren (virtue) and Man (humanity). Law is revealed as an ethical ring of return.

Diagram. Law of Final Words — The Ethical Origin of Law in Duty and Loyalty

Horatio Nelson (1758-1805)

World of Duty — The Theology of Horatio Nelson

"Thank God, I have done my duty."

Yi Sun-sin (1545–1598)

World of Loyalty — The Ethics of Action

"戰方急, 愼愼言我死."

"The battle is urgent; do not report that I have died."

Nelson's language is a theology of duty before God.

Yi Sun-sin's language is an ethics of action before the people.

One represents a transcendent law; the other, an immanent law.

Where they meet, law is reborn as the language of conscience.

Sources / Primary Accounts

Horatio Nelson (1758–1805):

Mortally wounded aboard HMS Victory during the Battle of Trafalgar off Cape Trafalgar, near Cádiz, on 21 October 1805, shortly after 4:30 p.m. His final words are recorded in William Beatty, The Authentic Narrative of the Death of Lord Nelson (1807), and in Robert Southey, The Life of Horatio, Lord Viscount Nelson (1813).

Yi Sun-sin (1545–1598):

Killed in action during the Battle of Noryang on 16 December 1598 (Seonjo 31, 11th month, 19th day by lunar record). The Veritable Records of Seonjo (선조실록, Book 131) records his final instruction:

"戰方急, 愼愼言我死."

"The battle is urgent; do not report that I have died."

Diagram 8. Personhood Structure of Law

Faith of Ren	↔	Loyalty of Man
Inner Law (內法)		Outer Law (外法)
Source: Conscience		Source: Command
Function: Reflection		Function: Enforcement

Mediation: Virtue as Ethical Personhood

Outcome: Law becomes Character (人格法)

This diagram proposes that law evolves from institutional norm into ethical personhood.

Nelson's Ren operates as interior faith;

Yi Sun-sin's Man operates as outward action.

In their intersection, law becomes living character.

viii. The Political Philosophy of Ren — The State as a Community of Virtue

The redemption of law implies the restoration of the State.

The State, in its highest form, is not merely an engine of command. It is a community of virtue.

Politics of Ren (仁政) transforms law from a technology of control into a language of coexistence.

Rule of Law guarantees order;

Rule of Virtue grants meaning.

Only when both principles are joined does the State become a moral being.

Diagram 9. State as Community of Virtue

Memory of Virtue (덕의 기억)

↓

Human Law (사람의 법)

↓

State Law (국가의 법)

↓

Community (공동체)

↓

Justice (정의)

Transformation:

The State becomes a moral community

when law internalizes virtue.

When State law absorbs the conscience of the human person, the State ceases to be a mere institution and becomes an ethical presence.

ix. Conclusion — The Law of Ren and the Humanity of Man

Law is born from virtue and fulfilled in Man.

The jurisprudence of the State is a delegated, secondary reason derived from the jurisprudence of Man;

the jurisprudence of Man is a delegated, primary morality derived from the memory of virtue.

Within this chain of delegation, law is elevated from control to redemption.

Nelson's final speech testified to duty before God.

Yi Sun-sin's final speech testified to responsibility before the people.

Where those two languages converge, law returns from institutional command to human conscience.

That return is the soteriology of law — the moment when legal ethics is completed in the union of virtue and humanity.

Diagram 10. Cross of Ren and Man — The Intersection of 仁 and 人

仁 (Virtue / Ren)

↑

Faith | Compassion

|

Justice | Conscience

←——→

|

Duty | Loyalty

↓

人 (Humanity / Man)

Equation:

Law = Conscience × Compassion

This crossing diagram expresses an ethical equation:

justice arises where Ren and Man meet, and law becomes the product of conscience and compassion.

Diagram 11. Delegation Chain of Law

Memory of Virtue (仁의 기억)

↓

Jurisprudence of Man (人的 法哲學)

↓

Jurisprudence of the State (國家的 法哲學)

↓

Justice and Redemption (正義와 救援)

Law returns to its origin

when the State recalls Man

and Man recalls Virtue.

This final diagram represents the full cycle of delegation and return.

When law returns to virtue, justice is no longer merely an outcome — it becomes a redemptive process.

x. Final Statement

State law is the shadow of human law.

Human law is the descendant of the memory of virtue.

When law does not forget its origin, the State ceases to be an organ of domination and becomes a trustee of conscience.

The final purpose of law is not order but redemption.

Justice is not the product of institutions alone; it is the state in which human virtue is made real within institutions.

"Beyond the State, Before God."

Law is the language of human conscience standing before the eternal.

So long as that language is not forgotten, the State will always move — not toward control, but toward redemption.

Chapter Ⅶ. CONCLUSION Ⅰ — Beyond the State, Before God and Before the People

〈Poem〉 Saint Yi Sun-sin(李舜臣)

"Admiral Yi Sun-sin(李舜臣), of the Republic of Korea (formerly the Kingdom of Joseon),

Supreme Naval Commander of the Three Provinces,

Prime Minister in virtue and command,

Is hereby proclaimed the Fifth Saint of the World."

Proclaimed at dawn,

on the 26th of October, 2025,

before Gwanghwamun Gate, Seoul, Republic of Korea.

— Pyeong-jeong (平靜) Ji Young-hwan (池榮鋎)

The encounter between the two souls — Horatio Nelson (1758–1805) and Yi Sun-sin (1545–1598) — is not a mere comparison but a restoration of human ethics.

Nelson's Duty was the language of prayer directed toward God,

while Yi Sun-sin's Loyalty was the language of life offered to humankind.

Their ethics transcended the commands of the State and elevated human conscience into the divine ethics of God.

The Philosophy of the Nation is not the philosophy of power, but the philosophy of moral testimony:

a human being standing before God in self-examination, and before the people in self-witness.

This definition represents the final culmination of jurisprudence and rewrites the relationship between State and Man, command and conscience, war and peace.

War is the record of the moment when the State usurps the place of God.

Nelson went to sea in the name of the Empire;

Yi Sun-sin sailed in the name of the people's survival.

Nelson's enemy was the Napoleonic Empire;

Yi's was the invasion of Toyotomi Hideyoshi (1537–1598).

Yet, at the moment of death, both transcended the role of instruments of the State and became ethical subjects.

Nelson returned as a man before God,

Yi Sun-sin as a man before his people.

Their deaths were not the victory of nations, but the birth of ethics.

From those seas, the philosophy of law was reborn in a new language.

"Thank God, I have done my duty."

"戰方急, 愼勿言我死."

Two sentences that converge into the same ethical horizon beyond nations:

the first a prayer to God, the second a command to life.

Their essence was one — the human conscience as the origin and completion of law.

The soteriology of law is a philosophy of return.

Law begins in virtue, passes through human action, is institutionalized by the State,

and returns again to virtue — thereby giving birth to justice.

The Law of the State is a Delegated Secondary Reason derived from the Law of Man,

and the Law of Man is a Primary Morality delegated from the Memory of Virtue.

When this chain of delegation is complete, law ceases to be a mere command

and becomes an ethical memory — the foundation of justice itself.

When law remembers virtue, justice is born.

Yi Sun-sin's ethics transcended the limits of loyalty and became the ethics of life.

He was not a proxy of God, but a final witness of humanity.

His sword was not a weapon of aggression but a shield of compassion;

his ship, not an engine of war but a sacred vessel of salvation.

Confucius taught virtue to order the world;

Jesus embraced humanity through love;

Śākyamuni dissolved suffering through enlightenment;

Socrates redeemed man through reason;

and Yi Sun-sin saved his nation through action.

Thus, the fifth light—the Saint of Action—rose upon the firmament of humanity.

His last words, "The battle is at its height; tell no one of my death,"

were not an order of death but a prayer for life.

That day, the sea became the mirror of the saint, and in that mirror, humankind saw its conscience anew.

Yi Sun-sin — The Fifth Saint of Humanity.

His ethics were the embodiment of divine morality within humanity.

His war was not the victory of an empire but the redemption of humankind.

His death was not the end of a nation but the awakening of humanity.

〈Figure 8-1. The Trinitarian Structure of Human Ethics〉

Duty (Nelson) → Faith → Salvation

Loyalty (Yi Sun-sin) → Life → Compassion

↓

Humanity → Sanctity → Eternity

This diagram illustrates how their actions expand from national ethics to divine ethics,

and ultimately to a saintology of humanity.

Ethics is not the agency of God but the self-awareness of Man —

the central axis of civilization that transcends the instrumentalization of the State.

Nelson and Yi were not merely soldiers but moral archetypes of being.

Nelson offered duty to God; Yi offered life to humankind.

One was Admiral of Empire, the other Commander of the People—

yet both souls were enshrined in the Temple of Humanity.

When man, born as an instrument of the State, completes himself as the ethics of God,

he becomes a saint.

Yi Sun-sin sublimated loyalty into action, action into ethics, and ethics into humanity.

His patriotism became universal justice;

his death, the birth of mankind.

When the blood of Trafalgar met the waves of Noryang,

a new sea of human ethics was born.

Nelson's sea was a prayer of duty;

Yi's, a vow of loyalty.

Yet both waves formed one ocean—its name was not State, but Conscience.

Yi Sun-sin was not a war god, but the Saint of Humanity proven through action.

He realized Immanuel Kant's Guter Wille (Good Will)

through the Confucian virtue of loyalty.

His sword was not a weapon of war,

but the final instrument sustaining the ethics of God.

Thus, law returns to man, the State to conscience, and ethics to salvation.

When law remembers virtue, justice is born; when justice remembers humanity, salvation begins.

Chapter Ⅷ. CONCLUSION Ⅱ — Beyond the State, Before God and Before the People

I. Preface — The Path of Five Saints

Each civilization has raised a single sacred light—

a light that transcends epochs, languages, gods, and men,

teaching the essence of law and love.

This conclusion records the moment when five such lights—Confucius, Jesus, Śākyamuni, Socrates, and Yi Sun-sin—

meet within a single circle of humanity.

These figures have traditionally been called Saints (聖人).

II. Philosophical Genealogy of the Five Saints

Confucius (孔子, Kǒng Zǐ, 551–479 BCE) — "仁者, 人也. 人不可以無仁." (Analects, Yan Yuan).

Jesus Christ (Ἰησοῦς Χριστός, c. 7–2 BCE – 30/33 CE) — "A new commandment I give unto you, that ye love one another." (John 13:34–35).

Śākyamuni Buddha (釋迦牟尼佛, 563–483 BCE) — "All conditioned things are impermanent." (Dhammapada).

Socrates (Σωκράτης, 470–399 BCE) — "Know thyself." (Apology).

Yi Sun-sin (李舜臣, 1545–1598) — "The battle is at its height; tell no one of my death." (Nanjung Ilgi).

III. Symbolic Structure — The Civilizational Mandala

Confucius — Institutionalization of Ethics (Founder of Virtue-Politics).

Jesus — Salvific Love (Agape connecting Man and God).

Śākyamuni — Compassion through Enlightenment.

Socrates — Reason through Self-Reflection.

Yi Sun-sin — Testimony through Action (Loyalty redeeming Life).

These five axes form the evolutionary line of human ethics—

Virtue → Love → Enlightenment → Reason → Action—

all united within the mandala of Law, Humanity, God, and Conscience.

IV. Mandala of Delegation

〈Figure 8-3〉 The Vertical Structure of Delegation — The Law Rises, the Love Descends

[North: God]

Divine Love (Agape)

↓ Descent

Salvation of Man (人의 救援)

↑ Ascent

Law of the State (國家의 法) ← Delegation → Law of Man (人의 法)

Conscience (良心) → Virtue (德) → Justice (正義)

↑ Humanity (人類 / Mankind)

Inscription

The law of the State is delegated upward from the law of Man,

while the salvation of Man is bestowed downward from the love of God.

— Pyeong-jeong (平靜) Ji Young-hwan (池榮鋎)

Ascent (上行): Delegated Secondary Reason—from human conscience to state institution.

Descent (下行): Delegated Primary Grace—from divine love to the soul of man.

Intersection (交叉點): The Plaza of Justice—the sacred space where law and love converge.

V. Return of Ethics

When the ascending law and the descending love intersect,
justice becomes memory, and memory becomes salvation.
When law remembers virtue, justice is born;
when justice remembers humanity, salvation begins.
Yi Sun-sin stood at that intersection, proving ethics through action.
His sword was not a weapon of war but a tool upholding divine ethics.
His death was not the end of a nation but the birth of mankind.

VI. Afterword

Confucius founded the basis of law through virtue;
Jesus opened its soul through love;
Śākyamuni expanded its compassion through enlightenment;
Socrates established its justice through reason;
and Yi Sun-sin inscribed its memory through action.
Thus, law is no longer the command of the State but the conscience of Man,
and love no longer a transcendence of God but a salvation within humanity.
Where these two lines of delegation converge lies the ultimate essence of the Philosophy of the State.

VII. Closing Epigraph

"He that loveth not knoweth not God; for God is love." (1 John 4:8)
This scripture responds to the following thesis:
"The law of the State is delegated upward from the law of Man, while the salvation of Man is bestowed downward from the love of God."

Thus law returns to virtue, and love returns to man—

the cycle of human jurisprudence, the mandala of justice where State, God, and Humanity become one.

Harvard-Oxford Annotated Edition

Beatty, W. (1807) The Authentic Narrative of the Death of Lord Nelson. London.

— Shipboard medical and eyewitness account of Nelson's death aboard HMS Victory at Trafalgar on 21 Oct 1805; principal source for "Thank God, I have done my duty."

The London Gazette (1805) No. 15858, "Dispatches from Vice Admiral Collingwood," October 1805. London.

— Official Admiralty dispatch; fixes "England expects that every man will do his duty" in the naval/imperial register.

The Naval Chronicle (1806) Vol. 14, p. 421; Vol. 15, p. 17, "Funeral of Vice-Admiral Lord Nelson." London.

— Early public dissemination of Nelson's last words and royal framing ("Saviour of the Nation") under George III.

The Times (London) (23 October 1805) "The Death of Admiral Horatio Nelson." London.

— Early metropolitan press account of Trafalgar and Nelson's death.

국사편찬위원회 (1990) 『宣祖實錄』 [Seonjo Sillok], 권131, 선조 31년 11월 19일조 [=1598.12.16 양력], p. 524. 서울: 국사편찬위원회 영인본.

— Records Yi Sun-sin's final words: "戰方急, 愼勿言我死" ("The battle is urgent; do not report that I have died.").

이순신 (李舜臣) (1795 [1592-1598]) 『李舜臣全書』 권5. 포함: 『亂中日記』(1598년 12월 기록).

— Field diary and compiled corpus of Admiral Yi; battlefield ethics and command decisions in real time.

Nelson, H. (1803) Signal Book for the Fleet. Admiralty manuscript. London: Admiralty Archives, Public Record Office Ref. ADM 51/1413.

— Contains the pre-battle signal logic later crystallized as "England expects …".

Nelson, H. (1845) The Collected Correspondence of Admiral Lord Nelson, ed. H. Nicolas. Vol. 7. London: John Murray, pp. 211–213.

— Includes Nelson's final private letters (e.g. to Lady Hamilton), situating "duty" in a theological–moral register.

Southey, R. (1813) The Life of Horatio, Lord Viscount Nelson. London.

— Romantic-national hagiography of Nelson; important for tracing how the ethic of "duty" became public virtue.

柳成龍 [Yu Sŏngnyong / Ryu Seong-ryong] (1604/2002) 懲毖錄 (The Book of Corrections), tr. B. Choi. Berkeley, CA: Institute of East Asian Studies.

— Statesman's war memoir on the Imjin War; political and moral framing of Yi Sun-sin's campaigns.

Modern Naval / Military / Statehood Analyses

Ballard, G.A. (1911) The Influence of Sea Power. London: John Murray.

— Early comparative appraisal of admirals; appendix identifies Nelson and Yi as "the two greatest admirals in human history who never lost a battle."

Ballard, G.A. (1928) Rulers of the Sea: Great Naval Commanders. London: Methuen, p. 314.

— Develops Nelson–Yi comparative naval leadership as a trans-civilizational standard.

Cannadine, D. (2001) Ornamentalism: How the British Saw Their Empire. Oxford: Oxford University Press, pp. 132–135.

— Interprets the performative imperial meaning of "England expects that every man will do his duty."

Corbett, J.S. (1911/1988) Some Principles of Maritime Strategy. Annapolis, MD: Naval Institute Press.

— Classic theory of sea command and fleet risk; useful to frame Nelson's acceptance of mortal risk at Trafalgar.

Hawley, S. (2005) The Imjin War. Berkeley: University of California Press / Korean Studies.

— English-language strategic narrative of the 1592–1598 Japanese invasions, including Yi Sun-sin's naval defense.

Parker, G. (2005) The Military Revolution. Cambridge: Cambridge University Press.
— Places naval-technical transformation and centralized state violence in early modernity.
Rodger, N.A.M. (2004) The Command of the Ocean: A Naval History of Britain 1649–1815. London: Penguin.
— Contextualizes Nelson's command culture and the Admiralty's moral economy.
Swope, K.M. (2009) A Dragon's Head and a Serpent's Tail: Ming China and the First Great East Asian War, 1592–1598. Norman, OK: University of Oklahoma Press.
— East Asian coalition warfare framing of Yi Sun-sin within broader Ming–Joseon resistance.
Tennant, A. (2002) Admiral Yi Sun-sin and His Turtle Ships. Seoul: Hollym.
— English-accessible treatment of Yi's naval engineering and command ethos.

Turnbull, S. (2008) Samurai Invasion: Japan's Korean War 1592–98. London: Cassell.
— Japanese-leaning framing of the Imjin War; useful for contrasting depictions of Yi in Japanese historiography.
김준배 (2017) "근대 일본 이순신 · 넬슨 비교 담론의 등장과 변화." 『일본언어문화』 38.
— Tracks how Meiji and later Japanese discourse appropriated and reconfigured Nelson–Yi comparisons for nationalist purposes.
이태진 (2019) "이순신의 국가윤리와 법철학." 『한국사상사학보』 48, pp. 117–142. 서울대학교.
— Articulates Yi Sun-sin's loyalty/virtue as a proto-constitutional ethic rather than mere royal service.
정성국 (2010) 『이순신 리더십과 국가안보』. 서울: 플래닛미디어.
— Modern Korean security-state reading of Yi as a model of "ethical command responsibility."
장학근 (2007) 『조선 수군과 해전』. 서울: 학고방.
— Operational and organizational analysis of the Joseon navy structure.
한명기 (2004) 『임진왜란과 한중관계』. 서울: 푸른역사.
— Diplomatic framing; Yi not only as admiral but as node between Joseon and Ming imperial legitimacy.
신병주 (2012) 『조선과 일본, 전쟁과 평화』. 서울: 민음사.

— Long-view examination of Joseon–Japan strategic memory.
정병설 (2014) 『징비록, 전쟁의 기록』. 서울: 문학동네.
— Critical modern Korean edition of Jingbirok (懲毖錄), focusing on narrative integrity and memory politics.
김영호 (편) (2005) 『임진왜란과 동아시아』. 서울: 역사비평사.
— Regional framing of the Imjin War as East Asian international war rather than "Korea vs. Japan" alone.
— Treats territory/survival/sovereignty as layered memory structures (land, people, institutional legitimacy). Forms an early scaffold for "the State as custodian of ethical memory."
東郷平八郎 [Tōgō Heihachirō] (1926) 海軍講話 ['Naval Reflections on Admiral Yi Sun-sin']. 東京: 海軍大学校講義録.
(인용: Kim, Young-hun (2015) The Ethics of Loyalty in East Asian Naval Traditions. Seoul: SNU Press, p. 93.)
— Japanese admiral Tōgō reveres Yi as model admiral; crucial for showing Yi's elevation across civilizations.
防衛研修所戦史室 (연차별) 『日本戰史 海戦史稿』. 東京.
— Internal Imperial/Japanese naval historiography; comparative reception of Yi in modern Japanese naval identity.
吉川弘文館 (1968) 『朝鮮征伐記』 (日本戰爭史料叢書 第14巻). 東京: 吉川弘文館.
— Japanese war chronicle material on the invasions of Korea; shows the adversarial gaze on Yi.
Foundational Legal Philosophy and Moral Theory
Aquinas, T. (1270/2006) Summa Theologiae, I–II, qq. 90–97. Oxford: Blackfriars.
— Basis for the derivation model: human law (lex humana) as a participation in higher reason (lex naturalis / lex aeterna).
Bentham, J. (1789/1996) An Introduction to the Principles of Morals and Legislation. Oxford: Oxford University Press.
— Instrumental/utilitarian frame of law as regulator of pleasure–pain; foil to virtue-based legitimacy.
Cicero, M.T. (52 BCE/1999) On the Laws (De Legibus), tr. C. Keyes. Cambridge, MA:

Harvard University Press.
— "Lex est recta ratio naturae congruens": law as right reason in harmony with nature; anticipates natural law.

Finnis, J. (1980) Natural Law and Natural Rights. Oxford: Clarendon Press, p. 23.
— Rearticulates natural law as practical reason aimed at basic goods; core modern support for law as moral participation, not mere command.

Fuller, L. (1964) The Morality of Law. New Haven, CT: Yale University Press.
— Internal morality of law as fidelity to purpose; relevant to "restoration" and the danger of purely procedural coercion.

Habermas, J. (1992/1996) Between Facts and Norms, tr. W. Rehg. Cambridge, MA: MIT Press.
— Law as discourse-dependent legitimacy; complements the "publicity" requirement of inner law becoming institutional.

Hart, H.L.A. (1961) The Concept of Law. Oxford: Clarendon Press, ch. 8.
— "Internal point of view": law is sustained by those who accept it as a standard. Critical for seeing State law as lived, not merely imposed.

Kant, I. (1788/1996) Critique of Practical Reason, tr. M. Gregor. Cambridge: Cambridge University Press.
— "The starry heavens above me and the moral law within me": grounds duty in autonomous moral law.

Kant, I. (1785/1998) Groundwork of the Metaphysics of Morals, tr. M. Gregor. Cambridge: Cambridge University Press, pp. 47–53.
— Universalization and autonomy: conscience as self-legislation.

Kelsen, H. (1967) Pure Theory of Law, tr. M. Knight. Berkeley, CA: University of California Press.
— Normativity without moral content; used in this dissertation as the counter-position to "delegated moral reason."

MacCormick, N. (2007) Institutions of Law. Oxford: Oxford University Press.
— Law as institutional fact structured by reason-giving practices; helpful for "institutional memory."

MacIntyre, A. (1981) After Virtue. Notre Dame, IN: University of Notre Dame Press, ch.

14, "The Virtues of Loyalty."
— Loyalty and narrative identity as moral intelligibility; directly supports the Yi Sun-sin reading of loyalty as ethical, not merely feudal.

Posner, R. (1998) The Problematics of Moral and Legal Theory. Cambridge, MA: Harvard University Press.
— Skeptical of moral foundations in adjudication; useful foil in arguing law is not morally empty.

Rawls, J. (1971/1999) A Theory of Justice, rev. ed. Cambridge, MA: Harvard University Press.
— Justice as fairness; institutionalizes moral claims into public reason.

Raz, J. (1979) The Authority of Law. Oxford: Clarendon Press.
— Authority as service conception: legitimate law helps subjects better conform to reasons that already apply to them — mirrors "delegation" logic.

Ricoeur, P. (1990/1992) Oneself as Another, tr. K. Blamey. Chicago, IL: University of Chicago Press.
— Narrative selfhood and responsibility; supports the reading of "law as personhood."

Sandel, M. (2009) Justice. New York: Farrar, Straus and Giroux.
— Communitarian challenge to purely procedural justice; aligns with "State as moral community."

Schmitt, C. (1932/2007) The Concept of the Political, tr. G. Schwab. Chicago, IL: University of Chicago Press.
— Sovereignty as decision over the exception; background foil for "State as custodian of memory vs. State as monopolist of violence."

Sen, A. (2009) The Idea of Justice. Cambridge, MA: Harvard University Press.
— Justice as realization rather than ideal blueprint; parallels "justice as event of return."

Shklar, J. (1986) Legalism. Cambridge, MA: Harvard University Press.
— Critique of moral emptiness in procedural legality; supports this work's warning against "institution without conscience."

Tamanaha, B.Z. (2004) On the Rule of Law. Cambridge: Cambridge University Press.
— Sociological genealogy of "rule of law," which this dissertation reframes as "custodianship of moral memory."

Weber, M. (1919/2004) "Politics as a Vocation," in H. Gerth and C. Wright Mills (eds), From Max Weber. New York: Routledge.

— The State as monopoly of legitimate violence; baseline that our "State as trustee of virtue" openly contests.

Waldron, J. (1999) Law and Disagreement. Oxford: Oxford University Press.

— Public justification under pluralism; resonates with "ethical legitimacy zone."

Weinrib, E. (1995) The Idea of Private Law. Cambridge, MA: Harvard University Press.

— Private law as corrective justice rooted in relational morality; supports "law as relational reason."

Luhmann, N. (1993/2004) Law as a Social System, tr. K. Ziegert. Oxford: Oxford University Press.

— Treats law as self-referential system; in this dissertation, contrasted with "law as memory of virtue."

Dworkin, R. (1986) Law's Empire. Cambridge, MA: Harvard University Press.

— Law as integrity: judges must interpret law so that it shows the legal system in its morally best light. This anticipates our "restoration" model.

Coleman, J. (2001) The Practice of Principle. Oxford: Oxford University Press.

— Positivism/moral theory dialogue; supports articulating law as both practice and justification.

Habermas, J. (again, see above) and Tasioulas, J. (2012) "Human Rights, Legitimacy, and International Law." American Journal of Jurisprudence 58(1): 97–116.

— Human-rights normativity as legitimacy claim, not mere treaty positivism; anchors the "State as trustee" argument in contemporary public law theory.

Fuller, L. & Winston, K. (1978) "The Forms and Limits of Adjudication." Harvard Law Review 92(2): 353–409.

— Adjudication as morally bounded craft; relevant to "interpretation = restoration of memory."

Gardner, J. (2012) Law as a Leap of Faith. Oxford: Oxford University Press.

— Law's normativity finally rests on an act of moral commitment; ties directly into "Beyond the State, Before God."

Green, L. (2012) The Authority of the State. Oxford: Oxford University Press.

— State authority as justified service; dovetails with "the State as custodian, not creator, of moral reason."

Shapiro, S. (2011) Legality. Cambridge, MA: Harvard University Press.

— The planning theory of law; clarifies how complex institutions operationalize shared moral purposes.

Agamben, G. (2005) State of Exception, tr. K. Attell. Chicago, IL: University of Chicago Press.

— The danger case: State claims to suspend law; foil for our insistence that law's legitimacy derives from conscience, not sheer command.

Classical East Asian Moral-Political Sources

Confucius (孔子) (1893) The Analects of Confucius (論語), tr. J. Legge. Oxford: Oxford University Press, esp. 12:22 ("Fan Chi asked about Ren … The Master said: 'To love others.'").

— Core textual basis for defining 仁 as relational normativity, not mere sentiment.

Mencius (孟子) (1970) Mencius, tr. D.C. Lau. London: Penguin, esp. 尽心篇 / Jin Xin ("仁者는 人也").

— Asserts that benevolence, righteousness, propriety, and wisdom are inherent, not externally implanted; supports "law as interior moral capacity."

Zhu Xi 朱熹 (1190/1983)『四書章句集注』. Beijing: Zhonghua.

— Canonical Neo-Confucian synthesis that systematizes 仁/義 as structural "inner law."

Wang Yangming 王陽明 (1527/2005)『傳習錄』. Shanghai: Shanghai Guji.

— Identifies 良知 (innate knowing) as immediately binding moral law; anticipates the idea of "self-legislated duty."

Xunzi 荀子 (c.3rd BCE/2001) Xunzi, tr. E. Hutton. Princeton, NJ: Princeton University Press.

— Argues for ritual and institutional cultivation of virtue; helpful for bridging inner morality and external order.

Dong Zhongshu 董仲舒 (c.2nd BCE/2010)『春秋繁露』. Beijing: Zhonghua.

— Early Han synthesis linking cosmic order, moral governance, and legitimacy of rulership; foreshadows "State as moral trustee."

黃仁宇 [Huang Renyu] (1983)『萬曆十五年』. Beijing: 生活・讀書・新知三聯.

— Macro-historical framing of late Ming governance logic, including the Ming–Joseon war environment of Yi Sun-sin.

牟宗三 Mou Zongsan (1962)『道德的理想主義』. Taipei: 學生書局.

— Modern New Confucian articulation of moral idealism as a live constitutional force.

唐君毅 Tang Junyi (1957)『中國哲學原論』. Hong Kong: 新亞.

— Human dignity and moral selfhood as the basis for political legitimacy.

梁啟超 Liang Qichao (1902/1996)『新民說』. Beijing: 中華書局.

— Transitions loyalty/virtue into modern citizenship discourse; bridges Yi Sun-sin's "loyalty for the people" with constitutional nationalism.

『明實錄 · 神宗實錄』卷308. 北京: 中華書局影印.

— Ming imperial records around the late Imjin War / Noryang context, for cross-checking Yi Sun-sin's final actions in alliance frameworks.

『皇明神宗實錄』(late 16th c. entries).

— Confirms Ming court perception of Joseon naval resistance as morally legitimated defense of civilians, not merely vassal obedience.

Authorial / Theoretical Contributions Cited in This Dissertation

Ji, Y.-h. (池榮錠, 平靜) (2025) Statecraft and the Wisdom of Wind: Symbols and Responsibilities of the Fan in East and West. Seoul: Future Governance Institute, ch. 3.

— Formally articulates the structural model "Law_State = Delegated(f_InnerReason)," i.e. State jurisprudence as delegated secondary reason.

Ji, Y.-h. (池榮錠, 平靜) (October 2025) "Beyond the State, Before God: Two Souls before the Nation — Horatio Nelson and Yi Sun-sin." Draft presented, Faculty of Law, University of Oxford.

— First public declaration of the core thesis: "The jurisprudence of the State is a delegated, secondary reason derived from the jurisprudence of Man."

부록

對談 : ChatGPT 對 평정(平靜) 지영환(池榮鋎)

평정(平靜) 지영환(池榮鋎) 왈(曰) 말하는바. '가로되', '가라사대'

ChatGPT 2025.6.15.09시판.

Ⅰ. 美 연방 수정헌법 제2조 총기권리 ChatGPT 의견?

1. 일반인의 총기 소지 허용 국가 현황

일반인의 총기 소지에 관한 국제 비교 연구

국가	총기 소지 가능 여부	규제 수준	주요 특징
미국	가능	낮음 ~ 중간	수정헌법 제2조에 따라 총기 소지 권리 보장
캐나다	가능	중간	허가제. 개인 소유 허용하나 사용 · 보관 규제. 공격 무기 금지
스위스	가능	중간	예비군 체계로 군 복무 후 총기 소지. 총기 등록 의무
핀란드	가능	비교적 낮음	사냥 · 스포츠용 총기 허용. 면허 필요. 정신건강 심사
체코	제한적 가능	높음	자위용 총기 허용. 매우 엄격한 허가제. 군 복무 운영
이스라엘	제한적 가능	높음	1996년 대량 총기회수 이후 강력한 규제. 특수 조건 등 필요
호주	매우 제한적	매우 높음	청기 소지 원칙적 금지. 일부 엽총 · 공기총만 허용
대한민국	원칙적 금지	매우 높은	총기 소지 불허. 일부 사냥용 총기 경찰 보관 하에 제한적 사용 가능

---

* 성균관대 국가전략대학원 겸임교수 · 중앙대학교 행정대학원 객원교수 · 국가공무원 · 서울대학교 객원연구원

총기 소지는 오랜 기간 동안 자유와 안전 사이의 갈등을 상징하는 주제였다. 각국은 역사적 경험, 사회적 신뢰 수준, 치안 환경, 정치 문화에 따라 상이한 총기 규제 정책을 시행하고 있으며, 이에 대한 비교 연구는 공공 정책과 형사사법 분야에서 중요한 의미를 갖는다. 본 논문은 세계 주요 국가들의 일반인 총기 소지 허용 여부 및 규제 수준을 비교하여, 총기 소지 정책의 특징과 그 사회적 함의를 분석하고자 한다.

가. 총기 소지 가능 여부와 규제 수준의 분류

국가별 총기 정책은 총기 소지를 전면 허용하는 국가, 조건부로 제한하는 국가, 원칙적으로 금지하는 국가로 나눌 수 있다. 미국은 수정헌법 제2조에 따라 총기 소지를 헌법적으로 보장하며, 주마다 규제가 상이하다. 자위 목적의 총기 소유가 일반화되어 있다. 캐나다, 스위스, 핀란드는 총기 소지가 가능하지만, 정부 허가, 면허제, 정신건강 심사 등의 통제를 동반한다. 체코는 유럽 내에서 자위 목적 총기 소지가 허용된 드문 사례로, 비교적 관대한 규제를 유지한다. 이스라엘과 호주는 특정 사건 이후 엄격한 총기 규제 정책을 도입하여, 총기 소지는 매우 제한적이며, 강력한 허가제가 시행 중이다. 일본과 대한민국은 총기 소지를 원칙적으로 금지하며, 일부 엽총 등에 한해 경찰 보관 하에 제한적으로 사용을 허용한다.

나. 규제 정책의 사회적 맥락과 배경

각국의 총기 정책은 특정 역사적 사건(예: 호주의 포트아서 사건, 이스라엘 내 안보 위협), 제도적 신뢰(예: 북유럽 국가들의 높은 공공 신뢰도), 문화적 가치(예: 미국의 자유 권리 강조) 등에 기초한다. 호주의 경우 1996년 총기 난사 사건 이후 대대적인 총기 회수와 법 개정을 통해 총기 소지를 강력히 통제하게 되었다. 이스라엘은 안보 상황과 군 복무 중심의 시민 구조로 인해 제한적인 총기 소지를 허용하면서도 강력한 심사를 병행한다.

다. 총기 소지 자유와 공공안전 사이의 균형

총기 규제 정책은 공공안전을 강화하면서도 개인의 자유를 존중해야 하는 균형점을 모색한다. 비교적 규제가 느슨한 국가들에서도 총기 범죄에 대한 우려가 제기되고 있으며, 반대로 강력한 규제를 시행하는 국가에서는 총기 관련 범죄율이 낮게 유지되는 경향을 보인다.

본 연구는 세계 주요 국가들의 총기 소지 정책을 비교함으로써, 총기 규제가 단순한 법적 문제를 넘어 사회 전반의 신뢰 구조, 국가 정체성, 공공 정책 전략과 밀접히 연결되어 있음을 밝혔다. 한국과 같은 고강도 규제 국가에서는 현 체계를 유지하면서, 합리적 예외 규정과 안전 교육 강화를 통해 제도적 신뢰를 더욱 높일 필요가 있다. 반면, 총기 자유가 보장된 국가에서는 규제의 사각지대를 보완하기 위한 정책적 접근이 요구된다.

1. State of the country allowing on Civilian Gun Ownership

International Comparative Study on Civilian Gun Ownership

Country	Civilian Gun Ownership Permitted	Level of Regulation	Key Characteristics
United States	Yes	Low to Medium	The right to keep and bear arms is guaranteed under the Second Amendment to the U.S. Constitution.
Canada	Yes	Medium	Permit system; personal ownership allowed but use and storage are regulated. Assault weapons are prohibited.
Switzerland	Yes	Medium	Based on a reserve military system; firearms possession after military service. Mandatory gun registration.
Finland	Yes	Relatively Low	Firearms for hunting and sport shooting allowed; license required; mental health checks mandatory.
Czech Republic	Limited Yes	High	Firearms for self-defense permitted under a very strict licensing system; military service in place.
Israel	Limited Yes	High	Strong regulation after a large-scale firearm recall in 1996; ownership allowed under special conditions.

Australia	Very Limited	Very High	Civilian firearm ownership generally prohibited; some shotguns and air rifles permitted.
South Korea	Generally No	Very High	Civilian firearm ownership prohibited; limited hunting firearms allowed under police custody for restricted use.

Introduction

Discussions on gun ownership vary significantly across countries, shaped by diverse historical, cultural, and social contexts. While some nations emphasize individual rights and self-defense by allowing firearm possession, others impose strict regulations in favor of public safety and crime prevention. This paper aims to compare and analyze the status of civilian gun ownership and regulatory frameworks in key countries, highlighting their policy characteristics and social implications.

Main Body

1. Typology of Countries Permitting Civilian Gun Ownership

Countries that allow civilian gun ownership can generally be classified into the following categories: Liberal Authorization: The United States is the most prominent example, where the right to bear arms is constitutionally protected. Regulations vary by state, with some maintaining minimal restrictions, reflecting a strong belief in individual liberty and the right to self-defense.[1]

Conditional Authorization: Countries such as Canada, Switzerland, and Finland allow gun ownership under strict conditions. These nations implement permit and licensing systems, with ownership primarily allowed for purposes such as hunting, sports, or national defense reserve forces.

Strict Regulation: Australia and Israel have adopted stringent firearm control policies, especially after significant gun-related incidents. Australia, for instance, launched a massive gun buyback program after the 1996 Port Arthur massacre.[2]

Prohibition by Principle: Japan and South Korea fundamentally prohibit civilian firearm ownership. Only under highly regulated circumstances, such as licensed hunting, are specific firearms allowed and strictly supervised by law enforcement.[3]

2. Level of Regulation and Social Context

The extent of gun control goes beyond legal measures and closely relates to factors such as social trust, law enforcement systems, and civic culture. Switzerland, for example, maintains low gun crime rates despite relatively liberal policies, attributed to robust military traditions, firearm education, and strict management. In contrast, the U.S. shows high levels of gun-related violence corresponding with its more permissive gun laws.[4]

Conclusion

As this study demonstrates, national gun policies reflect each country's social background, historical experience, and civic values. Rather than evaluating the effectiveness of regulations solely based on the legality of firearm possession, a comprehensive analysis that includes institutional infrastructure and social context is essential. In considering gun policy reforms in any context, especially in countries like South Korea, it is crucial to adapt international models to domestic realities rather than apply them wholesale.

Footnotes

1. U.S. Constitution, Second Amendment.
2. Chapman, S. et al. (2006). "Australia's 1996 gun law reforms: Faster falls in firearm deaths, firearm suicides, and a decade without mass shootings." Injury Prevention, 12(6), 365–372.
3. Krause, K. (2011). "Peace, Security and Development in Post-Conflict En-

vironments." Routledge. (Citing Japan and South Korea)

4. OECD (2022). Gun Violence and Public Safety Report.

References

1. Chapman, S., Alpers, P., Agho, K., & Jones, M. (2006). Australia's 1996 gun law reforms: Faster falls in firearm deaths, firearm suicides, and a decade without mass shootings. Injury Prevention, 12(6), 365–372.

2. Krause, K. (2011). Peace, Security and Development in Post-Conflict Environments. Routledge.

3. OECD. (2022). Gun Violence and Public Safety Report.

4. U.S. Constitution. Second Amendment.

https://chatgpt.com/c/68464c12-0538-8008-abd9-13558f3297bd 2025.6.9.검색.

Key Points on Civilian Gun Ownership and Regulation in the United States

Possession: Civilian gun ownership is permitted under the Second Amendment to the U.S. Constitution.

Regulation Level: Ranges from low to moderate, depending on the state.

Key Features:

The Second Amendment guarantees the right to keep and bear arms.

Federal and state laws vary — some states impose minimal restrictions, while others require stricter licensing and comprehensive background checks.

Firearms may be purchased for purposes such as self-defense, hunting, and sport shooting, but certain types (e.g., fully automatic firearms) are heavily regulated or prohibited under federal law.

2. 미국 일반인들의 총기 소지와 규제 핵심

미국 일반인의 총기 소지와 규제에 대한 고찰

구분	총기 소지 권리(찬성 측)	총기 규제(규제 측)
헌법적 근거	수정헌법 제2조: 무기를 소지하고 휴대할 권리 보장	수정헌법 제2조는 일정한 제한이 가능하다고 해석
문화적 배경	자위 및 사냥, 전통적 권리로 인식	대량 총기 사건 및 안전 문제 우려
정치적 입장	보수 성향 (공화당 중심), NRA 등 권리지지	진보 성향 (민주당 중심), 규제 강화 주장
법적 기준	많은 주에서 허가 없이 소지 가능 (특히 공화당 주)	일부 주에서는 등록, 교육, 심사 등 요구
배경 조사	제한적 신원조회 (일부 주만 강화)	범죄 이력, 정신질환 이력 조회 강화 주장
총기 종류	반자동 소총 포함한 다양한 총기 소지 가능	공격용 무기(AR-15 등) 금지 요구
총기 사고 대응	총기 소지가 범죄 예방에 도움	총기 접근 제한이 사고 예방에 효과적이라는 주장
규제 반대 논리	정부의 과도한 통제를 방지, 자유 수호	공공안전을 위해 최소한의 규제 필요

총기 소지는 미국 사회에서 오랜 역사와 전통을 지닌 민감한 이슈 중 하나이다. 수정헌법 제2조는 무기를 소지하고 휴대할 권리를 보장하고 있으며, 이는 미국 시민 개 개인의 자유와 권리를 상징하는 핵심 조항으로 여겨져 왔다. 그러나 현대에 이르러 총기 관련 범죄와 대량 총격 사건이 빈번히 발생하면서, 총기 소유에 대한 권리를 어디까지 허용하고 어떤 수준의 규제를 가해야 하는지를 둘러싼 논쟁이 첨예하게 대립하고 있다. 본 논문은 미국 내 총기 소지의 권리와 그에 대한 규제 정책을 정치적, 문화적, 법적 관점에서 고찰하고, 양측 주장의 핵심 논리를 비교 분석함으로써 이 복합적인 사회 문제에 대한 균형 잡힌 시각을 제시하고자 한다.

가. 법적 근거와 헌법 해석의 차이

총기 소지 권리의 가장 강력한 근거는 미국 헌법 수정 제2조이다. 이 조항은 “규율

잡힌 민병대는 자유로운 국가의 안보에 필요하므로, 국민이 무기를 소지하고 휴대할 권리는 침해받아서는 안 된다"고 명시하고 있으며, 총기 소지 옹호론자들은 이를 개인의 무제한적 권리로 해석한다. 특히 2008년 대법원 판결인 District of Columbia v. Heller에서는 개인의 자위 목적 총기 소지를 헌법상 권리로 인정하였다. 그러나 이 판결은 동시에 정부가 공공안전을 위해 합리적인 제한을 가할 수 있음을 명시하였다. 이에 따라 총기 규제론자들은 헌법이 총기 소지를 절대적 권리로 보장하는 것이 아니라, 사회 질서와 국민의 안전을 위한 법적 제약도 가능하다는 점을 강조한다.

나. 문화적 배경과 지역 간 인식 차이

총기는 미국의 개척 역사와 독립 정신과 밀접한 관련을 맺고 있으며, 특히 농촌 지역이나 남부, 중서부 지역에서는 총기 소지를 자위와 자유 수호의 상징으로 받아들이고 있다. 사냥, 스포츠 사격 등은 일상적인 여가 활동으로 자리잡고 있으며, 총기 소지는 생활의 일부로 간주된다. 반면, 도시 지역이나 진보 성향이 강한 지역에서는 대량 총격 사건과 총기 범죄로 인해 총기를 위험 요소로 인식하는 경향이 강하다. 이러한 문화적 · 지리적 요인은 총기 규제 법안에 대한 찬반 의견을 결정하는 데 큰 영향을 미친다.

다. 정치적 입장과 법제 차이

정치적으로는 공화당과 NRA(전미총기협회)를 중심으로 한 보수 진영이 총기 권리를 적극 지지하고 있다. 이들은 총기 소지가 범죄 억제 및 시민 자유 보호에 기여한다고 주장하며, 총기 규제를 정부의 과도한 개입으로 간주한다. 반면, 민주당은 총기 범죄와 사고 방지를 위해 강력한 규제를 추진하고 있으며, 특히 대량 살상용 무기의 제한, 배경조사 강화, 적정 소지 연령 제한 등의 정책을 지지한다.

실제로 미국 내 각 주는 총기에 대해 서로 다른 법률을 운용하고 있다. 예를 들어, 텍사스나 애리조나와 같은 보수 성향 주에서는 총기 구매 및 소지가 비교적 자유로운 반면, 캘리포니아나 뉴욕과 같은 진보 성향 주에서는 총기 등록, 교육 이수, 면허 발급 등을 요구하며 보다 엄격한 규제를 시행하고 있다.

라. 총기 사고 대응 논리의 차이

총기 소지 옹호론자들은 무장한 시민이 범죄를 억제할 수 있다는 '더 많은 총기 = 더 안전한 사회'라는 주장을 펼친다. 이들은 총기 소지가 자위권을 실현할 수 있는 유일한 수단이라고 강조한다. 반면 규제 지지자들은 총기 접근 자체를 제한해야 사고와 범죄를 줄일 수 있으며, 특히 안전 보관, 구매 시 대기 기간, 정신건강 상태 확인 등 구체적인 규제 방안이 필요하다고 본다. RAND 연구소 등의 연구 결과에 따르면, 총기 규제가 잘 시행된 지역일수록 총기 관련 범죄율이 낮은 경향을 보이는 것으로 나타났다.

총기 소지는 미국 사회에서 자유와 안전, 권리와 공공복지 사이의 균형 문제를 집약적으로 보여주는 주제이다. 총기 권리를 주장하는 측은 헌법적 권리와 문화적 전통, 자위권을 근거로 하며, 규제를 지지하는 측은 공공안전과 범죄 예방, 사회 질서 유지를 강조한다. 양측의 입장은 단순한 이념 대립을 넘어, 지역적 문화, 정치적 배경, 역사적 맥락이 복합적으로 작용한 결과이다. 미국 내 총기 규제 문제의 해결을 위해서는 양측의 주장을 이분법적으로 나누기보다는, 실증적 데이터에 기반한 중도적 접근과 정책적 조율이 필요할 것이다.[1]

---

1 https://chatgpt.com/c/684655fa-06e4-8008-9fb6-fee8dcd3a063 2025.6.9. 검색.
U.S. Constitution, Second Amendment.
Smith, J. (2021). Mass Shootings and Gun Control in the U.S. Public Policy Quarterly.
District of Columbia v. Heller, 554 U.S. 570 (2008).
Cornell, S. (2006). A Well-Regulated Militia: The Founding Fathers and the Origins of Gun Control in America. Oxford University Press.
Kohn, A. (2015). The American Gun Culture: Myths and Realities. Journal of American History.
Pew Research Center (2022). "Urban-Rural Divide on Gun Control."
NRA official platform and lobbying data, 2022.
Democratic National Committee (2020). "Gun Safety Reform Proposals."
Giffords Law Center. (2023). State Gun Laws Overview.
Lott, J. (2010). More Guns, Less Crime. University of Chicago Press.
Giffords Law Center (2022). "Safe Storage Laws and Public Safety."
RAND Corporation (2021). Gun Policy in America: The Effects of Gun Laws.

2. A Critical Review of Civilian Gun Ownership and Regulation in the United States

Comparison: Gun Ownership Rights vs. Gun Regulation in the United States

Category	Gun Ownership Rights (Pro-Gun)	Gun Regulation (Pro-Regulation)
Constitutional Basis	Second Amendment: Guarantees the right to keep and bear arms	Second Amendment interpreted as allowing certain restrictions
Cultural Background	Seen as a traditional right for self-defense and hunting	Concerns over mass shootings and public safety
Political Stance	Conservative (Republican-leaning), supported by NRA and similar groups	Progressive (Democratic-leaning), advocates for stronger regulations
Legal Standards	In many states, ownership allowed without a permit (especially in Republican-led states)	In some states, requires registration, training, and screening
Background Checks	Limited background checks (enhanced only in some states)	Advocates for stronger checks on criminal records and mental health history
Types of Firearms	Wide range of firearms allowed, including semi-automatic rifles	Calls to ban assault weapons (e.g., AR-15)
Response to Gun Incidents	Believes gun ownership helps deter crime	Argues that restricting gun access effectively prevents incidents
Arguments Against Regulation	Prevents excessive government control, protects individual freedom	Minimum necessary regulation is needed to ensure public safety

Introduction

Gun ownership remains one of the most sensitive and controversial issues in American society, rooted in a long history of constitutional rights and cultural traditions. The Second Amendment of the U.S. Constitution guarantees "the right of the people to keep and bear Arms," which has been widely interpreted by gun rights advocates as a foundational protection of individual liberty. However, the rise in gun-related crimes and mass shootings has prompted growing demands for stronger gun control measures. This paper aims to examine both the right to bear arms and the legal efforts to regulate firearms in the United States by analyzing their historical, cultural, legal, and political dimensions, thereby offering a balanced understanding of this complex societal issue.

Body

1. Legal Basis and Constitutional Interpretation

The Second Amendment provides the strongest legal basis for gun ownership in the U.S. It states that "a well-regulated militia, being necessary to the security of a free state, the right of the people to keep and bear arms, shall not be infringed". Gun rights proponents interpret this as guaranteeing an individual's unrestricted right to own firearms. This interpretation was supported by the landmark Supreme Court decision District of Columbia v. Heller (2008), which affirmed the individual's right to possess firearms for lawful purposes, particularly self-defense within the home.

However, the same ruling also acknowledged the government's authority to impose reasonable regulations for the sake of public safety. Advocates of gun control argue that the Second Amendment does not grant an absolute right and that constitutional rights must be balanced against the need for social order and security.

2. Cultural Background and Regional Differences

Gun ownership in the United States is deeply intertwined with the country's frontier history and ideals of personal freedom. In rural and conservative areas, firearms are widely accepted as tools for self-defense, hunting, and sport shooting. They are often viewed as part of one's cultural heritage and daily life.

Conversely, in urban and progressive regions, where mass shootings and gun violence are more prevalent, firearms are perceived as a significant threat to public safety. These regional and cultural differences play a major role in shaping public attitudes and policy preferences regarding gun ownership and regulation.

3. Political Stances and Legislative Divergence

Politically, the Republican Party and conservative groups — supported by organizations such as the National Rifle Association (NRA) — strongly defend gun rights. They argue that armed citizens deter crime and that gun control constitutes government overreach. On the other hand, the Democratic Party advocates for stronger gun control measures to reduce gun-related violence, including restrictions on assault weapons, background checks, and limitations on firearm access for high-risk individuals.

The divergence in state-level laws reflects this political divide. In conservative states such as Texas or Arizona, firearm purchases and possession are largely unrestricted. In contrast, progressive states like California and New York enforce strict regulations, including firearm registration, safety training, mandatory waiting periods, and licensing requirements.

4. Contrasting Arguments on Gun Incidents

Gun rights supporters maintain that increased firearm ownership leads to greater safety, citing the theory of "more guns, less crime". They emphasize the role of guns in deterring crime and protecting individual freedom. In contrast, gun control advocates argue that limiting access to firearms is essential to reducing gun violence and accidents. Measures such as safe storage laws, mandatory waiting periods, and mental health evaluations are proposed as effective means of prevention.

Research by organizations such as the RAND Corporation has shown that regions with stricter gun regulations tend to experience lower rates of gun violence. These findings support the argument that thoughtful regulation can enhance public safety without necessarily infringing on constitutional rights.

Conclusion

Gun ownership in the United States encapsulates the tension between freedom and safety, individual rights and collective responsibility. Proponents of gun rights invoke constitutional protections, cultural identity, and self-defense, while advocates of gun control emphasize public health, safety, and the need for legal boundaries. The polarized nature of this debate is not merely ideological but deeply rooted in historical, regional, and political contexts. Resolving the issue of gun regulation requires moving beyond binary arguments and adopting an evidence-based, balanced approach that reconciles constitutional freedoms with the imperative of public safety.

Ⅱ. ChatGPT 先生 미합중국 연방헌법(美合衆國 聯邦憲法) 수정 제2조 존속해야 할까? 폐지해야 할까?[234]

---

2 미합중국 헌법 수정 제2조(Second Amendment)의 존속 여부는 미국에서 가장 논쟁적인 헌법적 · 정치적 주제 중 하나입니다. 이 조항이 계속 유지되어야 하는가에 대한 질문은 단순한 법적 판단을 넘어서 역사적 맥락, 정치적 이념, 사회적 현실, 공공안전 등을 아우르는 복합적인 논의가 필요합니다. 아래에 대표적인 존속 찬성과 폐지 또는 개정 주장 양측의 주장을 요약해 드립니다.

존속 찬성 입장 ("Second Amendment Should Be Preserved")

개인의 자유와 자기 방어권 보호, 정부의 폭정으로부터 시민이 자신을 보호할 수 있는 수단으로 무장을 보장한다는 철학적 전제. 경찰이 도착하기 전 범죄에 대응할 수 있는 자위권의 일환. 미국 역사와 문화의 일부, 민병대 전통과 개척 시대의 역사 속에서 총기는 미국인의 정체성의 일부로 여겨짐. 독립전쟁과 초기 연방 형성 과정에서 시민 무장권은 핵심적 역할을 함. 총기 소유는 범죄율과 무관하다는 주장, 일부 연구는 총기 규제가 엄격한 지역에서도 범죄율이 높음을 근거로 총기 자체가 문제는 아니라고 주장. 헌법적 안정성, 기본권은 일시적 정치적 유행이나 충격에 따라 쉽게 변경되어서는 안 된다는 원칙론.

폐지 또는 개정 주장 ("Second Amendment Should Be Repealed or Revised")

현대 사회에 맞지 않는 시대착오적 조항, 18세기의 총기(머스킷)와 21세기의 자동화된 고성능 총기는 비교할 수 없으며, 조항의 원래 의도와 현 상황이 괴리됨. 총기 난사와 대량 살상 사건, 학교, 쇼핑몰, 교회 등에서 반복되는 총기 난사 사건이 더 이상 개인 권리의 문제로 보기 어려운 수준에 도달. 공공 안전을 이유로 규제 필요성 강조.

모호한 표현 "잘 규율된 민병대"의 의미가 불분명하여 해석에 따라 무한한 확장이 가능함. 대법원도 시대에 따라 상반된 판결을 내림 (예: 1939년 U.S. v. Miller vs. 2008년 District of Columbia v. Heller). 다른 선진국과의 비교, 총기 규제가 강력한 나라들(예: 일본, 영국, 호주)의 총기 사망률이 현저히 낮다는 점에서 교훈 가능. 결론적으로… 수정 제2조의 존속 여부는 단순히 "있어야 한다/말아야 한다"로 결론지을 수 있는 문제는 아닙니다. 이 조항은 미국의 정치적 이념, 자유에 대한 관념, 공공의 안전을 둘러싼 균형의 문제입니다. 보완적 제안: 어떤 이들은 완전한 폐지보다는 해석의 명확화나 합리적 제한(예: 고위험군 총기 소지 제한, 대용량 탄창 금지 등)**을 주장합니다. 시민사회와 입법, 사법부 간의 긴밀한 논의를 통해 현실적인 해법이 마련되어야 할 필요가 있습니다.

https://chatgpt.com/c/6846c10c-1a8c-8008-9ca4-bab611811096 2025.6.9. 검색.

3 미합중국 연방헌법 수정 제2조(Second Amendment)는 총기 소유의 권리를 다룬 조항으로, 다음과 같은 문구로 구성되어 있습니다: "A well regulated Militia, being necessary to the security of a free State, the right of the people to keep and bear Arms shall not be infringed." (잘 규율된 민병대는 자유로운 국가의 안보에 필요하므로, 국민이 무기를 소유하고 휴대할 권리는 침해되어서는 안 된다.) 이 조항을 존속시켜야 하는지, 폐지해야 하는지는 미국 사회에서 매우 뜨거운 논쟁거리입니다. 아래는 양측의 주요 논거를 정리한 것입니다.

- 존속해야 한다는 입장? 헌법상 자유의 상징, 총기 소유는 미국 독립 정신과 자유의 핵심 상징. 정부의 폭정에 맞서기 위한 마지막 방어 수단으로 간주됨. 자위권 개인이 자신과 가족을 보호할 수 있는 수단. 경찰의 즉각적인 대응이 어려운 상황에서 총기는 방어 수단이 됨. 헌법적 전통과 해석 : 미국 대법원(특히 District of Columbia v. Heller, 2008)은 개인의 총기 소유권을 헌법적으로 보호된 권리로 인정. 사냥 및 스포츠, 총기는 미국의 문화적 전통 속에서 사냥, 스포츠 사격 등의 활동과도 깊게 연결.
- 폐지하거나 대폭 수정해야 한다는 입장? 총기 폭력과 범죄 증가, 총기 난사 사건과 총기 관련 범죄가 계속해서 증가하고 있음. 총기 소지가 너무 쉬워 범죄자도 손쉽게 무기를 획득할 수 있음. 시대적 상황 변화, 수정 제2조는 18세기 상황(민병대, 무장 시민 중심)을 반영한 것으로, 현대 사회의 자동화 무기, 대도시 환경 등과 맞지 않음. 국제적 비교, 대부분의 선진국은 강력한 총기 규제를 하고 있으며, 그 결과 총기 관련 사망률이 훨씬 낮음. 공공 안전 우선, 개인의 자유보다 사회 전체의 안전과 생명이 더 중요하다는 입장.
- 중도적 입장: 폐지가 아닌 "규제 강화"? 수정 제2조 자체는 존중하되, 총기 구매 절차와 소유 조건을 대폭 강화해야 한다는 견해. 예: 신원조회 강화, 자동화 무기 제한, 정신건강 이력 확인 등. 이는 수정 제2조의 존속과 공공안전의 균형을 추구하는 절충안으로 제시됨.

결론

이 문제는 단순히 총기에 대한 논쟁이 아니라, 자유 vs 안전, 개인 권리 vs 공동체 보호, 역사적 전통 vs 현대적 현실의 가치 충돌입니다. 당신이 중요하게 여기는 가치가 무엇인가에 따라 입장은 달라질 수 있습니다: 자유와 자율성을 중시한다면: 존속 또는 부분 수정, 공공의 안전과 생명을 우선시한다면: 폐지 또는 강력한 규제

https://chatgpt.com/c/6846c5d9-d48c-8008-a697-d7606c8f2d39 2025.6.9. 검색.

4 Title: A Constitutional Dilemma: Should the Second Amendment to the U.S. Constitution Be Preserved or Abolished?

Author:

[Your Name]

[Institution or Course Name]

[Date]

Abstract

The Second Amendment to the U.S. Constitution remains one of the most debated provisions in American law and culture. While some view it as a sacred protector of liberty, others regard it as an outdated obstacle to public safety. This paper explores arguments for and against the continued existence of the Second Amendment and considers a moderate position advocating for reform rather than repeal. It concludes by emphasizing the need for a nuanced and balanced approach in addressing the complexities of modern gun ownership and regulation.

Introduction

The Second Amendment of the United States Constitution states:

"A well regulated Militia, being necessary to the security of a free State, the right of the people to keep and bear Arms shall not be infringed." (U.S. Const. amend. II)

Originally ratified in 1791, the Second Amendment was rooted in the post-Revolutionary context of citizen militias and distrust of centralized power. In the 21st century, however, its interpretation and application have become controversial, especially amid escalating gun violence. This paper examines the major perspectives surrounding the Second Amendment, highlighting the enduring tension between personal liberty and collective safety.

Arguments for Preservation

Constitutional and Historical Foundations

Proponents argue that the Second Amendment enshrines a fundamental right essential to American identity and democratic freedom. The Founding Fathers viewed an armed citizenry as a defense against tyranny (Halbrook, 2013). In District of Columbia v. Heller (2008), the U.S. Supreme Court ruled that the Second Amendment protects an individual's right to possess firearms, even outside the context of a militia.

Right to Self-Defense

Gun ownership is often justified as a means of personal protection. According to Kleck and Gertz (1995), firearms are frequently used in self-defense, sometimes preventing crimes that police could not have stopped in time.

Cultural Significance

In many regions of the United States, especially rural areas, firearms are associated with hunting, recreation, and family traditions. These cultural factors reinforce resistance to gun control efforts (Carlson, 2015).

Arguments for Abolition or Reform

Escalating Gun Violence

The U.S. suffers from disproportionately high rates of gun-related deaths compared to other developed nations. Studies link relaxed gun laws with increased rates of mass shootings and homicides (Grinshteyn & Hemenway, 2016).

Outdated Constitutional Context

Critics argue that the 18th-century rationale behind the Second Amendment—militias and muskets—has little relevance in a time of semi-automatic weapons and modern law enforcement (Winkler, 2011).

International Comparisons

Countries with strict gun laws, such as Japan and the United Kingdom, have dramatically lower rates of gun violence. This disparity fuels arguments that gun regulation contributes significantly to public safety (Chapman et al., 2006).

Moderate View: Reform Over Repeal

Rather than abolishing the Second Amendment, many experts suggest implementing evidence-based

regulations to reduce harm while respecting constitutional rights. These include:
Universal background checks (Everytown for Gun Safety, 2023)
Assault weapon bans
Mandatory training and safe storage laws
Red flag laws to temporarily remove firearms from individuals deemed dangerous
These measures aim to uphold the spirit of the Second Amendment while addressing 21st-century safety concerns.

Conclusion

The Second Amendment embodies a historic commitment to liberty but presents legal and ethical challenges in a modern, violence-prone society. Whether one supports its preservation, reform, or repeal depends largely on the values one prioritizes—individual freedom versus collective security. As gun violence persists, a nuanced, bipartisan dialogue grounded in both constitutional principles and empirical data is necessary to shape future policy.

References

Carlson, J. (2015). Citizen-Protectors: The Everyday Politics of Guns in an Age of Decline. Oxford University Press.

Chapman, S., Alpers, P., Agho, K., & Jones, M. (2006). Australia's 1996 gun law reforms: Faster falls in firearm deaths, firearm suicides, and a decade without mass shootings. Injury Prevention, 12(6), 365–372. https://doi.org/10.1136/ip.2006.013714

District of Columbia v. Heller, 554 U.S. 570 (2008).

Everytown for Gun Safety. (2023). Gun Law Rankings by State. https://everytownresearch.org/rankings

Grinshteyn, E., & Hemenway, D. (2016). Violent death rates: The US compared with other high-income OECD countries, 2010. The American Journal of Medicine, 129(3), 266–273. https://doi.org/10.1016/j.amjmed.2015.10.025

Halbrook, S. P. (2013). The Founders' Second Amendment: Origins of the Right to Bear Arms. Ivan R. Dee.

Kleck, G., & Gertz, M. (1995). Armed resistance to crime: The prevalence and nature of self-defense with a gun. Journal of Criminal Law and Criminology, 86(1), 150–187. https://doi.org/10.2307/1147618

U.S. Constitution, amend. II.

Winkler, A. (2011). Gunfight: The Battle Over the Right to Bear Arms in America. W. W. Norton & Company.

https://chatgpt.com/c/6846c5d9-d48c-8008-a697-d7606c8f2d39 2025.6.9.검색.

Ⅲ. 미합중국 연방헌법(美合衆國 聯邦憲法) 수정 제2조 총기권리 유지로 인해 총기난사가 지속 되는데, 미국과 세계 각국에 미치는 심리적 · 실질적 악영향이 존재할까?

1. 미합중국 수정헌법 제2조의 심리적 및 구조적 영향: 총기폭력과 정책 대응에 대한 세계적 분석

본 논문은 미합중국 수정헌법 제2조가 국내외 총기폭력 추세에 미치는 영향을 분석한다. 통계 자료, 심리적 영향, 정책 비교 분석을 통해 총기 소유권이 대규모 총기난사에 얼마나 기여하는지 평가하고, 효과적인 국제 대응 사례를 고찰한다. 또한, 전세계 모범 사례를 바탕으로 정책적 권고안을 제시한다.

(1) 서론

미합중국 수정헌법 제2조는 무기를 소지하고 휴대할 권리를 보장하고 있다. 이는 오랫동안 개인의 자유와 자기방어의 상징으로 여겨졌지만, 동시에 총기의 광범위한 접근성을 허용하여 심각한 공공 보건 및 안전 문제를 초래했다. 본 논문은 미국의 관대한 총기 문화가 초래한 심리사회적 및 실제적 결과, 특히 대규모 총기난사의 확산을 고찰하고, 그 여파가 국제 정책, 사회 규범, 공공 보건에 미치는 영향을 탐색한다.

(2) 미국의 총기폭력: 통계적 개요

Gun Violence Archive(2023)에 따르면 2014년부터 2023년까지 미국에서는 대규모 총기난사 사건이 크게 증가했으며, 2021년 한 해에만 689건이 발생했다. 2023년에는 총 754명이 사망하고 2,443명이 부상을 입었다. 미국의 총기 살인률은 다른 고소득 국가에 비해 현저히 높으며, 인구 10만 명당 10.6명으로 캐나다(2.1명), 독일(0.9명)보다 훨씬 높다(Small Arms Survey, 2016).

(3) 총기폭력의 심리적 영향

학교, 종교시설, 쇼핑몰 등 일상 공간에서의 총기 위협은 광범위한 심리적 고통을 유발하고 있다. 총격 훈련을 경험한 아동은 불안감과 외상 후 스트레스 증상(PTSD)을 경험하며(Cowan 외, 2020), 피해자뿐 아니라 지역사회 전체에도 우울증, 불신, 정신적 트라우마가 확산되고 있다.

(4) 국제적 인식 및 영향

미국 총기난사에 대한 언론 보도는 전 세계적으로 공포와 트라우마를 확산시킨다. 학부모들은 자녀를 미국에 유학 보내는 것에 대해 점점 더 우려를 표하며, 전 세계 시민들도 SNS 등을 통해 간접적인 외상을 경험하고 있다. 또한 미국에서 제조된 총기가 분쟁 지역으로 유입되면서 국제 안보에도 부정적인 영향을 미치고 있다(Alpers & Picard, 2019).

(5) 비교 정책 분석

여러 국가는 효과적인 총기 규제의 사례를 제시하고 있다: 5.1 호주: 1996년 포트아서 대참사 이후, 호주는 반자동 소총을 금지하고 총기 환수 프로그램을 도입했다. 이 조치는 총기 관련 사망률을 47% 감소시키고, 이후 대규모 총기난사가 재발하지 않도록 하는 데 기여했다(Chapman 외, 2006). 5.2 뉴질랜드: 2019년 크라이스트처치 모스크 총기난사 후, 뉴질랜드는 대부분의 반자동 무기를 금지하고 의무적 총기 환수 조치를 시행했다. 이 개혁은 신속하고 광범위한 정치적 지지를 바탕으로 통과되었으며, 이후 총기난사는 발생하지 않았다(New Zealand Parliament, 2019).

(6) 정책 제안

국제 모범 사례를 바탕으로 다음과 같은 정책이 권장된다: 보편적 신원조회 시스템 반자동 및 군용형 무기 금지, 총기 환수 및 자진 반납 프로그램, 고위험군을 대상으로 한 임시 총기 압수법(레드 플래그 법), 포괄적 총기 등록 시스템, 총기폭력에 대한 공공보건적 접근, 온라인 극단주의 콘텐츠 규제

(7) 결론

미국의 총기 정책은 심리적, 정치적, 사회적 측면에서 국제적으로 중대한 영향을

미친다. 수정헌법 제2조는 헌법적으로 도전이 되는 요소이지만, 무대응의 대가는 생명 손실, 공동체 붕괴, 국제 신뢰 하락으로 이어진다. 본 논문은 세계 모범 사례에 기반한 균형 잡힌, 증거 기반의 총기 규제 접근법을 제안하며, 국내외 시민 보호의 필요성을 강조한다.[5]

1. The Psychological and Structural Repercussions of the Second Amendment: A Global Analysis of Gun Violence and Policy Responses

Abstract

This paper examines the implications of the United States Constitution's Second Amendment on gun violence trends, both domestically and globally. By analyzing statistical data, psychological impacts, and comparative policy frameworks, this study evaluates the extent to which gun rights contribute to mass shootings and assesses effective international responses. The paper also outlines key policy recommendations grounded in global best practices.

(1) Introduction

The Second Amendment to the United States Constitution guarantees the right to keep and bear arms. While it has long been framed as a pillar of personal liberty and self-defense, it has also facilitated a climate where firearms are widely acces-

---

5 참고문헌 Alpers, P., & Picard, M. (2019). 미국 총기 수출의 세계적 영향. Small Arms Survey. https://www.smallarmssurvey.org Chapman, S., Alpers, P., Agho, K., & Jones, M. (2006). 호주의 1996년 총기법 개정: 총기사망률 및 자살률 감소, 대규모 총기난사 종식. Injury Prevention, 12(6), 365-372. Cowan, K. C., Vaillancourt, K., Rossen, E., & Pollitt, K. (2020). 학교 폭력 예방과 대응. 전미 학교 심리학자 협회. Gun Violence Archive. (2023). 미국 총기난사 연례 보고서. https://www.gunviolencearchive.org New Zealand Parliament. (2019). 무기(금지된 총기, 탄창, 부품) 개정법. Small Arms Survey. (2016). 고소득 국가의 총기사망률. https://www.smallarmssurvey.org The Guardian. (2024).
뉴질랜드 총기 개혁을 철회할 우려: 우파 연정의 움직임. https://www.theguardian.com/world/article/2024/jul/19/fears-rightwing-coalition-will-unwind-nz-gun-reforms 2025.6.9. 검색.
https://chatgpt.com/c/6846cf6e-fd44-8008-991c-b3b57661d4ad 2025.6.9. 검색.

sible, leading to significant public health and safety concerns. This paper explores the psychosocial and practical consequences of the United States' permissive gun culture, especially the proliferation of mass shootings, and considers its ripple effects on international policy, societal norms, and public health.

(2) Gun Violence in the United States: A Statistical Overview

Between 2014 and 2023, the U.S. saw a marked increase in mass shooting events, with 689 incidents recorded in 2021 alone, according to Gun Violence Archive (2023). These incidents resulted in significant casualties: 754 deaths and 2,443 injuries in 2023. Gun homicide rates in the U.S. remain significantly higher than those in comparable high-income nations (Small Arms Survey, 2016), standing at 10.6 per 100,000 people compared to 2.1 in Canada and 0.9 in Germany.

(3) Psychological Impacts of Gun Violence

The persistent threat of gun violence in everyday settings — schools, religious centers, shopping malls — has led to widespread psychological distress. Children subjected to active shooter drills report heightened levels of anxiety and trauma symptoms (Cowan et al., 2020). Beyond direct victims, community-wide exposure to such violence has been linked to increased prevalence of PTSD, depression, and social mistrust.

(4) International Perceptions and Impacts

Media coverage of U.S. mass shootings extends fear and trauma globally. Parents increasingly express concerns over sending children to study in the U.S., while global citizens are exposed to vicarious trauma through social media. Moreover, U.S.-manufactured firearms have been trafficked into conflict zones, exacerbating global insecurity (Alpers & Picard, 2019).

(5) Comparative Policy Analysis

Several countries offer instructive models of successful gun control:

5.1 Australia: Following the 1996 Port Arthur massacre, Australia implemented a national gun buyback program and banned semi-automatic rifles. These measures led to a 47% reduction in firearm-related deaths and the absence of further mass shootings (Chapman et al., 2006).

5.2 New Zealand: In the aftermath of the 2019 Christchurch mosque attacks, the government banned most semi-automatic weapons and initiated a mandatory buyback. The reforms passed swiftly and with broad parliamentary support, and no mass shootings have occurred since (New Zealand Parliament, 2019).

(6) Policy Recommendations

Drawing on international precedents, the following policy measures are recommended:

Universal background checks

Ban on semi-automatic and military-style firearms

Gun buyback and amnesty programs

Red flag laws enabling temporary confiscation from high-risk individuals

Comprehensive firearm registration systems

Public health framing of gun violence

Regulation of online extremist content

(7) Conclusion

The global repercussions of U.S. gun policy are profound, spanning psychological, political, and social domains. While the Second Amendment poses unique constitutional challenges, the cost of inaction is quantifiable in lives lost, communities fractured, and international credibility diminished. This paper argues for a balanced, evidence-based approach to gun regulation, inspired by global best practices, to safeguard both domestic and international populations.

References[6]

2. 미합중국 연방헌법 제2조 총기 권리 판례 분석: Bruen 판결 이후 하위법원 적용과 주별 규제 비교

(1) 서론

미합중국 연방헌법 제2조는 개인의 총기 소지 권리를 보장하는 조항으로, 총기 규제와 권리 사이의 긴장 관계에서 핵심적인 법적 쟁점이 되어왔다. 특히 2008년 연방대법원의 District of Columbia v. Heller 판결은 개인 총기 소지권을 명확히 확립하였으며, 이후 2010년 McDonald v. City of Chicago 판결을 통해 이 권리가 주정부에도 적용됨이 확인되었다. 최근 2022년 New York State Rifle & Pistol Association v. Bruen 판결은 '은폐 휴대 허가제'에 관한 심사 기준을 역사적 전통에 근거한 엄격한 기준으로 전환시켰다. 본 연구는 Bruen 판결 이후 연방 하위법원과 주별 규제법 판례를 분석하여, 제2조 해석의 변화 양상과 지역별 규제 차이를 비교하고자 한다.

---

6 Alpers, P., & Picard, M. (2019). The global impact of US gun exports. Small Arms Survey. Retrieved from https://www.smallarmssurvey.org Chapman, S., Alpers, P., Agho, K., & Jones, M. (2006). Australia's 1996 gun law reforms: Faster falls in firearm deaths, firearm suicides, and a decade without mass shootings. Injury Prevention, 12(6), 365-372. Cowan, K. C., Vaillancourt, K., Rossen, E., & Pollitt, K. (2020). Preventing and Responding to School Violence. National Association of School Psychologists.
Gun Violence Archive. (2023). Annual report on mass shootings in the U.S. Retrieved from https://www.gunviolencearchive.org New Zealand Parliament. (2019). Arms (Prohibited Firearms, Magazines, and Parts) Amendment Act 2019. Small Arms Survey. (2016). Firearm-Related Deaths in High-Income Countries. Retrieved from https://www.smallarmssurvey.org The Guardian. (2024). Fears rightwing coalition will unwind NZ gun reforms brought in after Christchurch massacre. Retrieved from https://www.theguardian.com/world/article/2024/jul/19/fears-rightwing-coalition-will-unwind-nz-gun-reforms

(2) 이론적 배경

• 제2조의 역사와 초기 해석

미국 독립 전쟁 이후 1791년 제정된 제2조는 “규율 있는 민병대의 필요성”과 함께 “총기 소지 및 휴대의 권리”를 명시하였다. 하지만 그 권리가 개인에게 부여된 것인지, 집단적 민병대의 권리인지에 관해서는 오랜 논쟁이 있었다.

• Heller 및 McDonald 판결

Heller (2008)는 “개인이 자기방어를 위해 집 안에서 총기를 소지할 권리”를 연방헌법상 보장한다고 판시하며 개인권 해석의 기준을 세웠다. 그러나 제한적인 규제는 합헌으로 인정하였다. McDonald (2010)는 이 권리가 14차 수정헌법을 통해 주정부에도 적용됨을 확립하였다.

• Brucn 판결과 새로운 심사 기준

Bruen (2022)는 휴대 권리를 집 밖까지 확장하였고, 종래의 수단-목적 분석을 폐기하고 “텍스트 · 역사 · 전통”에 근거한 엄격 심사 기준을 제시하였다. 이에 따라 하위법원의 판례 흐름과 해석이 재편되고 있다.

(3) 분석

• 하위법원 판례 흐름

Bruen 이후 연방 9th Circuit(캘리포니아)과 5th Circuit(텍사스)은 역사적 전통 해석에서 차이를 보인다. 9th Circuit은 역사적 쌍둥이(twin) 기준을 엄격히 적용하여 규제 허용 여부를 보수적으로 판단하는 경향이 강하다. 예컨대 Duncan v. Bonta 사건에서 대용량 탄창 제한을 합헌으로 판단하였다. 반면, 5th Circuit은 United States v. Rahimi 사건에서 Bruen 기준을 유연하게 해석하여, 가정폭력 보호명령 대상자의 총기 소지 제한을 합헌으로 보았다. 이는 역사적 전례가 명확하지 않더라도 현대 사회의 공익을 고려할 수 있다는 입장이다.

• **주별 법제 비교: 캘리포니아 vs 텍사스**

캘리포니아는 Peruta v. San Diego 판결 이후에도 여전히 "good cause" 허가제 및 탄창 제한 등 엄격한 총기 규제를 유지한다. 반면 텍사스는 2021년부터 Permitless Carry법을 시행, 휴대 허가 없이 총기 휴대를 허용하며 Bruen 판결을 적극 수용하는 모습을 보인다. 두 주의 입법과 판례는 제2조 해석에 따른 지역적 차이를 반영한다.

• **법조문과 역사적 영국법 비교**

초기 영국 권리청원(Bill of Rights, 1689년)은 의회의 승인 없이는 무기 소지가 금지되었으나, 미국은 제2조를 통해 개인 총기 소지 권리를 명시하였다. 20세기 워싱턴 DC의 전면 권총 금지법은 Heller에서 위헌이 되었고, 캘리포니아의 현행 탄창 제한법과 텍사스의 Permitless Carry법은 Bruen 판례를 통해 각각 다른 방향으로 정당화되고 있다.

(4) 결론

Bruen 판결은 제2조 해석에 중대한 변화를 가져왔으며, 하위법원에서는 역사적 전통에 근거한 엄격 심사 기준이 다양한 방식으로 적용되고 있다. 특히 캘리포니아와 텍사스는 총기 규제 및 휴대 허가제 측면에서 극명한 차이를 보이며, 이는 지역적 사회 · 정치적 특성의 반영이다. 앞으로도 연방대법원의 추가 판결과 주별 입법 변화에 따라 제2조 권리와 규제의 균형이 지속적으로 재조정될 것으로 전망된다.[7]

---

7 참고문헌 District of Columbia v. Heller, 554 U.S. 570 (2008). McDonald v. City of Chicago, 561 U.S. 742 (2010). New York State Rifle & Pistol Association v. Bruen, 597 U.S. ___ (2022). United States v. Rahimi, 61 F.4th 443 (5th Cir. 2024). Peruta v. San Diego, 824 F.3d 919 (9th Cir. 2016). Duncan v. Bonta, 19 F.4th 1087 (9th Cir. 2021). Bill of Rights, 1689 (영국 권리청원). 미합중국 연방헌법 제2조 (1791). 캘리포니아 대용량 탄창 제한법 (Cal. Penal Code § 32310). 텍사스 Permitless Carry 법 (HB 1927, 2021). https://chatgpt.com/c/6846e503-b0e4-8008-8c29-d3ef4ba98d12 2025.6.10. 검색.

2. Constitutional Interpretation of the Second Amendment: Post-Bruen Lower Court Applications and State Regulatory Comparisons

Abstract

This paper examines the evolving judicial interpretations of the Second Amendment of the United States Constitution, focusing on key Supreme Court rulings such as Heller (2008), McDonald (2010), and Bruen (2022). The study analyzes how lower federal courts, particularly in California's 9th Circuit and Texas's 5th Circuit, have applied Bruen's historical-traditional test, resulting in divergent rulings on firearm regulations. Additionally, it compares state-level regulations in California and Texas, reflecting differing approaches to firearm rights and restrictions. The paper concludes that while Bruen marks a significant doctrinal shift, substantial variation persists among lower courts and states, signaling ongoing constitutional and policy debates.

(1) Introduction

The Second Amendment of the United States Constitution enshrines the right of individuals to keep and bear arms, a provision that has historically sparked contentious legal and political debate. Landmark Supreme Court decisions — District of Columbia v. Heller (2008) and McDonald v. City of Chicago (2010) — affirmed an individual's right to possess firearms for lawful purposes, including self-defense, and incorporated this right against the states. More recently, New York State Rifle & Pistol Association v. Bruen (2022) reshaped constitutional scrutiny by introducing a strict historical-traditional test for evaluating firearm regulations. This paper explores the implications of Bruen for lower courts and state laws, focusing on the contrasting regulatory environments of California and Texas.

(2) Theoretical Background

• Historical Foundations of the Second Amendment

Enacted in 1791 as part of the Bill of Rights, the Second Amendment balances the necessity of a "well regulated militia" with the individual's right to possess and carry weapons. Early interpretations debated whether this right was collective or individual.

• Supreme Court Precedents: Heller and McDonald

The Heller decision decisively recognized an individual's right to possess firearms within the home for self-defense, albeit allowing for certain regulatory limitations. McDonald extended this right's applicability to state and local governments via the Fourteenth Amendment.

• The Bruen Decision and Its Impact

Bruen rejected the prior means-end scrutiny approach, mandating that firearm regulations must be consistent with the Nation's historical tradition of firearm regulation. This introduced a more stringent standard requiring historical analogues to justify modern regulations, prompting significant shifts in lower court rulings.

(3) Analysis

• Post-Bruen Lower Court Jurisprudence

The Ninth Circuit (California) adopts a strict "historical twin" test, demanding strong historical analogues to uphold firearm regulations. Cases like Duncan v. Bonta upheld California's large-capacity magazine ban under this framework. Conversely, the Fifth Circuit (Texas) embraces a more flexible interpretation, as demonstrated in United States v. Rahimi, where the court upheld restrictions on firearm possession by individuals subject to domestic violence restraining orders despite limited historical precedent.

• Comparative State Regulation: California vs. Texas

California maintains stringent firearm regulations including "good cause" permitting and magazine capacity limits, reflecting a cautious stance aligned with the Ninth Circuit's jurisprudence. Texas, responding to Bruen, has enacted permissive carry laws, exemplified by the 2021 Permitless Carry statute, emphasizing expansive individual firearm rights consistent with Fifth Circuit interpretations.

• Legal Textual and Historical Comparison

Comparing early English firearm regulation, such as the 1689 Bill of Rights mandating Parliamentary consent for weapon possession, with American constitutional and statutory frameworks highlights the evolution from collective control to individual rights. Modern regulatory measures reflect this complex legacy as courts grapple with balancing public safety and constitutional freedoms.

(4) Conclusion

The Bruen decision represents a pivotal recalibration of Second Amendment jurisprudence, emphasizing historical tradition as the foundation for constitutional review. Nevertheless, divergent interpretations across federal circuits and contrasting state laws in California and Texas illustrate ongoing contestation. This landscape suggests the Supreme Court will remain central in resolving future conflicts between firearm rights and regulatory interests.[8]

---

8 References

District of Columbia v. Heller, 554 U.S. 570 (2008).

McDonald v. City of Chicago, 561 U.S. 742 (2010).

New York State Rifle & Pistol Association v. Bruen, 597 U.S. ___ (2022).

United States v. Rahimi, 61 F.4th 443 (5th Cir. 2024).

Peruta v. San Diego, 824 F.3d 919 (9th Cir. 2016).

3. 미국 연방헌법 수정 제2조와 총기 소지 권리: 규제와 개정 논쟁의 정치적·사회적 고찰

초록(Abstract)

미국 연방헌법 수정 제2조는 국민의 총기 소지 권리를 보장하고 있으나, 이로 인해 총기 난사 사건 등 심각한 사회 문제가 지속되고 있다. 본 논문은 수정 제2조 존속의 법적 · 문화적 배경과 함께, 헌법 개정을 통한 총기 소지 금지 방안의 현실적 가능성과 한계를 검토한다. 또한 미국 내 총기 규제 관련 정치 역학 및 헌법 개정 절차를 설명하고, 해외 사례를 통해 대안적 규제 방안을 모색한다. 이를 통해 미국 총기 문제 해결의 다층적 접근 필요성을 논의한다.

(1) 서론

미국은 세계에서 가장 높은 민간 총기 보유율과 함께 잦은 총기 폭력 사건으로 인한 사회적 갈등을 경험하고 있다. 특히, 1791년 채택된 연방헌법 수정 제2조는 국민의 총기 소유 및 휴대 권리를 명시하고 있어, 이를 근거로 강력한 총기 권리 운동이 존재한다. 본 연구는 수정 제2조 폐지 또는 개정을 통한 총기 규제 강화 가능성을 탐색하는 한편, 헌법 개정 절차, 정치적 쟁점, 그리고 해외 사례 비교를 통해 현실적 정책 대안을 고찰한다.

(2) 미국 연방헌법 수정 제2조의 법적·문화적 배경

수정 제2조는 "잘 규율된 민병대가 자유로운 주의 안전에 필요하므로, 국민이 무기를 소유 · 휴대하는 권리를 침해하지 말라"고 규정한다. 이 조항은 미국 초기 독립 전쟁 당시 시민들의 무장권을 반영한 것으로, 현재까지도 '개인의 자기 방어권'으로 해

Duncan v. Bonta, 19 F.4th 1087 (9th Cir. 2021).

Bill of Rights, 1689 (England).

United States Constitution, Amendment II (1791).

California Penal Code § 32310 (Large-capacity magazine ban).

Texas House Bill 1927 (Permitless Carry, 2021).

https://chatgpt.com/c/6846e503-b0e4-8008-8c29-d3ef4ba98d12 2025.6.10. 검색.

석되어 왔다. 법원 판례 및 정치적 담론에서 이 권리는 강력히 보호되며, 총기 규제 반대 논리의 핵심 근거가 된다.

(3) 총기 문제와 수정 제2조 폐지 논의

총기 난사 및 기타 총기 폭력 사건은 사회적 충격과 인명 피해를 야기하며, 이에 대한 근본적 해결책으로서 수정 제2조 폐지 및 총기 소지 금지가 제안된다. 그러나 헌법 개정을 통한 폐지는 다음과 같은 현실적 어려움에 봉착한다.

• 헌법 개정 절차의 엄격성

미국 헌법 개정은 연방 상하원 3분의 2 이상의 찬성과 50개 주 중 3분의 4 이상의 주 비준을 요하는 매우 까다로운 절차이다. 이는 정치적 합의가 어려운 현안에서는 사실상 개정 불가능에 가깝다는 평가를 받는다.

• 정치 · 사회적 저항

총기 권리 옹호자, 특히 강력한 로비 단체인 NRA(National Rifle Association)의 영향력과 보수층의 총기 문화 수호 의지가 크다. 총기 소지는 개인의 자유권 및 자기 방어권으로 인식되기에, 수정 제2조 폐지 시도는 광범위한 사회적 분열을 야기한다.

• 총기 규제의 한계

총기 금지가 도입된 국가에서도 불법 총기 사용 문제는 지속된다. 따라서 총기 소지 금지만으로 모든 폭력 문제를 해결할 수 없으며, 사회적 · 경제적 요인과 정신건강 문제 해결도 병행되어야 한다.

(4) 미국 내 총기 규제 관련 정치 역학

총기 규제 논쟁은 미국 정치체제의 특성과 밀접한 관련이 있다. 상원과 하원의 정치적 균형, 주별 자치권, 이익집단의 영향력이 복합적으로 작용한다. 주별 규제 차이: 캘리포니아, 뉴욕 등 진보적 주는 강력한 규제를 시행하는 반면, 텍사스, 플로리다 등 보수적 주는 규제가 약하다. 이익 집단과 로비: NRA 등 총기 권리 단체가 막대한 정치자금과 선거 지원을 통해 입법 영향력을 행사한다. 정치 양극화: 총기 문제는 민주당과 공화당 간 이념 대립의 상징적 이슈로 자리 잡아 정책 합의가 쉽지 않다.

(5) 해외 총기 규제 사례

미국과 달리, 다수 국가에서는 총기 규제가 엄격하며 상대적으로 총기 폭력 사건이 적다. 호주: 1996년 포트 아서 총기 난사 사건 이후 공격용 무기 전면 금지, 엄격한 총기 등록 및 소지 허가제 도입으로 총기 관련 사망률이 급감했다. 영국: 총기 소지가 극도로 제한되며, 소유 시 엄격한 심사 및 목적 제한이 있다. 총기 폭력 발생률이 낮다. 캐나다: 총기 면허제 및 등록제를 운영하며, 일정 조건 하에 제한적으로 총기 소지가 가능하다. 이들 사례는 강력한 규제 정책이 총기 폭력 감소에 효과적임을 시사한다.

(6) 정책 제언

미국 연방헌법 수정 제2조의 기득권 유지가 가져오는 심각한 인명 피해는 단순한 국내 문제를 넘어 국제 사회에까지 영향을 미친다. 미국은 세계에서 가장 강력한 경제·군사 대국이자 글로벌 리더로서, 국제 인권과 생명 보호에 대한 책임을 함께 져야 함에도 불구하고, 자국 내 정치적 이익과 기득권 유지에 치중한 나머지 글로벌 차원의 생명권 보호에는 상대적으로 소홀한 모습을 보이고 있다.

• 기득권과 이중성의 문제

총기 권리 옹호 세력과 정치적 기득권은 수정 제2조를 기반으로 자신들의 이익을 지속적으로 방어한다. 이 과정에서 총기 난사와 같은 대규모 인명 피해가 반복적으로 발생함에도 불구하고, 근본적 문제 해결을 위한 헌법 개정이나 강력한 규제 추진은 지연되고 있다. 이는 미국 사회 내 민주주의와 자유의 이름 아래 '기본권'을 내세우는 한편, 동시에 시민의 생명권 보호라는 기본적 의무에는 소극적이고 모순적인 태도로 비춰질 수 있다.

• 국제적 책임과 글로벌 질서의 관점

미국이 세계 평화와 인권을 선도하는 위치에 있음에도 불구하고, 총기 폭력 문제에 대한 무책임한 태도는 국제 사회에서의 신뢰 저하와 책임 회피로 연결된다. 특히 총기 문제는 단순한 국내 사안이 아니라, 국제 테러, 범죄 네트워크, 무기 거래 등 다국적 문제와도 연결되어 있으므로, 미국의 내적 정책 변화가 세계적 안보와 인명 보호에도 중요한 영향을 끼친다.

• 제언

미국은 국내 정치적 기득권에 얽매인 좁은 시각을 넘어, 생명 보호와 인권 수호라는 국제적 가치에 부합하는 책임 있는 정책 변화를 모색해야 한다. 이를 위해서는 국내 총기 규제 강화뿐 아니라, 국제 협력과 다자간 무기 규제 체계 강화에도 적극 참여해야 한다. 국내외 생명 보호의 가치가 균형을 이루는 새로운 패러다임 정립이 시급하며, 이는 미국이 세계 리더로서 위상을 유지하는 데 필수적이다.

(7) 미국의 총기 규제 문제에 대한 국제법적·인권적 고찰

• 국가 주권과 국제적 인권 의무 간의 긴장

미국은 연방헌법 수정 제2조에 의해 개인의 총기 소지 권리를 헌법적으로 보장하면서도, 동시에 국제사회에서 보편적 인권의 수호자로서의 역할을 자임해왔다. 그러나 미국 내에서 발생하는 반복적 총기 난사 사건과 그에 따른 인명 피해는, 국제 인권 규범의 핵심인 생명권(right to life)을 심각하게 훼손하고 있음에도 불구하고, 이에 대한 적극적 조치가 결여되어 있다는 점에서 국제사회와의 규범적 긴장을 초래한다.

• 국제 인권법과 생명권의 보장

세계인권선언(Universal Declaration of Human Rights, 1948) 제3조는 다음과 같이 명시한다: "Everyone has the right to life, liberty and security of person."[1] 또한, 시민적 및 정치적 권리에 관한 국제규약(ICCPR, 1966) 제6조 제1항은 다음과 같이 규정한다: "Every human being has the inherent right to life. This right shall be protected by law. No one shall be arbitrarily deprived of his life."[2] 미국은 1992년 ICCPR을 비준[3]

하였으며, 이에 따라 국가로서 자국민의 생명을 보호할 국제법적 의무를 지닌다. 그러나 총기 규제 실패로 인해 연간 수만 명의 시민이 총기 관련 사건으로 사망하고 있음은, 미국이 국제 인권조약상 의무를 사실상 이행하지 않고 있는 것으로 해석될 수 있다. 유엔 인권이사회(UN Human Rights Council)는 총기 폭력과 생명권 침해 간의 연관성에 주목하며, 보편적 정례 검토(Universal Periodic Review) 절차를 통해 미국 정부에 총기 규제 강화를 권고한 바 있다. 특히 2015년[4], 2020년[5] 검토에서는 다수 국가가 총기 폭력에 대한 효과적 대응을 미국에 촉구하였다.

• 국제 정치질서와 미국의 신뢰성 문제

미국은 국제적으로 자유민주주의와 인권을 수호하는 국가로서 외교적 정당성을 주장해왔다. 그러나 자국 내에서 반복되는 총기 폭력 사태에 무기력하거나 무관심한 모습은, "국내에서는 자유를, 해외에서는 질서를" 주장하는 이중적 행태(double standard)로 해석될 수 있다. 이는 국제사회에서 미국의 도덕적 리더십에 대한 의문을 제기하며, 규범적 권위(normative authority)의 약화를 초래할 수 있다.

유엔총회는 무기무역조약(Arms Trade Treaty, ATT)[6]을 2013년에 채택했으며, 이는 국가 간 재래식 무기 거래에 있어 인권 보호와 민간인 피해 예방을 강조하고 있다. 미국은 2013년 오바마 정부 하에서 이 조약에 서명했으나, 2020년 트럼프 정부 하에서 조약 비준 의사를 철회하였다. 이는 미국이 총기 규제 문제에서 국제적 연대보다는 자국 내 정치 논리에 따라 입장을 선회해 온 대표적 사례로 볼 수 있다.

• 정책적 함의

미국은 생명권 보호를 국제 인권법의 핵심 의무로 인식하고, 헌법상 권리 보장과 인권 규범 간의 충돌을 조정하는 방향으로 법제 개선에 나서야 한다. 총기 규제 법안과 행정 정책은 ICCPR 및 유엔 권고안을 참고하여 생명권의 실질적 보장을 최우선 가치로 삼아야 한다. 미국은 무기 확산과 관련된 국제 협정, 특히 ATT와 같은 다자간 협약에 재가입함으로써, 국제사회와의 규범적 연대를 회복하고 총기 규제의 세계적 기준 형성에 기여해야 한다.

(8) 결론(통합 정리)

미국 연방헌법 수정 제2조는 역사적 · 헌법적 맥락에서 중요한 의미를 가지나, 오늘날 총기 난사와 같은 심각한 사회 문제를 야기하며 국민의 생명권을 위협하고 있다. 이에 대한 국제사회의 우려는 단지 미국 내 문제를 넘어 국제 인권 규범, 생명권 보장, 무기규제 노력 등과 긴밀히 연결되어 있다. 미국이 진정한 자유민주주의 국가이자 국제사회에서의 리더로서 위상을 유지하고자 한다면, 자국 내 기득권 정치 논리만을 앞세우는 것이 아니라, 생명권이라는 보편적 인권에 기반한 책임 있는 입법 및 정책 결정을 내려야 한다.[9]

---

9 각주(Footnotes)

United Nations General Assembly. (1948). Universal Declaration of Human Rights, Article 3.

United Nations General Assembly. (1966). International Covenant on Civil and Political Rights, Article 6.

United Nations Treaty Collection. (n.d.). Status of ICCPR Ratification by Country. 미국은 1992년 6월 8일 조약 비준.

UN Human Rights Council. (2015). Report of the Working Group on the Universal Periodic Review: United States of America. A/HRC/30/12.

UN Human Rights Council. (2020). Universal Periodic Review - United States (Third Cycle), Session 36.

United Nations General Assembly. (2013). Arms Trade Treaty. A/RES/67/234 B.

참고문헌(추가 포함)

United Nations. (1948). Universal Declaration of Human Rights.

United Nations. (1966). International Covenant on Civil and Political Rights.

United Nations Human Rights Council. (2015, 2020). Universal Periodic Review Reports: United States.

United Nations. (2013). Arms Trade Treaty.

United Nations Treaty Collection. (n.d.). Status of Treaties: ICCPR.

Alston, P. (2018). The US and the International Human Rights System. Oxford University Press.

Hathaway, O. A. (2005). Why Do Countries Commit to Human Rights Treaties? Journal of Conflict Resolution, 51(4), 588-621.

https://chatgpt.com/c/6846d7cc-99f8-8008-bf51-11f7ea40bb1a 2025.6.9. 검색.

3. Constitutional Gun Rights, Mass Violence, and the International Human Rights Framework: A Critical Analysis of the U.S. Second Amendment

Abstract

This paper examines the persistent gun violence in the United States in the context of the Second Amendment of the U.S. Constitution, critically analyzing the challenges of gun control in light of domestic political dynamics and international human rights obligations. By exploring the legislative history, political entrenchment, and international legal standards such as the right to life under the ICCPR and UDHR, this study evaluates whether the United States' domestic commitment to individual gun ownership is reconcilable with its global leadership in human rights. Comparative examples from other nations are also considered. The paper concludes with policy recommendations that integrate constitutional reform with international law compliance.

(1) Introduction

Gun-related violence in the United States continues to raise critical questions about the balance between constitutional rights and public safety. The Second Amendment of the U.S. Constitution guarantees individuals the right to "keep and bear arms," a principle that has been both historically celebrated and contemporarily contested. Amid increasing mass shootings and public health concerns, this paper explores whether the Second Amendment, in its current form, is compatible with international human rights obligations, particularly the right to life.

(2) Historical and Legal Background of the Second Amendment

Adopted in 1791, the Second Amendment emerged from a context of colonial resistance and mistrust of standing armies. Judicial interpretation, especially in District of Columbia v. Heller (2008), affirmed an individual's right to possess firearms unconnected with militia service. However, this jurisprudence has impeded comprehensive federal gun control efforts.

(3) Domestic Political Dynamics and Regulatory Challenges

Gun rights advocacy groups, most notably the National Rifle Association (NRA), exert significant influence on American politics, contributing to the preservation of expansive interpretations of the Second Amendment. Legislative paralysis at the federal level contrasts with varying state laws, resulting in inconsistent and often ineffective gun control across the nation.

(4) International Human Rights Obligations

The United States is a signatory to key human rights instruments, including:

The Universal Declaration of Human Rights (UDHR, 1948), Article 3: "Everyone has the right to life, liberty and security of person." [1]

The International Covenant on Civil and Political Rights (ICCPR, 1966), Article 6: "Every human being has the inherent right to life... No one shall be arbitrarily deprived of his life." [2]

The U.S. ratified the ICCPR in 1992, thereby assuming legal obligations to protect the right to life. However, the lack of effective gun control raises concerns about compliance with these obligations. The United Nations Human Rights Council has repeatedly urged the U.S. to adopt stricter gun laws in its Universal Periodic Reviews (2015, 2020). [3][4]

(5) Comparative Perspectives

Countries such as Australia, the United Kingdom, and Japan have enacted strict gun control laws following mass shootings, significantly reducing gun-related deaths. These examples demonstrate that democratic nations can reconcile individual freedoms with effective public safety measures without infringing on core human rights.

(6) Double Standards and Erosion of Normative Authority

The U.S. often positions itself as a global champion of human rights, yet its domestic inaction on gun violence reveals a normative inconsistency. While promoting international security and disarmament, the U.S. has failed to control civilian access to firearms domestically. This double standard weakens its credibility and moral leadership in the international human rights regime.

(7) Policy Implications and Recommendations

Constitutional reinterpretation or amendment of the Second Amendment should be considered to allow for clearer public safety regulations.

Federal gun legislation must reflect international standards, particularly obligations under the ICCPR.

The U.S. should re-engage with multilateral frameworks like the Arms Trade Treaty (ATT) and actively support international efforts to curb gun proliferation.

(8) Conclusion

The Second Amendment remains a formidable legal and cultural obstacle to gun reform in the United States. However, the persistent toll of gun violence, combined with international human rights norms, demands a critical reassessment of national priorities. Aligning domestic constitutional rights with global human rights obligations is both a legal necessity and a moral imperative.

Footnotes:

[1] United Nations General Assembly. (1948). Universal Declaration of Human Rights, Article 3.

[2] United Nations General Assembly. (1966). International Covenant on Civil and Political Rights, Article 6.

[3] UN Human Rights Council. (2015). Report of the Working Group on the UPR: United States. A/HRC/30/12.

[4] UN Human Rights Council. (2020). UPR: United States (Third Cycle), Session 36.

References:

Alston, P. (2018). The US and the International Human Rights System. Oxford University Press.

Hathaway, O. A. (2005). Why Do Countries Commit to Human Rights Treaties? Journal of Conflict Resolution, 51(4), 588–621.

United Nations. (1948). Universal Declaration of Human Rights.

United Nations. (1966). International Covenant on Civil and Political Rights.

United Nations Human Rights Council. (2015, 2020). Universal Periodic Review: United States.

United Nations. (2013). Arms Trade Treaty.

United Nations Treaty Collection. (n.d.). Status of Treaties: ICCPR.

주요 찾아보기

18세기(1791년 12월 15일) 권리가 미래의 안전을 설명하지 못할 때

"AI를 통한 변화는 세계적 흐름"이며 "AI를 규제하는 것은 시대에 역행하는 일"입니다. 19세기 영국에서 마차산업을 보호하기 위해 시행된 '붉은깃발법'('The Locomotives on Highways Act' 자동차 속도를 마차보다 느리게 규제해 자동차산업의 주도권을 빼앗김) 역사가 있듯이, AI를 외면하기보다 적극적으로 업무에 활용하는 자세가 필요합니다."

2025년 7월 9일

조재연(趙載淵) · 전 대한민국 대법원 대법관 · 법원행정처 처장 · 고위공직자범죄수사처장
후보추천위원회 위원장 · 現 성균관대학교 법학전문대학원 석좌교수

"지금 대한민국은 공동체 의식과 역사관(歷史觀)이 없는 정치인들의 리더십 빈곤이 가장 큰 문제입니다. 우리가 한 시대를 산다고 하는 것은 흐르는 강물 가운데 한 단계를 사는 것이며, 그 지점은 상류의 물이나 하류의 물과는 다른 곳이라는 걸 알아야 합니다. 지도자에겐 그 한 시대를 볼 줄 아는 지혜가 있어야 합니다."

2025년 2월 15일

김형석(金亨錫 · 107세) · 대한민국 철학자 · 수필가 겸 연세대학교 명예교수

『미국 헌법 쟁점론』을 출간함을 축하드립니다. 세계 석학들을 초빙 · 기획하여 인류가 꼭 풀어가야 할 미국 헌법 천년대계(千年大計)를 다루는 책을 본인 제자인 지영환 교수가 출판 협의한 것은 고무적성과(鼓舞的成果)가 아닐 수 없습니다. 앞으로 미국 연구 발전에 기여 하시길 바랍니다.

2026년 1월 7일

실보(實甫) 김영수(金榮秀) 성균관대학교 법학전문대학원 명예교수 ·
1999년 한국헌법학회 회장 · 전 미국헌법학회 / 한국헌법학연구소 이사장

"강대국 간의 경쟁이 심해질수록 한국과 같은 지정학적 중간 국가는 외교정책을 일관적으로 유지해야 합니다. 강대국은 상대적 약소국과 외교 전략을 수립할 때 자신들이 유리했던 시점만을 기준으로 삼기 때문입니다."

2025년 8월 13일

신범식(辛範植) · 서울대학교 정치외교학부 교수 · 서울대학교 국제문제연구소 소장

"굳건한 한미동맹을 통해 한반도 안보 상황을 안정적으로 관리하고, 우리에게 우호적인 한반도 주변 세력 균형을 유지해야 할 것입니다." 아울러 "중국과 새로운 소통관계를 정립하면서 일각의 '친중론'을 적절히 차단하는 것도 과제입니다."

2025년 8월 12일

민정훈(Min, Jeonghun) · 국립외교원 교수 · 미국 노스이스턴 주립대학교 정치학과 교수

When an 18th-Century Right (December 15, 1791) Can No Longer Explain the Safety of the Future

"Change driven by AI is a global trend. To regulate AI is to go against the flow of our time. Just as nineteenth-century Britain lost its automotive lead by enforcing the 'Red Flag Act'—slowing cars to protect the horse-carriage industry — we must learn from history and embrace AI as a tool for progress, not an object of fear."

— Jaeyeon Cho, Former Justice, Supreme Court of Korea; Former Chief Justice, National Court Administration; Former Chair, High-Ranking Public Officials Crime Investigation Nomination Committee; Distinguished Professor, School of Law, Sungkyunkwan University (July 9, 2025)

"The greatest challenge facing Korea today is the poverty of leadership among politicians who lack both community consciousness and historical perspective. To live in an era is to dwell in one stage of the ever-flowing river of time; that place is neither upstream nor downstream, but our own segment of history. A true leader must possess the wisdom to see the age in which he lives."

— Hyung-Seok Kim, Philosopher and Essayist; Professor Emeritus, Yonsei University (February 15, 2025)

"I warmly congratulate Professor Ji Young-Hwan on the publication of Controversies in U.S. Constitutional Law. It is an inspiring achievement to see my former student organize and edit a volume that brings together distinguished scholars from around the world to discuss the thousand-year questions of the American Constitution. I trust this work will greatly contribute to the advancement of American studies."

— Silbo (實甫) Kim Young-Soo (金榮秀), Professor Emeritus, School of Law, Sungkyunkwan University; President, Korean Association of Constitutional Law (1999); Former President, American Constitutional Law Society; Chairman, Korean Institute for Constitutional Law Studies

"As strategic rivalry among great powers deepens, middle-power states like Korea must maintain consistency in their foreign policy. Major powers tend to formulate strategies toward smaller states based only on the moments most favorable to themselves."

— Beom-Sik Shin, Professor of Political Science and International Relations; Director, Institute of International Affairs, Seoul National University (August 13, 2025)

"A stable security posture on the Korean Peninsula depends on a solid ROK-U.S. alliance and a balanced relationship with neighboring powers. At the same time, Korea must redefine channels of communication with China and prudently counter uncritical currents of 'pro-China' sentiment."

— Jeong-Hun Min, Professor, Korea National Diplomatic Academy; Former Professor of Political Science, Northeastern State University, U.S.A. (August 12, 2025)

Contributors / 공저자 약력(Bilingual Author Bio)

안경환(安京煥 | Kyung-Whan Ahn)

서울대학교 법학전문대학원 명예교수, 법무부장관 후보자, 제4대 국가인권위원회 위원장, 서울대학교 법과대학 학장, 제8대 한국헌법학회 회장, 미국 산타클라라대학교 법학대학원 초대교수, 아시아태평양 지역기구 국제조정위원회(ICC) 부의장, 미국 일리노이대학교 법학대학원 방문교수.

Professor Emeritus, Seoul National University School of Law; Former Nominee for Minister of Justice; Chairperson of the 4th National Human Rights Commission of Korea; Dean, College of Law, SNU; 8th President, Korean Constitutional Law Association; Founding Professor, Santa Clara University School of Law; Vice Chair, Asia-Pacific Forum of National Human Rights Institutions (ICC); Visiting Professor, University of Illinois College of Law (U.S.A.).

임지봉(林智奉 | Ji-Bong Lim)

서강대학교 법학전문대학원 교수, 제27대 한국헌법학회 회장, 한국입법학회 회장(2018-2020), 대검찰청 검찰미래위원회 위원, 헌법재판소 헌법연구위원.

Professor, Sogang University School of Law; 27th President, Korean Constitutional Law Association; President, Korean Association of Legislative Studies (2018-2020); Member, Prosecution Reform Committee, Supreme Prosecutors' Office; Research Commissioner, Constitutional Court of Korea.

손영호(孫永浩 | Young-Ho Son)

베트남 호치민 국립대학교 인문사회대학 교수, 청주대학교 교수 역임, 청주대학교 어학교육원장, 입학처장, 국제교류처장 역임.

Professor, University of Social Sciences and Humanities, Vietnam National University (Ho Chi Minh City); Former Professor, Cheongju University; Former Dean, Language Education Center; Former Director of Admissions and International Affairs, Cheongju University.

박창모(朴昌謨 | C. Mo Bahk)

미국 캘리포니아주립대학교 교수(학과장), 신시내티대학교 교수, 한미문학진흥재단 상임이사, 인랜드 미주한인회 부회장.

Professor and Department Chair, California State University, San Bernardino (CA); Former Professor, University of Cincinnati (OH); Executive Director, Korea-America Literary Promotion Foundation; Vice President, Inland Korean American Society.

지영환(池榮鋎 | Ji Young-Hwan, 號 Art Name 平靜 Pyeongjeong)

국가공무원, 성균관대학교 겸임교수, 중앙대학교 객원교수, 서울대학교 객원연구원, 중앙대학교 심리서비스대학원 겸임교수, 제주대학교 법학전문대학원 겸임교수, 전국지방변호사회장협의회 고문위원, 서울신문·통계청 자문위원, 제43·44대 한국시인협회 감사, 한국행정학회 학술정보위원회 이사(2014).

National Public Official and Adjunct Professor at Sungkyunkwan University, Chung-Ang University, and Jeju National University Law School; Visiting Research Fellow at Seoul National University; Advisor to the National Council of Local Bar Association Presidents, Seoul Newspaper, and the Korean Statistical Office; Auditor of the Korean Poets Association (43rd-44th terms); Board Member, Academic Information Committee, Korean Association for Public Administration (2014).

장인호(張仁豪 | In-Ho Jang)

경찰대학 법학과 교수, 미국헌법학회 감사, 전 경찰대학 치안대학원 공공안전학과장, 경찰대학 산단부단장.

Professor, Department of Law, Korean National Police University; Auditor, American Constitutional Law Association; Former Chair, Department of Public Safety Studies, Graduate School of Policing; Former Deputy Director, Police University Industry-Academic Cooperation Foundation.

윤대현(尹大鉉 | Dae-Hyun Yoon)
성균관대학교 경영학 학사·정치학 석사, FM 그룹 회장, 한국헌법학연구소 고문.
B.A. in Business Administration and M.A. in Political Science, Sungkyunkwan University; Chairman, FM Group; Advisor, Korean Constitutional Law Institute.

조현민(趙鉉珉 | Hyun-Min Cho)
서울특별시경찰청 특공대 전술교관, 범죄학박사.
Tactical Instructor, Special Operations Unit, Seoul Metropolitan Police Agency; Ph.D. in Criminology.

조기환(趙起煥 | Ki-Hwan Cho)
성균관대학교 경영학석사, ㈜ 에머티바이오 대표이사.
M.B.A., Sungkyunkwan University; Chief Executive Officer, EmertiBio Co., Ltd.

미국 헌법 쟁점론 – 美 연방 수정헌법 제2조 총기 권리 –

초판1쇄 발행 2026년 1월 13일

지은이 안경환·임지봉·손영호·박창모·지영환·장인호·윤대현·조현민·조기환
펴낸이 안종만·안상준

편 집 김선민
기획/마케팅 정성혁
표지디자인 벤스토리
제 작 고철민·김원표

펴낸곳 (주) 박영사
서울특별시 금천구 가산디지털2로 53, 210호
(가산동, 한라시그마밸리)
등록 1959. 3. 11. 제300-1959-1호(倫)
전 화 02)733-6771
f a x 02)736-4818
e-mail pys@pybook.co.kr
homepage www.pybook.co.kr
ISBN 979-11-303-9859-4 93330

정 가 38,000원